Becoming a College Writer

A MULTIMEDIA TEXT

Todd Taylor

The University of North Carolina at Chapel Hill

bedford/st.martin's
Macmillan Learning
Boston | New York

For Bedford/St. Martin's

Vice President, Editorial, Macmillan Learning Humanities: Edwin Hill
Senior Program Director for English: Leasa Burton
Program Manager: Molly Parke, Laura Arcari
Marketing Manager: Vivian Garcia
Director of Content Development, Humanities: Jane Knetzger
Developmental Editor: Sherry Mooney
Senior Content Project Manager: Kendra LeFleur
Senior Workflow Project Manager: Jennifer Wetzel
Production Supervisor: Brianna Lester
Media Project Manager: Rand Thomas
Editorial Services: Lumina Datamatics, Inc.
Composition: Lumina Datamatics, Inc.
Photo Editor: Angela Boehler
Photo Researcher: Krystyna Borgen
Permissions Editor: Claire Paschal
Design Director, Content Management: Diana Blume
Text Design: Laura Shaw Feit
Cover Design: William Boardman
Printing and Binding: LSC Communications

Manufactured in the United States of America.

1 2 3 4 5 6   23 22 21 20 19 18

For information, write: Bedford/St. Martin's, 75 Arlington Street, Boston, MA 02116

ISBN 978-0-312-48640-2
ISBN 978-1-319-24923-6 (Loose-leaf Edition)

Acknowledgments
Acknowledgments and copyrights appear on the same page as the text and art selections they cover; these acknowledgments and copyrights constitute an extension of the copyright page.

A Note to Students

On *Becoming a College Writer*

Our primary goal is straightforward: for you to improve and succeed as a writer, not only in your first-year composition course, but throughout college. A secondary but important goal is also straightforward: for you to strengthen your mind through writing so that you can become even more articulate and powerful in your academic life and beyond.

With these goals in mind, let's take a look at how *Becoming a College Writer* can help you succeed. This text provides you with

- **"No frills" advice on key concepts of writing.** Each brief, modular lesson first explains the "Why" and then the "How" of an essential aspect of college writing — such as writing for an audience and drawing on evidence. Why should you think about your audience? How can you keep them curious? Find out in Lesson 3: Audience.

- **Encouragement from other student writers.** You are not alone. In each lesson, hear from peers at community colleges and four-year universities across the country. Learn by listening: In brief videos and in bite-sized clips, students speak openly about their own approaches to writing for college. What have they struggled with? How have they improved and accomplished their goals? They've done it, and so can you.

- **Plenty of practice — and sample papers to learn from.** Each lesson includes a set of practice exercises and access to papers written by the students we interviewed for the book. Does the phrase "thesis statement" make your head spin? See the student video for Lesson 4: Topic and read through the thesis statements in the digital collection of student work.

***Becoming a College Writer* draws on interviews conducted with 100 college students.** We met with students at campuses across the United States to ask: What have you learned about writing for college? In their interviews, they share their backgrounds, challenges, strengths, and experiences. They talk about how they've come to think of themselves as writers and how they approach assignments that may have, at first, seemed daunting. Sometimes they talk about their transformations. We asked lots of questions and they generously answered. I'm grateful to each student who participated in this project, and I hope that as you read this text and watch the videos, you'll find some things in common. I hope that you'll say to yourself, "Yes, I've had that same problem. That might help me," or "Ah, that advice makes sense."

Why might interviews with college writers matter to you? The main reason is this: The students we interviewed have "been there" as college writers, and you, presumably, are just getting started. College writing — what it is and how to do it — might seem mysterious right now, or "inscrutable," as one student put it.

If so, who better than another student to help you get started? Who better to introduce you to college writing, in a down-to-earth way, than someone like yourself who has already learned how to succeed?

One hundred students helped me compose this text, which makes me more of an editor or movie director than a traditional "author." So, now is a good time to introduce myself: My name is Todd Taylor, and I am a university professor who is trying to capture, in a new way, the essentials of college composition. I've taught writing for over two decades and spent many years directing a large writing program. I live in North Carolina, and in my free time I like to play, coach, and watch a lot of soccer. Of course, like most parents, my children consume the majority of my free time, which leads to another introduction; namely, my two children, Max and Jake.

Max and Jake both entered college while I was working on this textbook, and they've read it in manuscript form. My writing students at UNC also responded to the manuscript (thank you, students!) and suggested areas for improvement. Because of the input of Max, Jake, and my many students, this book represents the very best I can do as a teacher and textbook author. Although you won't see their faces in *Becoming a College Writer*, I hope you can sense their influence. *Becoming a College Writer*, therefore, must have everything that they — and you — need. It must work exceptionally well.

What is your learning style? The diversity of the 100 student interviews highlights an important aspect of this text, which is that students learn in different ways. Do you learn well through traditional lectures and readings? Do you do best when you interact

hands-on with new ideas? Are you more visual, or perhaps more attuned to what you hear? Actually, each of us probably learns most effectively through a variety of ways, not just from one form of teaching and learning. That is why this text offers a wide "bandwidth" from which to learn: interactive text and video, student wisdom, focused, expert teacherly advice, and practical exercises. I hope that you and each reader of this book can find a personal connection, an individualized way in.

Have you ever wondered *why* you've been asked to learn something? Learning the *hows* of a given aspect of college writing makes a lot more sense when you understand *why* it matters. That is why each lesson in this book is divided first into a "Why" section that makes a case for why you will benefit from learning, for example, to organize your writing (Lesson 13), or to support what you say with evidence (Lesson 6). A couple of pages later, a "How" section gives you vital guidance for how to organize your paper or how to draw on evidence. Throughout both sections of each lesson, student interviewees pop up to offer their advice and encouragement.

Is there a "secret" to writing for college? Over the years, many students (and, in fact, many instructors) have asked me if I know of a secret or key to successful college writing. Something as rich and varied as college writing cannot be reduced to one absolute idea that will work for everyone; however, I must share with you an acronym that all of my students know that comes pretty close: **RRFF**

Revise
Repeatedly
From
Feedback

Revising Repeatedly from Feedback is the key, not only to college writing, but to all writing, including what you write in your personal and public lives and in your careers. (See Lesson 15: Revising, p. 206.) In fact, **RRFF** is what professional writers do. It's what I'm doing as I write these sentences. A wide array of readers are helping me develop these very words, to whom I am extremely grateful. I've already mentioned Max and Jake and my many students, but there's also a chain of editors at Bedford/St. Martin's who provided feedback, including Ellen, Sydney, Molly, Leasa, Adam, Beth, Shannon, Denise, and Joan — and copy editors whom I never met — and teachers in a variety of focus groups — and anonymous reviewers — and instructors who use the book — and students like yourself. It's a big, wide network, and it's the only way I know how to write.

Of course, **RRFF**, as a "key" to opening a lock on a metaphorical door, is just a beginning. Each of the lessons in *Becoming a College Writer* covers an essential dimension of college writing — and it's the activity of **Revising Repeatedly from Feedback** that makes everything come together. This textbook cannot make you **Revise Repeatedly from Feedback**; it can only point you in that direction and offer support. It's really your teachers, classmates, writing center tutors, and other readers who will help you integrate the essentials of college writing into practice. Your interactions with these key people — who make up your writing network — are what will help you improve your writing.

One last, introductory note: Throughout *Becoming a College Writer*, I encourage you to imagine that every use of the word "you" is aimed at you personally. I also encourage you to take another look at the book's cover. It features the faces of many of the students we interviewed for the project, but it could just as easily be your classmates on the cover. It could just as easily be you. "Becoming a college writer" is largely a matter of you seeing yourself as a writer. The ultimate goal for this text is for you to join the other student writers, for you to become the college writer you are so capable of being.

And so, this introduction is also a dedication, to you.

Preface for Instructors

NICOLE
California State University, San Marcos

I think college writing is worth the challenge, because it opens you up to a way to express your voice. You have your opinions, you have your voice; but then, with college writing, there's so much more to learn. It roots your voice. It grounds your voice.

What would happen if students wrote a college composition textbook for their peers? What would it look like if you collected the best advice from a wide array of students from all types of college campuses, from across the United States, and with different identities and experiences?

Five years before we met Nicole, we interviewed twenty-two leading college composition instructors for the Bedford/St. Martin's online video resource titled *Take 20*, a project that provided the inspiration for *Becoming a College Writer*. We asked each of the interviewees, "What have you learned from your students?" and there was a clear pattern among their answers, perfectly encapsulated by Andrea Lunsford at Stanford University: "They have over the years taught me to shut up and listen to what they had to say."

And so, *Becoming a College Writer* begins and ends by listening closely to the nearly 100 students we interviewed as the research foundation for the text. We travelled to every

region of the United States to interview as diverse an array of students as we could manage within budget and time. Everywhere we visited we proportioned the interviews between students in two-year and four-year programs. We asked local writing instructors to connect us with a diversity of students that represented their campus community, and we specifically asked to meet not just "A-students" and confident writers but those who would represent the experiences of students for whom college writing might not come easily. We did ask for students who seemed like they might be good storytellers and effective interview subjects.

Each stop on our college tour lasted four days, with us typically filming five one-hour interviews per day. At least once per day, I would start the interview and the student would just take off and I wouldn't say much of anything before the tape and time ran out. In *Take 20*, scholar and educator Mike Rose said that the lesson he had learned most from his students was "The extraordinary resilience and variability and majesty of the human mind." After one of those awe-inspiring student interviews would end, I would be speechless for a moment, in true awe of this amazing person, and then the coordinator and I would start to joke that we should publish the interviews uncut and forego corrupting the student voices by wrapping our words around theirs.

There's Nicole talking about the essential connections she sees between social justice and writing. There's Aime'e who says "I really do want to save the world, I just don't know how I'm going to do it yet," which I experienced as the deepest expression of grace and humanity after hearing parts of this student's heavy life story off camera. Crisosto talks about overcoming internalized negative stereotypes of Native Americans in academia, which we can also read in his paper, *Two-Spirit*, included in the book's LaunchPad. And I have one interview from which I learned more than any other — one which remains powerful and awe-inspiring even now after all of the hours of editing and revising and reviewing page proofs, in preparation for this book's publication. Stacy attended Roxbury Community College in Boston at the time, and she tells the story of overcoming, in her own words, a lot of "bad choices" in her life, to return to school. She describes how hard it was at times to swallow her pride and return to an educational level that her children had already passed. Stacy talks about wanting to quit and how the right authors and mentors got her through. I think I might have asked her one or maybe two questions before she began telling her story completely off (my) script. (You can see and hear her speak in the Essentials Video in Lesson 25.) The pages of the print book and the videos that come with this book share amazing insights from wonderful and talented students, many of whom we know endured struggles like Stacy. But there is no interview that for me captures as powerfully as Stacy's does what *Becoming a College Writer* is ultimately about: the dignity, power, and, in Mike Rose's term, "majesty" of the person who writes because it matters deeply to who they are. So, most importantly, in providing the inspiration for writing this book, I wish to acknowledge the Stacy in each of the student interviews and in each student I have ever taught. I am so grateful to them and honored to have heard their stories.

A Multimedia Guide from the Beginning

Like its prequel *Take 20*, this resource was "born digital" and was conceived since the very beginning as a multimedia guide more than a print-and-paper book. *Becoming a College Writer* offers lessons and model student work that enable instructors who want their students to write digital compositions. This text does not assume that writing is a print-bound endeavor, or that the essay is the only academic compositional form (though many of the students interviewed considered it that way). Instead, it offers models of writing across a variety of media, including Sarah's compelling project in Lesson 9: Media, which tells the story of a historic race-car track in North Carolina in six different media formats: print, podcast, film, presentation, website, and mobile application. This lesson also provides guidance for creating writing across those many media formats, while each of the other lessons in the book keeps multimedia composition as a key consideration.

Perhaps one of the best ways to support digital composition pedagogy is the example and design of the "born digital" online edition of the text itself which is available in LaunchPad. This digital component does not just supplement the book, it is a critical part of the pedagogy. While the LaunchPad, with its full e-book, 317 student videos, and nearly 100 models of student writing can stand on its own, the print book truly depends on the resources provided in the LaunchPad. LaunchPad enables the student voices and faces at the heart of this text to come alive in ways that traditional print alone cannot. In LaunchPad, your students can hear and see the students they've met in the pages of the book by viewing the student videos, while exploring and learning from examples of their actual work. This collection of student work is the largest available, and includes access to nearly 100 examples — from essays and research papers, to podcasts and other types of multimodal assignments — more than any other composition textbook. Sorted by discipline, type of writing assignment, and other useful categories, this collection is a powerful resource for students to compare and contrast writing across a variety of disciplines and genres, while learning from their peers. For this reason, the LaunchPad can be packaged with the print book for no additional cost.

Redefining the "Student Centered" Approach

Such a large, varied, and rich archive can be read, analyzed, sifted, and edited in a potentially infinite number of ways, but there do seem to be some fairly clear trends among the experiences of the college writers profiled in this book. First and foremost, students ultimately understand and value the invention-feedback-revision cycle and they are particularly interested in honest, productive feedback from their instructors. This is why the motto and theme **Revise Repeatedly from Feedback** (**RRFF**) is woven into every lesson and exercise throughout *Becoming a College Writer*. If nothing else, from the instructor's perspective, this text is designed to support as much revising from feedback as possible within the space of your course.

Becoming a College Writer is also very much committed to developing each student's identity and confidence as an educated, intellectual person, and as a college writer.

Lesson 2: Writer in particular focuses on such self-perception, and the students who field-tested this textbook consistently reported that beginning to see themselves as writers with something to say was (after **RRFF**) the second most important takeaway from the text. The student interviews that appear throughout this text serve to help students build confidence in themselves as writers, offering relatable advice about problems that are common to beginning college writers. They've done it, and so can your students.

The final key component is the notion of *reader-based prose* and the focus on writing as a dynamic relationship created by the rhetorical situation. Throughout this text, students are encouraged to consider themselves as the authors connected to their audience, topic, and context by bungee cords, so that each shift and pull in a new direction impacts the entire writing assignment. The author is not secondary in this arrangement — their identity is key to creating something new and compelling — but they are part of a larger whole, a unique writing situation, and are encouraged to make decisions accordingly.

The 25 lessons in this book include four key components that support these core goals:

- **An Essentials Video at the start of each lesson** collects the most focused advice from the student interviews about the topic of that lesson. Then throughout each chapter, additional **excerpts from the student interviewees offer advice and encouragement** that prompt the discussion that follows while encouraging students to join a writing community of their peers. All of the student quotes that appear on the pages of the book can be viewed in their original video form, along with the 25 Essentials videos, in LaunchPad.

- **Each lesson opens with a "Why" section that explains *why* students should approach college writing in particular ways** because learning the "how" of a given aspect of college writing makes a lot more sense when you understand "why" it matters and, in some cases. Later in the chapter, **a "How" section provides practical advice on achieving the aims of the lesson** and includes or points to models to illustrate that advice.

- **Practice Activities** appear throughout each chapter and actively demonstrate the ideas within the text by encouraging student interaction as they read the text. Then a set of **Exercises** at the end of each lesson extend, connect, and apply the reading to the student's own writing and development as a college writer. Both the Practice Activities and the Exercises provide connections between the students profiled in that lesson and the student writing that can be accessed in LaunchPad.

- **A dynamic graphic design** that leverages student "call-out" quotation boxes as well as colorful photography, both of which are designed to provide a visual narrative that reinforces the linguistic narrative in the writing.

Lessons 23 and 24 additionally offer **at-a-glance charts that break down the complexities of grammar and citation.** These quick, easy-to-reference resources make information visually appealing and easy to use so that students can get the support they need and get back to writing. Charts on grammar include important topics such as independent and dependent clauses, subject-verb agreement, and parallelism. Citations charts cover the basics of documentation in MLA, APA, and *Chicago*.

Finally, Lesson 25 highlights **six featured students who discuss their writing process in detail** and explain their thoughts on how they wrote the paper that is also included within this lesson. This lesson offers students the opportunity to follow six unique writing journeys and to consider how their own writing process compares.

These lessons have been designed to offer something for everyone in terms of not only different cognitive learning styles, but also different identities and experiences. We made a number of choices to ensure this representation and inclusivity, including the use of the singular *they* throughout the text and the approach we took in curating the student material. As we edited the student interviews — both the six included in Lesson 25 and the hundreds of video clips included in LaunchPad — we worked very hard to represent as many different perspectives and identities as possible for many reasons but, most specifically, because it is essential that we provide as many points of access — as many "ways in" — as possible, so that every student could see something of themselves reflected in these pages.

A Modular Design to Fit Your Course

The commitment in *Becoming a College Writer* to a variety of experiences leads to an intentionally modular design. You and your students might start in Lesson 1 and follow the text in numerical order. Or, you might start in Lesson 19: Thesis or

Part Five: Writers Like You and wind your way through the lessons along your own path. Either way, each lesson is designed to be a modular "turn-key" segment that could stand on its own. This modular structure arises from my experiences as the director of a large writing program that often employs instructors who are new to teaching college composition. In many ways, each lesson is a "greatest hit" in response to frequent questions from new instructors who have asked me many times over the years "How do you teach a lesson on _____?"

In fact, you'll notice that each segment of the text is called a *lesson* and not a *chapter*, because we wanted for you to be able to use them as more-or-less turn-key *Lesson Plans*. On a bad day, perhaps when traffic or domestic logistics disrupt your planning time, you could possibly start a class session cold by opening up to the first page of any lesson (plan) and roll right along. Each lesson defines and redefines key terms such as *audience*, *genre*, *research*, and *process* with an eye toward moving the needle from the most typical high school composition experiences toward college and pre-professional writing. Each lesson (plan) begins with discussion about "Why" students should expand their approaches to writing and then offers practical strategies for "How" to do so. You could begin every lesson plan by screening its corresponding Essentials video, using that screening to prompt discussion about developing as a college writer. Or you could follow along through the reading and use the embedded activities as part of the lesson plan. Students might respond some or all of the student call-out quotations to drive a particular class session. And, of course, you can use the Instructor's manual along with the LaunchPad version of *Becoming a College Writer* to structure your lesson

plans modularly. Either way, the lessons are designed to be easy for instructors use and arranged in a variety of ways that best suit you and your students.

To provide additional support, three "Pathways" in the front of the book offer ready-made syllabi for using *Becoming a College Writer* to teach intro composition, multimodal composition, and writing in the disciplines. These Pathways incorporate Practice Activities and Exercises, as well as suggesting writing assignments. They are a great out-of-the-box way to engage with the text, or a useful foundation for personalizing your course.

Mapped to Outcomes that Reflect Best Practices

Higher education is going through an important reexamination and refocus of its mission, purpose, and value as I write this preface in 2018. Colleges and universities have always provided great value to the communities and nations they serve, and much of this moment of reexamination requires all of us educators to make more explicit the incredibly valuable and powerful things we have always done with and for our students. Our mission has always been to help students develop as citizen-scholars. We have always helped prepare them to contribute to their professions, communities, institutions, and industries. We have always helped students grow stronger as critical thinkers and lifelong learners as capacities that will transfer beyond the immediate experiences of the classroom.

A lot of the conversation about the role and value of higher education at the moment pivots on the key words "learning outcomes," which is why *Becoming a College Writer* is mapped onto the Council of Writing Program Administrators Outcomes Statement. The WPA Outcomes Statement 3.0 identifies four types of primary outcomes for college composition: Rhetorical Knowledge; Critical Thinking, Reading, and Composing; Processes; and Knowledge of Conventions. Consequently, the table of contents in *Becoming a College Writer* is organized in four parts: Rhetoric, Context, Process, and Conventions. It's important to be aware that the WPA Statement does not conceive of any of these parts in isolation — even the outcomes related to conventions, rules, and formats are approached rhetorically and contextually. It's also important to note that the statement defines "composing" as referring "broadly to complex writing processes that are increasingly reliant on the use of digital technologies," which is why, whenever appropriate this text uses the words "compositions," "projects," and "assignments" rather than "papers" — although the student interviews themselves rarely varied from the traditional term.

The need to respond productively to conversations about outcomes and assessment influenced the way I framed the student interviews from the very beginning. Each interview prompt began with a generative question about a specific learning outcome such as "What have you learned about audience awareness?" and "Describe your writing process." The title of each lesson is stated in the form of a learning outcome that complements the WPA Outcomes Statement, and, again, the lessons are grouped according to the four-part structure of the statement. Each lesson has a keyword or key phrase in its title for clarity and focus, and, like the WPA Outcomes Statement, all of these key concepts are approached rhetorically and

contextually, including even (or especially) Lesson 23: Grammar and Lesson 24: Citation. Students might easily insert the words "By the end of first-year composition, you should be able to" in front of each lesson title, such as "By the end of first-year composition, you should be able to clarify your definition of *writing*" (Lesson 1) and "By the end of first-year composition, you should be able to conduct careful research to write with strong evidence" (Lesson 6).

By mapping each lesson title directly onto a learning outcome for college composition courses, *Becoming a College Writer* enables you, as an instructor, to draw direct lines between the text, your class, and increasingly prominent assessment practices. And by mapping these lessons to the WPA Outcomes Statement, we aim to support you and your writing program to better take control of the discussions regarding learning outcomes and assessments.

Gratitude for Many Collaborators

As I was writing this preface, it seemed only natural to use "we" whenever constructing a sentence about the makers/authors of *Becoming a College Writer*. That "we" begins with the nearly one-hundred students interviewed who are the heart and soul of this project. It was such a tremendous honor and experience to meet these former strangers for a brief hour in locations far from my home. I say "former" because, after spending hours screening the video recordings over and over again, I felt like I began to know them. The editorial team and I worked very hard to honor these students by representing them fairly and honestly. I know that I am terribly self-conscious about appearing in video myself (you won't find me anywhere in here), and so I am extremely grateful for their courage and their willingness to share. I hope that ultimately they feel like we enabled them to tell their story in their own terms.

Writing, editing, and publishing a textbook takes a village, or at least an incredible editorial team. I am so pleased to give foremost and heartfelt thanks to Sherry Mooney, who is simultaneously professional and magical. She's the one who really drove this project across the finish line. I have worked with many editors over my career, and none has come close to Sherry. She saved my life and this project in so many ways and on so many occasions that I can never thank her enough. Leaping back in time to the earliest days of *Becoming a College Writer*, I also want to deeply thank Denise Wydra and Joan Feinberg who believed in me and this project and had the vision and courage to innovate so many years ago. Leasa Burton has for decades been an unwavering ally to me professionally and to the field of composition studies. Beth Castrodale, Shannon Walsh, and Ellen Thibault each partnered with me editorially at different stages of the project. Adam Whitehurst has patiently worked with me through all kinds of crazy ideas for how the online edition might look. Kendra LeFleur managed the book's production process and Laura Shaw Feit designed the print book, which is gorgeous. Molly Parke was the Program Manager for the final two years of the push — in fact, she came up with the book's title, while Laura Arcari saw the project across the finish line as the new Program Manager. Vivian Garcia ably assisted with the marketing for this project and Edwin Hill was the Vice President who ultimately signed off on the project, and, I'm told, did a little art direction on the final version of the cover.

I also want to thank the staff at Bedford/ St. Martin's that contributed, especially the interns who transcribed interviews and had to manage the ridiculously large "Todd Taylor Project" cardboard box in the Boston office.

Thanks so much also to the dozens of focus group participants and anonymous reviewers who shared their honest feedback over years of development, as well as the many reviewers whom I would like to thank by name: Justin Atwell, North Dakota State University; Rebecca Babcock, University of Texas, Permian Basin; Laura Beasley, University of West Georgia; Jeanne Bohannon, Reinhardt University; Mark Collins, College of DuPage; John Danzinger, Pace University; Christine Day, Eastern Michigan University; Michael Donnelly, Ball State University; Anthony Edgington, University of Toledo; Richard Eichman, Sauk Valley Community College; Renee Field, Moberly Area Community College; Bryna Siegel Finer, Indiana University of Pennsylvania; Laurie Gries, University of Florida; Cynthia Haynes, Clemson University; Jennifer Hewerdine, Arizona Western College; Jana Hutcheson, Bay Mills Community College; Dennis Jerz, Seton Hill University; Paul LePrade, University of Texas, El Paso; Bonnie Markowski, University of Scranton; Meg Mikovits, Moravian College; Deepak Pant, Southern Illinois University; Erin Presley, Eastern Kentucky University; Deirdre Price, Northwest Florida State College; Jeff Pruchnic, Wayne State University; Allison Randall, Delaware Technical and Community College; Jenny Rice, University of Kentucky; Barb Rowland, University of Phoenix; Ilknur Sancak-Marusa, West Chester University of Pennsylvania; Shillana Sanchez, Arizona State University, Downtown Phoenix; Donna Strickland, University of Missouri.

I am eternally thankful for my mentors Gary Olson and Erika Lindemann whose patience

I tested but whose professionalism endured as I became more independent. As the first public university in the United States, I am extremely proud of and grateful to my home institution: The University of North Carolina at Chapel Hill. James Thompson, Beverly Taylor, and Mary Floyd-Wilson as Chairs of the Department of English and Comparative Literature supported my work in essential ways. Of course, Jill, Max, and Jake are the beginning and end to everything I do and that I am. So many weekends and evenings together were sacrificed for this project and this work that means so much to me, and I am beyond grateful for their support, understanding, and insight.

We're all in. As always.

Bedford/St. Martin's is as passionately committed to the discipline of English as ever, working hard to provide support and services that make it easier for you to teach your course your way.

Find **community support** at the Bedford/St. Martin's English Community (**community .macmillan.com**), where you can follow our *Bits* blog for new teaching ideas, download titles from our professional resource series, and review projects in the pipeline.

Choose **curriculum solutions** that offer flexible custom options, combining our carefully developed print and digital resources, acclaimed works from Macmillan's trade imprints, and your own course or program materials to provide the exact resources your students need. Our approach to customization makes it possible to create a customized project uniquely suited for your students, and based on your enrollment size, return money to your department and raise

your institutional profile with a high-impact author visit through the Macmillan Author Program ("MAP").

Rely on **outstanding service** from your Bedford/St. Martin's sales representative and editorial team. Contact us or visit **macmillanlearning.com** to learn more about any of the options below.

LaunchPad for *Becoming a College Writer: Where Students Learn*

LaunchPad provides engaging content and new ways to get the most out of your book. Get an interactive e-book combined with assessment tools in a fully customizable course space; then assign and mix our resources with yours.

- **Integrated videos** allow students to speak directly from the pages of the text

- **A database of student work** provides flexible models for every writer

- **Diagnostics** provide opportunities to assess areas for improvement and assign additional exercises based on students' needs. Visual reports show performance by topic, class, and student as well as improvement over time.

- **Pre-built units** — including readings, videos, and more — are easy to adapt and assign by adding your own materials and mixing them with our high-quality multimedia content and ready-made assessment options, such as **LearningCurve** adaptive quizzing and Exercise Central.

Use LaunchPad on its own or **integrate it** with your school's learning management system so that your class is always on the same page.

LaunchPad for *Becoming a College Writer* can be purchased on its own or packaged with the print book at a significant discount. An activation code is required. To order LaunchPad for *Becoming a College Writer* with the print book, use ISBN 978-1-319-22421-9. For more information, go to **launchpadworks.com**.

Choose from Alternative Formats of *Becoming a College Writer*

Bedford/St. Martin's offers a range of formats. Choose what works best for you and your students:

- *Print book with LaunchPad*   To order the print book with its LaunchPad packaged for free, use ISBN 978-1-319-22421-9.

- *LaunchPad*   To order the LaunchPad edition by itself, use ISBN 978-1-319-11182-3.

- *Paperback*   To order the paperback student edition without its LaunchPad, use ISBN 978-0-312-48640-2.

- *Popular e-book formats*   For details of our e-book partners, visit **macmillanlearning .com/ebooks**.

Instructor Resources

You have a lot to do in your course. We want to make it easy for you to find the support you need — and to get it quickly.

- *Resources for Teaching Becoming a College Writer* is available as a PDF that can be downloaded from **macmillanlearning .com**. Visit the instructor resources tab for *Becoming a College Writer*. Written by Todd Taylor, this instructor's manual provides guidance on how to find your ideal teaching pathway through *Becoming a College Writer* and breaks down each lesson, pointing to key elements, offering additional writing assignments, and suggesting ideal media accompaniments. Each lesson suggests student writing in the LaunchPad that would be an ideal model for that particular topic. Additionally, Resources for Teaching *Becoming a College Writer* provides a quick-start guide to using the Launch-Pad for *Becoming a College Writer* and suggestions for how to incorporate its rich student essay collection and video resources into your course.

Contents

PART ONE	RHETORIC

PART TWO	CONTEXT

PART THREE PROCESS

Pathway – Intro Composition

This pathway offers a suggested assignment sequence for first-year writing.

WEEK	ACTIVITIES
1	**Introduction** Introduction, Lesson 2, Writer *In Class:* First day materials; Defining a writer Practice activity (p. 3) *Homework:* Read "A Note to Students"; Read Lesson 5, Prompt
2	**Finding a Topic** Lesson 5, Prompt; Lesson 4, Topic *In Class:* Practice Activity (p. 56); Practice Activity (p. 45) *Homework:* Exercise 4e, Analyze student writing (p. 51); Read Lesson 10, Planning; Bring a planner or calendar to the next class
3	**Getting Started** Lesson 10, Planning; Lesson 11, Brainstorming *In Class:* Practice Activity (p. 151) *Homework:* **Rhetorical Analysis Paper**, rough draft
4	**Drafting** Lesson 14, Drafting *In Class:* Exercise 14f, Revise repeatedly from feedback (p. 205) *Homework:* Read Lesson 15, Revising; Rhetorical Analysis Paper, second draft
5	**Early Revisions** Lesson 15, Revising *In Class:* Screen Lesson 15 Essentials Video; Exercise 15f, Revise Repeatedly from Feedback (p. 217) *Homework:* Read Lesson 18, Reflecting; Rhetorical Analysis Paper, final draft
6	**Self-Reflection** Lesson 18, Reflecting *In Class:* Exercise 18f, Revise repeatedly from feedback (p. 261) *Homework:* Read Lesson 21, Paragraphs and Lesson 22, Sentences
7	**Research** Lesson 6, Evidence; Lesson 12, Researching *In Class:* Practice Activity (p. 174) *Homework:* Read Lesson 20, Introductions and Conclusions; **Proposal Paper**, first draft

WEEK	ACTIVITIES
8	**Structuring Your Paper** Lesson 20, Introductions and Conclusions *In Class:* Writing workshop *Homework:* Read Lesson 16, Proofreading; Proposal Paper, second draft
9	**Near-Final Revisions** Lesson 15, Revising; Lesson 16, Proofreading *In Class:* Proofreading journals; Exercise 16d, Invent your writing *Homework:* Proposal Paper final draft; Read Lesson 12, Researching
10	**Structuring Your Paper** Lesson 21, Paragraphs; Lesson 22, Sentences *In Class:* Select 1–2 student essays and work through the Practice Activities in 21.2 (pp. 303–311) *Homework:* **Research Paper**, first draft
11	**Research and Citation** Lesson 12, Researching; Lesson 24, Citation *In Class:* **Annotated bibliographies**; Practice Activity (p. 179) *Homework:* Select a research topic; Create a preliminary source list
12	**Media** Lesson 9, Media *In Class:* Sarah's multimedia project (pp. 127, 131, 139, 141) *Homework:* Research Paper, second draft; Multimodal component plan
13	**Finalizing a Project** Lesson 17, Publishing *In Class:* Exercise 17e, Analyze student writing (p. 248) *Homework:* Polish Research Paper; Apply the relevant "Safe bet" standards from Lesson 17
14	**Wrap Up** Presentations *In Class:* Presentations of final papers *Homework:* Research Paper final draft with self-reflection

Pathway – Multimodal Composition

This pathway offers a suggested assignment sequence for a multimodal composition course.

WEEK	ACTIVITIES
1	**Introduction** Introduction, Lesson 1, Writing *In Class:* First day materials, Writing as a dynamic relationship (pp. 7–9) *Homework:* Read "A Note to Students"; Read Lesson 3, Audience
2	**Audience** Lesson 3, Audience *In Class:* Exercise 3d, Invent your writing (p. 39) *Homework:* Practice Activity: Office hours appointment (p. 34); Read Lesson 7, Genre; View Lesson 7 Essentials Video
3	**Genre** Lesson 7, Genre *In Class:* Practice Activity (p. 89) *Homework:* Write 2,000 words in a chosen genre; Make an attempt to include relevant formatting
4	**Media** Lesson 9, Media *In Class:* Explore Sarah's project in different media formats *Homework:* Adapt your 2,000-word assignment to a different media format
5	**Planning and Research** Lesson 10, Planning; Lesson 12, Researching *In Class:* Screen Lesson 10 Essentials Video; Practice Activity (p. 179) *Homework:* Brainstorm topics and plan your multistage writing project
6	**Thesis** Lesson 19, Thesis *In Class:* Lesson 19 Practice Activities: Nicole's Thesis (pp. 269–275) *Homework:* First draft of multistage writing project in one of three formats: print, video, or audio
7	**Formatting for Print, Video, and Audio** Lesson 17, Publishing *In Class:* Discuss "Safe bet" standards; Exercise 17d, Invent your writing (p. 248) *Homework:* Final draft of multistage writing project, first format

WEEK	ACTIVITIES
8	**Drafting** Lesson 14, Drafting *In Class:* Exercise 14d, Invent your writing (p. 205) *Homework:* First draft of multistage writing project in a second format: website, social media site, or multimedia presentation
9	**Revision** Lesson 15, Revising *In Class:* Screen Lesson 15 Essentials Video; Exercise 15f, Revise repeatedly from feedback (p. 217) *Homework:* Second draft of multistage writing project in second format
10	**Online and In-person Presentations** Lesson 17, Publishing *In Class:* Exercise 17a: Integrate the video (p. 247); Discuss "Safe bet" standards *Homework:* Read Lesson 16, Proofreading
11	**Proofreading** Lesson 16, Proofreading *In Class:* Screen Lesson 16 Essentials Video; Practice Activity (p. 222) *Homework:* Final draft of multistage writing project in second format
12	**Presentations** *In Class:* Project presentations *Homework:* Read Lesson 18, Reflection
13	**Reflection** Lesson 18, Reflection *In Class:* Screen Lesson 18 Essentials Video; Exercise 18c, See yourself as a writer (p. 260) *Homework:* Exercise 18f, Revise repeatedly from feedback (p. 261)
14	**Wrap Up** Lesson 2, Writer *In Class:* Exercise 2c, See yourself as a writer (p. 26)

Pathway – Writing in the Disciplines

This pathway offers a suggested assignment sequence for a writing in the disciplines course.

WEEK	ACTIVITIES
1	**Introduction** Introduction, Lesson 1, Writing *In Class:* First day materials, Practice Activity (p. 3) *Homework:* Read "A Note to Students"; Exercise 1c, See yourself as a writer (p. 14)
2	**Writing in the Disciplines** Lesson 3, Audience *In Class:* Screen Lesson 3 Essentials Video; Practice Activity (p. 33) *Homework:* Exercise 3e, Analyze student writing (p. 39)
3	**Writing in the Disciplines** Lesson 6, Evidence *In Class:* Discuss 6.1 (pp. 65–68); Discuss what constitutes evidence in different disciplines *Homework:* Practice Activity (p. 80)
4	**Writing in the Disciplines** Lesson 8, Discipline *In Class:* Screen Lesson 8 Essentials Video; Exercise 8a, Integrate the video (p. 117) *Homework:* Read Lesson 8; Exercise 8d, Invent your writing (p. 118)
5	**Humanities** Lesson 25, Student Interviews and Sample Papers; Lesson 19, Thesis *In Class:* Look at models of humanities papers in the book and LaunchPad; Examine how the theses are similar and different *Homework:* Write a **Rhetorical Analysis** of one of the model essays
6	**Humanities** Lesson 22, Sentences *In Class:* Discuss 22d, Invent your writing (p. 325) *Homework:* Revise your Rhetorical Analysis using the Paramedic Method
7	**Humanities** Lesson 15, Revising *In Class:* Screen Lesson 15 Essentials Video; Discuss 15.2, How to Revise Repeatedly from Feedback *Homework:* Final revision of Rhetorical Analysis

WEEK	ACTIVITIES
8	**Social Sciences** Lesson 25, Student Interviews & Sample Papers; Lesson 4, Topic *In Class:* Narrowing a topic for the social sciences; Practice Activity (p. 48) *Homework:* Exercise 4e, Analyze student writing; Practice Activity (p. 176)
9	**Social Sciences** Lesson 12, Researching *In Class:* Practice Activity (p. 179) *Homework:* Collect 5–7 sources on your topic and use them to develop a thesis and outline for a research paper
10	**Social Sciences** Lesson 7, Genre *In Class:* 7.2: How to analyze and compare genres to meet audience expectations *Homework:* First draft, **Research Paper**
11	**Sciences** Lesson 25, Student Interviews and Sample Papers; Lesson 13, Organizing *In Class:* Practice Activity (p. 185); Discuss common formats in science writing *Homework:* Final draft, Research Paper; Conduct a **Literature Review** of three scientific sources on the same topic
12	**Sciences** Lesson 21, Paragraphs *In Class:* Practice Activity (p. 307) *Homework:* Draft the analysis/discussion of a report using your three sources, synthesizing their responses
13	**Sciences** Lesson 16, Proofreading *In Class:* Exercise 16f, Revise repeatedly from feedback (p. 232) *Homework:* Draft a full **Scientific Report**, including introduction, methods, results, analysis, and conclusion
14	**Closing Thoughts** *In Class:* Lesson 18, Reflecting *Homework:* Final Scientific Report with self-reflection due

How This Book Supports WPA Outcomes for First-Year Composition

NOTE: This chart aligns with the latest Writing Program Administrators Outcomes Statement, ratified in July 2014.

WPA Outcomes	Relevant Features of *Becoming a College Writer*
Rhetorical Knowledge	
Learn and use key rhetorical concepts through analyzing and composing a variety of texts.	Part One: Rhetoric guides students to clarify their definitions of key rhetorical concepts. The concept of the rhetorical triangle is introduced as a flexible model that adapts and flexes with each new rhetorical decision. This model, first introduced on page 7, resurfaces as a touchstone throughout the text and serves as an important framework for understanding the intricacies of the writing process.
Gain experience reading and composing in several genres to understand how genre conventions shape and are shaped by readers' and writers' practices and purposes.	Lesson 7, Genre introduces the wide range of genres in academic, popular, and career-oriented writing. It advises students on how to analyze and compare genres in order to meet an audience's expectations.
Develop facility in responding to a variety of situations and contexts, calling for purposeful shifts in voice, tone, level of formality, design, medium, and/or structure.	Part Two: Context provides five lessons that break down the rhetorical situation, prompting students to adapt their writing based on the prompt, genre, discipline, media, and evidence in use. This necessary adaptiveness is also addressed in Part One: Rhetoric, which discusses how audience and topic impact a writing situation.
Understand and use a variety of technologies to address a range of audiences.	Use of various technologies underpins all of *Becoming a College Writer,* from the video library to the many multimodal student essays. Additionally, Lesson 9, Media provides a thorough grounding in various media options and how to select the best fit for a particular context; Lesson 17, Publishing includes guidelines for polishing a variety of print, audio, and video assignments.
Match the capacities of different environments (e.g., print and electronic) to varying rhetorical situations.	Lesson 7, Genre and Lesson 9, Media most directly address the question of different environments and their suitability for differing rhetorical situations. In addition, the notion of rhetorical context is with students in every lesson of the book, often portrayed by a bungee-cord metaphor.
Critical Thinking, Reading, and Composing	
Use composing and reading for inquiry, learning, thinking, and communicating in various rhetorical contexts.	Each lesson in Part Two: Context encourages students to engage with reading and writing through the framework of a number of different contexts: their assignment prompt (Lesson 5), the evidence they discover (Lesson 6), the genre in which they are writing (Lesson 7), the discipline in which they are writing (Lesson 8), and the media with which they choose to present their writing (Lesson 9).

WPA Outcomes	Relevant Features of *Becoming a College Writer*
Read a diverse range of texts, attending especially to relationships between assertion and evidence, to patterns of organization, to interplay between verbal and nonverbal elements, and how these features function for different audiences and situations.	Lesson 25 features six students speaking at length about their writing processes and sharing their completed writing projects. The LaunchPad for *Becoming a College Writer* includes nearly 100 additional student works across a variety of genres, disciplines, and topics, inviting students to make comparisons and explore the variety of rhetorical choices available to them.
Locate and evaluate primary and secondary research materials, including journal articles, essays, books, databases, and informal Internet sources.	See in particular Lesson 6, Evidence (pp. 64–83), which offers a thorough discussion of how to locate and evaluate a variety of scholarly and nonscholarly sources.
Use strategies — such as interpretation, synthesis, response, critique, and design/redesign — to compose texts that integrate the writer's ideas with those from appropriate sources.	Taylor embraces the premise that good writing is evidence-based writing — whether that evidence comes from scholarly research or from the writer's own experience. Lesson 6, Evidence advises students on how to craft their evidence-based writing by responding to and critiquing their sources, while Lesson 14, Drafting and Lesson 15, Revising encourage them to design and redesign their work until it best meets the needs of their audience.
Processes	
Develop a writing project through multiple drafts.	Drafting and revision are at the heart of *Becoming a College Writer*. Part Three: Process guides students through the key (and recurring) phases of the process: Planning (Lesson 10), Brainstorming (Lesson 11), Researching (Lesson 12), Organizing (Lesson 13), Drafting (Lesson 14), Revising (Lesson 15), Proofreading (Lesson 16), Publishing (Lesson 17), and Reflecting (Lesson 18).
Develop flexible strategies for reading, drafting, reviewing, collaboration, revising, rewriting, rereading, and editing.	See the previous entry. Additionally, the "Practice" features throughout the book and the exercises at the end of each lesson prompt students to take specific key steps toward exploring their own writing processes and developing strong writing habits. Advice from nearly 100 students is also sprinkled throughout the book, offering insight into the many rhetorical and stylistic choices that are available.
Use composing processes and tools as a means to discover and reconsider ideas.	A focus on research and inquiry suffuses *Becoming a College Writer*, but composing processes are covered in detail in Part Three: Process (Lessons 10–18), including Lesson 18, Reflecting, which encourages students to pause and reflect on each element of their writing process and how it aids them in their intellectual growth and development. The text also points to model student writing in the book and the full LaunchPad to illustrate how different contexts and topics produce a variety of results.

WPA Outcomes	Relevant Features of *Becoming a College Writer*
Experience the collaborative and social aspects of writing processes.	Throughout the book, students are encouraged to talk to instructors and peers about their writing and writing process. One of the guiding principles of the book is to Revise Repeatedly from Feedback, with an exercise in each lesson reminding students of the importance of scholarly collaboration. Additionally, *Becoming a College Writer* provides students with the perspectives of nearly 100 college writers and encourages them to share with their peers their own insights, struggles, and breakthroughs. Lesson 17, Publishing also encourages students to consider a broader audience for their work and to remember that they have important contributions to make to ongoing discussions outside of academia.
Learn to give and act on productive feedback to works in progress.	See the previous rubric. Lesson 15, Revising, in particular, offers robust strategies for Revising Repeatedly from Feedback (pp. 209–215).
Adapt composing processes for a variety of technologies and modalities.	Part Two: Context provides guidance for considering the context of the writing situation and how to adapt the writing process accordingly. In particular, Lesson 9, Media addresses the best approach for different technologies and modalities. Lesson 17, Publishing also supports students in polishing their final work in whichever modality they have chosen.
Reflect on the development of composing practices and how those practices influence their work.	Lesson 18, Reflecting is built on the premise that reflection is a key component in growing as a writer. It provides students with strategies for considering their own composing practices and how those practices are situated within the larger framework of academic and writing communities. Additionally, Lesson 17, Publishing reminds students to consider their work in the context of a larger audience, and asks them to reflect on how each audience informs their writing process and compositional decisions.
Knowledge of Conventions	
Develop knowledge of linguistic structures, including grammar, punctuation, and spelling, through practice in composing and revising.	Revising Repeatedly from Feedback is a key principle in *Becoming a College Writer*, one that encourages students to consistently seek to improve their use of language. Lesson 23, Grammar provides at-a-glance grammar charts, giving students the information they need when they need it. Lesson 18, Reflecting also encourages students to use their composing and revising processes to intentionally and strategically grow and develop their skills.
Understand why genre conventions for structure, paragraphing, tone, and mechanics vary.	Although genre conventions are emphasized throughout the text, they are given particular attention in Lesson 7, Genre, which offers guidance on how to analyze and compare genres to meet audience expectations.

WPA Outcomes	Relevant Features of *Becoming a College Writer*
Gain experience negotiating variations in genre conventions.	Although considerations of genre are imbued throughout the book, Lesson 7, Genre introduces students to the concept and offers sound advice for navigating genre differences and the associated audience expectations.
Learn common formats and/or design features for different kinds of texts.	In Lesson 13, Organizing, students are introduced to approaches for structuring their writing to meet the demands of different kinds of texts. Lesson 17, Publishing completes the process, providing a set of "safe bet" guidelines for formatting and designing in a number of key genres.
Explore the concepts of intellectual property (such as fair use and copyright) that motivate documentation conventions.	Lesson 6, Evidence lays the groundwork for consideration of intellectual property and why it is so important to give credit to others for their work. Lesson 12, Researching provides guidelines for finding intellectual property and reiterates the importance of correct documentation. Lesson 24, Citation addresses the conventions behind documentation, while Lesson 9, Media addresses the concept of fair use and how it applies to the wide range of content students might choose to incorporate into their own writing (see p. 133).
Practice applying citation conventions systematically in their own work.	Lesson 24, Citation offers at-a-glance citation charts on each of the foundational concepts of citation in MLA, APA, and *Chicago*.

Rhetoric

The four lessons in Part One prompt you to build dynamic relationships between yourself, your audiences, and your work by redefining the elements of the rhetorical triangle.

Lesson 1 | **Writing** | Clarify your definition of writing.

Lesson 2 | **Writer** | See yourself as a writer.

Lesson 3 | **Audience** | Understand and interact with your audience.

Lesson 4 | **Topic** | Write about a topic that matters to you.

LESSON 1

Writing

Clarify your definition of writing.

lexilee/Getty Images

Visit the LaunchPad for *Becoming a College Writer* to watch the Lesson 1 Essentials Video.

1.1 [WHY]

Why you should clarify your definition of writing.

Each lesson in this text focuses on a specific key term. Lesson 1 asks you to focus on your understanding of the term *writing*. Why? So that you can strengthen the writing you do — in college and beyond.

A growth mind-set urges you to ask: "What do I already know about writing?" "What does it mean to write in college?" "How will *college writing* benefit me and add to my abilities?"

Think about the kind of writing you did in high school, and the deeper, more advanced writing that defines college composition. How does that reflection contribute to your working definition of the term *writing*?

PRACTICE Let's get started right away. Write down a single-sentence definition of the word *writing* in the space provided. You might imagine a dictionary definition of the word, although I don't want you to look at a dictionary for this exercise.

If it helps, try filling in one of the following blanks: "Writing can be defined as _____" or "Writing is _____." It's important that you do not lose track of this definition and that you literally and actually pause to write this down in your own words.

My definition of writing:

_____

_____

_____.

It will be interesting to look back at this definition at the end of the course to see how your perceptions have evolved. In this way, your definition can serve as a sort of time capsule for tracking your growth.

I've begun every writing class I've ever taught with this exercise because I believe it is crucial that each student have a clear sense of exactly what writing is or should be. Why? Because your definition of *writing* can function as a compass, guiding you as you head out for a long hike. If you have a well-defined focal point on the horizon, you are much more likely to travel efficiently and arrive at your destination comfortably. The same is true of writing.

Before you move on to the next section of Lesson 1, make sure you didn't just quickly toss off a definition to get through the previous exercise. Instead, you should have provided an *operational definition*, or one that reflects your instincts about what writing is. In other words, this definition should get across the notion of *writing* that you have deep in your heart or in your (previously) subconscious thoughts. This operational definition will be a compass that will set your direction and influence your choices as a writer.

Ninety percent of my students define *writing* as most dictionaries do: "Writing is putting your thoughts on paper," or "Writing is representing thoughts and words with letters." Since nine out of ten students agree with the dictionaries, they must be correct, right?

Actually, the answer is more complicated.

You are of course aware that dictionaries provide multiple definitions for each term — there's not just one definition of *writing*. For this lesson, I want you to consider three of the most common definitions of writing:

1) **Writing as a code**
2) **Writing as a process**
3) **Writing as a dynamic relationship**

PRACTICE As you read, consider which of these three definitions is closest to the definition that you just wrote at the beginning of Section 1.1.

Writing as a code.

Most dictionaries, and 90 percent of my students, first define **writing as a code**, as a noun, as the inscription of letters or characters to represent words. If your deeply embedded operational definition of *writing* is that it is a code, then you tend to focus on "getting the code right." With this definition of writing, imagine yourself on a desert island, with your best chance of survival being an SOS note, stuffed into a bottle and tossed into the ocean. You want to "code" your message so that some person at the other end of a vast sea will be able to decode it and rescue you.

VINH-THUY
Red Rocks Community College

An essay is not about following a math formula. . . . It's about writing about what you really, really like and writing passionately about what you really like and what you believe in. . . . So, when you do it the right way, you know you've done it the right way. When I write something that I did not put all of my mental capacities in, or I didn't put my heart and soul into, it doesn't feel like it's something that someone should read. Because if I can't even read through that and be proud of it, then it's not worth someone else's time, honestly.

As Vinh-Thuy suggests, a limitation of "writing as a code" is that if you're guided by this view, you can become so anxious about getting the code "right" that you lose sight of the bigger ideas you're trying to communicate. This approach can also be isolating: It might make you feel like you're all alone trying to translate your ideas into a code. This can make you focus too much on your own thoughts and not enough on your readers. As a student writer, you know that it is important to get the code right, to follow the rules, for example, by avoiding mechanical errors that will interfere with your meaning. But as Timothy reminds us, there is much more to writing than that.

TIMOTHY
Red Rocks Community College

After I took a formal English class, I realized that there's a lot more to words than just putting them on paper. There's meaning behind them, and you have to think about the reader — that's really the whole point.

Writing as a process.

Most dictionaries, and about 5 percent of my students, define *writing* as a verb as well as a noun. They think of writing as more of an action ("I write.") than an object ("Here is the writing I produced.") — as more of an experience than something you can hold in your hand, as more of a process than a product. If you wrote a research paper in high school, it's likely that your instructor required you to do so in stages, such as brainstorming, outlining, drafting, revising, and proofreading.

This approach defines **writing as a process**, in which teachers focus on the moves a student makes at each stage. The process approach to writing makes me think of footprints painted on the floor of a dancing class that illustrate the sequence of steps to follow for the tango, waltz, or fox trot.

Andrew Olney/Getty Images

Approaching writing as a process can help you improve your writing, and it is a focus of many high school writing classes. But, as Elizabeth points out, this operational definition has its limitations, too.

ELIZABETH
Palomar College

From high school I remember that you prewrite, you write, you edit, and revise, and then you're done, published. But, in college the difference for me has been that it's very specific: you have a class, you have a topic, and you write about that. And in high school you're writing just to write, just to do it. In college you're writing with a goal in mind.

Writing is a deeply human and creative thing, and learning how to do it by following prescribed steps can feel robotic. You might begin to learn the tango by following painted steps on the floor of a dance studio, but you are not really dancing the tango until you add flair, passion, rhythm, improvisation, and interaction with your partner — the human elements of dancing.

A robot can be programmed to follow steps on the floor, but it could never tango as beautifully as a human. Following a step-by-step process and getting advice on each step can be a great way to get started. But writing is really much, much more than a process.

ASHIA
Michigan State University

In our class we've been working on rhetorical analysis. To me that means making a connection with your audience. Making your audience believe that you are a reliable source, and that you really have a deep connection with what you are saying.

Writing as a dynamic relationship.

Here's the operational definition of *writing* that I strongly encourage you to drink in, the one that best gets at what I think writing is ultimately about:

> **Writing is a dynamic relationship between a writer, an audience, and a topic.**

Yes, writing is a code and a process, but it is most profoundly a relationship: between you, your audience, and the subject you are writing about. Like the key to writing that I discussed in the introduction to this text (**Revise Repeatedly from Feedback**), this operational definition is so essential that I hope you will never forget it. If you keep this definition fixed in your mind, and if this dynamic relationship is your steady compass, you will be a successful writer.

This definition of this dynamic relationship has been well established and field-tested over thousands of years. Teachers and thinkers have called it many things, but it is most famously known as Aristotle's "rhetorical triangle," which he lectured on 2,300 years ago. So, imagine a triangle, with you, the writer, at one point, your audience at a second point, and your topic at the third point. Now imagine some kind of connection between each of these points. I like to imagine rubber bungee cords because I think bungee cords are cool and because they are dynamic: They stretch, contract, link, relate, and *hold things together*.

In this definition, you are connected to your audience, your audience is connected to your writing topic, and your writing topic is connected to you. Each of these points in the rhetorical triangle pushes and pulls on the others in an active relationship.

To illustrate how this works, imagine that you are writing to a parent, grandparent, or former teacher about how you spent your first weekend in college. Take a moment and consider how you would write your message. How would it begin? What kind of highlights would you list? What kind of language would you use?

Now, imagine you were writing to your wildest, rowdiest friend about your first weekend in college. How different would your message be? Would you email your parent, but send your friend a text message? It's the same author (you) and the same topic (your first weekend), but as your audience changes, your writing is pulled in different directions because, again, *writing is a dynamic relationship between a writer, an audience, and a topic*. Can you feel the bungee cords pulling you around?

When Aristotle first described the rhetorical triangle, he was actually talking primarily about spoken communication because most people in ancient Greece exchanged information through speech, not writing. Now that writing is an essential form of communication, we need to add a fourth dimension to Aristotle's triangle: **context**.

If *context* seems like an unfamiliar idea, don't worry; we will cover this concept in Part Two. For the moment, think of context as the situation in which you are writing. Let's simplify the vast galaxy of potential contexts to the one that is most relevant to you right now: college writing. Nancy Sommers, a teacher, scholar, and colleague

I admire greatly, stated it very nicely when she said, "Academic writing as a genre is defined by its use of sources." I strongly recommend that you add Nancy's insight to your operational definition of "college writing":

> **College writing is a dynamic relationship between a writer/researcher, an audience/ discipline, a topic/question, and the sources/ evidence that support the writing.**

Like the elemental particles that make up a molecule, college writing is made from the relationship between four elements:

1) **Writer**
2) **Audience**
3) **Topic**
4) **Evidence**

Like the electronic forces that hold the elements of a molecule together, *context* is a specific arrangement that holds rhetorical elements together. In the "rhetorical molecule" diagram below, the red lines (the bungee cords in the dynamic relationship) are the context that arranges the elements and holds them together.

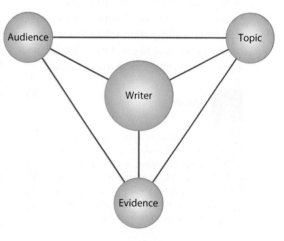

These four elements and their dynamic relationship are so important that the next eight lessons explore them in depth. Lesson 2 asks you to define and redefine your ideas about yourself as a **writer**. Lesson 3 explores **audience**, Lesson 4 discusses **topic**, and Lessons 5–9 consider different aspects of **context**.

PRACTICE But before we dive into these elements further, take a moment to solidify your true, operational definition of writing. How do you define writing now? How do you define college writing so far?

Writing is _____.

College writing is _____.

Hopefully, your approach to writing has already begun to grow.

1.2 [HOW]

How to clarify your own definition of writing.

A) College writing advances and improves your abilities beyond high school.

GRETCHEN
Boston University

The best thing about college writing is that you learn a lot and you become a better writer. The worst thing about college writing is it's college writing, so it's going to be difficult and you're going to have to rewrite things. You're going to have to write [about] books that you might not want to read. But, once it is over, you realize that you have become a better writer than when you started.

Because your success in college hinges on powerful writing and communication abilities, let's approach college writing in terms of building on your existing skills, the ones you acquired in high school. Let's take the foundation you already have as a writer and push it as far as you can go within a given course, academic term, or degree program.

PRACTICE In order to build upon your education, it's important for you to record and reflect on what you already know. Take a few more minutes to redefine the general term *writing* in the context of *high school writing*: What was the emphasis in high school writing? What was high school writing all about for you? What were the most important skills and concepts that you took from high school writing? Use the space below to reflect. Once you've reflected on the skills you have, you can begin to develop them.

High school writing was _____

_____

_____.

B) College writing draws on evidence and sources.

Earlier in the lesson I quote my colleague Nancy Sommers, who points out that college writing is defined by its reliance on evidence and sources. College writing is academic writing, and academic writing at the college level is built upon evidence and detail, which come from careful study and research. College writing is research-based writing; there is no separation between the two, as Yadirys recognizes on the next page.

YADIRYS
Boston University

My writing style has changed dramatically because in high school it wasn't as academic. In high school you don't have to use academic, scholarly papers when you reference people, but in college you do. You need to be as academic as possible, and you need to sound as professional as possible as an adult.

College writing stresses serious research, evidence, detail, and fact because that's how new knowledge is made. It's also how the professional world operates. The difference between an amateur and a professional is this: A professional works with highly refined and tested knowledge, whereas an amateur operates with limited knowledge and experience, which can include relying on assumptions and speculation.

College writing, therefore, is designed to transition writers from amateur approaches to professional ones. As you take a professional approach, you base your writing on advanced thinking, which requires research, evidence, detail, and the integration of expert perspectives.

⮌ Lesson 6: Evidence (p. 64) explores this idea more closely.

PRACTICE Take a glance at the body paragraphs of any of the model papers provided in Lesson 25. Write down the number of times the writer uses evidence, detail, serious research, or fact within one page of writing. Describe in a couple of sentences how the model's use of evidence and sources either does or does not seem to define college writing.

C) College writing prepares you to write well in your other classes and in your profession.

ELIZABETH
Palomar College

Seriously, the best class I ever took was English 100. I learned more in that class than in any [other] because I learned how to write. And that helped me everywhere else.

First-year composition is by far the most commonly required college course. You are most likely reading this text because you are currently enrolled in such a course and your instructor assigned it. College writing (or composition) courses are required because writing is central to every class, every discipline, and every profession. *Becoming a College Writer* prepares you to write successfully in your other courses and throughout your academic career.

College writing also prepares you to succeed in your career after graduation. Sure, academic writing practice is important for avoiding potentially embarrassing grammatical mistakes. But academic writing is even more important as a way to help you think, learn, communicate, and make meaning in any setting.

Too many people wrongly assume that some careers, such as engineering or medicine, do not require reading and writing skills, but that is not the case — just ask any engineer or health-care professional. Scientists and engineers do need to be exceptionally good at math, but as Frank reminds us, their work won't go anywhere if they cannot explain it to others.

FRANK
Michigan State University

I'm an electrical engineer and the more I've practiced writing, the more papers I have done, the [better] I can write a lab report, the quicker I can do it, the easier I can do it. . . . It's important to be a good writer in the professional world to successfully communicate with your boss and to describe the work you are doing to people who are going to use your object or design.

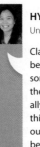

HYESU
University of Florida

Clarity is pretty important, especially because now we're not writing for some generic English course most of the time. Now, we're writing to actually communicate new ideas — the things we're supposed to think of for ourselves: independent thought. So, because these ideas we are trying to communicate become much more complex, clarity is a really big thing that college writers have to consider.

So, college writing prepares you, not only for your future coursework (where you will write many papers, exams, reports, and notes), but also for your future professional work, where you will need to develop and communicate your ideas through writing.

PRACTICE Compile a list of all of the writing assignments that you will complete this term in other classes beyond your college composition course. Share and compare your list with others. Describe in a couple of complete sentences some of the ways that your college composition course can prepare you for the writing assignments on your list.

D) College writing connects you with an audience and a writing topic.

I have asked you to imagine a rhetorical triangle with three points — a writer (you), an audience, and a topic — in a dynamic relationship that is a foundation for college writing. I'd also like to stress that moving away from a *writer-based* approach and toward *audience-based* composing is what college writing is all about.

Many of the students interviewed in *Becoming a College Writer* emphasized the importance of *clarity* in their writing, as Hyesu does.

Writers and readers talk about the importance of *clarity*, yet, ironically, it might not be perfectly clear what clarity is or how to achieve it. I would like to argue that clarity is the result of a close, dynamic relationship between a writer, a topic, and an audience. If these elements are tightly related, then there are *clear* connections among them. For example, the purpose of each lesson in this textbook is to help you strengthen the connections between you as a writer, the work that you write about, and your readers. Writing with clarity requires *reader-based* prose, as opposed to *writer-based* prose, which is in danger of being clear only within your own head. That is, your writing should aim to be integrated and connected in ways that your reader or audience understands.

PRACTICE *Clarity* is often an overused and under-defined term employed to describe effective writing. But what does it really mean? Can you describe a time when you have been asked to write with clarity or when someone asked you to "clarify" or "be clear" in your writing? Write down how you would have defined *writing clearly* before you began reading this lesson. Describe the ways that definition might be changing.

E) College writing educates you, the writer.

Remember the compass illustration from earlier in this lesson? It was meant to encourage you to focus your definition of writing so that you could head in the right direction. Now I'd like you to think about your purposes in completing college writing assignments. Why do you write in college? What is valuable about completing your assignments?

Unfortunately, some students think that college writing is a game that is mostly about giving teachers what they want. But the purpose of writing is not to please a teacher or to play a game; the reason you write is to grow intellectually. Getting an "A" out of your professor is a pretty empty goal in itself, but earning an "A" because you worked really hard and strengthened your mind is definitely worthwhile. Good grades happen on the road to good writing, not the other way around.

GREGG
California State University, San Marcos

When I started realizing that what I was doing at the academy was something that I could draw into all the parts of life and start[ed] sharing what I was learning, it became more powerful for me. I had a greater engagement and a greater desire to do the work in the first place because it's not just: "How can I keep my grades up and get done with my degree?" It's: "What can I actually take from my classes that impacts the world around me?"

Sometimes instructors assign writing for short-term purposes — to see if you read assigned material or paid attention to a lecture. However, the "big-picture" reason you write in college is to learn more and to deepen your education.

Defining writing as a dynamic relationship between an author, a topic, and an audience means that writing isn't something you do to demonstrate that learning already happened; writing is something you do to enable learning and intellectual growth to happen in the first place. Writing is not proof of learning; writing is the vehicle through which learning takes place. Yes, college writing is about learning to write, but college writing is also about writing in order to learn.

↰ **Lesson 6: Evidence extends this idea further.** See p. 64.

PRACTICE Now write down a few sentences that answer the questions at the beginning of 1.2 E. What do you see as the purposes of completing college writing assignments? Why do you write in college? What is valuable about completing your assignments?

F) College writing allows you to integrate the elements of writing, rhetoric, and learning.

If you look at the Contents for this textbook, you'll see that it's organized into twenty-five lessons. Each one focuses on a specific key element or term. Although it's helpful to break out specific terms into lessons, your success in college writing will depend on the degree to which you put all of these pieces back together for yourself. College composition courses break down and redefine writing one element at time, one day at a time, and one class session at a time. Ultimately, your evolution as a college writer will correspond directly with how well you integrate all of the pieces, lessons, and key terms covered in this textbook. College writer and artist Nanaissa compares writing an essay to sculpting a human figure to illustrate this principle.

NANAISSA
Lansing Community College

Writing is sculpture. And even when I sculpt, I kind of think about writing, too; they are linked together. . . . You really go into detail, and you try to understand why you put this here, put [each piece in place]. When I had to sculpt the human body, I didn't realize how much the neck muscles work to support the head. It's only when I tried to sculpt the head that I had to correct it. I do exactly the same thing in writing. You can't say "just write it and it's gonna work." You have to try it and check if it fits. And if it fails, just start it again. If you want to do it seriously, it's a lot of work—it's thinking about every word you write, every time you write.

At one point, I thought about naming this book *Writing with Integrity* to emphasize the importance of *integrating* the key dimensions of your definitions, purposes, and processes for writing. So, as the concluding idea in this opening lesson, I want to encourage you to create deeply dynamic relationships between you, your writing, your audiences, and your topics by integrating each of these twenty-five lessons into your approaches to college writing.

1.3

Exercises: writing

1a Integrate the video.

On page 7, Ashia defines writing as a dynamic relationship when she says, "In our class we've been working on rhetorical analysis. To me that means making a connection with your audience. Making your audience believe that you are a reliable source, and that you really have a deep connection with what you are saying."

Write a substantial paragraph or two, with a topic sentence or mini-thesis, through which you respond to Ashia and other videos in the chapter as you form your own definitions of *writing* and *college writing*. You can watch the Lesson 1 Essentials Video, or you can browse the embedded clips in the online edition of this lesson. You might begin by identifying the moments that stand out to you the most. Which student videos seem to make the most sense to you? With whom do you agree? Disagree? What patterns do you find among the student sound bites? Which ideas were the most instructive or helpful to you? What surprised you? How have your own ideas about "writing" come into focus through the videos?

1b Create a journal entry or blog.

Your instructor might ask you to keep a writer's journal throughout this class. This journal could be handwritten or composed on a computer; it could take the shape of a text-based blog or a video blog.

To prepare a journal entry on Lesson 1, define in your own words the key term *writing*, trying not to glance back at the material in this lesson, at first. Not referring to this material initially will help you see what you have internalized so far. After carefully composing your initial definition, look back at some of the definitions other students gave in Lesson 1 or in the online database of interviews. For example, in his interview, Deonta defines college writing as being about growth, improving from feedback, and making connections with readers:

What's helped me become a stronger writer is not necessarily the grade that I get on the paper but the feedback that I get from professors. And being able to sit down and talk about how I could do better on the next paper or what it was in the paper that worked or didn't work. So that's been a great help to me in improving my writing. And it also has enabled me to make relationships with people that I may not have been connected to before.

You might wish to disagree with some of this lesson, or you might want to modify or expand on some of its advice. For example, consider integrating additional thoughts, notes, and lessons from your instructor and your class meetings into your journal entry. It might help for you to imagine that you are giving advice to your future self about writing. What lessons from this chapter and from discussions about writing might benefit you down the road?

1c See yourself as a writer.

In a page or two, describe the evolution of your definitions of the word *writing* since you began writing. Where and when does your definition of *writing* begin? What major events, assignments, and papers have influenced your definition along the way? What particular teachers or classes have reshaped your definition? What was your definition before you began reading this lesson? What is your definition now that you have finished this lesson? In what ways can you imagine your definition of *writing* changing beyond college? How does your development as a writer compare with what other students said in their interviews, such as Vinh-Thuy, who has experienced a lot of freedom in his two college writing classes:

> I think college writing is being able to freely express who you want to be. In high school it's kind of hard to write about who you want to be because you're kind of discovering yourself. But, in college, you can really say whatever [you] want to say, because college is all about freedom of expression.

1d Invent your writing.

Section 1.2 of this lesson discusses six ideas (A through F) that define college writing. In six complete sentences, map out how each of these six concepts could be applied to a writing assignment you are working on in this class (or in another class, if you are not currently writing in this course). For example, section 1.2.E argues that "college writing educates you, the writer," and Kendra describes in her interview how she wrote a paper about Komodo dragons because she was curious about how they killed their prey; so, she used the principle in section 1.2.E to help drive or invent her scientific writing assignment.

1e Analyze student writing.

Study the opening two or three paragraphs or segments of a couple of model projects in Lesson 25 or in the LaunchPad. You might compare very different models, such as Dan's video and Nicole's paper, or you might read similar work, such as Nanaissa's and Vinh-Thuy's papers.

For each writer, describe in a sentence or two the kind of "college writing" each of these authors seems to offer. Based on the students' work, what definition of *writing* does each of them seem to hold? How does each of these definitions compare with the others? In what ways do they seem alike? Different? Which of the definitions of *writing*, as discussed in this lesson, does each piece of writing exhibit?

Your instructor might ask you to apply this analysis and these questions to your class-mates' writing instead (or in addition to the model projects).

1f Revise repeatedly from feedback.

Examine a writing assignment you are currently working on or one that you wrote recently, perhaps in another class or in high school. What definition of *writing* does your assignment seem to hold? What aspects of the writing support that definition and why? Describe some specific ways that you can use the ideas from Lesson 1 to revise your writing and improve as a college writer.

Writer

See yourself as a writer.

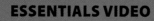

> **Visit the LaunchPad for** *Becoming a College Writer* **to watch the Lesson 2 Essentials Video.**

2.1 [WHY]

Why you should see yourself as a writer.

Close your eyes and meditate for a few moments on the picture that comes to mind when you think of a writer.

No, really, take a moment and do this.

Really.

What did you see?

If you're like many college students, you might have pictured a professional (i.e., paid) or famous writer. But why not picture yourself as a writer? In fact, that is the first step toward becoming a successful college writer. Don't let a lack of confidence or experience get in your way. You are probably not as good a writer as Shakespeare, but neither am I. That does not mean that we're not writers.

Mike Palmquist is a scholar and a professor of writing at Colorado State University. Before becoming a writing teacher, he was a college track and cross-country coach at the University of St. Thomas in St. Paul, Minnesota. As a new writing instructor, he was shocked to meet so many students who lacked confidence in themselves as writers. In his analogy, cross-country runners are racers like college students are writers: If you are in the race, you can run; so, if you are in college, then you can write. It doesn't make sense to be in a race thinking that you can't run, just as it doesn't make sense to be in college thinking that you can't write.

A writer can be defined as someone who writes and who has something to say.

MIKE
Colorado State University

Before I went to graduate school, I had been a college cross-country and track coach for several years, and it never occurred to me that one of my athletes would go out into a competition thinking, "I don't really have what it takes to be successful at this." But when I walked into the writing classroom, so many of my students said, "You know, I'm really not a good writer. I really don't have the gift for writing." And it just floored me.

NICOLE
California State University, San Marcos

To call myself a writer has been a struggle for me. I remember when I first arrived at the four-year university that I transferred to, I was in a creative writing class, and my teacher said, "You know, we're all writers." . . . I guess I kind of linked it to [the idea that] a writer has to be published — a writer has to be accomplished. Through my journey, I've come to this: If you're speaking about a writer in terms of a "professional" or a "profession," [then] no, I'm not yet a writer. But if you're speaking about *writer* as a verb [as in, *to write*], then yes, I'm a writer.

In many ways, as Nicole, a student at California State University, points out, it might be more helpful to think in terms of the verb *to write* rather than the noun *writer*, since the act of writing makes you a writer.

Do you think of yourself as a writer? If not, you may be buying into dysfunctional myths about writers and writing, as shown in the following examples. **Becoming a college writer** can mean getting beyond such myths.

What makes someone a writer? Some myths and facts.

Myth: A writer is a literary genius working alone in a marble tower, an oak-paneled study, or a hipster coffee shop.

CRISOSTO
Metropolitan State University of Denver

I'm Mescalero Apache and I grew up on that reservation in New Mexico. I'm the only person in my family that has a high school diploma. I'm also the only one in my family that has a college degree under my belt, and I'm looking forward to getting my second degree. I grew up in a family of eight, and we were sort of considered impoverished. So those experiences I think definitely play into a lot of what I've transformed into as far as [being] a writer. . . .

Because of the stigma that a lot of Native Americans grew up with . . . I think that is internalized. That certainly happened with me [in terms of what] academic work should look like and how it should be accomplished. So in my whole journey, I've never asked [if I was a "writer"] because I never wanted to be deemed an idiot or be seen as stupid or whatever.

Fact: Actually, what defines all writers, professional, famous, or not, is the simple act of writing. When you write, you are a writer. Furthermore, most writers work in collaboration with readers, editors, and other writers; they do not work in isolation. In Lesson 1, *writing* was defined as a dynamic relationship between an author, an audience, and a topic. As for being isolated, while you might be physically alone when you write so that you can concentrate, the act of writing is intrinsically about connecting with other people. The myth of the solitary "literary genius" denies the vast majority of us the power and experience to make connections and meaning through our writing.

Myth: Some students are writers and some students are not.

Fact: Language is fundamental to being human, and reading and creating written language are fundamental to being an educated person. Thus, all students are writers. Maybe you have a friend who gets better grades than you on her school papers. Maybe, like Crisosto, you struggle with negative ideas about yourself or your writing abilities. Or maybe you admire a famous author and feel as if your own writing does not compare. Even so, that doesn't mean you are not a writer. You can think, you can read, and you can write: abilities that define you as an educated person and a college student.

RYAN
Palomar College

Yes, I do consider myself a writer because writing is important for everything that I do [and has been] ever since I was in high school. Writing is something that you do all of the time, in most every class you're engaged in, whether it be English or physics or anthropology.

Myth: Some students are "naturally" good with language, while others are "naturally" good at math.

Fact: If you subscribe to this myth, it's possible that divisive ideas about learning have skewed your perception of yourself as a writer. The idea that you cannot be good at both language and math is not supported by research or science, yet it is reinforced by many schools and institutions. The language arts classrooms in my high school were at opposite ends of the building from math and science. This idea is also reinforced by standardized tests that have separate scores for reading, writing, and mathematics.

Myth: So-called "right-brained" (creative) people tend to be better writers than so-called "left-brained" (analytical) types.

Fact: A second divisive idea is that our brains are hardwired into two separate hemispheres, namely, the right (creative) side versus the left (analytical) side. In practice, we need to write both creatively and analytically, because writing is fundamental to all kinds of disciplines and ways of thinking and is essential to learning in all classes, as Ryan points out on the previous page.

Presumptions about gender are often built into the myths around right- and left-brained people. Too often we're encouraged to associate mental "splits" as follows: Women are supposed to be more creative, whereas men are allegedly more analytical. While it's true that parts of the brain have different functions and purposes, it's also true that higher-order thinking happens precisely when many parts of our brain work in concert. In other words, we are at our intellectual best when we exercise both creative and analytical abilities *at the same time*. Writing does

this, requiring us to be linguistic and creative and also logical and analytical. Do not allow gender or cultural biases to prevent you and your classmates from using all of your mental capacities to their fullest.

Myth: Writing comes easily for some people.

MATT
Metropolitan State University of Denver

The difference in the approach from high school to college is that, for one, I'm not cranking papers out the night before. I'm definitely putting a lot more time into my writing, so I'm not handing in first-draft stuff. It's definitely a process. [I] start with a thesis, and I continually change my thesis to support my grounds and then from there move on — and it's just definitely a good process that takes three weeks or so.

Fact: It's true that some writers have an easy time filling pages, but they are the exception rather than the rule. Writing requires concentration and effort, and the biographies of most world-famous authors are filled with stories of sweat and struggle. Writing is a complicated intellectual activity that activates many parts of your brain, and it's definitely work. In fact, the ability to produce a lot of writing quickly isn't necessarily a good thing. As Matt reports, college writing takes concentration and effort. Like most things, the more you practice, the better you become.

PRACTICE Take five minutes and write down a list of myths or presumptions that you previously held about yourself as a college writer. Compare your list with others in your class. Cross out the ideas that you no longer believe to be true or that are likely to interfere with your development as a college writer.

Becoming a college writer requires persistence (and perhaps a selfie).

I've identified a few of the common myths that can get in your way as you work to become a stronger writer. Can you think of other misperceptions that cloud your image of yourself as a writer? If so, try to get at the falsehoods and assumptions built into those ideas. You will see that they lack foundation.

While seeing yourself as a writer might not happen immediately — it didn't for Gina — it will happen with persistence. Once you begin to define *a writer* as *someone who writes* and *someone who has something to say,* you should find, like Gina, that you are indeed a writer. This self-perception is powerful.

GINA
Metropolitan State University of Denver

I do consider myself a writer. It took me awhile to get there. [From] my first college writing class, when I re-entered school, I knew that I wanted to be a writer. I knew that writing was something that I loved to do. But I couldn't quite bring myself to call myself a writer. That was a question that we had to address at the end of the semester, and it felt like such a big thing to be able to say: "I'm a writer."

The next part of Lesson 2 asks you to further embrace your identity as a writer and outlines concrete habits for improving your craft. But before we move on, think to yourself: "A writer is: ____"; then close your eyes again and visualize yourself.

Now, imagine you're looking at a dictionary entry for the word *writer*. Imagine yourself (and not Shakespeare this time) portrayed in an illustration beside that entry, in an image

of you at work, writing. Take a selfie of you working on a college writing assignment. Now imagine that the definition in that dictionary is "a writer is a person who writes" and paste your selfie next to that definition. Maybe convert your selfie into a meme that includes the word "writer" or "college writer."

Really.

Then turn the page.

2.2   [HOW]

How to see yourself as a writer.

Writing is an essential, fundamental intellectual activity that defines you as an educated person. Don't let anyone take writing away from you. Instead, begin with a positive self-image of yourself as a writer. Following are five essential habits of successful writers. The more you practice these habits, the more you will see yourself as a writer.

A) Develop a network of readers and writers who can respond to your writing.

In the introduction to this text, we established that the key to success in all writing, not just college writing, is to **Revise Repeatedly from Feedback (RRFF).** To get such feedback, you need an inner circle of people to respond to your writing so that you can improve it. Ideally, this circle will include the following:

- **Your instructor:** Sometimes instructors are available to respond to drafts of papers, often during their office hours. If your instructor is available to provide such help, take advantage of that opportunity!

- **Class peers:** Often, your writing classes will be organized as a workshop, in which students respond to each other's drafts. Is there someone in your class who seems to be able to give you good advice about writing? If so, you might comment on each other's writing even outside of the class workshop.

- **Writing center tutors:** Most colleges and universities have a writing center staffed with people who are trained to give students productive feedback. In the professional world, you might have to pay hundreds or thousands of dollars to get this type of help from an editor or writing coach. At writing centers, however, tutors typically offer feedback for free.

- **Friends or relatives:** Many of the students interviewed for this text describe a particular person — often a parent or close friend — who gives them feedback on their writing before it's handed in. Consider whether you have a parent, friend, or sibling who could give you honest, informed, and helpful feedback.

In addition to building an inner circle of people who respond to your writing, you also need to think of yourself as positioned within a larger, outer circle of people whom you may not know but who are interested in your topic.

Your writing will inevitably address an issue or question that is important to this larger group and will build upon ongoing conversations about the topic. For example, when writing in college, you will often need to base your thoughts on what others have said or published about your topic. You will also want to add something new to the wider debate or discussion that others are having about your topic.

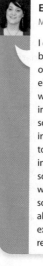

ERIENNE
Metropolitan State University of Denver

I consider myself to be a writer because I think that it's more of a way of being in the world than anything else. . . . A real writer is also someone who devotes themselves to translating this immutable and ambivalent sort of very abstract world of ideas, into language that we can all relate to. You think of a writer as a very introspective person, and they're very solitary. But a good writer is someone who [has] their introspection and their solitude, but they know how to take all of these moments of solitude and express them in a way that people can relate to them.

So, your network includes not only the people you consulted before writing, but also others who might be interested in what you discover and what you have to say. Social media now make it easy to visualize and connect with networks of people who can respond to your work. The quotations from college writers embedded throughout this text are formatted to resemble social media posts to help you envision a network of writers with whom you are connected. Cultivate audiences who can respond to your work.

↰ **Lesson 3: Audience (p. 27) explores writing networks in more depth.**

PRACTICE Take five minutes to write down a list of people who you might ask to respond to your writing in this class. Try to name some people from each of the four listed categories. Also, remember that this text

introduces you to many college writers like you. Throughout this course, you should browse their interviews for advice and insights and consider them part of your writing network too.

B) Express your ideas.

HANNAH
California State University, San Marcos

[Writers are] responsible for creating and imagining and revising new ideas, and that's what any writer is going to do. So if you can do that — and if you can challenge other people through your writing — I think that's what makes a writer. And since I do that, that classifies me as a writer.

Writers of novels, screenplays, and songs will often describe a burning desire to tell a story. It's as if their story is an about-to-be-born baby just beyond the due date, who is kicking to get out into the world. In academic settings, finding that kind of inspiration might seem tricky, especially if you're given an assignment that you don't connect with at first. But keep this in mind: Any idea worth writing a college paper about ultimately connects to you and the human condition in some way. Try to find those connections.

What aspects of the topic do you relate to particularly? How does it affect your life and the lives of others? Successful writers are able to find such connections, even when doing so is hard work. As Hannah points out, writers don't simply capture ideas that are already in circulation; she argues that writers are "responsible" for the development and rethinking of ideas in the first place. So, as a writer, you're not merely packaging thoughts into words; you also have something to say that will influence your world.

MAYA
Massachusetts Bay Community College

I feel very strongly connected to the things that I want to write about. It's very emotional and personal for me to write about these things, and [doing so] really makes sense of the thoughts in my head, you know? It makes me understand who I am and make sense of the world. It's weird, because before this class, I was so confused about myself and I was so confused about other people in the world. I couldn't understand anything. And it was hard. And because I feel so strongly about it, it's making it easier for me to write and research.

Writers create and revise new ideas and critical thought; they also use words to make sense of their own experiences, as Maya and Aime'e do. As a writer, you position yourself in the world through what you write. And as a successful writer, rather than "telling" your audience what to do or think, you use writing to locate yourself within your own experience, connect with others, and gain understanding of your world.

AIME'E
Red Rocks Community College

I think of myself as a writer because in order for me to remember or be able to look back on most of the things that I've done, I would have needed to have documented it. And, I like to know what's going on in my life. I like to know what's going on around the world, in my country, and other countries. What's going on with other people? Because I really do want to save the world. I just don't know how I'm going to do it yet.

To sum up, writing is at its best when you have something that you're burning to say. In fact, writing tends to become much more effortless when you have ideas to express and discoveries you are working to make.

↰ Lesson 4: Topic (p. 41) and Lesson 5: Prompt (p. 54) explore connecting to writing and responding to writing prompts in more depth.

PRACTICE Hannah uses writing to be "responsible for creating new ideas." Maya uses it to understand her world, and Aime'e uses writing to try to change the world. Can you describe a time when you used writing to accomplish one or all three of these goals? If not, describe how you can imagine that using your writing to accomplish those goals would impact your writing assignments.

C) Develop your voice.

In spy and crime movies, a "voice print," like a fingerprint or signature, is sometimes used to identify a person because each person's voice is unique, at least when analyzed mathematically. The analogy between an orator's spoken voice and an author's written voice isn't much of a stretch because both are based upon words, language, tone, style, and idiosyncrasies. Everyone has a unique, personal spoken voice, just as everyone has a unique, personal written voice.

NICOLE
California State University, San Marcos

I think college writing is worth the challenge, because it opens you up to a way to express your voice. You have your opinions, you have your voice; but then, with college writing, there's so much more to learn. It roots your voice. It grounds your voice. And it's a way for people to comprehend what you are actually thinking and what you're trying to get out there — the message you're trying to push. When I think of "voice," I think of the individual. Voice is linked to the individual. It's a piece of you. It's your personal style. It's your rhetoric.

Hogie/Getty Images

For Nicole, college writing is very much about finding your voice. Just as a professional singer takes lessons to develop and improve a musical voice, you, as a college writer, are working to develop and improve your written voice. Developing your written voice is a matter of preparation (reading and studying other writers), practice (exercising and experimenting with your voice), and performance (delivering your words to an audience and gaining confidence based on your impact).

In the introduction to this text, I said that the secret to writing is **RRFF**. The more often you draft, get feedback, and revise, the better your written voice will become. Perhaps the best way to develop your written voice would be to first read your draft aloud to yourself and see how it sounds to you. Does your written voice feel natural to you, like your spoken voice? If not, you might be writing with a voice that is not authentic to you. It's okay — crucial, actually — that you be and sound like yourself.

PRACTICE Read the first three paragraphs of Nicole's magical realism paper in Lesson 25. Locate two or three sentences when her voice seems to come through distinctly. Discuss and compare the sentences you located with what others in your class found. Do these sentences seem particularly strong or weak? How are Nicole's thoughts about voice reflected in the sentences you read?

Lesson 22: Sentences (p. 314) explores voice and style in more depth.

D) Identify and interact with your readers.

In Lesson 1: Writing, we defined writing as a dynamic relationship between a writer, an audience, and a topic. We've established that a writer is a person who has something to say to others. Although writing requires some solitary time to get words down, writers need to keep in mind the audiences they're writing to. As Erienne pointed out: "A writer knows how to take moments of solitude and express them in a way that people can relate to them." As a writer, think of the needs and expectations of your readers. Interact with those readers in order to better understand them. This idea is so important that all of Lesson 3: Audience focuses on understanding and interacting with your readers.

For your college papers, your instructor is often your initial reader on the way to reaching larger audiences. Regardless, the more interactions you have with your readers, the better you'll understand audience expectations. That said, you may have other layers in your audience — inside and outside the classroom. Interacting with anyone in your writing network will help you improve. As Nicole mentions in her interview, a classmate helped her successfully redirect her paper on magical realism (p. 461).

VINH-THUY
Red Rocks Community College

When I write, I'm much more opinionated than I am in person. It might not seem like it at the moment, but I'm a pretty quiet person at school, at college, and at home. I don't really have much to say and I don't really want to say much. But when I write, it allows me to put my thoughts and all the opinions that I don't get to just say to a person, or maybe I don't get to just voice my opinions out to a crowd. I get to put it on paper and I can put it in a way that I can edit it to a point where it's just a very fluid and very effective argument.

Vinh-Thuy talks about being socially reserved and keeping his thoughts to himself, except when it comes to writing, where the creative opportunities drive him to express his ideas passionately. He uses writing to connect with people in important ways.

PRACTICE As a writer, it's a good idea to get to know a little bit about your readers, especially if they're going to be grading or otherwise commenting on your work. If your audience is larger than the class, take five minutes online and research what you can about your external audience. If your first reader is your instructor, take five minutes and see if your school's website includes a biography, résumé, or information on research or publications for your instructor. If your secondary audience is a specific academic community, do some research on that as well. Now take five minutes to write down three to five sentences that describe how your readers' backgrounds might shape their expectations regarding your writing.

When instructors give you a prompt for a writing assignment, pay careful attention to each word they write and say about the assignment because they are telling you what they expect and defining your audience (also see Lesson 5: Prompt). Ask any questions you have about the assignment prompt as soon as possible. Take a draft of the first page to your instructor during office hours and well ahead of the deadline. Get as much feedback as you need. Some questions you may want to ask are: "What do we know about the audience for this assignment?" (see Lesson 3: Audience), "What kind of genre is appropriate for this assignment?" (see Lesson 7: Genre), and "What might be some helpful sources for my research?" (see Lesson 6: Evidence).

E) Exercise your writing muscles.

MARK
Palomar College

I constantly write in my notebook, and I'm constantly writing verses with the aspirations to write a book or to actually sit down and write something bigger. But I consider myself a writer because I always write. You know, I would not feel like myself without a notebook or without having something to write my ideas down.

Your writing ability is very much like a muscle. When you use it regularly and exercise it intelligently, it becomes stronger. Mark, a student at Palomar College, carries a notebook and writes down his ideas constantly — he's always exercising his writing muscles. Mark exemplifies how writing can become much more than something you do in school for a grade. It can become a "way of being in the world" as Erienne said earlier. It can be a way to find meaning and connection, as Aime'e and Maya described.

While writing to participate in the world, find meaning, and connect with others requires focus and practice, well-crafted writing doesn't have to be painful or scary. Just remember the secret to successful college writing: **RRFF**. To strengthen your writing muscles, you need to go to "the gym of RRFF" as often as you can.

Each part of your practice is supported by this text, from planning to brainstorming to drafting to reflecting (see Part Three). If **RRFF** is the gym, then each part of your process is a different exercise machine on which to build your writing muscles.

As any gym trainer will tell you: Use it or lose it. Research on college writing shows that abilities can decline after a student's first-year composition course because instructors and students sometimes avoid writing assignments. So it's a very good thing to have gym buddies. With the support of your network, you can be a lifelong writer, making improvements along the way, well beyond your first year in college. Because writing will become a part of your life, you will keep toning the muscles you're building right now.

PRACTICE Remember that at the beginning of this lesson a *writer* is defined as *someone who writes*, and we encouraged you to take a selfie as you worked on a college writing assignment so you could *see yourself as a writer*. Now take out your calendar and write down actual "appointments" for the next two weeks. How many days per week will you write? How many sessions per day? How many minutes per session? How often will you go to the "writing gym" to strengthen your muscles? Write down the names of the "gym buddies" or "personal trainers" who will help you exercise your writing muscles in each session.

2.3

Exercises: writer

2a Integrate the video.

Early in this lesson, Nicole, Crisosto, and Gina describe their struggles to see themselves as writers. They eventually overcome those struggles by redefining the term *writer* to be more inclusive. Write a substantial paragraph or two, with a topic sentence or mini-thesis, through which you respond to Nicole, Crisosto, and Gina, as well as other videos in the lesson, as you form your own definitions of *writer* and *college writer*. You can watch the Lesson 2 Essentials Video, or you can browse

the embedded clips in the online edition of this lesson. You might begin by identifying the moments that stand out to you the most. Which student videos seem to make the most sense to you? With whom do you agree? Disagree? What patterns do you find among the student sound bites? Which ideas were the most instructive or helpful to you? What surprised you? How have your own ideas about the word *writer* come into focus through the videos?

2b Create a journal entry or blog.

Your instructor might ask you to keep a writer's journal throughout this class. This journal could be handwritten or composed on a computer; it could take the shape of a text-based blog or a video blog.

To prepare a journal entry on Lesson 2, define in your own words the key term *writer*, trying not to glance back at the material in this lesson, at first. Not referring to this material initially will help you see what you have internalized so far. After carefully composing your initial definition, look back at some of the definitions other students gave in Lesson 2 or in the online database of interviews. For example, in his interview, Dan defines *writer* in terms of producing and circulating content that impacts audiences in more practical and less "lofty" or "snooty" ways:

> [For me], originally a writer was someone who sat in their loft apartment in New York and typed on their typewriter and sent their book in every couple of years and made a bunch of money. . . . Now I'm realizing that's not a writer — that's a "snooty writer," I suppose. But what the people who are actually producing writing [do is strategize] how to produce content, how to deliver content, and eventually how to continue to maintain content.

You might wish to disagree with some of this chapter, or you might want to modify or expand on some of its advice. For example, consider integrating additional thoughts, notes, and lessons from your instructor and your class meetings into your journal entry. It might help for you to imagine that you are giving advice to your future self about writing. What ideas from this lesson and from discussions about writing might benefit you down the road?

2c See yourself as a writer.

In a page or two, describe the evolution of your definitions of the word *writer* since you began writing. Where and when does your definition of *writer* begin? What major events, assignments, and papers have influenced your definition of *writer* along the way? What particular teachers or classes have reshaped your definition? What was your definition before you began reading this chapter? What is your definition now that you have finished this lesson? In what ways can you imagine your definition of *writer* changing beyond college? How does your development as a writer compare with what other students said in their interviews, such as Nanaissa who experienced dramatic improvements in her self-perception as a writer as she moved from one school system (in France) to another (in the United States):

> In France, [instructors] don't care about what you think. That's what I really like in [my US school]. I thought, "Whoa! I can write what I think, and I won't be punished for that?" I got punished a lot [in the French schools] because I wrote with too much passion. So, I really prefer the American freedom when [writing].

2d Invent your writing.

Section 2.2 of this lesson discusses five ideas (A through E) that define college writing. In five complete sentences, map out how each of these five concepts could be applied to a writing assignment you are working on in this class (or in another class, if you are not

currently writing in this course). For example, section 2.2.A asks you to develop a network of readers and writers who can respond to your writing, and sections 2.2.E encourages you to write regularly. Take a moment and write down the names of people who can help you on a current college writing assignment. Then write down on a calendar specific appointments with each of those readers to improve your self-perception as a writer as you invent and develop your own writing assignment.

2e Analyze students like you.

Study the opening three to five paragraphs of two interviews in Lesson 25 or in the Launch-Pad. You might choose interviews from students who seem a lot like you or different from you — or one of each. You could also search through two interview transcripts for the word *writer* to see what they say. Or you could study their interview videos to get a sense of that person as a writer.

Describe in a paragraph how the students define themselves as *college writers*. What definition of *writer* does each of them seem to hold? How does each of these definitions compare with others? In what ways do they seem alike? Different? Which definitions of *writer* discussed in this lesson does each interview reflect or reject?

Your instructor might ask you to apply this analysis and these questions to your classmates' autobiographies (or in addition to the featured students).

2f Revise repeatedly from feedback.

Examine a writing assignment you are currently working on or one that you wrote recently, perhaps in another class or in high school. Describe some specific ways that you can use the ideas from Lesson 2 to revise your writing and improve as a college writer.

LESSON 3

Audience

Understand and interact with your audience.

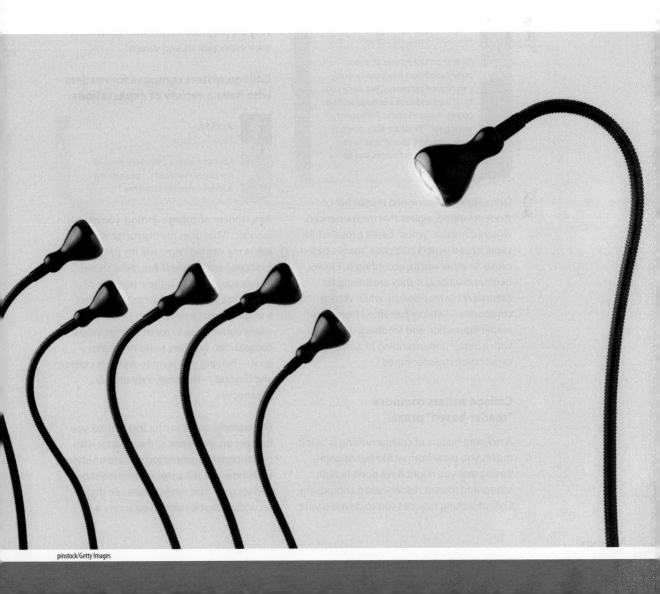

ESSENTIALS VIDEO

Visit the LaunchPad for *Becoming a College Writer* to watch the Lesson 3 Essentials Video.

3.1 [WHY]

Why you must understand and interact with your audience.

TIMOTHY
Red Rocks Community College

[In high school,] it was all about myself and how I processed words and created sentences. But once I got to college and took a college writing course, it was all about: "Who am I writing to?" "What are they going to think about my ideas?" and "Is my point going to get across and be powerful?"

Linda Flower, a renowned researcher of student writing, argues that inexperienced writers compose "writer-based prose" while experienced writers compose "reader-based prose." In other words, according to Flower, beginners write as if they are talking to themselves (writer-based), while veteran composers — who've benefited from more reader interaction and feedback — write with a better understanding of audience expectations (reader-based).

College writers compose "reader-based" prose.

A defining feature of college writing is that it moves you away from writer-based composing that you might have done in high school and toward reader-based composing. College writing requires you to develop your audience awareness. It puts you in situations with a variety of audiences and asks that you pay attention to how your readers respond to your writing. To become a reader-based writer, ask yourself: Who are my readers? Why are they reading my writing? What are their expectations and values?

College writers compose for readers who have a variety of expectations.

ALYSSA
Santa Fe College

I became aware that every piece of my paper mattered . . . because my audience doesn't know me.

As a student of college writing, you may wonder: What does my instructor want to see in my writing? How will my projects be evaluated and graded? Are these things purely subjective or is there more to it? Let's break that down. Just as there is not a single correct way to write, there is not a single correct way to teach writing. While composition teachers share the same goal — helping you learn to write for college and beyond — they may vary in their approaches.

For example, some instructors will ask you to make an argument and support it with evidence, while others focus more on style or on how you tell a story. Some insist on perfect grammar, while others see that as secondary to your ideas. Some care a lot about the research behind your writing, while others want to see how well you integrate course material. Most writing teachers care about all of these things to some extent, but they choose to focus on specific aspects of your compositions.

Every writing teacher I know works hard to define expectations clearly and to grade fairly and consistently. Likewise, there are clear patterns that define good college writing. This textbook explains those patterns, and you can learn them and succeed.

At the same time, the variety and subjectivity of your readers (especially as you branch out and write for other courses and disciplines) is good for you — it's healthy — precisely because it helps you learn how to connect and communicate with a wide range of people. It helps you learn how to appeal to ever-widening audiences. It teaches you how to negotiate the real world beyond school, where there is no answer key in the back of the textbook. It gives you practice writing for audiences as you become an experienced, reader-based writer.

College writers and readers are dynamic and diverse. You and your fellow students represent a variety of backgrounds, personalities, and values — as well as different learning preferences and writing styles. You are responding to an equally diverse set of assignments and writing for a variety of purposes and instructors. For those reasons, we have drawn on numerous interviews with students from across the United States, whose experiences as college writers will enrich the discussion of writing for an audience.

PRACTICE Take five minutes to describe three different instructors who required you to write an assignment (either in college or high school). What did each emphasize? How were their expectations different and the same? How did the nature of the course seem to influence the type of writing that each instructor valued? How were the writing assignments different and similar?

College writers *Revise Repeatedly from Feedback.*

As I write in the introduction and repeat in almost every lesson, the key to college writing is to **Revise Repeatedly from Feedback (RRFF)**. Where does that informed feedback come from? It comes from your readers. The more readers you face, the better you'll become at meeting most any expectations. I invite you to embrace this challenge. There are rewards: As you compose for different audiences in college, your writing and critical thinking skills will grow. Further, if your instructor asks you to participate in peer editing for your papers, you will not only learn from the work of others and become a better reader yourself, but also get to see how others experience your writing.

The more carefully you listen to someone as they read and share their thoughts about your writing, the better you will become as a writer. As you listen, try to let go of any defensiveness you may feel and focus on what is constructive. Do your best to find as many different readers as you can in the time you have — and do your best to capture everything they say.

The best way to become a reader-based writer is to get feedback in a face-to-face environment where you can listen and concentrate. Other kinds of feedback can work too, including online interchanges, notes written in the margins or at the end of your papers, and even voice- or video-recorded responses.

Lesson 1: Writing defined *writing* as **a dynamic relationship between a writer, an audience, and a topic**. It asked you to imagine a triangle — with the writer, audience, and topic positioned at each of the three points respectively. Imagine if you didn't think about your reader. One of those points would be missing and your whole writing triangle would collapse. To become a reader-based writer, and to keep your writing triangle strong, take into account all of the reader feedback you can get.

PRACTICE Spend at least five minutes sitting with an informed reader as they read through a draft of your writing line by line. Write down at least three things that either you noticed yourself or that they pointed out to you that could improve the draft. If you have never had an instructor read a draft of your writing line by line, then make an appointment during office hours to have that experience for at least fifteen minutes — or go to the writing center. Write down what you learned.

3.2 [HOW]

How to understand and interact with your audience.

As a college writer, you must know your audiences and interact with them so that you can write with their needs in mind. In this section you will find nine concrete practices that will help you understand, interact with, and write for your audiences.

A) Talk with your instructor. Share drafts of work in progress.

YADIRYS
Boston University

The advice I would give to others about succeeding in college writing would be: See your professors a lot. Honestly. First semester, I did not see my professors. And then I learned; second semester I became best friends with my writing professor.

There is one thing that each of the students I interviewed agrees upon: The most helpful thing a writing instructor can do is to give specific, constructive feedback. I recommend meeting with your instructor during his or her office hours. A one-on-one, face-to-face conference in a quiet environment can be very effective. Remember: In order to **Revise Repeatedly from Feedback**, you need to know what your instructor expects, what you need to focus on and improve, and how your final work will be evaluated.

B) Research your audiences — especially your primary audience.

DAN
Michigan State University

More than just researching the topic, I also think that researching your audience . . . is vital to really writing well and writing effectively.

You know that cliché "You can't understand someone until you walk a mile in their shoes"? As a reader-based writer, not only do you need to walk in your readers' shoes, you need to walk through their neighborhood, speaking their language while doing so.

Each of our perspectives is strongly influenced by the physical and cultural world we encounter every single day. As a reader-based writer, you want to learn to see the world through your reader's eyes as best you can.

In the context of college composition, each class meeting gives you the opportunity to improve your audience awareness. Your instructor might be your primary audience, but it's more likely that you should aim for an audience beyond the class; your instructor is there to help you reach a larger, external audience. Either way, your instructor is likely to model or explain audience expectations, so you want to study and interact with your instructor to best understand your readers.

What do you know about your readers' writing and scholarly interests? For example, college professors publish articles and give conference presentations about their research, and these materials are often available online or in libraries. You can learn a lot about someone, especially about them as a reader, in just ten minutes of studying their professional profile, résumé, or published work on your college's website.

Get to know your readers, not only through research, but also through interactions in class. Most of what your teachers say — and everything they ask you to do as part of their course — reveals something about their expectations as readers of your writing. Make a study of these clues. As Dan suggests, pay careful attention to the ideas, key words, and activities that your teacher emphasizes and you will develop a better understanding of what they will value in your writing.

To make the most of your class sessions, train yourself to ask thoughtful questions. Be present and engaged. You learn more about your instructor and fellow students as readers, and you will retain more information. Avoid shying away in the back row and retreating into your own thoughts. Active learning is more effective than passive listening and will help you on your way to becoming a reader-based college writer.

In becoming a college writer, you will also want to connect confidently and effectively with audiences beyond your class and instructors. As you read the following sections, imagine your sense of audience expanding in ever-widening circles beyond your classmates and instructors.

PRACTICE If you didn't already do so in Lesson 2, take five minutes and conduct a quick online search for your writing instructor; look on your college's website to see if your instructor has a biography, résumé, research profile, or publications. Now do some research on any secondary audiences. Take five minutes to write down three to five sentences that describe how your audience's background might shape their expectations regarding college writing.

C) Interact with your peers.

ASHIA
Michigan State University

In high school the only audience we had was basically the teacher, because she was grading [our writing]. But now I feel like our audience is our class — everybody looked at our papers. So, now I know how to approach different subjects differently with different audiences.

Lesson 2: Writer, section 2.2 outlines the habits of successful writers. Number one on that list is: "Develop a network of readers and writers who can respond to your writing." Among the students I interviewed for this text, many value and depend on their writing networks. They describe an array of readers who give them feedback, readers including peers, writing center tutors, friends, and family members.

While writing instructors are typically the very best source of feedback for a given assignment, they may not be available at the exact moment you need help. For a quick response, a classmate will be able to give you informed feedback. They have a good sense of your course work and instructor's expectations. In a pinch you can seek the advice of a parent or sibling, but unless they are in the class too, they will lack insights into your audience and the assignment.

Part of your work in most writing courses these days is to provide your peers with informed feedback too. When you respond to the writing of others, most typically as part of an in-class draft workshop, you naturally place yourself on the other side of the desk. That is, assuming your instructor is the primary audience for you and your peers, you will try to see your classmates' work from your instructor's perspective when you give them feedback. In a sense, you are finding out what it's like "to walk in your instructor's shoes." For example, nearly every day in one of my writing classes, students whose work we will read together in class will notice mistakes they made before the discussion even begins because they suddenly see their writing from the point of view of their readers.

PRACTICE The activity at the end of section 3.1 asked you to spend at least five

minutes sitting with a reader as they read through a draft of your writing line by line. Now spend at least five minutes reading through and responding to a peer's draft. Write down at least three things that you noticed that could improve the draft. Did your peer notice improvements to make as you were reading, even before you pointed out a recommendation for revision?

D) Know your audience, especially if it extends beyond your instructor and peers.

Decades ago, college professors rarely discussed the audience for the papers they assigned because it was assumed that students were writing for their professor and their professor only. These days, while your instructor is your initial audience most of the time, assignments often ask you to write for readers outside your course. For example, you might write a letter to the editor of a newspaper, put together a public service brochure for your community, create a grant or fellowship proposal to help fund a research project, or even create a video that makes an argument to a public audience.

And, of course, you won't be doing college writing forever, so knowing how to write for audiences beyond the classroom will be equally important for whatever you pursue after your degree.

DEONTA
University of North Carolina, Chapel Hill

In college it's more like your writing is based on the prompt, and [your writing] may not be just for your professor. . . . They may give you the audience, or you may have to think about the topic and what kind of audience would be reading something of that nature.

When your instructor gives you an assignment prompt, the prompt should indicate for whom you are writing. If this is not clear, then ask questions about the audience to learn more (see also Lesson 5: Prompt). Some useful ways to frame your questions might be to ask:

> **What should we know about the audience for this assignment?**
> **What particular things do you think this audience might value or expect?**
> **Where can I go to learn more about this audience?**
> **Is the audience for this assignment specific or general?**

Ideally, your teacher will provide a grading rubric along with the assignment, which will give you information about the audience, what they value, and how your writing will be assessed. Even if you do not have a rubric, be sure to begin every assignment by learning everything you can about your intended audience.

PRACTICE Write a paragraph in which you describe the audience for the specific college writing assignment that you must complete. Use thick description to capture this audience, as if they are characters in a novel, play, or film. Try to get inside this character's head: How do they see the world? What kind of writing are they looking for? What are their expectations?

E) Engage your audience. They want you to succeed.

It's been said that some people are more afraid of speaking in public than they are of dying. One of the best ways I know to relieve anxiety about public speaking is to turn the tables and ask would-be orators to put themselves in their audience's chairs for a minute and consider, "From the audience's perspective, what do I want in a speaker?"

The first thing most of us want when we are in the audience is to be engaged or entertained. We want the speaker to succeed, and it's uncomfortable to listen to someone who is anxious. In fact, from our seats in the audience, we want the speaker to connect and talk with us. It's the same way in writing. No reader wants to be bored. They want to engage with you and be interested in what you're telling them. *The audience is on your side.* The audience *wants* you to perform well. They are not there because they want to see you stumble or because they want to tear you down.

Likewise, the teachers in your audience *want* you to succeed. They do their job because they want you to improve, grow, and learn. While it's also your teacher's job to point out mistakes so that you can learn to avoid them, they are still on your side. More important than any minor mistakes you make is that you engage your audience. Your teachers want to see fresh ideas, clever connections, personal energy, and dynamic development. They want to hear what you think. Rather than reading a stack of papers that are all alike, or listening to a string of presentations that are dull and forgettable, the instructors in your audience are looking for intriguing work — and words that are lively and vibrant.

As you begin to draft and revise, ask yourself and your readers:

> **Is my writing engaging?**
> **Does it have energy and enthusiasm?**
> **Do I have unique ideas and observations?**

Is it bold without being too "out there"?
Does it take reasonable risks?
Did I craft my work carefully because it matters a great deal to me?

At the same time, also consider the difference between being engaging and flashy. College audiences are not looking to be entertained as if attending a circus. They want writing that *says* something interesting, not just writing with a lot of fancy language.

PRACTICE Take an early draft of a writing assignment to your instructor during office hours or to the writing center. Ask the appropriate questions in the list above. If you can do this early in your writing process, the overall development of the paper will be much more successful.

F) Persuade your audience with evidence.

In Lesson 1: Writing, I referenced Nancy Sommers who said: "As a genre [college writing] is defined by its use of sources." Your audience wants you to convince them that what you have to say is insightful, logical, and accurate. In order to convince them, you need to know your topic well and provide evidence to explain and support your perspectives.

Your readers will expect you to draw on what others have said about your topic and to integrate these sources in your writing. They are more interested in your thoughtful responses to what others have said than in ideas you brainstormed within your own head the night before your paper is due. Your readers are skeptical, but not in an antagonistic way; they simply need you to support what you say with evidence. And

your evidence needs to be presented in such a way that a more general audience of readers could follow your reasoning, as Brad describes.

BRAD
University of Florida

Obviously, if I'm writing in college, I'm going to try to impress my professor as much as possible. So that is my primary audience. But [I] also understand that if my paper is picked up by someone else that I'm clearly defining certain terms, so that even if the person hasn't read the book or the article that I am writing [about], they won't be completely lost.

The evidence that you draw on will depend on the context of each assignment you are given. For example, if you are asked to write a literary analysis, quotes from and references to the literary text itself will be essential. If you are writing a problem/solution proposal, then references to what professionals and other experts have written or said will be most convincing. If you are writing a lab report, then careful documentation of your procedures and data will please your readers. If you are producing a video or podcast, you will often want to include commentary from experts, whom you will want to introduce and name explicitly.

When you are in the early stages of researching and drafting an assignment, ask yourself: "What kinds of evidence and sources will be most convincing?" The answer to this question will, again, teach you a lot about your audience.

⮑ **Lesson 6: Evidence (p. 64), Lesson 12: Researching (p. 170), Lesson 21: Paragraphs (p. 296), and Lesson 24: Citation (p. 362) discuss in more detail using evidence in your writing.**

G) Make your writing flow.

While your teacher might not consciously think this way when faced with a large stack of student assignments, anyone will look for and appreciate writing that is clear and easy to read. The same is true of general readers. How many times have you left a website or stopped reading an article because the writing was convoluted or the format didn't make sense? Thinking about design and language will help you to reach your audience.

HUSSAIN
University of Florida

I read this author recently, Kurt Vonnegut, and he says that . . . you should write with only one person in mind. . . . If you do . . . your writing flows together [because it has focus].

Readers mainly want writing that flows smoothly, writing that moves along and does not slow down their progress. "Flow" is one of those qualities that everyone says that they want: We all know it when we see it and notice when it's missing. However, flow can be difficult to define because it's a holistic quality, an umbrella term that covers many features of your writing.

Let's start with this: **Writing that flows is writing that is easy to read**. What factors go into making a piece of writing readable? First is formatting. Being careful and neat in how you set up your document boosts readability. Organization, structure, continuity, and coherence impact the flow of your writing. Does your thesis tie your ideas together? Does your introduction map out what's to come? Do your paragraphs connect and transition from one to the next smoothly? Flow is also created through sentence structure and style: Do your sentences have a comfortable or natural rhythm? All of these components of "flow" are examined more closely in their own lessons.

John Taylor/EyeEm/Getty Images

For more on structure and coherence, see p. 183; for thesis, see p. 265; for introductions, see p. 279; for paragraphs and transitions, see p. 297; for sentence structure and style, see p. 315.

What are other ways to assure flow in your writing? And how do flow and readability connect with your sense of your audience? See the advice from Hussain. Would narrowing your audience to a specific person help your focus and flow? The quality and abundance of evidence can also influence your flow, especially when you are trying to stretch a thin amount of material a long way. What about taking a look at your sentence structure or transitions? Often your sentence begins to break down when your flow is hampered by lack of organization and logic.

PRACTICE Define what *flow* means to you in terms of your writing. Describe in a short paragraph the kinds of things that have the biggest impact on your writing in terms of *flow*.

H) Know your audience's purpose in reading your work.

MAYA
Massachusetts Bay Community College

I worked in peer groups in my English class and, at first, it was kind of traumatizing . . . because I never liked public speaking. I was always very shy about talking in front of people. I guess because I felt so strongly about the topic that I was writing about I felt like I wanted to know what people thought. . . . So it's nice to know that . . . [your writing] makes sense for the rest of the world and not just for you.

People go to the theater to be entertained. Students listen to lectures to gain new knowledge. Congregations attend religious meetings for spiritual inspiration and moral direction. Subscribers browse news sites, journals, and newspapers to be informed. Maya feels so strongly about her writing topics that she is eager to get feedback from her audience, even though she was initially scared of peer review. Likewise, your audience will have a purpose in mind as they read your writing, and you will want to understand that purpose.

Actually, the audience that assigned your work (your instructor) might have a variety of purposes for your writing in mind, including one or more of the following:

- **To be persuaded**
- **To gain new knowledge**
- **To solve problems**
- **To exercise, improve, and evaluate your specific skills, including your comprehension of course materials, your critical thinking abilities, your skill at research, and your familiarity with punctuation and grammar**

As a writer, you have purposes in mind when you write. On a basic level, you want to get good grades on your assignments, receive course credit, and graduate from college, right? But your larger purpose is to gain knowledge and learn to communicate.

So how do you achieve those purposes? Your composition instructor defines the audiences for your written assignments and knows the purposes behind each one. If these purposes are not obvious, ask questions such as: What is the main goal of this assignment? What does a successful response to the assignment look like, and what should it accomplish? What skills and objectives should we work to gain from this assignment?

PRACTICE Make a list of three to five different kinds of writing assignments that you either completed or will complete in your coursework (in college or high school). Now list the corresponding purpose for each assignment. How are they different and similar? How does a change in audience impact a change in purpose in these writing assignments?

I) Meet your audience's standards for tone and correctness.

TOREY
Lansing Community College

When I think of audience, I think of standing in an auditorium with millions of people watching me, listening to me. So, I think that when I write, I don't want to be too biased or too rude.

Often, the questions my students ask when I give them their first writing assignment include: "Can we use the first-person 'I'?" "How many sources do we need to have?" and "How much do you count off for grammar errors?" Students have learned that each teacher has slightly different expectations in terms of grammar, punctuation, and tone, just as different audiences have different expectations.

If you are writing a cover letter and a résumé for a job application, your audience demands that your writing be flawless. If you are writing a personal narrative, then your audience will expect your tone to be less formal and more like your natural, spoken voice. If you are writing a research paper that explores solutions to civil war and genocide, then your readers will expect your tone to be more serious than it would be if you were telling a light-hearted story. War and genocide are heavy, complex topics that have to do with the value and treatment of human beings. Those topics dictate that your tone be respectful and your style very clear.

To understand your audience for a particular writing assignment, you need to have a sense of their expectations in terms of grammar, punctuation, and tone. Some writing should be loose and casual. Some writing needs to be precise and formal. But most writing falls on a spectrum between the two extremes.

⤶ Lesson 1: Writing (p. 2) defined writing as a dynamic tension between a writer, an audience, and a topic — a tension that also depends on context.

In this discussion about audience, correctness, and tone, you can see this tension at work. Different audiences will have different expectations, which are influenced at the same time by the topic of the writing and the genre in which you are working.

But tone can be much more than simple mechanical correctness or the use of informal language. College audiences most typically expect a "professional" or "pre-professional" tone, which is thoughtful, serious, and confident without being extreme or highly emotional. This means that you should aim to be decisive without being dogmatic. And, in terms of your readers, this means that you should work diligently to connect with them — without selling out, losing your own voice, and focusing only on pleasing your readers.

NANAISSA
Lansing Community College

It may sound a little selfish, but, if I really like what I am doing, I believe that I can touch most of my audience. In my class, I was told the contrary, that I had to pay a lot of attention to my audience. . . . But it's you; you are the one writing the paper, not the audience.

It's perhaps too easy to fall into the trap of thinking that "writing is all about pleasing your audience." In the context of college composition, this translates into "writing is all about giving my teachers what they want." Nanaissa expresses more confidence in her individual tone and voice than Torey does at the beginning of this segment — but notice how both of them are thinking about audience.

Remember that we are defining writing as a dynamic relationship (between writer, audience, and topic, in various contexts). You definitely need to connect with your audience, but you don't want to lose yourself and only think about "pleasing your boss," your reader. That's called being obsequious, and it will make your writing triangle collapse because the writer (you) has disappeared too far into the background. However, now that I've warned you of the risk of obsequiousness, I want to remind you that inexperienced writers often improve a great deal by developing audience awareness. And what's the best way to develop audience awareness? **Revise Repeatedly from Feedback** from a variety of audiences.

3.3

Exercises: audience

3a Integrate the video.

Yadirys testifies that interacting with her instructors during office hours was the key to her improvement as a college writer. And Dan argues that researching your audience is almost as important as the topic itself.

Write a substantial paragraph or two, with a topic sentence or mini-thesis, through which you respond to Yadirys, Dan, and other videos in the lesson as you form your own definitions of *audience* and develop strategies for interacting with and understanding your readers. You can watch the Lesson 3 Essentials Video, or you can browse the embedded clips in the online edition of this Lesson. You might begin by identifying the moments that stand out to you the most. Which student videos seem to make the most sense to you? With whom do you agree? Disagree? What patterns do you find among the student sound bites? Which ideas were the most instructive or helpful to you? What surprised you? How have your own ideas about audience come into focus through the videos?

3b Create a journal entry or blog.

Your instructor might ask you to keep a writer's journal throughout this class. This journal could be handwritten or composed on a computer; it could take the shape of a text-based blog or a video blog.

To prepare a journal entry on Lesson 3, define in your own words the key term *audience*, trying not to glance back at the material in this lesson, at first. Not referring to this material initially will help you see what you have internalized so far. After carefully composing your initial definition, look back at some of the definitions and strategies other students gave in Lesson 3 or in the online database of interviews. For example, in his interview, Deonta compares his sense of audience awareness in oral presentations versus written papers:

> Oral presentations are good because they train you for real world experiences where you may not be doing just written assignments. And they also allow you the opportunity to see an audience and how they're going to react to what you're saying while you're talking to them.

You might wish to disagree with some of this lesson, or you might want to modify or expand on some of its advice. For example, consider integrating additional thoughts, notes, and lessons from your instructor and your class meetings into your journal entry. It might help for you to imagine that you are giving advice to your future self about writing. What lessons from these discussions about writing might benefit you down the road?

3c See yourself as a writer.

In a page or two, describe the evolution of your sense of audience awareness since you began writing. Where and when does your sense of audience awareness begin? What major events, assignments, and papers have influenced your sense of audience along the way? What particular teachers or classes have reshaped your awareness of audience? What was your sense of audience before you began reading this lesson? What is your approach to audience now that you have finished this lesson? How does your development as a writer compare with what other students said in their interviews, such as Deonta?

> I have progressed as a college writer in terms of thinking about audience, because

in high school you're only writing for your teacher. And now that I'm in college, it's more that you're writing based on the prompt that may not be just for your professor. The prompt may give you the audience or you may have to think about the topic and what kind of audience would read something of that nature. So you have to think about the audience that [is interested in your topic] that you're writing about — how they perceive it; how they might think about.

3d Invent your writing.

Section 3.2 of this lesson discusses nine strategies (A through I) for understanding and interacting with your audience. In five complete sentences, map out how five of these nine concepts could be applied to a writing assignment you are working on in this class (or in another class, if you are not currently writing in this course). For example, in her interview, Yadirys emphasizes how valuable bringing drafts of her writing to her instructor's office hours was, which is strategy 3.2.A. Share drafts of work in progress. Can you foresee using that strategy too? If so, write down a plan for 3.2.A (and four others like it).

3e Analyze student writing.

Study the opening two or three paragraphs or segments of a couple of model projects in Lesson 25 or in the LaunchPad. You might compare very different models, such as Dan's video and Nicole's paper, or you might read similar work, such as Nanaissa's and Vinh-Thuy's papers.

For each writer, describe in a sentence or two, the kind of audience each of these authors seems to address. Based on the students' work, what audience expectations does each project seem to value and emphasize? How do each of these audiences compare with the others? In what ways do they seem alike? Different? List a couple of specific choices each writer makes to meet their readers' expectations.

Your instructor might ask you to apply this analysis and these questions to your class-mates' writing instead (or in addition to the model projects).

3f Revise repeatedly from feedback.

Examine a writing assignment you are currently working on or one that you wrote recently, perhaps in another class or in high school. Now, answer the questions from Exercise 3e in terms of your draft and your assignment instead of someone else's writing. Describe some specific ways that you can use the ideas from Lesson 3 to revise your writing and improve your sense of audience awareness.

LESSON 4

Topic

Write about a topic that matters to you.

ferrantraite/Getty Images

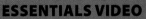

ESSENTIALS VIDEO

Visit the LaunchPad for *Becoming a College Writer* to watch the Lesson 4 Essentials Video.

4.1 [WHY]

Why you should write about a topic that matters to you.

The word *topic* comes from the Greek word *topos*, which means most literally a place or location. Over two thousand years ago, Aristotle had a lot to say about topics, or *topoi*, in his language. In fact, he describes over one hundred different types of *topoi*. For him, different topics were not so much things you write about as much as they were different ways of arguing that depended upon the metaphorical "place you are standing" (your rhetorical position).

Of course, in Aristotle's time, the place from which you spoke publicly made a big difference. You would talk one way if you were speaking in a political forum, a different way if you were teaching in a school (as Aristotle was), and you would talk still another way in the public marketplace. In ancient Greece your rhetorical triangle (see Lesson 1, p. 7) depended a great deal on the ground, or the location — the *topos* — underneath your sandals.

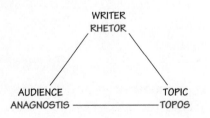

WRITER
RHETOR

AUDIENCE
ANAGNOSTIS ——————— TOPIC
TOPOS

What is a topic?

VINH-THUY
Red Rocks Community College

There's always a theme, but within that theme, there's a huge amount of freedom and a huge number of directions in which you could take [your topic]. I have never actually had a class where you write about one thing and one thing only.

For college writing, the word *topic* likely has a meaning related to, but different from, Aristotle's. For you, a topic is most often what your instructor has asked you to write about, and it's your job to select a *subtopic* within the assigned topic. Your prompt might be to write a research paper about environmental issues on campus. Within that larger topic you might select the smaller subtopic of "paper products and recycling in the dining hall," or maybe "using local and sustainable produce in the cafeteria."

This definition of a topic as *the thing you are writing about* is sometimes called the *subject* of your writing. *Subject* can be a confusing word because it can get mixed up with the subject of a course such as English, European history, or biology. In our example, "environmental science" would be the subject, "environmental issues on campus" being a subdivision of that topic, and your report on "cafeteria paper products" being a subtopic further down the chain. Sometimes college assignments are also called "themes," which can also be defined as "the thing you are writing about."

However, sometimes college instructors assign you *a way of writing* rather than *a thing to write about*. For instance, you might be asked to research a problem and propose a solution, and it's up to you to pick a specific problem. You might be asked to compare and contrast two poems, and it's up to you to pick the poems. A teacher might assign an autobiographical narrative, and you decide which aspect of your life you wish to share. When your teacher assigns a topic as *a way of writing* more than *a thing to write about*, they are getting closer to what Aristotle had in mind when he tried to define *topics* as ways of making an argument, within specific contexts. **Your writing will be stronger.**

Often a writing assignment prompt does both: It asks you to write about a topic and it tells you *how* to write about it. For example: "Write a well-researched proposal to the dean in which you identify an environmental problem on campus and offer a reasonable solution."

Therefore, your focus and concern regarding the topic of your college writing is, first, about locating possible topics and, second, selecting a topic that will work for you. Of the thousands of pieces of advice in the student interviews I conducted for this text, there is one clear message that almost every student shared, and here it is:

ERIENNE
Metropolitan State University of Denver

The process is usually an epic journey, and it begins with finding a way that I can relate to and identify with the assignment that I've been given. Oftentimes I feel like students feel apathetic about their work or are unmotivated to do it because they haven't figured out why this piece, this assignment resonates with them. Once I identify [how] the project speaks to me personally, I know that it will motivate me throughout the process and I will want to write this paper.

Lesson 1 defined *writing* as **a dynamic relationship between an author, an audience, and a topic** — all within a specific context, and it asked you to imagine a triangle as representing this relationship, as in the figure below. If you, as the author, are disconnected from your topic, the triangle collapses. So, as you work to determine the subtopic you'd like to address within the larger topic assigned by your instructor, think positively and refuse to settle until you find some kind of personal connection with your topic. You must find an angle or a way into the topic or your writing will not be engaging — and everyone will be unhappy. **The choices are yours to make.**

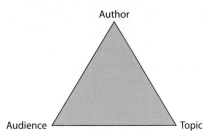

Once you have a selected a topic (or subtopic) that you find engaging, a second principle emerges: You, as a writer, will have chosen the first relationship among many that will define the context of your writing. In other words:

> Selecting a topic is the first of many *choices* you make as a writer, and, from this point, your writing is very much about *making choices*.

When you have chosen your topic, even if your focus changes as you revise, you have established the foundation of your rhetorical triangle. You have placed the writer, your audience, and your topic in a relationship. From this moment on, you will build your rhetorical context by making choices about your writing, similar to the ways architects make choices about a building as they work from the ground up. In the Three Little Pigs fairy tale, one pig *chose* to build a house out of straw, the second pig *chose* wood, and the last pig *chose* bricks. How did those choices work out for the pigs?

The next section in Lesson 4 gives you practical, step-by-step advice on how to locate, select, and refine a topic, beginning, of course, with the first principle, which is that you must connect with your topic. When you begin to search for, select, and refine a topic, you begin making *choices*, even if you haven't written a single word yet. As represented in the metaphor of a writing triangle, the various choices you make will build the dimensions of your writing toward the other aspects of the context, including genre, discipline, and media, as discussed in the following five lessons:

↳ Part Two: Context, Lesson 5: Prompt, p. 54; Lesson 6: Evidence, p. 64; Lesson 7: Genres, p. 84; Lesson 8: Discipline, p. 105; and Lesson 9: Media, p. 120.

PRACTICE Either write down or verbally describe to a classmate one of your very best or most favorite writing assignments that you completed in school — at any level, even as far back as elementary school. Have your classmate describe the same to you. What was the topic or subtopic that you wrote about? After exchanging stories, discuss how you felt connected to the topic of your writing. Was your project successful because you cared a lot about your topic?

4.2 [HOW]

How to write about a topic that matters to you.

A) An effective topic connects with you and energizes your writing.

HANNAH
California State University, San Marcos

Writing is about life, and, if you can't connect [your topic] to your life, then you shouldn't be writing about it.

The "Why?" section of this lesson defines the word *topic* in terms of college writing and identifies the most common piece of advice from the nearly one hundred students interviewed for this project. That advice is: *Write about topics that matter to you.* Here in the "How" section of this lesson are six steps to help you do that. When you connect your topic with your own interests, it shows in your writing and makes a big difference to you and your readers.

Connecting to your topic begins with a positive attitude. The word *academic* can have a negative connotation as in "related only to school," "disconnected," or "not real." If you approach your coursework as "academic" in this negative sense of the word, then you won't learn much and you and your readers will be miserable. The more positive and accurate way to approach "academic" work is to focus on building and gaining new knowledge and sharing fresh ideas that are worth careful study.

CHATIANA
Lansing Community College

In high school, you really don't have to focus on your topic. You can just write about whatever. You don't even have to have an emotional attachment to the paper. . . . But, when you are in college, you really have to have that emotional connection to your paper.

If you find yourself desperately clawing your way to reach an assignment's word count or page length, then your writing is probably just empty busywork—not "academic" in the positive, true sense of the word. Don't do this to yourself or your readers. Life is too short to spend your time on papers that you do not want to write and that no one wants to read. (See Lesson 3: Audience, p. 27.)

You must work to find a topic that's not just easy to cover, but worth your time. Energetic, dynamic, enthusiastic writing can compensate grade-wise for a lot of accidental typos. Better yet, engaged writing is your best chance to avoid mistakes in the first place because you will concentrate more easily, craft your words more carefully, and, as a result, write with greater ease and smoothness.

So, to begin with a positive, constructive mind-set, the voice inside your head needs

to cheer you toward finding a topic that sparks your interest. You must proudly refuse to give up until you discover what it is. Beginning an assignment this way will save you time and energy because you won't be swimming against the current as you write. Once you practice this attitude a few times and experience the positive results, you will never write another way.

PRACTICE Make a T-chart like the one below about the last three writing assignments that you completed. On the left side of the chart sketch out the task or prompt as you understood it. On the right side of the chart list the topics that you chose. Then rank the topics according to the ones you liked most and the ones you liked least. Compare your T-chart with a classmate's and discuss why you found certain topics more engaging than others. Lastly, brainstorm a way that you might have made your least favorite topic more compelling for you, and, if you can't come up with a new angle on your own, ask your classmate for suggestions.

assignment prompt	selected topic
nutritional report	weekly sugar consumption
community member profile	cashier at the dining hall
literary analysis	symbolism in a Conrad novel

B) An effective topic connects with your audience.

We know that writing is a dynamic relationship between author, audience, and topic, and in Lesson 3 we took a close look at audience. Here in Lesson 4: Topic, the principle still applies: The more you understand your audience, the more your writing will meet their expectations and the better you will connect.

ASHIA
Michigan State University

When I'm picking a topic, I'm looking for a personal connection. Because I feel like I can get more feeling into the paper and create more pathos and ethos in the paper. I [want to] get my audience to feel what I am saying and to feel what I feel.

An effective topic is one that interests your readers just as much as it interests you. The topic connects you with those readers. Think of something that bonds you to a friend or family member. You both might love the same sports team or the same food. You might be connected to family members through special traditions or holiday meals. Sometimes you bond through shared experiences, like roommates or teammates do. Likewise, a topic bonds or connects writers and their audiences because they each share the same interest — and that shared interest is the topic.

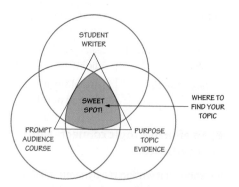

You can assume that your instructors are already interested in the topic they've assigned to you. With that in mind, and when you think positively as described

earlier, then . . . bingo! you are bonded to your audience. Ask yourself, "What will my readers gain from my writing and research?" If, like Kendra, you aim to discover something new for yourself and your readers, then you are potentially rewarding your audience and definitely building connections.

KENDRA
Michigan State University

I think [that] taking the risk and trying to find something that hasn't really been known or is still a question is a good way to go, because then you're learning from [what] you find and from your writing process — and others might learn from it too.

PRACTICE To understand your readers so that you can select a topic that connects your rhetorical triangle, follow the advice in Lesson 3: Audience (p. 27). Ask yourself, "What kinds of topics seem to be interesting to my audience?" Or, better yet, write down your answer to that question. It's not enough to answer this question superficially, as in, "My professor and classmates are interested in American literature." Within that subject, for example, you would want to consider which authors, which types of literature, which historical moments, which particular aspects of literature are energizing to you and your audience. Very often, teachers will give you a list of topics from which you can choose. You won't write on every topic on that list, but if you study the list, you can find a pattern to the kinds of topics that your audience is particularly interested in. Locating such patterns will help you select a topic that connects you and your writing with your readers.

C) An effective topic connects with your course.

CHASE
Santa Fe College

I recommend finding something in your own life and then finding an element in class where you can relate the two and then bring them together.

It's easy, at first, to think that your instructor is synonymous with the course itself, that they are practically the same thing. After all, you will hand in your assignments to a teacher, not to a course. But selecting a topic that connects your work to the specific objectives of the course, as well as to readers, can help you write efficiently and successfully.

The syllabus almost always defines the objectives for the course—the things that you, as a student, will master by the end of the semester. These might include gaining critical thinking skills, research skills, and an understanding of rhetorical contexts for writing. Sometimes an instructor will identify specific themes on the syllabus—for example, writing about climate change—and purposes—persuading audiences to take action. As you think about a topic, remember that the overarching goal of any college writing assignment is not just to give you practice; the aim is always to advance one or more of the course objectives.

So, now would be a good time to go back and read the syllabus again and ask, "What topic could I select to meet the goals of the course?" and "How can a topic that interests me connect various aspects of this course together?" While the syllabus

defines basic goals and objectives, your instructor further defines the course focus every day in class. "What key themes, key terms, and big ideas does my instructor emphasize repeatedly?"

PRACTICE Write down connections between these points of emphasis to the topic you select. Explore key terms from the course in your writing in more depth.

Select a topic not because you have to. Select a topic that connects your writing to the course as a whole. Even when the prompt for an assignment is comprehensive and thorough, you can gain a lot by spending even five minutes looking back over the course's main goals as you select a topic. If you do so and if the course has a final exam, you will double the benefit because you will prepare yourself for the exam as you write and research. Double prizes!

D) An effective topic offers potential for investigation and insight.

DEONTA
University of North Carolina, Chapel Hill

When it comes to picking a topic, I normally think about what I'm interested in, how that relates to the [assigned] text, whether or not it will require research, and how many sources I will need. Also, I try to keep in mind the [assigned] page limits that we're given. That way I know I'm not . . . broadening the topic to a point that I can't make a conclusive argument about it.

Your topic must have potential in three ways. First, it must be compelling to you, as we have already discussed in this lesson. Second, it must explore something new. Third, its scope must be wide enough so that you can present plenty of ideas, but narrow enough so that you can manage and focus. (See the table below.)

Your topic must have potential for new discovery, even if that discovery is new only to you. The point of education and research is to pursue new knowledge. What would you like to learn and discover as you complete your current writing assignment? How does your topic extend from the lessons and goals of the course? Many of the most familiar topics (like capital punishment, legalizing marijuana, gun laws, or recent wars) can have limited potential because they have been widely debated and written about already, and because you will already be familiar with all sides of the issues. If there is a recent, important development regarding one of these subjects, then that might be worth looking into. Otherwise, stay clear of topics that may lack potential for new insight.

The topic you select also needs to have an appropriate scope. Think of your topic as a container that must be large enough to hold a lot of good ideas, sources, information, and evidence. But, if the topic is too large a container, then you won't be able to fill it up. If your topic is too broad, you won't be able to explore key ideas in enough depth to be convincing because you will not have enough space, time, and words to establish and support your ideas. In general, inexperienced writers almost always need to narrow the scope of their assignments because it can initially seem easier to write something that is a very large, easy target. For more on scope, see Lesson 5: Prompt (p. 54).

PRACTICE Work with a partner and each write down an extremely large topic — as big and all-encompassing as you can imagine. Then swap topics and narrow the giant topics down just a little, but not too drastically. Then swap again and further narrow the scope. Once you have tried two or three

SCOPE	ARISTOTLE'S RHET. THEORY	CAMPUS SUSTAINABILITY	SHAKESP. HAMLET
TOO BROAD	HOW TO PERSUADE AN AUDIENCE	HOW TO STOP GLOBAL WARMING	THE MEANING OF HAMLET
JUST RIGHT	THE USE OF REPETITION IN MLK'S SPEECHES	CAMPUS-WIDE PLAN FOR RECYCLED PAPER PRODUCTS	ROLE OF WOMEN IN HAMLET
TOO NARROW	USING 1ST PERSON IN A EULOGY	THE PRICE OF 100% RECYCLED NAPKINS	HAMLET'S COSTUME

times for each initial topic, then go online and search for a recent event that might focus and connect the topic into a final subtopic. Discuss how the scope of the final sub-sub-subtopic might be easy or difficult to manage as a writing project.

E) An effective topic is born from brainstorming and early research.

HANNAH
California State University, San Marcos

I start with questioning what my passion is about the topic. And then I do research. And then after the research, I write. And then I write my thesis.

There is a lot to consider if you want to select a topic that will work effectively. As this lesson suggests, the best topic is one that connects with you, your audience, and your course objectives, and that allows you to discover something new and interesting. You might hope that this topic will come to you easily, but it's most likely going to take some effort.

PRACTICE The best way to begin — in addition to practicing a positive attitude — is to write down quickly the first thing about the writing assignment that attracts your attention. What might be intriguing about it? Many of the one hundred students interviewed for this text say that they begin their writing with brainstorming lists. Ask yourself: What seems cool to you? What do your readers seem to like? How can you connect the topic to the course objectives? See how long you can make your brainstormed list of potential topics.

This is also the moment you want to begin to research your topic. Browse a few resources online to see what experts are talking about. What key terms are people defining and redefining in the conversation about your topic? What are the different perspectives people seem to have on your topic? Write down some particularly interesting quotes or examples that you find.

For more on research, brainstorming, and reading, see Lesson 6: Evidence, p. 64; Lesson 11: Brainstorming, p. 158; and Lesson 12: Researching, p. 170.

Try to respond to as many of these preliminary questions and ideas as you can, and then look back at your brainstormed list and pursue what seems most promising to you. I don't know why exactly, but I always do this kind of brainstorming on a pad of legal paper. And then I look back at the list and I think to myself, "What looks really juicy?" Yes, "juicy" is a silly word, but it has always worked for me. And don't just brainstorm alone. Share your thoughts, lists, and brainstorms with others. You will be surprised how your messy lists come into clear focus within minutes of sharing them with somebody.

And this might be the most important point in this section: When writing in college, **you cannot just pick a topic off the top of your head, because your writing must respond to research.** Therefore, you must do some preliminary research before you select a final subtopic. Yes, you want to begin with what appeals to you personally and naturally, but then you must also connect that with what other people are thinking and saying.

F) An effective topic is revised and refined in response to additional research, drafting, and feedback.

KENDRA
Michigan State University

I think that when you are writing in a class that a lot of people come up with a first idea and they just run with it. But if you're going to put the effort in to write a paper, you might as well make it interesting.

The introduction to this text claims that the key to writing is to **Revise Repeatedly from Feedback (RRFF)**. You might at first think that **RRFF** applies only to your writing once you begin to draft, or once you get feedback on a draft. But revision is a constant process, and you will get many new ideas and want to revise your focus and aims throughout a writing assignment.

HYESU
University of Florida

It's fairly difficult for me to find an appropriate scope [when picking a topic]. . . . If my scope is too broad, I have to go back and change it and revise the essay to fit the new scope. So [picking a] topic is surprisingly difficult.

PRACTICE You will inevitably revise your topic, too. You will select a topic at first, and it's important that you do so with intent and commitment. But you are likely to narrow, expand, and even redirect your topic as you read and write further. Get feedback from your classmates, instructor, or writing center tutors as you choose and then refine your topic. You can ask: "Does my topic seem to respond to what I have been reading?" and "Does my scope seem appropriate?" and "Does my topic seem headed in a clear direction?"

4.3

Exercises: topic

4a Integrate the video.

Ashia has a well-designed, strongly connected, and ideally balanced rhetorical triangle when she says, "When I'm picking a topic, I'm looking for a personal connection. Because I feel like I [can] get more feeling into the paper and create more pathos and ethos in the paper. I [want to] get my audience to feel what I am saying and to feel what I feel." Notice how Ashia is connected to her topic, and her topic is connected to her audience, and, thus, her audience is connected to her, as a writer.

Write a substantial paragraph or two, with a topic sentence or mini-thesis, through which you respond to Ashia and other videos in the lesson as you form your own approaches to selecting and refining a topic for your writing assignments. You can watch the Lesson 4 Essentials Video, or you can browse the embedded clips in the online edition of Lesson 4. You might begin by identifying the moments that stand out to you the most. Which student videos seem to make the most sense to you? With whom do you agree? Disagree? What patterns do you find among the student sound bites? Which ideas were the most instructive or helpful to you? What surprised you? How have your own ideas about *topic* come into focus through the videos?

4b Create a journal entry or blog.

Your instructor might ask you to keep a writer's journal throughout this class. This journal could be handwritten or composed on a computer; it could take the shape of a text-based blog or a video blog.

To prepare a journal entry on Lesson 4, describe your thoughts and approaches to the key term *topic*, trying not to glance back at the material in this lesson, at first. Not referring to this material initially will help you see what you have internalized so far. After carefully composing your initial thoughts, then look back at some of the ideas and strategies other students gave in Lesson 4 or in the online database of interviews. For example, in his interview, Dan echoes the discussion from early in this lesson about narrowing a topic into a subtopic, and he also anticipates other lessons in the book such as genre, media, and sentence style:

> Keeping in mind what your topic is [is] vital. Understanding what you need to cover is vital. But more importantly you need to figure out what you want to say about that within that topic and then how you're going to say it.

You might wish to disagree with some of this lesson, or you might want to modify or expand on some of its advice. For example, consider integrating additional thoughts, notes, and lessons from your instructor and your class meetings into your journal entry. It might help for you to imagine that you are giving advice to your future self about writing. What ideas from this lesson and from discussions about writing might benefit you down the road?

4c See yourself as a writer.

In a page or two, describe the evolution of your sense of *topic* since you began writing. Where and when did you start to develop strategies for topic selection? What major events, assignments, and papers have influenced your sense of *topic* along the way? Which teachers or classes have reshaped the ways you select a topic? What was your sense of *topic* before you began reading this lesson? What is your approach now that you have finished this lesson? In what ways can you imagine your sense of topic selection changing beyond college? How does your development as a writer compare with what other students said in their interviews, such as Nicole:

In high school they give you your topic. Always! In college they let you choose your topic, which is even harder than having a teacher give you your topic. Because, when you get to college and your teacher says, "Write on whatever you want to write," now, you have the process of finding all of your passions and then narrowing down that passion to one topic that you want to write about — and then narrowing that down [further] to categories that you want to address. And for me I found that just nerve-racking because I had never had so much freedom in my writing — that would be the biggest difference that I see between high school and college writing.

4d Invent your writing.

Section 4.2 of this lesson discusses six principles (A through F) to keep in focus as you select and develop a topic. In five complete sentences, map out how five of these six concepts could be applied to a writing assignment you are working on in this class (or in another class, if you are not currently writing in this course). For example, in her interview, Hyesu talks about her struggles to narrow her scope and strategy. Section 4.2.F describes ways to get feedback to help adjust the scope of your topic.

4e Analyze student writing.

Study the opening two or three paragraphs or segments of a couple of model projects in Lesson 25 or in the LaunchPad. You might compare very different models, such as Dan's video and Nicole's paper, or you might read similar work, such as Nanaissa's and Vinh-Thuy's papers.

For each writer, describe in a sentence or two the kind of topic each of these authors seems to choose. Based on the students' work, what kinds of connections can you sense between the writer and the topic? How does each author/topic connection compare with the other? In what ways do they seem alike?

Different? List a couple of specific choices the writers make to suggest connections between their topics and themselves. Also evaluate the scope of each project. Does the writer manage the scope of their chosen topic effectively? How do they do so?

Your instructor might ask you to apply this analysis and these questions to your classmates' writing instead (or in addition to the model projects).

4f Revise repeatedly from feedback.

Examine a writing assignment you are currently working on or one that you wrote recently, perhaps in another class or in high school. Now answer the questions from Exercise 4e above in terms of your draft and your assignment instead of someone else's writing. Describe some specific ways that you can use the ideas from Lesson 4 to revise your writing and improve your sense of connection to your topic. Perhaps most important, to complete this exercise, take an early draft of your writing to the writing center, a peer workshop, or your instructor's office hours and document the responses to the questions at the end of 4.2.F: "Does my topic seem to respond to what I have been reading? Does my scope seem appropriate? Does my topic seem headed in a clear direction? Do I seem connected to this topic through my writing?"

PART TWO

Context

The five lessons in Part Two encourage you to consider your writing situation and how it sets the stage for each of the decisions that you, the author, will make.

Lesson 5	**Prompt**	Answer the assignment prompt and respond to the grading rubric.
Lesson 6	**Evidence**	Support your writing with evidence.
Lesson 7	**Genre**	Analyze and compare genres to meet audience expectations.
Lesson 8	**Discipline**	Understand that a discipline is a methodology applied to a subject.
Lesson 9	**Media**	Select the appropriate media for your context.

LESSON 5

Prompt

Answer the assignment prompt and respond to the grading rubric.

Tim Robberts/Getty Images

5.1 [WHY]

Why you should answer the assignment prompt and respond to the grading rubric.

Each writing assignment that you complete in college will likely be a response to a prompt from your instructor, so be sure to study the prompt and respond to it directly. An assignment prompt is more than just a list of things you need to do to complete a college paper. It defines your rhetorical context, establishing a dynamic relationship between you, your audience, and your topic.

HUSSAIN
University of Florida

A great college writer is someone who understands the prompt very well, who has a great understanding of the prompt, and who's talked it over with the professor. So someone who's got a great understanding of the prompt and thus their writing adheres pretty close to what the professor wants to see. Because, at the end of the day, the professor is the one who is judging your writing.

An assignment prompt provides instruction for the writing you will do.

Let's take a look at an assignment prompt. This one is from a course that Hyesu, a student at the University of Florida, is taking, called the History of Law.

ASSIGNMENT: Legal Brief Write a legal brief that summarizes the relevant facts and findings regarding a famous, historic American legal case from the last one hundred years. You are writing this brief as a legal research intern who has been asked to capture the important details of the case for a judge who is preparing to hear a similar, contemporary case. Base most of your summary and analysis on the published case documents and rulings, but also include at least one or two critical commentaries from legal scholars to verify that your analysis addresses the most important aspects of the case. Use proper legal documentation style and limit your brief to 2,000 to 3,000 words.

The assignment prompt above defines the context that Hyesu will need to consider as she plans and writes her paper. Specifically, the assignment informs Hyesu about the **audience** (a judge), the **topic** (a historic case to be selected), her role as the **writer** (legal intern), the **genre** (a summary brief), the **medium** (text document, 2,000 to 3,000 words), the **sources of evidence** (the case documents), and the **discipline** (legal studies).

The first three boldfaced terms above are the focus of the three previous lessons, and the last four terms are the focus of the following four lessons. The assignment prompt serves as a kind of hinge that leverages the rhetorical context for college writing. So, the best way to begin a writing assignment is to make sure that you clearly understand the seven dimensions of your rhetorical situation.

55

PRACTICE Make a list, and number it from 1 to 7. In as few words as you really need, and on no more than seven separate lines, write down your analysis of an assignment prompt for one of your college writing projects, ideally one that you have just begun to address. On the first line, write *audience* = and then define the audience for the project. Follow the same approach with *topic, writer, genre, medium, evidence,* and *discipline.* If you need to read more about any of those seven dimensions, there is a nearby lesson to help explain it to you. If you cannot figure out one of these seven dimensions because the prompt lacks that information, then asking your instructor to further discuss or explain that aspect of the assignment will be critical to launching your writing and research, and ultimately to your success.

An assignment prompt is designed to help you succeed.

To complete any writing assignment successfully, pay close attention to the instructions you're given. Your teachers have built into their assignment prompts specific guidelines and details to help you do your best work. For example, the legal brief assignment from Hyesu's History of Law professor directly states the purpose of the paper (to summarize and analyze a legal case), the sources to be consulted (case documents), and the length of the paper (2,000 to 3,000 words). Your instructors want your writing to be the best it can be, so they design prompts that create possibilities.

Some writing assignments will be more open-ended, giving you a lot of choice and leaving many decisions up to you. On the one hand, more freedom can open up exciting possibilities for your writing. On the other hand, too much freedom can be confusing and might make you feel that you're lacking in direction. Whenever you are in doubt about what a writing prompt is asking you to do, ask your instructor for more specifics. Your instructor is just as much a resource as the assignment prompt itself.

MASON
Boston University

I think a lot of people find that professors can be kind of the enemy, really — they're giving you the assignment, the thing that you are having so much trouble with. But really, they're there to help you — most of the time. And they can be a great resource for writing a paper, in my experience.

An assignment prompt helps determine the scope of your writing.

An assignment prompt usually says something about the scope of your writing — that is, how narrow or wide your field of vision will be as you write. Think of scope this way: A microscope sees things up close and a panoramic lens captures a wide landscape. The things you see under a microscope look very different from the vision you get through a wide-angle lens. As a writer, you need to figure out how close or far away you will position yourself in relation to your topic. In other words, your scope must be wide enough to offer a complete picture but narrow enough for you to be focused and specific.

Hyesu's History of Law assignment prompt is narrowly focused in its scope: Her instructor asked her to choose a single legal case and analyze and summarize it for a legal expert. The instructions also suggest depth of coverage; for instance, Hyesu probably won't be able to cover the topic sufficiently in three or four pages.

When a prompt is broad in scope, you will need to narrow it. Let's say that a prompt asks you to evaluate the effectiveness of your campus recycling program. It's likely you'll have a tough time considering every area of campus: the dorms, dining halls, classrooms, athletic facilities, and so on. And you would be overwhelmed if you tried to consider every part of the recycling program, which might include public awareness and participation, policy and enforcement, maintenance and staffing of recycling centers, and so on. In this scenario, you might narrow your scope to "student participation in the dorm recycling program," or "encouraging recycling during athletic events," to make your writing and research manageable.

PRACTICE Analyze a current or specific college assignment prompt in terms of scope by applying the "microscope versus wide-angle lens" analogy above. Write down what a "microscopic" scope for the prompt would include, and then imagine the other end of the spectrum: What might a panoramic or wide-angle lens approach to the prompt look like? Discuss your two approaches to the prompt with a peer. Then imagine a more manageable scope in between the two and discuss that as well.

An assignment prompt is good for your writing and future grade.

You might be shocked by how often students submit writing assignments that do not follow the original prompt. As a result, they may receive no credit or a failing mark. From an instructor's point of view, a student who ignores a prompt might be someone who isn't paying attention, doesn't care, or is perhaps submitting work from another course (or worse, by another student).

I think students make this mistake *not* because they are lazy or they don't know how to follow instructions; I think it's because they may be afraid to ask their instructors for clarification, so they resist the prompt subconsciously or they're intimidated. If you ever have feelings like these, make a special effort to focus on the prompt's instructions, ask questions, and, if possible, try to find an angle on the assignment that especially interests you and that you can connect with (see Lesson 4: Topic).

TIMOTHY
Red Rocks Community College

If I had to give advice to someone that I knew or wanted to help in a college writing course, the first thing I would probably tell them is to take a breath and that it's going to be ok. And I would probably start by going over the actual assignment. In my own experience I've done this. I've completed an assignment in writing in a composition course and maybe didn't catch part of the writing assignment or I missed the point of the writing assignment. So I may have written a great paper, but I missed the whole point so in the end it's not a great paper.

Like Timothy, I think that following the prompt is one of the most critical pieces of advice for you to be deeply in touch with. If there were 10 commandments for college writing, the first one would be "Thou shalt answer the prompt." Of course, "Thou shalt Revise Repeatedly from Feedback" is just as important, but that comes later in the writing process (Lesson 15, p. 206). If writing is a dynamic relationship between the author, the audience, and a topic (see Lesson 1), then, in a college writing assignment, that relationship begins with the assignment prompt.

Why you should answer the assignment prompt and respond to the grading rubric

An assignment prompt might include a grading rubric that indicates how your writing will be evaluated.

LINDSEY
Michigan State University

It's important to follow the guidelines that the professor gives you just because they're all looking for something different, they're all coming from different backgrounds. Like, every professor wasn't necessarily an English major. So I think you can use your own style but you really need to do what they ask as far as topic and references and things like that.

A rubric is typically a single-page document that defines standards for each grade on a particular assignment. Rubrics often say "An 'A' paper will accomplish X. A 'B' paper will do Y," and so on, and they are usually arranged as checklists. If you are given a rubric, think of it as an extension of the assignment prompt and follow it closely. To succeed as a college writer, you will need to read and respond to any rubric that accompanies an assignment prompt. Rubrics are so important to answering the prompt that, if you are not given an actual rubric, I strongly encourage you to write your own, as described in 5.2.E.

5.2 [HOW]

How to answer an assignment prompt and respond to a grading rubric.

A) Study the assignment prompt immediately and thoroughly.

A natural instinct is to not pay close attention to the requirements of a writing task until you actually sit down to work on it. But the sooner you understand its requirements, the more effective your writing will be.

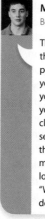

MASON
Boston University

The first thing I would do, or that I think is necessary to write a good paper, is to be attentive in class and do your assignments because inevitably your paper is going to be about what you are discussing and talking about in class. So that's kind of the first step. The second step is receiving the prompt, the topic of your paper, the assignment, and then start brainstorming — looking at the prompt and saying, "What do I want to write about? What do I want to say here?"

One of the best ways to really "get" an assignment prompt is to write a quickly brainstormed response to it. For example, if you were given the legal history assignment on page 55, you might jot down a few paragraphs about the most memorable case you've studied so far in class, and even include some questions you have about it or the judge's decision.

PRACTICE Analyze a current or specific college assignment prompt by writing down a quick, initial response of less than 50 words. Then discuss with a peer or instructor how your "quick response" can

- allow you to ask insightful questions about the prompt from "inside" the assignment.

- increase the likelihood that you will stumble across material that can support your writing.

- give you more time to draft and Revise Repeatedly from Feedback.

- reduce anxiety and boost efficiency by establishing early momentum.

B) Take notes and ask questions about the assignment prompt.

NIA
University of Florida

I feel like it's always good to take notes. I'm a very avid note taker, definitely. Love to take notes. So whenever I get a prompt, I always jot notes down about what my first thoughts are — what I could say, what might be moving, especially if it's interesting.

If your instructor devotes class time to discussing the prompt, take Nia's fantastic advice and write down any additional details about the assignment. If your instructor does not devote class time to discussing the prompt, study it on your own and write down questions such as the following.

According to the assignment prompt:

- **Who is my audience? (For more on identifying and engaging your audience, see Lesson 3.) What expectations does my audience have?**

- **What is the context of this assignment in terms of: genre (Lesson 7), discipline (Lesson 8), and media (Lesson 9)?**

- **What kinds of evidence and sources (Lesson 6) will be most effective?**

- **How narrow or wide should my scope be?**

- **What are possible pitfalls to avoid in this assignment?**

You will probably be surprised by how much additional detail your instructor will provide about the prompt in response to questions like these in class, during office hours, or through email.

MARC
Boston University

I would tell these students to definitely go and just ask the teacher, after class or during class. It would probably be better to do it during class — that way, other students get to hear it. While you might feel like you're annoying the teacher or asking too many questions, it's worth it. You shouldn't care, it's your grade, so you need to do what you have to do to get a good grade.

C) Ask a reader to evaluate your first draft in terms of the prompt.

Two common ways to bomb a writing assignment are (1) to fail to answer the prompt, and (2) to fail to acknowledge your sources (see Lesson 24: Citation). When you get feedback on your drafts, ask readers to first read the assignment prompt to see how well you have responded to it. Whether you bring your assignment to your instructor's office hours, the writing center, or a peer workshop for feedback, begin your session by asking your readers to review the prompt and assess whether or not your draft answers it effectively. When you conference with your instructor, peer reviewer, or writing center tutor about your first draft, ask specific questions such as: "How well am I responding to the prompt?"

PRACTICE Exercise 5.3.F may be one of the most important exercises in this entire book because it literally gets you to follow the advice above. So, if you are just beginning a college writing assignment, this exercise is an ideal way to start. It will make your work much more efficient and successful. Most important, once you get in the habit of getting early feedback on your initial directions in a writing assignment, you will have

developed a strategy that will serve you well in any situation, in college and beyond. This approach is pivotal to *Becoming a College Writer.* Take a moment now and complete exercise 5.3.F.

D) Ask a reader to evaluate your first draft in terms of your scope.

When getting feedback on early drafts, have your readers look at the assignment prompt and ask: "Does my scope seem to fit the assignment? Is my scope too broad or too narrow?" Inexperienced writers tend to enlarge the scope of their writing too broadly so that they make sweeping generalizations rather than carefully detailed observations.

Let's say that, for a world affairs course, you are assigned to write about efforts to curb the use of chemical weapons. You might be tempted to examine these efforts across several decades and countries, but you would probably need to write an entire book to do justice to such a broad topic. A more manageable approach might be to focus on one effort, such as the recent push to eliminate chemical weapons in a particular country.

Of course, a scope that is too narrow — for example, the 1988 Halabja mustard gas attack — might not connect to larger ideas about the topic, which most writing aims to do on some level. Either way, broad or narrow, adjusting your scope to fit an assignment prompt is essential, so be sure that you ask for feedback on your scope from your readers or, as Deonta suggests, from your instructor, as you draft and revise.

DEONTA
University of North Carolina, Chapel Hill

Some professors [say], "Here's the prompt. Go do this." Some professors are really, really strict about what they want. And they know exactly what they want, how they want it, and that's a lot easier because you know what they expect. But when the professor just gives you a broad topic, you don't really know what to expect or what they're looking for — that can be a daunting task to college students. So then students have to go to office hours and ask a bunch of questions.

E) If you are not given a rubric, write your own.

NANAISSA
Lansing Community College

I'm always afraid of assignments because there are many things to do and I want to make sure I don't miss anything, so I always underline the most important points. Then I write — I even write those points down to make sure I really get what I have to do.

Many students, like Nanaissa, use the wise strategy of cutting and pasting the assignment prompt and the rubric into an outline that shapes their drafts so that they "don't miss anything." But what happens when the prompt is short or there is no rubric that outlines specific expectations? The answer is to write your own rubric — or adapt the one I've provided below.

To write your own rubric, you can begin with the generic categories on the list below that in most cases define a strong college writing. From this generic rubric that describes excellent writing, you can imagine other letter grades matching performance levels from excellent (typical A) to successful (typical B) to adequate (typical C) to poor and below.

To earn an "excellent" score on this assignment, your writing needs to:

- ☐ Address all of the requirements described in the assignment **prompt**.

- ☐ Have a clear focus stated through an insightful **thesis**.

- ☐ Draw on evidence or **research** that directly supports your thesis.

- ☐ Use an appropriate **genre** for conveying your ideas.

- ☐ Use an appropriate **medium** for reaching your **audience**.

- ☐ Match the expectations of your **discipline's** audience in terms of method, tone, and formality.

- ☐ Present a logical **organization** of **paragraphs**.

- ☐ Demonstrate careful attention to **conventions** of **style, grammar**, punctuation, correctness, format, and citation.

The above generic rubric is a checklist that you can use for any assignment, regardless of whether or not your instructor provides a rubric. As Hussain argued earlier in this lesson, a successful college writer is someone who "has a great understanding of [a given assignment] prompt." Think of the generic rubric above as a component of every assignment. If you get into that habit—and **Revise Repeatedly from Feedback**—you are bound to do your best work.

PRACTICE The online version of this textbook has an easy-to-print version of this checklist. Print out this checklist and tape or pin it right above your desk or workstation so that it can help you focus and succeed throughout every step in your college writing assignments.

F) Complete a contextual list.

An assignment prompt provides context for the writing you will do. Ask yourself: Who is my audience? How can I connect my audience with my topic? What is my role as an author in this situation? The beginning of this lesson suggested that you make a list of the seven rhetorical elements of each writing prompt you are assigned. If that advice was too early for you to complete until you read to this point, now is the time to actually follow it. Either way, every writing assignment that you complete should begin with an actual list that you write out yourself that documents the seven rhetorical elements described in more detail in Lessons 1–9.

PRACTICE If you did not already, take a moment now to make the list outlined on page 56. This contextual list will set you on the right track for writing a paper that meets your instructor's (and your own) expectations.

5.3

Exercises: prompt

5a Integrate the video.

Timothy describes two aspects of his experience toward becoming a college writer. He acknowledges some initial anxiety about dealing with a prompt for a writing assignment, and he admits that he's made the mistake of failing to answer the prompt because he did not read it carefully. This lesson urges you to learn from Timothy's advice and mistakes. We both urge you to always answer the prompt; other writers in this lesson give you specific strategies for doing so.

Write a substantial paragraph or two, with a topic sentence or mini-thesis, through which you respond to Timothy and other videos in the lesson as you form your own approaches to always answering the prompt. You can watch the Lesson 5 Essentials Video, or you can browse the embedded clips in the online edition of Lesson 5. You might begin by identifying the moments that stand out to you the most. Which student videos seem to make the most sense to you? With whom do you agree? Disagree? What patterns do you find among the student sound bites? Which ideas were the most instructive or helpful to you? What surprised you? How have your own ideas about assignment prompts come into focus through the videos?

5b Create a journal entry or blog.

Your instructor might ask you to keep a writer's journal throughout this class. This journal could be handwritten or composed on a computer; it could take the shape of a text-based blog or a video blog.

To prepare a journal entry on Lesson 5, describe your thoughts and approaches to the key term, *prompt*, trying not to glance back at the material in this lesson, at first. Not referring

to this material initially will help you see what you have internalized so far. After carefully composing your initial thoughts, then look back at some of the ideas and strategies other students gave in Lesson 5 or in the online database of interviews. For example, in his interview, Deonta describes how his entire writing process begins with the prompt and with questions for his instructor about the prompt:

> When I have to start [writing], I normally go in my room. I like to sit on my bed and listen to 90s R&B and hip-hop. And I get out a notepad and pen and the prompt, and I'll start to think about the things that interest me and how they relate to the topic. I write that down, and then I ask, "Am I going to need to do research?" So I also ask, "Is the paper allowed to have research as a component of it?" If so, then I think "Should I email the professor to make sure the research is okay for the paper before moving any further?"

You might wish to disagree with some of this chapter, or you might want to modify or expand on some of its advice. For example, consider integrating additional thoughts, notes, and lessons from your instructor and your class meetings into your journal entry. It might help for you to imagine that you are giving advice to your future self about writing. What lessons from this chapter and from discussions about writing might benefit you down the road?

5c See yourself as a writer.

In a page or two, describe the evolution of your sense of *prompt* since you began writing. Where and when did you start to develop strategies for *assignment prompts*? What major events, assignments, and papers have influenced your sense of *prompt* along the way? What particular teachers or classes have reshaped the ways you answer a prompt? What was your sense of *assignment prompts* before you began reading this lesson? What is your approach now that you have finished this lesson? In what ways can you imagine your sense of *prompt* changing beyond college? How does your development as a writer compare with what other students said in their interviews, such as Kendra? Does her advice contradict other voices in this lesson?

> I guess when I first entered college I thought writing was just [about completing] an assignment you were given, and you had to do it more toward how the teacher wanted it. But I found that in college you're following more what you want to do and that's why you're in college: to further your passion so you can get a career. So pick topics that you are interested in and answer your own questions rather than a teacher's.

5d Invent your writing.

Section 5.2 of this lesson discusses six strategies (A through F) to help you answer assignment prompts effectively. In five complete sentences, map out how five of these six concepts could be applied to a writing assignment you are working on in this class (or in another class, if you are not currently writing in this course). For example, in his interview, Ansel describes how he gains insights about assignment prompts while concentrating on a lecture. Strategies 5.2.A and 5.2.B encourage you to answer the assignment prompt immediately, especially with the help of class notes as Nia (from earlier in the lesson) and Ansel suggest. According to Ansel:

> One of things I've noticed is that if I think about the paper prompt or what I'm writing about ahead of time, then sometimes I'll be sitting in the class that the paper's due and during the lecture I'll hear my professor say things and I'll think about my paper and I'll be able to come up with ideas. So a lot of

my brainstorming that's been happening is that I'll write it down during class and then I'll go back later and think about it.

5e Analyze student writing.

Study the opening two or three paragraphs or segments of a couple of model projects in Lesson 25 or in the LaunchPad. You might compare very different models, such as Dan's video and Nicole's paper, or you might read similar work, such as Nanaissa's and Vinh-Thuy's papers.

For each writer, describe in a sentence or two the kind of prompt each of these authors seems to respond to. Based on the students' work, what connections can you sense between the writer and the prompt? How does each author/prompt connection compare with the other? In what ways do they seem alike? Different? List a couple of specific choices the writers make to suggest connections between their assignment prompts and themselves.

Your instructor might ask you to apply this analysis and these questions to your classmates' writing instead (or in addition to the model projects).

5f Revise repeatedly from feedback.

Examine a writing assignment you are currently working on or one that you wrote recently, perhaps in another class or in high school. Describe some specific ways that you can use the ideas from Lesson 5 to revise your writing and improve your instincts for always answering the prompt. Perhaps most important, to complete this exercise, take an early draft of your writing to the writing center, a peer workshop, or your instructor's office hours and go through each aspect of the assignment prompt, word-by-word, asking "How effectively do I answer each aspect of the prompt?"

Evidence

Support your writing with evidence.

6.1 [WHY]

Why you should support your writing with evidence.

To quote Nancy Sommers again, "Academic writing as a genre is defined by its use of sources." This means that as a college writer, you need to draw upon sources and evidence, not just on your own thoughts and ideas. College writing is mainly *evidence-based writing*, which means that it should be based upon careful, systematic study.

DAN
Michigan State University

Research is the first step of every production, of every piece of writing. You always have to start with research.

Research is a strategic way to gather strong evidence — and evidence is valuable to your audience.

Some people think of the term *research* in only the most formal, stereotypical ways: You need a white lab coat and a PhD to conduct it. But what *research* really means is *to look closely and systematically*. The purpose of looking closely and systematically is to gather evidence to support your claims — and, in our case, to support your academic writing.

Any time you slow down and examine something carefully and methodically, you are conducting research. When you read reviews of movies that you are thinking about watching, you are conducting research. When you read a consumer report about a car, appliance, or television that you might buy, you are looking for evidence. When you ask your friends about the latest hot gossip, that is a form of light research, too. In all these cases you are, to some extent, digging for evidence instead of letting information come to you passively or accidentally. In these examples, you are motivated to look closely and systematically at topics that matter to you. Lesson 4 urges you to find a writing topic — or an angle on an assigned topic or issue — that you can connect with personally for many reasons, including the motivation to dive into your research, as Nia describes below:

NIA
University of Florida

If I'm interested in it, I'll read about it — I'll read what other people have to say. . . . I feel like a good paper is when you really take the time to know what you're talking about. That way you're not worrying about how many words you need until you have to stop writing. . . . You did your research, you did your homework, and there's a lot to put in the paper.

Professional researchers (think of the folks in white lab coats) add new knowledge to the chain of human progress that others have yet to discover or articulate. They use specific strategies for gathering evidence to build new knowledge, and these strategies for gathering information are called *research methodologies*. These are discussed in more detail in Lesson 8: Discipline (p. 105).

As a college writer, you are likewise a researcher because you will apply specific strategies, also known as methodologies, to use strong evidence to pursue new knowledge. However, the knowledge that college writers pursue is most typically new to them but not to professional researchers. Consider your academic writing as a chance to get started or catch up on the knowledge that professional researchers have been putting together, and as an opportunity to begin to add to it.

Through research, you create new knowledge and connect with an ongoing conversation about a topic.

MAYA
Massachusetts Bay Community College

I love to put quotes in my work. I love it!—especially when you're writing about something that's close to where you're from or things that your community has experienced—and to show that there's a person from the other side of the world that's in a different situation in a different time that dealt with the exact same thing, it really makes you feel human. . . . It just makes you feel part of something bigger, I guess. I love that you can connect to different people at different times in history.

As a college writer, you will use the evidence you gather to establish and support your thesis or claim. (A claim is the main idea or thesis statement of an argument paper. See Lesson 19: Thesis, p. 263 for more on thesis

statements and claims.) While the research you do may not be aimed at discovering a cure for cancer or finding Aristotle's lost manuscripts, it will connect you with an ongoing exchange of ideas around your topic.

For example, as you draw on the research of others, you may make a fresh connection or conclusion. At the very least, you will uncover information that is new to you and others like you who are not yet professional researchers. For Salhuana, whose native language is not English, reading research is also a way to build her vocabulary and explore topics that are new to her:

SALHUANA
Red Rocks Community College

Because I have to read a lot, I learn a lot of new words. I use research for two purposes, I use it for myself to learn more words, my vocabulary, and I learn about the topics. I like to learn and discover new things that I never imagined, so sometimes when I'm starting to write something, I have some ideas, [but] when I do my research I find out it's more than I expected. And sometimes I have to change my view because it is not how I [used to] think. I don't try to persuade the reader, "Ok, think like me." No. I want to say "This is my point of view based on this or this."

Salhuana also points out a fundamental purpose of college writing and research that is often misunderstood: Your aim as a writer is for readers to *understand* your perspective based upon the evidence you use. That is not necessarily the same thing as getting readers to agree with you 100 percent of the time.

For professional researchers, progress can be slow and incremental. Giant progressive leaps, like the cure for a major disease or the development of a new technology, are actually built upon thousands of much smaller discoveries. In other words, most "new" knowledge is achieved through research that uncovers only small and sometimes contradictory pieces of much larger puzzles.

KENDRA
Michigan State University

Research for a scientific paper could be taken both ways: You have to do research on a topic to find out more about it to see if it's a topic that you want to look more into, but then you have to personalize the research and do your own so that you can write a paper that is exciting, and that is a fresh idea and looking at something a different way than other people. So you want to do previous research to find out what's been done so you know that your research is significant and it is fresh and new and exciting.

For you, as a college writer, gaining knowledge might mean that you interpret a poem or a novel by carefully analyzing imagery or symbolism, an approach Nicole uses. Or you might analyze your personal history of becoming a digital writer, as Dan does. (See Lesson 25 for more from Nicole and Dan.) You could write a news report based upon personal interviews and library research, as Gretchen does. Or you could work as part of a laboratory team to develop new cancer treatments, as Dan does. You might research case studies of real-life journalists and then base a script for a play on that research, as Samantha does. All of these students discovered (through their research) and articulated (through their writing) something that was small but nonetheless new and purposeful to them. And they based all of their discoveries on strong evidence.

Academic writing and the research it requires are sometimes assigned without enough context. You may be asked to go to the library and return with three sources, with little explanation as to why you are doing so other than "to support your claims," "to learn how they do it in college," or "to learn to cite properly."

A more effective research assignment is one that helps you learn *how to learn*. Research can help you develop the intellectual skills to find relevant information about a question or issue, to solve problems, and to learn new things throughout your life, not to back up preconceived notions or beliefs.

Strong evidence differentiates a professional from an amateur.

KIMBERLY
California State University, San Marcos

I do believe that college writing consists of a lot of research because then you know your information, you know what you're talking about. You're not just sitting there and rambling on about something that you have no idea what it is. And what I've learned is that a scholarly source is by a professional who knows that topic and who's done their research and knows every aspect of it.

The defining characteristic of professionals is that they are paid for their expert abilities, abilities that are based upon systematically developed knowledge. An amateur does things without careful preparation and thought, whereas a professional operates from established, methodical approaches. Becoming a college writer requires you to become a researcher, to become a professional as you move through college toward graduation.

See the LaunchPad for more from Gretchen, Dan, and Samantha.

Being a professional means being able to explain your educated perspective based on patterns you find within the most relevant evidence. It doesn't matter whether you are a professional car salesperson, a nurse, a teacher, or a textbook author. Professional careers are defined by the ability to do three things in combination:

1) **To gather the most relevant and persuasive evidence**
2) **To identify a pattern among that evidence**
3) **To articulate a perspective supported by your analysis of evidence**

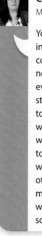

CATHERINE
Michigan State University

You have to be able to find patterns in what you're reading. So, say you're comparing two separate texts. You need to be able to look at them, and even though they may be different stories or different theories, you need to be able to look at them and see where they connect and where they weave into one another. . . . You have to find patterns; you have to find the way that [readings] bounce off of each other. It's really interesting, and that makes academic writing a lot easier, when you can find the pattern in something.

As a college writer, you pursue new knowledge through research. You understand that writing is a dynamic relationship between you, your audience, and your topic. You learn to make new connections for yourself, the way Catherine describes in her quote about finding patterns in reading and research. Notice how she defines research as a relationship among the source or sources that she consults. Once you identify connections and patterns in the evidence you have gathered,

you must explain your perspective in a way that allows your audience to understand.

Nathan begins his writing process by first locating evidence (step 1), then relating his findings to one another (step 2), which is a research process that establishes his credibility as a college writer, so that when he presents his analysis (step 3), his audience will trust his work. Bingo!

NATHAN
Massachusetts Bay Community College

I draw material from the database, and then the way [research] gets into my paper is based on similarities between multiple papers. They have to be kind of saying the same thing. I don't like to use just one source in one point. I like to take from two different ones, two different researchers or two different research papers to talk about one point because I think that really supports it better. It shows that even though they're not the exact same study, they had similar results or they quoted some similar findings. And I think that really says that different types of research have come up with these same results. So it's not biased.

PRACTICE For about three to five minutes each, "speed interview" at least three classmates or college friends about their approaches to research. What is their first reaction to the word *research*? Do they find research intriguing, miserable, or somewhere in between? How do they define it? What is their research process? Then analyze patterns among your speed interviews. What perspective about student research can you share as a result of your interviews? How do your interviews compare with the students' comments in this lesson? (And, once you have completed this activity, does it seem like *research* to you? Why or why not?)

6.2 [HOW]

How to support your writing with strong evidence.

1. Begin with a research question.

ELIZABETH
Palomar College

I start with the purpose, the assignment, the question, the prompt, whatever it is that the professor is asking me to write about. I start there and I try to make everything relevant to that and relate it to that, that initial question or that prompt. So that's how I organize my papers, I start with the question.

When you conduct research, you also create and acquire new knowledge. An easy way to grasp the idea of new knowledge is to think in terms of a gap in your current understanding or a question that needs to be resolved. What's missing that you could help investigate? What current problem might you help solve?

Elizabeth says that she starts her writing and research with a question. The best advice for *how* to conduct research is to begin by framing a *research question*. Asking a question naturally moves you toward investigating information, toward pursuing new knowledge. A research question focuses your examination of evidence and helps you use your time wisely.

In fact, college writing prompts are often formulated as questions for students to address. (See Lesson 5: Prompt, p. 54.) If you are given an assignment prompt that is not formulated as a question, it may help for you to frame or reframe it as a question to be answered.

In her featured essay on magical realism in a Gabriel García Márquez novel, Nicole does not specifically frame a question in her title or introductory paragraph. However, she might have used a question to focus her research and writing, asking, for example: "What literary approaches explain the novel?" or "What is magical realism and how does it influence Márquez's writing?"

 To read Nicole's entire paper, see page 461.

PRACTICE If you haven't done so already, frame your response to a current writing assignment in the form of a question, and then use this question as a starting point for your searches and research. Share this question with others and discuss its strengths and weaknesses.

2. Select a method for gathering evidence.

EMILY
Boston University

My greatest strength as a college writer is being able to gather a lot of research materials. I know a lot of other students get really impatient when it comes to researching and I think they become impatient because they become frustrated with Google. I'm the type of person who searches Google last. I go straight to my library's database resources and straight to the library, and try to start my research stages there because Google is so overwhelming. Even Google Scholar might not be helpful. So that's why I go to the library first. I think that's one of my strengths: I know [where and] how to start researching.

To get started, decide on a *method* you will use to gather evidence. (For guidance

69
How to support your writing with strong evidence

about specific methodologies, see Lesson 8: Discipline.) In this case, a *method* or *methodology* is a deliberate and systematic way of gathering and analyzing evidence. If you were farming a vineyard, your method might be to go through the entire vineyard and harvest only the ripe fruit each day. Or, you might completely harvest each row of the vineyard in order, regardless of whether or not each row is completely ripe. The method used to harvest the grapes and process them together will determine the kind of wine that comes from the vineyard. Likewise, a research method is a way of gathering and processing evidence that directly shapes the knowledge produced as a result.

Often, your research methodology will depend on the discipline (branch of academic knowledge) in which you are working. Here are some of the most common methodologies by discipline:

- **All disciplines:** Conducting online research by entering topic-related keywords into an Internet search engine.

- **Literary studies:** Reading a work of literature closely to interpret meanings and patterns as part of a literary analysis.

- **Hard sciences:** Developing a replicable, or repeatable, procedure for a laboratory experiment. This procedure should produce a reliable set of data to help prove or disprove a hypothesis.

- **Social sciences and business:** Developing a survey with questions for human subjects to respond to. By compiling the responses to surveys, researchers can draw larger conclusions about the questions they've posed.

- **Social sciences, business, and other disciplines:** Comparing and analyzing a number of case studies to try to determine a larger pattern and to help solve a problem.

- **History:** Closely examining historical archives to locate information relevant to a research topic. This information is then put into context through a historical narrative.

Once you have framed your research with a question that needs an answer and have selected a method for gathering evidence, research becomes a four-step process:

1) **Gather abundant, relevant evidence (see pp. 71–75)**
2) **Evaluate your evidence (see pp. 75–76)**
3) **Integrate your evidence into your draft (pp. 77–80)**
4) **Acknowledge the sources of your evidence (p. 179)**

The following discussion explores the first three steps more closely, with an emphasis on the most common methodology for college writers: reading and responding to sources found online and in academic libraries. The fourth step is also addressed in Lesson 24: Citation, p. 362.

You have probably written a lab report in high school or college. Lab reports should include a methods section that describes the exact steps and methods that will be followed to conduct an experiment and produce data. However, it's unusual for academic essays or research papers to require or discuss specific descriptions of the methods to be used, other than general directions for which primary texts to read or the kind of secondary sources to consult.

PRACTICE It can be very helpful to actually write down a sentence or two that fills in the following blank: "In this writing assignment, the method I will use to gather and analyze evidence to support my writing will be _____." If you struggle to fill in that blank, then you have a great question to ask a writing center tutor or your instructor to help you focus your writing and research.

3. Use search tools to gather abundant, relevant evidence.

Your assignment prompt might require you to consult secondary sources for your analysis, but it might not. There are a variety of potential sources, so you will need to confirm which type you should be using, if your prompt does not specifically say. Sources can be categorized as either primary or secondary.

A primary source is direct, firsthand evidence, such as an interview that you conducted, a diary, or an eyewitness account of an event. The most familiar type of primary source is a text or a book. If you are asked to analyze Steinbeck's novel *The Grapes of Wrath*, the novel is your primary source for evidence. A secondary source is one that presents information or analysis on a topic or event originally documented elsewhere. If you use literary critics to help you analyze *The Grapes of Wrath*, then those critics are secondary sources.

For his assignment on the effectiveness of the AVID program (see p. 443), Deonta was not required to conduct experiments or to administer surveys, and his secondary sources were not the central evidence in his work. Instead, he was asked to use his own classroom observations to analyze the effectiveness of the program. In this case, Deonta began by looking to his own experiences. Even though he conducted in-depth secondary research, he needed to gather other relevant evidence for his paper. Deonta's use of observations is one example of the many ways to gather and draw on evidence.

There are a number of ways to gather evidence, but let's start with the most common way to begin your research: with online search tools.

These days, *lack* of information is not the problem; if anything, the problem now is *too much* information. The challenge you face as a researcher is finding the *best* and *most relevant* material on your topic. Becoming a skillful electronic investigator is, therefore, an important talent to develop. It's an important one to maintain, too, because the digital landscape is evolving so rapidly. While it is likely that some of the research strategies you use today will become outdated within a year or two, there are some key tools and strategies that are likely to remain for a long time:

- Your library's website
- Internet search engines
- Keyword searches
- Advanced search functions
- Patience and skill
- Librarians

Your Library's Website. Typically, this site will allow you to search your library's holdings for respected scholarly resources — everything from print books and e-books to journal articles (both print and electronic) to videos. On the next page is an example of just one library website, from Amherst College.

As you can see, this site offers access to the college's online catalog, to databases and journals, and to archives, among other resources. There are also "Research guides" that allow students to find online resources by discipline.

Using discipline-specific databases from your college library is a more targeted approach than searching the Internet for information related to your topic. While a Google search may produce irrelevant or sketchy results, library databases will connect you with vetted books, journals, archival materials, and other reliable sources of scholarship. Library databases will lead you to the kind of information that will be most relevant for college writing assignments.

Internet Search Engines. Although they cast a wide net, giant search engines such as Google and Yahoo have different subdivisions that can be used to browse scholarly resources. For example, Google offers Google Scholar, which provides access to professional and academic articles, books, and other sources across a variety of disciplines. Yahoo also allows users to do cross-disciplinary searches for information.

Whether you are searching your library's digital resources or the Internet, it is helpful to have a grasp of keyword searches and advanced search functions.

Keyword Searches. You have probably conducted thousands of digital searches for all kinds of things: videos, news, music, celebrities, events, and sources for your academic papers. So you probably already know that if you use effective keywords for your searches, you are more likely to get good results. Still, there may be ways to improve your strategies.

One way to conduct effective keyword searches for college assignments is to think of the process in stages. Following is a four-stage search strategy using Google.

Follow these steps for any research question:

1) **Do a trial-and-error test of about a half dozen search terms. For example, if your research question is "Which novels and short stories can teach us about autism and the experiences of the autistic?" then you might begin the search with some of the key terms underlined above.**
2) **Then see which ones return the most helpful or relevant results. Let's consider just the terms *autism fiction* and *autism nonfiction*. Entering them into Google turns up information about specific novels that feature autistic characters and about nonfictional works that discuss autism. It also turns up more specific "consensus" terms that people have used to label information on the topic. Some of the consensus terms are *autism novels* and *autism autobiographies*. These consensus labels are frequently known as *tags*.** 🔁
3) **Search again, using the consensus terms (or tags). Using the terms *autism novels* and *autism autobiographies* produces information about additional fictional works and about books in which people with autism describe their experiences. The search also leads to articles that directly address the sample research question. If you turn up additional consensus**

terms that help you narrow your search, you might repeat step three.
4) **Introduce fresh search terms to the existing ones to make sure that you are not missing important information. For instance, adding the term *insights* to *autism novels* turns up additional articles on what the fiction of autism can teach us.**

Advanced Search Functions. Search engines have a variety of advanced functions that can help you focus your searches, returning the best and most relevant information. The most common advanced search strategy is to use quotation marks around search terms, which will find instances of those exact words in that exact order.

For example, go online and see the differences between searching for the words *autism fiction* (without quotation marks) and "*autism fiction*" (with quotation marks). You can also make searches more targeted by specifying dates of publication and media types (such as images, videos, or maps).

Academic search engines enable you to restrict and combine searches according to a number of particular "fields" relating to publication, such as author, date, title, journal, publisher, document type, and keywords. In advanced search functions, you can often combine searches using modifiers like *and*, *or*, *not*, and *near*. (By the way, these modifiers are known as Boolean operators.) These modifiers work according to a very specific logic that can seem counterintuitive at first.

For example, if you search for "autism novels" AND "autism autobiographies," your results will be much smaller and narrower than if you searched for "autism novels" OR "autism autobiographies." The first search will return only results that include both the first search

⬇ **See the LaunchPad for a video showing a search using consensus terms.**

How to support your writing with strong evidence

string AND the second one, whereas the second search will return any results that include the first string OR the second one.

Patience and Skill. Imagine that you have thoroughly defined and refined your search strategies, which have produced a few dozen sources. Now you must take a closer look at those resources, trying to identify those that you might want to use in your writing and those that suggest additional sources to pursue. (Additional sources of interest might appear, for instance, in bibliographies of scholarly articles.) This stage in the research process is like digging for gold. You search until you find a promising streak, and then you follow that streak to find additional results, digging deeper as branches and veins of reward emerge, combine, and separate. The most valuable sources are often nearby or linked to the initial prospects you sought to find. The bibliographies at the end of a good source, or the links the author included throughout, can often lead to even better research material, but this process takes time, patience, and flexibility.

↰ See Lesson 12, Researching for more on how to use research to find evidence.

MONICA
Palomar College

A lot of the kids who don't want to do a lot of research just go on Google Scholar and type in whatever their subject is and use whatever first comes up. But I'll usually search through a million abstracts, and those are the best way to research critically. Just read the abstracts; see when it was written. If it's from within the last five years, it's probably a bit more credible when it comes to science because things are changing all the time.

Librarians. Remember that a major purpose of librarians is to help you find what you are looking for. So, don't hesitate to ask them for help if you are having trouble finding sources or using research tools. Additionally, information science is changing so rapidly that only professional librarians can truly keep up with the latest strategies. Even your professors now need help from librarians to figure out new information technologies. If you need research help when you are not at a library, visit your college library's website. There, you should be able to get online help from a librarian or make an appointment for such assistance — these online resources often have a live chat function!

When people first learn to drive a car, they almost always have an experienced, knowledgeable instructor in the passenger seat to teach them how it's done. Navigating your way through the highways of information available to you can be complex and difficult at first, and too often students try to do it alone.

PRACTICE Make an appointment with an expert "information instructor," such as a librarian, and spend at least ten minutes together searching for evidence and sources online for a current writing assignment. Your information instructor should not touch the keyboard or mouse as you take this journey because you must have your hands on the wheel the entire way if you are going to learn how to drive your own research. Do take note of the steps and advice that your information instructor gives you, but don't let them do all of the thinking. The goal of this activity is not so much about finding evidence for a current assignment as much as it is learning how to find evidence in the future, so that you become an excellent driver on your own.

4. Generate your own primary evidence.

In some cases, it can be powerful for you to generate your own data. Instead of relying completely on ideas or information that other researchers have published (secondary research), you might discover important knowledge on your own (through primary research). Conducting original research might make sense within an appropriate methodology (which is why the beginning of section 6.2 began by talking about *method* and Lesson 8 covers methodology in more detail). It might be appropriate to conduct an experiment or create a survey to create your own primary evidence. Or, you might consider interviews or conversations with experts on your subject as a kind of living library book or scholarly article. College campuses are full of experts on many things, and professors are generally eager to share their life's work with others who are sincerely interested.

THERESE
Santa Fe College

I started out with the Internet, with finding out everything I could read [with] articles, journal articles, things that I could find in virtual space. Then I progressed to people. I started talking with people. I talked with the bee lady at the farmer's market; I talked with the UF professor, the entymologist, who gave me a lot of information. And I stopped and I let myself be late to work to speak with the man who tends the bee boxes down the road, and those were really enriching experiences for me and they got me really enthusiastic about my work, much more so than the Internet articles, which tend to be more dry. And I think because I talked to people I got a livelier perspective, a living perspective on my paper.

Important: Before you create a survey or start interviewing live sources, do your homework. You have to read and research so you know what questions to ask and how to approach your topic. Therese describes how her Internet research led to conversations with experts in her local community that informed her paper on bees.

Therese got a lot out of her interviews, and you can as well, particularly if you find the right person to interview and ask them questions based on your research. Is there anything from your research that an interview might help clarify? Are there any gaps in your research that an interview could fill? Consider how this in-person source will fit into your paper and help you determine the types of questions you will ask. Just remember that professionals — like students — are often very busy, so you will want to leave yourself plenty of time to prepare your questions, schedule your interview, and then incorporate your living source.

Therese's interviews function in her paper as a kind of living source. It's as if the experts she interviewed are "publishing" their knowledge verbally instead of in a conventional scholarly journal — which makes it doubly important for Therese to cite these interviews (see Lesson 24). You could also find yourself going one step further than Therese. You might generate original, primary evidence in a laboratory science class as you write up a report about an experiment you completed or in a social science course where you gathered data from a survey that you created.

PRACTICE In a group of two to five students, brainstorm a list of the kinds of writing and research projects that might encourage you to generate your own

primary sources of evidence (even if you might also use secondary sources elsewhere in the writing).

5. Evaluate your evidence.

By now, at least one teacher has probably told you not to use Wikipedia as a source for papers, and you probably know why: You cannot trust Internet sources that have anonymous authors because the information could be highly unprofessional or biased. Yet, sometimes Wikipedia entries are fantastically well-written and researched; it's just that it's difficult to know which ones are trustworthy. Either way, it is your responsibility to evaluate the quality and the credibility of the sources you include in your college writing. One of the best ways to evaluate a source is to examine the types of evidence it uses. Is the source itself comprised of serious and carefully researched information, facts, data, and statistics? Notice how important the use of rigorous evidence is to Chatiana's approach to her own research.

CHATIANA
Lansing Community College

When I do research, I look for articles with hard facts. I want statistics. I want percentages, you know, and I want great quotes. If you're doing research, you're going to need stuff like that because, if you don't have statistics on something, then how can you tell that it's actually accurate?

Another way to assess the quality of a source is to check the backgrounds of its author and publisher. If the author has professional, expert credentials, then the source is likely to be reliable. If the publisher is a professional organization with a reputation to uphold, like a university press or government institution, then the materials it produces are likely to be credible. However, you should also consider the relationship of the author or publisher to the topic. Are they likely to be objective or biased toward the subject?

Consider an article on the benefits of a dietary supplement that appears not in a medical journal but on a website that sells such supplements. The author is identified vaguely as a "wellness coach," not as a doctor or medical researcher. In this case, the author and the publisher (i.e., the website) may be more interested in promoting the supplement than in sharing scientifically sound and unbiased information.

If the author is anonymous, or it is unclear who is taking responsibility for publishing the resource, you should also be suspicious about the integrity of the information. If the resource is located within an institutional domain (with a URL ending in .edu or .gov), then it is likely more reliable than, say, a .com source aimed at selling a product or service.

You should also examine textual clues that can indicate a source's credibility. Professionally researched publications will most often be free of errors and cleanly formatted, and they almost always include thorough bibliographies. In fact, perhaps the best way to use Wikipedia is to check out the academic sources in the bibliographies at the end of the entries rather than using the entries themselves.

PRACTICE Make a list of three to five sources that you might use in a current or upcoming writing assignment. For each source, list the author's name, the organization for which the author works,

and the name of the publisher. Also list in ten words or less the kind of evidence, facts, or research that each source uses to support its author's claims. Is there a clear pattern among your lists? Was it easy or difficult to generate this list? What does this evaluation reveal about the quality of your sources?

6. Integrate your evidence into your draft.

DAN
Michigan State University

It makes you more effective as a communicator to both prove to yourself and prove to your audience that you've done your research and that you understand the topic and that you're bringing in other people's thoughts. You're not just: "Here are my thoughts." It's: "Here are my thoughts and here are some experts and some research that agrees with my thoughts." So it should never be, "Oh, this paper doesn't have enough resources. I need to go get three more sources." It should never be that. . . . It's no longer just, "Let me throw a source in that paragraph because I have to."

It's one thing to know *how* to integrate sources *mechanically* in terms of choosing words, punctuating quotes, and formatting citations. Lesson 24: Citation describes how to integrate your researched evidence into your paper *mechanically*. This evidence may come in the form of direct quotations, paraphrases, and summaries of source material that are noted in parenthetical citations and on Works Cited pages. However, it's a very different thing to know *how* to integrate sources *logically* and *rhetorically*. As Dan

points out, inexperienced writers and researchers might lightly read a few sources, draft a paper consisting mostly of their own thoughts, and then sprinkle a quote or two into each body paragraph to try to support their claims.

In this approach, the research process amounts only to cherry picking, which means that you skim only the easy-to-reach sources without diving in deeply. When you only put three or four cherries on top of your pie at the end, you haven't made a cherry pie. In college writing, your research and sources are integral to every word, every sentence, every paragraph, and every subtopic throughout your drafts. To make a cherry pie, you start with cherries, the cherries are incorporated throughout the pie, and you can't take a bite without tasting delicious fruit.

DILLON
University of Florida

It's best to have it feel as natural as possible to quote something or put something in. In some of my earlier papers, I would just have sources to take up space. I would just put large quotes just to take more page space, but it never made sense, really, to have it like that. And it's much nicer to frame a quote as "this person said this from this book," — to integrate the source . . . more conversationally — [to] incorporate sources like talking, in a very natural way."

Many researchers think of their enterprise as a conversation, either literally or metaphorically, which is an approach that Dillon describes as "like talking, in a very natural way." Imagine a series of cascading "talk-bubbles" that you might find in a

cartoon or in the student quotes throughout this text.

> Taylor discovered X in 2014.

> Professor Mooney said Y about Taylor's research in 2016.

> Professor Burton added a new perpective in 2018.

Lesson 19: Thesis (p. 263) encourages you to use a research-based thesis statement in your writing. In this statement, you are, in effect, entering into a conversation with what other people have said or written in their research. When you are integrating sources into the rest of your writing, a conversational approach is ideal.

Imagine that you are entering such a conversation. At first you outline what others have written on the subject, and then you add your own perspective in a dialogue with the others. If you approach research as entering into a conversation, then integrating what others have said into your writing is central and essential — integrating sources and evidence into your writing is the very substance of college writing, not an afterthought. Notice how Cara uses the words *natural way, marrying, weave,* and *context* to describe how she integrates sources deeply — every bite is full of cherries.

The word *integrate* means to bring things together in a very close, essential way. To *compose* means to combine different pieces into a unified whole. So, college *composition* is really about *integrating* ideas into a piece of writing. This textbook, for example, integrates the voices from more than one hundred college students to offer you collective advice on becoming a college writer.

CARA
Metropolitan State University of Denver

If I read an essay or read an article, at the end I'll just jot down my responses, jot down what stuck out most to me in that article. And then those little free-writes can pop into my essay sometimes. It's just a natural way of marrying my thoughts with the articles and with my sources. The second way that I often weave them in is I'll write out questions for myself about my subject and then part of my answers will include my source material. So all these answers to all the questions about the subject slowly weave together to form my essay.... From there, you fill in around the source material and explain the context. Why is that source there? What does that source mean to the overall argument or to the overall message?

VINH-THUY
Red Rocks Community College

When I'm writing a traditional research paper, like my botany paper, I do have to really pay attention to the resources. I'm really against — when I read a newspaper or when I read a magazine — when people use factual things or they use wording to get [the source to say] what they really want to say. So when I do a research paper what I have to do is, I usually read through the primary literature and I pay attention to the context from the actual content that I'm extracting from the work. And once extracted, are the ideas still loyal to the original work? So I spend a lot of time making sure that everything that I've extracted retains the original intention of its writer.

But *integrate* is also related to *integrity*, which is another critical part of weaving evidence and source material into your work. You know that your integrity as a college writer and a student requires you to acknowledge your sources through proper citation (covered in Lesson 24). And your integrity is also a function of how honestly you represent the original context of a source that you use.

Vinh-Thuy is very careful not to pull a quote out of its original context or to distort it to fit his argument. Misrepresenting what someone else has written or said for manipulative purposes is known as "spin" in broadcast media, and it is a significant problem in mainstream culture that each of us needs to resist and reject, beginning with our own use of research, sources, and quotes.

This segment on integrating evidence began with a quote from Dan that was very wise in many ways, but might mislead you on one very important account: You do not want to integrate only sources that "agree" with your thoughts. If research writing is like an unfolding textual conversation, as we have said, then that conversation will have more integrity if it includes different, thoughtful perspectives and is not one-sided. If you ignore or conceal reasonable objections to your points and conclusions, then your readers will find *you* less credible as a source. And, if you do include counterpoints in your writing but you dismiss them or do not consider the issues in their full complexity, then your composition will not hold together as well. As you work to integrate multiple perspectives into your writing and analysis, especially in an argumentative piece, work hard to differentiate simple nay-sayers and rants from thoughtful opposing views. All ideas are not of equal merit, especially ones that are not based upon evidence and careful research. Thus, integrating sources with integrity is not just finding and citing credible sources, it's also how you integrate them to be fair to context and to different viewpoints.

PRACTICE Analyze a sample piece of writing, ideally a recent college paper you have completed or a classmate's paper. Next to each body paragraph, count the number of different sources or quotes used in that paragraph. Does the paragraph seem to integrate evidence effectively, given the number of sources? Also look closely at one sample paragraph; are the sources used with integrity, and are they woven into the writing naturally and conversationally?

7. RRFF your evidence.

AMANDA
Palomar College

So I kind of skim over [an online resource] or I read it and see if it's what I want. If it's something that I feel might be pertinent, I bookmark it and then I start [to drift into] "research nowhere-land." Something is on the screen, you click on it, and it takes you to another page and another page and another page and another page. And all of a sudden you're all, "Wait a minute, this doesn't pertain to where I need to be." So you back up and you start again — well, not start the process again, but you go back to where it was essential to what you want to write about.

Lesson 12: Researching discusses research as one of the steps in your college writing process. Like most other steps in this process, research is recursive, which means that you keep working at it and returning to it throughout the process until you finally submit or publish your work. In other words,

you don't just conduct research once, stop, and then move on to drafting your paper. You continue generating and collecting new or different evidence.

As you research and draft, let new questions and ideas emerge. These will deepen your understanding of your topic and lead you to new key terms to search for, new voices in the conversation, and more evidence to make your writing coherent. If writing effectively means **Revising Repeatedly from Feedback**, and college writing is based upon research, that means that you will also want to Revise your Research Repeatedly from Feedback. To get more insights for that revision process, ask readers of your

HUSSAIN
University of Florida

I would say there's a stage before I start writing anything and there's a stage after I'm done writing everything [when] I look at the research again. Most of the papers I've written for my own [scientific] research begin with an abstract or an introduction where I'm introducing the audience to the reading I've done and to my own experiment. So you have to cite the literature that's available on the research that I'm doing. So, when I'm writing the actual paper, that research, most of it comes in the beginning, but before I actually write the paper. After I'm done with the paper and I've written everything and have my conclusions, I look for other things in the literature that support what I've written, or I just look for other connections that could be there. So, I think there's a phase where you look at the research in the beginning before you start writing and then you go back to it in the end.

drafts-in-progress to evaluate your use of sources and evidence. Ask them to identify places in your draft where they would like to find more evidence, or where the support seems flawed or illogical. And, of course, you need to revise your search and study strategies along the way as you conduct research — getting lost in what Amanda describes as "research nowhere-land" and then finding your way back is part of revising your research process.

PRACTICE Quickly list on paper or on a chalkboard the various stages and drafts of a writing assignment that you are working on at the moment or this term, or you can diagram the process Hussain describes above. Put a star next to every step that involves either gathering or integrating evidence. Now draw lines from one star to the next, like links in a chain. Define in a single sentence how each line, each link in the chain, revises in some way your processes for gathering or integrating evidence. How does each new line revise or add to previous evidence, perhaps in ways similar to Hussain's approach?

6.3

Exercises: evidence

6a Integrate the video.

Lesson 1 of *Becoming a College Writer* defines *writing* as a dynamic relationship between an author, a topic, and an audience. This means that you want your readers to sense substantial connections and integrity between all aspects of your writing, especially your use of evidence. Notice how supporting her writing with evidence is so essential to Nia's definition of *good writing*:

I feel like a good paper is when you really take the time to know what you're talking about. That way you're not worrying about how many words you need until you have to stop writing. You did your research, you did your homework, and there's a lot to put in the paper.

Write a substantial paragraph or two, with a topic sentence or mini-thesis, through which you respond to Nia and other videos in the chapter as you form your own approaches to gathering and integrating evidence. You can watch the Lesson 6 Essentials Video, or you can browse the embedded clips in the online edition of this lesson. You might begin by identifying the moments that stand out to you the most. Which student videos seem to make the most sense to you? With whom do you agree? Disagree? What patterns do you find among the student sound bites? Which ideas were the most instructive or helpful to you? What surprised you? How have your own ideas about evidence and research come into focus through the videos?

6b Create a journal entry or blog.

Your instructor might ask you to keep a writer's journal throughout this class. This journal could be handwritten or composed on a computer; it could take the shape of a text-based blog or a video blog.

To prepare a journal entry on Lesson 6, describe your thoughts and approaches to the key term *evidence*, trying not to glance back at the material in this lesson, at first. Not referring to this material initially will help you see what you have internalized so far. After carefully composing your initial thoughts, look back at some of the ideas and strategies other students gave in Lesson 6 or in the online database of interviews. For example, in her interview, Nicole describes how she uses evidence to support her claims:

When I think about integrating sources into my writing, it's more so of an internalized thing where I'm not so much aware of what I'm doing or what I'm choosing. When I choose a quote from a source, I make sure that it backs up my claim in my paper. You don't want to just drop a quote into the paper. You want to introduce your quote. Why are you using this quote and why is it relevant to the [nearby] point?

You might wish to disagree with some of this lesson, or you might want to modify or expand on some of its advice. For example, consider integrating additional thoughts, notes, and lessons from your instructor and your class meetings into your journal entry. It might help for you to imagine that you are giving advice to your future self about writing. What ideas from this lesson and from discussions about writing might benefit you down the road?

6c See yourself as a writer.

In a page or two, describe the evolution of your sense of *evidence* or *research* since you began writing. Where and when did you start to develop strategies for gathering, analyzing, and integrating evidence? What major events, assignments, and papers have influenced your approaches to evidence along the way? What particular teachers or classes have reshaped the ways you use evidence in your writing? What was your sense of *evidence* and *research* before you began reading this lesson? What is your approach now that you have finished this lesson? In what ways can you imagine your sense of *evidence* changing beyond college? How does your development as a writer compare with what other students said in their interviews, such as Dan? Have your approaches to evidence, research, and sources evolved since high school like Dan's?

Including resources was always the most frustrating thing for me in high school because I used to think "I've written this paper, it's pretty good. Aw, now I need to quote the author three times somewhere. OK, I'll throw that quote in there and that quote in here." But now it's more important to me. It's not just, oh yeah, I need to make this look better so I'll throw in some resources. In college writing, [you are more] effective as a communicator when you prove to yourself and prove to your audience that you've done your research.

6d Invent your writing.

Section 6.2 of this lesson discusses seven strategies to help you support your writing with evidence. In five complete sentences, map out how five of these seven concepts could be applied to a writing assignment you are working on in this class (or in another class, if you are not currently writing in this course). For example, in his interview, Deonta describes how he uses search engines and consults with librarians (strategy 6.2.3) to build the evidence that supports his writing:

I typically [begin by] using Google Scholar or school search engines. But sometimes I'll go to the library and search through the selves, or ask the librarians for help looking for a certain book. After that, I normally read through the books or download the articles that I found and take out the points that I think are important, including direct quotes that I plan to use for my paper. I compile a list of that stuff [for] later on when I make my citations.

6e Analyze student writing.

Study the opening two or three paragraphs or segments of a couple of model projects in Lesson 25 or in the LaunchPad. You might compare very different models, such as Dan's video and Nicole's paper, or you might read similar work, such as Nanaissa's and Vinh-Thuy's papers.

For each writer, describe in a sentence or two the kinds of evidence each of these authors uses to support their claims and ideas. Based on the students' work, what kinds of connections can you sense between the evidence and the prompt or the audience for the writing? How does each evidence/prompt/audience connection compare with the other? In what ways do they seem alike? Different? List a couple of specific choices the writers make to suggest connections between their use of evidence and their prompt or audience.

Your instructor might ask you to apply this analysis and these questions to your class-mates' writing instead of, or in addition to, the model projects.

6f Revise repeatedly from feedback.

Examine a writing assignment you are currently working on or one that you wrote recently, perhaps in another class or in high school. Describe some specific ways that you can use the ideas from Lesson 6 to revise your writing and improve your instincts for generating, analyzing, and integrating evidence in your writing. Perhaps most important, to complete this exercise, take an early draft of your writing to the writing center, a peer workshop, or your instructor's office hours and ask, "Where am I integrating evidence effectively? Where can my use of evidence be improved?"

LESSON 7

Genre

Analyze and compare genres to meet audience expectations.

Gandee Vasan/Getty Images

Visit the LaunchPad for *Becoming a College Writer* to watch the
Lesson 7 Essentials Video.

7.1 [WHY]

Why you should analyze and compare genres to meet audience expectations.

As a college writer you will expand your ability to write in a variety of genres and contexts. You will go beyond the basic academic essay and generic research paper and learn to compose arguments, reports, and presentations in an array of genres as you take more advanced courses in a variety of academic departments and disciplines.

Genre is a massive umbrella term that covers a lot of ideas. For many, the concept can seem pretty abstract. That's why it's common to oversimplify or reduce *genre* to mean a composition's physical form or format — because doing so makes the concept of *genre* easier to grasp. But there's much more to genre than mere form, and fully understanding the term will help you to become a stronger writer.

Getting practice writing in a variety of genres will build your confidence throughout your college career and beyond.

Terryn describes how he moves among contexts and forms in his writing. As you read Terryn's advice, substitute in your head the word *genre* every time he uses the word *form*.

TERRYN
Santa Fe College

I've been using [the traditional essay] form for a long time, since I [was] taught in middle school by one of my teachers. And, you know, basically when I'm assigned an essay I usually think about using that form. Of course, I get in a little trouble if you go into another subject, such as journalism, where you're going to have ten or eleven paragraphs and most of them are going to be quotes. It's completely different because the paragraphs are just going to be stating facts. So that form doesn't really have any ground in that subject. . . . For English classes I definitely use that form. But for other classes you just have to find another form.

DEONTA
University of North Carolina, Chapel Hill

Throughout my college career I wrote lab reports, English composition papers, literary analyses, sociology papers, proposals. And starting this semester, I'm writing philosophy papers. [But] moving among the genres is sometimes kind of hard for me. Sometimes I'll be writing a lab report and it looks more like an English composition paper, so I have to start back over to make sure that I get all the statistics that I need in the paper.

Terryn's comments show that he sees a connection between the physical form of a genre and the need to negotiate among different genres rhetorically, as a writer. As you analyze and compare genres, it's likely that you'll first notice their different physical forms. You may notice differences in the look of the composition, and in the purpose, style, length, and arrangement of paragraphs. But it's important to keep the horse in front of the cart.

A *genre* is defined by the relationship between an author, audience, and topic. The demands of that relationship determine the physical format of the writing, and not the other way around. Meaning and connection come before the format. The context determines the form. The form does not shape the context.

If, like Deonta, you find yourself struggling to understand and move among genres, ask yourself, "What are my audience's expectations regarding genre, and why do they have those expectations?" rather than "What is the correct physical format for the genre I have been assigned?"

The most familiar definition of *genre* is that it is a type of writing. For example, literature includes the genres of poetry, novels, short stories, and drama. In these genres, the physical shape of the written words — a poem broken into stanzas, a play written as dialogue — are part of what define it, at least on the surface. But novels, for example, can be classified into various other genres — comedy, tragedy, romance, or thriller — and look pretty much the same on the page.

Let's look at film. When you want to watch a movie with someone, you might ask, "What kind of movie are you in the mood for tonight?" Comedy? Drama? Action? And then you browse film titles based upon genre to find what you want. So, *genre* can

first be defined as *classification* for different types of writing.

However, if you think more closely about genre, the definition becomes more complicated. Let's say that you want to watch a film drama tonight. Which kind of drama are you looking for? Romantic? Historical? Science fiction? Crime? You're in the mood for some crime, but which kind of crime? Thriller? Heist? Modern gangster or classic mafia?

Let's say you pick *The Godfather*. What genre is it? Hollywood classic? Action/adventure? Crime drama? Historical epic? If you had to put *The Godfather* on a shelf or in a database according to genre, where would you put it? If you were looking for *The Godfather* to download from a streaming service, under what category would you look?

Like the discussion of topics and subtopics in Lesson 4 (p. 41), understanding a particular genre is also a matter of genres (plural) and subgenres. The term *genre* is applied to many things beyond writing, including movies, visual art, architecture, music, and even styles of clothing.

You can see how messy it can be to try to define a genre precisely, or to locate a particular work within a genre. This messiness is no reason to avoid thinking about genre, however. Consider how your own expectations about genre influence the ways you and your friends select and watch movies. If your friend hates horror movies, you're unlikely to suggest the latest slasher flick for your Friday night entertainment. In other words:

Audiences have expectations about genre. As a writer, knowing those expectations will help you succeed.

Let's narrow the potentially enormous discussion of genre down to "college writing" as a genre. Under the genre of college writing you will encounter many subgenres, including formal essays, research papers, journals, reports, oral presentations, essay exams, reaction pieces, blogs, position statements, podcasts, documentary films, summaries, and narratives. And within those subgenres lie additional sub-subgenres; for example, the report genre includes lab reports, book reports, news reports, literature reviews, and many others.

In the middle of Lesson 4: Topic (p. 41), I said that once you, as a writer, select a topic, you trigger a series of choices that need to be made. These choices define your writing and establish a dynamic relationship between you, your audience, and your topic. Consequently, it's helpful to *think of genre as a pattern that guides the choices you make.*

Your instructors will often define the genre of your assignment for you. They might ask you to write a research paper or a four-page essay or an opinion blog. They might even define a subgenre for you, such as "Write a movie-critic blog about three recent films."

Even when you are assigned a specific subgenre, you will still make choices about whether to accept or reject the "rules" for a particular genre. More important, when you find yourself choosing a genre without the guidance of an instructor (or a boss), experience and practice with genres will be key to writing successfully on your own.

Approach your chosen or assigned genre in ways that *balance* your writing.

JENNA
California State University, San Marcos

There are differences, and you need to recognize those differences because that can radically change the way you approach a certain assignment. I mean, at the heart of things, your thesis is still your argument, your body paragraphs are still going to connect to each other, your conclusion is still going to wrap everything up. But it depends on what mode of thought you should be concentrating on while you're writing. I think that's why they call it a mode. It's a mode of thought. Say you're writing a literary analysis. It's a different mode than if you're writing a cover letter for a résumé. And it's different than an essay that specifically compares and contrasts two different things.

Think of practical ways that you can use genre to balance your writing. Section 7.2, which follows, describes the kinds of choices that tend to "fit" each of the most common genres of college writing. As you think about genre and balance, imagine that you are an architect hired to design and construct a building.

pryzmat/Shutterstock.com

Why you should analyze and compare genres to meet audience expectations

In this analogy, the foundation depends upon the relationship between you (the architect), your composition (your building), and your audience (the people who have hired you). As the architect, you have many decisions to make before you can raise the roof. You want your building to be sturdy and attractive. Will you build the exterior walls out of masonry, wood, steel, or glass? If you choose masonry, then which kind: brick, stone, or concrete? And how will you stack the stones: in rows, columns, or steel-reinforced slabs? Which style will make sense for your building: traditional, minimal, or decorative? You want your design to *balance* form and function, which means you want it to look nice and also withstand the weather. You want all of your choices to balance your building.

In this analogy, one choice that you will make about your building (okay, your writing) is your use of *material*, of evidence (which is the focus of Lesson 6: Evidence). You will select and align evidence like you might select and stack bricks. Of course there are many kinds of bricks and many ways to stack them; this is also true for the evidence you choose and arrange in your writing. In this analogy, the *way* you stack the bricks might be called your *method* (which is part of the focus of Lesson 8: Discipline).

As you build, you will also make choices about the style and tone of your paper (see Lesson 22: Sentences, p. 314). You might consider which medium would work best: paper, oral presentation, video, website, podcast, blog, etc. (see Lesson 9: Media). In college you often write in the context of a particular department or discipline (see Lesson 8: Discipline). There will be a pattern to the way you respond to these variables for each writing assignment, and that pattern can be called your *genre*. You make choices, not only about *what* you include in your writing, but also about *how* you arrange the parts; these choices determine your *genre*.

Ranch House

Chalet House

Alpine House

Cottage House

Imagine that your building is complete. Now step back and look at it. The architectural choices you have made define it: the building materials, the shape of the roof, the colors and textures of the surfaces, and more. Your building has a style that reflects the way that you selected and arranged all of the materials. Look at your building. It has an architectural genre. It has a relationship to the space around it and to the people who will inhabit it. *It's a composition.* And if you chose and assemble all of the pieces thoughtfully and harmoniously, it has *balance*.

PRACTICE In a group of two-to-five students, brainstorm a list of all the genres of writing projects you have been assigned or completed in high school or college. Make this list as long as possible and compare it to other groups in the class. The longest list wins! Or you might make your own list and compare it with the essays of the featured students in this textbook or in the online database. How comfortable has it been for you and your classmates to negotiate successfully between different genres? Has it gotten easier?

The way you assemble your writing can also help balance your relationship with your reader.

Section 7.2 analyzes the most common genres for college writing. What is the genre for a piece of writing you're working on now? To see samples of college writing, examine the student papers on pages 422–93. Additional samples are also available in the LaunchPad edition of *Becoming a College Writer,* where they are searchable and indexed by genre.

LINDSEY
Michigan State University

When you get your first paper back from that professor you really need to look at the criticism and adjust to what they said. You really need to be flexible and adaptable depending on who you're writing for. . . . I started out writing just typical English papers, like argumentative and persuasive and research and things like that and then I switched to more scientific research papers. . . . What's kind of similar about all of them is [that] you really have to see who you're talking to and that is probably one of the most important things about writing: to cater to the right audience.

Notice how Lindsey learned to negotiate different genres by responding to feedback from her professors. In other words, she learned about genres by **Revising Repeatedly from Feedback**. The kind of adaptability that Lindsey developed through **RRFF** is one of the ultimate goals of a college writing course. Genres are often combined and blended, so there are no absolutely black-and-white rules for meeting the demands of a particular genre. For example, you might be asked to write a research paper in the form of a narrative essay, which demands that you combine and recombine genres that are conventionally separated. Vinh-Thuy took a risk with his paper by combining a personal narrative with photographs, and he was rewarded with an A because his audience appreciated his experiment, but a different audience might not respond the same way to his hybrid genre (p. 472).

Why you should analyze and compare genres to meet audience expectations

7.2 [HOW]

How to analyze and compare genres to meet various audience expectations.

Ask specific questions about what your audience expects in terms of that genre.

Before you begin a writing assignment, ask yourself: "Who is my audience?" "What is my genre?" and "What are my audience's expectations about this genre?" While an assignment prompt will typically identify your target audience and a preferred genre, inquiring about your audience and their expectations will help clarify the specific context for your writing. To find out what your audience may be expecting, take some time to analyze some ideal examples of the genre you've been assigned. For instance, if you are writing a zoology paper (like Kendra's), you might study a scientific zoology journal that actually publishes in that genre and see if you can identify and list the specific characteristics of that genre.

KENDRA
Michigan State University

I think the variety is good. You may not like a certain type [of writing], but if you play around with other types of writing you might find one you do like. Going in between them is different. You have to change your mind-set and approach for different types of papers. But you can ask other people who may have just written that type of paper; or [ask] your teacher how to set yourself up for that type of paper you're writing.

As you "set yourself up" (in Kendra's words) for analyzing specific examples in a genre, consider these defining questions:

- **For this genre, what is the situation of the audience in relation to the author and topic?**

- **What seems to be the defining purpose or function of this genre?**

- **What kind of evidence is presented in this genre and how is the evidence arranged?**

- **What is the organizational structure and function of this genre's paragraphs, parts, and other segments?**

- **What seem to be the conventions for formatting?**

- **What kind of language, tone, voice, and sentence style are conveyed through this genre?**

DAN
Michigan State University

When I first came to college I did my first couple of papers by following the rules because I thought that's how I'd be judged, and I did terrible on the papers. . . . I realized that you can't just write an intro with your thesis in it, a few paragraphs, and a conclusion. I think that [formula] was a great place to start because it helps you start thinking about the writing process and how to organize your thoughts. But now if you stick to that sort of format, whether you're writing a paper or doing something digitally, it's not going to go well because no one wants to read that no matter what it is, even if it's an academic paper. So writing has sort of evolved for me from understanding the rules, really understanding the rules, not understanding why I'm following the rules, and then breaking the rules and breaking them really effectively.

As you study examples of genres, be sure to reflect critically on what you observe. Avoid blindly adhering to "rules" you see in the examples, especially if they don't make sense for your particular context. In fact, one of the best ways to understand and work with genres is to question a genre's conventions, after you understand their assumptions in the first place, as Dan does. In fact, you could say that Dan becomes fully developed as a college writer the very moment he learns to successfully challenge static notions of genre.

Explore the differences among approaches.

Negotiating between different academic genres is both a healthy practice and an ultimate goal of a college writing course and this textbook. Part of why we interviewed nearly one hundred students and gathered sample papers is so that you can compare a variety of approaches to college writing and academic genres. An effective way to learn about genres is to spend some time comparing the sample writing assignments on pages 424–93, as well as the ones in the accompanying online version of *Becoming a College Writer*. For example, among the featured students you will find a literary analysis essay (Nicole), a hypothesis-research paper and oral presentation (Kendra), a sociology research paper (Deonta), a rhetorical reflection film and transcript (Dan), a hybrid personal narrative essay (Vinh-Thuy), and a problem-solution argumentative essay (Nanaissa).

I sorted through those sample papers to identify the most common genres that students are assigned in college writing courses. In the examples that follow, you'll find some concrete ways to differentiate among those genres — and to approach the particular genres you chose or are assigned in college.

As you read through the following "Top 10" list, please be aware that your instructor might assign writing that combines one or more of the genres described below, in which case you will need to think critically to determine which characteristics of each genre will work best for you, your audience, and your topic. You always want to consider expectations regarding genre, but you will also make critical choices based upon what you, as a writer, believe will work best in a particular situation. You want to be aware of established genres but not be rigidly bound by them.

Top 10 college writing assignments by genre.

1) Argumentative essay. The argumentative essay combines the genre of argument with the very familiar institution of the essay. Argumentation requires that you clearly define and explain your debatable position on the issue in question. It begins when you take a stand, which you must then support with abundant evidence. In the form of an essay or an oral presentation, structure your argument with a beginning, a middle, and an end. The beginning announces your position, which cannot be either a fact (which is not arguable) or an unsupported opinion (which is a rant, not a structured argument). The middle carefully supports your argument, often by also exploring or refuting counterarguments. And the end drives home your argument emphatically.

The argumentative essay features:

- **A clear, emphatically stated main idea, position, or thesis**
- **Abundant evidence from appropriate source material to support and explain your position**
- **A deliberate, logical organization**

How to analyze and compare genres to meet various audience expectations

The advantage of this genre is that it's familiar and easy to access for both the writer and reader. The argumentative essay directly prompts evidence-based research writing and mirrors the type of analysis and problem solving required in most professions. The downside of the argumentative essay, as the most popular of college writing genres, is that the approach can become static, robotic, and formulaic.

Most of the best argumentative essays have broken away from the five-paragraph essay format. Although the structure is straightforward, you have a lot of room to play with the number of paragraphs and the relationships between paragraphs to make your case as compelling as possible.

PRACTICE Nanaissa's paper in Lesson 25 is clearly an argumentative essay. Which of the features discussed above, particularly the three bullet points, can you locate in her essay? Discuss these features in class or in a written analysis of her essay.

2) Rhetorical analysis. This genre requires you to look at the work of another author and analyze the choices that author has made in a piece of writing, in speech, or with their presentation of visuals. However, if that author is writing literature, you might want to consider the "literary analysis" genre below instead of this one.

To conduct a rhetorical analysis, you can start by applying what you learned about the dynamic relationship of an author, audience, and topic in Part One: Rhetoric. You want to critically examine the choices that authors make to appeal to their audiences and explore their topics. You might analyze the way the authors select and combine evidence. You might notice if they

appeal to emotions (pathos), logic (logos), or morality (ethos).

The rhetorical analysis features:

- **A generalized insight into the choices an author makes to persuade an audience**
- **Specific, concrete references to the author's text (whether print or visual)**
- **Identified patterns in the author's choices that explain how the text works overall**

The advantage of the rhetorical analysis as an academic genre is that it urges you to dig into the ways language and communication work. And, if you've ever read something and thought, *Why did the author do that?*, this is your chance to try to answer that question.

Further, you can apply this critical awareness to your own writing and communications. The disadvantage of this genre is that the approach may lead writers to focus on superficial or obvious concerns. For example, if you are analyzing an advertisement and it includes an attractive person, you might too easily conclude that the author is using sex appeal to sell the product, when that conclusion is too obvious and does not go deep enough.

PRACTICE Yadirys's visual/textual paper is an in-depth rhetorical analysis of a television advertisement. The paragraph below is from her essay.

The eye level shot makes the viewers seem as if they are sitting behind the family on the bed, even though the viewers cannot see their reflections in the mirror; this feeling that the viewers are immediately behind the family makes the viewers feel claustrophobic

and feel as if they are imposing into this family's personal space. **Their reflection in the mirror seems to make them even closer together, and adds to the feeling of claustrophobia that comes from five people sitting on the bed. This lack of space shows that the television set is far too small for this family.** Yet, the advertisers indicate that the size of the television does not matter because the quality and color make it so that everyone will want to watch it.

Which of the features discussed above, particularly in the three bullet points, can you locate in this paragraph? Which features can you find elsewhere in her essay (available in the LaunchPad for *Becoming a College Writer*)? Discuss these features in class or in a written analysis of her essay.

3) Literary analysis. This genre requires that you analyze a work of literature by either reading the text closely or by applying a critical framework to the text (or both). You might read a particular work or compare a number of works. You might discuss a particular author or compare authors. You might examine a genre (like poetry), a literary device (like symbolism), or a historical era (like the Renaissance).

The most common way to analyze literature is to select a text or a group of texts for a particular reason and then read those texts carefully, almost microscopically, in order to see how they work and to analyze the choices that the literary authors make. Literary criticism also requires writers to evaluate the more general qualities of a work. For example, such criticism can involve applying a particular critical, theoretical lens (such as feminism, formalism,

postcolonialism, or new historicism) to a text, author, or group of texts. The range of potential approaches to literary analysis is very broad, but at its heart is always a very careful, close reading of text.

Examining giant themes in literature such as "man versus nature" or "individual freedom versus social constraint" can be tempting, but these may be too broad for a college paper. If you do choose a large theme, be sure to ground it in the text to make sure that you are not being too general. Most often you will be asked to be meticulous and to examine a text carefully, as you might examine a rare specimen in a biology lab. This type of writing is not about how the text makes you feel. It is a type of analysis that hinges on what you can prove by drawing on evidence from the text itself.

Literary analysis features:

- **An insightful main point, thesis, explication, or interpretation about literature or literary authors**

- **Abundant evidence that comes from, and refers to, specific, careful reading of literature**

- **The application of a consistent, cohesive method or critical lens for reading and interpreting literature**

- **Connections between the literature analyzed and a deeper understanding of the human condition**

The advantage of this genre is that many students begin to learn to write academically through the study of literature, so literary analysis is familiar and well matched to the traditional form of the academic essay. Literary analysis, of course, focuses

How to analyze and compare genres to meet various audience expectations

on language, which can influence your own linguistic abilities. The disadvantage of this genre is that it may limit developing writers from recognizing or practicing other ways of writing in other contexts.

PRACTICE Nicole's model paper (in Lesson 25) offers a postcolonial literary analysis of a novel by Gabriel García Márquez. Which of the features discussed above, particularly the four bullet points, can you locate in her essay? Discuss these features in class or in a written analysis of her essay.

4) Research projects. All college writing draws on evidence, to varying degrees. For example, a rhetorical or literary analysis assignment may not require research, but it does require that you draw on evidence and quote from the article, poem, story, or text that you're examining.

However, as a specific genre, the "research paper" (or better yet, the "research *project*" because the format might not be on paper) has some defining characteristics, despite the wide array of types and presentations of research done at the college level. At the heart of this genre is, of course, the careful research you conduct. The discussions of research in Lesson 6: Evidence and Lesson 12: Research prompt you to think of research as a kind of "conversation" around a specific topic. Your task as a researcher is first to study what other researchers have written or said on a given topic and then to add your own ideas to that conversation.

Consequently, a college research project should be packed with the evidence you have collected and combined from researchers, but you must also declare your own view on the issue — and you must use research to support your view firmly. If the topic is worth researching in the first place, then there must be an issue, problem, or question that begs for a response. As such, a research question can frame and introduce a research paper, and your contribution to the conversation, your particular answer to the research question, can be called your thesis, which should be supported throughout the paper.

↰ For more on thesis, see Lesson 20, p. 278.

Research papers feature

- **A unifying question, idea, thesis, or main point that brings together a rich collection of sources and information — although analysis, synopsis, or summary may be as valued as argument or persuasion**

- **An organization that unfolds in incremental or cumulative ways, so that each piece of research builds on previous ideas to create a cohesive, structured perspective**

- **Deliberate, careful methods for locating, evaluating, and integrating high-quality source material**

- **A sense of closure about the research topic that conveys that the writer has addressed the topic or question thoroughly**

The advantage of the research project is that it allows you to educate yourself on a particular topic while you practice and improve your writing. But the genre can be confusing if it's not made clear whether the writer should merely report on established information or critically examine the topic to argue for a new perspective.

PRACTICE Kendra's model research paper and oral presentation examines published zoological articles to test her hypothesis about the Komodo dragon. Which of the features discussed above, particularly the four bullet points, can you locate in her research project? Discuss these features in class or in a written analysis of her presentation.

5) Technical and scientific reports. The lab report is the most familiar example of this genre. Students in applied sciences such as engineering and information science use the report genre to share data, findings, and inventions.

In technical reports, presenting your data with clinical, scientific, and mathematical objectivity is your first priority. The second concern is explaining the precise method you used to generate or gather your data. You almost want to think, write, and report like a robot would because your goal is to describe precisely what you did so that other scientists can follow your procedure exactly and produce the same results.

Technical and scientific reports can include sections that are more subjective or interpretative, such as an introduction or background discussion, that provide context for the information in the report. A report writer can also include thoughts on the implications for additional research based upon the findings of the current report. Even so, the data and the method sections are most important.

Technical and scientific reports do not argue for a new understanding as much as they report on new data and facts that have been uncovered through an experiment or research. A lab report that describes an experiment and reports the results is a familiar example. But a technical report could also describe the development of a new computer component or an improved solar energy cell. Such reports are likely to include visual elements such as figures, tables, charts, graphs, illustrations, diagrams, and photographs.

Technical and scientific reports feature

- **An educated hypothesis that responds to previous research**
- **The presentation of data and information for practical application and replication to prove or disprove the hypothesis**
- **Objective, clinical writing based upon data and facts**
- **Document structure with modular segments, each of which have a separate function**
- **The easy, direct, and expedient distribution of knowledge**
- **Precise, technical descriptions of methods so that others can replicate, confirm, or deny the data and findings**

The forms for reporting scientific and technical information are universally established and understood, so readers know precisely how to read them and where to locate what they are looking for. The disadvantage of this static form is that it conceals the interpretative aspects of understanding the data. Scientists might use a passive voice because it suggests that a completely objective person did the work; but even the most clinical of scientists is a human being whose thoughts and opinions had influence on the research.

How to analyze and compare genres to meet various audience expectations

HUSSAIN
University of Florida

The structure of the lab report is a tried and true method where you don't really want to alter much. You have your introduction or abstract. You have your hypothesis. You state your materials and methods that you used. You have an observation section that includes your tables, graphs, and figures. You have a results section saying the results you got from your lab, from your experiment. Then you have your conclusion or discussion, stating your findings and the problems you had and where you're going from there. The structure of the lab report is very set in stone, and you don't want to fiddle with that because that's what your audience expects.

PRACTICE Kendra's paper is a hypothesis-driven research report, not a lab report, but it uses the scientific method just the same. Which of the features discussed above, particularly the six bullet points, can you locate in her research project? Discuss these features in class or in a written analysis of her presentation.

↰⌐ **See Lesson 25 for Kendra's paper and the LaunchPad for her accompanying oral presentation.**

6) Narrative essay. A narrative is a story. As such, the narrative essay might be considered more appropriate as a purely creative writing genre than as an academic writing genre. For one thing, creative writing is not defined by its use of evidence and sources the way academic writing is.

However, creative writing, literature, and composition instructors tend to work very closely together — sometimes they are the same person. As a result, hybrid narrative assignments are fairly common in college

writing classes, partly because they are comfortable and familiar to your teachers. For example, you might be asked to write an autobiographical narrative essay that uses your life experiences as the evidence to support your point. You'll see the third exercise (or "C" exercise) in most every lesson of this book asks you to tell the story of your development as a writer.

The narrative essay can also be classified as creative nonfiction, a genre that draws on elements of literature, including character, theme, and dialogue. The genre is also closely related to journalism, and journalism is definitely writing based upon sources. In general, creative writing does not prove or argue a point, but when you try to overtly make an argument with a story, then you are writing a narrative essay.

The narrative essay features

- A thesis, argument, or main point presented more subtly than in an argumentative essay

- Concrete but creative images, anecdotes, characters, events, and descriptions that combine in the form of a story or a portrait to support the main point

- An essay structure with a beginning, middle, and end that is not as deliberate or predictable as a conventional academic essay but does provide a shape, arc, and sense of progress from start to finish

PRACTICE Vinh-Thuy's narrative essay in Lesson 25 is a hybrid of many genres, including autobiography, photo-essay, and even a little poetry. Which of the features discussed above for a narrative essay,

particularly the three bullet points, can you locate in his paper? Which significant dimensions of other genres beyond the narrative essay can you also find in the paper? Discuss these features in class or in a written analysis of his presentation.

7) *Proposal or application.* Proposals and applications can be simultaneously the easiest and most difficult college writing genres. They are easy in the sense that your purpose and audience is exceptionally clear. You are writing to obtain a specific thing: admission, funding, acceptance, approval, a sale, or a job. However, applications are also difficult because your future is on the line, and there can be money or an important opportunity at stake. Emily describes how the transition to real-world writing genres was difficult for her but ultimately rewarding.

EMILY
Boston University

A lot of my classes are in the College of Communication and those classes are very practically based. For example, in my Corporate Communications class almost all, if not all, of our assignments were writing that I would be doing out in the workplace: writing a "pitch letter" or memo letter to a boss or writing a blog post. That writing has been more career focused. I've liked it a lot because I know it's preparing me for the real world, once I graduate.

Your instructor might ask you to write a hypothetical proposal or application, which is obviously less pressure than if a real acceptance depended on your writing. But you get the point: Proposals and applications demonstrate just how essential writing is to your life and your future.

Approach a proposal or application by putting yourself in the shoes of the people who will read your writing and decide whether or not to select you. Imagine how your audience will see your proposal. Your readers are looking for applicants whom they can trust with whatever investment is at stake. They're looking for applicants who present themselves as professional and mature, applicants who will reflect well on the organization that is offering the opportunity. Your goal is to describe logically, but not arrogantly, why you are a good match for the organization.

Applications and proposals are like all college writing because they spring from research. If your thesis for every proposal or application is that you are a good match, then you must first research the position and organization to describe how you would contribute and how you would fit in. Get your hands on previously successful proposals and study them to figure out why they were winners.

As always, discuss your preliminary draft with someone who can give you informed feedback. Student fellowships and admissions committees often have staff members whose job is to help find and develop good applicants. If so, run your ideas by these people *well ahead of time.* Do *not* use these people to help you gauge your chances for success — don't ask them if they think you will "get in." Do ask them about previously successful applications and how your ideas might match the target.

If you are asked to include a budget, be fanatically meticulous. You are proposing that somebody invest money in you and your ideas, and your readers will read your budget to see if you can be trusted with their money. A budget is another opportunity to demonstrate your maturity and thoughtfulness.

The proposal features

- **Writing that demonstrates a good match between the applicant and the opportunity**
- **Abundant, concrete, factual examples and evidence that support connections between the applicant and the opportunity**
- **Logical structure, most typically arranged chronologically**
- **Extremely concise and direct language**
- **Perfection and precision in correctness and document preparation**
- **Positive assertions without exaggeration or fluff**

As Emily points out, the advantage of the proposal is that it applies to professional contexts beyond college. The downside is that it can be difficult for students with only conventional academic writing experience to make the stark transition to a very different kind of writing.

PRACTICE Daniel provides a cover letter and an application, which you can study in the LaunchPad for *Becoming a College Writer*. Which of the features discussed in the section above, particularly the six bullet points, can you locate in Daniel's writing? Discuss these features in class or in a written analysis of his writing.

8) Essay exam. Essay exams are either in-class or take-home. Both are timed, and you probably do not have the option to **Revise Repeatedly from Feedback**. Since the most common essay exam is taken in class, we'll focus on that. The best advice is to prepare yourself by completing a practice exam one or two days ahead of time, upon which you can get feedback, before you take the actual exam.

In your exam answers, be decisive and direct; you don't have time to wander. It's often impossible to revise substantially, so investing about 5 to 10 percent of your time to sketch out a quick outline is essential to organization and success. If you have ten minutes for an answer, spend thirty seconds writing down key terms or examples on scratch paper. As you move toward writing your response, reread the question to be sure that you respond to each component of the prompt with a specific item in your outline.

Begin with a single, declarative thesis sentence. Then offer as many concrete, specific details as you can to support your opening claim. Weak essay exam answers are desperately rushed and stream-of-consciousness, composed of vague generalizations that lack real evidence.

Your last sentence must wrap everything up, so never stop mid-sentence. Your thesis will often evolve or come into focus as you write a timed essay exam, which means that you often need to reconnect the end to the beginning.

Time management is essential. Allocate a specific number of minutes for each question, make an outline that will fit within your plan, and watch the clock. Taking a practice exam will help you gauge the scope of what you can accomplish within the allotted time. If you practice and plan, you are more likely to feel composed and convey confidence, which will improve your grade. Neat handwriting or typing also helps, if you have that ability.

If you have available time, proofread and neatly make changes. If your answer includes two or more paragraphs, and you still have time, add an informative title because it will point to your thesis and make what feels like a mad scramble read more like a sculpted essay.

Essay exams feature

- A direct, clear, obvious thesis that responds directly to the question or prompt and is located in the very first sentence of the essay

- Abundant, coherent, concrete evidence, support, or details that directly support your thesis

- Simple, coherent, predictable organizational structure that can be managed under time pressure without the opportunity to revise

- Well-composed, correct sentences and handwriting that convey confidence and composure (versus sloppy, desperate scribble)

- A satisfying concluding sentence

- An informative, not creative, title, if time and scope permit

The advantage of the essay exam is that it can prepare you to think and talk extemporaneously — conversationally without a script or preparation — which is how most communication actually happens, even in professional contexts. The downside is that a timed essay can be a genre with no specific future application; you will almost never have to write under severe time constraints after graduation.

PRACTICE If you must take a timed essay this term, why not practice right now, perhaps when things are not as stressful as exam week? Ask your instructor or a writing center tutor to give you a practice prompt. Then write an essay under timed conditions and have them give you feedback ahead of the actual exam. As you and your readers evaluate your practice exam, ask which of the features discussed above, particularly the six bullet points, are in your writing?

9) Oral presentation. Oral communication is often an entire course in itself, but students are commonly asked to make formal, oral presentations in composition classes too, primarily because writing, speaking, thinking, and reading are closely connected. Writing and speaking can both be founded upon the study of rhetoric.

Anxiety is one of the first concerns when it comes to making a speech in front of an audience. The principle of **RRFF** applies to public speaking, too: the more experience, feedback, and practice you have making oral presentations, the more comfortable and confident you will become. College classes that require you to develop this skill are relatively safe places for you to practice, if you compare them to public speaking in the professional world, where your job and paycheck might depend on the quality of your presentation. You can work on this skill almost daily in college by consistently engaging in discussion and by asking and answering questions in class. The benefits of regularly and actively participating in class discussions are many!

In Lesson 9: Media, the presentation tools subsection examines oral communication more closely, particularly in conjunction with presentation software such as PowerPoint and Prezi. The key idea in that discussion is to engage your audience by talking *with* them, not *at* them. Talk extemporaneously. Think in terms of *dialogue* rather than *monologue,* and try to imagine ways for your audience to *interact* with your presentation rather than just listening.

How to analyze and compare genres to meet various audience expectations

Speeches often begin with a joke or an amusing anecdote because laughter connects the speaker with the audience and because it loosens the stiffness and anxiety of a public address. Use media elements to highlight key terms and to offer visuals such as charts, graphs, diagrams, and photographs. Never take the shortcut of cutting up a written paper and pasting it into note cards or projection slides — and try never to read directly from your note cards or slides.

Because an oral presentation is primarily heard by your audience rather than seen, organizational elements such as paragraphs and section headings are often lacking, so you must be more deliberate in presenting a quick overview of your talk at the beginning for your listeners to follow. You should also repeat key terms and points consistently to provide structure and coherence. Sentence structure in oral presentations cannot be as complex as a formal academic essay because it's more difficult to keep a long, complicated sentence in mind as a listener without the visual clues (see Lesson 22: Sentences).

You must also carefully acknowledge and document your sources in an academic oral presentation by providing either a print bibliography or a bibliography slide. You must consider copyright and fair use for any media elements included in your presentation, which amounts to using your bibliography to indicate when images or other media elements were the result of someone else's work. (See also Lesson 24: Citation.)

Perhaps most important, try to enjoy the experience of an oral presentation. Public speaking can often seem threatening, especially if you are being evaluated for a grade. At the same time, you have a captive audience that is eager for you to engage them. Show them and yourself what you can do!

You have probably written dozens of school papers, but likely have not had nearly as many chances to present your academic work in your more natural, spoken voice. As nervous as you might be, your enthusiasm as a public speaker will always make a huge difference in terms of everyone's experience — yours as well as your audience's.

Oral presentations feature

- **A clear introduction of the main idea and purpose**
- **A quick overview of what the presentation will cover**
- **An extremely deliberate structure that can be easily followed or intuited**
- **Presenters who convey composure and confidence because they have thoroughly prepared themselves, not by rehearsing a script but through careful research**
- **Effective audiovisual support that complements rather than complicates the oral information**
- **Presentation of direct, easily digestible ideas, facts, figures, and illustrations**
- **Careful, respectful management of the audience's time and attention**
- **Engaging body language**

Although the oral presentation may not seem like a genre to practice in a college composition class, verbal communication can be deeply linked with writing. The vast majority of the communication that you will convey in academic and professional contexts is likely to be oral. In other words, college writing will also improve your speaking skills. The disadvantage of covering oral communication within a writing class is that there are already so many concepts and lessons to cover that it can be difficult to focus effectively on becoming a college speaker at the same time that you are also becoming a college writer.

PRACTICE Dan's model rhetorical presentation is a hybrid combination of oral presentation, personal narrative, rhetorical analysis, and multimedia genres. Kendra's model oral presentation was delivered as a conventional classroom or conference speech with visual slides. Analyze one or both of these presentations according to the features discussed above, particularly the eight bullet points. Or, if you have an upcoming oral presentation, pick either Dan's or Kendra's model, depending on which one is more similar to yours. You can find their presentations in the LaunchPad for *Becoming a College Writer*.

10) *Multimedia project.* In the past, college composition was almost always written on paper and only sometimes delivered in a speech. However, instructors are increasingly assigning digital work in a variety of forms such as websites, blogs, videos, podcasts, and even virtual worlds and video games. Lesson 9: Media examines these new, emerging, digital forms of composition more closely. (And, obviously, you are currently immersed in a multimedia textbook.)

DAN
Michigan State University

I think in academia genre is vital, and I think when you come to the digital world, genre becomes exploded and vast. It also becomes something that you can readily change. . . . You write something and the genre is a press release, and then all you've got to do is parse that out a little bit and then you can reproduce it as a featured story on your website. So digital technology makes genres and weaving between genres really easy.

A still from Dan's multimedia project

How to analyze and compare genres to meet various audience expectations

A multimedia author faces a wide array of decisions, beginning with which media format(s) to use. Like any choice you make as a writer, you want to carefully consider which digital format will work or fit best for you, your topic, and your audience — which genre will balance your writing. Would a radio essay in the form of a podcast make sense for your project? Or do you need a companion visual track to complement the podcast, and so maybe you should make a video? Perhaps it would be better for your audience to browse their own way through your project individually, in which case an interactive website or clickable animation might work best.

Regardless of the choices you make as you begin to compose with electronic media, I encourage you to think of print forms (or really, the text itself) as your base, your foundation, at least in your college composition classes.

Most filmmakers begin their projects with an intense focus on the quality of a typewritten screenplay. Actors, directors, and producers are constantly and feverishly searching for great scripts. The script or screenplay is almost always the backbone or foundation of any movie, and moving pictures are one of the most important forms of multimedia composition, since the visual track and the sound track work together so essentially in every film.

The screenplay is an effective concept to keep in mind with multimedia projects, especially if you have abandoned pen and paper for keyboard and computer screen, because it's far too easy to become distracted by flashy visual and digital elements. At the heart of even the most visually dynamic multimedia project lies well-crafted conventional writing. If you begin with a solid screenplay, then many good things will follow.

Multimedia genres feature

- Dynamic interactivity between the audience and the author's media objects
- Compositions that take advantage of the full bandwidth available by presenting in a variety of sensory modes (reading, seeing, hearing, interacting, etc.)
- Media objects that provide organization and navigation structures for readers to follow, such as subheadings, menus, and maps
- Application of selected media according to the purposes and nature of the composition
- Careful writing and informative research at the heart of the composition (substance before flash)

Dan points out that digital presentation technologies, such as websites or online videos, explode the possibilities for writing, rhetoric, and communication, expanding the boundaries and potential of almost every genre. On the other hand, this rapid expansion of possibilities can also be disorienting for authors and their audiences. Choose wisely and stay focused.

PRACTICE Dan's model rhetorical presentation is a hybrid combination of oral presentation, personal narrative, rhetorical analysis, and multimedia genres. Analyze his presentation according to the features discussed, particularly the eight bullet points of an oral presentation. Does he choose the right genre? And the best media format for what he wants to say? Is his rhetorical triangle (writer, topic, audience) well connected?

7.3

Exercises: genre

7a Integrate the video.

In 7.1, Jenna points out how there are very important differences between genres of college and writing, saying that "you need to recognize those differences because that can radically change the way you approach a certain assignment." She then compares writing a literary analysis with a cover letter and résumé, and describes each genre as a completely different "mode of thought." Thus, *Becoming a College Writer* is about gaining experience with different genres of writing and different modes of thought. Kendra agrees with Jenna:

> I think [it] is good to play around with all different types of writing. You may not like a certain type of writing; you might find one you do like. Going in between them is different. You have to change your mind-set and approach for different types of papers. But you can ask other people who may have just written that type of paper, or ask your teacher how to set yourself up for that type of paper you're writing.

Write a substantial paragraph or two, with a topic sentence or mini-thesis, through which you respond to Jenna, Kendra, and other videos in the lesson as you form your own thoughts about writing in a variety of college genres. You can watch the Lesson 7 Essentials Video, or you can browse the embedded clips in the online edition of this lesson. You might begin by identifying the moments that stand out to you the most. Which student videos seem to make the most sense to you? With whom do you agree? Disagree? What patterns do you find among the student sound bites? Which ideas were the most instructive or helpful to you? What surprised you? How have your own ideas about genre come into focus through the videos?

7b Create a journal entry or blog.

Your instructor might ask you to keep a writer's journal throughout this class. This journal could be handwritten or composed on a computer; it could take the shape of a text-based blog or a video blog.

To prepare a journal entry for Lesson 7, describe your thoughts and approaches to the key term, *genre*, trying not to glance back at the material in this lesson, at first. Not referring to this material initially will help you see what you have internalized so far. After carefully composing your initial thoughts, then look back at some of the ideas and strategies other students gave in Lesson 7 or in the online database of interviews. For example, in his interview, Deonta describes how some academic genres are more challenging to him than others:

> Moving between the genres sometimes is kind of hard for me. Sometimes I'll write a lab report and it looks more like an English composition. So I have to start back over to make sure that I'm making an analysis of the statistics instead of just talking about what we did in the lab. And then moving back to the English papers, it's usually literary analysis in which I "put texts in conversation with one another." Philosophy papers so far have been reconstructions of arguments and then [critiquing] something that you found wrong in the argument — that's been a little more complicated.

Describe your experience with different academic genres. Like Deonta, do you find some genres more challenging than others? Include in your entry on *genre*, additional thoughts, notes, and lessons from your instructor and your class meetings. It might help for you to imagine that you are giving advice to your future self about writing. What lessons from this chapter and from discussions about writing might benefit you down the road?

7c See yourself as a writer.

In a page or two, describe the evolution of your sense of *genre* since you began writing. Where and when did you start to develop a sense of genre awareness? What major events, assignments, and papers have influenced your approaches to genre along the way? What particular teachers or classes have reshaped the ways you approach different writing genres? What was your sense of *genre* before you began reading this lesson? What is your approach now that you have finished it? In what ways can you imagine your sense of genre changing beyond college? Dan discusses how the number of genres from which a writer might choose has exploded in the digital age:

> Back when all you had was stone tablets and things like that, the genre was, well, whatever you were recording. There's not really much "genre." But when you move to the digital world, you're opening up all these new genres — vast amounts of genres. And genre in academia is really important: to understand what your genre is and how it needs to look. That's vital. Because if you're not living within the purposes of that genre, of the rules of that genre, then your content is not going to work for your audience.

You might also feel like the number of genres from which you might choose has exploded after high school, as you entered college. Describe how your awareness of and approaches to *genre* are currently evolving for you as a college writer.

7d Invent your writing.

This lesson includes ten elemental genres of college composition. Map out how some of these ten genres might be applied to the writing assignment you are currently working on in this class (or in another class, if you do not have a writing project at the moment in this course). Many of the ten elements might simply be irrelevant, but at least three or four of them are likely to be close neighbors to your assignment, even if your instructor's prompt names

only one of these genres specifically. As this lesson points out a number of times, genres are often combined and recombined, and their boundaries may not be perfectly clear. How might a number of the elemental genres listed in this lesson combine or recombine to influence your current writing assignment?

7e Analyze student writing.

Study the opening two or three paragraphs or segments of a couple of model projects in Lesson 25 or in the LaunchPad. You might compare very different models, such as Dan's video and Deonta's paper, or you might read similar work, such as Nanaissa's and Nicole's papers.

For each writer, describe in a sentence or two the kinds of genres each of these authors seems to follow. Based on each student's work, what kinds of connections can you sense between the genre and the prompt or the audience? How does each genre/prompt/audience connection compare with the other? In what ways do they seem alike? Different? List a couple of specific choices the writers make to suggest connections between their genre and their prompt or audience.

Your instructor might ask you to apply this analysis and these questions to your classmates' writing instead (or in addition to the model projects).

7f Revise repeatedly from feedback.

Examine a writing assignment you are currently working on or one that you wrote recently, perhaps in another class or in high school. Describe some specific ways that you can use the ideas from Lesson 7 to revise your writing and improve your approaches to genre. Perhaps most important, to complete this exercise, take an early draft of your writing to the writing center, a peer workshop, or your instructor's office hours and ask, "Is my approach to this genre working?" and "Do I seem to meet audience's expectations for genre as set up in the assignment prompt?"

Discipline

Understand that a discipline is a methodology applied to a subject.

ESSENTIALS VIDEO

Visit the LaunchPad for *Becoming a College Writer* to watch the Lesson 8 Essentials Video.

8.1 [WHY]

Why you should understand that a discipline is a methodology applied to a subject.

1. An understanding of disciplines will help you succeed in college and beyond.

Academic disciplines will probably be most familiar to you in terms of the branches, departments, or majors at your school, such as art history, biology, chemistry, English, geology, history, and political science. And in any college writing situation, you are as likely to think as much about discipline ("I've got a *poli sci* paper to write") as genre ("My *lab report* is due tomorrow").

The disciplines in which you work influences your writing so heavily that you will want to consider this influence very carefully. At first glance, you might expect that a discipline is defined by *what* it studies, by the *subject* of its focus. Biology studies living organisms. English studies literature. Political science studies politics. But a discipline is more accurately defined as a combination of not only *what* researchers study but also *how* they study it.

Another word for *what* is being studied is *subject*, and another word for *how* something is being studied is *methodology*. So, in order for you to understand how to write successfully in a variety of different college classes, you should understand that a discipline is defined as a methodology applied to a subject — a way of using evidence to study a topic.

There is a two-way, dynamic relationship between the subject being studied and the methods for studying it, which defines each discipline. It follows that there is also a two-way, dynamic relationship between the discipline being studied and the genres and conventions for writing about it, which defines your task in becoming a college writer.

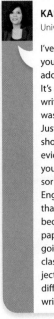

KARINA
University of Florida

I've taken criminology classes and, you know, the style that I have to adopt there is completely different. It's a lot more scientific. I'm used to writing very wordy and the professor was just "No, cut straight to the point. Just tell me what you're writing about, show me the research, show me the evidence, and that's all I want." Maybe your audience is a psychology professor or an engineering professor or an English professor, and those are things that you always have to keep in mind because you're not going to write a paper for English the same way you're going to write a paper for a biology class. So, if you keep in mind the subject that you're writing for, it makes a difference as to how you're going to write and fill out your paper.

Understanding the methods and conventions of various disciplines — the central concern of this lesson — will help you write effectively in *every* college course, not just in a first-year composition class. Also, as I have said many times in this book, **Revising Repeatedly from Feedback** will be the key to figuring out how to write well in any discipline, as Lindsey discovered when she first moved from English composition to science writing.

LINDSEY
Michigan State University

It was pretty hard for me to figure out how to write scientifically because nobody taught me. After I read enough scientific papers and talked to enough of my teachers and professors, then I kind of got the hang of it and got it down. I figured out how to do it mostly through the feedback that I got on my papers, whatever [the teachers] had written. The first lab report I did in a class, they would mark it up and actually explain to me why I did things wrong. If I didn't understand what was wrong, I actually went up and asked them, "Hey, what did I do wrong here?" I used to write like I was writing a research paper for English and it was, you know, trying to write to an audience of people who know nothing about [the subject], a general audience, like someone reading the newspaper. But as I switch to [science] writing, I know I'm writing to scientists and that's who I try to make my audience.

As noted in Lesson 7: Genres, becoming a college writer means figuring out how to compose in a variety of academic genres. This is something Lindsey discovered as she began to write lab reports. Because *what* you write about is so connected with *how* you write about it, becoming a college writer also means figuring out how to write for a variety of academic audiences and disciplines. These experiences prepare you for writing beyond college, as you negotiate changing professional landscapes, contexts, and situations.

2. An understanding of disciplines allows you to learn the customs, practices, and languages of disciplinary communities.

Thanks to Stephen North,[1] another influential researcher on student writing, I can't help but think about disciplines anthropologically. North taught me to recognize that each group of people within each discipline acts like a community. As discussed in section 8.2, the "How to" section of this lesson, each of these communities has its own culture, values, language, and practices, as well as a particular way of seeing the world. So, as you travel from class to class, from building to building, and from one department to the next, try to get to know and understand each of these different communities or cultures, just as you might try to understand different places or cultures as you travel across the country or the globe.

Crisosto's description from an anthropology class reveals the anthropological nature of disciplinary communities on the next page. He points out how essential it was for him to base his writing on researchers who were members of the very culture being studied (Native Americans). Crisosto emphasizes

[1] Stephen North, *The Making of Knowledge in Composition: Portrait of an Emerging Field* (Boynton/Cook Publishers, 1987).

how important it was for him to consider not only *what* the researchers were writing about (the subject), but also *how* they were writing about it (the methodology).

CRISOSTO
Metropolitan State University of Denver

Some of the information I really wanted to look at for this particular paper was [written by] Native American anthropologists because I think that it's very important to try to gain a perspective from which the subject is being written.... So that's where I tried to look for the most information because there's a lot of books written on that topic by non-Native people. But I think it's also encouraging to have academic work presented by the indigenous culture from which they're writing. I think that really encouraged me to try to look at what they were writing and how they were writing it so that I could somewhat translate it. There's a certain thing I noticed when looking at that: There's a specific language that a lot of this type of writing requires. One of the things we were encouraged in that class to do was [to keep track of] words that we didn't understand. My list was very long with all these words that I didn't know [how to define].

Also notice how this disciplinary community of anthropologists is defined by the language it uses, like any culture or community. Developing a glossary of disciplinary vocabulary and learning to "speak" the discipline's language was key to Crisosto's writing and research in his anthropology course. Therese also tells the story of how learning the language (in this case scientific language) allowed her to find better research and sources to integrate into her writing.

THERESE
Santa Fe College

I took a science class the year before, and we were forced to learn scientific names for plants and animals — and everyone thought it was the biggest waste of time. Why do we have to know these scientific names? But I pulled up a lot more reliable information when I used the scientific name for the bee. And I was able to pull up a lot more information for a specific type of bee. The honeybee has a specific scientific name, so when I entered that name for the bee, I often came up with journals that were peer reviewed and researched by scientists at universities.

As you choose a major for your degree, you will eventually join at least one of these communities yourself, and learn to speak its language. When you select and complete a particular major, you move from a novice speaker of that language to a more fluent member of that discipline. Along the way, you will try out the languages of a number of disciplines through your writing. Negotiating these differences is healthy for you because it broadens your abilities to relate and communicate.

GREGG
California State University, San Marcos

But the bottom line is, when we do research, no matter what the topic, the important thing is that we know the vocabulary around the discipline, know the discourse, and know the people and know the sources to grab a hold of what would give what we're saying power.

And there's more to it than learning the vocabulary or jargon of each discipline. A methodology is defined as a way of putting evidence together (see also Lesson 6: Evidence and Lesson 7: Genre). For example, Hyesu talks about important differences between writing for English and writing for history, even though those two disciplines are often closely related within the humanities.

HYESU
University of Florida

Something else that I noticed was (this was my first history class in college) the expectations were different from high school. I was used to writing English papers so the formatting was a little difficult. You're not supposed to use literary present tense in history papers. It sounds intuitive now, but as I was writing I just didn't think about it. So, I had to rethink a lot of how I wrote, or how I thought I should be writing. It was more difficult than I thought to shift gears from an English paper perspective to a history paper perspective.

When Hyesu mentions the "literary present tense," she is talking about the convention in literary studies to write as if an author is working in the present day, as in "Shakespeare *examines* guilt and morality in Macbeth." But in a history course you would use the past tense: "Shakespeare *examined* guilt and morality through Elizabethan drama."

Literary researchers tend to see their work as more timeless, applying to any age, whereas historians are more connected to date and chronology. The different use of tense that tripped up Hyesu at first might seem like a small issue, but it illustrates an important point, namely: *What* you write about influences *how* you write about it. Becoming a college writer means learning to negotiate disciplinary differences.

3. An understanding of disciplines will help you work within and across a variety of fields.

ALEXANDRA
University of Florida

For me, because I'm an English and environmental science double-major, the types of papers I write for each major are very, very different. For anything I write in my environmental science classes, I try to make it dry, with as little voice as possible, very to the point, no expressive language. I try to make sure that everything is straightforward, and I try to keep out my own opinions and feelings about the subject. In English classes, the rules of the game are much different. It's difficult to try to write in a different mode for each class. They're very distinct in my mind.

Like genres, disciplines can be difficult to define neatly because, within any academic department, researchers can have different methodologies. Many departments of psychology, for example, grant two types of undergraduate degrees: a bachelor of science (BS) and a bachelor of arts (BA). The BS students are more likely to emphasize quantitative data, whereas a BA in the same department might be more qualitative. Likewise, sometimes a history class leans toward a social science approach, using data and statistics as evidence, but other history classes might be more humanistic, using texts, stories, and interpretations as evidence.

Quantitative methods argue using numbers and data. Qualitative methods argue with

Why you should understand that a discipline is a methodology applied to a subject observations and interpretations. The "hard sciences," like math and physics, rely most purely on numbers, which is why Kendra characterizes scientific writing as objective and tightly structured.

KENDRA
Michigan State University

The difference between scientific writing and normal composition or English is the audience and the structure. With English writing, you have a lot more freedom and ways to make it creative and make it different. With scientific writing you have to do a lot of that beforehand and make sure that it's interesting before you start, because once you're filling in the data, it's very exact — you're filling in blanks of an outline, where with English essays it's more free to your own interpretations of how you want to mold it.

At the other end of the spectrum, interpretive methods are used in disciplines where numbers and data tend to be difficult to apply, especially when working in the arts and humanities. You could use mathematics and quantitative methods to study Picasso, Mozart, or the French Revolution, but that will typically not reveal as much as if you used more interpretive kinds of evidence, such as texts, events, people, ideas, themes, and historical movements.

Lastly, it's important for you to understand that many academic writers and researchers see their work as interdisciplinary and not strictly confined within departmental borders. My own work is interdisciplinary. I'm an English professor, but I'm also interested in rhetoric, education, documentary film, and digital media. It's likely that your areas of interest and study represent multiple disciplines, too.

Throughout your college career, as you work in different disciplines, approach each writing assignment by making sure you understand the conventions, methodologies, and genres of that discipline, and whether the assignment draws on multiple disciplines. Ask yourself

- **What kinds of evidence do writers prefer in this discipline? How do they gather that evidence? What's their methodology, and how is it different from other methodologies?**

- **How do researchers in this discipline arrange the evidence they use?**

- **What style and tone of writing does this discipline use? For example, is the tone formal, or is some casual language acceptable? Is technical terminology common and accepted, or should the writing be accessible to a general audience?**

- **What writing genres are most common in this discipline, and why?**

- **Is this particular writing assignment interdisciplinary, and, if so, how and why?**

Writing in a variety of academic contexts requires that you negotiate the differences and similarities between disciplines. You may encounter two professors from two seemingly different departments who, in fact, share a methodology and discipline. For instance, if a biologist is interested in the history of science, her work may be more like a historian's than a laboratory researcher's.

You may also encounter two professors within the same department who use different methodologies. You might find an archaeologist whose work is scientific and based upon chemical experiments with artifacts. But a different archaeologist might be interested in ancient texts and look for evidence in words more than in chemistry.

Also, be especially conscious of the fact that although writing tends to be taught primarily in departments of English, communication, and rhetoric, the world of college writing is much larger than the familiar essays or generic research papers written in one discipline (such as English).

First-year composition courses can help prepare you for this larger world, and part of that preparation is to study a variety of academic disciplines and how they work. The following "How to" section guides you in this study in practical ways, describing key goals of five of the most common disciplinary "continents," which are home to many subdisciplines.

PRACTICE Write down a list of the last five courses from five different departments that you have taken. Then apply this lesson's definition (discipline = subject + method) to each of those courses. Be specific. For example, don't write English = literature + reading. Instead, perhaps your class was English 225 = Shakespearean tragedies + analyzing live performances on video. If you can be specific about the methods, you can begin to get a picture of how different disciplines use different research methods, genres, and approaches to college writing. Compare your five listings with each other, and compare your list with others in your class, if possible.

Why you should understand that a discipline is a methodology applied to a subject

8.2 [HOW]

How to understand that a discipline is a methodology applied to a subject.

1. Be aware of a key goal of the arts and humanities: To study the human condition by analyzing art, literature, music, and history.

Although people working in the arts and humanities use a variety of strategies to analyze human culture, thought, and experience, they share some common practices.

They do not tend to use empirical or numerical data very much, as scientists do, because it is impossible to accurately control the conditions and variables regarding such broad questions as "What is moral or evil?" "What explains our history?" and "What does it mean to be a human being?"

Also, most aspects of human culture and experience resist numbers and quantification. So, instead of looking to data to understand human beings in broad terms, people working in the arts and humanities (called *humanists*) look to artifacts, texts, events, and records to try to understand our individual identities and our relationships to others.

Consequently, the research methods of humanists are more interpretive and less objective than the methods of scientists. Humanists study primary materials (such as texts or artwork), and then they publish secondary commentary, analysis, and interpretation of those materials. They might even create their own primary texts, including sculpture, musical compositions, and creative writing.

Humanists who work with written texts are often called scholars. Those who study historical records are, of course, historians. And those who evaluate visual and performing arts or written works are critics.[2] Furthermore, individual disciplines may be divided into subdisciplines. For example, the discipline of English literature includes the subdisciplines of literary studies, literary history, and literary criticism, and these subdisciplines may have their own methodologies.

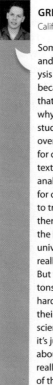

GREGG
California State University, San Marcos

Some people think that, in literature and writing departments, the analysis that we do is not "real" research because it's not mathematical. And that's not the case at all — which is why the research we do for literary studies can be just as easily paralleled over into other areas. We are looking for concrete information in a literary text that we're trying to tie into our analysis. With physics, we're looking for concrete information in our data to try to tie into our analysis. So there's this parallel, and unfortunately the humanities get a bad rap at the university because, "Oh they're just really the fluffy stuff, the aesthetics." But that's not the case at all. I know tons of people who do serious, critical, hard-core research on a daily basis for their classes that is on par with the scientific research that's going on. And it's just as applicable because it talks about the nature of humanity. We really have to see them as two forms of the same thing, two different areas of expertise.

[2] Stephen North, *The Making of Knowledge in Composition: Portrait of an Emerging Field* (Boynton/Cook Publishers, 1987).

PRACTICE Nicole's model paper in Lesson 25 offers a postcolonial literary analysis of a novel by Gabriel García Márquez. Which of the features of the arts and humanities previously described can you locate in her essay? Discuss these features in class or in a brief written analysis of her essay.

2. Be aware of a key goal of the physical and applied sciences: to analyze and engineer the physical world.

The scientific method involves these steps:

- Coming up with a question or problem to investigate. To give a simple example, "Why is my cell phone not charging?"

- Making observations related to the question or problem. In the case of the cell phone, you would have observed that the phone doesn't charge after being plugged in for several hours. You might also have noticed that nothing seems to be wrong with the charging jack.

- Developing a hypothesis — for example, "My battery is dead."

- Conducting an experiment to test the hypothesis. You might test the cell phone hypothesis by asking a friend who has the same model of phone if you can try her battery in your phone.

- Accepting or rejecting the hypothesis based on the results of the experiment. If you try the friend's battery and it doesn't work in your phone but still works in hers, you will need to reject your hypothesis.

- Figuring out next steps. In the case of the cell phone, you might change your hypothesis to "Something is wrong with my phone's circuitry," and then test that.

Abraksis/Shutterstock.com

How to understand that a discipline is a methodology applied to a subject

As you can see from the cell phone example, the scientific method involves close, objective observation and experimentation. And in the case of the physical and applied sciences, it often involves collecting and analyzing numerical data. Although mathematics is often regarded as its own discipline, it is actually an essential part of many other disciplines in the physical and applied sciences. In fact, many branches of math (such as geometry and calculus) were created in order to understand and explain the physical world.

The physical sciences include chemistry, physics, astronomy, and earth science, and the applied sciences consist mostly of engineering and its many subdisciplines. Both are built almost exclusively on mathematics. Engineering *applies* physical sciences like chemistry and physics to address human problems and needs.

For example, mechanical engineers use physics to figure out how to build strong bridges; electrical engineers use physics to design utility plants and to power your digital devices; and chemical engineers use chemistry to create new or better compounds, such as less toxic household cleaners.

Although physical and applied sciences are more data-driven and objective than arts and humanities disciplines, they do not lack a human element. For example, mathematics is often correctly described as a language of numbers instead of words, which reveals its essential human dimensions. Engineering involves the design of new and better products and infrastructure by humans and for humans. And because all of the sciences

have consequences for humans, writing is actually very important to those disciplines, even though some naive science students wrongly think they do not need to write, as Vinh-Thuy points out.

VINH-THUY
Red Rocks Community College

I really do think that there is a subset of [students] who are in science, and they seem to think that because they are in science that they don't have to write. But then I ask them, "When you become a PhD and you go out and work for the National Science Foundation, how are you going to get people to agree with you?" You have to write a proposal. You have to get up there and deliver a multimedia presentation. Science majors, like myself, should see the value in writing, the value in composition class. Because most people I talk to, especially the engineering students, they're always saying that, "you know, once I'm done with community college, once I'm at another school, I'm done with writing. That's it, no more writing from then on." But then they don't see that writing is such an important part of your life and it's something that's life-long, right?

PRACTICE Billy's lab/technical report about the Alcoholics Anonymous treatment community explores the question of how certain clinical values changed based on participation in a values-based program. Which of the features of the applied sciences described above can you locate in Billy's research project? Discuss these features in class or in a written analysis of Billy's report.

You can find Billy's paper, "Test/Retest with MMPI-2" in the LaunchPad for *Becoming a College Writer*.

3. Be aware of a key goal of the life and health sciences: to analyze living organisms.

ALICE
University of Florida

I had to write a nine-page lab report on every single lab, and it was ridiculous, and there had to be at least three pages of introduction, your discussion had to be well thought-out. You had to go through all of the theory and all of the concept of why this particular biological thing happened and it was extremely difficult....I couldn't just fluff through it. I really had to think about what I was saying, and it was challenging in a way that I hadn't ever been challenged before. It really shaped me in terms of how I write scientifically now. That was really meaningful to me.

Life and health sciences — such as anatomy, biology, medicine, and public health — involve the study of living organisms and/or the conditions that affect them. People in these fields gather knowledge through the use of the scientific method (see more on page 113), and often collect and analyze numerical data. For instance, epidemiologists gather data on how common certain diseases are in particular populations and analyze the numbers to uncover trends.

However, because living organisms and populations are much more complicated than the atoms, molecules, and compounds studied in the applied sciences, there is more uncertainty in the life and health sciences regarding which research questions to ask and how to interpret the results of experiments and studies. You might be able to prove that a vaccine can make a particular set of laboratory rats immune to a particular virus, but that doesn't mean that the vaccine will work exactly the same way on humans, or on a mutation of that virus.

Increasing numbers of college students are being drawn to the life and health sciences, in part because of the growing number of health-care jobs. But even if you're not a health-care professional, it's good to have an understanding of how the life and health sciences use data, statistics, and the scientific method to uncover knowledge about living organisms, particularly humans.

PRACTICE Kendra's zoology oral presentation tests her hypothesis about Komodo dragons and their methods for killing prey. Which of the features of the life sciences described above can you locate in her research project? Discuss these features in class or in a written analysis of her presentation. ⬇

⬇ See the LaunchPad for *Becoming a College Writer* to listen to Kendra's presentation.

4. Be aware of a key goal of the social sciences: to analyze how people function and behave, particularly in groups.

Compared to hard sciences like chemistry and physics, the social sciences — such as psychology, sociology, history, economics, and public policy — are sometimes labeled "soft" sciences because they are more interpretative and do not rely so strictly on numerical evidence and mathematical proof. There's a good reason for this difference: Human behavior and relationships are so varied and complex that it's impossible to control social variables according to strict scientific methods. You can't prove that a particular person, or a group of people, behaves in a certain way by using only data and numbers. The best you can do is provide evidence that suggests explanations for complicated human behaviors.

However, some social scientists' methods are just as data-driven as those of medical researchers. Within departments of political science or history, for example, you will find researchers who study historical texts as a humanist would, others who conduct interviews or survey people's experiences or opinions qualitatively, and still others who use purely numerical data to help explain the political landscape. In an economics department, you will also find a lot of researchers who rely on quantitative research and numerical data.

HANNAH
California State University, San Marcos

I'm definitely able to connect my life to papers outside of literature and writing. I've taken many psychology classes, and it is important to put in your own opinion because psychology is so not concrete. They have concrete ideas, but the manner in which you apply them is going to be your own [educated perspective]. In psychology papers, I focus more on concept. I remember in one psychology paper I had to write about "attachment theory" in children, so I had to go into each attachment theory and then evaluate the child and which attachment theory they fall into.

PRACTICE Nanaissa's paper in Lesson 25 provides background research to support an educational policy statement. Which of the features of social science disciplines, such as public policy, described above can you

locate in her essay? Discuss these features in class or in a written analysis of her essay.

5. Be aware of a key goal of professional disciplines: to prepare students for their careers.

Professional disciplines — such as law, education, business, journalism, social work, and urban planning — prepare students for their professional lives by giving them practice and by examining current trends and issues facing these fields. This preparation can happen through a number of methods:

1) *Hands-on practice*, **which gives future professionals practice in the kind of work their careers will require. For example, in a course in entrepreneurship you might be asked to create a business proposal, and in a public-relations class you might be asked to write a press release.**
2) *Research*, **which critically examines questions, issues, and problems, such as the role of standardized tests in education or the ethics of publishing a news story that includes information gathered from computer hacking. Such assignments involve investigating the background or history of a particular issue or problem and then presenting specific solutions or responses, based on evidence gathered through careful research.**

In the undergraduate setting, most courses in the professional disciplines are intended for majors. However, students are increasingly being assigned writing and research projects grounded in the professional disciplines, even in the earlier years of their college education. The practical, relevant nature of these writing assignments can make them especially gratifying.

FRANK
Michigan State University

It's definitely important to be a good writer in the professional world. You have to be able to successfully communicate with your boss and write lab reports and to describe what work you're doing to people who are going to use your object or design. So, it's pretty important.

Instructors and researchers in the professional disciplines use a variety of approaches to gather evidence and publish research, even within a particular discipline. For example, some academics in the education field are highly scientific, using numeric data, statistics, and metrics to measure student learning. Others focus on teaching philosophy, theory, and methods.

PRACTICE Daniel provides a cover letter and an application, which you can study in the online edition of *Becoming a College Writer*. Which of the features of the professional disciplines described above can you locate in Daniel's writing? Discuss these features in class or in a written analysis of his presentation. ⊡

8.3

Exercises: discipline

8a Integrate the video.

Lesson 1 of *Becoming a College Writer* defines writing as a dynamic relationship between an author, a topic, and an audience. This means

that you want your readers to sense substantial connections and integrity between all aspects of your writing. This lesson emphasizes the substantial connections between the subjects, methods, and conventions of college writing and research. Greg sums up the power in these connections for college writers when he argues that "the bottom line is, when we do research, no matter what the topic, the important thing is that we know the vocabulary around the discipline — that we know the discourse, and know the people and know the sources to grab hold of that would give what we're saying power."

Write a substantial paragraph or two, with a topic sentence or mini-thesis, through which you respond to Greg and other videos in the lesson as you form your own approaches to writing in a variety of disciplines. You can watch the Lesson 8 Essentials Video, or you can browse the embedded clips in the online edition of this lesson. You might begin by identifying the moments that stand out to you the most. Which student videos seem to make the most sense to you? With whom do you agree? Disagree? What patterns do you find among the student sound bites? Which ideas were the most instructive or helpful to you? What surprised you? How have your own ideas about writing in a variety of disciplines come into focus through the videos?

8b Create a journal entry or blog.

Your instructor might ask you to keep a writer's journal throughout this class. This journal could be handwritten or composed on a computer; it could take the shape of a text-based blog or a video blog.

To prepare a journal entry on Lesson 8, describe your thoughts and approaches to the key terms *discipline* and *research methodology*, trying not to glance back at the material in this lesson, at first. Not referring to this material initially will help you see what you have internalized so far. After carefully composing

⊡ **See the LaunchPad for *Becoming a College Writer* to read Daniel's cover letter and application.**

your initial thoughts, then look back at some of the ideas and strategies other students gave in Lesson 8 or in the online database of interviews. For example, in her interview, Karina describes her insights on writing for different disciplines, classes, and professors:

> I've taken criminology classes and, you know, the style that I have to adopt there is completely different. It's a lot more scientific. I'm used to writing very wordy and the professor was just "No, cut straight to the point. Just tell me what you're writing about, show me the research, show me the evidence, and that's all I want." Maybe your audience is a psychology professor or an engineering professor or an English professor — those are things that you always have to keep in mind because you're not going to write a paper for English the same way you're going to write a paper for a biology class.

You might wish to disagree with some of this lesson, or you might want to modify or expand on some of its advice. For example, consider integrating additional thoughts, notes, and lessons from your instructor and your class meetings into your journal entry. It might help for you to imagine that you are giving advice to your future self about writing. What lessons from this chapter and from discussions about writing in different disciplines might benefit you down the road?

8c See yourself as a writer.

In a page or two, describe the evolution of your awareness of the differences in writing for a variety of disciplines that use an array of methodologies. Where and when did you start to develop strategies for disciplinary writing? What major events, assignments, and papers have influenced your approaches to disciplines along the way? What particular teachers or classes have reshaped the ways you write in different disciplinary contexts? What was

your sense of *discipline* and *research method* before you began reading this lesson? What is your approach now that you have finished this lesson? In what ways can you imagine your sense of disciplinary contexts changing beyond college, perhaps morphing into a sense of professional contexts? How does your development as a writer compare with what other students said in their interviews, such as Hyesu? Earlier in the lesson, she describes the moment in an introductory history class in which she began to recognize that college writing is different from high school writing because disciplines and research methods are so varied:

> Something else that I noticed was (this was my first history class in college) the expectations were different from high school. I was used to writing English papers so the formatting was a little difficult. You're not supposed to use literary present tense in history papers. It sounds intuitive now, but as I was writing I just didn't think about it. So, I had to rethink a lot of how I wrote, or how I thought I should be writing. It was more difficult than I thought to shift gears from an English-paper perspective to a history-paper perspective.

8d Invent your writing.

The "How" section of this lesson covers five broad disciplinary areas, each of which includes a number of subdisciplines. In a detailed paragraph, describe what you know about the particular discipline and subdiscipline for a current writing assignment. What are the preferred methodologies and genres for your subdiscipline? Why are they preferred? Conduct some brief, preliminary online research about your subdiscipline. What defines your subdiscipline, and how does this definition influence your writing for that disciplinary audience? Finally, describe in a short paragraph how your new understanding of this particular subdiscipline will impact your writing.

8e Analyze student writing.

Study the opening two or three paragraphs or segments of a couple of model projects in Lesson 25 or in the LaunchPad. You might compare very different models, such as Dan's video and Nicole's paper, or you might read similar work, such as Nanaissa's and Vinh-Thuy's papers.

For each model, fill out the formula from earlier in the lesson: discipline = subject + method. Be as specific as you can for each model. Based on the students' work, what kinds of connections can you sense between the discipline and the audience for the writing? How does each discipline/audience connection compare with the other? In what ways do they seem alike? Different? List a couple of specific choices the writers make to suggest connections among their discipline, research methods, and audience.

Your instructor might ask you to apply this analysis and these questions to your classmates' writing instead (or in addition to the model projects).

8f Revise repeatedly from feedback.

Examine a writing assignment you are currently working on or one that you wrote recently, perhaps in another class or in high school. Describe some specific ways that you can use the ideas from Lesson 8 to revise your writing and improve your awareness of discipline, subject, method, and audience in your assignment. Perhaps most important, to complete this exercise, take an early draft of your writing to the writing center, a peer workshop, or your instructor's office hours and ask "Is this draft well matched to the discipline, subject, method, and audience? How can my approach to this discipline be improved?"

Media

Select the appropriate media for your context, and use it appropriately.

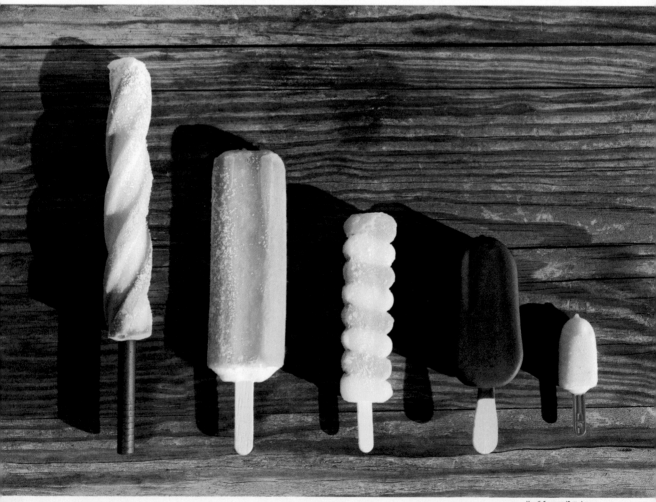

ESSENTIALS VIDEO

Visit the LaunchPad for *Becoming a College Writer* to watch the Lesson 9 Essentials Video.

9.1 [WHY]

Why you should select the appropriate media for your context, and use it appropriately.

Write a set of instructions for making your favorite sandwich so that someone could follow them and make the sandwich. Go ahead and do this. Really. I'll be here when you get back.

I have asked my students to complete this exercise hundreds of times. Only one in ten will include a diagram in their instructions, but nearly all will choose to structure their instructions in a numbered, step-by-step list. Did you?

Why?

My students reply by saying "You told us to *write* a set of instructions, not *draw* them." I then ask, "When was the last time you read a set of instructions that did *not* include a diagram?"

As composers in a digital age you have tools for collecting, creating, and editing images, videos, animations, audio, and multimedia content that you can use in your writing. These different media are a great opportunity to better connect with your audience.

Choosing appropriate media makes your writing appealing to your audience.

JENNA
California State University, San Marcos

One of the ways that we can [write] across genres and modes and film and essays and screenwriting and podcasts or blogs or anything like that is to find the commonalities between them. I think one of the biggest commonalities is going to be your focus on your audience. That's going to really determine how you approach things. Say, for a film you want to accomplish a certain thing through it. You want to consider who's going to be viewing it. . . . Who do you want to reach through this? Who are you talking to? It's going to be the same thought process whether you're writing an essay or doing some sort of technological variation on that sort of thing.

Think of the biggest, most popular soft-drink company you know. Now consider how extensively this company markets its brand. You can barely walk down a city street without seeing the soft drink's logo, and you can't watch television without the brand appearing somewhere as advertising, product placement, or sponsorship.

Now, think of all the senses that the product appeals to: You *see* the bright colors and familiar type of its logo; you *hear* the soft drink's jingle in your head long after a

YouTube advertisement is over; you *feel* the seductive shape of the cool bottle; and you *smell* and *taste* the beverage.

The soft-drink company demonstrates that the *more times* and the *more ways* it can connect with consumers, the *more successful* it will be. Likewise, you can appeal to as many of your audience's senses as possible in the writing and multimedia projects you create. (You'll learn more about this strategy in section 9.2.) The more you do so, the more successful *you* will be as well.

FRANK
Michigan State University

In college I've done a lot more digital writing and I honestly think it's more interesting and more captivating for me, rather than just the normal writing. Technology is going crazy right now with its advancements; so it's good to [be creating] podcasts and digital newsletters and staying in touch with advancing software and technology — making it more interesting than just writing a paper about a book, which is still important.

The digital technologies available to you encourage you to compose with a variety of media, including words, photographs, illustrations, audio recordings, movies or videos, audiovisual slide shows, computer graphics, virtual worlds, and interactive websites and hypertexts — and this list will keep expanding as new technologies emerge.

Choosing appropriate media helps you achieve your purpose.

Just because you *can* include a photograph, audio recording, or movie clip in your college writing assignments does not mean that you necessarily *should*. For example, a photograph in the middle of a conventional essay might distract some readers, especially if it's not clearly connected to the content. However, if you are writing about the construction of the Panama Canal for a history course, a photograph of the construction might be quite relevant.

A good way for you to figure out the best approach in a given context is to **Revise Repeatedly from Feedback**. Make a draft, experiment with media elements, and see how your readers react. This approach will not only help you figure out what works best on a particular assignment, it will also develop your instincts as a successful media producer in other contexts. Nanaissa describes the lessons she learned about sculpting from feedback and revision, which demonstrates how becoming an artist and becoming a college writer both depend on **RRFF**.

NANAISSA
Lansing Community College

When I had to sculpt an entire body, I didn't realize how much this part [the back of the neck] was important to support the head. It's only when I had to sculpt it and it didn't fit that I had to correct it. It's exactly the same thing in writing. You can't say, "Just write it. Just try that and it's going to work." You have to try it and check if it fits. And if it fails, start it again.

Also, pay close attention to your context, especially your writing prompt, as discussed in Lesson 5. Some assignments may specify visuals or other media to include in your writing. Other assignments may be more fully multimedia, like those in the following chart.

Course	Assignment	Purpose	Successful Features
American History	Create a one-minute trailer for an imaginary movie about a historical figure.	To encourage the audience to learn more about the historical figure.	• It uses images (still or moving), sound (speech, music, or sound effects), and text to briefly tell a compelling story. • It fulfills the assignment's purpose.
English Composition	Compose a literacy narrative (the story of how you learned to read and write) as a blog post, including images and audio.	To interest audience members in your story and prompt them to reflect on their own history with reading and writing.	• It tells an interesting textual story and gives specific examples of your past experiences with reading and writing. • It goes beyond straight text to engage the audience. For example, you might include a video clip showing a younger you reading a favorite storybook to your grandmother. • It fulfills the assignment's purpose.
Introduction to Professional Communication	Create a thirty-second public-service announcement, designed for radio broadcast, on the need to avoid text-messaging while driving.	To convince listeners that they shouldn't text while driving.	• It hooks listeners quickly, perhaps with facts or statistics about the dangers of texting while driving. • It uses sound (speech, music, or sound effects) to engage the audience. • It fulfills the assignment's purpose.

Why you should select the appropriate media for your context, and use it appropriately

Course	Assignment	Purpose	Successful Features
Marketing Communications	Design an online micro-website for an imaginary business.	To garner interest in the business's products or services.	• It hooks the audience through appealing slogans, headlines, or visuals, or with an intriguing message about what makes the business's products or services distinctive. • It has a clear, uncluttered design that doesn't get in the way of the main message(s). • Its visual elements (whether still pictures or videos) contribute to the marketing message(s); they're not just window dressing. • It fulfills the assignment's purpose.
Mechanical Engineering	Deliver a half hour PowerPoint, Prezi, or Spark presentation on a current challenge in the field.	To help the audience understand the challenge and what is being done to address it.	• It explains the challenge and possible remedies clearly and within the time limit. • It uses audio (the speaker's voice) and visuals (such as text and inserted photographs and diagrams) effectively. • It fulfills the assignment's purpose.

Choosing and producing appropriate media helps you develop a critical eye.

As you move from media consumer to media producer, you learn how multimedia elements can contribute to the substance of your writing and help you make connections with your topic and audience. In other words, using various media becomes not an end in itself, but a new way of making meaning — a new way of seeing, encountering, explaining, and reshaping the world.

MICHAEL
Michigan State University

I'm really curious to find out what happens in the next few years for writers and students who are trying to understand these [new digital] spaces as they try to legitimize them. It's a really intriguing thing to see happen. . . . The reason I'm a writer is because I like to watch and experience other media and [first] lay it out in writing — to understand [digital media] and review it critically through writing.

Like Michael, you will need to reflect critically on the choices you make as you compose with media. The first question will be: Which media elements to use? Which media are appropriate for the context of your topic, audience, genre, and discipline? Which media might enhance the dynamic relationship in your writing context? At the same time, knowing which media to use in a particular situation depends on a critical understanding of the possibilities and limitations of each medium.

So, in order to select the appropriate media and to then use those media effectively, you must appreciate the advantages and disadvantages of each medium. Section 9.2 explains how to use media critically and appropriately by weighing the benefits and drawbacks of six primary media: text, sound, image, presentation tools, video, and online/social media.

Throughout the next section, we feature Sarah, a college writer who tells the same story about a historic race-car track in Hillsborough, North Carolina, in six different media formats: print, podcast, film, photography, website, and mobile application. Since one of the goals of this lesson is to help you select the appropriate media and use it correctly, comparing Sarah's different approaches and uses of each media for the same story can help deepen your understanding of how these media work. Of course, you will need to follow the links to Sarah's project in the LaunchPad, since most of her work is digital.

9.2 [HOW]

How to select the appropriate media for your context, and use your media appropriately.

Your audience is more likely to connect with your work if you appeal to more than one of their senses through a combination of media. Be aware that each medium has particular possibilities and limitations. Understanding how individual media work will help you combine them effectively when appropriate.

1. Make the most of written words.

Written words are visual media. This is why the physical formatting of your writing is important, as discussed in more detail in Lesson 17: Publishing.

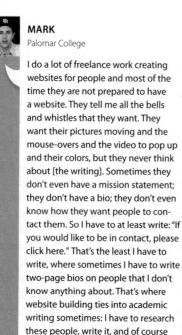

MARK
Palomar College

I do a lot of freelance work creating websites for people and most of the time they are not prepared to have a website. They tell me all the bells and whistles that they want. They want their pictures moving and the mouse-overs and the video to pop up and their colors, but they never think about [the writing]. Sometimes they don't even have a mission statement; they don't have a bio; they don't even know how they want people to contact them. So I have to at least write: "If you would like to be in contact, please click here." That's the least I have to write, where sometimes I have to write two-page bios on people that I don't know anything about. That's where website building ties into academic writing sometimes: I have to research these people, write it, and of course everything has to be correct.

As a web designer and builder, Mark has found that his clients may focus too much on the appearance of their sites instead of the written content. He says his work isn't about flashy design so much as it is about conveying words and meaning. Even in the visually saturated space of the Internet, textual writing may still be king because it has particular advantages that other media do not.

In your composition course you may be asked to create print texts only — or you may be encouraged to experiment with creating work that incorporates multiple media. Keep in mind, though, that text offers significant advantages for academic work that other media cannot match.

A writer can typically pack more ideas, more complicated ideas, and more specific ideas into textual writing than other media formats because text is easier to browse

and review than other forms; if you don't understand something or if you lose track of an idea, it's easy to go back a paragraph or a page and figure it out. Readers can actually comprehend more information from a printed text in a much shorter time than they can from a live speaker.

So the possibility of presenting more information more clearly is an advantage that textual media offer, and you should be conscious of that possibility and use it to your benefit. On the other hand, text alone can be visually limiting — like only looking at one color band within the spectrum of a rainbow. Very often images and illustrations can more effectively connect with readers than pure text, so keep that in mind when thinking about the limitations and opportunities of conventional writing.

PRACTICE Name and discuss two or three specific choices that Sarah makes in her magazine article (on the next page) that seem to make especially good use of written words. List some important differences between Sarah's magazine version of her project and other versions, such as her podcast, film, or mobile app.

2. Use sound to connect with your audience — intellectually, emotionally, and physically.

Hearing and speaking are auditory experiences, though we can also "feel" sounds, as when we sense vibrations from drums during a rock show. We feel sounds because they come from *physical* entities, sound waves. Listening to music can also be a *cerebral* experience, affecting our thoughts and feelings. It is therefore a good idea to make careful choices about the sound in any work that you produce.

Visit the LaunchPad for this book to study Sarah's print version of her digital story in the genre of a popular magazine feature article. Sarah tells the same story in five additional media formats, and you can compare these versions to deepen your understanding of how media work and to help you make effective choices in your own digital projects.

CARA
Metropolitan State University of Denver

If I were to develop a story for radio, like public radio or a news outlet, first I myself would want to have a deep understanding of the issue and get whatever information I could. . . . The second step would be to, in a concise way, give that information to my listeners, viewers, readers because if they don't have a little background information, they'll be asking "Why does this matter? Why is this relevant?" So you have to give them that picture of where your story fits into their world.

Cara's first concern when making a podcast is structure. A disadvantage of creating an audio composition without a visual component is that your audience has no way of knowing how the recording is organized. Further, in the context of academic writing, an audio-only composition may limit you in terms of how in-depth your communication can be. However, there are distinct advantages for writing with sound. Keep the following in mind:

1) **Be aware of the sound of your writing.** Read your writing aloud once you've finished a draft, or better yet, have someone else read it aloud to

How to select the appropriate media for your context, and use your media appropriately

you. Does your writing have rhythm, or are there a lot of short sentences that give it a choppy sound? Are there specific words or phrases that should be emphasized? Does anything sound odd or flat? Mark any problem areas while you listen. Then go back and see where you might combine sentences, revise or add punctuation, or make other improvements. (See also Lesson 16: Proofreading.)

2) **Tap the power of the human voice.** The human voice conveys a tone and a lot of feeling, which can be powerful. When creating an oral presentation, podcast, video voice-over, or any other work that requires you to speak aloud to an audience, have someone else listen to your work. Make sure that you are speaking loudly and clearly enough, and that your tone suits your purpose. For example, if you are creating a news podcast, you should establish a serious tone.

NIA
University of Florida

Because I am very dramatic, I have a voice — maybe I'm spitting a poem or something. I like everything in 3D, if that makes sense. I just applied to film school, and I really wish I could have sat down with all the people that read my application and read them my admissions letter because I feel like I could [get admitted] if I could read it to them. . . . I just feel like my voice makes it better because you know how you sound and you know when your heart *feels* a certain word. . . . Whereas, reading [text] could be anything. Someone could send you a text message, and they could be mad, but you thought that they were sad.

3) **Use the power of music.** We all know how powerful music can be, with or without lyrics. When you are selecting music to, say, introduce a podcast or serve as a background score for a video, make sure that it is in keeping with the purpose and style of the larger work. For instance, consider the ways Vinh-Thuy describes how happy- versus evil-sounding music can impact your message.

VINH-THUY
Red Rocks Community College

I selected music because I feel like if [my film] was just words across a projector screen it would get a little boring. But also music can really influence your mood, right? So imagine you see a grown man and a child walking down the street, and if you hear happy music, you think, "Oh, it's a father and child on his day off!" But if you hear this really hairy music you think, "Oh, this kid's being kidnapped!" So music can really change your mood, and music can really shape what you think, and what the author wants you to think. So I wanted to add the music [in my film] to wake [the audience] up a little bit, but also have the music guide them toward the point I wanted to make. But I didn't want the music to be overpowering, so they were mainly instrumental. . . . I wanted them to focus primarily upon the visual cues and the textual cues.

4) **Understand the practical aspects of recording sound.** Whenever you are delivering sound to an audience, ask yourself the following questions: "Where, when, and how will my audience hear my audio composition?" "Will I be speaking and performing live?" "Will the audience listen to a

recording through headphones? In a classroom with underpowered speakers?" With headphones, for example, your listeners should be able to distinguish nuanced sounds, so you can layer multiple voices, music, and soundtracks more easily. But if your work will be heard through speakers or in a room with poor fidelity, you might need to simplify the recording and make each of its components clear and distinguishable.

When planning any audio composition, begin by studying models of the kind of thing you aim to produce. For example, listen to Sarah's podcast, and identify the different layers in her soundtrack, imagining how you could record, edit, and produce something similar. Be sure to practice with your equipment before capturing actual recordings. Test-drive your microphones, editing software, and publication tools to make sure that you are ready to produce the work you have in mind.

If your instructor has given you a multimedia assignment, they should direct you to the equipment and software you need to complete it, which might be available through a library or media center. If you are experimenting with multimedia on your own, do some research into your college's resources and the tools that are available for free online.

TIPS FOR RECORDING

- Try to use headphones to listen to the recording while you are making it so that you know right away if there's a problem.

- Try to record indoors to limit possible background sounds (e.g., from airplanes or passing cars) that might interfere with your recording.

- Moving air, whether from an open window or from a heating/cooling system, can interfere with a recording, although placing a windscreen over the microphone can help.

- Try to use an external microphone instead of microphones built into other devices, like video cameras, which will often capture mechanical sounds of the device that you probably don't want.

- Most microphone systems have meters to indicate the decibel level of a recording. If the level is either too low or too high, your recording cannot be fixed. So check the levels and stop if there is a problem.

- Some microphones and systems have decibel "boosts"; use your sound meter to check your decibel levels and to determine whether or not you should use the boost.

- Position your source (typically a person or a musical instrument) as close as possible to your microphone so that the sound is projecting directly toward the center of the microphone (unless it is a clip-on lavalier microphone). But do not place subjects so close to the mic that they bump into it, or create a burst of distracting air when they pronounce an "ess," "pah," "tah," or "dah" sound.

- If your subject makes a mistake, leave at least a two-second pause between the mistake and a second take to give yourself space to make a clean edit later.

TIPS FOR EDITING

- If you are new to editing audio, a good rule of thumb is to keep it simple with

129

as few layers, voices, instruments, songs, and effects as possible.

- It is easy to correct an audio recording by editing out chunks of sound, such as "ums," lip smacks, and misstatements, but it is more difficult to fix recording errors such as low volume or background noise.

- You should adjust the pieces of your recording so that they have a consistent volume and so that various segments seem coherent when mixed together. Adjust the volume so that background tracks (such as music) do not overwhelm the foreground of your mix (such as narration). Again, it is more difficult to adjust the volume of a recording dramatically after it is captured without creating other problems, so work hard to get the initial recording right.

- If you want to create a simple podcast, put each of your vocals and sound files on a different track and then merge them only when you export, if possible. If your software is very limited, you can edit one track in the left stereo channel and a second track in the right channel and then merge the two channels when you export.

- Add a half-second or so of silence at the beginning and end of your sound file. If you have opening or closing music, you will typically want to fade those in at the beginning and out at the end.

TIPS FOR PUBLISHING/SHARING

- Consider file size when exporting your final work to share it with others. When you export a sound file, you will have a number of choices for format and compression, which will determine the size of your file. Most email or upload options require files to be no more

than 5 MB or so, although some upload options will compress your file additionally when it is shared. A CD holds about 700 MB, and a DVD holds about 4 GB. Thumb drives and solid-state flash drives hold anywhere from 2 GB to 4 TB.

- If you need to compress your sound file to share it, the first consideration is sample rate: the number of samples of a sound signal taken per second. (The higher the sampling rate, the better the quality of the sound.) CD-quality sound is sampled at about 44 kHz, radio broadcasts at about 22 kHz, and basic voice podcasts at 11 kHz. With audio-editing tools, try exporting at these different sample rates (and listening to the export) until you find the one you want.

- The length of your file will of course determine the size of the export: the longer your recording, the larger the sound file.

- There are a number of file formats for exporting, many of which are proprietary to specific software applications and computer systems. The WAV, MP3, and AIFF formats are currently the ones most widely used for college projects.

- If you are using any copyrighted material (such as a recording of a popular song), be aware of what constitutes permissible uses of such material under the Fair Use doctrine of U.S. copyright law. (See page 133 for more on Fair Use.) Also, be sure to give credit to the source.

PRACTICE Name and discuss two or three specific choices that Sarah makes in her podcast that seem to make especially good use of that format. List some important differences between Sarah's podcast version of her project and other versions, such as her magazine, film, or mobile app.

Visit the LaunchPad for this book to study Sarah's audio version of her digital story in the genre of a streaming podcast. Sarah tells the same story in five additional media formats, and you can compare these versions to deepen your understanding of how media work and to help you make effective choices in your own digital projects.

3. Understand when images can enhance or replace written text.

As the cliché goes, "A picture is worth a thousand words," which suggests at least two important ideas: (1) Images can communicate a lot in a brief amount of time, and (2) photographs are often more convincing than words. Let's look at an image of an abandoned classroom. What does this photograph achieve that a textual description couldn't?

Visuals can make ideas easier to understand or remember, especially if they are used in combination with words. For example, notice how the diagram on page 132 uses words and visuals to illustrate a mining process.

Combining images and texts can be more effective than using text alone because different media activate different parts of the brain, and the more dynamic your brain is, the more engaged you are. Aside from photographs and diagrams, you might also use maps when you want your audience to, say, visualize the geographical features of a desert or track troop movements in a historical battle.

On the other hand, providing an image might sometimes get in the way of what you are trying to accomplish. For example, John Keats's famous poem "Ode on a Grecian Urn" is probably more effective *without* an accompanying image of a Grecian

Sean Gallup/Getty Images

131

How to select the appropriate media for your context, and use your media appropriately

urn because the poem is about using imagination to animate the objects on the urn beyond their still and static forms. (It's interesting to note that in this poem Keats suggests that the three-dimensional visual art form of the Grecian urn is more effective than his written poem at telling its story.)

In the context of college writing, the important thing to remember is that any images you use should serve your purpose, whether that is to portray the physical impact of poverty or crisis or to explain how fracking works. Images should not be used purely as decoration. They need to do part of the work of conveying your ideas.

PHILLIP
Santa Fe College

One of the requirements for a technical communication paper was that it had to have images. Whenever I was selecting an image for a certain part of the paper, I tried to think of myself as the reader, put myself in the reader's shoes, as a reader who may not even know anything about this topic. I would pick a picture that, when the reader looked at it, it would give them an idea of what that paragraph or set of paragraphs was going to explain.

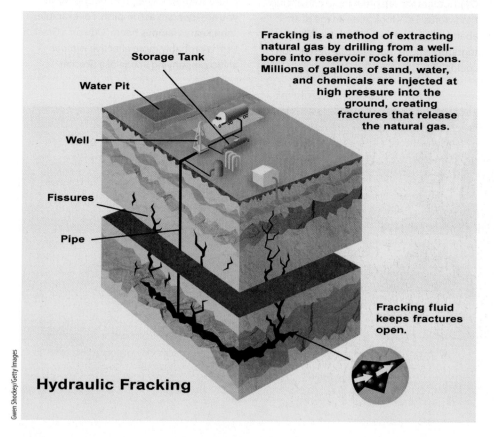

Storage Tank

Water Pit

Well

Fissures

Pipe

Fracking is a method of extracting natural gas by drilling from a well-bore into reservoir rock formations. Millions of gallons of sand, water, and chemicals are injected at high pressure into the ground, creating fractures that release the natural gas.

Fracking fluid keeps fractures open.

Hydraulic Fracking

Gwen Shockey/Getty Images

[In] my History of Jazz class I was required to write a concert review. So I went to this jazz venue and watched the show and took some notes and wrote my report later. But I also got a picture at the end [during] this ballad song that they were playing. There were these two people in the audience, husband and wife, maybe in their eighties, and I was able to get a picture of them dancing to the closing song of this jazz performance. I attached that to my paper and my instructor, who was also at the concert, said that I had really captured the theme of the concert by throwing the picture in there, and I got extra credit for that. So I wish that I could attach more pictures to my writing in college.

It is also important that you have permission to use the images and other visual elements you include. For your academic writing, the material you use will often fall under the Fair Use doctrine of U.S. copyright law, which says that creators of noncommercial works that include small extracts of others' works for educational purposes (or as the basis for critical review or commentary) may not have to get permission. Even if your images are Fair Use, however, you should still cite the source. For more details on Fair Use, visit www.copyright.gov.

There are oceans of material about how to compose and interpret visual materials. Even so, there is consensus on key elements and principles of visual composition.

ELEMENTS OF VISUAL COMPOSITION

- **Line:** a path between points that can vary in width (thick or thin) and direction (straight or curved).

- **Shape:** a two-dimensional space that has a length and width and a boundary to define it. Circles, triangles, squares, and rectangles are familiar shapes.

- **Form:** a three-dimensional space that has length, width, and depth. Spheres, pyramids, cubes, and cylinders are familiar forms.

- **Texture:** the real or implied tactile, three-dimensional surface of an object. Rough, smooth, glossy, matte, stony, sandy, and glassy are familiar textures.

- **Color:** a part of the visible range of light, often represented by a rainbow. Different colors can have different associations and connotations: The sky is blue, grass is green, blood is red, and so on.

- **Value:** how light or dark something is. We think of white as light and black as dark, but each color can be darker or lighter, too.

- **Frame:** the space contained within a two-dimensional visual, including the perspective from which the image is established. Frame may be the most relevant consideration for the purposes of integrating images into college writing because you are likely to consider first the point of view (where the viewer is positioned by the composer) and second what is cropped (included or excluded) within the frame you select.

PRINCIPLES OF VISUAL COMPOSITION

- **Focal point:** the object(s) that seem most important in a visual composition. The focal point is not necessarily at the dead center of the composition; in fact, the "rule of thirds" suggests that it is more effective for the focal point to be located one-third of the way from one edge of the frame.

- **Unity and balance:** the relationships among the dominant and subordinate

How to select the appropriate media for your context, and use your media appropriately

objects in a visual composition. If the various objects in the image seem to have a "weight," those weights can be distributed throughout the frame to suggest balance and unity.

- **Contrast:** the tensions and differences between the objects in a visual composition. The objects in the image might be of contrasting or complementary color or shape, thus creating or eliminating tension and contrast. Or the foreground and background could work together or pull against each other.

- **Pattern and variety:** repetition and variety of objects, shapes, colors, and so on within a visual composition. If an object, shape, or color is repeated, the composer usually is trying to convey something with the pattern.

- **Scale and proportion:** the geometric relationships among the objects in the composition as well as the location of the viewer in relationship to the composition (which determines perspective). The objects in the frame may be large or small in relation to each other, or they might be skewed for effect beyond what we might perceive as natural proportion. Also, the proximity of the viewpoint to the objects in the frame establishes perspective through scale.

- **Movement:** either (1) implied motion within the visual composition (such as blurring images to suggest action) or (2) the movement of the viewer's eye through the composition.

4. Understand the strengths and weaknesses of presentation tools.

In college you have probably sat through a number of PowerPoint presentations.

A business executive friend of mine once sent me some information about a class reunion in a PowerPoint document. I asked why he didn't just send an email or a Word document, and his reply was, "Everything I do ends up in PowerPoint anyway, so now I just begin there."

The popularity of PowerPoint and other presentation applications is probably subsiding somewhat as people get tired of those formats, but, as you can tell from your college lectures, this multimedia approach to communication is here to stay for the foreseeable future. Sometime in college you will likely be asked to give a presentation yourself, so you will want to become familiar with presentation software at some point.

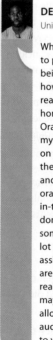

DEONTA
University of North Carolina, Chapel Hill

When I compare oral presentations to papers I think about actually being able to see the audience and how they're going to perceive it and react to what you're saying. And, honestly, I get a little frightened. Oral presentations aren't really my thing. I prefer to put my ideas on paper. They flow easier and they come out a lot smoother, and I can also revise that. With an oral presentation, it's more of an in-the-moment kind of thing. You don't really get an attempt to redo something if you mess up. So, I'm a lot more comfortable with written assignments, but oral presentations are good because they train you for real world experiences where you may not be [able to write]. They also allow you the opportunity to see the audience and how they're reacting to what you're saying.

Here are a few key advantages of presentation tools like PowerPoint, Prezi, or Spark:

- They make it easy for you to incorporate multimedia elements into your presentation: photographs, charts, graphs, video clips, sound files, and more. (For more on how images can enhance words, see the previous section.)

- They allow you to appeal to multiple senses, helping to engage your audience.

- They make it easy for users without much experience with the elements and principles of visual composition to make something attractive in a short time. For example, predesigned templates offer different combinations of colors, design formats, and fonts, suggesting various styles: "contemporary," "executive," "modern," "western," "sunset," and the like.

- Presentation software, like word-processing software, makes it simple to add headers, bulleted and numbered lists, and other design elements.

- The slide-based and outline-based structure of presentation software can help organize and balance your presentation.

Each segment of an electronic audiovisual presentation is most typically called a *slide* because late in the last century slide projectors were one of the easiest ways to make a colorful audiovisual presentation. Textual information and images are placed on each slide, and the arrangement of all of the slides together provides a deliberate, linear structure to the presentation, somewhat like the paragraphs in an essay.

Most often, the slides progress simply from one to the next, but the composer can create transitional effects like "dissolve" and "wipe" that animate the presentation, or they can create a web of slides instead of a linear progression. However, these effects often come across as more cheesy than effective, unless there seems to be a specific purpose to them.

Presentation software has evolved significantly since its earliest days. For instance, this software can be used to make mini-movies and clickable hypertexts. Also, electronic presentations can be looped to play continuously at conference booths or kiosks, standing in for human presenters.

In making an audiovisual presentation, consider what's most effective for your purpose and your audience.

- Do not read from or talk directly to the projection screen/monitor, especially if you must turn to face the screen momentarily.

- Do talk naturally and conversationally, using the presentation as an outline to prompt your thoughts, and use the "presenter's mode" to read a brief transcript from your laptop only when necessary.

- Do not transfer a document made to be read on paper onto presentation slides.

- Do build your slides from select keywords that organize the sections of your presentation and highlight your most important ideas.

- Do not use complicated visual elements with low resolution or cheesy clichés.

- Do selectively employ bright, clear, straightforward images to complement your spoken words.

- Do not present complicated charts, tables, and graphs with fine print and details too tiny to discern from the back of the room.

How to select the appropriate media for your context, and use your media appropriately

- Do use large, bold, cleanly formatted geometric charts, graphs, and illustrations to support the points or facts you are making verbally.

- Do not design a presentation so that it can substitute completely for listening to an oral presentation, if you plan to deliver it live.

- Do try to take advantage of what your spoken voice can accomplish that visual support cannot, and vice versa.

- Do not use flashy or cheesy visual, sound, or animation effects just because you can.

- Do rely on the quality of your research, words, and thoughts to engage your audience.

- Do not use copyrighted material without fairly attributing your sources.

- Do provide a bibliography in the final slide, or hand one out on paper.

5. Use film or video to bring a subject to life.

Movies can seem like magic: They transport us to places and into adventures that we may not be able to otherwise experience. The stories they tell can be transformative when they expose us to new ideas. Movies can also provide straightforward entertainment or social opportunities to connect with others.

As a college writer, when might it be more effective for you to make a movie instead of writing a paper or giving a live presentation? In some cases, an assignment prompt will make decisions about format for you. But when you have more leeway, you should first consider the nature of motion pictures and what they offer that other forms of media cannot.

Vinh-Thuy explains his crude composing method for storyboarding and making a rudimentary film. Notice how, even as a novice filmmaker, he understands the essential relationship of the visual and audio tracks in movies.

VINH-THUY
Red Rocks Community College

[To make my film], I opened up a Word document (it wasn't anything fancy), and I dragged all of the images into there. I had two pictures per page and I was going to write three sentences per two pictures, and that was how I got my captions. I split the screen, and I had my essay on the right and I had the pictures on the left. And I just read through the essay and looked through the pictures to see "How can I match this with this?" And, if I couldn't, I'd move the pictures to another place. I would take two or three sentences out of the paragraph, and that would be my caption for each of the pictures — that was how I put it together. At the end, the actual iMovie part was incredibly simple because I had the pictures already lined up. All it took was pasting the pictures into iMovie and pasting the words on there, putting music to it — and then just clicking "Create."

The art of filmmaking is hugely complex and forever evolving, making it far beyond the scope of this textbook. However, here are some tips to help you avoid the most common and frustrating problems with academic filmmaking.

TIPS FOR FILMING

- Plan your shoots on paper before the day you film, including a checklist of things to bring, such as charged batteries, extra tape/disks/media, power cords, microphones, tripods, cables, earphones, lighting, and release forms (discussed next). Always bring duct tape.

- The people in your movie should sign release forms giving you permission to film them for the purposes that you spell out in person and on the forms. In addition to getting permission in writing, get it on film as a backup. Also, be aware that parents must give permission for anyone under the age of eighteen to appear in a film, and you might need approval from your school's institutional research board to interview people in your film.

- Test your microphones ahead of your shoot and wear earphones during filming to make sure there are no recording problems. (For more information on audio recording, see pages 129–30.)

- Begin each shot by using a written slate to indicate the date, location, and project name, or just say this information into the camera as you begin to roll.

- Always make sure that you are recording and that the film is "rolling" before you begin shooting your live action. (The time counter should be moving, and a recording indicator on the viewfinder should be on.)

- Plan your background and foreground carefully so that neither is disrupted nor distracting.

- Avoid backlighting, in which the light *behind* your subject is stronger than the light *on* your subject, creating a silhouette effect. For example, do not place your subject in front of a bright window.

- Adjust the white balance before shooting, if you can. When the balance is correctly adjusted, white objects come out looking white on the film, instead of being tinged with some other color.

- Whenever possible, use a tripod to avoid the shaky footage that can result from filming with a handheld device.

- Leave at least two or three seconds before and after every take, shoot, scene, or filming session so that you have clear places to make editing cuts.

- As the director, prompt your interviewees to answer in complete sentences that contain the question in their response.

- Don't be afraid to interrupt a shot or make multiple takes to get the shot right.

- Film with calm and composure. Avoid rushing while filming, and check your planning notes to make sure that you've covered everything before wrapping up a shoot.

- Label your media/disks/cards carefully and immediately lock them to prevent accidental erasure, if you can.

TIPS FOR EDITING

- Most personal computers include movie-editing software that is adequate for a very first project. However, by the second or third project you can hopefully find a media lab on campus where you can edit your film with more advanced software because the free, stripped-down version is often too limiting. Software manufacturers often offer a midrange "light" or "academic" version of their products, which is more affordable and fairly powerful, compared to the sometimes expensive and cumbersome professional editions.

137

- The first step in editing video is getting all of the necessary settings and preferences correct before you begin to work with any footage. Ask for help or check online for tutorials if you have never used a particular computer or application before. You want to be sure that all of your work is being saved to a secure and designated space as you go along, and you want to establish essential settings such as frame rate and aspect ratio before you proceed.

- The second step in editing video is "capturing," which means duplicating the footage from your original storage medium onto the hard drive of the computer (or onto an external hard drive). Never edit your only copy of your film. Make backup copies and edit those instead. To give just one example of why you should take this advice, say that during the editing process you delete some footage that you later wish you hadn't. If you don't have a backup copy, that footage is gone for good. If you do, you get a second chance.

- Once you have saved all of your footage onto a hard drive, allocate at least one hour of solid editing for each minute of footage in your final project. Double the time allocation for your first project or when using new software.

- If you have never edited a movie before, find a friend or media lab consultant who can help you learn as you go, but keep their hands off the keyboard and mouse as much as possible because if they do the work, you will never learn how to edit.

- In most student academic movies, the simplest approach is almost always the best, which means that you should avoid gimmicky treatments and effects, especially if you do not have a lot of experience making movies.

- In most student academic movies, the audio track is the spine on which the film is built; so get the sound right first and then adjust the visual track to complement the audio.

- Add effects like texts and transitions after cutting the entire piece together based first on the audio track and second on the visual layer.

- Use effects like texts and titles consistently throughout your project to provide cohesion and continuity.

- Include a title card in the introduction of your movie, and provide credits and reference information at the end.

TIPS FOR PUBLISHING/SHARING

- You must cite any outside sources of content, such as video or audio clips, that you use in your film, just as you cite sources in a written paper. However, citations for a film might be better presented in an accompanying textual document than in the film itself. (For more on how to cite and document sources, see Lesson 24: Citation.)

- Especially in commercial contexts, people or institutions that want to use copyrighted works created by others must get permission to do so. For instance, say that a commercial publisher wants to include a magazine article on fracking in an anthology on environmental policy. This means that the publisher would need to get permission for the article from the copyright holder — either the journalist who wrote the article or the magazine. However, under the Fair Use doctrine of U.S. copyright law, creators of noncommercial works that include small extracts of others' works for educational purposes (or as the basis for critical review or commentary) may not have to get permission. This means that a student who includes, say, a brief TV news clip in a documentary that will be screened solely within a classroom is most likely protected under Fair Use. However, the student should cite the source of the news clip. For more details on Fair Use, visit www.copyright.gov.

- Preparing your film for viewing, whether by burning it onto a disk, saving on a flash drive, or uploading it online, often takes around thirty minutes, even if you have experience doing so. Plan this final step of your project carefully, and allocate enough time for glitches because you do not want your hard work to be wasted by rushing or stumbling at this last step.

- Determine the context in which your audience will view your movie, and choose a suitable export format and file size. At one end of the spectrum, a movie that you share through email or social media should probably be compressed in size to less than 5 MB. Different online video-hosting sites have different limitations in terms of file size and clip length, and most of these sites will compress your movie file as it uploads. At the far end of the spectrum, a full-quality, one-hour film will often consume 15 GB or more of disk space but will be compressed to 4 GB or less when formatted or burned onto DVD or for streaming. If you plan to share your work on a solid-state flash drive, check with your reader ahead of time to make sure that will work.

- Most movie-editing software has preset options for exporting films so that they can be viewed by others. Experiment with these options until you find the right one.

- You should consider whether or not your audience might have access issues, which can include needing a high-speed Internet connection or having disabilities regarding hearing or sight. Closed captioning is standard for commercial video projects, but it is typically too difficult for college students to provide that service, even though they should be aware of such considerations. A printed transcript of the text of the film might be a more manageable alternative.

A Track Through Time

Visit the LaunchPad for this book to study Sarah's video version of her digital story in the genre of a short film. Sarah tells the same story in five additional media formats, and you can compare these versions to deepen your understanding of how media work and to help you make effective choices in your own digital projects.

How to select the appropriate media for your context, and use your media appropriately

PRACTICE Name and discuss two or three specific choices that Sarah makes in her film that seem to make especially good use of that format. List some important differences between Sarah's film version of her project and other versions, such as her magazine, podcast, or mobile app.

6. Make the most of social networks.

Social media have enabled new connections among users who are both consumers *and* producers of digital content. By sharing texts, video, and the like through social media, you are collaborating to make and remake knowledge and meaning. In choosing digital media for your work, consider which format best suits your context and audience: It might be a basic website or a blog, or it might be a more social Facebook site, Twitter feed, or YouTube account.

TIPS FOR ONLINE CONSUMERS

GRETCHEN
Boston University

It really annoys me when people don't use capital "I"s in their [Facebook] statuses. I think those should be illegal. And I hate when people text me and say like, "R U awake?" So I'm definitely kind of old school in that I'm almost a luddite. . . . But I do use the computer a lot for finding good writing and I think social media is a good way to find good writing and for writers to [publish] themselves. Because, before social media, you couldn't really be your own publisher or your own editor, but with Facebook and Twitter and blogs, people are posting amazing work that would have never really reached a broader audience. So in a way I'm thankful for that.

Gretchen uses social media to find quality writing, which is important to her and her career as a journalist. Her distaste for text-speak in the form of abbreviations does not go so far as to kill her willingness to wade through bad writing to find the work that she deeply values. In other words, being a critical media producer begins with also being a critical media consumer.

TIPS FOR ONLINE PRODUCERS

CHASE
Santa Fe College

The first post [in my custom blog] was something I had written before that I threw up there — but then I went into really high density, quality content, like, Tim Ferris's blog or other CEOs' blogs. That's where that came from. . . . I wrote it for my friends, actually. I saw that a lot of my friends would struggle to get As or they would struggle to do well in school and they didn't know what to do. They didn't know how to study. And there were key things that they weren't taking full advantage of or they just didn't know anything about. And I wrote it really for them as a reference guide. And surprisingly I've had not just them read it but a lot of people come to read it.

Chase and his blog demonstrate how you can make meaning with your writing, respond to rhetorical context, and manage genres and media. His most popular post was written to help out his friends, and his evident relationship with his topic and audience also attracted other readers. Chase lacked experience with blogging, but he had the wise instinct to study a model of the genre and media (Tim Ferris's blog) to get him started. What moves did Chase make that can help you too?

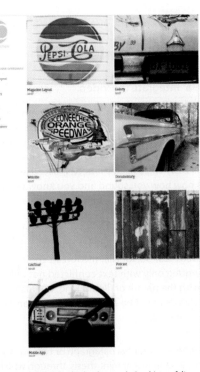

DANIEL
Roxbury Community College

Well, a couple of friends of mine last year, in November, we were interested in doing some community service, and we really didn't have any idea who to go to. First of all, this wasn't a class assignment. This was just something that my friends and I kind of talked about, and I came up with the idea of creating a newsletter that could give us an opportunity to mentor and create more like a family of writers. So, my friends and I we went to communities here in Roxbury and Allston and Jamaica Plain and we recruited some of the high school students. We asked them "Do you need help in English or history — any writing assignments that you're doing for school?" We drafted this idea of "Real Talk Boston" [as an online newsletter], which deals with creating a family of writers where we can talk about our pieces, critique each other, and also give feedback on how we can improve ourselves as writers.

Visit the LaunchPad for this book to study Sarah's portfolio version of her digital story. Sarah tells the same story in five additional media formats, and you can compare these versions in her portfolio to deepen your understanding of how media work and to help you make effective choices in your own digital projects.

As emphasized throughout this textbook, the key to college writing is to **Revise Repeatedly from Feedback**. What is the best way to use media to develop your writing? A good beginning is to build yourself a network of other writers and producers to exchange, critique, develop, revise (RRFF), and promote your writing, as Daniel did.

PRACTICE Name and discuss two or three specific choices that Sarah makes in her portfolio that seem to make especially good use of that format. List some important differences between Sarah's portfolio collection and other versions, such as her magazine, podcast, or film.

9.3

Exercises: media

9a Integrate the video.

Earlier in this lesson, Nia talked about applying to film school and how unnatural it felt for her not be able to use her actual voice as part of the application. She said, "I just feel like my voice makes it better, because you know how you sound and you know when your heart *feels* a certain word. Whereas, reading [text] could be anything. Someone could send you a text message, and they could be mad, but you thought that they were sad." So, for Nia, the forced choice of writing only with text conflicted not only with the nature of filmmaking, but also with Nia's desire to be authentic, human, and even emotional.

Write a substantial paragraph or two, with a topic sentence or mini-thesis, through which you respond to Nia and other videos in the lesson. It will help you form your own approaches to selecting the appropriate media and then using that media appropriately. If possible, try to capture your response as a video selfie or voice recording instead of in sentences and paragraphs.

You can watch the Lesson 9 Essentials Video, or you can browse the embedded clips in the online edition of this lesson. You might begin by identifying the moments that stand out to you the most. Which student videos seem to make the most sense to you? With whom do you agree? Disagree? What patterns do you find among the student sound bites? Which ideas were the most instructive or helpful to you? What surprised you? How have your own ideas about writing in a variety of media come into focus through the videos?

9b Create a journal entry or blog.

Your instructor might ask you to keep a writer's journal throughout this class. This journal could be handwritten or composed on a computer. Since you are working on media in this lesson, now would be a great time to compose a video blog, using either a smartphone or built-in recorder on a computer to capture a video selfie.

To prepare a journal entry on Lesson 9, describe your thoughts and approaches to the key term *media*, trying not to glance back at the material in the lesson, at first. Not referring to this material initially will help you see what you have internalized so far. After carefully composing your initial thoughts, look back at some of the ideas and strategies other students gave in Lesson 9 or in the online database of interviews. For example, in her interview, Kendra talks about the importance of the visual elements in writing, even in a conventional textual format, such as the conventional genre of a lab report: "When putting your data into your paper it's good for the visuals to be self-explanatory, where everything is clearly labeled."

What insights have you gained from the advice of students like Kendra? You might wish to disagree with some of this lesson, or you might want to modify or expand on some of its advice. For example, consider integrating additional thoughts, notes, and lessons from your instructor and your class meetings into your journal entry. It might help for you to imagine that you are giving advice to your future self about writing. What from this lesson and from discussions about writing in different media might benefit you down the road?

9c See yourself as a writer.

Describe the evolution of your awareness of the differences in writing for a variety of media that use an array of media. Ideally, you might do so in a simple video selfie using a smartphone or a computer to record your story (instead of using a conventional word processor). Take a glance at Dan's film in which he describes his evolution as a digital writer. Where and when did you start to develop strategies for multimedia writing? What major events, assignments, and papers have influenced your approaches to media along the way? What particular teachers or classes have reshaped the ways you write in different media? What was your sense of "media" before you began reading this lesson? What is your approach now that you have finished this lesson? In what ways can you imagine your sense of media production changing beyond college, perhaps morphing into a sense of professional media production? How does your development as a writer compare with what other students said in their interviews, such as Dan? Dan describes his evolution as a college writer in terms of the ways he learned to productively challenge static "rules" for academic writing through experimentation with a variety of media forms in his writing:

> When I was initially taught how to write there were sort of these rules that I'd follow. And you were graded and you were judged based on how well you followed those rules — not how well you changed the rules, not how well you came up with new ways to do things, but how well you stuck to a guideline. And I did that for, probably, from the moment I knew how to write until the middle of high school, end of school. And then as I sort of started to fall in love with writing and really enjoy communicating — writing those rules sort of became extremely evident to me. I sort of saw those rules in a new way, and I delved into breaking them.

9d Invent your writing.

The "How" section of this lesson covers six broad media forms, from writing to podcasts to video, each of which includes a description of some potential advantages and disadvantages of each media. In a detailed paragraph, describe what you know about the particular media for a current writing assignment. What is the preferred media for the assignment? Why is it preferred? Review what is written in 9.2 about that media form, and then conduct some additional brief, preliminary online research about using that media to write in college. Does the preferred media form seem like the best or only way to achieve the purposes of the assignments? Why? Finally, describe in a short paragraph how a different multimedia approach to the assignment might impact your writing. If it were only up to you, which of the six media discussed in 9.2 would you choose?

9e Analyze student writing.

Study the opening two or three paragraphs or segments of a couple of model projects in Lesson 25 or in the LaunchPad. You might compare very different models, such as Sarah's video versus her magazine article (in LaunchPad), or you might read work that is similar in its use of visual elements, such as Vinh-Thuy's paper and Kendra's PowerPoint presentation.

Based on the students' work, what kinds of connections can you sense between the media and the audience for the writing? How does each media/audience connection compare with the other? In what ways do they seem alike? Different? Describe a couple of specific choices that the writers seem to make in the ways they "write" with media. How do these specific choices suggest connections between their media, genre, and audience?

Your instructor might ask you to apply this analysis and these questions to your classmates' writing instead (or in addition to the model projects). Ideally your classmate is working on a multimedia project, and you could use the questions above to analyze that work. Connect your feedback to your classmate's composition as a link or an embed, if that project has an annotation or comment function.

9f Revise repeatedly from feedback.

Examine a writing assignment you are currently working on or one that you wrote recently, perhaps in another class or in high school. Describe some specific ways that you can use the ideas from Lesson 9 to revise your writing and improve your awareness of media, genre, and audience in your assignment. Perhaps most important, to complete this exercise, take an early draft of your writing to the writing center, a peer workshop, or your instructor's office hours and ask, "Does this draft use the right media, and does it approach that media effectively? How can my approach to this media be improved?"

PART THREE

Process

The lessons in Part Three explore different stages of the writing process. Even though each step is presented as its own lesson, they are all closely related. There is no one correct order for completing these stages, and some of them will likely come up more than once over the course of a single project.

Planning

Plan your writing process.

ESSENTIALS VIDEO

Visit the LaunchPad for *Becoming a College Writer* **to watch the Lesson 10 Essentials Video.**

10.1   [WHY]

Why you should plan your writing process.

MATT
Metropolitan State University of Denver

The difference in the approach from high school to college is [that] I'm not cranking papers out the night before. I'm definitely putting more time into my writing, so I'm not handing in first draft stuff. It's definitely a process.

TARA
Boston University

Freshman year I had a hard time writing because I was so stuck to the way of writing in high school that was definitely more basic. I was used to not spending a lot of time writing — editing and working on my papers. So I think my first assignment I probably got a C because I just wasn't used to all the time and effort you actually need to put into a paper to get a good grade.

Matthew and Tara let you know straight up what all of the student interviews reveal: Becoming a college writer requires more of a time investment than writing in high school. It requires self-discipline and planning skills and makes demands on your schedule, often on days when you have less available time than ever — which is where this lesson comes in.

Each lesson in **Part Three: Process** is designed to help you improve upon a specific step in your writing process:

LESSON 10	Planning (You are here!)
LESSON 11	Brainstorming
LESSON 12	Researching
LESSON 13	Organizing
LESSON 14	Drafting
LESSON 15	Revising
LESSON 16	Proofreading
LESSON 17	Publishing
LESSON 18	Reflecting

This lesson on *planning your writing process* is the gateway to the other lessons. Where should you begin your process? You might assume that a first step would be to begin writing or researching as fast as you can — which isn't a terrible idea. However, I recommend that you first do this: Look at your calendar and jot down a plan — a strategy for how you will get your writing done. One that includes concrete goals. This lesson will explain why it's a good idea to plan and will show you how to create a solid one.

By now, you know that the key to college writing is to **Revise Repeatedly from Feedback**. So, it's worth noting up front that the primary purpose of careful planning, as recommended throughout this chapter, is to schedule plenty of time to draft, get feedback, and revise based upon that feedback. In my decades of

147
Why you should plan your writing process

teaching college writing, I have found that students who dedicate substantial time to getting feedback and revising based upon that feedback always improve and succeed—this is how you become a college writer. The essential part of a successful plan—as Matt and Tara suggest—is to set aside time to **Revise Repeatedly from Feedback**.

PRACTICE Brainstorm a vertical list of three to five names of people who could give you good feedback on your writing. Next to each of those names, write down a realistic estimate of the number of calendar days it would take you to schedule an appointment with that person, gather good feedback from them, and then deeply revise your draft to incorporate their advice. Be realistic about your schedule and theirs. Sure, you might walk down to the writing center this very minute, get an open appointment, gather some feedback, and revise immediately, all within the space of a single day. But how likely is it that your schedule is that open, and, more important, how likely is it that each of these people will be immediately available? RRFF takes planning.

Writing is magic. Declaring your goals helps you achieve them.

I doubt there exists a self-help book on any topic, whether it's losing weight or succeeding in business, which does *not* require you to begin by putting your goals in writing. There's something magical about seeing your plans in writing that helps to make them come true. When you do this, you take a positive step forward by visualizing what you want. For example, Lesson 2 asks you to see yourself as a writer. If you were to write "I am a writer" on a Post-it note to yourself, and if you were to look at that note every day, you would likely come to see yourself as a writer. There's good

cognitive research on why this is the case, but for our purposes, let's just say that writing down your goals is a very helpful sort of magic.

So, writing is not just something you do in school for a grade. Writing can change your life in positive ways because it can help you realize your ambitions, in college and beyond college.

PRACTICE Write down a single, important goal for your writing and post it in a prominent place where you will see it every day or multiple times throughout the day. Your goal might be, "Write for thirty minutes before going to class (or going to bed)" or "Get feedback twice on each paper before handing it in," or even "I am a writer." You could list two or three smaller goals for a specific week and a specific project, such as "Write 250 new words and find three good sources for five days in a row." You could use a Post-it note, your computer desktop, a whiteboard, a bulletin board, or even a bathroom mirror. After at least a week of this practice, ask yourself, "Did seeing this goal in writing help me reach that goal, even if it was only partially?"

Metawriting is magic. Journaling as you write gives you a playbook for your process.

DAN
Michigan State University

As humans, we're just so used to writing. We've done it our entire lives—just writing things out and actually seeing them visually and being able to move them with our hands . . . We need to use this tactile ability. We have to write things. That's how we figure things out.

Metawriting can be defined as writing about writing. In this case, I mean writing about *your own* writing. When you metawrite, you reflect upon your strengths, weaknesses, and experiences as a writer. If writing down goals for physical fitness helps you get into better shape, then documenting goals for your writing can help make you a better writer. As Dan says, writing is "how we figure things out." The more aware you are of yourself as a writer, the more efficient you will be as you work to improve.

The second exercise in each lesson of this book (the exercises labeled "b") asks you to keep a journal or a blog in which you write to your future self. Imagine rereading your journal/blog in your junior year as a way to help you perform well on an important writing project in your major. If you maintain a thorough, thoughtful writing journal, then you will, in fact, have two college composition textbooks: The one I wrote and the one you created with your own hands. Which one will eventually mean more to you?

What should you metawrite about your writing process in your journal/blog? Think of your writing process as the steps you take as you complete a writing assignment. These steps form a writing plan. In high school, students are often required to submit a different document for each separate step they take as they complete a research paper. For example:

STEP 1: Page(s) of free-writing = brainstorming

STEP 2: Collection of note cards = researching

STEP 3: Formal outline = organizing

STEP 4: Rough draft = drafting

STEP 5: Second draft that responds to feedback = revising

STEP 6: Red-lined version with sentence-level corrections = editing

STEP 7: Final draft = publishing

Writers who document each stage of their writing processes take deliberate, strategic steps over time to complete an assignment. That means they avoid the stress of trying to complete an assignment in one sitting, late on the night before the paper is due. Inexperienced writers can benefit by separating each step of their process discretely, allotting ample time to take each step thoroughly, and developing customized strategies for each step. Consider how Chase designates a specific time and date to a specific step in his writing process:

CHASE
Santa Fe College

I pretty much use Parkinson's law: "Work fills the time that you allot it." So I try to give myself very short, concise deadlines. Usually, a lot of the time, within a day. Like, I want my first draft written for that day. So I'll give myself milestones: "By 4:00 pm I want to have this done. I want to have written all of these topics, done all the research. By 4:00 pm I want this done. By 7:00 I want to have X amount of my paper written. By 8:00 I want to have it all written. And by 9:00 I want to have it edited." And I'll usually do that in almost an unrealistic manner in the time that I allot myself because it forces me to think and focus really hard on one specific thing, which [makes] my writing a lot better.

PRACTICE Exercise 10.3.b asks you to keep a writer's journal. It encourages you to create a double entry for each step in your writing process: one entry that plans or envisions a step you are about to take, and a later entry that reflects back on how effectively each step was completed. With Chase's advice in mind, take a moment to complete the planning entries in your writer's journal now.

Being aware of your individual process makes you a better writer.

The comedian Steve Martin once joked, "Not many people know this, but the *Mona Lisa* was painted with just one stroke." The truth is that not even Leonardo da Vinci, who is considered one of the greatest geniuses of Western civilization, could crank out good work in one draft; in fact, he worked on the *Mona Lisa* portrait for four years or longer and never fully completed it. Leonardo da Vinci did not finish many paintings, but he did produce incredible volumes of sketches, studies, and plans in his notebooks and journals. He was very good at the early stages of composing, but not so good at completion. However, he was very good at journaling. If you take the time to document or journal insights about your writing process, then you will be surprised at how much you will learn about yourself and how much you will improve as a writer.

GINA
Metropolitan State University of Denver

Break the process down to its most basic level and get [students] to understand that everyone comes at writing a little bit differently. And what works for me won't necessarily work for everybody. Everybody's writing process is unique and whatever it is that works for you is okay. Whatever it is that gets you to that place where things start to come together. Whether that's prewriting or it's brainstorming or it's taking a walk in the park and sitting under a tree and writing because that's a great place. It's different for everybody.

Experienced writers are comfortable in their individual processes. They know which stages are key and the best order in which to take them. They have played with different writing strategies over time and figured out how to negotiate each one through trial and error. The students interviewed for this book describe their writing processes, but none of their descriptions are identical. You can learn a lot by comparing your process to others. For example, I particularly like the way Nicole structures her drafts in deliberate stages, and am fascinated by the way Billy arranges his workstation with a dry erase board and no Facebook in order to be productive.

As you work through the lessons in Part Three, you will find ways to customize the writing strategies that work best for you. As Gina points out, every writer is different. And, because every assignment is unique, you will inevitably adapt your processes in different contexts, as well. The more comfortable you are with your process, the easier it will be to adapt to different situations, and the stronger your writing will be.

10.2 [HOW]

How to plan your writing process.

1. Create a writer's journal.

A writer's journal is like a diary in which you are both author and audience — so your entries can be informal and brief. As you will likely find, when you observe, document, and reflect on your writing process, you will integrate specific strategies and learn a lot about yourself as a writer.

Many of the students interviewed for *Becoming a College Writer* report that they keep writer's journals. Their journals give them a personal space to record experiences, questions, thoughts, and insights. Daily journaling, in which you might record the time and effort you've spent on the project, can help you be more disciplined and efficient. You may even beat your deadlines. All it takes is jotting down a few sentences each day that you work on a project.

As noted earlier in this lesson, completing the end-of-lesson exercises labeled "b" will prompt you to maintain a productive journal.

2. Plan each assignment in writing, on a calendar, working backward from the due date.

DANIEL
University of Florida

I think that in college, you have to come up with a plan and try to manage your life, basically — from the morning through whatever it is I have to do [along with] having to go to school. I try to organize in terms of what is study time and what is writing time and research time. . . . You should do this the first day of school: make a personal schedule, not [just] a college schedule, make a personal schedule of your life, of what you're going to do every day.

Notice that Daniel begins his planning with things that he *has* to do in his day-to-day life as a student, including setting aside time to study, research, write, complete assignments, and attend classes. Assignment deadlines can be frightening because they apply pressure. But due dates also help you focus and place limits on tasks that might otherwise haunt you indefinitely. Begin your plan by plotting it out on your calendar.

Mystery novelists often compose their intricate, twisting plots backward, beginning their writing with the moment that the detective solves the crime. They then unwind the story backward toward the crime itself. I urge you to plan like a mystery novelist. Once you receive a due date for a writing assignment, get out your calendar and write that date down. Then, work backward from the due date, scheduling ample time to complete each stage of your writing process.

PRACTICE I urge you to get out your calendar, and write down the due dates for *all* of your writing assignments. Go ahead. Do it. Right now. I can wait. I'll be here when you get back. . .

. . . And, now that you have returned from your calendar, do you feel a little better? Do you feel a little more in control of your time and assignments? If not, I think you will appreciate the reminders in the future. Asking you to mark your due dates on your calendar isn't a Jedi mind trick. It's practical advice that will make your academic life much better. I promise.

3. Give yourself a due date for each step of your process.

TIMOTHY
Red Rocks Community College

It's a bit daunting when you think about writing, especially [since I hadn't] written a lot prior to taking a composition class. It's daunting to think of all these things I need to do; so put them in order. What do I need to do first and last? Make sub-notes of each [task] and find out what's going to make this easy for me?

If you follow Timothy's advice, your next step (after marking your due date on your calendar) is to evaluate the scope of your assignment and estimate how many days and writing sessions you will need to do your best work. If you've been assigned a major paper, you will need at least two weeks and at least four or five work sessions on four or five different days. If you're assigned a shorter paper, you might compose only two drafts and finish the assignment in three days or fewer.

when you will be unable to work on your assignment. For example, most of us are unlikely to get much done on Halloween or over a holiday weekend, even if you do take your books with you over a break. You might also have work or social events that conflict with potential writing and research days. Preparing for a big exam in a tough science course might interfere with your ability to concentrate on your writing on a particular day.

DEONTA
University of North Carolina, Chapel Hill

So when I'm given a prompt and I start planning my process for writing my paper, I typically look at my calendar and the things I have planned out for the next week or two weeks or however long before the paper's due. And I look at my pockets of free time, like when I'm done with my homework or when I'm done with recreational activities. So I try to use that time well for my paper writing process. I normally try to schedule brainstorming one day and then organizing the next day — that way I don't feel overwhelmed from doing it all in one day. I normally try to write the paper after brainstorming, planning, and organizing. I try to write the paper three or four days in advance. That way I can make edits and revise, possibly go to the writing center to get another person's point of view on the paper. And if there's anything else that I'm missing, I [have the time to] make additions to it.

KARINA
University of Florida

I give myself these little increments: write 500 words and see how that goes. Even if I just write 250 words the first day, it's fine. I give myself 500-word increments because sometimes you have a fifteen-page paper, and if you say in your head, "I have to write a fifteen-page paper, or a twenty-page paper," you're never going to get started. You're thinking, "Ugh, I have seventeen more pages to write." I find that's really important to help me say, "Oh, I'm going to do a 500-word limit today or 1,000-word limit today." And that really has helped me.

As you plan your writing dates, begin, like Deonta does, by being honest and crossing out on your calendar the hours and days

Once you have documented your due date and known conflicts on your calendar, look at the remaining days, working backward from the due date. Karina's strategy is to break a large, complicated task down into manageable, methodical, bite-sized chunks, to make it seem less "daunting" (in Timothy's word). Reserve the day (or night) before an assignment is due for final proofreading (see Lesson 16: Proofreading) and final formatting and printing (see Lesson 17: Publishing). One way to schedule your writing is to work with the nine lessons in Part Three: You could schedule one day per strategy, again working backward from your due date. Another possible two-week writing calendar might look like this:

DAY 1:	**Write a plan on calendar.**
DAY 2:	**Write a quick, short response to the prompt.**
DAY 3:	**Research and gather evidence.**
DAY 4:	**Brainstorm loose draft of a page or two.**
DAY 5:	**Organize brainstorm and research notes.**
DAY 6:	**Complete first draft.**
DAY 7:	**Get informed feedback on first draft.**
DAY 8:	**Gather additional research and evidence.**
DAY 9:	**Revise first draft into second draft.**
DAY 10:	**Get informed feedback on second draft.**
DAY 11:	**Revise second draft based on feedback.**
DAY 12:	**Proofread, format, and print final draft.**
DAY 13:	**Publish or submit a day early.**
DAY 14:	**Smile at the deadline, while others might be fretting.**

4. Schedule at least two dates to receive feedback on at least two drafts.

Notice on the calendar above that drafting, getting feedback, and revising consumes *six days*. As you know, the secret to college writing is to **R**evise **R**epeatedly **f**rom **F**eedback. **RRFF** takes time. **RRFF** takes discipline. **RRFF** takes scheduling and your calendar. You have to designate time to draft. You have to designate a separate time for getting feedback, especially since getting informed feedback often requires making an appointment to meet with a writing center consultant or your instructor during office hours. And, of course, revising your drafts based upon feedback requires a big chunk of time and attention too.

CARA
Metropolitan State University of Denver

My greatest weakness as a writer is when I overbook myself and don't have the time to devote to doing that intense research or to really doing as many drafts as I should do. Sometimes it is really difficult to devote the time to getting it done right, especially when, you know, you have work and school and so many other things that you have to be doing. But, when it's complete and I'm done with the essay, I feel really good about it because, if I've put in the time, I *want* my teacher to read it because I worked hard on this. Please, read it! . . . No one wants to say, "Yeah, I turned in an essay. It was awful." It doesn't feel good.

In addition to your assignment due date, the most important dates on your calendar will be the *separate* dates and sessions that you designate for *drafting*, *getting feedback*, and *revising*.

5. Be on time and under budget.

Dan Kitwood/Getty Images

RICHARD
Metropolitan State University of Denver

When you start writing in college, I think it's important to not procrastinate when an assignment is given out. I think it's important to, right then and there, get in there and do it. And the more you do it, at least for me, the easier it gets. I think putting off writing if you're not very apt at it is going to do nothing but shoot yourself in the foot because then you start to get the stress built up, and when you actually try to do the assignment, everything's falling apart at the seams and the next thing you know, you're burnt out, going crazy, losing hair, and you're still a freshman.

The mantra for a successful project manager is "on time and under budget." Contractors who build roadways, renovate houses, or design computer chips are in high demand

when they are "on time and under budget." Like successful contractors who impress their clients and are rewarded with a great reputation and additional business, you want to schedule your writing projects to be "on time and under budget." In other words, commit to a schedule you've written on your calendar that completes your assignment *ahead of the due date.*

Imagine that your assignment is due on a Friday. If you schedule a meeting with your instructor a week before the due date, and you have a second, nearly complete draft of your paper for them to give you feedback on, you will be in good shape. Maybe you can even turn in your paper a few days early. How would you feel? You've written a series of careful drafts. You have not crammed your entire writing process into one pressure-packed, sleep-deprived binge during the night before. When writers are rushed and anxious, their thinking can become confused and tangled; consequently, their sentences, style, tone, and grammar deteriorate too. Fixing these problems will take time. The day following an all-nighter is a waste because no one can be at their best after losing that much sleep.

Aiming to complete your assignment before the due date will actually *reduce* the number of hours and the amount of energy that you will expend on the project. As a professor, I have never known a student to perform poorly on a writing assignment completed ahead of schedule. In fact, work submitted before a due date is usually my students' best work. If you have an assignment, give yourself a break and work *ahead* of schedule rather than *behind*. Doing so further benefits you because you'll have created a space in which you can deal with any possible conflicts and misdirection.

If you find you're the sort of writer who needs pressure to get words onto paper, create your own deadlines and stick with them. This will help you to feel the crunch-time inspiration that some writers crave, while leaving you with room to refine your paper before turning it in.

Remember, though, that for all the goal setting and scheduling you may do, in-depth intellectual work almost never goes exactly according to plan. Messiness and recursiveness (starting over) is a natural part of college writing. If your plan is too strict and your writing process too rigid, then you might be unable to follow inspiration, which is an important aspect to Aime'e's writing process:

AIME'E
Red Rocks Community College

It actually starts really organized and then gets messy and then gets back in slow organization. It's like, I start with a plan, a beautiful plan, and then I go crazy and find all this inspiration and then I've got to get back to the subject at hand.

Stress is bad for you. It's toxic and can damage your health. So, the difference between a literal assignment deadline and completing your work a day or two earlier is (1) perception, (2) maturity, (3) success, and eventually (4) your life expectancy. Schedule your calendar *in writing* to complete your assignments *ahead of the due date* to give yourself space to breathe, write, **RRFF**, and do your very best work.

10.3
Exercises: planning

10a Integrate the video.

One of the primary purposes of *Becoming a College Writer* is to deepen your awareness of audience, research, genre, and media — all of which are covered in Part One and Part Two. The purpose of Part Three is to deepen your awareness of your writing process so that you can work strategically to improve your approach to each step. And, of course, *Becoming a College Writer* emphasizes the essential value of **Revising Repeatedly from Feedback** as the center of your process. All of the student sound bites in this lesson discuss how important time management and planning are for successful college writing.

Write a substantial paragraph or two, with a topic sentence or mini-thesis, through which you respond to the sound-bite videos in the lesson as you form your own approaches to planning and process. You can watch the Lesson 10 Essentials Video, or you can browse the embedded clips in the online edition of this lesson. You might begin by identifying the moments that stand out to you the most. Which student videos seem to make the most sense to you? With whom do you agree? Disagree? What patterns do you find among the student sound bites? Which ideas were the most instructive or helpful to you? What surprised you? How have your own ideas about planning and process come into focus through the videos?

10b Create a journal entry or blog.

This lesson urges you to get out your calendar and begin planning your writing process for an upcoming college writing assignment. This exercise asks you to write in a journal, which is often organized with a different entry for each day. For this exercise, combine your calendar with your journal by first writing down a different step for each day, as described in 10.2.3. Then, write two short paragraphs for each step: (1) one that describes your plan for that stage ahead of time, and (2) one that reflects on your experiences with that stage after it's completed.

Each of the following lessons covers a different step or stage in your writing process. So, for now, you might just want to list the plan for each stage but complete the full journal entry for the planning stage only, which you should complete immediately. Then, you can add subsequent entries after you read the next lessons and complete those steps.

You could keep this calendar/journal using only print/text, or you could make an online blog, a video blog, or an audio podcast that captures your unfolding thoughts and experiences in your actual voice.

10c See yourself as a writer.

In a page or two, describe the evolution of your sense of "planning" and "process" since you began writing. Where and when did you start to develop intentional strategies for beginning and scheduling a writing assignment? What major events, assignments, and papers have influenced your approaches to planning and process along the way? Which teachers or classes have reshaped the ways you plan your writing process? What was your sense of planning and process before you began reading this lesson? What is your approach now that you have finished this lesson? In what ways can you imagine your writing process changing beyond college? How does your development as a writer compare with what other students said in their interviews, such as Nicole, who seems to have a clear sense of her writing process, even though she sometimes cannot fully develop each step:

> Usually I freewrite a lot before an essay and this semester has been really, really busy. So with this assignment I didn't do as much freewriting as I could've done. But for the most part yes, [this paper followed] the process that I usually do: the freewriting, the outlines, the sentence break, the reading out loud, the peer review, the rough drafts—the whole nine yards.

10d Invent your writing.

Section 10.2 of this lesson discusses five recommendations for planning and strategizing your writing process. In five complete sentences, map out how each of these recommendations could be applied to a writing assignment you are working on in this class, or in another class, if you are not currently writing in this course. (These five sentences are a simplified version of Exercise 10b above, for those who are not keeping a writer's journal.)

10e Analyze student writing.

Read at least one of the featured student interviews in the text, and study in particular their discussion about their writing process in general or the steps they followed to complete their model assignment. Or you might choose to browse the LaunchPad for a student who seems like you or is interesting to you. Compile a list of five or so different things the student said in their interview about their planning and process. Then compare their interview, your list, and, their writing sample. Can you see connections between their discussion of their writing process and written product?

Your instructor might ask you to interview a classmate instead of reading one of the interviews in the text or online. Or you might compare what you found in one of the textbook interviews to an interview with your classmate. If you interview a classmate, ask them about their planning process for a writing assignment. Do they use a calendar or journal to plan? What are the most prominent stages of their writing process? What aspects of their process are they confident about? When do they struggle? And, most important, can you identify connections between their planning and their written products? Can you see how planning impacts the quality and experience of their writing?

10f Revise repeatedly from feedback.

Examine a writing assignment you are currently working on or one that you wrote recently, perhaps in another class or in high school. Describe in a written paragraph, video selfie, or audio podcast some specific ways that you can use the ideas from Lesson 10 to revise your writing and improve your process. The best thing you can do is take a current draft of your writing to the writing center, a peer workshop, or your instructor's office hours and ask, "What are the weakest aspects of this draft, and how could I have planned my process more effectively to address those weaknesses?"

LESSON 11

Brainstorming

Develop a brainstorming strategy.

11.1   [WHY]

Why you should develop a brainstorming strategy.

Lesson 10 emphasized how important a written plan and schedule are for your writing process. Planning is considered to be part of the prewriting phase of the process because you have not yet begun to draft or write in the conventional sense. You have, however, begun the intellectual work of writing.

Now we move on to *brainstorming*, the most common second step in the prewriting phase. It happens after *planning* and before *drafting*. Writing processes vary from writer to writer and from one project to another. For many college writers *researching* comes before *brainstorming*; so, if you think that *researching* should come first, skip ahead to Lesson 12 and come back to this lesson later.

Most of the students interviewed for this book do not think of their writing process as a static, fixed, linear experience — many writers go back-and-forth between steps and stages. So the point of Lesson 11 is not to insist that you adopt one approach to brainstorming, once-and-for-all; instead, I encourage you to experiment with different approaches and select the one that seems like it will work best for you in a particular assignment, in your particular context.

PART THREE: PROCESS

PREWRITING PHASE

WRITING AND BEYOND

If you look at the table of contents, you will see that Parts One and Two (Lessons 1–9) of this textbook focus on context. Establishing your context is also a fundamental aspect of prewriting because, before you can either brainstorm, research, or organize, you need to understand the dynamic relationship between yourself as a writer, your audience, and your topic. Furthermore, you need to have a sense of the research methods, genre, media, discipline, and scope established through the assignment prompt before you can begin to brainstorm. You might consider these rhetorical and contextual concerns pre-prewriting, although they should remain in focus throughout the entire writing process.

KENDRA
Michigan State University

I think a good emphasis [is] the work you do *before* you start writing. It's not something that you can just sit down and start. You have to look into the topic, you have to put thought into it, write it out, brainstorm it, think of the bigger picture, and how it will look before you start. There's a lot of brainstorming and [preliminary] work before you can actually start writing.

Brainstorming gets you started on the intellectual work of writing.

Brainstorming is a prewriting activity that has a great influence on your final product. And while it may not directly produce conventional paragraphs and pages, it can help you wrangle your preliminary thoughts, get your ideas on paper or screen, and build a sense of progress and momentum. For Erienne, brainstorming can happen during discussion: A question raised in class helped her shape ideas for her writing assignment.

ERIENNE
Metropolitan State University of Denver

The professor would ask us questions like, "Do you think that this character is acting selflessly when he's helping the other characters?" And I remember that was one of the questions that really stuck out to me and would eventually shape my paper. There were a lot of questions that the professor would ask, and I think the students would oftentimes get caught up in the discussion and not really realize that the professor was constantly giving them little seeds for a thesis, little questions that they could pursue all the way to a wonderful thesis. So, [be] alert....It's really important to take notes and be aware of all the ideas you're having, when you're having them.

Brainstorming gets your writing moving by reducing pressure.

Brainstorming can overcome the dreaded problem of writer's block. Writers can become blocked when they feel overwhelmed by what they need to accomplish. But breaking down a complicated task (like writing a college paper) into smaller, manageable steps can reduce the pressure and get your writing moving. Many writers are helped by low-stakes brainstorming strategies because they remove the pressure of filling pages with perfect writing. Brainstorming helps many writers move from anxiety to action.

Writing is a creative, intellectual activity. Many well-known writers and scholars emphasize creativity as the key to writing. I have always thought of *creation* and *invention* in terms of *making connections*, first within the writer's thoughts and second with an audience. To practice this, I encourage you to complete Exercise d in each lesson of this textbook, which prompts you to "Invent your writing" in different ways.

CATHERINE
Michigan State University

Some people are like, "No, no, I'm not going to put it down on the computer until I know it's right." I mean, it's a computer and it has a backspace key. Get everything out that you can. Get it out of your brain . . . because once something's physically in front of you, it's a lot easier to manipulate.

Brainstorming gets your writing moving by stimulating creative connections.

Consider the term *brainstorm*: It suggests a messy, cognitive eruption of thoughts and ideas. I've always thought of a brainstorm as an electrical tempest going off in my skull, a wild storm in which bolts of lightning connect previously isolated areas of my brain into networks of meaning. So, the term *brainstorm* can be a metaphor, but it might even describe what is happening in your brain neurologically when thoughts are connected and learning, creativity, and invention take place.

BILLY
University of Florida

Brainstorming is actually something I don't have a problem with. It's turning it off that I have a problem with. I use a dry erase board now for, I guess you call it, "cluster diagrams." I write a circle and connect the lines all around to see where the thoughts go. I also free write. I have a paper due next week and I just wrote three pages of non-sense, and I know I'm going to be able to pick it apart and use sections of it. Now it's marinating in my brain....I had all these ideas and every time I settled on one, I came up with a better idea, so it was turning it off that was the issue.

Because writing is creative and creativity tends to be a very personal thing, writers have their own approaches to getting started. Some of the students we interviewed brainstorm by writing in notebooks or recording ideas on their phones or other devices. Some need to lock themselves away in a quiet place where they won't be interrupted, while others need the energy of a crowded coffee shop. Billy can't write in bed because he falls asleep, but that's where Nanaissa is comfortable and focused. The key is for you to try a variety of approaches until you find the ones that work best for *you*.

Brainstorming helps you achieve confidence, flow, and momentum.

Dan left high school thinking that there was a limited number of ways to prewrite and brainstorm, and, even though these approaches worked well for him, he has since figured out that every aspect of his writing should be a response to a particular context.

DAN
Michigan State University

In high school you're taught there are four or five ways you can brainstorm. You can create a web that connects things, you can get things all in a list or in a Venn diagram, and that's how you brainstorm. Then, it seemed like there are only a couple ways you can brainstorm and there's only a couple ways you can do it right. Those principles that are taught are really valuable. [But] the actual brainstorming process changes every time, and I think it changes based on what I'm producing [and the research].

Perhaps there is no step in the writing process that is more personal than brainstorming. The following section surveys the most common techniques for you to consider and experiment with. Like all aspects of your writing, you can improve by revising your approaches to brainstorming based upon previous successes and failures. You can also improve your approach by doing as Dan does, by adapting to each assignment.

11.2   [HOW]

How to develop a brainstorming strategy.

Following are nine of the most familiar brainstorming strategies that college

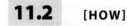

writers have been using for many years. Keep in mind that different types of writing assignments may call for different brainstorming strategies. You might be frustrated by freewriting (11.2.1), but your classmate can't live without it. Or you might be very comfortable using note cards (11.2.4) to brainstorm for an oral presentation in political science, but then you discover that applying a heuristic (11.2.8) works better for launching a scientific report.

You will want to customize your brainstorming according to your assignment in the way that best strengthens connections between yourself, your audience, and your topic. What will work best for you? What approach might help you respond most effectively to the prompt?

ANGELA
Red Rocks Community College

I like to make a bubble. I like to have my main topic and draw the lines off it, trying to [generate] ideas. If that doesn't work for me, I'll do something like a "pros and a cons" list. And I'll write down what I'm talking about — what are the good things about it and what are the bad things about it. And then I also get help from my peers.... [Y]ou need to have engagement with others [when writing].

Mix and match the following strategies as you like. For example, Angela brainstorms by placing a key term in a central bubble (11.2.2); but, if that fails, she makes a T-chart of positives and negatives (11.2.6), and she also consults with peers (11.2.5). Professional authors brainstorm in the same ways. The table of contents to this

textbook began as a phone conversation I had with Leasa Burton (an editor) (11.2.5) while looking at the white board on my office wall (11.2.9).

1. Freewrite.

NICOLE
California State University, San Marcos

My approach to writing a college assignment paper is lots of freewriting. A lot of freewriting. Literally, I dump my thoughts onto the page. I don't worry about grammar, I don't worry about mechanics, I don't worry about logic, clarity, comprehension, nothing. So I do a lot. A LOT of freewriting. And then I go back to the freewriting and organize.

To *freewrite* means to write free of the concerns and obstacles that can keep a writer from flowing productively. It means writing without an immediate concern for quality. Most freewriting exercises require writers to write as much as possible within a given time frame without stopping and without reading back over any of the words. Even if you write: "I don't know what to write at the moment," the idea is to keep your fingers flying. When you finish with a freewriting exercise, you may feel a little tired from your writing sprint, but pleased that you've generated some words, sentences, and pages. Your next step will be to sift through the freewriting to find your best ideas so that you can build from there. Freewriting encourages you to play with your writing and to indulge and enjoy the freedom and messiness of creativity and invention, as Gregg's freewriting on the next page demonstrates.

6: B. While it is clear that the definition of the "frontier" has changed and developed significantly over time, ~~the~~ no single definition is sufficient in itself to fully characterize the "frontier" as studied in early ~~American~~ literature. In fact, ~~the best way to utilize the many definitions would be~~ we must learn to view each definition ~~that~~ as a separate lense coloring and enhancing different aspects of the Frontier uniquely.

First if we take ~~an~~ examples like John Smith's Virginia narrative, the Spanish conquest ~~as~~ depicted in the Florentine codex, or ~~on~~ the interaction of Columbus upon landing ~~and~~ we must ~~note~~ that the classic definition expressed in the O.E.D. becomes salient. Each of these instances exemplify conflict and borderlands to be ~~gained~~ as ~~lessed~~ geographically. But going further, if we take the ~~frontier~~ ~~as~~ texts like Last of the Mohicans or The production of texts like The Popul Vuh or Florentine Codex, we find a definition more like Anne Kolodny's to be appropriate. ~~As~~ With Kolodny's, the ~~complexity~~ ~~the~~ ~~many~~ poly used aspects ~~these~~ are clarified ~~as~~ ~~seen~~ ~~the~~. The Spanish and Nahuatl Florentine codex displays a cultural heritage along the lines of what Gloria Anzaldua ~~called~~ the mestizo, where the Frontier becomes less external and more the internal struggle of the inhabitants to embrace both cultures or live in dichotomy.

2. Map key terms.

TOREY
Lansing Community College

I like the "concept map" idea. I do that a lot. I write a lot of lists — just like random topics, and then I'll start just writing little sentences and branch off one sentence to another — and usually I come up with a pretty good topic.

Mapping key terms is a technique that's also known as *clustering* and *idea mapping*. To experiment with this method, think of your current writing assignment. Begin by writing down a word that is central to it. Then, think of terms that relate to your central (key) term, and jot them down. You might diagram your word cluster like a star map, drawing lines between the terms — the way constellations diagram relationships between stars — and adding notations. Because this technique focuses on key terms, it will also help you focus your topic and thesis, as well as your research. Key terms are doubly helpful when you use them as starting points for electronic research. Another benefit of mapping key terms is that what you produce is more of a doodle than a conventional paper, like Nick's map about food on the following page. This can free you from some of the prewriting pressure you may be feeling.

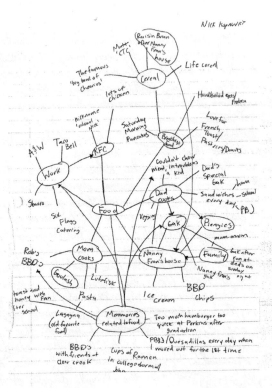

3. If your assignment requires research, keep notes as you begin your preliminary search for sources.

HYESU
University of Florida

I find I brainstorm better when I have a paper and a pencil. I can't brainstorm on a computer. I'll just start by making lists of things I feel like I need to talk about — and [find] information in the books that can help me. My brainstorming process is pretty messy, actually. I don't think anyone can read what I write afterward. They're just scribbles all over a piece of paper. I'll draw lines from one to the other and see if they can make a paragraph.

Hyesu's brainstorming includes doing some preliminary research on her assignment topic. She gets started by laying out books and other potentially useful sources and taking notes, a common prewriting technique. Many writers begin by taking a couple of hours to create a page or two of notes that include summaries of the most promising sources. You might even jot down some direct quotes from your sources — many students like to make vertical lists of quotes. Once you have one or two pages of material, step back and look for connections among what your sources are telling you. You might draw lines between ideas in your notes, as Hyesu does, which can identify emerging directions and additional questions to drive your writing.

This technique boosts your sense of productivity from an early point in your process. If you do some preliminary reading, take some notes, and produce a few pages of material, you've made progress and gained the momentum that will move you forward.

As noted elsewhere in this text, academic writing is defined by research and the integration of sources — this technique begins your writing process by making your approach research-based. Important: As you gather sources and take notes (especially if you cut-and-paste), it is *essential* that you track and record each source carefully, right from the beginning. (See also Lesson 24: Citation.)

4. Record your brainstorming and any preliminary research on note cards.

Recording your brainstorming on note cards breaks down the complex task of writing into manageable chunks. It can also be less intimidating than filling a blank page. Once you have a stack of note cards completed, you can shuffle and reorganize them as you begin to give structure to your ideas. One method is to do something different on each card. For example, one card may include your freewritten spontaneous thoughts; another may include major statements from your sources, including direct quotations; another may contain the key requirements of your assignment prompt, and so on.

Using note cards can smooth the transition to the next stages in your writing process as you sequence the cards to organize and revise your work. If one card does not connect tightly with another, then you might need to do more research and create a new card. As your structure emerges and your research accumulates, you might discover that some of the cards are dead ends — and it's often easier to discard a note card or two than a paragraph or a page of writing. Some writers use paper "sticky notes" when notecarding, and some writers use digital versions of note cards and sticky notes in a similar way. Writer Hunter S. Thompson used thumbtacks to hold an array of plastic baggies on a bulletin board, and then he would stuff bits of writing and clippings into each bag as a way to first generate and gather thoughts before drafting.

5. Talk to others about your ideas and take notes on their feedback.

SAMANTHA
California State University, San Marcos

I have to have that inspiration, and once I get it, you can't stop me. So that is normally when I'll have my discussion period: I go talk to my friends, professors, family, and just say, "Okay. I've got this idea, let's talk about it. What do you think?" And then once I get that inspiration and [that] different feedback, that's when I can get past the writer's block.

What's another way to get started? Discussion. Samantha takes this approach and **Revises from Feedback** even before she begins to write when she bounces her ideas off others. Conversation is a low-stakes way to brainstorm ideas for a writing assignment: Sometimes it's easier to talk through what you're thinking than to write it down. Another strategy is to have someone interview you about your assignment and record it. Or, if you have a smartphone that records voice memos, you can try a verbal brainstorm that way.

6. Create a T-chart for your brainstorm.

A T-chart is similar to a keyword map but it formats ideas into tables, columns, and cells and can also offer a kind of structure to your brainstorm. The T-chart's graphic shape compels you to move forward by structuring relationships between ideas and then generating thoughts by filling in the empty spaces in the form. When you're asked to make an argument, prepare for a debate, or even make an important decision, it helps to make a T-chart with a column for pros on one side and cons on the other, as Angela describes in the opening of this section. You simply draw a vertical line down the middle of a page (or a whiteboard, like I do), and list positive reasons on one side and negative reasons on the other. The T-chart can have horizontal relationships, too; for example, each point in the left column might have a direct counterpoint in the right column.

North	South
Ulysses S. Grant	Robert E. Lee
Control of Mississippi = major strategy	Privateering
Numerical advantage	Defending their own territory

But the columns in a T-chart do not necessarily have to be structured according to contrast; the left column might contain a list of heuristic questions (see number 8 below) and the right column might brainstorm preliminary answers to those questions. You could have multiple columns instead of just two; for example, if you were writing a research paper on literature around the American Civil War, you might have a table with three columns titled "Before," "During," "After"; and two rows titled "North" and "South." You could use computer software to create tables with columns.

7. Try role-playing as a technique for brainstorming.

Role-playing is a theater-inspired approach that can seem strange at first but has actually helped many college students immerse themselves in a writing project. This technique almost always requires collaboration with a classmate, which is mutually beneficial. When role-playing, assign yourself the role of a character to play in a particular situation. The most common roles to play involve acting in the role of another writer. If you are analyzing literature, you might play the role of the author of a novel, or better yet, a particular literary critic. If you are researching political science, you might play the role of a leader or a citizen from a particular place.

When writing in the sciences, you might play the role of a scientist who is also working on the same topic. You can imagine that this scientist is being interviewed by a granting agency considering her application for research funding, or you can role-play that the scientist is explaining the importance of their work to students in a lecture. By improvising and role-playing a person who is important to your topic, you will psychologically locate yourself with the ideas, issues, questions, and answers that define your topic, which can be an especially effective brainstorming technique because it strengthens the connections between you, your topic, and your audience.

8. Apply heuristic questions.

CRISOSTO
Metropolitan State University of Denver

I think a majority of my ideas come from [freewriting]. It sets up the scope in which I'm going to develop a paper. And then from there, I start to question a lot of what I've written and start to answer those questions so I can start to formulate a thesis about what I want to address.

Crisosto begins his brainstorming with free-writing, but he also asks heuristic questions that emerge from his freewrite. A *heuristic* can be defined as a learning aid; so, a *heuristic question* prompts or aids further learning. Crisosto then brainstorms answers to those questions, and these answers help drive his first draft. Based upon the previous lessons, the most fundamental heuristic questions for college writers are

- **What connections can I establish with my assignment topic?**
- **What do I know about the members of my audience for my assignment, and how can I connect with them?**
- **What can I do to connect the interests of my audience with my topic?**

Perhaps the very best heuristic questions to answer as you begin include:

- **What is the significance of my topic?**
- **What questions can my topic address?**
- **How can I work my perspective and the perspectives of others into a research question that I can address in my writing assignment?**

If you intend to use a research-based thesis (see Lesson 19), then you might brainstorm by answering these heuristic questions:

- **What does everyone already know about this topic? What can I learn about the topic within just a minute or two of online browsing about the topic?**
- **What are experts investigating on this topic? What are they discussing?**
- **What gap in our understanding or perception on the topic might my writing help to fill? How can I connect my writing to the current conversation on this topic?**

9. Brainstorm with whatever tools work for you.

DAN
Michigan State University

I work with storyboarding a lot and I think storyboarding is brilliant, and my brainstorming process for everything now is more or less a storyboard — when I'm designing a website, they call them "wireframes." Scene 1: What needs to appear? When does it need to appear? What does it need to look like? That's like paragraph one, you know, that's like point one. You just sort of get everything out on your storyboard — whether it's on your computer or actually drawing it — get that on your storyboard and figure out the moves I need to make to transition between those storyboards.

I am going to end this section on brainstorming strategies by acknowledging my favorite tool: whiteboarding. For me, whiteboards are especially vivid, colorful, and erasable/revisable; and now that I have a smartphone camera, they are also easy to capture and refer back to. If you don't have a whiteboard available to you, maybe you can find an empty classroom with one (and with fresh pens, hopefully).

With a whiteboard, you can combine a variety of the brainstorming strategies. I tend to begin by listing key terms and then drawing boxes and arrows to connect the ideas. I often use a black pen for the most important ideas and then I use colored pens to subordinate and coordinate supporting concepts. My addiction to whiteboarding began in the 1990s when I was planning and building a lot of hypertextual websites, like Dan. Then, in the 2000s, I began using whiteboards to "storyboard" the videos I made, also like Dan.

I like to have a collaborator or editor dialoguing with me as I sketch and modify my whiteboard brainstorms. I used to be very nervous about someone erasing my sketch before I was completely finished with the project, but these days I just snap a photo of it to preserve it. When I consult with graduate students who are writing dissertations, I have to use a whiteboard to help map their projects.

In the movie *A Few Good Men*, Tom Cruise's character, Lieutenant Kaffee says, "I need my bat. I think better with my bat." And the moment Kaffee finds his missing softball bat, he has a brainstorm. I can't brainstorm without my whiteboard. I think better with my whiteboard. Of course, you don't have to use a whiteboard like I do, or a bat like Kaffee does. What's your best brainstorming technique? Maybe making a video selfie or voice recording is your favorite tool.

11.3
Exercises: brainstorming

11a Integrate the video.

In his interview, Chase describes his brainstorming approach:

> Just have a purge from what's in your head onto the paper. Then, after you have it there and it's a little more concrete, it makes you more comfortable as far as finishing the rest of the paper because you feel like you have the puzzle pieces, now you've just got to put the puzzle together.

Write a substantial paragraph or two, with a topic sentence or mini-thesis, through which you respond to the sound-bite videos in the lesson, like Chase's, as you form your own

approaches to brainstorming. You can watch the Lesson 11 Essentials Video, or you can browse the embedded clips in the online edition of this lesson. You might begin by identifying the moments that stand out to you the most. Which student videos seem to make the most sense to you? With whom do you agree? Disagree? What patterns do you find among the student sound bites? Which ideas were the most instructive or helpful to you? What surprised you? How have your own ideas about brainstorming come into focus through the videos?

11b Create a journal entry or blog.

This lesson urges you to develop your own individualized approaches to brainstorming as part of your writing process, and this exercise asks you to use a journal to do so. Write two short paragraphs in your journal: one that describes your plan for brainstorming on an upcoming writing assignment and a second one that reflects on your experiences after you have brainstormed. Describe some past experiences with brainstorming that will influence your plans for the upcoming assignment. Do you have a specific brainstorming approach in mind, like those listed in 11.2, that you think is well suited for the assignment? After the assignment is complete, upon reflection, evaluate how well your brainstorming plan worked and what you can learn from the experience for next time. You could keep this journal using only print/text, or you could make an online blog, a video blog, or an audio podcast that captures your unfolding thoughts and experiences in your actual voice.

11c See yourself as a writer.

In a page or two, describe the evolution of your approaches to brainstorming since you began writing. Where and when did you start to develop intentional strategies for brainstorming? What major events, assignments, and papers have influenced your approaches to brainstorming along the way? What particular teachers or classes have reshaped the ways you brainstorm? What was your sense of brainstorming before you began reading this lesson? What is your approach now that you have finished this lesson? In what ways can you imagine your brainstorming process changing beyond college? How does your development as a writer compare with what other students said in their interviews, such as Nicole, who relies heavily on freewriting to brainstorm, even though she has increasingly limited time to do so because of her busy college schedule:

> Usually I freewrite a lot before an essay and this semester has been really, really busy. So with this assignment I didn't do as much freewriting as I could've done. But for the most part yes, [this paper followed] the process that I usually do: the freewriting, the outlines, the sentence break, the reading out loud, the peer review, the rough drafts — the whole nine yards.

11d Invent your writing.

Section 11.2 of this lesson discusses nine different brainstorming techniques. In five complete sentences, map out how these nine recommendations could be applied to a writing assignment you are working on in this class, or in another class (if you are not currently writing in this course).

11e Analyze student writing.

Read at least one of the featured student interviews in the text, and study in particular their discussion about their approach to brainstorming and prewriting. Or you might choose to browse the LaunchPad interviews for a student like you or who is interesting to you. Compile a list of five or so different things the student said in their interview about their brainstorming and invention processes. Then compare their interview, your list, and, their writing sample. Can you see connections between their discussion of their writing process and their written product?

Your instructor might ask you to interview a classmate instead of reading one of the interviews in the text or online. Or you might compare what you found in one of the textbook interviews to an interview with your classmate. If you interview a classmate, ask them about their brainstorming technique for a writing assignment. Do they use the same approach for each assignment? What are the most prominent benefits of their approach to brainstorming? What aspects of their brainstorming are they confident about? When do they struggle? And, most important, can you identify connections between their brainstorming technique and their written products? Can you see how brainstorming impacts the quality and experience of their writing?

11f Revise repeatedly from feedback.

Examine a writing assignment you are currently working on or one that you wrote recently, perhaps in another class or in high school. Describe in a written paragraph, video selfie, or audio podcast some specific ways that you can use the ideas from Lesson 11 to improve your writing through better brainstorming. Ideally, you can take a current draft of your writing to the writing center, a peer workshop, or your instructor's office hours and ask, "What are the weakest aspects of this draft, and how could I have brainstormed more effectively to address those weaknesses?"

LESSON 12

Researching

**Research before you draft, and cite as
you research.**

Andrew Kornylak/Getty Images

ESSENTIALS VIDEO

Visit the LaunchPad for *Becoming a College Writer* to watch the Lesson 12 Essentials Video.

12.1 [WHY]

Why you should research before you draft, and cite as you research.

CARA
Metropolitan State University of Denver

If I could give someone one piece of advice about both college writing and college, I would say to get your reading done first. Because, in the writing process, if you get all of your reading done first, you will have such a strong grasp on your subject matter that writing down what you have to say will feel natural.

ANSEL
Lansing Community College

When I was in high school, we didn't really learn how to do research....But what I've learned in college is that the very best way to write is to get all of your data and then look at it and then figure out what the data is saying and then explain what the data is saying. I always do the research before I do any writing at all.

My first step in writing this book was to interview student writers. After I had defined my context (I'm a teacher/scholar writing a multimedia textbook for students about becoming a college writer), the first stage of my own process was to conduct research.

As I interviewed students, one of my biggest surprises was that nearly all said that research is *the most crucial* part of their early writing processes. For Cara, Ansel, and almost all of the interviewees, research defines college writing and sets it apart from the work they did in high school. And so it deserves careful attention (and *three* lessons in this text).

Research is introduced in Lesson 6 as a method for finding evidence, which is fundamental to college writing. In Lesson 6, we covered **why** you should support your writing with evidence and **how** to gather and draw on evidence. This lesson builds on Lesson 6 and focuses more on research as action and as a specific stage in your college writing process. Lesson 24: Citation is also related — it covers the principles of documenting your sources and how to do so effectively.

Earlier in this text, we established four principles about research and college writing:

- **College writing is primarily *evidence-based writing*, which means that it should be based upon careful, systematic study (research).**

- **College writers are also researchers.**

- **College writers draw on evidence to pursue new knowledge to benefit themselves and others, most typically in small, incremental ways.**

- **College writing emerges from strong evidence. Evidence is not added later onto what you have already written.**

171

To do your best researched, evidence-based writing, I recommend that you conduct your research **after initial planning** and **brainstorming** (Lessons 10, 11) but **before organizing and drafting** (Lessons 13, 14). However, because the process of writing is not linear—you don't just walk a straight line from beginning to end—you may find yourself going back to research during your drafting and revising stages as well. As Deonta describes, there may be times when you need to gather additional evidence to incorporate into your paper during final revisions.

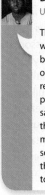

DEONTA
University of North Carolina, Chapel Hill

There have been a couple of papers when I've found myself having to go back and do more research. In this one paper, I was writing and did some research. And, as I was writing and putting the [primary] text in conversation with the [secondary] research that I found, a new topic came to mind. So, I had to go back and do some more research five hours before the paper was due and figure out how to incorporate that into the paper.

Conducting research before you draft, and citing as you research, will make it easier to draw on evidence when you start writing.

Think of research as the beginning and the end of your college writing assignments. At the start of your process—during your planning stage—marking your calendar for specific dates for research will help you stay on track. As you conduct your research, keeping an accurate record of your sources will make it easier to for you to integrate them as you draft and revise. Keeping track of your sources will also make it easier for you to cite them in the body of your paper and list them correctly at the end in a works cited or bibliography. These strategies will allow you

to do your best evidence-based writing and will actually save you time as you write.

PRACTICE Write down the name of something you know how to do very well, such as preparing a favorite recipe or traveling a familiar route. Explain that knowledge verbally to a partner in thirty seconds or less and listen to your partner explain their areas of expertise. Now, write down something you do not know how to do well but would like to learn. Try to explain the unfamiliar thing to your partner in thirty seconds, and notice the difference between the two explanations. What does this comparison demonstrate about the importance of knowing your topic before writing about it?

Capturing source information from the start will make it easier to draft and will ensure the accuracy of your citations.

As you gather evidence by collecting sources, you also need to collect bibliographic information about your sources. Doing so will allow you to include accurate citation information in all of your future drafts, from the very first rough draft to the final submission. Citation generators—available online and also a feature of Microsoft Word—can be a big help in this task. For more on this topic, see Lesson 24: Citation.

12.2 [HOW]

How to research before you draft, and cite as you research.

Following are six habits that characterize how successful college writers approach research. These habits represent an attitude — a frame of mind — for making research a foundational moment in your writing process. While it is important to know the mechanics of how to research (see Lesson 6: Evidence), there is also a psychological component of research to consider.

Throughout this segment, I will use a hunting metaphor that isn't so much about hunting in a forest for food. I'm thinking more of the hunting you might do in an interactive game: Let's say you are the protagonist in a video game who needs to gather food and tools to prepare for a journey through a forest, materials that will make you strong as you prepare for climactic moments in your writing process, moments when you must prevail. Here we go.

1. Hunt in your audience's forest.

Part Two: Context focuses on the situations in which you will find yourself as a college writer. What determines context? Several things do, including the assignment prompts you're given (Lesson 5), the genres you will compose in (Lesson 7), the discipline in which you're writing (Lesson 8), and the media that will best connect your topic and audience (Lesson 9). You will, of course, write in your first-year composition course, but you will also write in disciplines outside of college English courses. Let's focus on the idea of a discipline for a moment.

Discipline, which can be thought of as an area of study, an area of specialization both in and outside of college, is made up of a community of researchers and scholars. Think of each discipline as a tribe of people with their own preferred diet and ways of hunting for and gathering food. According to this analogy, your instructor is a native of a particular tribe (a discipline), and in the forest where the tribe lives, there are particular things to eat (evidence), and, consequently,

preferred ways to find food (methodology) and prepare it (genre, media).

So, how should you begin your research? By hunting in your audience's forest, which means that you will search for particular things in particular ways in particular places. If your research will be based upon a search of materials found in libraries and online, then you will want to focus on the shelves where the books on your topic are grouped and within electronic databases for your discipline (such as the sciences, social sciences, humanities, etc.). Begin the "search" within your research in the places that are familiar to your audience. For example, Kendal knows that to find food for a particular tribe, she needs to hunt in the forest of college libraries and academic databases.

KENDAL
Red Rocks Community College

If it's a mainly researched-based paper, I want to find my sources first because that also helps me figure out where I'm going to go in my paper and how I want to integrate the sources that I've found. We have databases through [the college library] that I use often — EBSCO and a few other ones — [with] reputable sources. It's not like Wikipedia where everyone can go in there and change [the information].

However, searching for and studying documents (online or on a shelf) is not the only way to gather evidence or conduct research. In a class on religious studies, you might be asked to study a literary or scriptural passage and write a personal response without referring to outside sources. In this case, the "forest" in which you would "hunt" would be the passage itself: You would read the text very closely and use words, phrases, and ideas as the evidence from your research. In a sociology class, you might help administer

How to research before you draft, and cite as you research

a survey to determine college students' changing attitudes about a specific topic. You might first need to do some background research to design your survey and study, but the most important evidence in your research will be the data produced by the survey.

Begin your research process by searching for sources in the places where your audience resides.

PRACTICE Examine an assignment prompt for this course or, better yet, another college course for which you must write. Compare that prompt to the syllabus and to the "big ideas" covered so far in the course. Perhaps you could conduct five minutes of online research about the instructor and discipline/ department. Now describe the "forest" in which the course, instructor, and discipline/ department reside. How do they hunt for evidence and research? What kind of evidence/research do they like to "consume"? What are their methods for gathering research? How do they prepare or share in writing the research they find?

2. Be organized.

Time management is a critical concern for you as a college student, and the work habits you develop now are likely to continue after graduation. Quality writing and research simply take time, and the more organized and disciplined you are with your research strategies, the more efficient you will be — and the more time you'll save.

It is beyond the scope of this textbook to teach you how to manage your time, work habits, paper documents, and computer files. However, I will give you these pointers for managing your research process:

1) **Capture all of your writing and research in a single computer file (which might be a Microsoft Word or Google document).**
2) **Name this computer file with a keyword from your topic and the current date (for example, Uganda091219 or Nanorobotics112419).**
3) **Resave this file with a *different name* according to the current date *every time you work on the project* (Uganda091219 would become Uganda091419 if you worked on the project again, two days later, on September 14, 2019).**
4) **Store every version of the file online as well as offline on your hard drive so that you can recover from computer problems (store each version in an online "cloud" or send each version to yourself as an email attachment).**
5) **Include citation and bibliographic information in this singular file from the very first moment of your research process. Do not create a separate file that separates citation from your research.**

This means that *all* of your electronic brainstorming, researching, citation, cutting-and-pasting, drafting, and revising will be held in one file that gets resaved as a new version every time you work on it. This file will swell in the early stages when it contains *everything*, but it will gradually get trimmed down as only the final product remains toward completion. The earlier copies and versions of the file will protect and preserve the material that you delete along the way, in case you make a mistake or want to go back and recover something.

CATHERINE
Michigan State University

My first stop [for my research process] is a computer so I can have access to online journals, but after that, I write down all my notes on paper. I do need a specific pen. I have a crappy seventy-page, one-subject notebook for every class I take. I keep all of those notebooks. More than I keep the papers, I keep the notebooks because there's a lot of good stuff in those. . . . I feel like research has to be sort of a tangible process for me. I have to have a tactile experience with these things, and it helps me remember what I read. I don't know why; it's a neat trigger, I think.

You need to be organized to make the most of your research process. If you were to hunt for wild berries in a forest, you would need to bring a proper container to put them in; likewise, as a protagonist hunting for food in a video game, you might collect magical berries to get to the next stage, something that requires saving your progress along the way. Catherine organizes her research through an archive of cheap, paper notebooks. In fact, she keeps her notebooks to feed future writing assignments down the road. These days, cloud-based document and file management systems are becoming standard, and most cloud-storage systems track previous drafts of your documents automatically. If you use such a cloud system, spend at least ten to twenty minutes learning how to recover earlier drafts of research and writing so that these powerful functions can make your work more efficient. Catherine's method may not be as sleek as digital cloud storage, for example, but as long as it works for her, that's all that matters.

3. Be curious.

I have often joked that being a teacher should be easy. After all, my job is to get students to think and learn, something I do by showing up to class and repeatedly asking them: "Why is that?" In theory, a teacher could take any issue, ask students to respond, and then ask "Why is that?" over and over to prompt students to dig deeper into the causes of the issue. Intellectual progress happens when you post interesting questions and then work diligently to answer them. As a researcher and writer, it's in your interest to cultivate a habit of curiosity. Be your own teacher by asking yourself an ongoing series of questions about your assignment topic, with each leading to further research, deeper understanding, and additional questions to address.

Most of the students I interviewed for this project emphasized how important it is for them to connect with the topics of their writing assignments (Lesson 4). To establish connection, it helps to be genuinely interested in discovering answers to the questions within the assignment prompt. Even if your topic is one that has been assigned to you (and you don't have much choice), try to find some aspect of it that you can connect with personally. When you do so, you'll *want* to conduct research because *you will want answers*. You will find that one question leads to another, especially if you approach your research with sincere curiosity.

For example, Kendra describes in her interview (pages 429–30) her experience researching and writing about Komodo dragons for her zoology class. She began with a research question: "Is the species venomous, and has it adapted to become decreasingly venomous in the present day?" She accumulated an array of scientific articles that explored the question, and she became fascinated to learn that scientists are still unsure about whether or not the dragon is actually venomous.

Kendra was surprised that research had not yet figured this out, which prompted her to keep digging to locate a definitive study. In the end, she made a conclusion based upon weighing and comparing the evidence across a number of studies, which then led to the possibility of new research ideas to try to settle the question. Kendra actively engaged her topic by being continually curious about responses to her research questions. She was eager to solve a puzzle, and she was driven by a genuine curiosity to discover how the puzzle pieces fit together, how the puzzle might be solved, and what she would discover as a result.

If research is a process like hunting in a forest, then you have to be curious about finding tracks, clues, and answers.

PRACTICE Brainstorm a list of three to five thoughtful questions you have about a topic you have been assigned to research. After writing down those questions, rank them in order of which ones seem most compelling or interesting to you. Then, list two or three follow-up questions that will extend your curiosity from the issues that you find most interesting. As you move from one question to the next, you might ask yourself "Why is that?" after each new question that you find.

4. Be patient.

SAMANTHA
California State University, San Marcos

A lot of times, you start looking and you can't find anything. You're like, "Okay no one's thinking this way? Am I missing something?" At that point, you maybe start finding dissenting opinions or you find other information that makes you change your original perspective. In doing research it's very important . . . to keep an open mind so that, if you do find something that's different [from what you expected], you're receptive to maybe changing your perspective.

Research requires patience, an open mind, and a sense of adventure, as Samantha suggests. If hunting were easy and did not require skill and patience, then it would not be very interesting or worth talking about—and you probably wouldn't learn much. The research process takes time and persistence, which means that you must plan your writing process carefully (Lesson 10) to provide enough time for a thorough hunt.

Prepare yourself to follow trails that might eventually become dead ends. Know that you may need to back up and change directions, which in itself is useful because you're thinking critically and gaining insight as you work. Patience will help you through the inevitable problems you will encounter; it will keep you from freezing in your tracks and allow you to return to research, as needed, throughout your writing process.

Consider the scientists who are the subject of Charlie's documentary film on the Ugandan Space Association. They are a study in patience and persistence, having worked on their spacecraft for many years. Their curiosity about space exploration drove them to work on the puzzle of building a space program with extremely limited resources. And, if they had lost their patience and given up, they would not have learned so much from their ongoing work to solve incremental problems, regardless of whether they were able to launch their aircraft into space.

PRACTICE In a short paragraph or through a quick verbal story, describe a time when you were rewarded for being patient and persistent. Then describe a situation in which impatience got you into trouble. Why does the research process require patience? Describe what you imagine will be the consequences if you rush through the research process.

5. Be strategic.

When hunting in your audience's forest for evidence to use in your writing, study the methods other hunters have used. Be deliberate in your research; don't let yourself wander off, hoping to get lucky without a strategy. Be aware of the methods other researchers have used to produce results. While you will improve your research skills through trial and error, be sure to ask for help when you need it, as Emily does.

EMILY
Boston University

The area that I need most help on — and seek the most help on — is the research stage. [So] I go to the librarian and I go to my professors to ask them for help on books I can read and articles to find.

Let's look again at the researchers featured in Charlie's documentary. These scientists are strategic and collaborative in their research. Their method of operation or modus operandi (MO) is to assemble a

See the LaunchPad for *Becoming a College Writer* to view Charlie's documentary.

Still from Charlie's Documentary, "African Skies"

team of scientists and engineers who meet regularly to discuss issues, problems, and solutions (often in the evening), then to build and test prototypes (in the daytime). Their research method is based upon their strategic analysis of what other scientists and engineers have done to succeed, namely: study, discuss, plan, experiment, evaluate, and then repeat the problem-solving process.

Be strategic about the way you conduct your research by analyzing and applying success-ful methods used by others, perhaps using the model previously described.

6. Be persistent.

Part of the inspiration for this textbook was a famous documentary film called *Hoop Dreams* (1994) by Steve James, Frederick Marx, and Peter Gilbert. These filmmakers collected over 250 hours of film footage by following two young basketball players, Arthur Agee and William Gates, across four years of high school and into their first year of college. The final cut of *Hoop Dreams* distilled 250 hours of footage into a three-hour film. The critical acclaim and success of the film is due to the Herculean persistence of the filmmakers working so hard over such a long period of time.

No one expects college students to commit every waking moment to a single class or a single project like professional filmmakers or researchers do. But these professionals help illustrate the importance of persistence and diligence in your research process. It's of course unlikely that you will work on a sin-gle research project for your entire college career. Even so, like the creators of *Hoop Dreams*, Cara also invests herself deeply in the research process.

CARA
Metropolitan State University of Denver

I've become a lot more disciplined about my research process. Especially if it's a ten-page essay or something. I can't afford not to know what I'm talking about. In the past I might have just kind of been like, "Oh, I need five sources for this, so I'll just find five sources and pull out some quotes." But now, I just try to read anything I can get my hands on. . . . I know the research [process] is done . . . when I have almost too many resources to handle.

One of my college professors, Lee Pederson, was the lead researcher on a project called the *Linguistic Atlas of the Gulf States*, which mapped changes in language patterns and pronunciation according to geography. Pederson and his team recorded over 900 audio interviews with people across the southern United States and compared the way that locals used and pronounced certain words — nine hundred interviews from Georgia to Florida to Texas over *fourteen years*! Now, that's persistence!

You will not have the time, resources, or expertise (yet) that professional researchers like Professor Pederson or the makers of *Hoop Dreams* do. But these exemplary researchers illustrate an essential point about the research process: the importance of diligent work and persistence, for which there is no substitute. Thorough research simply takes time (and "elbow grease") to succeed. Your success is almost always a direct result of your effort.

In short, the quality of your writing will depend upon the quality of your research, and the quality of your research will depend on the time and energy you invest in that stage of your writing process.

PRACTICE Lesson 11: Planning urges you to plan your writing process out on a calendar carefully. Take a moment and zoom in closely on a plan for your research process in particular. Imagine, and then write down, the number of minutes each of the following steps will take for the research process of a current or upcoming writing assignment: locating or generating evidence, scanning and evaluating each potential source, studying each source closely, taking notes on each source, integrating ideas from each source into your draft. Add up the number of minutes that your research plan will take and compare your tally with those of your classmates. After that discussion, return to your calendar and revise your schedule in writing accordingly.

7. Leave a trail of breadcrumbs as you hunt: Cite your sources early and often.

HANNAH
California State University, San Marcos

Once my research is done, I go and write my Works Cited page before I do any writing.

Hannah's research process requires her to cite sources before she begins writing, and I strongly encourage you to do the same. Lesson 24: Citation discusses the mentality and mechanics of citation in detail for you, but I must cover an essential aspect of citation right now so you can incorporate it from the very beginning: You must leave an obvious trail of breadcrumbs for you and your readers to follow. This means that you must collect and preserve citation data the very moment that you begin research. Your very first draft should contain this citation data (a trail of crumbs for others to follow), even though the citation information doesn't need to be perfectly formatted right away.

Take a minute to think about the answer to this question: Why is it essential for college writers in the information age to cite *during* researching and drafting rather than after?

I am not going to directly answer that question for now, but I will share two things:

1) Nothing will disconnect an audience more immediately than broken trust in the research and evidence used by the writer.
2) Writers who do not cite correctly have usually erred because they failed to keep track of their sources from the very beginning of their projects.

So, cite sources from the start of your research and writing process — and aim to cite them often throughout your process. The more frequently you cite sources, the more readily you are thinking and behaving like a researcher and becoming a college writer. If you are going to be curious, patient, strategic, and persistent as a researcher, how will you convey all of that work without documenting your findings? Why hunt in the forest and then drop everything you found?

For the time being (until you get to Lesson 24: Citation), please trust me on this piece of advice which I mentioned earlier in this lesson: Use a citation generator to gather citation and bibliographic information during your research process, *but be aware of their limitations*. Most college libraries now offer online citation-generator applications, and many word processors now include built-in bibliography features.

12.3

Exercises: researching

12a Integrate the video.

Karina describes how researching comes before drafting in her writing process:

> After I get my idea, the first thing I do: I actually go to the library and I take out a million books. I know this is ridiculous, but I've taken out like twenty different books because I see everything, and I want to do a lot of different research. I think you have to have good research. So, after doing my research, I start to write.

Write a substantial paragraph or two, with a topic sentence or mini-thesis, through which you respond to the sound-bite videos in the lesson, like Karina's, as you form your own approaches to researching. You can watch the Lesson 12 Essentials Video or you can browse the embedded clips in the online edition of this lesson. You might begin by identifying the moments that stand out to you the most. Which student videos seem to make the most sense to you? With whom do you agree? Disagree? What patterns do you find among the student sound bites? Which ideas were the most instructive or helpful to you? What surprised you? How have your own ideas about researching come into focus through the videos?

12b Create a journal entry or blog.

This lesson urges you to develop your strategic, disciplined approaches to researching as part of your writing process, and this exercise asks you to use a journal to do so. Write two short paragraphs in your journal: one that describes your plan for researching on an upcoming writing assignment and a second one that reflects on your experiences after you have researched. Describe some past experiences

with researching that will influence your plans for the upcoming assignment. Do you have specific researching strategies in mind, like those listed in 12.2, that you think will help you with your assignment? After the assignment is complete, reflect on and evaluate how well your researching plan worked and what you can learn from the experience for next time. You could keep this journal using only print/text, or you could make an online blog, a video blog, or an audio podcast that captures your unfolding thoughts and experiences in your actual voice.

12c See yourself as a writer.

In a page or two, describe the evolution of your approaches to researching since you began writing. Where and when did you start to develop intentional strategies for researching? What major events, assignments, and papers have influenced your approaches to researching along the way? What particular teachers or classes have reshaped the ways you approach research in your writing process? What was your sense of researching before you began reading this lesson? What is your approach now that you have finished this lesson? In what ways can you imagine your "researching process" changing beyond college? How does your development as a writer compare with what other students said in their interviews, such as Hannah, who has a love-hate relationship with that part of the writing process: "My least favorite part is research. It's tedious, it's long, it's time-consuming, um, but it's the most important part."

12d Invent your writing.

Section 12.2 of this lesson discusses seven different principles to guide your research process. In five complete sentences, map out how at least five of these recommendations could be applied to a writing assignment you are working on in this class, or in another class (if you are not currently writing in this course).

12e Analyze student writing.

Read at least one of the featured student interviews in the text, and study, in particular, their discussion about their approach to researching. Or you might choose to browse the LaunchPad interviews for a student like you or who is interesting to you. Compile a list of five or so different things the student said in the interview about their researching processes. Then compare their interview, your list, and their writing sample. Can you see connections between their discussion of their research process and their written product?

Your instructor might ask you to interview a classmate instead of reading one of the interviews in the text or online. Or you might compare what you found in one of the textbook interviews to an interview with your classmate. If you interview a classmate, ask them about their researching technique for a writing assignment. Do they use the same approach for each assignment? What are the most prominent benefits of their approach to researching? What aspects of their research process are they confident about? When do they struggle? And, most important, can you identify connections between their researching technique and their written products? Can you see how the research process impacts the quality and experience of their writing?

12f Revise repeatedly from feedback.

Examine a writing assignment you are currently working on or one that you wrote recently, perhaps in another class or in high school. Describe in a written paragraph, video selfie, or audio podcast some specific ways that you can use the ideas from Lesson 12 to improve your writing through better researching. Ideally, you can take a current draft of your writing to the writing center, a peer workshop, or your instructor's office hours and ask, "What are the weakest aspects of this draft, and how can I improve my research process to address those weaknesses?"

LESSON 13

Organizing

Organize your preliminary writing according to patterns.

fStop Images – Larry Washburn/Getty Images

13.1 [WHY]

Why you should organize your preliminary writing according to patterns.

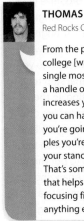

THOMAS
Red Rocks Community College

From the perspective of a first-year college [writer], I would say that the single most important thing to get a handle on is organization. It really increases your efficiency so much if you can have a clear path about what you're going to write and what examples you're going to use and what your stance is before you start writing. That's something that I've learned that helps me with all of my classes: focusing first on organization before anything else.

Our brains are hardwired to seek patterns. Perhaps the most important pattern of all is the human face, with its eyes, nose, and mouth framed by hair, ears, and chin. This pattern is so deeply ingrained into the way we encounter the world that we may rarely think about how much essential information it conveys. How do we instinctively know that babies, puppies, and kittens need to be treated gently and are no threat to us? How do we recognize our mothers, our leaders, and our role models? The patterns of their faces cue our thoughts.

Patterns are everywhere: They shape and are shaped by ideas and perceptions. Even if you are not a musician, you can easily anticipate upcoming melodies in a pop song because music is arranged according to patterns. Even if you have never watched a Shakespearean play, you can expect it to be structured according to scenes that establish the setting, then present a conflict, leading to a climax that is resolved at the end. To get a new job, you expect to apply, be interviewed, agree to terms, and then begin an orientation or training.

By now you have figured out (either consciously or intuitively) that this textbook is structured according to lessons and that each is further organized into three parts: (1) how, (2) why, and (3) exercises. These patterns enable your brain to anticipate and integrate learning. They are essential for intellectual growth.

Your writing also has structures and patterns. Sentences are composed of subjects and predicates (Lesson 23). Paragraphs are patterns of sentences (Lesson 21). Academic writing assignments are typically organized with an introduction (Lesson 20), followed by a body (Lesson 21), followed by a conclusion (Lesson 20).

Your readers will expect you to structure your writing according to patterns, and they will be frustrated if they are unable to find an organizing pattern that makes sense to them. In fact, every rubric I have ever seen for evaluating an academic writing assignment has emphasized clear and appropriate structure.

There is no single, standard structure for all college writing (although the "five-paragraph theme" might seem like it is). In fact, expectations for organizing your sentences and paragraphs tend to change depending on genre, methodology, discipline, and media (see Part Two). Nonetheless, your readers will expect you to organize your writing according to patterns that they can "follow," which means that your structure will help them process your writing. **Patterns provide frameworks that help us learn and understand.**

Because patterns are essential to thinking and learning, you'll want to integrate them into your writing process from the start. If you are reading this textbook sequentially as you work on a specific writing assignment, then you began by planning (Lesson 10), followed by brainstorming (Lesson 11), followed by researching (Lesson 12). If so, you should now have many pages of pre-writing, perhaps including your calendar, freewriting, brainstorming, note cards, and notes from your research. At this point it's a good idea to begin to structure and organize that preliminary material into a pattern before you dive into a first draft.

YADIRYS
Boston University

Outlining your papers is very, very important. I didn't do that first semester and then I learned. In my second semester I'd have the most detailed outlines, so that I knew what each paragraph was about. Because my professor, she stressed that a lot: Know what your paragraphs are going to develop into.... Put your paragraphs down and know what academic work you're going to use in the paragraph. Write it down, your main idea for that paragraph. Outline your entire paper so when you go to write it ... you won't be wasting time sitting at a computer and staring at a screen. [With an outline] you have something to look back at.

Your initial motivation to organize your writing is to connect with your audience. You want to be understood. I've just described how structures and patterns make it easier for readers to comprehend your writing — organization makes it easier for your readers to "connect the dots." Organized writing connects an audience with the topic they're reading.

But organization also connects you with the topic you are writing. So there's an equally important second reason to organize your brainstorming and research notes logically: Organizing messy, preliminary thoughts into logical patterns helps you figure out what you want to say. Applying structure to your preliminary ideas is an essential step toward finding meaning in your writing. In the early stages of writing, your ideas are often fragmented and collected loosely. It's like you have a bunch of pieces of broken tile all mixed up and now you want to put them together in a mosaic design. Analyzing the fragments and organizing them into a shape is a critical, intellectual process through which you deepen your understanding so that you can communicate that understanding to others.

Organization, patterns, and structure can also make your writing process more efficient, manageable, and focused. Yadirys describes how important outlines are for connecting her writing with her professor. But she also uses outlines to help make her process efficient, instead of "wasting time sitting at a computer and staring at a screen." When you organize your brainstorming and research notes logically, you make it easier to respond to your assignment prompt (see Lesson: 5: Prompt) and complete your writing assignment, as Cara notes.

CARA
Metropolitan State University of Denver

You can't really think too much about your structure when you're in a time crunch and you have to turn [your paper] in in twelve hours. But if you spend time beforehand structuring it, making sure it all flows correctly, then the drafting almost takes care of itself because you're constantly thinking and revising as you structure it, [which helps you to] put all the little pieces into place.

Structures help you complete a first draft efficiently because they can break the job down into manageable chunks. Once you have an overall sense of the structure of your writing, then it is often much easier to flesh-out each task, each segment, and each paragraph so that it will add up to a complete, coherent draft.

PRACTICE Make a list of two or three things in your life outside of school that are organized with a clear structure, such as a favorite recipe, a storage space, or a procedure you follow at work. Then pick one of those things and describe its structure and how that structure helps you. Why do think that structure works? What would happen if there was no pattern? Can you imagine a different pattern that might work as well or better? Describe that thing to someone else who might be unfamiliar with it. Does the structure make it easier for you to explain and your listener to understand?

13.2 [HOW]

How to organize your preliminary writing according to patterns.

If you have followed the advice in Lessons 10, 11, and 12 (Planning; Brainstorming; and

Conducting Research), then you are well prepared to begin organizing for your first draft. At this point, you should have a lot of material in front of you: some brainstorming and a lot of notes from your early research. Now it's time to organize all of your prewriting into a logical structure that will pave your way into the first draft.

Following is advice on how to organize your early writing into a draft. The first group of strategies offers four ways to physically structure your ideas: by creating cluster maps, outlines, and note cards, and by cutting and pasting. The last group of strategies offers five different patterns you might use for organizing your writing.

Structure your ideas.

1) Create a cluster map. With this technique, you would:

a) Read through your brainstorming and research notes and then circle, underline, or highlight key terms, ideas, and quotations from your sources.
b) Transcribe from your highlights a pivotal word, idea, or phrase and place it at the center of the map and circle it.
c) Surround your central idea with supporting terms and phrases arranged in a cluster.
d) Add graphic shapes and lines to map the relationships between the ideas in the surrounding cluster and your central idea.
e) Evaluate your cluster map. Has it helped you think more clearly about your ideas? To what extent has it suggested a logical organizing structure?

Cluster maps can benefit you, especially if you like thinking visually. Further, as a low-stakes way to begin to get words on a page, cluster mapping can help overcome writer's block. If you used key-term mapping (p. 163) as a brainstorming strategy, then cluster mapping would naturally follow as an organizational strategy in your writing process.

The downside of cluster mapping is that most college assignments require you to write in a straight line from the first paragraph and page to the last. You are not often asked to submit final work organized in circular clusters, although you are expected to coordinate related ideas in clusters known as paragraphs. If your assignment asks you to compose a presentation using Prezi software or a digital website or hypertextual document, then a cluster map is ideal for organizing within that genre and media. Otherwise, you must convert your web-shaped map into sequential blocks of text as you begin to draft. See also how to "Organize with a nodal pattern" in section 13.2.5 on page 191.

See Lesson 11, page 164 for an example of Nick's cluster map.

2) Create a formal outline. Creating a formal outline (like Gregg's, below) compels a writer to coordinate and subordinate ideas, thereby creating a logical structure that supports the main idea. To create a formal outline, identify your major subtopics and format each of them as a level-one heading, in capital letters, preceded by a Roman numeral, and aligned flush-left. Each *sub*-subtopic is formatted as a level-two heading, preceded by an alphabetic letter, listed under its corresponding subtopic, and indented to the right, indicating that the level-two topic is subordinate to the level-one headings. An advantage of a formal outline is that you can glance over an entire project in a page or two to determine if your plan is organized effectively.

Formal outlines are useful because they help you think structurally. Outlines are organized according to big topics and little topics—main topics and subtopics.

I. INTRODUCTION

II. ETYMOLOGICAL ASSOCIATION

    a. "Behold, I have made your face strong against their faces, and your forehead strong against their forehead." Ezekiel 3:8

    b. French word for forehead, *le front*. Outer interaction where two different people interact in conflict.

III. PHYSICAL ASPECT/JOHN SMITH

IV. PHYSICAL ASPECT/MARY ROWLANDSON

V. TRANSITIONAL PARAGRAPH/INTERNAL ASPECT OF FRONTIER

    a. Recontestualization of Frontier to the Interior

    b. "The frontier, in McMurtry's Westerns, is a place where world views meet and collide." 193

    c. "… the captive, who is suddenly removed from a familiar world and placed in a world where language and representation operate according to unknown principles, crosses a frontier that is less geographical and racial than it is epistemological. The captive is placed in a world where meaning and knowledge are in suspension." 200

    Discourses of Frontier Violence and the Trauma of National Emergence in Larry McMurtry's Lonesome Dove Quartet, Deborah L. Madsen, *Canadian Review of American studies*, Volume 39, Number 2, 2009, pp. 185–204 (Article), Published by University of Toronto Press

VI. INTERNAL ASPECT/JOHN SMITH

VII. INTERNAL ASPECT/MARY ROWLANDSON

VIII. CONCLUSION

This hierarchy, or ranking, of big ideas and supporting ideas is called *subordination*. Outlines can also pull related ideas closely together, which is called *coordination*. Deonta makes a formal outline, but he uses "big" bullets and "little" bullets in his outline, instead of numbers and letters, to organize and subordinate his points. But then he switches to a "bubble diagram" to bring ideas together — to coordinate his topics and subtopics.

DEONTA
University of North Carolina, Chapel Hill

When I'm brainstorming, I get a notebook and I just write out ideas. I make bullet points and little subpoints underneath each bullet point of how the idea will relate to the paper, what I could possibly talk about. And then I choose one or two ideas and I try to map it out with bubble diagrams. I normally go with the one that interests me most — the one that had the most substance when I was brainstorming. . . . Once I have the idea that I want to talk about, I don't really like the strict outline format. So I normally do just bullet points and a couple of ideas under each bullet point. And then, after making my bullet points, I might try to go ahead and write my thesis. Just as a rough draft.

Some writers find it easy to create a formal outline using presentation software. For example, PowerPoint offers an outline function that allows you to see your topics and subtopics on each slide at a glance. I know students who have used PowerPoint to outline their writing assignments before drafting. In fact, a student once said to me, "I don't know why, but I just learned to think in PowerPoint, and then I have to move all of my ideas into the paper."

What's most important is that you find an approach that works for you. Based upon what Deonta said about his struggle with strict outlines, his version of Gregg's outline would probably use only bullets instead of organizing numbers and letters. If you find strict, formal outlines frustrating or unhelpful, you might try Deonta's version of big, main bullet points and small, subordinate bullet points under each big, main idea. Either approach can naturally grow from an outline to the paragraphs in your draft.

3) Create note cards. College writers sometimes prepare note cards before beginning to write a research paper. Typically writers use note cards to jot down direct passages from source material, and then arrange and rearrange the cards to provide a structure for their writing to follow. If you used note cards to brainstorm your project (see Lesson 11), then note cards can be a natural transition from prewriting to organizing to drafting. I like how note cards can offer writers a sense of crafting their work by trying different sequences and looking for patterns and relationships among the cards.

4) Cut and paste (physically or electronically). Friends have told me that paper-and-scissors cutting and pasting is their preferred organization technique. With this technique, the writer prints out all of their prewriting materials and then uses scissors to cut the printout into blocks of text. You could use a tabletop or a bulletin board to arrange and rearrange the text blocks, but my friends say that they like to use the floor to spread things out and move them around. Once you discover a structure that works, tape the pieces back together.

How to organize your preliminary writing according to patterns

When cutting and pasting electronically, simply copy the paragraphs or outline segments that seem out of place and re-paste them in your document in a better location. Or you can start with your brainstorming (as Chase does) and rearrange those pieces into a workable structure.

CHASE
Santa Fe College

I'll usually take my [freewrite], and then I'll go down to the very bottom of the document . . . and I'll write down my [sub]topics. Then, I'll just copy and paste [chunks of text] under each topic . . . and I'll figure out what logically flows from there: What should come first and what should come last, how does one topic segue into the next topic. It's usually done through Word, just like that: Copy, paste, write, titles, bold, underline, all that to organize it.

At first, it might seem silly to use scissors and waste paper by creating an extra step on the floor that you will have to repeat on your computer. But there is something potentially effective about seeing the entire project laid out in front of you on the floor. There also seems to be something productive about having to commit the scissors to the paper as well as the tactile experience of holding and moving the chunks of text in your hands. Taping or gluing the pieces back together again can likewise give you a unique perspective on your writing process, and it can heighten your sense of how your ideas are organized and connected. You could use a variety of computer applications, such as sticky notes or PowerPoint, to mimic this technique electronically. Chase uses his word processor to cut-and-paste key words, topics, and quotes to organize the structure of his writing. But the feeling probably

wouldn't be the same as getting down on the floor with your paper.

Organize your ideas by patterns.

As you organize your writing project into topics and subtopics, consider the relationships *between* these topics. What structural pattern will make your writing most effective and create connections with your audience? Each of the patterns below offers you a different way of sequencing your paragraphs to create different perceptions for your readers. As a college writer, make the most of every opportunity you have to establish meaning by showing relationships and patterns within the structures of your writing projects. Take advantage of structural patterns — perhaps one of the ones that follows — to connect with your audience.

1) Organize with a sloping pattern.
A sloping pattern of organization presents main points in an increasing or decreasing trajectory from the beginning to the end of your paper. The most common sloping patterns are to either (1) place your strongest point first (to make a powerful first impression) or (2) locate your strongest point last (to conclude with emphasis).

It may be more effective for you to put your most complicated idea first (when the reader has more energy), or you might put your densest material in the end (after you have established a rhythm and a familiarity with your reader). You might also try switching between an increasing slope and a decreasing slope to see what makes more sense before ultimately selecting one approach or the other.

Inexperienced writers who sometimes get tired near the end of their writing processes might benefit from experimenting

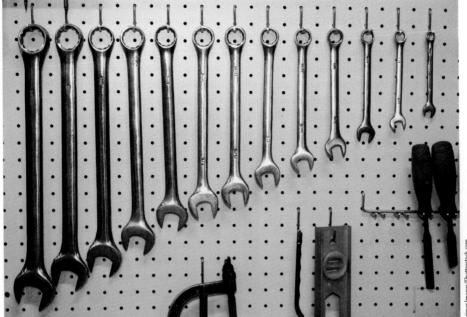

Lorimer Images/Shutterstock.com

with sloping organization. Some genres (see Lesson 7) have expected conventions for a sloping pattern. For example, newspaper articles put the most important information up front to grab the reader's attention. Brad uses a sloping pattern to start with his most engaging material first.

BRAD
University of Florida

When it comes to structuring paragraphs . . . I always start with a topic that I feel not only that I have the most information on, to build from, but I'm most excited about. Because my excitement will translate to that very first paragraph, and that's why I put it first because I want my reader to be initially engaged. And then I will play around with the paragraphs and see where my excitement level is, to see where the flow is.

A sloping pattern might also move from general to specific, rather than from most prominent to less prominent (like Brad). You might have seen a geometric diagram of an essay that begins with an inverted triangle, which suggests that the introductory paragraph "slopes" from general to specific. Your entire draft might move from general to specific or from specific to general, too, in a sloping pattern.

2) Organize with a linear pattern. A linear pattern of organization presents ideas in a sequence. One idea leads to the next, like links in a chain. The most familiar linear pattern is chronological, based upon time. When writing a history paper, you might organize your ideas in chronological order, according to a sequence of events. If you are storyboarding a video, you will place your frames linearly, in the order they will appear in the film.

This section of this book (Part Three, where you are now) is structured in a linear fashion, according to a sequence of steps you might take from brainstorming to drafting to finalizing and reflecting. While you do not need to follow the lessons in order, doing so can make it easier to find what you need to improve your writing process.

YADIRYS
Boston University

The most helpful thing that a writing teacher has ever done for me was [to teach] me to list paragraphs — to put paragraphs in chronological order. He had us . . . write our introductory paragraph and then what each paragraph was going to be after that, [focusing on] the main point in each paragraph.

3) Organize with a variable pattern. While sloping and linear patterns of organization march your ideas in only one direction, a variable pattern can be the right choice for some writing. The most familiar variable pattern is the point-counterpoint structure: Every other paragraph argues in favor of a point, and the paragraphs in between explore counterpoints.

You could also compare things according to different criteria as you move through your paper. For example, you might begin by pointing out the differences between two poems, but then you conclude by analyzing their similarities. You can structure your writing into repeatedly rising and falling qualities, like a sine wave, by discussing an admirable character in a movie, followed by

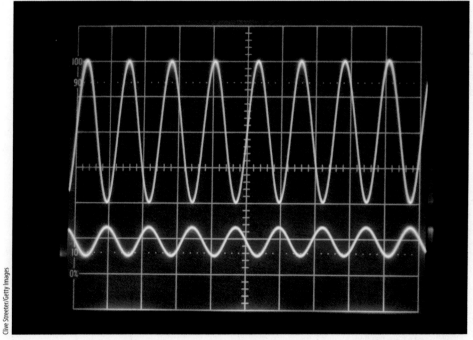

Clive Streeter/Getty Images

a villain, followed by a comedic character, and ending with a tragic victim. If your writing involves solving a puzzle of sorts, you might begin by providing basic background information, then set up a tension, reveal a solution in the climax, and then reflect back on lessons learned in the conclusion. Ashia finds the flexibility of variable structures freeing.

ASHIA
Michigan State University

I was originally taught to write an outline, basically, roman numerals, topics for each paragraph. Now I don't use an outline. I'll read over it, copy and paste, switch things around . . . moving things to see if it sounds right. If it doesn't, then I move it back. I do a lot of playing around with my papers — versus writing an outline and just having one set outline.

4) Organize with a formal pattern. Certain genres require specific, formal patterns of organization (see Lesson 7), including some genres of college writing, as Kendra acknowledges. One of the most common examples of a formally-structured format is the scientific lab report, which often follows the IMRAC acronym: Introduction, Methods and Materials, Results, Analysis, Conclusion. At my university, biology professors give students very specific instructions for each of these organizational elements. However, not all scientists and scientific disciplines follow these patterns exactly; many have variations on the IMRAC structure.

A research project proposal, like Charlie's Uganda film proposal, uses formal structures indicated with subheadings, such as "experience," "plan of work," "budget," and

"recommendations." However, even when you're asked to organize according to a specific formal pattern, you will still make some organizational choices. For example, if you are asked to submit a proposal for undergraduate research (like Charlie's), how would you organize your autobiographical experiences: chronologically? Or according to relevance to the proposed project?

 See the LaunchPad for Charlie's final film on the space program in Uganda.

KENDRA
Michigan State University

With scientific writing you have to do a lot of [organizing] beforehand and make sure that it's interesting before you start because once you're filling in the data it's very exact, it's like filling in blanks of an outline. English essays [allow you to be] more free to your own interpretation and of how you want to mold [your organization].

5) Organize with a nodal pattern. The World Wide Web is an example of a nodal pattern of organization. Each individual site is a "node" and each clickable link is a hypertextual connection between nodes. Cities and towns are geographical nodes connected by a pattern of roadways. Utility systems, like power lines and telephones, are organized by nodal structures, although mobile phones now make the nodal telephone network more invisible. Cluster maps, recommended earlier in this lesson, follow a nodal structure, too.

Paper and print technology is essentially linear and sequential. The first page necessarily leads to the second page, and so on. Because print technology is so familiar, it can be difficult to imagine a different kind of literacy. Nodal, networked computer structures have begun to change these

How to organize your preliminary writing according to patterns

trigga/Getty Images

tendencies, although it will probably take a couple of generations to alter these patterns and expectations deeply.

You might be assigned a specific genre (Lesson 7) or media (Lesson 9) that prompts you to write with nodes and links rather than a conventional sequence of text blocks. You might be asked to create a website in which the relationships between individual web pages (the nodes) are not necessarily hierarchical. The pattern here might be nodal and weblike rather than linear or sequential, although you can easily make a website as sequential and hierarchical as a book, if you choose.

PRACTICE It might be interesting to consider that the print version of the textbook you are reading is linear, but the electronic version is nodal/hypertextual. What difference(s) does it make to you as a reader that you can click on a link only in digital versions of this book? What is the effect as you interact with the video elements in this textbook compared to the experience of reading ink on paper? Take your experiences as a reader of nodal patterns into consideration as you make choices about organizing your electronic documents.

13.3

Exercises: organizing

13a Integrate the video.

In her interview, Nicole describes her transition from brainstorming (Lesson 11) to organizing (Lesson 13).

My approach to writing a college assignment paper is lots of free writing. A lot of
free writing. Literally, I dump my thoughts
onto the page. I don't worry about
grammar, I don't worry about mechanics,
I don't worry about logic, clarity, comprehension, nothing. I do a lot, a lot of free
writing and then I go back to the free
writing and organize and do somewhat
of a "post-outline" to my free writing. That
kind of sets up the outline for where I'm
going to take it from there. And that's
how I organize.

Write a substantial paragraph or two, with a
topic sentence or mini-thesis, through which
you respond to the sound-bite videos in the
lesson, like Nicole's, as you form your own
approaches to organizing. You can watch the
Lesson 13 Essentials Video, or you can browse
the embedded clips in the online edition of
this lesson. You might begin by identifying
the moments that stand out to you the most.
Which student videos seem to make the most
sense to you? With whom do you agree?
Disagree? What patterns do you find among
the student sound bites? Which ideas were
the most instructive or helpful to you? What
surprised you? How have your own ideas
about organizing come into focus through
the videos?

13b Create a journal entry or blog.

This lesson urges you to develop your own
individualized approaches to organizing as
part of your writing process, and this exercise
asks you to use a journal to do so. Write two
short paragraphs in your journal: one that
describes your plan for organizing an upcoming writing assignment and a second one that
reflects on your experiences after you have
organized. Describe some past experiences
with organizing that will influence your plans
for the upcoming assignment. Do you have

a specific organizational approach in mind,
like those listed in section 13.2, that you think
is well suited for the assignment? After the
assignment is complete, upon reflection, evaluate how well your plan for organizing worked
and what you can learn from the experience
for next time. You could keep this journal using
only print/text, or you could make an online
blog, a video blog, or an audio podcast that
captures your unfolding thoughts and experiences in your actual voice.

13c See yourself as a writer.

In a page or two, describe the evolution of
your approaches to organization and structure
since you began writing. Where and when did
you start to develop intentional strategies for
organizing? What major events, assignments,
and papers have influenced your approaches
to organization and structure along the way?
What particular teachers or classes have
reshaped the ways you organize? What was
your sense of organizing before you began
reading this lesson? What is your approach
now that you have finished this lesson? In what
ways can you imagine your organizing techniques changing beyond college? How does
your development as a writer compare with
what other students reported in their interviews, such as Nanaissa, who says in her interview that her high school in France demanded
formal and deliberate organizational structures. She prefers the organizational style in her
U.S. college, which is more relaxed.

13d Invent your writing.

Section 13.2 of this lesson discusses nine
different organizational ideas: four techniques
for organizing your ideas and five different
structural patterns. Pick one of the four techniques and one of the five structural patterns
and apply them to a writing assignment you
are working on in this class, or in another class
(if you are not currently writing in this course).

13e Analyze student writing.

Read at least one of the featured student interviews in the text, and study in particular their discussion about their approach to organization and structure. Or, you might choose to browse the interviews in the LaunchPad for a student like you or who is interesting to you. Compile a list of five or so different things the student said in their interview about organization and structure in their writing. Then compare their interview, your list, and, their writing sample. Can you see connections between their discussion of their writing process and their written product?

Your instructor might ask you to interview a classmate instead of reading one of the interviews in the text or online. Or you might compare what you found in one of the textbook interviews to an interview with your classmate. If you interview a classmate, ask them about their organizing technique for a writing assignment. Do they use the same approach for each assignment? What are the most prominent benefits of their approach to organizing? What aspects of their organizing are they confident about? When do they struggle? And, most important, can you identify connections between their organizing technique and their written products: Can you see how organizing impacts the quality and experience of their writing?

13f Revise repeatedly from feedback.

Examine a writing assignment you are currently working on or one that you wrote recently, perhaps in another class or in high school. Describe in a written paragraph, video selfie, or audio podcast some specific ways that you can use the ideas from Lesson 13 to improve your writing through better organizing. Ideally, you can take a current draft of your writing to the writing center, a peer workshop, or your instructor's office hours and ask, "What are the weakest aspects of this draft, and how could I have organized more effectively to address those weaknesses?"

LESSON 14

Drafting

Generate momentum in your first draft.

ESSENTIALS VIDEO

Visit the LaunchPad for *Becoming a College Writer* to watch the Lesson 14 Essentials Video.

14.1 [WHY]

Why you should generate momentum in your first draft.

DAN
Michigan State University

We learned in college that everything's a draft. You never, ever have a final draft. Everything's always in process, you know? . . . So drafting is vital. . . . Drafting is a forever process, I'd say.

The word *draft* has many applications. For example, a *draft* is airflow: When you are indoors and feel the movement of cold air, it's called a *draft*. Beverages pumped from a keg are called *draft* (or *draught*). And, of course, the word *draft* describes an early version of an important document, such as the Declaration of Independence or a work by Shakespeare.

The word *version* comes from the Latin verb meaning *to turn*; so, both of these words — *draft* and *version* — are about movement, especially from one place or one form to another. I imagine a cartoon depiction of a snowball rapidly growing larger and gaining momentum as it rolls down a wintery incline. That's what you're doing in your first draft: You're trying to kick-start a small snowball over the edge of a mountain so that it builds substance and gains force as more material accumulates on the way to something big.

If you have followed the sequence of this text, by now you have scheduled a writing plan on your calendar (Lesson 10), brainstormed (Lesson 11), begun your research (Lesson 12), and mapped a structure for your writing project (Lesson 13). Those steps, which might be considered prewriting, have led to this moment. It's time to write the first true draft.

Your goal for your first draft is to generate momentum and to establish a core upon which you will build subsequent drafts. If you are going to **Revise Repeatedly from Feedback** (Lesson 15), then thinking of your writing as a series of drafts is fundamental. As Dan says, writing is drafting, and drafts are meant to be improved.

PHILLIP
Santa Fe College

Whenever I write anything, whether it's for science class [or] English class, the first thing I do is make sure I let [everybody] know not to bother me. I make sure I have something to drink right there, so I don't have to get up, and I actually try to get all my resources together, especially the online ones. . . . To get temptation out of the way before I write, I will check my email and then turn the Internet off. . . . Usually that process will go on until I run into a big problem and I feel like I need to review something else. Or if it just gets to the point where I'm exhausted.

So drafting is about movement, flow, momentum, and improvement. You are certain to have your own, customized approach to the drafting stage that helps you build momentum, although it can be helpful for you to hear from other college writers, like Phillip, who describes the "isolation booth" technique on the previous page.

Hyesu does a lot of preparation and prewriting (Lessons 10–13) so that she feels confident when she sits down to draft, even though she might not have a thesis statement yet. For her, drafting momentum begins with an interior body paragraph and does not stop until the paper is due.

HYESU
University of Florida

When I start to write my first draft is when I actually start using a computer, and I just start writing. I tend not to start with the introductory paragraph because at that point I'm pretty confident about what I want to say, but I'm yet unsure as to how to make that an argument, and I kind of need a thesis statement. Since I don't have [a thesis] yet, I have to kind of start in the middle, with the first body paragraph, right after the introduction. . . . For me, drafts are a continuous thing: no first draft is the "rough draft." . . . It's more of a continual process. . . . It's a very fluid thing. . . . For me there's no distinction between first, second, third, or final drafts.

You may find that you prefer Hyesu's style over Phillip's, or that some combination of their advice works best. The rest of this lesson will help you to develop your own personalized approach to drafting a writing assignment.

PRACTICE Brainstorm a list of things, other than academic writing, for which you have produced a draft. Maybe it was a diagram for something you planned to make, a step-by-step plan that you eventually followed, or an important email or proposal. Describe some of the things those drafts had in common with drafts of your writing for school. Also consider some of the ways they might be different.

Drafting early and gaining momentum offers rhetorical benefits.

When you produce multiple drafts well ahead of your deadline, you give yourself multiple opportunities to interact with your audience and gain helpful feedback along the way. The earlier you produce a draft, the earlier you can gather responses from readers, including your instructor or a writing center tutor, and the more time you will have to effectively integrate their feedback into your writing. Remember, of course, that the key to college writing is to **Revise Repeatedly from Feedback**, which the next lesson describes in detail. Feedback is primarily about developing your ideas and the substance of the paper, whereas convention and correctness are often best addressed at the end of your writing process (see Lesson 16: Proofreading).

As Lesson 3: Audience stresses, interacting and connecting with your readers is key to doing your best work — and the most effective way to interact with your readers ahead of a deadline is to discuss your drafts-in-progress. Drafting early and often provides the ideal opportunity to build connections with your audience.

When Abigail drafts, she does so with her audience in mind, especially her peer reviewers. She defines each different draft according to the feedback she has received to move it beyond the previous draft. Unlike Hyesu, Abigail does think in terms of distinct drafts. Also, Abigail likes to refine her first draft before she shares it, unlike Karina later in this lesson, who gains momentum through loose, messy first drafts. Putting a lot of effort into an advanced first draft helps Abigail gain momentum. What approach to drafting might work best for you?

ABIGAIL
Santa Fe College

In the first draft, I want to do the best that I can, but I know that I'm going to have more than two or three drafts. I was taught in high school and in college writing that you need to have people review your paper — that's when the drafting comes into play. You have your own thoughts, you have your own draft, but you need someone else to look at it to form another draft. . . . Personally, I don't want to [share a first draft] with one of my peers and make myself look like an idiot because I didn't go as far as I possibly could with that first draft. . . . That's why I strive to do excellent [work] in my first drafts, so that [my workload] goes downhill from there. Most people think that their final draft is the hardest — the worst, most dreaded draft. But I think of my first draft [as the most challenging].

Drafting early and often offers cognitive benefits.

The earlier you produce a first draft, the earlier your mind can begin to accumulate ideas and solve problems within your writing. When a friend purchases a car, suddenly I begin to notice that model of car all over the place. Of course, it's unlikely that my friend's purchase had much to do with the number of those cars on the road — it's my sudden awareness of that model that has changed.

When you draft early, your mind begins to be more aware of the issues and questions connected with your topic, so that as you casually skim newspapers or browse the Internet, you are more likely to notice related information to incorporate into your writing. Additionally, if you have an early first draft, you also have a mental or cognitive framework that can help you understand, organize, and integrate relevant information as it falls into your lap. Thanks to your first draft, you now have a place to put a lucky piece of information that you just happened to come across. This makes your research more efficient because your radar is always turned on, seeking out connections and sources.

On many occasions, creative ideas and solutions have come to me when I'm alone and concentrating on other tasks, like driving or taking a shower. If I have an early draft, I find that it allows my subconscious and conscious minds to process ideas, so I'm thinking through writing even when I'm not sitting at a keyboard. In her interview on page 455, Nicole describes how reading for pleasure or reading for other classes can provide surprising insights for writing assignments that were not directly connected at first.

Drafting early and often offers emotional benefits.

Creating an early first draft can be emotionally healthy and relaxing because it reduces the pressure to try to get everything right in just one try, which is difficult or impossible to do. An early first draft helps me sleep better at night, which helps me think more clearly, because it gives me confidence and momentum toward a successful final version. Sure, most of us need a little bit of pressure and anxiety to help focus and motivate our work, but too much pressure can make us freeze up or fail. You are less likely to work efficiently when you're in a panic or under a lot of pressure.

Writing is a deeply personal activity, which means that your state of mind almost always comes through in your voice, tone, and in the quality of your words. When you create an early first draft, you are much more likely to write with composure and to convey a feeling of thoughtfulness and clarity. Gretchen describes how one sentence leads to another, incrementally building to the point that she feels good about seeing some paragraphs, which is when her drafting momentum takes off.

GRETCHEN
Boston University

I'll start to type on my computer — and it's usually one sentence. I'll sit there with one sentence. And then I'll have a couple sentences, and then once I get the first paragraph, I just keep going and going. It doesn't always connect. But as long as I have writing, I'll feel good, like I'm getting somewhere. I just have to have something written down.

Drafting early and often offers concrete benefits.

Writing is work. It requires labor, concentration, and effort; and it doesn't help to deny the mental and physical energy that's required. So, once you have invested yourself in your writing, you want to be able to see the results of your hard work. An early first draft can also be a concrete, physical representation of all the preliminary exploration, brainstorming, researching, and planning that you have accomplished. You have been diligent, and now you begin to hold in your hands the rewards of your efforts.

For Gretchen, seeing sentences grow into paragraphs encourages her and gets her draft flowing. The reality of words on a page (or screen or whiteboard) can help organize and clarify your thoughts. For Michael, drafting offers a way to work through a conflict.

MICHAEL
Michigan State University

As I started [drafting, I felt] an internal conflict . . . something that I couldn't sort out in any other way [than through writing]. [Drafting] is like a puzzle where not all the puzzle pieces fit. You can't sort them out by thinking. Your mind can't put all the pieces together by banging them in with a hammer. You have to reshape everything, and have to put it on a page to make everything make sense.

As you move from high school writing to first-year college writing, to writing in your major as a senior, to writing as a professional beyond college, your writing tasks tend to become more complex. It becomes no longer possible to complete a writing project in a day or two. You will find, if you are writing at the last minute, that "the last minute" begins to move further and further away from your actual deadlines — you will need much more time to draft and revise. So, managing the pace at which you produce words, pages, and drafts becomes more important and more deliberate (see Lesson 10: Planning).

Get into the early drafting habit now and your life will be easier. An early first draft is necessary, not only as your writing tasks become more involved, but also as your efforts become more dependent on delivering your best work on time.

14.2 [HOW]

How to generate momentum in the first draft.

Let's assume that you have followed the advice in Lessons 10 through 13 and that you have not rushed to begin drafting (or writing the paper itself) until you are fully prepared. You should have a lot of material in front of you: some brainstorming and a lot of notes and thoughts and a preliminary structure from your early research. So, what are some ways to get drafting?

The following section offers six recommendations for developing an early first draft, the goal of which is to generate momentum and flow without worrying too much about the final version. Your final version is likely to be significantly revised and reworked based upon feedback on multiple drafts.

1) Brainstorm a paragraph or two of a first draft on the day you first receive an assignment prompt.

On the first day that I commit to a writing project, I like to blast out a brainstormy first draft in the form of a title and an opening paragraph or two. At this point, I haven't yet done any careful research, so it's unlikely that much of this brainstorm draft will survive as I revise. However, there's something comforting in knowing that I already have a page of material in hand, which is much better than an anxious feeling that I'm starting completely from scratch. When I return to this preliminary writing after researching and organizing my ideas, I am often equal parts amused by my mistakes, impressed that the naïve brainstorm helped,

and reassured that I have some material to use to build momentum.

2) Respond to your research in your first draft.

GRETCHEN
Boston University

[When I begin drafting] I usually hop in my bed with my laptop, and I get out my notes that I scribbled on a notebook or on the back of an assignment, or even on a receipt or whatever I have. I will start to type up notes and type up quotes, and I might have quotes organized on a page, one by one. I'll come up with some kind of connection. . . . Then I'll start to write.

Gretchen's drafting process begins with a list of quotes that she responds to, which is a strategy that she no doubt learned as a journalism major. News writers build their reports from quotes so that their writing becomes a dialogue of comments woven together.

If college writing is defined by the integration of source material (Lesson 6: Evidence), then beginning your first draft by responding to the evidence you have gathered builds connections with your audience (Lesson 3) and context (Part Two). Imagine each of your sources is a person sitting in the room with you. Write down the main point or argument that each source makes, and organize each source and its main point as a separate paragraph.

To begin building each new paragraph in your first draft, write down your response to each source, remembering that your responses must be based upon evidence, not unsupported feelings or opinions. In this way, your first draft could be generated conversationally, as if you were engaged in a dialogue with your sources. This drafting strategy helps ground your writing in research, support, and evidence. It also encourages you to explore important questions, offer specific answers, and advance knowledge and understanding.

However, as Vinh-Thuy mentions in his interview (see page 466), in most situations, it would be too simple and robotic to just use one source or one quote in each paragraph. Eventually, each paragraph in each draft needs to be centered on an idea or point to more than a single quotation or piece of evidence. Lesson 6: Evidence discusses how evidence-based writing should be conversational and more like a dialogue than a monologue. Notice how this lesson (and every lesson in this book) includes multiple quotes and multiple sources on each topic and subtopic. As you move from first draft to more developed later drafts, you will probably add more complexity and variety to the evidence used to make each point and subpoint.

3) Structure your first draft according to a pattern.

Lesson 13: Organizing encourages you to structure your drafts according to patterns and lists a variety of patterns that you might apply. If you structured an outline of your project according to a pattern, then simply following the pattern can allow you to generate your first draft. For example, if you want to use a variable pattern (such as point-counterpoint or comparison-contrast), then the first body paragraph would examine research from one perspective and the

second paragraph would counter or contrast with the first, and so on.

But maybe your writing context requires that you write about your topic linearly or chronologically, where you begin with early history and move toward the present. Or perhaps you'll generate your first draft from a discussion and analysis of key terms, where each paragraph or section examines a different term. In other words, if you have organized your preliminary writing, thoughts, and research according to a logical pattern, then use that same logical pattern to prompt each paragraph of your first draft. Basing your first draft on a logical structure makes your writing flow more efficiently, makes your sentences clearer and more direct (Lesson 23), and makes it easier for readers to follow your thoughts.

When Chase drafts, he cuts and pastes between two word-processing documents: his prewriting notes and a fresh, empty first draft. He structures his draft topically, so that each paragraph addresses a different subtopic. He doesn't use an outline, but he does use the topical structure to generate momentum as he "fills-in" each paragraph.

CHASE
Santa Fe College

When I'm drafting . . . I'll just start writing the first paragraph based on whatever topic that I want to be first. I'll be looking at that topic as I write and filling in all the research, all the thoughts, all the interesting things about it. . . . Then I go to the next topic, and I just fill that in — and just go back and forth between the draft and my research.

4) Write in chunks and modules, especially if the assignment seems too big at first.

"One step at a time" is clichéd but sound advice. When a writing task seems overwhelming, break it down into smaller pieces. Think of your first ten-page paper as a combination of two related five-page papers. Think of twenty-pages as five four-page papers. Approach your difficult six-page paper as accomplishing a set of two or three specific tasks, and then tackle the drafting one task at a time. This is why an early first draft is so important: It's the simple first step that leads to a second one, and so on.

If a particular step or task is giving you trouble, skip over it and address something else on your list. In many of the interviews, students discuss how their writing process begins with an introduction that they are likely to revise later, but just as many of these students skip writing an introduction until after they have a draft of the body. Remember, the goal for your first draft is momentum; whatever generates momentum is the right approach for you.

I have directed many large, intimidating doctoral dissertations, which are typically two hundred or more pages. Every single one of them, including my own, was written modularly; that is, they each were a collection of four or five related, smaller pieces connected together to add up to a whole. Additionally, 75 percent of the effort on these dissertations was completed by the end of the first chapter, because once the first module was finished, then it was a much easier task to replicate that module. A vast majority of the writers I have worked with have benefited greatly from drafting in modular chunks, including yours truly as I write these very words.

5) Write a lot (too much, even) and trim excess later.

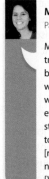

MONICA
Palomar College

My English 100 teacher was really trying to get down to bare bones because so much of [my drafting] was filler. He wanted us to start out with maybe a few hundred words, even a thousand words, and then just strip it from there. Because if we write too much, we can just go back and [remove everything except] what is necessary and that'll be our final [draft]. [We learned to] just cut down a lot.

Most (but not all) writers benefit from generating too many paragraphs and pages and then cutting back to only the most effective, powerful material. This way, only your strongest ideas survive and the filler is sifted away. If you are given a specific page or word length by your instructor, I recommend targeting about 50 percent more writing than the guidelines suggest. For example, I suggest that you write a fifteen hundred-word draft for a thousand-word paper. This approach helps you build fluency, rhythm, and confidence as a writer. It's like training with leg weights so that you run faster when the actual race is on the line.

Writers too often can't help but think that their task is defined by a word count, which leads to problems like inflated openings and faded closings. All track coaches train their runners to accelerate beyond the finish line. Professional photographers shoot hundreds of images in order to select the very best material worth sharing. If you use this approach when writing your first draft, your next step would be to ask for feedback that identifies your strongest ideas as the ones to keep. Feedback also helps you identify your weakest segments, the ones to delete. For some writers, including Karina, it's productive to have a sense of experimentation about drafting, especially early drafts.

KARINA
University of Florida

When I begin the drafting process, I just write and I let my first draft be terrible — because it is my first draft, and I know I'm going to have to go back and edit it and proofread it, all those things. I'm not going to write horribly, but I let it go — let it flow. [When] I feel like I'm done with my draft, I don't read it that same day. I like reading it the next day, with fresh eyes.

6) Revise your plans after your first draft.

Do not put a lot of pressure on your first draft to be finished or perfect. As Karina points out, a first draft is exploratory, and only after you have tried to go through a first draft will you be able to see missing pieces. Because the key to college writing is to **Revise Repeatedly from Feedback**, a first draft is an experiment that will almost always be reenvisioned from different perspectives. Eventually discarding 50 percent or more of your first draft is usually a good thing, especially if you do so in response to informed feedback.

A first draft often prompts writers to reorganize their plans and revise their calendars (see Lesson 10: Planning). It is common to discover that you may need to gather more research and evidence: First drafts raise new

Arctic-Images/Getty Images

questions and expose incomplete answers. The beauty of an early first draft is that it allows you time to improve your approach if need be. Again, don't put too much weight on your first draft, and, assuming you have given yourself enough time to do so, don't be afraid to rethink your approach.

You will begin to feel confident in your drafting process once you have figured out what works for you. Comparing your approach to others can help you reflect on your process, but you'll find that everyone is different. Yadirys and Hyesu think in terms of one continuous, rolling draft, but Karina and Abigail draw clear distinctions between drafts. However, all of them remain open and flexible, using early drafting as a basis for revision and experimentation toward a final, high-quality product.

YADIRYS
Boston University

When I think about drafts, I don't think [of] a first, second, and third draft, and then a final draft. I feel like there is a flow to the whole thing. Let's say that one day you start your first draft and you write it down. But then, a minute later, you start to change things — you're going to constantly be changing things throughout the week. So there really isn't a specific point where [I think] okay, this is my first draft, I'm done with it. This is my second draft. . . . I'm always changing my ideas, I'm always changing my sentences.

14.3

Exercises: drafting

14a Integrate the video.

Gretchen sums up the big idea of this lesson on drafting when she says,

I'll start to type on my computer — and it's usually one sentence. I'll sit there with one sentence. And then I'll have a couple sentences, and then once I get the first paragraph, I just keep going and going. It doesn't always connect. But as long as I have writing, I'll feel good, like I'm getting somewhere. I just have to have something written down.

Gretchen's first draft is all about developing confidence and "feeling good." And yet the other students in this lesson have a slightly different approach to building momentum in their first drafts. Write a substantial paragraph or two, with a topic sentence or mini-thesis, through which you respond to the sound-bite videos in the lesson, like Gretchen's, as you form your own approaches to drafting. You can watch the Lesson 14 Essentials Video, or you can browse the embedded clips in the online edition of this lesson. You might begin by identifying the moments that stand out to you the most. Which student videos seem to make the most sense to you? With whom do you agree? Disagree? What patterns do you find among the student sound bites? Which ideas were the most instructive or helpful to you? What surprised you? How have your own ideas about drafting come into focus through the videos?

14b Create a journal entry or blog.

This lesson urges you to develop your own individualized approaches to drafting as part of your writing process, and this exercise asks you to use a journal to do so. Write two short paragraphs in your journal: one that describes your plan for your first draft on an upcoming writing assignment and a second one that reflects on your experiences after you have drafted. Describe some past experiences with drafting that will influence your plans for the upcoming assignment. Do you have a specific drafting approach in mind, like those listed in section 14.2, that you think is well suited for the assignment? After the assignment is complete, upon reflection, evaluate how well your drafting plan worked and what you can learn from the experience for next time. You could keep this journal using only print/text, or you could make an online blog, a video blog, or an audio podcast that captures your unfolding thoughts and experiences in your actual voice.

14c See yourself as a writer.

In a page or two, describe the evolution of your approaches to drafting since you began writing. Where and when did you start to develop intentional strategies for drafting? What major events, assignments, and papers have influenced your approaches to drafting along the way? Which teachers or classes have reshaped the ways you draft? What was your sense of drafting before you began reading this lesson? What is your approach now that you have finished this lesson? In what ways can you imagine your drafting process changing beyond college? How does your development as a writer compare with what other students, such as Matt ("The difference in the approach from high school to college is for one, I'm not cranking papers out the night before. I'm not handing in first-draft stuff. It's definitely a process."), said in their interviews?

14d Invent your writing.

Section 14.2 of this lesson gives you six recommendations for building momentum in a first draft. In five complete sentences, describe how five of these recommendations could be applied to a writing assignment you are working on in this class, or in another class (if you are not currently writing in this course).

14e Analyze student writing.

Read at least one of the featured student interviews in the text, and study, in particular, their discussion about their approach to drafting. Or, you might choose to browse the interviews in the LaunchPad for a student like you or who is interesting to you. Compile a list of five or so different things the student said in their interview about their approach to drafting. Then compare their interview, your list, and, their writing sample. Can you see connections between their discussion of their drafting and their written product?

Your instructor might ask you to interview a classmate instead of reading one of the interviews in the text or online. Or you might compare what you found in one of the textbook interviews to an interview with your classmate. If you interview a classmate, ask them about their drafting technique for a writing assignment. Do they use the same approach for each assignment? What are the most prominent benefits of their approach to drafting? What aspects of drafting are they confident about? When do they struggle? And, most important, can you identify connections between their drafting technique and their written products? Can you see how drafting impacts the quality and experience of their writing?

14f Revise repeatedly from feedback.

Examine a writing assignment you are currently working on or one that you wrote recently, perhaps in another class or in high school. Describe in a written paragraph, video selfie, or audio podcast some specific ways that you can use the ideas from Lesson 14 to improve your writing through better drafting. Ideally, you can take a current draft of your writing to the writing center, a peer workshop, or your instructor's office hours and ask "What are the weakest aspects of this draft, and how could I have drafted more effectively to address those weaknesses?"

LESSON 15

Revising

Revise Repeatedly from Feedback.

15.1 [WHY]

Why you should Revise Repeatedly from Feedback.

You have scheduled a plan on your calendar (Lesson 10), brainstormed (Lesson 11), begun your research (Lesson 12), mapped a structure for your writing project (Lesson 13), and written a first draft (Lesson 14). So you are probably more than halfway through your current writing assignment in terms of the mental investment, physical energy, and number of hours required to do your best work. Congratulations! But now is the moment of truth: It's time to revise your first draft.

Unless you happened to start reading this textbook with this lesson, you are probably aware that every lesson and every piece of advice hinges on **Revising Repeatedly from Feedback**. From the introduction of this book to its end, **RRFF** is discussed as *the* key to college writing. It's the single most essential thing for you to do in order to become a college writer. But don't just take my word for it:

GRETCHEN
Boston University

The most helpful thing a writing professor has ever done for me was to push me to re-edit papers over and over again. Even when I thought they were perfect, even if I did get an okay grade, [my teacher] would push me to look at it in a different way, or add more, take parts out. It taught me that nothing's ever perfect, and even the best writers have edited many times. We went to the archives that Boston University has of old notes from journalists, and we saw how many times they rewrote, and rewrote, and rewrote books. It was kind of fun to see that they mess up, too!

KENDRA
Michigan State University

I think a writer, a good writer, has to be able review their papers and not just sit down and write a final [draft]. They have to get peer edits and other people to look at [their work]. When you're [writing], it'll make sense to you when you reread it, but other people might not have the same train of thought or background knowledge that you have. So it's good to get other input, so that when you do share it, other people can follow your writing.

PHILLIP
Santa Fe College

Any college paper I've ever written [has] always been multiple drafts. . . . In this particular assignment, I went through about five drafts, which is very important. That's how you catch your mistakes, that's how you hone [the draft], that's how you confront problems of style, sometimes discarding entire paragraphs if they didn't make sense. There are definitely multiple drafts.

DAN
Michigan State University

In high school the process was always: Produce your first draft . . . proofread it, and turn it in. [Then] get some notes from your teacher, make those changes, and then turn your paper back in, and you get a 100 percent. That was "revising." . . . Now revising is more like [this process]: Get something on the page and start reading through it all. I go through it all [and say to myself]: "Yeah, that's a good point, let me figure that out a little more, let me kick away some of the weeds around it, delete some stuff." . . . So, revising is very much a systematic thing. I'll put something on the page, read through it, cut what I can, bring out what I can, get to the bottom of the page. Do it again, and just keep doing it, and keep doing, and keep doing it.

MARCUS
California State University, San Marcos

The process that I went through developing this essay was to do peer editing, peer revising. For example, if we have an essay that's a six-page requirement, we would be given a day to come up with two pages, which would be an introduction and two body paragraphs. We'd bring it to class; we'd meet up with two different classmates, and we would go over it. The professor would give us something to [focus our] notes on the side of the paper: Is the intro a narrative? Is it a stat[istic]? Does it relate to the assignment? Does it connect to the thesis? So we would start off there, and then go to the body paragraphs, to the [evidence]. Is it relating to the text? Or is it just [an unrelated] fact? We would bring in two copies so that [two readers] could edit it. We would get different, multiple views about it. . . . [This process] allows us to be concrete and to not have to do everything at the end.

ANGELA
Red Rocks Community College

I love criticism . . . honest criticism. I think it helps me see where I need to go. Being able to go back in the classroom among peers, sharing our writing, and not being able to see something yourself and having somebody else see — it is key. Being able to go back and sit in front of the computer and rewrite something that, to you made sense, but really didn't make sense to anybody else [is how I've] learned to develop [my] writing through other people.

NANAISSA
Lansing Community College

I mostly look for feedback when it's closer to the end. I'm not a [native] English speaker; so I know I won't understand anything and it will be frustrating just to have someone saying, "Okay, what are you trying to say?" So, I'm going to work a lot on myself, work on my English, work on my structure, and it's only after that that I'm looking for feedback.

SALHUANA
Red Rocks Community College

When I lived in Peru, I had the great opportunity to work with a linguist who was [also] my boss. She wrote some books, and I saw how hard it was for her to write the books. She wrote a lot of drafts, and I never understood why. And she told me, "Salhuana, you have to do this!" . . . She had many, many, many, many drafts.

PRACTICE Section 15.1 [Why] is comprised almost completely of student sound bites. Why did we make that choice? Each sound bite is somewhat like a mini-manifesto on the connections between revising and becoming a college writer. What does your mini-manifesto sound like? Write a lengthy sound bite or short paragraph that represents your position on the role of revision and feedback in your writing.

15.2 [HOW]

How to Revise Repeatedly from Feedback.

So, assuming you have developed a first draft through a series of careful stages in your writing process, you have reached a big moment: It's time to **Revise Repeatedly from Feedback**.

But what does it really mean to *revise*? What kind of *feedback* is most effective, and how can you get it? Why *revise repeatedly* and not just once to fix typos and turn in your assignment?

1) Revise.

CARA
Metropolitan State University of Denver

If you're writing or doing any kind of editing, you get so close to what you're doing that it's impossible to see the big picture. Having a little break can allow you to see [your paper] with fresh eyes. I do that and have somebody else [read it]. . . . Other people's perspective[s] give me ways to improve and strengthen it so that [my writing] is the best it can be.

To *revise* your writing means to *re-vision* it—to see it again, or *see it from a different perspective*. An inexperienced writer might equate revision with spell-checking and looking for typos, but revision is more than that. Fixing mistakes is important, but it occurs later in the writing process, as explained in the next lesson on proofreading. *To deeply revise, you must work to see your draft from a different viewpoint*, which is why feedback is integral to revising effectively.

Revising is large scale and global (across the entire writing project). Proofreading is small scale and local (within the tiny grammatical unit of each sentence). If you were to film an experienced writer revising from feedback, it's

likely that you would see 50 percent or more of a first-draft change as a result. Revision often requires entire paragraphs to be rearranged, deleted, moved around, rewritten, and significantly reworked. It might require that completely new paragraphs be written.

Proofreading merely fixes words and sentences. If your second draft physically looks a lot like your first one, then you probably did not *re-vision* your work; you did not deeply reshape its thoughts and structures. You probably only polished the surface—which is *not* revision. Revision is seeing your

writing from a new perspective. Michael talks about starting a paper over again from the beginning, once he realizes that his draft is "structurally unsound." For him, becoming a college writer means making mistakes and learning from them. It means committing to large-scale revision.

Seeing your writing from a different angle requires feedback. Feedback also makes the work of substantially revising your writing much easier. Substantial revision requires courage because it can be scary in the short term to discard entire sections or paragraphs of your work (although, you should save previous drafts electronically in case you need to recover something). Substantial revision requires grit because it can mean that you have to return to research and study to develop new approaches to problems or gaps in your earlier draft.

MICHAEL
Michigan State University

One of the more difficult processes of writing is [knowing and] accepting [when] a paper is structurally unsound. It's the same as when you lose a paper to a computer. You have to start again [like] it's a new paper. You just have to accept that process because if you don't, you're going to get either a bad grade or become a stubborn writer and keep on making [the same] mistake.

So, to revise is to change a draft substantially based upon seeing your writing from a different perspective, based on the feedback you get from readers.

2) Revise Repeatedly.

MATTHEW
Palomar College

Once I have the [draft] paper done, I do share it with my friends. They read it and then I just keep making more copies [until], at the end, I have at least five or six copies with everybody's comments. Then, finally I condense it, and that's the draft. Then, I turn the draft in, and my teacher gives it back to me, and I fix whatever he says [needs fixing]. I keep doing it again. I go and do more research because you can always improve. Once I'm done with that, I turn in [my final paper]. But it's a long process. It doesn't take one day. I do not procrastinate when it comes to writing.

Matthew writes a rough draft with multiple readers, a second draft reviewed by his instructor, and a third and final draft. Earlier, this book addressed the idea that there is no one single writing process: Each writer has a slightly different approach to each step in his or her process.

Another reason that it makes sense to talk about writing processes (plural) is that *writing is a recursive process*, which means that it is neither linear nor lockstep. When something is *recursive,* it loops back on itself and is interconnected. The word *recursive* is defined by repetition. Notice how many of the central ideas in this textbook (like **RRFF** and research-based writing) are repeated throughout the lessons. When a process is recursive, it is also integrated, meaning that the parts are connected and repeated. Matthew's revision process involves a lot of readers giving him a lot of feedback on a lot of different drafts. It's recursive.

Writing processes are individual (different for everyone) and recursive (repeating). Writing does not happen one absolute step at a time, with each stage, from brainstorming to organizing to drafting to revising, only happening once and only happening in one order. As you revise, you will likely repeat earlier steps that you took in your writing process. For example, Matthew returns to research before he revises his final draft.

When you eventually proofread (Lesson 16), you are almost certain to resee and reshape parts of paragraphs, which means that you may return to revision as well. While separating out stages of the writing process can be helpful conceptually, the process is never completely linear, from one starting point, in one direction, to a finish line. You will inevitably repeat different steps of your writing process as you revise, and that is a good thing.

Hopefully, you are now convinced of the benefits, wisdom, and effectiveness of **Revising Repeatedly from Feedback**. But I suspect that you have probably been mostly focused on the words *Revise* and *Feedback*. Because writing is a nonlinear, recursive process, true revision often requires multiple rounds of drafting, getting feedback, and then more revising. It's like a filtration process: The more often you run water through a filter, the cleaner it will become.

For a college writing assignment of substantial length (perhaps four pages or more), I recommend at least four drafts: first draft, second draft, third draft, final draft. The second and third drafts are substantial revisions of the previous drafts, and these revisions should respond to substantial feedback from an informed audience, ideally in a writing conference. The more often you revise a project through a series of drafts—the more

times you revise *repeatedly*—the better your writing will be. Revision itself is a recursive process.

Effective revision is rarely a one-step process. Revising repeatedly not only improves your current writing performance, it also strengthens your overall writing abilities—it makes you a better writer in general because **RRFF** is the most effective and efficient exercise for building your writing muscles. Period.

3) Revise Repeatedly from . . .

Unlike inexperienced writers—who sometimes base their writing on their own thoughts and feelings without thinking of readers (*writer-based* prose)—experienced writers create *reader-based* prose, which takes into account the reader's point of view (see Lesson 3: Audience). As a college writer, aim to write *reader-based* prose: Make sure your insights, claims, and arguments are based upon concrete evidence (Lesson 6). One of the purposes of this textbook is to

Gandee Vasan/Getty Images

help you develop your writing so that you become a pro. As you become a college writer, you mature from an amateur to a professional who can perform a job based upon talent, expertise, and education.

Becoming a pro at college writing means becoming a pro at revising. Becoming a pro at revising means making revisions based on something concrete: feedback. As you've read earlier in this text, college writing is defined by its use of sources. It is based on concrete evidence and support. Amateur writing is based on ideas that flow easily or accidentally from the novice writer's stream of consciousness or from easy-to-find, low-quality resources. Professional writing is built on careful evaluation and integration of high-quality sources. For Michelle, each new draft is defined by the new ideas she adds, ideas that come from feedback. Each new draft is based upon specific advice or evidence.

MICHELLE
California State University, San Marcos

The difference between drafts for me is [how much I've] improved on my ideas. How far did I come from the first draft to the second draft? Did I make a better point? Did I expand on my idea? Did I make a new point? I always figure out what needs to be improved [by] giving my papers and edits to different people to read. I always want to get more opinions, and, the better the opinion, the better my draft is going to become.

Serious revision is based on serious feedback, so *revising* also means basing your revisions on strong, specific reasons. Specific, pointed feedback is key for your development as a writer.

4) Revise Repeatedly from Feedback.

If you ask your roommate to give you feedback on your draft, he or she may compliment your writing because they like you and see the best in you. Or your roommate might dismissively say: "Looks great, nice font, let's go out." To your *uninformed* roommate, your draft may look impressive because you have no doubt put a lot of thought into the assignment, the research, and the class. Your draft *will* look great to someone who doesn't understand the contexts of the assignment, which is why their feedback is unlikely to help you revise substantially. Your roommate, friend, or parent is more likely to be helpful when it comes to proofreading and fixing errors because that generally requires only the ability to locate mistakes in terms of readability on the sentence level. But, in order to revise based upon something solid and helpful, your readers need to be *informed*.

HARLEY
Red Rocks Community College

When revising drafts, I spend a lot of time going from my computer, to the writing center, to my friends and family, back to the writing center. There are [times] I've spent three or four days in the writing center. . . . So, I like feedback and criticism from everybody. But sometimes, it's not as good getting feedback from people like your brother, or your mom, because they're biased, or they're giv[ing] advice that really doesn't relate. . . . But the writing center is one of the best resources because you get an unbiased approach from an instructor who doesn't know you.

Typically, the most informed reader for a college writing assignment will be your instructor. I encourage you to visit your instructor during office hours. Most instructors I know are thrilled when students stop by for help to think through questions and challenges. In addition, most college campuses have writing centers staffed by tutors who are specifically trained to provide informed feedback. Your instructors and writing center tutors are *professionals* at giving feedback; it's what they are *paid* to do. You can't get much more informed than that. Beyond college, you often pay hundreds of dollars an hour for professional feedback and editing on your writing, so why not use this resource in college? (After all, you most likely have already paid for these services through your tuition and student fees.)

Ideally, your writing class involves peer workshop sessions in which your instructor helps train the class on ways to respond to each other's drafts effectively. Regardless, your classmates are also *informed* readers who can provide effective feedback because they, too, are integrated in the contextual network of the assignment, including audience, prompt, rubric, genre, and so on. Feedback in writing workshops among your classmates is by no means a one-way street, either. That is, you will learn a lot about your own writing and your own draft through the process of evaluating your classmates' writing, as Michael has found.

MICHAEL
Michigan State University

I have moments of clarity, understanding, and self-realization when I'm teaching somebody else, or when I'm [suggesting] revisions to somebody else. When I'm explaining a revision, I feel more competent because I can say a specific thing that will make sense. I'll remind myself that I'm a fairly competent writer.

If writing is defined as a dynamic relationship between a writer, audience, and topic, then you will need to gather feedback from *informed readers. Informed readers* are those who have knowledge of the specific contextual relationships of the assignment and who have some training and direction when it comes to giving college writers feedback on their work. The more professional and the more informed your readers, the better the feedback and, therefore, the better your revision will be.

Once you have scheduled a session with an informed reader, the next task is to manage the very valuable time you have together to work on your draft. You will want to (1) plan ahead for the session, (2) make the most of the session in progress, and then (3) integrate the feedback into your revised drafts.

Lesson 3: Audience offers effective strategies for *interacting* with your readers. The key is to prepare and to ask questions that strengthen and integrate the relationships between you, your audience, your topic, and context. To make the most of a writing conference and to get helpful feedback from your readers, ask specific questions about the particular context of your writing. For example:

- Does this draft seem to respond to the prompt/rubric?

- What do we know about the audience for this assignment and does my draft seem to connect with that audience?

- What do you think my main point is, and is that claim either too broad or too narrow?

What's most important is that you begin a writing conference with specific questions that you are genuinely thinking about.

Deonta has learned to focus his writing conferences on the structure, organization, and flow of his papers, so he asks his readers to focus their feedback on those issues specifically.

DEONTA
University of North Carolina, Chapel Hill

When it comes to revising, I like to revise my papers at least twice, sometimes three times if possible. I will typically go to the writing center or I'll talk to the professor or the TA about the paper to get their feedback. When revising I'm looking for how well paragraphs flow, how they connect to each other, making sure the organization of the paper [works] well—and also making sure that my thesis is strong and my conclusion is also pretty strong.

Gathering high-quality feedback doesn't happen by accident. It is often the result of a well-prepared writer who comes to a draft workshop with a printout of the prompt and specific, critical questions about the draft in hand.

If you are invested in your writing, then it may sting a little when you recognize problems in your draft. After all, you put in a lot of hard work and want to be understood. For example, when I was new to publishing, it took me about three years of having readers and editors challenge me with their feedback before I could get my own ego out of the way. We all have emotional ties to our writing. When you are in a workshop session, my strong advice is to do your best to *only capture* what your readers are saying during the session itself. Do *not* try to defend or disagree with their criticism; during the conference, just record that

feedback so you can evaluate it later, alone, when the atmosphere will be less emotionally charged.

BRAD
University of Florida

I appreciate it when teachers reveal to me something about my point [in my draft] that I didn't recognize while writing. . . . I think it's also important to realize that when getting feedback, that you can be offended sometimes. It's your baby, especially if you take writing seriously, and you've agonized over your paper for, say, three weeks. But [I] also realize that [giving feedback] is the professor's job and that they come from a good place. If [you've made] a personal, creative choice [in your writing] and your teacher doesn't like it, that doesn't mean it's bad; it could just mean that's not her personal taste; so, you don't have to completely abandon it.

Remember, the *entire point* of revision is to *re-vision* your draft from a new perspective. So after getting your readers' feedback, take a second pass through their comments and sort out the ones that make sense to you, as opposed to the ones that don't add up, as Brad suggests. Not all feedback will be perfectly on target, so it's up to you to decide which recommendations to integrate into your revised draft and which ideas to disregard. If you have a second workshop session on the assignment, then you can ask questions about the new draft based upon previous feedback. For example, you might ask, "Does the new approach seem to address the concern that my last reader had?" Gather feedback without being defensive during a draft workshop, and then sort through the suggestions later as you revise.

15.3

Exercises: revising

15a Integrate the video.

In his interview, Vinh-Thuy describes his revising approach:

> Sometimes I can [write] the [first] draft and feel really good about it. And then I'll do my second draft, and then I'll go into the writing center for the third draft, for the very final draft. Sometimes I go in the middle [of my process]. So there's no[t] really one time in which I go into the writing center. It's all about how well I can write that particular essay or paper. I'll go in at the point where I really do need help starting the paper or ending the paper, or gathering enough evidence. So it depends: I don't only have one single location in my writing process that I need to visit the writing center for.

Write a substantial paragraph or two, with a topic sentence or mini-thesis, through which you respond to the sound-bite videos in the lesson, like Vinh-Thuy's, as you form your own approaches to revising. You can watch the Lesson 15 Essentials Video, or you can browse the embedded clips in the online edition of this lesson. You might begin by identifying the moments that stand out to you the most. Which student videos seem to make the most sense to you? With whom do you agree? Disagree? What patterns do you find among the student sound bites? Which ideas were the most instructive or helpful to you? What surprised you? How have your own ideas about revising come into focus through the videos?

15b Create a journal entry or blog.

This lesson urges you to develop your own individualized approaches to revising as part of your writing process, and this exercise asks you to use a journal to do so. Write two short paragraphs in your journal: one that describes your plan for revising on an upcoming writing assignment and a second one that reflects on your experiences after you have revised. Describe some past experiences with revising that will influence your plans for the upcoming assignment. Do you have a specific revising approach in mind, like those listed in 15.2, that you think is well suited for the assignment? After the assignment is complete, upon reflection, evaluate how well your revising plan worked and what you can learn from the experience for next time. You could keep this journal using only print/text, or you could make an online blog, a video blog, or an audio podcast that captures your unfolding thoughts and experiences in your actual voice.

15c See yourself as a writer.

According to Dan,

> In high school, the process was always: Produce your first draft, proofread, and turn it in. [Then] get some notes from [your] teacher, make those changes, and then turn your paper back in, and you get a 100 percent. That was "revising." Now revising is more like: Get something on the page and start reading through it all. I go through it all [and say to myself]: "Yeah that's a good point, let me figure that out a little more, let me kick away some of the weeds around it, delete some stuff." So, revising is very much a systematic thing. I'll put something on the page, read through it, cut what I can, bring out what I can, get to the bottom of the page. Do it again, and just keep doing it, and keep doing, and keep doing it.

In a page or two, describe the evolution of your approaches to revising since you began writing. Where and when did you start to develop intentional strategies for revising? What major events, assignments, and papers have influenced your approaches to revising along the way? What particular teachers or classes have reshaped the ways you revise? What was your sense of revising before you began reading this lesson? What is your approach now that you have finished this lesson? In what ways can you imagine your revising process changing beyond college? How does your development as a writer compare with what other students said in their interviews, such as Dan, who approaches revision differently in college?

15d Invent your writing.

Section 15.2 of this lesson discusses four aspects of **RRFF**. In four complete sentences, map out how each of these four recommendations could be applied to a writing assignment you are working on in this class, or in another class (if you are not currently writing in this course).

15e Analyze student writing.

Kendall reports:

> I find it extremely helpful to have peer feedback inside the classroom, especially when [my readers] want to help. A lot of people will just look through [a paper] and say, "Oh, it's fine." [However,] if you actually have a student who is really good and giving you true feedback, then you do get a lot from it. [It's helpful when] they can say, "Well, I'm not really understanding what you're trying to get across right here. Can you go a little bit more in depth? Or, can you give me a little bit more [of an] introduction right here before you go into ideas that aren't really backed up?" The [writing] center does really help, [too], but having someone who is in your class day-to-day, who's with you, who knows what you're going through—I find that really helpful.

Read at least one of the featured student interviews in the text, and study, in particular, their discussion about their approach to revising and feedback. Or, you might choose to browse the interviews in the LaunchPad for a student, such as Kendall. Compile a list of five or so different things the students said in their interview about their revising and feedback process. Then compare their interview, your list,

and their writing sample. Can you see connections between their discussion of their writing process and their written product?

Your instructor might ask you to interview a classmate instead of reading one of the interviews in the text or online. Or you might compare what you found in one of the textbook interviews to an interview with your classmate. If you interview a classmate, ask them about their revising technique for a writing assignment. Do they use the same approach for each assignment? What are the most prominent benefits of their approach to revising? What aspects of their revising are they confident about? When do they struggle? And, most important, can you identify connections between their revising technique and their written products? Can you see how revising impacts the quality and experience of their writing?

15f Revise repeatedly from feedback.

Matt observes:

> In my nutrition class I went through the same [writing] process as I did in English, going through numerous drafts with classmates. I went to class with copies so they could read them and give me their feedback. I ended up tweaking a lot of things [and learned] how to put an equation into a paper. Peer feedback definitely brought my writing together and made it make a lot more sense. Having peer review as part of revision was key.

This lesson presents four pieces of advice in section 15.2 How to Revise Repeatedly from Feedback. Follow as much of that advice as you can for a current writing assignment, perhaps in a class outside of English or composition, like Matt does. Ideally, you can take a current draft of your writing to the writing center, a peer workshop, or your instructor's office hours and ask, "What are the weakest aspects of this draft, and how can I revise effectively to address those weaknesses?"

Proofreading

**Use professional proofreading techniques
to help you find errors.**

ESSENTIALS VIDEO

Visit the LaunchPad for *Becoming a College Writer* to watch the Lesson 16 Essentials Video.

16.1 [WHY]

Why you should use professional proofreading techniques to help you find errors.

SALHUANA
Red Rocks Community College

My grammar is the last part that I check. First are my thoughts.

Lesson 15 defines **revision** as *re-vision*: seeing your writing from a new perspective and making large-scale changes to your draft, primarily at the paragraph level or larger. This lesson defines **proofreading** as: copyediting correcting surface errors and mechanical mistakes, primarily on the sentence level or smaller. Both lessons urge you to separate revision and proofreading as distinct steps in your writing process because, when you confuse the two, you are less likely to do either one effectively.

Salhuana, a native Spanish speaker, knows that the quality of her thoughts comes *before* grammatical correctness, even when writing in another language. Proofreading happens *after* you have done substantial revision and are close to turning in your final paper. It is typically one of the last steps in the writing process. Likewise, once Hyesu knows that her argument and ideas are sound, she turns her attention to sentence-level concerns like diction and punctuation.

HYESU
University of Florida

Once I get to a point that I know my argument is coherent, then I start looking for more language-related [issues], like, "Did I use the correct word in this instance? Is this verb tense the correct one? Could I change the verb tense in this sentence to make it more impactful to the reader?" So that's my proofreading stage. It's very minute details. My revision is more for structural things, and the proofreading is more for diction, punctuation, and how one sentence flows into the next one.

Of course we all fix our writing on the fly as we type or write — that's only natural. You might not know any other way to work, and you might be relatively successful at proofreading-as-you-go. On the other hand, worrying too much about mechanical correctness as you draft and revise can hang you up and disrupt your flow. The most important thing is to be deliberate, conscious, and focused during each development stage as you work.

No singular approach will be perfect for every writer, and no singular approach will work for you on every occasion. But approaches that encourage strong connections between an author, audience, and topic (Part One) and strategies that compel you to **Revise Repeatedly from Feedback** (Lesson 15) are worth the investment.

Because writing can be a complex pursuit, many writers find it helpful to focus on one goal at a time. This is why I suggest you break your writing down into a series of manageable tasks, setting aside time specifically for proofreading: "Monday I will read and research. Tuesday I will organize. Wednesday I will draft. Thursday I will get feedback. Friday I will revise. Sunday I will proofread."

Proofreading brings you closer to your final product.

Proofreading is the beginning of the endgame of your writing process. You can now see the light at the end of the tunnel — the finish line is in your sights. Keep the following principles in mind so you can sprint across the finish.

- **First principle:** Proofreading requires great concentration. This means that you should plan your official, final proofreading for the end of your writing process: You don't want to have to do it twice.

- **Second principle:** Proofreading can be a challenge because after looking at your writing for so long, you may not be able to see the mistakes. As you reread your draft, the voice in your head tends to correct typos so that you don't notice them.

- **Third principle:** Proofreading is mostly (but not exclusively) focused on sentence-level concerns. Proofreading concentrates primarily on sentences as grammatical and logical units.

- **Fourth principle:** You can sometimes introduce new errors as you revise; so think of copyediting as a final, pristine, perfect cleaning. You don't want to

sweep your floor before house guests arrive if the soccer team hasn't come home yet after a muddy workout.

When I teach my students about proofreading as one of the final stages in their writing process, I begin by asking: "How many of you have been taught that you need to proofread carefully to eliminate mistakes before you turn in your paper?" Nearly everyone raises their hands. My follow-up question is then: "How many of you have been taught *specific techniques* for how to proofread?" Rarely do students raise their hands in response to that question.

"So how do you proofread your paper?" By far, the most common answer is "I just read over it, looking for errors," or "I just use grammar checker." But those routine, almost unconscious approaches don't address the first and second principles in the list to the left. You need a conscious strategy to see beyond the voice inside your head in order to notice what you have literally written. Developing a conscious proofreading strategy is part of becoming a college writer. Follow, for example, Deonta's routine and designate a specific time late in your writing process for proofreading.

DEONTA
University of North Carolina, Chapel Hill

When I was in high school I didn't do a lot of proofreading. I had a bad habit of writing papers the day before they were due. So proofreading wasn't really something I could do. But now that I've been in college, since I've been planning out papers and doing them in advance, I've started to do proofreading after I've made final revisions. So once I make sure that everything is the way I like it, I go back and proofread the paper to see if there are any errors I made, like spelling, grammar, punctuation.

You owe it to yourself and your readers to be as error-free as possible.

As a writer, proofreading is ultimately your responsibility — a worthwhile task that can benefit your final paper and better connect you with your readers. Spell checkers and grammar checkers can point you in the direction of correctness, but you still have to do the legwork to get things right.

CATHERINE
Michigan State University

The paper that I [just completed] could have been better proofread. I relied too much on Microsoft Word and not enough on "Oh, that doesn't make sense." For example, you leave a letter off a word, but Microsoft Word doesn't know the difference."

You may have experimented with proofreading techniques such as reading your draft aloud or reading it backward from the last sentence to the first. Those are helpful strategies, but there are other strategies that can be even more reliable so that when you get to the final stages of your process, you can work confidently and efficiently. They are based on the techniques that professional copyeditors use, which are described in detail in section 16.2. But, before we get there, a few more points about the value of proofreading and why the nature of making errors is so often misunderstood.

Proofreading helps you identify places where you need to sort out your thoughts.

GREGG
California State University, San Marcos

When [your readers] stumble and get confused, no matter where it is, it gives you something to go back and look for places you need to clarify.

While proofreading, when you come across a sentence that causes you or your reader to stumble, your first thought should be "How can I straighten out the *thoughts* behind this sentence?" rather than "How can I change a word or two to make this problem go away quickly?" My technique is to *speak* the idea in the sentence out loud to the ceiling *as simply and directly as I can*, without looking at the words I have written down in front of me. Then I replace the confused sentence with a clear one, which is almost always shorter than the original. Most writers approach proofreading as a way to tidy up surface errors, but proofreading is also an effective way to clarify your thoughts.

So, like all stages in the writing process, proofreading is recursive — it loops back on itself. If proofreading can point out places where your *thinking* needs improvement, then you might need to do a little more research, drafting, and revision to solve a problem or to fill a particular gap in your writing. Consequently, you cannot put off proofreading until just an hour or two before the assignment is due because you may find that it takes time to rethink, research, and revise a particular paragraph, section, or segment in your writing.

Errors may distract readers and upset the relationship between you, your audience, topic, and context.

DAN
Michigan State University

You can make people completely lose your point if you're not polished, if you haven't made the right moves in terms of the small things.

Why you should use professional proofreading techniques to help you find errors

You want to make your final drafts (see Lesson 17) as error-free as you can because mistakes will distract your readers, especially if errors pile up. As you move through college writing and into writing as part of your career, you will no doubt conduct your work with increasing care and professionalism. Likewise, your motivation to proofread will grow even more positive as you invest in your writing and take pride in your finished work.

Of course we are all a little afraid of making an error that will make us look bad. That is a motivator, too, but a negative one. Don't let that anxiety overwhelm you and lead you to focus too much on the wrong things — or to obsess over perfection. Your goal is to proofread your papers carefully in order to connect with your audience.

Identifying the kinds of errors you tend to make will help you prevent future errors.

The title of Lynne Truss's book *Eats, Shoots and Leaves* is a light-hearted play on the importance of commas to differentiate between the diet of a panda bear and someone who robs a diner at the end of their meal. When writers make mistakes, it's not necessarily because they are slacking off. In fact, research shows that we make mechanical mistakes for a variety of reasons, and all errors are not the same.

Individual writers tend to have their own weaknesses when it comes to grammar and punctuation. I personally have been perfectly clear on the differences between the three homonyms *there*, *their*, and *they're* since before high school, but, when typing in a hurry, I frequently type the wrong thing. I don't make this mistake

because I am illiterate or careless; I'm just a lousy, self-taught typist, which means that my keyboard fingers don't agree with the words in my head. I even sometimes type "no" when I mean "know" (and vice versa) because I learned to type more by sound than by sight. I have taught myself to proofread for these particular problems after seeing this pattern repeatedly in my writing.

So, we each have our little quirks, and we should identify them and take responsibility for them by working diligently to improve. However, college-level writers (an enormous, diverse population) tend to make errors for two reasons: (1) They punctuate sentences according to spoken language rather than written principles, and (2) their sentences break down grammatically when their thoughts are unclear. Therefore, the best techniques for proofreading are those that prompt you to notice the differences between what you literally typed and the "voice" inside your head.

Two sentences ago, I typed "there" when I should have typed "their," and I caught this mistake as soon as I reread the sentence. Lessons 22 and 23 on sentences, grammar, and punctuation focus on the most common problems college writers make when writing and punctuating sentences. This lesson is focused on helping you understand the relationship between mechanical error and logical thinking: Most of the mistakes inexperienced writers make are caused by unclear thoughts, not because the writer suddenly forgot the English language.

PRACTICE Write down a list of at least five grammatical mistakes that have been pointed out to you in your writing. Then list

or explain to someone verbally what you believe to be the cause of each mistake. Why do you think you trip up? When you step back and look at this list, does it add up to a lack of confidence in yourself as a writer? If so, then now is a good time to browse through Lesson 2: Writer. After reading about the causes of errors and some initial ideas on how to fix them, write down a specific strategy that might help you overcome errors like the ones on your list.

16.2 [HOW]

How you should use professional proofreading techniques to help you find errors.

Each of the following strategies are based on a central principle: To notice your errors, it helps to decontextualize your writing so that it looks or seems strange or different or "new" to you — even if you've been looking at it for days or weeks. It's possible to see your writing with fresh eyes and through your reader's perspective — to counter the natural "voice inside your head" that might cause you to overlook errors and to counter any writer's fatigue you may feel at this stage of the process.

PRACTICE Like the other "How to" sections in this textbook, the advice that follows offers methods that I encourage you to mix and match according to what works for you. As the student interviews we conducted make clear, we each have different, individual approaches to writing. So, reflect on the tips and experience of others to determine what is best for you.

That said, there are two essential approaches to proofreading that are likely to be the same for everyone.

1) When you are writing something that must be mechanically correct (like a résumé or college paper), then you should separate *revising* from *proofreading*, which means that proofreading should be the last thing you do before submitting or publishing your work. (See also Lesson 17: Publishing.)
2) Proofreading requires significant concentration, so it cannot be rushed, which means that you want to schedule a specific time to proofread. (See Lesson 10: Planning.) Ideally you will proofread at least 24 hours before you intend to turn in your writing.

1) Finish your draft and sleep on it.

Once you finish revising (Lesson 15), leave your text alone while you sleep and then begin proofreading the next morning. Your writing may seem different to you in the light of day after a night of hard work. You are more likely to notice errors that were difficult to see while you were caught up in the demands of drafting and revising. As noted earlier, scientific evidence suggests that your mind will continue to process problems unconsciously while you sleep or dream.

"Sleep on it" may seem like such an obvious piece of advice that we often overlook it, but it could be the very best and most universal approach to seeing your writing freshly, so that you can proofread (or revise) effectively. Sleeping on it is like rebooting your computer to clear the memory and optimize its functions (rebooting seems to solve about 90 percent of computer problems).

CHASE
Santa Fe College

When I proofread, I usually go through it a couple times throughout the day. At the end of the day I'll stop looking at it for a couple of hours and give myself some time to do something else, and I'll come back to it. I think that's a big strategy because when you're so in the forest, you can't really see the trees. . . . So I take myself out of the situation, out of the writing environment, and I come back to it later.

2) Read your draft aloud.

KARINA
University of Florida

To proofread, I read out loud because I hear what's wrong. I [think]: "That does not sound right. That sounds really weird. I'm wording this completely wrong." I read it aloud maybe two or three times, and until it starts sounding a little bit better. I think writing, even if it's academic writing, is like a song or a poem: It has to have a certain ring to it.

As you read your draft aloud, errors that you miss when you read silently will seem to jump out. As you read aloud, pay attention to moments when you pause or stumble: That almost always indicates a problem or mistake. You may need to reread a sentence that you stumble over a couple of times before you can finally locate the problem that caused you to trip. When you get hung up reading your own writing aloud (even for a split second), it's most likely because there is a conflict between your spoken voice, the overpowering "voice inside your head," and the words you wrote down. The whole point

of proofreading is to locate such conflicts so that you can fix problems; so, read slowly and deliberately, paying special attention to snags as you read. Glossing over bumps and hiccups because you are too eager to get to the end defeats the purpose of proofreading.

3) Have someone else read your draft aloud.

Hearing someone else read your draft aloud is a powerful way to identify problems and mistakes in your writing. Asking someone to read your work aloud is also an opportunity to connect with a member of your audience and to get feedback. Your reader doesn't need to be an informed reader or a proofreader, as we suggest for the revising stage. Almost anyone, such as a roommate, parent, or friend can read your words back to you for the purpose of catching mistakes.

Your reader's job is simply to verbalize what's on the page and perhaps point out any errors in punctuation, spelling, or grammar that they notice. During the reading, follow along on your own copy of the text. If your reader is patient, you might ask them to also "speak" each punctuation mark, too (literally saying "comma" or "period" or "quotation mark" and so on). "Speaking" punctuation marks will help draw attention to those mechanics in particular.

Listen carefully for disruptions and circle, highlight, or flag that moment in the text so you can fix the problem later, on your own, once the reading is complete.

It may seem almost magical how readily you will notice errors when someone else speaks your words aloud. So many times I have had students foresee errors in a sentence of theirs that I was *about to read*. I have students read each other's work aloud in class almost daily. Inevitably, within seconds of beginning, the author says something like, "That mistake was so obvious! Why didn't I see it until just now?" Of course, this experience is not magical; it's logical if you define writing as a connection between an author, an audience, and a topic, and if you focus on writing "reader-based prose" (see Lesson 3: Audience). However, your readers will not be perfect; for example, it's easy for them to "read over" and miss problems. After all, they are merely assisting you. Correctness is ultimately the writer's job.

4) Use a ruler or other straight edge to focus on each sentence.

A fantastic high school mentor of mine demonstrated how to use a simple ruler to read closely. Thanks to him, every desktop, backpack, and briefcase of mine since the tenth grade has included a ruler. I use the ruler to focus my visual attention on each sentence, one at a time, flowing down the page, and I use this ruler to underline key phrases and passages to return to later. I pull the ruler with my left hand while I have a pen in my right hand to draw lines and write notes and questions in the margins. I don't use colored highlighters for close reading like this because then I would have to change pens and it would slow me down.

Obviously, this type of slow, methodical reading is for close, study purposes — you probably wouldn't read for pleasure or the daily news this way. And, you don't want to drag a ruler across a computer screen either, which is why I can only proofread on paper, not on a screen.

Readers absorb much more than a single word at a time: We actually read and comprehend more in "word clusters" than in singular sentences. We're adept at anticipating, putting pieces together, and filling in missing elements to help us make meaning as we read. For example, I can conceal most of the vowels in the following phrase, but most likely you will have no problem deciphering it: J*hn k*cked th* s*ccer b*ll.

Proofreading, however, is unlike normal reading. Proofreading is meticulous and slow-paced because, to locate surface errors, you need to focus on distinct grammatical units, not clusters of words. Proofreading requires that you study each sentence on its own, without anticipating what comes next or remembering what came before. Using a ruler to conceal the lines that follow the sentence you're examining helps you focus and attend to surface errors and mechanical correctness. You work line by line and sentence by sentence instead of reading "clusters of meaning." If you want to conceal the sentences surrounding the one you're working on, you might use a ruler to read that sentence in reverse order, as described in the technique that follows.

5) Proofread backward: Read each sentence, beginning with the last one.

HUSSAIN
University of Florida

For grammar and spelling errors I read from the end. I go to the last sentence in my paper and just read backward. I found out when you read forward, you tend to miss a lot of the mistakes you make in spelling or grammar. But if you go backward there's no flow, so you focus on each sentence. . . . And you force yourself to go sentence by sentence instead of skimming.

How you should use professional proofreading techniques to help you find errors

Novelists, journalists, and writers who publish professionally have people whose job it is to correct their surface errors and mechanical mistakes. This textbook and these words you are reading were, in fact, fine-tuned by a team of editors and copyeditors. Professional copyediting is a special skill and professional copyeditors are a rare breed. I don't have the talent to proofread at the level they do, but that doesn't mean I can't learn from them and do a pretty good job locating errors. In fact, I learned to use a ruler to read in reverse order from a professional copyeditor because that's what I watched her do as she helped prepare my manuscript for publication. Hussain doesn't use a ruler to isolate each sentence, but he does read

backward to accomplish the same focus on each grammatical unit.

While you may not have access to a professional copyeditor, you can use the same techniques that they do. Furthermore, pushing yourself to become a better copyeditor of your own work will strengthen your understanding of language and your ability to use writing to make meaning and connect with readers. Proofreading your own work is also an important step in your intellectual development as you take increasing responsibility for your own work — as you come to *own* your work.

Reading backward is a technique that productively disrupts your typical reading

David Butow/Getty Images

pace. To take this disruption one step further, use a ruler to focus on one sentence at a time beginning with the *last sentence* of your paper and working backward to the beginning. With this technique, you hold the ruler *above* the current sentence you are reading, moving the ruler *up* the page, instead of down. If you read from top-to-bottom, your thoughts can't help but linger on the previous sentence you just read as you move to the subsequent one. But if you read backward, against the grain of your typical reading and the "voice inside your head," then you can focus exclusively on each sentence as an isolated grammatical unit.

This technique is the very best advice I have for you as a writer who wants to proofread as carefully as possible. It's the technique I applied once, and only once, on the final draft of this very paragraph before I submitted it to the publisher. Copyediting backward with a ruler sentence by sentence is time-consuming and tedious. It requires extraordinary concentration and patience, which is why I take a quick break every other page or so as I work. I like to get up from my desk and walk around for a minute before plunging back in. Proofreading also requires isolation and quiet. You can't concentrate with precision on your words while also hearing musical lyrics, television dialogue, or a nearby conversation.

6) Proofread on hard copy, and tap each word and punctuation mark.

To be completely honest, not only do I proofread each sentence with a ruler (see #4) reading backward from the last sentence (see #5), I also use a pencil to tap each word and punctuation mark as I say

it out loud. In essence, this combines all of the techniques (#2, #4, #5). Not only do I tap each word as I say it aloud, I also "say" each punctuation mark aloud, too, ("comma," "period," etc.). The result is a small dot above each word or punctuation mark.

Whenever I stumble, my tapping goes out of rhythm and I know there is an error. My mind has wanted to tap a word or punctuation mark that is not there. So I circle the spot and take a moment to find the problem. The tapping technique slows your reading down even more than a ruler alone does. It focuses your attention on each word you have actually typed, as opposed to what the voice inside your head thought it had written. Michael doesn't tap on each word and punctuation mark, but he does focus microscopically on each piece and has a physical interaction with each sentence as he places a check mark between each sentence.

MICHAEL
Michigan State University

[Right before I submit a paper,] I look just at the words and try to stop at each one and assess each sentence as its own organism — like a single-cell kind of thing. If it doesn't have a nucleus, like a verb, it's not going to function. It's not a sentence without a verb. . . . You're not focusing on the paper's cohesion any more, you're just thinking about each letter, . . . scanning sentences, and making check marks. That's a nice way to do it: Checkmark every sentence. And I'm thinking, "This sentence makes sense. All words are there. All words are spelled right or are the correct usage."

How you should use professional proofreading techniques to help you find errors

You can use proofreading techniques to attend to many kinds of mechanical and grammatical problems, not just typos and the conflict between your fingers and your thoughts. If you use the tapping technique in combination with technique #9 (p. 230) you will begin to improve upon your familiar mistakes. As I mentioned earlier, I know the difference between the homonyms *there*, *their*, and *they're*, but I often mistype them when I draft. However, I have trained myself to be aware of this particular problem so that I always do a double tap (a double take) on these words when I proofread.

7) Save a backup copy — and then reformat your paper so it looks very different.

In Lessons 12 through 15, I've urged you to save duplicate copies of your writing in separate, dated electronic files throughout your process. These days, you should also save backup copies online, in the cloud, or by emailing a copy to yourself. I now strongly encourage you to create a new copy of your file to begin your proofreading stage. I like to put the word FINAL (all caps) in the title of this new file. You'll want your previous version(s) to serve as backup in case anything goes wrong.

Much of the advice in this lesson requires you to proofread printouts of your paper. This particular strategy, however, is one that you would apply on-screen. I almost hesitate to share it with you because it risks losing your work or introducing new errors if you do not save a backup copy first and proceed very carefully. **Before you try this technique, triple-check to make sure you have saved a backup copy.**

To make your text look "strange" to you on-screen, change the font to one that you don't like or that you rarely use. While you will submit your final copy in a professional font (see Lesson 17), playing with an unusual font for the purposes of proofreading can help you see your writing differently.

My favorite technique for on-screen proofreading is to temporarily add extra white space between sentences, and then read backward from the last sentence to the first. Use your word processor's search-and-replace function to search for every period and replace it with a period and two paragraph breaks.

The code for a paragraph break is typically ^p. So input ". " for the period in the search window and replace all of the periods with a double paragraph break ". ^p^p" to visually separate each sentence into its own paragraph. Then you will be able to scroll to the end of the document and read each sentence in reverse order, looking for mechanical mistakes. If you used a period in an abbreviation (like Mr. or St.), that will create an accidental break there, but you can just ignore that problem. When you are finished reading through and making corrections, then you *reverse* the search-and-replace (search ". ^p^p" replace all with ". ") to restore the original formatting, although you will need to scan through for any glitches.

Some students like to use this technique and then print out the results rather than using a ruler to read backward, but printing out a text with so much empty white space can consume a lot of paper.

8) Mark corrections on hard copy, input them electronically, and double-check to avoid new errors.

SAMANTHA
California State University, San Marcos

I do my best proofreading when I print [my paper] out and mark it, which sounds so silly because you would think, "Oh, you just do it on your computer. It's easy, it's done." But there's something about [reading my paper] on a computer. I kind of think that it's already done, so I don't look at it as I should. But when I print it out, I can see, "Oh, there are problems." . . . Printing it out is definitely something that's helped me with my proofreading process.

Samantha proofreads more effectively on paper than on-screen, perhaps because it's easier to interact physically with a pencil compared to a keyboard. Or maybe it's just comforting to hold the document in your hands. Another reason to use hard, paper copy is that it can act as kind of a "receipt" or record of the changes you make. Word processors have a "Track Changes" feature (under "Tools") that can accomplish a similar purpose, though it can be cumbersome to read if you are not used to it.

It may surprise you to learn that it is common to introduce *new mistakes* into your final draft while you were trying to fix an earlier problem. This happens because the word processor betrays you, or you focus on only one part of a sentence and fail to reread the sentence as a whole. As a teacher, I often read sentences with entire phrases missing, typically with the end of the sentence completely lopped off. When I point this out to students, they have no idea how it happened, but this is usually caused by the word processor's auto-select function that grabs too many words as you are cutting and pasting: You intend to select just one word or two and then delete or move the words, but the auto-select function grabs and mangles everything up to the end of the sentence.

Therefore, as you input your proofreading changes, you should double-check the new sentence to make sure that you did not accidentally cause a new problem while trying to fix an old one. You might change a word in the beginning of your sentence that does not agree in number or tense with the end of your sentence, and you could very easily overlook the new problem if you do not reread the corrected sentence carefully and entirely.

The best solution I know to the problem of introducing new errors is to mark all of your edits on hard copy, input them electronically, and then go back and double-check each of the edits on paper against what you see on your screen. You are likely to be shocked at how often you make a new mistake while correcting a small thing like adding a comma, moving a misplaced modifier, or deleting an unnecessary phrase. I have often added a comma *before* a particular word instead of *after* where it belongs, just because I am thinking about too many things at once and I fail to concentrate on my typing.

Taking this final step is like sprinting across the finish line in a race: You don't want to undermine all of your effort by letting up at the end. It would be a shame to work so hard on copyediting only to introduce new errors while trying to fix others.

9) Create a journal identifying your typical error types and refer to it before you proofread.

Writing is an open-capacity skill, which means that you are never done improving as a writer. You never close the door on developing as a writer. You need to be open to improvement. There is always another level to aspire to. Many of the most accomplished, award-winning authors talk about constantly refining their craft. Writing is like athletic development: If you continue to train (run, lift weights, practice, etc.), then you will grow stronger. But if you stop working (or if you train improperly), your abilities will decline.

As a college student, you are focused on your development as a writer. You will get better and grow stronger. And the best way to do that is to learn from your mistakes so that you don't repeat them. However, in the frantic rush to meet a deadline, you can often forget to take the time to deeply learn from the assignment you are working on. You can get so caught up in the pressure to finish a paper or earn class credit that you lose sight of the big picture: The larger goal is to improve as a writer. On page 469, Vinh-Thuy describes how his professor drew his attention to problems he was having with colons, semicolons, and dashes. Once he was made conscious of his particular grammatical problems, he learned solutions that he was able to apply.

Lesson 18: Reflecting emphasizes the importance of taking a few minutes after you have completed a college writing assignment to *write down* in a journal the lessons you learned. In order to make the most of your effort, you should methodically note the mechanical mistakes you made so that you do not repeat them. As a teacher, I tell my students that it's okay for them to make a mistake as long as they improve on the problem in their next paper. But if you don't deliberately document the kinds of mistakes you tend to make, then you are likely to forget about the problem in the flurry of writing your next paper.

The first question I ask my students as I begin to give them feedback on their writing is "What kinds of problems were you having on the last assignment that you are working to improve this time?" The purpose of college writing is learning and improving, and learning from your mistakes by writing them down is a shockingly effective way to grow.

As you proofread, look for patterns to the kinds of mistakes you make: What types of mistakes do you make frequently? It is probably not a good idea to list every single mistake you make because that becomes overwhelming. Ask your readers, and especially your instructor, to help you locate patterns to the mechanical errors you make, so that you can study them, practice them, and improve. You will be surprised how quickly you can almost permanently correct a mistake you have been making for many years with just a few minutes of documentation, discussion, practice, and attention! Once you identify a problem, commit to yourself (and to your instructors) to specific improvement on the next paper.

Each writer has his or her own set of individual weaknesses and misunderstandings about grammatical and mechanical issues; so the best way to grow is to identify your particular concerns and then customize intentional strategies to improve upon them. For example, Nanaissa puts English adjectives in the wrong place (after the noun) because that's grammatically correct in her native French language. Once she is aware of her tendency to make that mistake in English, her radar will always be "on" while proofreading.

NANAISSA
Lansing Community College

In French you don't say "the blue car." You say "the car blue." I'm always inversing that, and they're always catching it: "Mm-mm, this goes the opposite. This goes the other way." I have a really hard time finding it because when I read it, I can't see it.

To fully integrate the lessons you learned from careful copyediting, you should document the patterns of errors you make by *writing them down in a journal*, even if this journal is simply an email that you send to yourself. So, the next time you begin to proofread, the first thing you should do is review your journal to focus your attention on learning from your previous mistakes. (Funny story: In the rough draft of the previous sentence, I typed "mitakes" instead of "mistakes." Even professional writers regularly make errors. You just have to learn how to catch them before publishing the final product.)

16.3

Exercises: proofreading

16a Integrate the video.

Write a substantial paragraph or two, with a topic sentence or mini-thesis, through which you respond to the sound-bite videos in the lesson as you form your own approaches to proofreading. You can watch the Lesson 16 Essentials Video, or you can browse the embedded clips in the online edition of this lesson. You might begin by identifying the moments that stand out to you the most. Which student videos seem to make the most sense to you? With whom do you agree? Disagree? What patterns do you find among the student sound bites? Which ideas were the most instructive or helpful to you? What surprised you? How have your own ideas about proofreading come into focus through the videos?

16b Create a journal entry or blog.

This lesson urges you to develop your own individualized approaches to proofreading as part of your writing process, and this exercise asks you to use a journal to do so. Write two short paragraphs in your journal: one that describes your plan for proofreading on an upcoming writing assignment and a second one that reflects on your experiences after you have proofread. Describe some past experiences with proofreading that will influence your plans for the upcoming assignment. Do you have a specific proofreading approach in mind, like those listed in section 16.2, that you think is well suited for the assignment? After the assignment is complete, upon reflection, evaluate how well your proofreading plan worked and what you can learn from the experience for next time. You could keep this journal using only print/text, or you could make an online blog, a video blog, or an audio podcast that captures your unfolding thoughts and experiences in your actual voice.

16c See yourself as a writer.

Chatiana explains:

When I proofread, I reread my paper about three or four times just to make sure there are no misspelled words, no incorrect sentences, no comma splices, no imprecise language — and to make sure my details are accurate. Then I read it backward, from the last paragraph, to make sure that my sentences are flowing correctly. In college I was taught to read backward so I can check my sentences.

Chatiana also says that learning to proofread was part of her development as a college writer. In a page or two, describe the evolution of your approaches to proofreading since you began writing. Where and when did you start to develop intentional strategies for proofreading? What major events, assignments, and papers have influenced your approaches to proofreading along the way? What particular teachers or classes have reshaped the ways you proofread? What was your sense of proofreading before you began reading this lesson? What is your approach now that you have finished this lesson? In what ways can you imagine your proofreading process changing beyond college?

16d Invent your writing.

In section 16.1, I encouraged you to avoid significant proofreading until the last the steps of your writing process. But once you have experience and confidence in your own approach to proofreading, that confidence might help you in the earliest stages of your writing process. Write a short paragraph that begins with this sentence: "My plan is to proofread my next writing assignment on [indicate date here] by using [indicate technique from section 16.2 here], and doing so will help the early stages of my writing process in the following ways: [brainstorm a list of benefits here]." This exercise is meant to illustrate what Part Three has been saying all along: Your writing process is recursive and interconnected, which means that the earliest stages and the final stages all work together like the reciprocating parts of an engine.

16e Analyze student writing.

Read at least one of the featured student interviews in the text, and study, in particular, their discussion about their approach to proofreading. Or you might choose to browse the LaunchPad interviews for a student like you or who is interesting to you. Compile a list of five or so different things the student said in their interview about their proofreading processes. Then compare their interview, your list, and their writing sample. Can you see connections between their discussion of their writing process and their written product?

Your instructor might ask you to interview a classmate instead of reading one of the interviews in the text or online. Or you might compare what you found in one of the textbook interviews to an interview with your classmate. If you interview a classmate, ask them about their proofreading technique for a writing assignment. Do they use the same approach for each assignment? What are the most prominent benefits of their approach to proofreading? What aspects of their proofreading are they confident about? When do they struggle? And, most important, can you identify connections between their proofreading technique and their written products? Can you see how proofreading impacts the quality and experience of their writing?

16f Revise repeatedly from feedback.

Examine a writing assignment you are currently working on or one that you wrote recently, perhaps in another class or in high school. Section 16.2 of this lesson discusses nine different proofreading techniques, and in section 16.2.6, I admit that I combine three of these techniques in my personal approach to proofreading. List the technique or combination of techniques you will apply on a current draft, and then analyze and discuss with a writing center tutor or your instructor the errors you located and the lessons you learned from using your (new) proofreading technique!

LESSON 17

Publishing

Publish your writing with pride and purpose.

ESSENTIALS VIDEO

Visit the LaunchPad for *Becoming a College Writer* to watch the Lesson 17 Essentials Video.

17.1 [WHY]

Why you should publish your writing with pride and purpose.

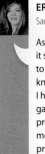

ERICA
Santa Fe College

As I started to compile the paper and it started to come together, I started to be impressed with myself, you know? And the day that it was due, I held the paper in my hand and I gave it to my professor and I said, "I'm proud of myself." And he looked at me and said, "What?" And I said, "I'm proud of myself." And he said, "I don't hear that often. Usually I hear kids say 'Oh, this is awful.'" So I was pleasantly surprised that he was proud of me, too, after he read the paper. He asked me to submit it for a research award, and he referred it to the Honors professor and put it into the mix to have it presented at a conference, which is next weekend.

Think of *publishing* as the moment in which you physically deliver your work to your audience. Writers (and not just college writers) are often required to *submit* their work for approval at the end of their writing process, but the word *submit* seems negative. I prefer the term *publish* because it more directly indicates *an author connecting to an audience about*

a topic. After all, what is the larger purpose of all the work you put into your writing? Is it submitting to an authority for approval? Or is it having something to say and joining a conversation? I argue that the big picture is learning to publish your ideas to an audience, perhaps not in the sense that you are paid to publish, but in terms of relating your work to a *public*.

The English word *publish* derives from a Latin term that translates as "to make public."

The endgame of chess is to capture your opponent's king, the endgame of a soccer match is to score more goals than the other team, and the endgame of legislation is to make laws. In each of those cases, the endgame determines how you approach your process. So, if you define the endgame of your writing process as fixing errors and submitting your work to an instructor, then you are not realizing the full potential of writing. If you conceive of *publishing* as the endgame of your writing process, then you will strengthen your abilities to connect with large and varied audiences. Publishing your writing to a public audience can naturally compel you to make effective choices throughout your writing process, including formatting your final draft carefully and professionally because you begin to see your writing from the perspective of real readers.

You've done great work and want to present it in the best light.

NIA
University of Florida

"Then it was time to turn [my paper] in, and so, I'm sweating. Of course the printer doesn't work. And then . . . I need to get to my professor's office hours. . . . I'm late. I run up her stairs and I have the folder and I have the little disk which is my final project movie. I have all this for her, and I hand her the folder and it's almost like I didn't want to let go. I'm like, "Oh, this is my life I'm handing to you.""

If you have worked hard on your writing, you will naturally want it to look good when you hand it in. The primary reason to format and publish your final draft with care is that you want to have a dynamic relationship between yourself, your audience, and your topic (see A Note to Students and Lesson 1).

In Lesson 6: Evidence, you read how important it is to use high-quality evidence from reputable sources. One of the ways that you can evaluate the credibility of a potential source is the quality of document preparation: Is it professionally written? Error-free? Does it include a thorough bibliography? Does it match the expectations of the appropriate genre? Likewise, the quality with which you prepare your documents indicates that you can be trusted as a writer-researcher, and that you are seriously invested in your work (as argued in Lesson 4: Topic). Publishing with pride, therefore, deepens the connections between you, your audience, and your topic, and shows your respect for your readers.

MARCUS
California State University, San Marcos

I work to pay for school, so I'm busting my butt. When I hand a paper in, it feels great because I know I've taken another step toward achieving my degree. I've taken a step toward obtaining my goal. . . . So, I feel accomplished after every essay I turn in.

You're contributing to an ongoing conversation — and connecting with academic and public audiences.

GREGG
California State University, San Marcos

The best thing about college writing is sharing it with others. And the worst thing about college writing is that so much of the work we do . . . will never be realized. In your composition course your audience is your teacher most of the time. . . . You're thinking, "Okay, my teacher's taking my writing and I'm going to get a grade and then I'm done." . . . [But] if you're doing work that you plan on publishing, your stakes are higher because there's a larger audience. You're not just going for the A. If you shoot for a publishable work, the A is going to happen.

Ultimately, your purpose as a college writer and researcher is to say something to your readers (see Lesson 1: Writer and Lesson 12: Researching). This makes publishing a big part of your writing process. You're ready to add your contribution to the ongoing conversation about your topic. You're ready to publish your work, perhaps not in a professional book or magazine, but at least in the sense of putting your findings in circulation with other writing and research.

You also have the ability to share your writing with public audiences thanks to online networked technologies and social media. Many campuses, including my own, are promoting undergraduate research and publication increasingly. As a result, your teachers may not be the final audience for your writing. They may become coaches or mentors of your writing. (My writing students often call me "Coach Todd," not "Dr. Taylor.")

So, as you complete your writing process and submit your final draft, it's important to stay focused on the "big picture." Stay motivated by what you have to say and your desire to be understood by your audience. At the same time, remember that you're writing within the context of a class and for a grade: There are expectations about how to format your final draft, in terms of correctness and document layout. Which brings us to the goal of this lesson: to help you negotiate the tension between the big picture of sharing your work and the more mundane aspects of publishing your writing when you complete a class assignment.

You have invested a lot of effort into your writing and you want that effort to be apparent to your audience. Format matters. Before your audience reads a single word, they will form a first impression about your final draft based upon how professionally it is presented. In the previous two lessons (15: Revising and 16: Proofreading), I argued that if you have high-quality thoughts, then correct grammar and mechanics are more likely to follow. If you have pride and purpose in your writing, then correct format and document preparation are more likely to follow.

CHASE
Santa Fe College

As far as formatting goes, [no matter] what class it is and how formal the topic is, I'll make sure that my paper is stapled and on clean paper. . . . I format it so that it's very readable — double spaced, easy for my professor to make comments in.

It helps to put yourself in your reader's shoes and to focus on writing "reader-based" prose (Lesson 3: Audience). Imagine the experience of a typical instructor with a stack of papers to grade. If your paper is wrinkled, carelessly formatted, lacking organization, poorly proofread, or fails to respond to the assignment prompt, then your reader has to struggle to overcome the obstacles you have put between your writing and their reading. Sloppiness suggests that you did not care, which will affect your grade and your learning. How would you react if you read something that was meant to be taken seriously but was unfortunately messy or careless?

The physical appearance of your writing establishes an important first connection with your audience.

I urge my students to get in the habit of formatting their documents from the very first draft. I tell them that even a first draft of a college writing assignment needs to include a complete header, a title, page numbers, professional formatting, and a bibliography. Every time we read a student draft in class on the projection screen, I zoom out to the size of the first page so that we can't really make out the words, and I ask, "So, what's your first impression of this document? Is it headed toward a C or D? Or does it look carefully prepared, like an A or B paper?"

Even though publishing or submitting your final draft to your audience happens at the end of your writing process, it's very helpful to get into the habit of cleanly formatting your drafts from the very beginning. That said, I urge you not to get distracted early in your process by all the details of formatting, such as every parenthesis in every citation or the perfect indention of your bibliography. Rather, apply basic formatting from your very first draft: header, title, page/section numbers, font, margins, justification, line spacing, subheadings, and a bibliography.

Different situations call for different formatting standards. If writing is a dynamic relationship between an author, an audience, and a topic (as noted in Lesson 1 and onward), then different relationships can call for different approaches to formatting. If specific contexts like genre, method, discipline, and media further define the relationships between author, audience, and topic, then the formatting choices you make should respond accordingly.

For example, page numbers are essential to conventional paper documents, but technical manuals are often organized by section numbers rather than page numbers because users read such manuals according to indexed topics rather than front-to-back, one-page-after-another. And if your writing is published and read on-screen, then the use of color will be an important formatting concern, whereas a conventional college paper primarily uses black ink. As a writer, you are constantly making choices about your work, and how to format your document is one of them.

BRAD
University of Florida

I think formatting is important. . . . It's part of your grade. . . . And it's exciting, especially when you've dedicated so much time to your writing. Why mess up when it comes to formatting? Why desecrate your own sort of masterpiece?

Many instructors have specific guidelines for you to follow, which makes formatting straightforward for you. *Definitely follow the guidelines you are given.* If your audience has gone to the trouble of spelling out exactly what they expect, then pay careful attention to those expectations. Whether or not you are handed formatting specifications, you should still consider how formatting and publishing define a relationship between you and your audience. What formatting will be best for your reader? What types of connections between you and your reader does the formatting style establish? How do the instructor's formatting guidelines set up a dynamic relationship (Lesson 1), define scope (Lesson 5), address genre (Lesson 7), suggest a method (Lesson 8), and affect mode (Lesson 9)?

Each reader and each writing situation is unique and calls for you, the author, to be responsive to the formatting expectations of your audience. For example, most writing instructors do not care which font you use, as long as your choice is mature and professional, rather than comical or highly stylized. Times or Helvetica are the safest bet. Most writing instructors will not appreciate it if you change fonts within a paper, or if you use a giant font to stretch your words out to fool an assignment's

Why you should publish your writing with pride and purpose

page requirement. (I use word-length guidelines in my assignment prompts to discourage playing with fonts and margins for the purpose of gaming page-length requirements.)

If your instructor provides you with formatting guidelines, great. You know what to do. Otherwise, you can use the "safe bet" formatting guidelines in Section 17.2 to format your document.

Formatting is professional.

Throughout Part Three of this textbook, you have been encouraged to separate each distinct phase of your writing process and to focus deliberately on the strategies that can best help you in that particular moment. Most student writers tend to think of publishing as the final stage in the process, and it usually is. The point of this lesson, however, is to encourage you to focus on formatting as an important, distinct moment in the process as well — a stage that is often overlooked.

When I was in elementary school I was terribly eager to use a brightly colored, clear plastic report binder to hand in my paper — it just seemed cool. More important, it made my writing assignment look and feel professional, which isn't a bad thing as long as the impulse to look professional also works its way into the quality of the writing inside. However, most college writing instructors don't want to see colored plastic report covers anymore. They are much more concerned with the professionalism of the writing and the way the content itself is presented, as Alyssa recognizes.

ALYSSA
Santa Fe College

Sometimes I get nervous once I see everybody else's essay and I think, "Oh, mine doesn't look as cool" or "mine doesn't have a shiny folder on it." But if the content of my essay is good, then I don't need to stress out. I had a paper in my Technical Writing class, and the minimum was seven pages and I did eight. I got to class and my classmates had done like twelve, fifteen pages. And I thought, "This is not going to go well for me." But I wound up getting an A. I was confident in what I had written, and I knew that, had I continued writing just to make my paper longer, it wouldn't have been [as successful.]

When you aim to *publish* for a public audience, you improve your writing.

Throughout your writing process, you might imagine that you will publish your paper in an online blog simultaneously as you submit it to your instructor. You might limit in some ways the readers of your blog, or you might ultimately decide not to publish your work at all. But if you at least *target* a public audience throughout your writing process, your work will almost always be more relevant, engaged, and connected — by definition. If there's a secondary key to successful college writing beyond **Revise Repeatedly from Feedback**, it would be: *Write with a bigger purpose than merely completing an academic assignment. Intend to share your final draft with readers beyond your instructor and classmates.*

PRACTICE Describe either verbally or in writing your emotions when presented with a list of formatting standards for a writing assignment. In the past, what were your thoughts and feelings when an instructor

gave you a list of rules for preparing a paper? What are your thoughts and feelings when you are given an assignment without explicit instructions for formatting? Describe how those past experiences impact your sense of pride and purpose in your writing. How do format instructions impact the earliest stages of your writing process? Are you aware of them at first, or do you ignore them until later? In the past, how have formatting instructions shaped the "endgame" of your writing process?

17.2 [HOW]

How to publish your writing with pride and purpose.

Publish your writing assignments with pride and purpose by asking yourself "What formatting choices will make my work look as *professional* as possible?" Section 17.1 encourages you to begin formatting your documents with care from the first draft, following your instructor's guidelines as indicated in the assignment prompt or on the syllabus. If your instructor does not give you specific guidelines, then you can apply the guidelines in this section. Each formatting aspect discussed below concludes with a bulleted list of "safe bet" standards, meaning that almost every instructor will find these formatting specifications acceptable because they will make your document look professional.

Remember, your document formatting is typically the first impression and first connection you will make with your audience, so make sure your formatting reflects the effort you invested in your work and how good you feel about what you've written.

Africa Studio/Shutterstock

Few writers ever feel like their final draft is perfect, but it is relatively easy to format your document cleanly, which can convey a positive impression of precision and professionalism.

1) Choose your paper/medium.

CATHERINE
Michigan State University

Times New Roman, twelve-point font, one-inch margins all around. I think that's MLA format. Funny story: Lab reports are written in eleven point font, and I was like "What?" I just recently got a printer . . . I usually don't have a staple, but I have gone so far as to go out to a corkboard in the hallway and just pull a staple out and force it through the paper and kind of bend it back. I always print out three copies of my paper. Why? Professor loses one, you can say "This is it." I always email one to myself, too. . . . [But usually] just to cover myself I print out three copies, email it to myself, and I save it on my computer so it's in a lot of different places.

Most college writing assignments are published on paper from a computer printer, very often from a campus printing station. The quality of paper that college writers used was a consideration when typewriters were dominant, but those days are over. If you have your own printer, use a medium-grade paper, perhaps paper with significant recycled content. If you are preparing a very important document like a résumé, then use high-quality paper. Be sure to purchase paper that is optimized for the kind of ink or toner you will use, since ink jet and laser toner printer ink will adhere differently to different types of paper.

"SAFE BET" PAPER STANDARDS

- **Use 8.5 x 11 inch medium-grade white paper.**

- **Match your paper style with the designated ink/toner style, if possible.**

- **Hold documents together with a sturdy paper clip, not staples or a binder.**

- **Printing on only one side of the paper is the safest approach, but printing on both sides is more environmentally friendly.**

In professional settings, writers often exchange and publish their documents electronically. In college, you will probably provide an electronic file and a printout. Ask your instructor for the preferred file format for exchanging documents. The most widely accessible electronic file formats are preferable, if you have the software to prepare your document that way. The preferred formats below are examples of the most popular formats at the time of publication, but these preferences can change quickly as new technologies and software editions emerge:

"SAFE BET" ELECTRONIC FILE STANDARDS

- **Text documents: MS Word is best, but Google docs and PDF can also work.**

- **Movie clips: Quicktime MOV format is best, but MP4 can also work.**

- **Audio files: MP3 format is most universal, but WAV files can also work.**

- **Images: JPG is preferred, but GIF, TIFF, and PNG can work.**

- **Presentation projects: PowerPoint files are most universal, but Prezi and Adobe Spark can also work.**

- **Online documents: HTML files are standard, but WordPress can also work.**

2) Include document headers.

There are two types of document headers: (1) one that you place at the top of the first page in the *body of your document* and (2) a second one that goes at the *top of each page*. The header in the body of your document identifies the author (you), the date, the course, and the instructor. Be *very careful* to spell your instructor's name correctly, and apply his or her proper titles — the safest approach is to use "Professor" as the title, in case you do not know whether your teacher has a PhD. If the assignment is part of a course sequence such as "Unit Two" or "Reader Response #4," also include that in your header. Sometimes an instructor will prefer a student ID number in this header, too, either alongside or in place of your name. The function of the in-body header is to identify this particular document in the event that it gets shuffled in a stack of other papers.

You should also provide a header at the top of each subsequent page of your document. This header should contain a verbal link back to the main header on the first page, in case the pages get shuffled or confused with other papers. Use your word processor's "header" function to insert your last name (or student ID number) and the page number, separated by a single space, at the top-right corner of your document. You can also use your word processor's header function to conceal or suppress the header and page number on the first page of your document, since the main body header already provides all of the necessary information. Use the "insert page number" function to paginate your pages; do not manually insert a header or page numbers to paginate your document.

"SAFE BET" DOCUMENT HEADER STANDARDS

- Use the word processor's "header" function to create a header on each page that includes your last name (or student ID number) and the automatic page number function, separated by a single space.

- Use the word processor's "header" function to suppress the header with automatic page numbering on the first page of your document only.

- In the body of your document (not in the "header"), create a vertical list that includes (double-spaced): (1) your full name and/or student ID number, (2) the date, (3) the course number and name, (4) the instructor's name, and (5) if available, the assignment sequence number/name.

- Use the standard font for the header: Do not enlarge or shrink the size, do not change fonts, and do not use bold-face or italics.

3) Choose a title.

I beg my students to include a title on every draft they write, beginning with the very first rough draft. The title is one of your first opportunities to connect with your reader and lead them to your main ideas or your thesis statement. The title announces the topic and purpose of the document, and a strong title can compensate for a weak introduction in terms of orienting your readers and preparing them for what will follow.

Writers too often get hung up on titles, but even a placeholder title is better than no title — so include a title immediately after completing your body header and before your first paragraph. A title for an academic paper is similar to, but not exactly like, a newspaper headline. The first purpose of a college paper headline is to *inform* the reader about the writing that will follow, not to grab their attention in a dramatic or cutesy way. There is a common convention within academic titles to have a more colorful or poetic prefix followed by a more informative suffix, separated by a colon. For example, the title of this textbook is *Becoming a College Writer: A Multimedia Text*. Some writers (and readers) need the poetic prefix to energize the title, but, when in doubt, the safe bet is always the informative title.

Do not use one-word titles or simply the name of the assignment (like "Unit One"), because neither will help fully connect your audience to the central ideas in your paper. If your instructor gave you an assignment prompt, consider using keywords from the prompt in your title. Remember to correctly punctuate and capitalize words in your titles when they include proper names and the titles of other works, like a novel, movie, song, or poem. Consider revising your title as you develop your project through multiple drafts to reflect the changing directions of your main points and thoughts. Capitalize the first word in your title and all of the subsequent words, except for conjunctions and prepositions.

"SAFE BET" TITLE STANDARDS

- **Always include an informative title in every draft of your college papers.**

- **Use your word processor's alignment function to center your title (do not use spaces or tabs for this).**

- **You can boldface your title, but do not otherwise change the font in the title.**

In fact, it's best to just leave the title plain and visually separate it by centering it. Check your style guide (MLA, APA, etc.) for additional guidance on formatting the header.

4) Provide a bibliography.

A bibliography is a list of sources that you used to compose your writing assignment. There are different citation styles that have different rules for formatting your bibliography, and these differences are carefully detailed in Lesson 24: Citation. Depending on the citation style you use in a particular assignment, the bibliography will go by a different name, such as *Works Cited, References, Bibliography,* or *Works Consulted*. Either way, each of these bibliographies is a list of works provided at the end of the document that should be linked using in-text citations within the body paragraphs. Each text cited in your paper (even if it's a song or a movie) needs to appear in your bibliography.

As I've mentioned throughout this book, academic writing as a genre is defined by its use of sources. That is why I require my students to include a bibliography in their documents from their very first drafts. Citations and a bibliography are fundamental, and you typically cannot complete a college assignment without them. Furthermore, it is too easy to lose track of your sources as you advance from draft to draft if you do not include a bibliography from the beginning. Use your word processor's "insert page break" function to create a space for your bibliography at the end of your document. Do not create a separate document for your bibliography because you do not want it to get lost or disconnected from everything else.

- Always include a bibliography in every draft of your college papers.

- Format your bibliography according to the citation style of your assignment (see also Lesson 24).

- Insert a page break at the end of your document and place the bibliography after the page break. Do not create a separate file for your bibliography.

- You must include a bibliography for any academic writing you do that references even one outside source — whether you've written a paper, a movie, a web page, a slide presentation, and so on.

5) Select a font size and style.

DANNY
University of Florida

If you just print [your paper] out, however it is [without proper formatting] it looks like you don't care as much. I think a lot of people just get sloppy with the end. It's like, Why do you spend all this time writing this paper, and then at the end, when you turn it in, you don't even make it look good?

In general, academic documents are supposed to be classic, simple, and conventional. This means that as a college writer, you should probably stick with the Times family of fonts, or you can venture into something sans serif, like Helvetica, if you want to be daring.

More important than worrying about a preferred font, academic readers emphasize substance over style. For the time being, the content matters most, and an exaggerated or overstylized font is seen as a gimmicky distraction. When you write in alternative genres and modes, the standards shift a little, but only a little. In brochures, web pages, and on screens, your audience expects you to vary font style, size, and color — but still within fairly narrow standards. The size of the font varies to separate headings from body text, and generally muted colors can be used to connote tone and symbolism. But in general, digital readers expect a modern sans-serif font from the Helvetica family or nearby.

- For print publication the Times font family is the safest, and the Helvetica family should be okay, too.

- For print publication, 12 point font is the safest, and 11 point font can be acceptable, but 10 point is too small and 13 point is too large.

- Maintain the same font style, size, and colors (black for print) throughout your document.

- Use boldface sparingly, only for your document's titles and subheadings. Use italics, instead of underlining, to indicate the titles of books, to emphasize certain words, and to indicate foreign-language words.

6) Choose ink and color.

Black ink on white paper has the highest resolution and contrast, which means it is easier to read than other font colors. And, by the way, the resolution of black ink on white paper is much higher and easier to read than black letters against a white background on any computer screen, monitor, television, or projection. So, obviously, black ink on white paper is the standard for academic writing.

The two primary exceptions to this guideline are hypertext links and the text sometimes used with a chart or a graph. Your word processor will often automatically format a URL in blue, and, if you use a color printer, that text will print in blue, which may be acceptable. Sometimes the labels on colored charts and graphs will automatically print text that is colored to correspond with elements of the graph. Otherwise, you should stick with black ink.

If you are printing your own documents, you need to have backup toner cartridges so that your print does not fade if you are running out of ink. However, students are often at the mercy of public print stations, and sometimes those ink and toner qualities are out of your control. Either way, plan ahead so that you can deal with any printer, ink, or toner problems. Do *not* print out your document at the very last minute, in case there is a problem.

- **Use black ink exclusively, except in rare, unavoidable circumstances.**

- **It is often acceptable to print the URL of online resources in blue ink, if your printer and word processor default to that option.**

- **Plan to print out your document well ahead of the deadline so that you can adjust if there is problem with ink/ toner or the printer itself.**

7) Set margins.

If your instructor provides margin requirements, be sure to follow them. In the absence of guidelines from your teacher, one-inch margins all around are the default. It's also generally acceptable to have a 1.25 or 1.50 inch top margin to make room for a page header. Sometimes an expanded

inside margin of 1.25 or 1.50 (typically left margin) is a good idea to create what's known as a *gutter*, which is space on the inside of the page to be bound together or three-hole punched.

"SAFE BET" MARGIN STANDARDS

- **Provide one inch on all four margins: left, right, top, bottom.**

- **Provide 1.25 or 1.5 inches on the top margin only if it creates appropriate room for a header.**

- **Provide 1.25 or 1.5 inches on the inside/left margin only if it creates appropriate room for binding.**

8) Use standard line spacing.

Double spacing is standard because it gives readers ample space to write responses and to indicate any editorial changes clearly. As always, follow your instructor's or your writing program's guidelines for line spacing. Sometimes you will be asked to single-space parts of the document, like the first page header, block quotes, and footnotes that might take up too much room if they were double-spaced.

You or your instructor might be conscientious about the environment and agree that conserving paper by reducing the line space to 1.5 is a good idea. You might also have a particular document that needs to be limited to one page that cannot accommodate double spacing (like a cover letter or résumé).

"SAFE BET" LINE SPACING STANDARDS

- **Double space.**

- **When required or appropriate, use single-space for the document header on the first page, lengthy block quotes, and/or footnotes.**

9) Include white space.

White space is an essential design element for professional publications, but it's unusual for a conventional academic paper to need to create empty white space intentionally. Notice how each page in this textbook, particularly at the beginning of a new lesson or section, uses white space to guide the way your eye travels across the page or screen. Inserting tables, graphs, illustrations, and photographs (see section 17.2.10) will almost always introduce regions of empty white space in a conventional academic paper. The rule of thumb is to try to avoid "trapped" white space, which means that you generally do not want empty white space between your left margin and a graphic element to the right. Word processors allow you to wrap text around graphic inserts, but it's safer and more straightforward to break the text on separate lines before and after a graphic element.

The next most common white space considerations come from documents that are formatted with distinct, separate sections, like a lab report. If page-length requirements are not a concern, then the rule of thumb is that using white space to separate different segments of a document is often a good idea because it creates a sense of calm and composure; generous white space can make a complicated document feel less crowded, giving the reader the feeling of room to breathe.

Some style formats require extra line spaces to indicate certain levels of subheadings, which creates empty white space. If you have a specific document style that requires white space, you should, of course, follow those guidelines.

- **Conventional academic documents do not require extra graphical white space.**

- **Crop, expand, contract, format, or align your graphic elements (see section 17.2.10) to avoid large fields of empty white space in the left margins and at the tops or bottoms of printed pages (online and screen-based publications are more forgiving in this regard).**

- **Complicated documents, especially ones with multiple segments, can use graphical white space between sections to create a sense of structure, composure, and breathing room.**

10) Provide photographs, tables, graphs, and illustrations.

AMY
Boston University

Designing is important and should reflect what you're trying to say. . . . Where the indents are on the page and . . . where and how you place [photographs] within the text is really important because these choices evoke certain feelings.

Principles of document design—guidance for presenting graphical elements, including photographs, tables, graphs, and illustrations—can be very complex; in fact, that's an entirely different textbook in itself. The best "safe bet" rule to keep in mind in terms of conventional academic writing is to *keep it clear and simple*. That means, too, that you should never shy away from including a graphical element that can help clarify your writing. For example, I am often puzzled when students choose not

Goldilocks' Review of Bear Accommodations

	porridge	chair	bed
Papa Bear	★	★	★
Momma Bear	★★	★★	★★
Baby Bear	★★★★	★★★★	★★★★

Porridge Temperature per Minutes of Cooling

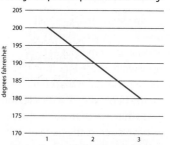

Rocking Chair Dimensions

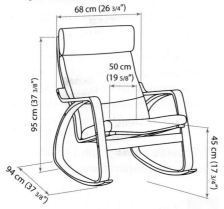

Grizzly Bear: *Ursus Arctos*

Alex Bondarenko/EyeEm/Getty Images

Table 17.1   How to Label a Graphical Element

to include a diagram when writing a set of instructions, simply because "It's an English class . . . you're only supposed *to write*." At its root, the word *composition* means "to put things together," and if a photograph helps your composition integrate your rhetorical contexts and convey your ideas, then you should absolutely include one.

There still exists in the academic world some prejudice against writing with images. So it might be difficult for you to incorporate them effectively and professionally at first because you lack experience getting feedback from informed audiences about your use of images alongside your paragraphs and sentences, which is why it is safest to keep it clean and simple at first.

↰⤷ **See also Lesson 9: Media**

A second principle for including graphical elements is that *they must be clearly cited and labeled*. Just like integrating any outside source into your writing, it is essential that graphical elements complement, rather than disrupt, the flow of your writing and your readers' experiences. And, of course, when you use any graphical element from another source, then you must cite that source the same way that you would a direct quote, paraphrase, or summary. Lesson 24 on citation provides detailed guidelines for attributing graphical elements, but it is very important to make the point that these elements must be carefully cited because so many writers make the mistake of overlooking this information.

The key to integrating graphical elements is simply to label them clearly. Number and perhaps provide a caption or title for each of the graphical elements you use so that you can refer to them in the body of the text. Doing so can make it easier to place the element physically within your document in a way that does not disrupt the layout or lead to empty, wasted white space. You can put a well-labeled image almost anywhere near its in-text reference so that the placement results in a clean layout. Careful and consistent labeling and captioning of your graphical elements will also encourage you to provide citations. For example, I could cleanly place *Table 17.1: How to Label a Graphical Element* either before or after this current paragraph, depending upon the least disruptive physical layout, because I labeled it so clearly. Notice how the corresponding caption also creates a natural space to indicate the source of the graphic (although, in this case, I created the table myself).

"SAFE BET" GRAPHICAL ELEMENT STANDARDS

- **Clearly, logically, and sequentially label all graphical elements so that you can refer to them directly in your sentences and paragraphs.**

- **Be sure to attribute all graphical elements: Provide citation for outside sources and take credit for any graphical element that you create yourself.**

- **Do not shy away from using graphical elements to integrate your writing, but try to keep them clean, simple, and complementary — do not use them for decoration, filler, or distraction.**

17.3
Exercises: publishing

17a Integrate the video.

For Chatiana, formatting is an important part of the dynamic relationship between the writer, audience, and topic:

> Format is a good way to show how much you care about the paper. If you care about the paper you want people to know: "I wrote this and this is my feeling toward it, so I'm going to have a good format for it." That's format for me.

She defines formatting as an expression of the care and pride she invests in her work. Write a substantial paragraph or two, with a topic sentence or mini-thesis, through which you respond to the sound-bite videos in the lesson as you form your own approaches to formatting. You can watch the Lesson 17 Essentials Video, or you can browse the embedded clips in the online edition of this lesson. You might begin by identifying the moments that stand out to you the most. Which student videos seem to make the most sense to you? With whom do you agree? Disagree? What patterns do you find among the student sound bites? Which ideas were the most instructive or helpful to you? What surprised you? How have your own ideas about formatting come into focus through the videos?

17b Create a journal entry or blog.

This lesson urges you to increase your awareness of publishing and formatting as part of your writing process, and this exercise asks you to use a journal to do so. Write two short paragraphs in your journal: one that describes your plan for publishing and formatting on an upcoming writing assignment, and a second one that reflects on your experiences after you have published your writing. Describe some past experiences with formatting that will influence your plans for the upcoming assignment. Do you have a specific formatting approach in mind, like those listed in section 17.2, that you think is well suited for the assignment? After the assignment is complete, upon reflection, evaluate how well your formatting plan worked and what you can learn from the experience for next time. You could keep this journal using only print/text, or you could make an online blog, a video blog, or an audio podcast that captures your unfolding thoughts and experiences in your actual voice.

17c See yourself as a writer.

For Harley, seeing his well formatted, publication-ready document is gratifying, and it promotes his self-confidence and self-esteem as a writer. He explains:

> I prefer to write about subjects that I'm interested in. I also really like to get my thoughts down on paper. It feels really good to have an organized paper to show everything that I know or think or have researched. So, uh, I really like seeing the end product. So I take a lot of pleasure in just knowing that I've done a good job.

In a page or two, describe the evolution of your approaches to publishing and formatting since you began writing. Where and when did you start to develop intentional strategies for formatting? What major events, assignments, and papers have influenced your approaches to formatting along the way? What particular teachers or classes have reshaped the ways you prepare your final documents? What was your sense of formatting before you began reading this lesson? What is your approach now that you have finished this lesson? In what ways can you imagine your publishing and formatting process changing beyond college?

17d Invent your writing.

In section 17.1, I encouraged you to format the basic aspects of your first drafts, but not obsess about the fine points of formatting until the last the steps of your writing process. Early formatting can set a professional tone and feel to your writing, even in the early stages, as long as it doesn't disrupt your research-drafting-revision loop. Write a short paragraph that begins with this sentence, completed by you: "On my next writing assignment, my plan is to initially format an early draft on [indicate date here] and to prepare the final formatting for publication on [indicate date here] because doing so will help the early stages of my writing process in the following ways: [brainstorm a list of benefits here]." This exercise is meant to illustrate what Part Three has been saying all along: Your writing process is recursive and interconnected, which means that the earliest stages and the final stages all work together like the reciprocating parts of an engine.

17e Analyze student writing.

Read at least one of the featured student interviews in the text, and study, in particular, their discussion about their approach to formatting and publishing. Or you might choose to browse the interviews in the LaunchPad for a student like you or who is interesting to you. Compile a list of five or so different things the student said in their interview about their formatting and publishing processes. Then compare their interview, your list, and, their writing sample. Can you see connections between their discussion of their writing process and their written product?

Your instructor might ask you to interview a classmate instead of reading one of the interviews in the text or online. Or you might compare what you found in one of the textbook interviews to an interview with your classmate. If you interview a classmate, ask them about their thoughts on formatting for a writing assignment. Do they use the same approach for each assignment?

What are the most prominent benefits of their approach to formatting? What aspects of their formatting are they confident about? When do they struggle? And, most important, can you identify connections between their formatting technique and their written products? Can you see how formatting impacts the quality and experience of their writing?

17f Revise repeatedly from feedback.

Examine a writing assignment you are currently working on or one that you wrote recently, perhaps in another class or in high school. Section 17.2 of this lesson discusses ten "safe bet" formatting standards. Use section 17.2 as a checklist to see if your draft meets the "safe bet" standards. Then analyze and discuss with a writing center tutor or your instructor any struggles or differences you found between your draft and the "safe bet" publishing standards. What lessons did you learn about writing and publishing as a result?

LESSON 18

Reflecting

Reflect on each completed assignment, in writing.

Mieke Dalle/Getty Images

Visit the LaunchPad for *Becoming a College Writer* to watch the Lesson 18 Essentials Video.

18.1 [WHY]

Why you should reflect on each completed assignment, in writing.

DEONTA
University of North Carolina, Chapel Hill

What's helped me to become a strong writer is not necessarily the grade that I get on the paper, it's the feedback that I get from the professors — being able to sit down and talk with them about how I can do better on the next paper or what it was in this paper that didn't work and why it didn't work. So that's been a great help to me in improving my writing, and it also has enabled me to make relationships with people that I may not have been connected with before. So, when I'm writing papers in other courses, I can go talk to them, and they'll be able to give me feedback and tell me what they've done throughout their writing process and give me tips.

NIA
University of Florida

An effective college writer is someone who is not too shaken by critique. A good college writer knows how to not be too proud and to look at the C, D, F, A — whatever it is you got on your paper, it's probably in red ink, unfortunately — and to take that and get better. . . . To be a good college writer you need to be humble, you need to be able to listen, and you need to be open for criticism so you can build.

Congratulations! You have worked hard to develop and publish your writing assignment, and you deserve to exhale for a moment. Since college writing is academic and developmental, however, the final, finished product is neither the end of the process nor the ultimate goal, so after you take that moment, it's time to get back into the game. The purpose of college writing is for you to grow as a writer and to strengthen your critical writing, reading, and thinking skills.

The paper you just completed is a means to an end, and that end is your long-term development and learning. So what matters most — what's most important — is *what* you learn from completing a college writing assignment that you can *apply* or *transfer* to other writing situations, in college and beyond. Deonta and Nia each have a growth mentality about their writing that allows them to be open to feedback, which they claim is responsible for their development and eventual success.

Written reflection maximizes the lessons and experiences you've gained from completing a writing assignment.

Writing down your thoughts about a completed writing assignment is a high-reward activity. You may be formally assigned to write a reflective essay as part of a larger assignment, for example, for a multipart project or for a portfolio of work. Or you might draft an informal reflection for yourself in order to grow as a writer. Even if you invest just five or ten minutes to jot your thoughts down anywhere (in a journal, in an email to yourself, even on the back of your graded paper), you can realize enormous payoffs integrating the lessons you just worked so hard to learn. Reflection is so important to your success that the third exercise in each lesson prompts you to be reflective. In the composition classes at my university, each course has three major writing assignments, and many of the instructors assign a specific journal or blog entry to encapsulate takeaways from each unit that ask:

- **What did the feedback you receive focus on?**

- **What did you learn in particular from this assignment?**

- **What did you accomplish in your writing that you want to repeat?**

- **What weaknesses did you identify to improve upon?**

- **How does this particular assignment relate to the purposes of the class as a whole?**

- **What goals for your future writing can you set after learning from this assignment?**

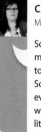

CATHERINE
Michigan State University

Sometimes at the beginning of class my professor will say, "You're welcome to revise any of these papers you want." Sometimes I've asked: "This paper, even though it's pretty good and it's what I turned in, I know that I can do a little bit better, so can I revise it?"

If **Revising Repeatedly from Feedback** is the key to producing a successful college writing assignment, then written reflection is the key to continuing that success. After you receive a grade and final feedback from your instructor, you are unlikely to revise the draft again (unless it will be part of a future portfolio or unless you have Catherine's mentality and her professor). If you will not revise again, then you will not fully integrate the things you learn from the final feedback unless you reflect purposefully.

In Lesson 10: Planning, I argued that "writing is magic" because writing things down, particularly on paper, seems to have the power to help you realize your goals in almost every aspect of your life. For Arely, writing in a journal helped her cope with the transition to becoming a college student. Reflection allowed her to see her progress.

ARELY
California State University, San Marcos

The transition from high school to college was [a challenge]. College is so different. I was having trouble with trying to keep in contact with friends back home. I just felt really, I guess, homesick, you could say. But writing that allowed me [to see:] "Oh, wow, I've really developed as a person. I've learned a lot." It's just something I can look back to, and it's nice seeing the difference.

The life of a college writer can be frantic. When you pour yourself into completing an assignment, you may find yourself ignoring other classes and areas of your life. So, when you finish and turn in your project, the urge to move on to the things you've put on hold is understandable. However, I urge you to take just a little time more time to reflect.

Reflection is crucial — more important than your grade — because it allows you to take stock of your learning and growth as a thinker and writer. Reflection solidifies your experiences. If you fail to reflect, you are coasting instead of sprinting across the finish line. You are letting up at the most critical moment. Take ten minutes or so to evaluate your experience. It really is worth it. For Alexandra, failing to plan her project so that she could make the most of reader feedback is something that she would do differently next time. Her reflection is valuable because in the future, she is likely to learn from feedback.

ALEXANDRA
University of Florida

[A] downfall of procrastinating and not doing my best work [is that] the feedback that I get isn't useful.

A final reflection is good therapy for the future writer in you because you look back and specifically identify everything that you accomplished. Some writers have a tendency to be too self-critical when it comes to their own work. However, identifying the ground you've gained, the lessons you've learned, and the rewards you've received through your writing is critical, too. This kind of positive reinforcement is valuable. As you identify and replicate the successful moves you made in your writing, you will inevitably improve your instincts as a writer as your best sentences increasingly take space away from weak ideas.

Written reflection allows you to improve by avoiding future pitfalls and replicating successes.

The point of reflection is to maximize your learning by staying in the moment, by critically focusing on the work you've just completed. It is a time to consider the big picture. This means identifying, as Elizabeth says, both the "good and bad" in your writing. When you reflect, you create a unique moment to use your recent experience to set specific, manageable goals to propel you forward.

ELIZABETH
Palomar College

Feedback is so important, direct feedback, good and bad. It's so much more useful than just a grade . . . it has forced me to be self-reflective, which is good and I'm happy for the opportunity. . . . The questions made me think about my process and about things I probably wouldn't have thought about otherwise.

The next time you complete an assignment and reflect, I urge you to review your previous reflections; when you do, you will be pleased to see how very effective written reflection and specific goals can be. But reflection and improvement also require commitment and effort. As Erienne points out, after she has received constructive feedback, she has to work to integrate those lessons into her future writing process.

ERIENNE
Metropolitan State University of Denver

You improve your writing by sharing it with people and by being unafraid. You have to develop the courage to be able to give your pieces away and honestly ask someone what they think not expecting a certain response. If all you wanted to hear was "Wow, this was great! I loved it, I know exactly what you're talking about," then you're not going to improve. You have to be ready to hear, "This was unclear. I don't know what you're talking about. This was frilly. This was grotesque." And then you have to work with that and modify your writing accordingly.

Why you should reflect on each completed assignment, in writing

1. **Make a quick list of a few of your earliest childhood memories before reading the next step.**
2. **List the mental and literal (photographic) images that you associate with each memory.**
3. **How often are these thoughts and memories associated with or documented by a photograph, video, or written record?**

These connections, between your experiences and the documents that represent them, demonstrate the essential power of reflection. Describe an important event, celebration, accomplishment, or experience in your life that you reflected on in a journal, scrapbook, story, video, or presentation. Why did you document that experience? What does that reflection mean to you now? How do you think the experience was enhanced by your reflection?

18.2 [HOW]

How to reflect on each completed assignment, in writing.

Notice that this last lesson of Part Three: Process is **not** revising, proofreading, or publishing, although most writers tend to think that those stages define the end of their writing processes. It is reflection. As noted in Section 18.1, *written reflection* is the very best way to maximize what you have learned from a recently completed writing assignment. Written reflection is the best way to transfer that experience to other writing contexts, both within and beyond your college career.

Most lessons in this text conclude with an exercise that prompts you to reflect (Exercise f). The lessons also include an exercise that asks you to keep a writer's journal or blog (Exercise c). So, when you reflect in a journal about what you have learned and the progress you've made, you have a very powerful combination. The following five strategies offer advice on how to reflect productively in a writer's journal (whether it is written, an audio library of reflections, or even a vlog) so that you can drive your progress toward becoming a college writer.

1) Capture and preserve feedback without emotion.

ALYSSA
Santa Fe College

Getting feedback is kind of terrifying because you're afraid that your teacher is going to say, "This is the worst paper I've ever read." But really you can't write the worst paper your teacher's ever read, unless you really didn't try. . . . In one of my papers this semester, my teacher took off points because he thought my opinion was "too naive." So, I understood that I have to be careful that I consider all sides of someone's story and perspective. When I get feedback, there [are] two sides to it: There's knowing what you have to do to make a better grade, and then there's understanding what you are doing wrong fundamentally and knowing that you need to take your professor's advice and apply it to your writing.

Alyssa and Billy admit an important reality about feedback and criticism: Our natural instinct may be to feel afraid and defensive, at first. But becoming a college writer, according to every student quoted in this lesson, is a direct function of getting beyond negative emotions so that you can grow. Section 15.2.4 in Lesson 15: Revising describes how to integrate insights from informed feedback into your revision. You might want to (re)read that section now. If you follow the advice in Lesson 15, you can resist a natural defensiveness when receiving feedback. This allows you to hear your readers' advice and to actually begin reflecting during your revision stage. (Remember that writing is a recursive process. See Lesson 14: Drafting and Lesson 15: Revising.)

BILLY
University of Florida

When someone would give me feedback in the past, and I really thought that what I was writing was the most important thing in the world, I couldn't take the feedback. I couldn't hear it because it was hitting my ego. . . . So, I really started to improve when I could hear the suggestions, when I could listen to my teachers. I had a teacher tell me that I write really hyperbolically, so when I was able to nurse my wounds and could hear that advice, I started taking out all of my adverbs and adjectives.

As you begin to write down your reflections after submitting/publishing an assignment, begin by reviewing all of the feedback you received throughout the process. And by "all of the feedback," I mean *all* of it: positive, negative, substance, style, intellectual moves, typographic errors, your writing process, as well as the final product. If you heard and captured that feedback without emotion, it's likely that you can learn even more from it at this moment of closure. If you had multiple readers at different stages in your writing process, it's likely that their feedback was different. Even if readers disagree, reflecting on their feedback is

helpful as you sift through, evaluate on your own, and move forward. This does not mean that you should agree with each and every criticism or compliment, but if you don't take the time to reflect, you may not be able to sort out the good advice from the bad.

Ask yourself: In what ways did earlier feedback teach me something new? How did it influence my writing? What pitfalls did I avoid (or suffer) based upon informed feedback? What would I do differently next time, and why?

You might already have final feedback and a grade from your instructor in hand. If so, try to hear that feedback and learn from it without being resistant or frustrated. Writing down the points you gather from final feedback as objectively as possible helps you learn, and ideally you will learn a lot from compliments in the feedback, too.

2) Begin your reflection immediately after turning in your assignment.

CHASE
Santa Fe College

When I get feedback or when I'm waiting for feedback, I'm generally pretty tense. There [are] obviously bound to be a couple of things my professor did not like about what I've written. I think meeting with them after or taking a couple of minutes to figure out what they thought about it — and what you could do to be better — is a great strategy to compound your success in writing throughout college.

Chase has a positive attitude about how to transfer the lessons he learns from one writing assignment to future assignments as a college writer. But he could be even more productive if instead of waiting tensely for

255

the feedback to come, he used that moment to begin his reflection. If possible, spend ten or even five minutes writing down your thoughts immediately after handing in your final draft, even if it's tentative, such as: "I wonder if my revised introduction was too long?" or "Writing a scientific document was surprisingly difficult, given that the format was so well established." Hopefully you are neither exhausted nor sleep deprived and you can capture important reflections while you remain in a mental state of deep concentration on this piece of writing. I like to capture moments of reflection by sending myself a quick email so that I won't lose track of important lessons that I need to retain.

Depending on your personality and schedule, however, you might want to wait for a quiet moment later in the day for deeper reflection. Ask yourself:

- **What do you perceive to be the highlights of your experience?**

- **What do you think are the major strengths and weaknesses of your final draft?**

- **What defining moments or snags in your writing process heavily influenced your final version?**

- **What do you anticipate your audience's response will be?**

- **What did you learn from the entire assignment?**

- **What did you learn that you will want to integrate into your future writing?**

For example, Billy learned to avoid hyperbole and overstatement (see section 18.2.1), and Vinh-Thuy learned to tie his paragraphs together more carefully (see section 18.2.3).

By beginning your written reflection on your own terms, perhaps before you receive final instructor comments and a grade, you take control of and responsibility for your own development as a writer — and you are preparing yourself to make the most of the final feedback once you receive it.

3) Extend your reflection after receiving feedback and a grade.

If you followed the advice above, you are now well positioned to reflect for a final time. Ideally, you worked hard on your assignment, published it with pride and purpose, and received feedback and a grade that rewarded your success. Now it's time to reflect on and integrate that feedback. Doing so will set you up well for future writing assignments so that you can draw on what you've done well and build on your success.

Because the nature of giving informed feedback is to offer a critique, readers, including your instructor, may gravitate toward identifying problems. As a writer, being open to feedback can be a challenge — but you will benefit most from honest feedback that identifies problem areas and offers ways to address them. Do your best to process the criticism you get, including the strengths that your readers have identified. As the final step in your writing process, reflection is the moment when you can learn from experience.

After Vinh-Thuy received a grade and feedback on one of his papers, he chose to reflect on that feedback. He learned a valuable lesson about how to respond to an assignment prompt and about working with style, language, and genre. He learned that while poetic language is appropriate in

Lightspring/Shutterstock.com

many contexts, and experimentation is exciting, these choices were not the best ones for the assignment he describes.

VINH-THUY
Red Rocks Community College

In my original draft . . . I had ten different paragraphs, ten different stories. It wasn't really good. But when I first read it I thought: "Wow, this sounds awesome, it's really poetic. It's going to get a really good grade." After [my instructor] graded it, and after I took two weeks to not look at the paper, I read it again and thought: "Wow, this is terrible. What was I thinking?"

If you began your reflection before receiving a grade and final comments, especially if you specifically considered how your instructor might respond, then you are in a great position to learn from final feedback. And if you continue that reflection weeks after you receive the grade, like Vinh-Thuy did, you will learn even more from your experience and become a better writer.

4) Document repeated mistakes.

Section 16.2.9 in Lesson 16: Proofreading recommends that you create a journal or log where you identify the types of errors and patterns of errors that you tend to make.

257

How to reflect on each completed assignment, in writing

That lesson also recommends that you refer back to your error log before you proofread your current assignment. If you have not read that section, I invite you to do so now.

HUSSAIN
University of Florida

I wrote a paper for [my] Women's Poetry class, and we had a writer's workshop where [my instructor] shared snippets out of different students' essays. She took a body paragraph out of mine that was heavily loaded with quotations at the beginning. Not only did I [introduce] a quotation, but I also quoted that quotation afterward. In this course, not only am I getting feedback on the quality of my writing, but I'm also getting time with my professor that's dedicated to improving my writing.

Hussain was able to improve the way he integrates sources in his writing because his professor identified a specific problem in his writing. This is fairly straightforward when it comes to mechanical problems and mistakes. Years ago I remember writing down the difference between the words *compliment* and *complement* because I kept confusing them, but I never make that mistake anymore, thanks to writing it down as a note to myself.

Of course, all writers repeat mistakes that are more complicated and difficult to fix than simple mechanical or grammatical confusions. You might have been told repeatedly that your introductions are too long and indirect. Your readers might have asked you to integrate a deeper variety and complexity of evidence in your writing. It can be overwhelming, or impossible, to try to take to heart *every* piece of feedback you receive; so you have to be strategic and look for specific patterns to the current weaknesses in your writing.

In other words, if you receive a specific criticism multiple times, especially from multiple readers on multiple assignments, then you should write it down and also begin to write down specific techniques and strategies for improvement. The cartoon character Wile E. Coyote was doomed to repeat his mistakes trying to catch the roadrunner because he failed to reflect on and learn from them. Michael, on the other hand, uses reflection on earlier projects to avoid previous mistakes and to inspire his current writing.

MICHAEL
Michigan State University

I really like looking back at my old [writing assignments]. . . . Sometimes, when I'm in the moment, I'm too into a current project to understand all the little details, all the little decisions I'm making unconsciously or even consciously. You just don't reflect as well as you will when you look at it maybe a few months later. It's really helpful to look back at your writing and really helpful to understand who you are as a writer. If you're lost on a current project, just sit and read or watch what you've already made. Contemplate what you could do to one-up yourself, to just understand what mistakes you made. It's very helpful. It's enjoyable.

5) Discuss your reflection, revisit earlier goals, and identify new goals for how to improve for future assignments.

Like Michael, Terryn looks back on past essays to mark his improvement. This allows him to appreciate his progress and set new goals for improvement. Getting started by reflecting in solitude can help you concentrate, as Michael does when he reflects on his previous work. However, once you have done so (in writing), consider asking for help to transform your reflections into a plan of action. It can be overwhelming to address the complex challenges of writing all at once. So, work incrementally, one step at a time, using feedback and reflection to set manageable goals for improvement.

TERRYN
Santa Fe College

I've definitely improved over the years since high school and since a year ago. With every English class I've taken, they've all incorporated different strategies. I've been using them to build up what I'm writing now, the style that I write in. I've definitely improved. I definitely write a little bit different because I still have my essays saved on my laptop. I actually just looked at them last week to see how I've improved, and it's definitely come a long way.

Hannah is diligent about becoming aware of her mistakes and working on them. She is deliberate about reflecting back on her old work so that she can make plans for future improvement. If she writes down what she has learned from conferences with her teacher and from her reflection of her past papers, then her development as a writer will be even more efficient and dramatic. I often hold writing conferences with my students, each of which begins with this question: "What specific goals for improvement did you write down last time?" Then we read the current draft together looking for specific improvement. Each conference concludes with, "Now, what goals do you have for your next draft?" How often do you imagine that one of my students writes down goals for improvement, but then fails to progress on the next draft? (It has never happened.)

HANNAH
California State University, San Marcos

I correct weaknesses by talking to the people who are going to help me proofread my paper before I turn it in, reminding them where my weaknesses lay: "These are the points that you need to focus on with me. Not *for* me, but *with* me. Because I'm trying to focus on them, too, trying to be consciously aware of my weaknesses as I'm writing." I'll explain to my professor when I get my first paper back: "Okay, I know this is a weakness of mine, and I'm trying to work on it. So if you can focus on this with me, we can work on this together to make me a better writer." It's a matter of working together with multiple people.

The way I noticed weaknesses was through my professor. Professors are really good at pointing out where you're weak in papers. That's their job. They're supposed to make you better writers. So when a professor points out: "Hannah, this is where you're weak," I think, "Oh, okay, I need to improve on that." Then I'll go back to my old papers and try to find evidence of what they're saying. More often than not, I do find plenty of evidence. Once I'm made aware of a problem, I focus on it in my next papers and really work to improve.

Discuss your written reflections with your instructors or writing center tutors. Ask them to help you better understand the nature of the problem and to work with you to address specific ways to improve. The ideal way for you to set an impressive tone for a writing conference is to begin by saying, "On my last assignment I was struggling with problem X, but I have been working to improve by using strategies Y and Z. Does this draft seem like an improvement in terms of problem X?" Written reflection is the key to such improvement, and asking for help is wise.

How to reflect on each completed assignment, in writing

18.3

Exercises: reflecting

18a Integrate the video.

For Amanda, feedback is essential to her improvement, and her positive growth mentality will serve her well as she reflects on the lessons learned with every draft and every paper. She says:

Practice makes perfect. So as you continue to write and get feedback, things become easier. Even if you turned in a paper and it's slaughtered with red pen and you got a horrible grade, that paper's going to help you more than the paper that was marked "Good job" on the top. As my college career has progressed, my papers have improved and the feedback I have gotten has helped.

Write a substantial paragraph or two, with a topic sentence or mini-thesis, through which you respond to the sound-bite videos in the lesson as you form your own approaches to reflecting. You can watch the Lesson 18 Essentials Video, or you can browse the embedded clips in the online edition of this lesson. You might begin by identifying the moments that stand out to you the most. Which student videos seem to make the most sense to you? With whom do you agree? Disagree? What patterns do you find among the student sound bites? Which ideas were the most instructive or helpful to you? What surprised you? How have your own ideas about reflecting come into focus through the videos?

18b Create a journal entry or blog.

This lesson urges you to use reflection as part of your writing process, and this exercise asks you to use a journal to do so. Write two short paragraphs in your journal: one that describes your plan for reflecting on an upcoming writing assignment and a second one that

looks back on your experiences after you have published your writing. Describe some past experiences with reflecting that will influence your plans for the upcoming assignment. Do you have a specific reflecting concept in mind, like those listed in section 18.2, that you think is well suited for the assignment? After the assignment is complete, evaluate how well your reflection plan worked and what you can learn from the experience for next time. You could keep this journal using only print/text, or you could make an online blog, a video blog, or an audio podcast that captures your unfolding thoughts and experiences in your actual voice.

18c See yourself as a writer.

Arely used a journal to document her learning and progress as she transitioned from high school to college, and reflecting on that progress helped develop her confidence and self-esteem in ways that might not have happened if she had not written them down. She explains:

The transition from high school to college was a challenge. College is so different. I was having trouble with trying to keep in contact with friends back home. I just felt really, I guess, homesick, you could say. But writing allowed me to see: "Oh, wow, I've really developed as a person. I've learned a lot." My journal is something I can look back to, and it's nice seeing the difference.

In a page or two, describe the evolution of your approaches to reflecting since you began writing. Where and when did you start to develop intentional strategies for reflecting? What major events, assignments, and papers have influenced your approaches to reflecting along the way? What particular teachers or classes have reshaped the ways you reflect? What was your sense of reflecting before you began reading this lesson? What is your approach now that you have finished this lesson? Can you use a written reflection, like Arely, to document your progress as a college writer? If so, what does it show?

18d Invent your writing.

Lesson 10: Planning, at the beginning of Part Three: Process, urges you to map your writing processes on your calendar. As such, writing down a plan on a calendar is actually a first step toward reflection. Now that you are at the end of Part Three: Process, you should reflect on your entire writing process all the way back to Lesson 10: Planning. Did you write down a date for reflecting on your calendar back in the beginning? If so, how did an awareness of a final reflection influence your research-brainstorming-drafting-revision loop along the way? If not, describe how you might reimagine the earliest stages of your writing process being enhanced by systematic reflection.

18e Analyze student writing.

Read at least one of the featured student interviews in the text, and study, in particular, their discussion about their approach to reflecting and improving. Or you might choose to browse the interviews in LaunchPad for a student like you or who is interesting to you. Compile a list of five or so different things the student said in their interview about their reflecting and improving processes. Then compare their interview, your list, and their writing sample. Can you see connections between their discussion of their writing process and their written product?

Your instructor might ask you to interview a classmate instead of reading one of the interviews in the text or online. Or you might compare what you found in one of the textbook interviews to an interview with your classmate. If you interview a classmate, ask them about their thoughts on reflecting for a writing assignment. Do they use the same approach for each assignment? What are the most prominent benefits of their approach to reflecting? What aspects of their reflecting are they confident about? When do they struggle? And, most important, can you identify connections between their reflecting technique and their written products? Can you see how reflecting impacts the quality and experience of their writing?

18f Revise repeatedly from feedback.

Examine a writing assignment you are currently working on or one that you wrote recently, perhaps in another class or in high school. Section 18.2 of this lesson discusses five ideas for reflection, and you should follow as many of them as possible for a recently completed assignment. Then analyze and discuss your reflection with a writing center tutor or your instructor. What lessons did you learn about becoming a college writer as a result of your reflection?

PART FOUR

Conventions

The six chapters in Part Four will help you to refine your strategies for some of the key elements of a writing project.

LESSON 19

Thesis

Focus your thesis through evidence and research.

Visit the LaunchPad for *Becoming a College Writer* to watch the Lesson 19 Essentials Video.

19.1   [WHY]

Why you should focus your thesis through evidence and research.

The first form of thesis statement that most students learn is what I call the *terrier thesis*: Sink your teeth into your claim and don't let go for any reason.

As a means to an end, the strident terrier thesis is a good way to encourage inexperienced writers to establish and support a specific point. As writers move from middle school to high school, their academic writing often transitions from writing reviews and reports to making insights and claims, and the terrier thesis can help with this move away from summaries toward arguments.

In this transition, students evolve from writing that primarily synthesizes what others have said to writing that says something original, and the terrier thesis prompts writers to be emphatic in their claims. The limitation of the terrier thesis is that, in exchange for being clear and convincing, the writer will overstate or oversimplify the case. Here's a terrier version of the thesis in the Note to Students in this book:

The only way to improve as a writer is to revise repeatedly from feedback.

Ashia identifies the next commonly taught form of the thesis beyond the terrier thesis, which is what I call the *composite thesis*.

ASHIA
Michigan State University

I've been taught that a thesis statement is the last sentence in your intro paragraph that describes what you're [going] to write about. If you have three body paragraphs, it's going to be basically your first sentence in each body paragraph all condensed into one main sentence.

The composite thesis formula goes something like this:

The point of this paper can be explained by considering subtopic #1, subtopic #2, and subtopic #3.

This approach to making a thesis is part of the famous five-paragraph essay. The primary aim of the five-paragraph theme is to give inexperienced writers a simple way to learn about organization and structure.

This formula provides a deliberate and reliable format for making sure that the paper has three body paragraphs, each with a subtopic that supports the overall thesis. Again, as a means to an end, the five-paragraph paper and its companion composite thesis can be helpful. It can teach

Introduction

Subtopic #1

Subtopic #2

Subtopic #3

Conclusion

students how to move beyond the terrier thesis, and it's especially helpful at teaching organization and structure. Here's a composite version of the thesis in the introduction, and you can see how this might easily lead to a five-paragraph essay:

Writers need to understand three key terms in order to improve: revision, repetition, and feedback.

However, like all formulas, the five-paragraph theme and the composite thesis have limitations. You might have heard by now from more advanced writing teachers that the five-paragraph essay is too predictable, too mechanical, or too formulaic for most college writing. Writing is an essentially human endeavor, and the five-paragraph essay and the composite thesis are often too robotic, too much like merely filling in blank spaces on a form. Maybe you've tried to add a sixth paragraph and subsequently a fourth subtopic in your composite thesis, which is a small step in the right direction. But there are other ways to approach a thesis.

NICOLE
California State University, San Marcos

To develop a thesis you need your topic and you need your opinion on that topic and you combine both the topic and your opinion to create your thesis. And I've kind of always just flowed with that formula for the thesis.

Nicole's formula for a thesis sentence is one part topic and one part opinion, which is an important lesson to learn to make sure your thesis is stated clearly as a claim and not a fact that stands alone and does not require support.

I am going to provide you with a new, more advanced thesis formula to consider

as a way to break out of stale approaches. Like the composite thesis, this new model is also a formula, so it has limitations, too. But the new model, which I term a *research-based thesis*, can be nimbler and more adaptable than either the terrier thesis or composite thesis. Hopefully, this new research-based thesis will work for you. Here it is as a fill-in-the-blank form:

Most people assume _____,
but closer study reveals _____,
and in this paper I will add or argue
_____ to further our understanding.

CUYLER
Metropolitan State University of Denver

My approach to a thesis now is less mechanical. … Now, the reason you write a paper is because there's something about the topic you don't understand. And so the thesis is oftentimes for me the question itself, or maybe the question rephrased as an answer. And then I take the reader through all the different arguments to show them how I answered that question, or how I arrived at the answer.

The *terrier thesis* teaches writers to be clear and assertive. The *composite thesis* helps writers learn to structure and organize their writing. The *research-based thesis* drives writers to base their argument on careful, systematic study (in other words, on evidence and research). It also prompts writers to enter into a conversation with experts on the subject and to explore aspects about the topic that "you don't understand," in Cuyler's words. A formula for the composite thesis is shown on the following page.

MOST PEOPLE ASSUME X.
(X is common knowledge.)

BUT CLOSER STUDY REVEALS Y.
(Y is what research has shown.)

AND IN THIS PAPER I WILL ADD OR ARGUE Z TO FURTHER OUR UNDERSTANDING.
(Z is a gap in our understanding. Z is an answer to a question that has arisen in the conversation about this issue.)

An evidence-based version of the thesis in the Note to Students in this book reads like this:

> **Many writing students and perhaps some of their teachers believe that writing is an innate talent, where some gifted students can write, but the majority are probably better in other areas of their college work. However, years of teaching college students and volumes of research on student writers suggest to me that every student can and should write. It might be that the real difference between successful and unsuccessful college writers is more a matter of experience and exercise, rather than natural ability or talent. In fact, the defining characteristic of successful writers is that they have more experience revising their work in response to feedback from their readers.**

You could argue that the final sentence in the paragraph above is the thesis statement, but you could also argue that this thesis is actually distributed across these four sentences. Note how the sample follows the "formula" for a research-based thesis, but it does not slavishly use exactly the same words in the X-Y-Z template above.

You might begin a draft of your current paper by filling in the X-Y-Z blanks above; however, as you then revise based upon feedback, your words and voice should evolve differently.

In order to focus your ideas for an academic audience in college, you will want to base your thesis statements on evidence and research (see Lesson 6: Evidence and Lesson 12: Researching in particular). In order to connect with college readers to address a college topic, your thesis statements should respond to research, not precede it.

Framing your topic, at least initially, as an answer to a research question (see pages 112–17 in Lesson 8: Discipline) will naturally encourage you to focus your thoughts. You might want to start out with an exploratory thesis to help guide your research, which would be more like a hypothesis that you are testing as you gather evidence to prove or disprove your idea, as Gretchen argues below. A *research-based thesis* is thus defined as a guiding statement that directly responds to the evidence the writer uses to contribute a new perspective.

GRETCHEN
Boston University

The important thing to remember about a thesis is that it's your own idea and you're proving it with examples from a text or from a play or from any topic you choose to write about. The thesis is technically your hypothesis that you're proving in an assignment, in a writing assignment. And it should be clearly stated in your introduction so that your reader is clearly aware of what statement you're trying to make with your paper. A thesis should always be clearly identified. The reader should know right away when they see your thesis that that is what you're going to talk about. And your thesis should always be something that you can get an answer to through your writing.

PRACTICE **In order to really learn the power of a research-based thesis, try creating one on your own. Create or revise a thesis statement for a current project. Begin by filling in the formula for a research-based thesis outlined above.**

19.2 [HOW]

How to focus your thesis through evidence and research.

1) State your thesis clearly and support it consistently throughout your writing.

GREGG
California State University, San Marcos

Usually the thesis has to be something that's generally complicated enough [so] you can write the size of the paper you need to write but clear enough for people to get where you're going to go. It acts as a contract with your reader [for] what the next pages of writing are going to be about.

SHERSHAH
Boston University

When I think about my thesis, I think about argument. That's the first word that comes into my mind because that's basically been nailed into my head since high school.… And then in college, when I took that to another level, I noticed that a thesis has to be complex in order for it to be surrounded by a lot of work.… If my thesis is complex, it's still strong enough to withstand a lot of criticism and absorb a lot of other ideas.

If the purpose of a relay race is to carry the baton from the starting line across the finish line, then the point of any college paper is to support or carry your thesis from your first paragraph to your last. You can't drop the baton during the run, and the judges must agree that the baton was delivered.

Your readers should be able to locate and comprehend your thesis in less than a minute — or, as Gregg says, you want them to understand the "contract" you have with them before they get too far in. You also want them to nod in agreement at the end of your paper that your thesis was well supported throughout. Your paper will make many points, or "absorb a lot of other ideas" to use SherShah's words, but the logical end of all of your secondary, subordinate points is to uphold a singular, main point: your thesis.

PRACTICE Locate the thesis in Nicole's magical realism paper in Lesson 25 and consider each paragraph. Does each paragraph support her main point, her thesis? Does she carry the baton through each leg and across the finish line? Which paragraphs most strongly support her thesis? Which are the weakest in this way?

2) Frame your thesis as a claim that answers a research question.

MARCUS
California State University, San Marcos

In college I've learned that [a thesis] needs to be an argument, it can't be a fact.

KIMBERLY
California State University, San Marcos

Well, in high school I used to think that a thesis was just a special sentence. I didn't know why it was special. I just thought it was this special sentence and now that I'm in college I kind of more so think that it's an argument.

Your job as a college writer is to explore new territories of ideas and plant your flag when you discover something new, as small as your new plot may be. You are like Neil Armstrong, who left the American flag on the moon as a symbol of his country's accomplishment. Your thesis is like an explorer's flag in this analogy because it declares and represents your claim.

The words *thesis*, *claim*, *argument*, and *point* are therefore similar: They are your assertion about an issue in question. So a thesis must claim something new or original, and it must assert a point that responds to an ongoing argument or conversation. Others might disagree with your thesis or your claim — that's okay — but you have to make a claim nonetheless; you have to plant your flag. Kimberly's sense of a thesis in high school was probably more along the lines of a main idea summarized in a "special sentence," but until she became a college writer, she didn't fully understand that the purpose and function of a thesis is not just to state a big idea but to argue a claim.

By contrast, a thesis statement cannot be an already established fact, as Marcus has learned in college. For example, this statement cannot be a thesis: "Napkins can be made of paper or fabric." Further, a thesis must be arguable or worth exploring. This statement cannot be a thesis because it is inconsequential: "Napkins should be folded once at lunch but at least twice at dinner." This statement is not a thesis because it asks a question instead of asserting a claim: "Should the dining hall only use napkins made from 100 percent recycled paper?"

Student writers often use rhetorical questions to frame their thesis or argument, but the question itself cannot be a thesis because it does not make a claim and it does not "plant a flag."

PRACTICE Look at Nicole's thesis again: "The magical realism elements in Gabriel García Márquez 'The Handsomest Drowned Man in the World' work as a postcolonial narrative serving as a decolonizing agent." Is Nicole's thesis arguable? Is it important? Does she plant a flag and make a claim?

3) Focus your thoughts and your readers' attention with a research-based thesis.

NANAISSA
Lansing Community College

The thesis in France is [called] a *problématique*. It's a question you ask yourself and you ask to the audience so they can think about it through the essay. We also have a topic sentence, we call it *le introduction du paragraph*. I still think in French when I'm structuring my paper because I really like the idea of a question to make sure it sticks to my thesis: "So why is it so …" And I always come back to my thesis after each paragraph to make sure it sticks to and answers my questions… In French we call it a *problématique* because it's a question you're trying to ask. Here, we call it a *thesis*, [but] it doesn't have to be a question.

PHILLIP
Santa Fe College

I learned in my first college English class that it is a good idea to have an outline, and I think the outline comes from your thesis statement. Before I start writing my first draft, I come up with my thesis statement first and that will serve as a guide to writing the rest of the paper. It serves as something you can always go back to, like a compass, to refer to and keep you going — keep you focused on your main point. … And that's how I start writing.

Nanaissa and Phillip use their thesis statements to focus attention throughout their essay, for themselves as writers as well as their readers. It's interesting to note that Nanaissa's expectations for academic writing in France are slightly different than in her U.S. college. In both places, a question could be used to focus attention; but in the United States, Nanaissa's thesis statement needs to assert an answer, not just ask a question.

Since your thesis must be arguable or debatable, it will necessarily address a complicated issue, involving a variety of people, variables, contexts, and perspectives. Because there are so many moving parts and various ways to approach the topic of your writing, your thesis must help your readers focus attention on the concrete, specific dimensions you will address. A thesis helps determine the scope of your writing.

Flags help focus attention because they are designed to catch your eye and because they symbolize or represent larger ideas and peoples. Flags are very colorful, graphic, and symbolic. They are composed of bold colors, shapes, and icons, which are simple and easy to understand. Likewise, your thesis will help focus your reader's attention if your claim is easy to locate and read.

Flags succinctly symbolize large, complex ideas (like liberty or a religion), and they represent territories, citizens, and governments. Likewise, college writing should explore complicated ideas, and so your thesis concisely needs to represent or stand in place for your many subtopics, abundant evidence, and intricate analysis.

PRACTICE   Nicole's magical realism paper in Lesson 25 includes many complex subtopics. How does her thesis focus the reader's attention and "represent" her many subtopics? How does her thesis define the scope of her claim? Does Nicole's "flag" focus your attention?

Pisit Rapitpunt/Getty Images

4) Employ your thesis to establish a theme repeated in your writing, thus providing structure, continuity, and rhythm.

HYESU
University of Florida

When you get the topic and you read the materials, you start to get a feel for what's interesting. I guess the qualification for what's interesting is if it makes me ask why or how did this happen? The thesis then would usually come to be something like, "This happened because …"—an answer to the question I had while I was reading. You would arrive at that answer through analysis of the documents you've read.… I guess after writing all the body paragraphs, I find that I have this common thread of thought that you can kind of see throughout the paragraphs, so that's where I get my thesis.… I guess usually people say start with an argument so that you can support it with details later, but I can't do that for some reason.

MICHELLE
California State University, San Marcos

If there was one thing I could tell all college professors to help their students [it would be] to help them develop a better thesis. A thesis is basically what your argument is going to be all about. If you have a good thesis, your essay is obviously going to have better flow—a better argument, better essay. But if your thesis isn't strong enough, then you're going to have trouble with writing.

Michelle begins writing with a clear thesis, but Hyesu develops her thesis after writing the body paragraphs. Even though their initial approaches are different, they both agree that a thesis provides structure throughout their documents. Michelle links a clear thesis

to flow and ease of writing. Hyesu finds a "common thread" between the body paragraphs that eventually becomes her thesis.

The primary origins of the word *thesis* are twofold:

1) **As the downbeat in a musical composition (what the bass drum typically plays)**
2) **To place or put an object down or in front of someone**

So you can think of a thesis as putting your foot down, figuratively, as you make your point or establish your ground. Like stomping on the pedal of a bass drum, the repetition of your main ideas and the repetition of key terms from your thesis provide a structure and cohesion throughout your work.

Jazz compositions, symphonies, movies, and even television shows have musical themes that are repeated for similar purposes. To be coherent, all of the parts and paragraphs of your writing need to return to and recall your thesis.

If a national flag is the visual symbol of a country, then its national anthem is its musical representative. Notice how national anthems often repeat both lyrical words and musical notes throughout the composition. These repetitions establish a theme for listeners to follow and identify. And of course an *anthem* is by definition thematic because it unifies ideas and focuses listeners through repetition. Likewise, your thesis will establish central ideas and key terms that will be repeated throughout your assignment. In fact, college writing assignments that are now called *papers* or *essays* were commonly called *themes* not too long ago.

PRACTICE What themes and key terms does Nicole repeat throughout her paper

in Lesson 25? How does her thesis establish these themes and key terms? Could her thesis be improved to better echo key themes and terms?

5) Present your thesis most often, but not always, as a single sentence located in your introduction.

MARC
Boston College

For a thesis, I was always taught that it [should] be one sentence, not two sentences. But, this year, a couple of my friends were telling me how their thesis is four or five sentences long. And I guess it just varies depending on the teacher. Usually, for my papers, my thesis is a sentence or two, never more, just because that's how I was taught. But I know you could do it differently than that.

DANNY
University of Florida

In high school they tell you, "Last sentence of your introduction paragraph. That's where your thesis should be. That's how it should be in every paper." . . . But I kind of always disagreed. I don't think there's a problem with the thesis not being in that same spot. I think it can be wherever it's most fitting, and I think that's probably what a lot of kids don't realize, if they're still depending on that high school style of writing.

The rudimentary five-paragraph theme has conditioned college writers and readers to place a single, declarative thesis sentence at the very end of the introductory paragraph. On the one hand, this convention is so well established that writers take a slight risk when they experiment against the convention. On the other hand, you must make creative, artistic choices in your work based not on pressures of convention but on the rhetorical contexts of your writing.

The *research-based* thesis discussed in this lesson distributes the thesis across a number of sentences, although the final sentence could still satisfy readers expecting to find a conventional thesis.

Regardless of where you place your thesis, your readers should be able to identify it. Most of the time, flags are placed on a pinnacle at the top of a flagpole, or they do not work so well. However, sometimes a flag may also be painted on a wall, worn on a badge, or printed on paper. Likewise, you do not always need to place your thesis in the most obvious place, but you take a risk if you break with convention.

PRACTICE What does Nicole say in her interview in Lesson 25 about her preference for locating a thesis? Why do you think she does or does not follow her own advice in her magical realism paper in Lesson 25?

6) Use your thesis to respond to the research you conduct and the evidence you find.

SAMANTHA
California State University, San Marcos

I would say that the different pieces of a college paper are pretty much the same as I learned in high school, you know: thesis, introduction, body paragraphs, supporting sources, and then you have your conclusion, then typically your bibliography, your footnotes, and all that. . . . I would say that what's changed, though, is definitely my approach, how I put it all together. Before, it used to be: come up with my thesis first and find a bunch of stuff to support it, and I found that became very difficult sometimes because my [initial] thesis may not be as relevant as I thought it was. Now, what I do when I'm first writing an essay is to do as much research as I can … and then say, "Okay, I have all of this information. What do I want to do with it?" From there the thesis normally becomes very, very obvious.

Lesson 1 established that college writing is defined by its use of sources, which is a key idea that has been repeated throughout almost every lesson. Your task as a college writer is to investigate a question or a problem and articulate a solution or an approach in the form of your thesis. Thus, until you first consult what others have said regarding your topic, you cannot formulate a true thesis.

This change from "thesis-before-research" to "research-before-thesis" is one of the defining characteristics for becoming a college writer, as it was for Samantha. You might have a tentative or exploratory thesis as you begin your research (like a *hypothesis*), but you cannot totally nail the thesis until you have studied what others have been saying recently about your topic.

PRACTICE **What is Nicole's primary source of evidence in her magical realism paper in Lesson 25? Does it seem likely that she gathered this evidence before or after formulating her thesis? Why do you think so?**

7) Revise your thesis statement in response to the evidence you find throughout your researching process.

DEONTA
University of North Carolina, Chapel Hill

Well, throughout high school I always thought the thesis was this strict thing that had to be perfect, it had to be done at the start of the paper, and I used to spend too much time on it. But now that I'm in college I've learned that the thesis, it may not be perfect the first time. You can always redo it, you don't have to do it the first thing. As long as you have an idea of what you want to talk about, you can write the rest of the paper and come back to the thesis later.

CONNOR
Boston University

My thesis statements have become more complex, and it was really hard in the beginning when you're writing difficult papers to come up with a thesis statement. I ended trying to reverse-engineer it. So, I would go in to look at all of my evidence and then say "What does this prove?" and "What's something common about all of these?"…I came up with this [approach to a thesis] mainly by proofreading because I can get off on a tangent.… It was just constant revision, constant consultation with the professor.

Connor brings the discussion of thesis statements full circle back to the beginning of this text and **RRFF** when he describes how "constant revision" in "consultation with the professor" defines his approach to developing a thesis. Deonta describes how becoming a college writer has made thesis statements easier for him to write, since he is confident in the revision process.

ERIENNE
Metropolitan State University of Denver

You don't have to be completely certain about whatever you're arguing to begin with. You ask the questions, then you get the evidence, and then maybe you'll get a clearer thesis. I think that it puts a lot of pressure on students to think that they have to start with something that is completely solid and completely gold. It's a process. All of these things are often happening simultaneously. You're developing your thesis while you're researching and you're keeping some little seed of an idea in the back of your mind while you're doing all this. But it's not that all-encompassing, grand, and glorious couple of sentences that says exactly where you're going. Yet.

If you use a research-based thesis, then your main point will evolve throughout the writing process in response to research, feedback, and revision. You may find yourself even reversing your initial thesis as you collect additional research throughout your writing process.

For example, you might have begun your research on the ecology of napkins for the dining hall by assuming that 100 percent recycled materials would be the best choice. So, your tentative thesis was:

> **The dining hall should only use napkins made from 100 percent recycled material.**

But as you researched the issue in more depth, you discovered that the ecological impact of shipping 100 percent recycled napkins from their source to your campus was severe, and that a better overall solution was to use a product from a local mill with sustainable wood and 75 percent recycled contents. Your final thesis became:

> **The dining hall should use napkins manufactured in a neighboring county because the overall carbon footprint of this product is much less than shipping napkins from across the country to our campus.**

PRACTICE In Lesson 25, Nicole describes a classmate's advice that helped her redirect her paper on magical realism. In what ways can you speculate that her preliminary thesis was different from her final version (according to the evidence in her interview and sample paper)?

19.3

Exercises: thesis

19a Integrate the video.

Notice how Cuyler uses the thesis to connect to his topic and then connects his "arguments" and "answers" with his readers. Cuyler has a well-designed, strongly connected, and ideally balanced rhetorical triangle when he says,

> My approach to a thesis now is less mechanical. Now, the reason you write a paper is that there's something about the topic you don't understand. And so the thesis is oftentimes for me the question itself, or maybe the question rephrased as an answer. And then I take the reader through all the different arguments to show them how I answered that question, or how I arrived at that answer.

Write a substantial paragraph or two, with a topic sentence or mini-thesis, through which you respond to Cuyler and other videos in the lesson as you form your own approaches to developing research-based thesis statements. You can watch the Lesson 19 Essentials Video, or you can browse the embedded clips in the online edition of this lesson. You might begin by identifying the moments that stand out to you the most. Which student videos seem to make the most sense to you? With whom do you agree? Disagree? What patterns do you find among the student sound bites? Which ideas were the most instructive or helpful to you? What surprised you? How have your own ideas about *thesis* come into focus through the videos?

19b Create a journal entry or blog.

Your instructor might ask you to keep a writer's journal throughout this class. This journal could be handwritten or composed on a computer; it could take the shape of a text-based blog or a video blog.

To prepare a journal entry on Lesson 19, describe your thoughts and approaches to the key term *thesis*, trying not to glance back at the material in this lesson, at first. Not referring to this material initially will help you see what you have internalized so far. After carefully composing your initial thoughts, then look back at some of the ideas and strategies other students gave in Lesson 19 or in the online database of interviews. For example, in his interview, Dan criticizes obsessive approaches to a thesis statement, like the terrier thesis discussed in section 16.1:

> I hate the idea of a "thesis" because writers all too often think, "Okay, here's my thesis, all I've gotta do is make sure everyone understands what my thesis is and then I have to give a little bit of proof for my thesis and I'm done, I got it." *Thesis* is way bigger than that, and *writing* is way bigger than that.

You might wish to disagree with some of this lesson, or you might want to modify or expand on some of its advice. For example, consider integrating additional thoughts, notes, and lessons from your instructor and your class meetings into your journal entry. It might help for you to imagine that you are giving advice to your future self about writing. What from this lesson and from discussions about writing might benefit you down the road?

19c See yourself as a writer.

In a page or two, describe the evolution of your sense of *thesis* since you began writing. Where and when did you start to develop strategies for thesis development? What major events, assignments, and papers have influenced your sense of *thesis* along the

way? What particular teachers or classes have reshaped the ways you develop a thesis? What was your sense of *thesis* before you began reading this lesson? What is your approach now that you have finished this lesson? In what ways can you imagine your sense of thesis development changing beyond college? For example, as a writing center tutor, Jenna works with students who do not see themselves as writers and lack confidence, which can lead to tentative thesis statements. She encourages students to write affirmatively: "In the end, your thesis should be a statement of your claim. Whatever you're claiming: claim it, know it, be confident. I hate when people use 'I think,' 'I believe,' all those sorts of things, because that just weakens it. You don't want to weaken your thesis because it's your words. Be confident; you know it."

19d Invent your writing.

Section 19.2 of this lesson discusses seven strategies for developing a thesis statement. In five complete sentences, map out how five of these seven concepts could be applied to a writing assignment you are working on in this class (or in another class, if you are not currently writing in this course). For example, in his interview, Connor talks about how he uses the research and evidence he has gathered to launch his thesis statements.

19e Analyze student writing.

Study the opening two or three paragraphs or segments of a couple of model projects in Lesson 25 or in the LaunchPad. You might compare very different models, such as Dan's video and Nicole's paper, or you might read similar work, such as Nanaissa's and Vinh-Thuy's papers.

For each writer, describe in a sentence or two the kind of thesis each of these authors seems to write, compared to the descriptions of the terrier, composite, and research-based thesis statements described in Section 19.1. In what ways do they seem alike? Different? Also evaluate the scope of each project. Does the writer manage the scope of their chosen thesis effectively? How do they do so?

Your instructor might ask you to apply this analysis and these questions to your class-mates' writing instead of (or in addition to) the model projects.

19f Revise repeatedly from feedback.

Samantha deeply revises her thesis statements as a critical part of improving her writing:

> I think that a thesis statement is ever-evolving in the process of writing your paper. I [never] think, "Okay, cool. I have my thesis statement and now I'm going to write the rest of my paper and it's going to stay the same from the first time I write it to the time that I turn it in." I think that the thesis statement is something that should always be adapted as you are finding more research.

Examine a writing assignment you are currently working on. Describe some specific ways that you can use the ideas from Lesson 19 to revise your writing and improve your thesis state-ments. Perhaps most important, to complete this exercise, take an early draft of your writing to the writing center, a peer workshop, or your instructor's office hours and ask, "Does my thesis seem to respond to the evidence I use? Is it research-based? Does my scope seem appropriate? Does my thesis seem headed in a clear direction?"

Introductions and Conclusions

Design the right introduction and conclusion.

ESSENTIALS VIDEO

Visit the LaunchPad for *Becoming a College Writer* to watch the
Lesson 20 Essentials Video.

20.1

Why you should design the right introduction and conclusion.

Writers make many choices that help connect them with a topic and an audience. When it comes to thinking about the more conventional and physical aspects of writing, you might want to think in terms of *design* — making choices about your composition so that everything fits together. This means that the kind of thesis you write *fits* the kind of assignment you have been given, the kind of introduction you write *matches* the genre in which you are working, and the kind of conclusion you write *is designed* to satisfy your readers' disciplinary expectations. Your choices should also be well designed for your mode and medium: words on paper, interactive digital format, audio-visual communication, and so on.

At first glance, it might seem like following a convention is easy and does not require thought or craft. The most famous convention in academic writing is probably the five-paragraph essay, which is conventional because you don't have to think about it much anymore — just follow the rules and fill out the form.

You have probably sensed by now, however, that becoming a college writer depends on moving beyond forms and formulas, which means that you need to think strategically about conventions like introductions and conclusions. The word *design* is used throughout this lesson and in other lessons on writing conventions to urge you to be thoughtful about such choices, making the most out of them by not following the "rules" blindly. Writing conventions, such as introductions and conclusions, are a way for you to make meaning throughout your writing process, rather than a merely mechanical, surface concern to consider as an afterthought (or not at all).

Introductions and conclusions that are designed to fit the context of your specific assignment will engage your audience.

This concept of *designing* your writing is perhaps most obvious when it comes to the more physical components of your writing, such as introductions, conclusions, paragraphs, and thesis statements. But it can be very helpful to also think in terms of the *rhetorical* design of your writing, which emphasizes the choices you make to connect with a topic and an audience. The next lesson, on paragraphs, continues this concept of design to help you shape your writing, while this lesson focuses on two design conventions that my writing students have lots of questions about: introductions and conclusions.

The easiest way to begin to understand *designing your writing* in this way is to talk about the most familiar, elementary approach to designing introductions and conclusions: the *mirrored triangles* of the five-paragraph essay. The mirrored triangles design has four guidelines:

1) **The introduction begins broadly, with a generalization.**
2) **Each of the middle sentences in the introduction restates a topic sentence from each of the body paragraphs.**
3) **The final sentence in the introduction narrows and announces the focus in the form of a thesis sentence.**
4) **The conclusion is a mirror, or an inverse of the introduction, moving from specific to general, providing the thesis first, then a recap of topic sentences, and finally ending in a relevant generalization.**

As a first lesson on essay format, the five-paragraph theme with its mirrored-triangle introductions and conclusions can be quite effective because it teaches you to design your writing with structure, organization, and a clear focus. The common problem with the mirrored triangles approach is when it becomes too thoughtless, when writers follow the form slavishly without thinking critically about how it actually works. If you decide to adopt a mirrored triangles approach, try to break away from other elements of a strict five-paragraph essay format. Include more or fewer paragraphs, place an engaging thesis somewhere other than the end of the first paragraph, or find some other method of reimagining the format to make your writing fresh and compelling.

Emily follows the form for a conclusion, but she is beginning to recognize that it doesn't make sense for her. So, for Emily, becoming a college writer means finding new

approaches to conventions like a conclusion, approaches that help her to get the most out of her writing. When you follow a prescribed approach without thinking deliberately about how it works and how it matches your particular assignment context, you are filling out a form, not *designing* your writing. I admire how Hannah makes deliberate choices about academic conventions like introductions by studying the moves that other writers make. Hannah is actively designing her writing.

EMILY
Boston University

I have such a hard time on conclusions because I feel like "Oh well, I'm just repeating what I wrote in my paper. Why do I really need to write this?"

HANNAH
California State University, San Marcos

I read so many of my friends' papers and they have these long introductions and it just feels overwhelming. So I decided with my own papers, I just want to state what I want to state. Everything else is unnecessary.... I don't add fluff, I don't add lead-ins; it's just not my style.... I used to think that an introduction had to be an inverted triangle, that it had to have a hook at the very beginning and then narrow down into what your thesis was going to be. And then I felt like the conclusion had to be the mirror opposite of that. You start with your thesis, and then you reformat your essay in short sentences and then you end. I thought that's what it was. Now, I think that an introduction is more of, "This is what I'm going to talk about. Here it is. I'm presenting it to you. You've read two sentences now. If this is what you want, keep reading. If it's not, go find something else."

Writers and readers are both likely to be bored by forms.

In other words, avoid thinking that each sentence in an introduction and conclusion has a rule that governs it. Instead, think about the big picture: What do introductions and conclusions aim to accomplish for college writers? What work do they do? On the simplest level, an introduction is a preview, and a conclusion is a review, which is an important function in every type, genre, mode, and medium of academic writing. Even a lab report has an introduction and a conclusion! One of the most common analogies for an introduction is that it is like a road map for your readers, outlining the route the writing will follow, especially the starting point, key landmarks along the way, and, of course, the destination. If an introduction is like a road map, then a conclusion is like a scrapbook that reflects back on the journey.

Michael writes conclusions that help him make sense of all his thinking, writing, research, and analysis in new ways, now that the experience is complete. He talks about the "shapes" of his thinking that he could not see until the end, until all of the pieces of the puzzle were put together in the conclusion.

MICHAEL
Michigan State University

These shapes before didn't seem all too concrete. As I started writing about them, as I started fleshing them out, I could kind of make my conclusion. Sometimes people just say reiterate your introduction, but I think, for a conclusion…you're trying to encapsulate the real idea, not just the evidence, not just the introduction. You get [the solution] to that puzzle that you couldn't see before. That's where the real conclusion comes from, trying to shape that.

koya979/Shutterstock.com

For Michael, the conclusion has enormous purpose because it's the place where all of the ideas he has been working on so diligently finally come together and pay off. He doesn't write a conclusion because someone told him that he had to. Catherine also designs her introductions and conclusions to provide coherence to her thoughts and writing. She emphasizes the functions of her introductions and conclusions so that she can design them accordingly.

CATHERINE
Michigan State University

Say you're taking pieces of cloth and you're trying to weave them together into a rope or whatever. There's a knot up [top], and that's your introduction, it's culminating everything that's going on, and this is its function. From there on out, you have six or seven strands, and you're trying to weave them into this thing that's very tight and very useful. They come in and out of each other to be this cohesive piece. And at the end you tie it in a simple knot. It's going to probably be almost the same as your introduction, but you'll have some sort of revelation at the end. For it to be satisfying, this piece of rope has to be pretty tightly woven.

Cuyler uses a weaving metaphor like Catherine to design linkages between all of the parts of his writing, and the purpose for the knots at the beginning and end of the weave is to hold everything together. Cuyler uses the conclusion as a kind of test or diagnostic for the entire work: If writing the conclusion is a struggle, then perhaps the ideas lack cohesion and need more revision throughout.

CUYLER
Metropolitan State University of Denver

When I'm writing a conclusion, I want to make sure that all of those threads that I've been weaving throughout the paper have been resolved. As I'm writing, I kind of keep my eye on the thesis, and then once I hit the conclusion, I make sure that all the threads wind themselves into the conclusion and match the thesis. If you have to really, really, work hard to make a conclusion, then there's something wrong either in the thesis or in the body of the paper and you need to go back and figure out where it went wrong. I think conclusions should come pretty naturally for a functioning paper.

So, as Micheal, Catherine, and Cuyler demonstrate, introductions and conclusions can do much more than merely preview and review topics and subtopics. Introductions establish context, connecting with the audience, by describing to the readers what they will get from your writing. Conclusions extend context by suggesting ideas or actions that your readers might pursue in response to your writing.

Academic writing typically addresses complicated issues that are unlikely to begin or end within the limited boundaries of your drafts. Therefore, academic introductions often trace what other writers and researchers have said leading up to your work, and academic conclusions often suggest follow-up issues and questions to explore as a result of your writing.

Vinh-Thuy compares his introductions and conclusions in his academic writing to those in fictional stories. The typical narrative story begins by establishing the setting and the context: "Where are we, and how did we get here?" The conclusion, in Vinh-Thuy's narrative comparison, resolves most of the immediate questions and comments, but provokes readers to continue to think.

VINH-THUY
Red Rocks Community College

For me, an introduction kind of sets up the entire story. An essay is a story that has an argument. So, an introduction should set up the story, kind of telling your reader where you are at. Or maybe ask your reader to ask that question as they read: "Where are they? What point of the story are they at?" And your conclusion should be something to wrap up, but it doesn't necessarily have to be the end-all happy ending. It can be the terminal point of your argument, but it can continue to ask questions.

Part One: Rhetoric and Part Two: Context argue repeatedly that successful writing responds to the specific relationships within a specific writing situation, including the relationships among writer, audience, topic, assignment prompt, genre, mode, media, and discipline. When you watch a movie, you have expectations regarding the beginning, middle, and end. You expect the opening to identify the setting and establish the characters, which is a principle that Vinh-Thuy applies to his academic writing, too. The middle develops dramatic conflict, and the closing resolves the tension in some way.

However, consider how disappointing it is when a movie provides exactly the same kind of story that you have seen many times before. How do you feel when filmmakers seem to be following a familiar formula rather than crafting, shaping, or designing something at least slightly original and genuine? Also consider how

disappointed you might be when a movie fails to provide you with a coherent introduction or conclusion. We have come to expect movies and stories to have at least some kind of a beginning, middle, and end — with the opening being a transition into the depths of the work and the closing being a transition back out.

Scientists will have expectations about the reports they read that will be different from the expectations moviegoers have about films, but they both expect those three key components: a beginning, a middle, and an end. Newspaper readers will have different expectations compared to poetry critics or historians. You might browse the first paragraphs in each of the six featured model papers to examine how different they are because they are responding to such different contexts.

Take a look at Nicole's first paragraph for her paper on magical realism and compare it to Kendra's abstract from her report on Komodo dragons. What important differences do you see between these introductions?

NICOLE

Magical realism is a blend of magical-like elements rooted in the foundation of reality. This binary blend borders the uncanny, while placing emphasis on the supernatural. The culturally-hybrid genre is infused with elements oscillating on the seam of reality and fantasy; however, these transcendent elements also serve in challenging the meta-narrative. Within this process, the magical realism genre becomes a lens of decolonization. Magical realism is "postcolonial writing" created by one "who learns the master's language," and then uses this language "to undermine some of its master's assumptions" (Faris 28). The magical realism elements in Gabriel Gárcia Márquez's "The Handsomest Drowned Man in the World" works as a postcolonial narrative serving as a decolonizing agent.

KENDRA

Abstract

Using three key sources on the topic to stand in for field or laboratory research, this paper examines the question of how Komodo dragons successfully subdue their prey. The close examination of the mechanics of the reptile's teeth and jaw, combined with a chemical analysis of blood, saliva, and mouth swabs, all combine to indicate that it is the combination of tactics rather than a single, principle factor that allow for the effectiveness of the Komodo dragon as a hunter.

GREGG
California State University, San Marcos

I consider it opening a frame in the introduction that I plan on closing in the conclusion. . . . What that does is give your writing a clear beginning and a clear end, so that you come full circle and tie up loose knots with the final conclusion paragraph.

PRACTICE No matter the context, your readers will expect you to design your writing to have a strong introduction and a solid conclusion. An emphasis on the idea of *design* can help you intimately connect the contextual relationships in your writing because it encourages you to shape, craft, and sculpt your words thoughtfully. Describe in a few sentences how you want to *design* a current or upcoming draft of an introduction. Then list some ideas for *designing* a conclusion for that writing assignment.

20.2 [HOW]

How to design the right introduction and conclusion.

Because introductions are like road maps to orient your readers, and conclusions are like scrapbooks that look back on the ground that was covered on the trip that you and your reader have taken together, introductions and conclusions serve important cognitive functions. They preview and organize your thoughts so that readers can adequately process your insights. Drafting and revising introductions and conclusions also serve an important developmental function for the writer because working through these two elements helps you focus, organize, and evaluate your thoughts through writing.

Introductions and conclusion do similar things, but they are also different in important ways. Introductions map out an intellectual pathway for readers who have not yet taken that journey. Conclusions look back on an intellectual journey from the unique perspective of having gone through the experience. If the sentences in your introduction and conclusion are mostly identical, even if they are in a different order or use synonyms, then their functions are not differentiated, which is to say that they are probably not well designed.

Introductions and conclusions are not only different from each other; different audiences, prompts, genres, disciplines, and contexts also call for different approaches to writing introductions and conclusions. It helps to avoid thinking in terms of a single, universal format for introductions and conclusions because it's more effective to design these elements in terms of the right match for a particular writing assignment. The nine pieces of advice below can help you to design the right introductions and conclusions for your academic writing projects.

1) Provide context and application for your readers.

KENDRA
Michigan State University

An introduction gets the reader interested in why your question needs to be answered. If you were to just start with this question and not give it context to the bigger picture, or the human population, it may not get as much attention from the reader. The reader might just think, "Well I don't really need to know about pH levels in this river or…" So, if you put it in the context of a larger picture of how other people could use it for their research, then you can gain more readers.

The first and perhaps most important job for any introduction or conclusion is to provide connection, context, and application for your readers. In your opening, you want to establish the relevance of the writing that will follow. In the closing, you want to underscore that relevance by encouraging readers to apply your insights. Kendra explains to her readers how her scientific research impacts their lives, even if they are not scientists themselves. Most college-level introductions

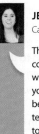

JENNA
California State University, San Marcos

The introduction should be used to contextualize your thesis. Say you're writing about an issue in society, and you're arguing that something should be changed, you're going to want to tell us what the issue is. You're going to want to maybe set up how you feel about the issue, what's going on, and then lead us into what should be changed and that would be your thesis.

aim to draw connections between the audience's current knowledge and the advanced, discipline-specific material that follows.

Since academic writing is so heavily based upon sources and evidence, people often describe it as a textual conversation that you, as the writer, are contributing to. If so, an introduction establishes context by giving a sense of the conversation that has been leading up to this moment when you join it. Likewise, a conclusion builds application by identifying your specific contribution to the conversation and anticipating new directions that the conversation might take as a result. When Jenna says that an introduction should tell readers "what's going on" and "what should be changed," she designs an introduction that enters an ongoing conversation and adds something to it.

In Lesson 19: Thesis, we describe a research-based thesis statement that stretches out over three or more sentences. The design of the research-based thesis is to ground your writing firmly in previous research. The essential move of that research-based thesis statement is to identify what others have been saying about your topic so that you can contribute additional, incremental ideas. That move and the multiple sentences it requires can serve as an introductory paragraph in itself — an introduction that establishes context and leads to the eventual application of your contribution to the conversation, after you have explored and supported your main point throughout.

PRACTICE Locate the introduction in Dan's film about communication and writing (the transcript is on page 488). Describe how his introduction provides context and connection for his audience. Is it effective in this regard? How might it be improved?

2) Move from general to specific in the introduction, establishing scope and providing focus.

MARCUS
California State University, San Marcos

What I've learned in college is the triangle formation: you start out very broad, you narrow down into your subject, leaving off with your thesis before you dive into the writing.

BRAD
University of Florida

I don't want to say you can completely do away with an introduction, but you can almost start with your main point. Rather than deductive reasoning, you can do inductive reasoning, where you're actually thinking of a paper as broad starting off and you slowly siphon down to your main point at the end.

Since the first job of an introduction is to establish relevance, most introductions begin broadly, casting a wide net to connect with a wide range of readers with diverse experiences and perspectives, as Marcus has learned. However, you can only manage to

research and support a limited number of ideas thoroughly within any academic writing assignment. You will have to narrow your focus to specific areas and a particular main point. Introductions are often represented geometrically like a triangle that is wide and flat at the top, with a narrow point at the bottom, because that suggests moving from general to specific. To continue the conversation metaphor: The context of your writing begins by connecting with an array of voices in a discussion, but then it narrows to your specific contribution. A well-designed introduction follows the same shape: It provides context and connection by moving from a broad, general perspective to your specific main point.

PRACTICE Revisit the introduction in Dan's film about communication and writing. Does the introduction move from general to specific? Which sentences establish the scope and focus? Does he seem to manage the scope and focus effectively?

3) Announce your main point.

GRETCHEN
Boston University

A good introduction should make it clear to the reader what you are about to talk about, not just, "I'm going to talk about this play or this book," but *what specifically* about the play or the book you want to examine in your essay.

Most U.S. high school graduates have taken a timed essay exam, and the very first piece of advice they are given is "Be sure to state your main point clearly." The idea that the introduction is a sort of container for a thesis statement, most typically in the form of a single sentence, should be familiar. (See Lesson 19 for more on the thesis statement.)

You have probably also been taught to begin a concluding paragraph with a restatement of your thesis in some form. Your readers are very likely to expect your main point to be located in these ways in your introductions and conclusions; consequently, an undeniable, essential function of these two elements is to announce your thesis statement.

But introductions and conclusions can accomplish so much more than merely providing a parking space for your thesis, and they can suffer if you design them primarily for that limited purpose. Yes, you should be sure that you point to your big idea, but design your introductions and conclusions to take every opportunity to make connections and respond to context by following the other advice listed in this lesson.

Nicole, who admits that she likes to "go against the grain," puts her thesis in the second paragraph on longer papers. She can't explain why, but I am certain it's because she wants to be thoughtful and intentional about designing her written work.

NICOLE
California State University, San Marcos

I don't really like to include my thesis at the end of the first "introduction" paragraph as we were taught. If it's a three- to four- possibly five-page paper, I will because it's such a short assignment that you have to include your thesis at the end of the introduction. But I usually like to include my thesis in a second paragraph. I don't know why, maybe it's just me trying to go against the grain.

PRACTICE Revisit Dan's video introduction. Does he announce his main point? Does his introduction steadily build to the main point, or is it inconsistent? How does Dan announce his main point and make it apparent?

4) Begin to define and redefine key words in your title and introduction.

Academic, research-based writing is intended to explore answers to difficult problems. This means that academic writing often revolves around the definition and redefinition of key terms: exploring what is going on in depth, beyond and behind simplistic ideas and definitions. For example, Dan explores the terms *writer* and *writing* throughout his film. He is wise to introduce these key terms in the title and introduction, although it will take the balance of the film to examine these definitions more fully.

Consider beginning to define your key terms in your introduction, since so much of your writing will hinge on words and definitions that are being contested and that are evolving. In fact, one way to design an effective introduction is to discuss how key terms have evolved over time and why they are currently of interest and worth examining in your research. Dan's film describes the evolution of his *writing* as a *writer*. Be careful, though, because beginning an introduction by citing a dictionary or simply paraphrasing the etymology of a word can often be a tiresome cliché that most academic readers will dislike (see section 20.2.9).

PRACTICE Previously I described how Dan explores the key terms *writer* and *writing* in his film. How does he establish those terms in the opening of his film? How do those terms evolve throughout the film? Does he return to those terms in the conclusion?

5) Preview your structure.

TOREY
Lansing Community College

[The introduction] gives a map of the essay, I think. You can tell what the essay is going to be about: it [foreshadows] the body paragraphs and eventually the conclusion.

Speech coaches are famous for saying, "Tell the audience what you are going to say. Say it. And then tell them what you just said." That deliberate and redundant approach works much better when it comes to oral rather than written communication because remembering the structure of spoken words is much more difficult than remembering textual words. (Textual words have many more structural cues, such as punctuation, sentences, paragraphs, headings, etc.) However, that advice does bleed over into written discourse when we think of *introductions as previews* and *conclusions as reviews*. On the one hand, it can be very effective to give your readers cognitive clues about what they are about to encounter because it gives them a place in their brains to store and orient the ideas as they accumulate. You do not want to surprise your readers to the point that they do not know how to handle your ideas.

Torey aims to preview the structure and main concepts in her introductions, which she describes as a "map" to her composition. Doing so increases the chances of her ideas connecting on the first try, which improves flow and readability. You probably should avoid having a single sentence in your introduction that corresponds directly with each paragraph in the body because that's too robotic and formulaic. But you do

want to help your audience anticipate the key terms, ideas, research, and subtopics you will visit, most typically in the order in which they appear.

PRACTICE Locate the introduction in Dan's film about communication and writing. Does the introduction preview the structure of the work? If the film were delivered as a "paper," do you imagine the introduction would be different, especially in terms of previewing the structure? Is the introduction in the film well designed for that context and mode? Why or why not?

6) Use the conclusion to reflect on the ground you have gained.

JENNA
California State University, San Marcos

Conclusions are sometimes the hardest part of the essay, and they can be different for any sort of essay you're writing. But, typically, you're going to be wrapping it all up. You're going to be tying enough loose ends that readers feel that it's complete. We can exit the tour and think, "Oh, I feel good about that." It's not going to be just a cut and paste of your thesis. Once you've reached that final body paragraph, go back, look to see what ideas developed throughout the essay, see what new things came up, how did the direction change? There should be a point where you're looking back, all the way up to your thesis through the body paragraphs and saying, "Okay, where am I now? How do I regroup?"

If a conclusion is like a scrapbook, then your readers should look back from the unique perspective of having just read the entire piece of writing, as Jenna concludes. Your thesis and the evidence used to support it should seem different to your readers after they have thoroughly reviewed all of your writing. There should be progress of some kind in your audience's perspective, even if that movement is small or incremental. If nothing has changed from the beginning to the end of your writing, what was the point? Therefore, your conclusion should not be identical to your introduction because, at the end, your readers have had more experience with your ideas, research, sentences, and thoughts.

A scrapbook that pulls together and summarizes all of the experiences of a journey could not possibly have been made before the trip took place. A highly effective conclusion says in so many words, "Dear Reader, now that we have shared this research together, you can better appreciate my main point from the perspective of seeing the entire argument and all of its support, in its full complexity." Design your conclusion to emphasize the ground that has been covered *from the unique perspective of having gained that ground*. In other words, how does the view from the end of your journey compare to the perspective from the starting point? Jenna frames this different view as she designs her conclusions by asking "what ideas developed throughout the essay" and "how did the direction change?"

PRACTICE Locate the conclusion in Dan's film about communication and writing. Does his conclusion effectively reflect on the ground gained in the film? Why or why not?

7) Underscore your thesis statement in the conclusion.

CARA
Metropolitan State University of Denver

I feel like the conclusions I used to write were a lot more like summaries and not quite as powerful. … I feel like in the conclusion I want to, yes, summarize the points that I've made, but kind of suck out the essential power of the essay and put it in that conclusion. You want to leave people thinking, "Wow. She had some awesome points! I totally see where she's coming from." I feel like the conclusion is that final punch in your argument that shows just how right you are.

Most readers expect a restatement of your main idea in your conclusion so you should give it to them. However, this convention does not mean that reiteration is the only purpose or function of your conclusion; underscoring your thesis statement is just a bare minimum. Perhaps the best way to underscore your main point isn't just to restate it but to synthesize a combination of key ideas and support as you conclude. Design your conclusion so that you do not merely substitute a couple of words from a previous statement.

If you used a single-sentence thesis before, try to distribute the idea across a number of sentences, as we suggest in the research-based thesis statement earlier in Lesson 19 (p. 267). Your main point might now have been explored in more complexity, prompting you to state it in a number of sentences, instead of one. Your conclusion might focus on your evidence and how it holds together. A well-designed conclusion can be much more than a mere container to hold one last blast of your thesis statement.

PRACTICE Revisit the conclusion in Dan's film about communication and writing. Does his conclusion effectively underscore the thesis in the film? Why or why not?

8) Suggest additional applications and implications in your conclusion.

ALICE
University of Florida

I want to talk about conclusion, because I'm okay with thesis and introduction. Conclusion for me is pointless in the way that it is taught. It's just like you restate your thesis, which I think is important. That's what a conclusion should do, it wraps everything up. But, at the same time [I've been taught], "Don't bring anything else into it," like "Don't, don't be creative about it." It's just basically a filler paragraph and I don't like it. It's a bookend and it's not doing anything, and I feel like everything in your paper should have some sort of purpose. … People just end up copy-pasting their entire introduction into the conclusion, changing a couple words, and that's their [final] paragraph, and it's not acceptable for me. I don't like that. I feel like it's useless.

NICOLE
California State University, San Marcos

I learned this in school and I still look at it this way. I look at the conclusion as the "So what?": Why does this matter? What's the point? That's how I work with my conclusion, on that "So what?" factor.

Alice wants her conclusions to have purpose, and what Nicole calls the *"So what?"* factor might offer just what she's looking for. Nicole designs her conclusions to answer the question "So what?" This sets her up to explain the implications of her writing, which is a thoughtful, respectful way to end by connecting with her audience. If introductions explain what the readers will gain from the writing, then a conclusion should identify what the readers can take away. Introductions move from general to specific and conclusions can do the reverse, moving from your specific main point to generalizations that extend from it. Beginning your conclusion with a different version of a thesis statement is safe and conventional. But the truth is, there is not a lot of consensus on what to do next. A conclusion can go in a number of different directions as it unfolds, so there are a number of different approaches.

The most familiar design is to review your primary subtopics in more or less the order they were presented, but that approach can be somewhat empty. Many professional researchers design conclusions to explore the implications and new questions that emerge in response to their research. However, some readers dislike conclusions that pose new questions, since they feel like the job of the draft is to put a lid on an issue by providing a definitive answer. Many conclusions finish with a call to action, including some version of "Dear reader, now that you have seen my research and understand my main point, please consider doing something more to continue to address this problem."

BRAD
University of Florida

Try different formulas. If you want to leave your conclusion as a question — if there's something that is plaguing you — or you feel like there is opportunity to explore [or] expand, [you can] say: "You know, I have done this, but there are the questions that I've answered that other scholars can pick up." That's a completely viable way of having a conclusion that [opens] up a gap for further studies to leap from.

NANAISSA
Lansing Community College

In French you called it an *ouverture*, [which] makes the person think about your essay even after they read it, finished with it. [In the conclusion, an *ouverture*] is a tiny question, not opening a new subject, but making the person want to think about your writing after they read your essay.

If research-based writing is a kind of conversation, then an effective way to design the very end of your conclusion is to begin to anticipate where the dialogue goes from here, as Brad suggests: What comes next? What new questions now arise? What additional research does your writing pave the way for? Scientific reports often include an error analysis section to reflect on possible problems within the study. Other forms of academic writing can likewise be reflective and self-critical by considering gaps in your research that might be filled through additional investigations to follow. Almost all scientific reports begin with a discussion of the previous research to which it is responding and conclude with a call for additional studies along the same lines. And most college-sized writing assignments demand a fairly limited scope to be manageable, meaning that a follow-up project might be begging for attention at a later time.

Regardless of the specific function that is right for your particular writing context, you will want to design a conclusion that considers the applications and implications of your research, which means that you should close your hard-fought draft with much more than a simple parroting of things you have already said.

PRACTICE Does the conclusion in Dan's digital project effectively lead you to consider "what's next?" for Dan — and perhaps yourself, in terms of digital writing?

9) Avoid clichéd and dysfunctional approaches to introductions and conclusions.

Fluffing and *fading* are very common phenomena when it comes to college writing. Frequently opening paragraphs are overly long, delaying the real start of the analysis. (It's easier to generate a lot of fluffy words in an introduction, compared to meaty, well-stated, and well-supported words in a body paragraph.) Very often the final paragraphs in the body and conclusion become thin and underdeveloped as the writer runs out of energy, ideas, and/or words near the deadline. The cure to both fluffing and fading is to design your introductions and conclusions with specific purposes beyond simply parking or reparking your thesis statement.

Do not write an introduction or conclusion primarily because you feel like you have to. Just going through the motions will disconnect you from your audience and topic. Identify specific, meaningful goals for your introductions and conclusions; then design them to meet those specific aims. Your introductions establish your first impression, and your conclusions stamp a lasting impression, so make them count!

ABIGAIL
Santa Fe College

My teachers always told me, "You need something catchy, but you don't want to make it cheesy either." So, my introduction has definitely gotten more professional. You know that guideline: "Tell them what I need to tell them, tell them, and then tell them what I told them." You need to make [it] more sophisticated and not just blatant. I feel that's how my introduction has evolved.

In your introductions, avoid the cliché of a cutesy "attention grabber" for your opening sentence, and try to establish connection and context through serious thought and professional sources instead. Puns and alliteration in your titles and opening sentences will be less effective than an emphasis on key terms from your assignment prompt, sources for support, and your research. The most clichéd opening is to begin: "According to Webster's dictionary. . . ."

At the end of your conclusions, avoid the cliché of a melodramatic, overreaching benediction along the lines of "Now that we have studied this question, let us all go forth and make the world a better place for everyone."

Perhaps the most common dysfunction when it comes to introductions and conclusions is your process and experience writing them. So many academic writers claim to either love or despise writing introductions. Those who love them can invest too much time and too many words on them. Those who struggle with introductions often skip them and jump straight into composing the body, but they risk lacking direction by leaping over the framework. Neither loving nor hating introductions is essentially bad or good. Many very successful writers use each approach.

What *is* essential is that you become aware of what does or does not work for you. Pay attention to what happens to your writing as you design and compose your introductions and be sure to reflect on it. The most effective common approach that I know of is to write a tentative introduction before writing a complete first draft; then go back, deleting the original introduction and writing a new one from the more coherent, experienced perspective of having worked your way through most of your ideas.

HUSSAIN
University of Florida

The majority of my effort in my first draft is spent on getting a really good introduction down — a really good introduction and a pretty good conclusion. For me, the hardest part is to actually start and get a good intro, not only for my readers, but also so I can formalize where I'm going with this paper. So, I spend most of my time trying to get a good intro before I go on to the rest of the body paragraphs.

CARA
Metropolitan State University of Denver

I used to spend a ton of time writing my introduction before I would let myself get further in the essay, [thinking,] "Oh this has to be perfect because this is the foundation of my whole essay." Now, I've allowed myself to just write anything down, just get out the introduction and get it done. And then write the rest of my essay and look over it and see, "Does this introduction still fit? Does this thesis still fit?" And if it doesn't, then I just tailor it to the rest of the essay that I've written.

I like that Cara expects to revisit her introduction after a first draft because, as this text has said in every lesson, the key to becoming a college writer is to **Revise Repeatedly from Feedback**. But this doesn't mean that Hussain's approach is wrong — in fact, if it works for him, it's the right way to go.

Writers experience a lot of confusion about designing and crafting introductions and conclusions because, to be honest, few writing instructors emphasize their development significantly beyond (re)stating the thesis and transitioning in or out with a generalization. The cure to this dysfunction is to identify the intention and purpose for these conventions beyond mere formality.

PRACTICE Locate the conclusion in Dan's film about communication and writing. Is his approach to a conclusion predictable or clichéd? Why or why not? If not, describe what Dan does to design his conclusion thoughtfully and effectively.

20.3

Exercises: introductions and conclusions

20a Integrate the video.

Dillon says, "I don't know how to introduce a paper that I haven't written yet," while Hyesu notes, "The conclusion is the hardest part for me, by far. I think it's because, by the end, you're already pretty worn out by writing the paper and I've probably said everything I had to say. It's a hard balance between not wanting to repeat yourself and wanting to introduce new ideas but not too new."

Dillon and Hyesu identify some of the struggles that accompany writing effective introductions and conclusions at a more advanced level. Write a substantial paragraph or two, with a topic sentence or mini-thesis, through which you respond to Dillon, Hyesu, and other videos in the lesson as you form your own approaches to developing introductions and conclusions. You can watch the Lesson 20 Essentials Video, or you can browse the embedded clips in the online edition of this lesson. You might begin by identifying the moments that stand out to you the most. Which student videos seem to make the most sense to you? With whom do you agree? Disagree? What patterns do you find among the student sound bites? Which ideas were the most instructive or helpful to you? What surprised you? How have your own ideas about introductions and conclusions come into focus through the videos?

20b Create a journal entry or blog.

Your instructor might ask you to keep a writer's journal throughout this class. This journal could be handwritten or composed on a computer; it could take the shape of a text-based blog or a video blog.

To prepare a journal entry on Lesson 20, describe your thoughts and approaches to the key terms *introductions* and *conclusions*, trying not to glance back at the material in this lesson, at first. Not referring to this material initially will help you see what you have internalized so far. After carefully composing your initial thoughts, look back at some of the ideas and strategies other students gave in Lesson 20 or in the online database of interviews. For example, in his interview, Gregg describes his trick of using a metaphor to launch his introduction:

> With an introduction, I usually try to think of a metaphor to start, to draw people in [so] that anybody could really connect with [my writing]. That way, anyone who's reading it would be able to get started, even if I get deep into the conversation and start using elevated language or jargon specific to the field of study I'm writing about.

You might wish to disagree with some of this lesson, or you might want to modify or expand on some of its advice. For example, consider integrating additional thoughts, notes, and lessons from your instructor and your class meetings into your journal entry. It might help for you to imagine that you are giving advice to your future self about writing. What from this lesson and from discussions about writing might benefit you down the road?

20c See yourself as a writer.

In a page or two, describe the evolution of your sense of introductions and conclusions since you began writing. Where and when did you start to develop your strategies for introductions and conclusions? Phillip uses his conclusions to affirm his voice and identity as a college writer:

> I always find the concluding paragraph to be the most fun out of the entire essay. I really love the conclusion because this is the part where I usually have the least amount of citation. It's a part of the entire

essay where I'm wrapping up everything, putting a real, nice, strong spin on it. So you want to summarize, you want to have some [strong] sentences that reinforce what has been said, reinforce your argument. I also think the concluding paragraph is a great platform for the author's voice.

What major events, assignments, and papers have influenced your sense of introductions and conclusions along the way? What particular teachers or classes have reshaped the ways you develop introductions and conclusions? What was your sense of introductions and conclusions before you began reading this lesson? What is your approach now that you have finished this lesson? In what ways can you imagine your sense of introductions and conclusions changing beyond college?

20d Invent your writing.

Section 20.2 of this lesson discusses nine ideas for developing introductions and conclusions. In five complete sentences, map out how five of these nine concepts could be applied to a writing assignment you are working on in this class (or in another class, if you are not currently writing in this course).

20e Analyze student writing.

Study the opening and closing paragraphs or segments of a couple of model projects in Lesson 25 or in the LaunchPad. You might compare very different models, such as Dan's video and Nicole's paper, or you might read similar work, such as Nanaissa's and Vinh-Thuy's papers. For each writer, describe in a sentence or two the kind of introductions and conclusions each of these authors seems to write. How do these models compare to the more predictable and robotic approaches critiqued throughout this lesson? In what ways do the model papers seem alike? Different? Which approaches to introductions and conclusions in the models seem most effective?

Your instructor might ask you to apply this analysis and these questions to your classmates' writing instead (or in addition to the model projects).

20f Revise repeatedly from feedback.

Hussain and Cara have different approaches to revising their introductions (as discussed at the end of section 19.2.9). Cara makes a rough draft of her introduction that she overhauls later, after she has written her body paragraphs. Hussein develops and revises his introduction thoroughly before writing the body paragraphs. Examine a writing assignment you are currently working on, and consider when and how you should revise your introductions and conclusions. Describe some specific ways that you can use the ideas from Lesson 20 to revise your writing and improve your introductions and conclusions. Perhaps most important, to complete this exercise, take an early draft of your writing to the writing center, a peer workshop, or your instructor's office hours and ask: "Do my introductions and conclusions fit this particular prompt, assignment, genre, and mode? Are my introductions and conclusions well designed for the particular context? Are there places where my introductions and conclusions are formulaic and could be improved?"

Paragraphs

Design your paragraphs and pack them with evidence and detail.

Visit the LaunchPad for *Becoming a College Writer* to watch the
Lesson 21 Essentials Video.

21.1 [WHY]

Why you should design your paragraphs and pack them with evidence and detail.

DEONTA
University of North Carolina, Chapel Hill

When I was in high school, I used to think papers were introduction, three paragraphs, conclusion. But since I've been in college, I've learned that a paper is going to have more than three paragraphs. And in writing paragraphs, I've learned that you also need to make sure there's a connection from one paragraph to the next and that they're well organized in a way that makes sense for the paper, and also that makes sense to the reader. I've also figured out that paragraphs are going to be somewhat long because they're the meat of the paper.

You have been writing for many years, and you have been writing serious, intellectual assignments in school for years, too. So you are very familiar with the idea of a paragraph. Perhaps you are so familiar with the idea that you haven't thought precisely about *what paragraphs are* and *how they work*.

You are probably so used to writing paragraphs that you might be unaware of how important and fundamental they are, especially since your college paragraphs can be so much more than your high school paragraphs — and not just in terms of

physical length. Paragraphs are the primary *form* or the *structure* that your college compositions are made of. Paragraphs are the fundamental units with which you build your writing assignments, regardless of genre, mode, or media. College writing is a matter of *paragraph design* or *paragraphing*.

Since college writing is defined by its use of sources, then college writing is also *evidence-based paragraphing*, at least in terms of generating the actual composition or assignment. Thus, it makes sense that Gregg has found that becoming a college writer has lot to do with his ability to craft paragraphs:

GREGG
California State University, San Marcos

If we can learn as writers to write paragraphs well, then we ultimately can learn to write essays well. Structuring a small piece makes it easier to structure the big piece because it's a microcosm of the larger essay. So then, if we've talked about individual paragraphs, now we have to figure out how to connect them. There is this idea that you only use three body paragraphs, but that doesn't work, unless you only have three primary topics you're going to talk about. Ultimately, it doesn't matter how many paragraphs are in your body, it matters that you can communicate what you're saying in a way that people understand.

Gregg insists that connecting with your audience is the purpose of writing paragraphs. He also draws attention to the dual nature of writing paragraphs, since they are simultaneously individual and collective things. This lesson examines paragraphs *microscopically* and *macro-scopically*: We look at how each paragraph works internally (micro) as well as how paragraphs function in relation to each other (macro).

You are probably familiar with the section of your compositions known as the *body*, which is defined as a collection of core paragraphs that serve a similar purpose and function. You might also be familiar with the format for a scientific lab report that is organized by different sections such as introduction, methods, results, analysis, and conclusion, where each of these sections is identified by a bold-faced subheading. The sections in a lab report can contain multiple paragraphs, which is an example of designing your writing to consider not just individual paragraphs (micro), but paragraphs in relationship to each other (macro).

Sections, then, are defined as a group of paragraphs that serve a particular function and purpose, and they are often, but not always, identified by a subheading. Notice how this lesson is designed in large-scale sections (21.1 **Why**, 21.2 **How**, 21.3 **Exercises**) and small-scale sections (each boldface idea separates a collection of paragraphs).

College compositions are most often the act of composing evidence-based paragraphs.

CUYLER
Metropolitan State University of Denver

A paragraph to me is a small collection of related sentences that form one complete idea. … The relationship of paragraphs to each other in an essay is that each one should be building on the one that came before it.

A paragraph is defined, by Cuyler and by academics, as a group of sentences that gather around a central idea — and this definition applies to almost every form, format, mode, and media of writing. In the case of lengthy academic writing, each paragraph addresses a subtopic that in turn connects with an overarching thesis or main idea for the entire composition. The main topic for Kendra's zoological analysis is the source of a Komodo dragon's effectiveness as a predator, and her paragraphs each explore a different subtopic, or aspect of the predator, including the bite, the venom, and the bacterial composition of the saliva (see pages 434–38).

A *paragraph* is also defined as a conventional form that conveys meaning and structure, which is why we are examining it in Part IV, along with other conventional forms like introductions, conclusions, and sentences. The physical shape of the paragraph is established using formatting: The convention of using white space by indenting the first line and subsequent white space between paragraphs establishes the form of the paragraph. (Increasingly, paragraphs like the one you are reading are established not with indention but with extra line spaces, primarily as a result of reading text on screen instead of paper.) So a paragraph is most important an *intellectual* design, but it is also a *physical* shape that influences readers, too, as Chase points out below. This form of intellectual "chunking" tends to look roughly the same whether you are writing a speech, a literary analysis, or a storyboard.

CHASE
Santa Fe College

So as far as paragraphs, I would say space 'em out between, anywhere between, four to ten sentences. You don't want some paragraph to be huge, to where you're looking at it like, "Wow, I don't want to read that; it's hard to look at." You want it spaced evenly or in a nice rhythm to where it's easy on the eyes.

Like each of the other lessons and pieces in Part Four: Conventions, it is perhaps easy to misunderstand *paragraphs* as empty, mechanical, inorganic things: They can seem like physical forms simply to be filled in without much thought and attention. However, experienced, successful writers actively shape, craft, and design their paragraphs as fundamental to the ways they make meaning, articulate their ideas, and connect with their readers. Experienced writers actively shape their paragraphs with intention; these writers approach the *form* of the paragraph in terms of meeting very important *functions* in their writing. Paragraphs are an essential form for writing in all genres, contexts, formats, modes, and media.

Effective writers employ the paragraph *form* to achieve important *functions* in their compositions.

MARCUS
California State University, San Marcos

In my first semester writing class, we were taught to use an "AXES outline" to organize our body paragraphs. The "A" part of the AXES is the Assertions we use to say what the whole paragraph was going to be about. The "X" portion would be the eXample, like a scholarly source or text from an actual book. The "E" part would be the Explanation in which we would explain the quote. And then the "S" would be the Significance, which we would use to conclude the whole paragraph and say why it's significant to the prompt that we were writing about.

If college compositions are made up of paragraphs, then we also know that paragraphs are made up of sentences. Marcus describes an "AXES" formula that assigns a role to each of the sentences in a college paragraph. The next two lessons on sentences explore working with those more elemental forms, but we are intentionally looking at *paragraphs before sentences* because paragraphs are more critical to college writing and to making meaning. They allow for the development of thought, which allows the ideas you present to be complex and powerful.

If sentences are the building material of your writing, then paragraphs are the spaces you design for your readers to occupy — the rooms you build with

Why you should design your paragraphs and pack them with evidence and detail different functions and shapes. These rooms, with their different purposes and locations, provide organization and structure to the design. This concept of *designing* your writing is perhaps most obvious when it comes to the more physical components of your writing, such as introductions, conclusions, paragraphs, and sentences.

Of course, when you are formatting a document for page or screen, you are also aware of visual design — the way it looks in terms of color, font, graphics, and so on. But it can be very helpful to also think in terms of the *rhetorical design* of your writing, which emphasizes the choices you make to connect with a topic and an audience. For instance, the length of your paragraphs can make or break an oral presentation or the usability of a website. For Cara, becoming a college writer means becoming the architect of her paragraphs because she now bases her *design* choices on a deep understanding of structure and purpose.

CARA
Metropolitan State University of Denver

In high school, you have to have three paragraphs, and each paragraph has to have so many sources and it's very, very structured. But I feel like once you get to the college level, you have a better understanding of what the purpose of that structure is. So you can tailor that structure to your subject matter, to the sources you're using. You can just make it your own because once you understand how that structure works, you can own it, and use it, for powerful writing.

BRAD
University of Florida

[Before,] if I had a long paragraph, I would break it down so all my paragraphs looked the same. But, if you think about it, that's really stupid because not all your points are going to be the same length. You're going to have some points that are really succinct, to the point, and you're going to have some points that take longer to develop — so you're going to have longer paragraphs. All of those are okay, as long as you can read over your paper and say, "Wow, I did a really awesome job, and I'm proud of it."

Brad's comments get at two central ideas in this lesson:

1) **Preconceived notions about what a paragraph should look like can interfere with the larger purposes of your writing;**
2) **You should shape your paragraphs to your specific writing situation.**

Front doors and entryways are like introductions and conclusions designed to greet or say farewell to houseguests, and they have a shape and position within the design for those functions and purposes. Bedrooms, bathrooms, kitchens, and closets are each planned and composed as different physical shapes. Placement within each house and each floor plan is designed uniquely to respond to the needs and nature of the people who will come inside, as well as the location in which it is situated.

Like rooms in a house, paragraphs provide structure. Your readers will travel through the physical spaces of your paragraphs to find their way. Like buildings that are defined by the collection of rooms that make up a floor plan, your written compositions are defined by the collection of paragraphs in your design. If so, ask yourself:

- **Which different functions should each of my paragraphs fulfill?**

- **How do each of my paragraphs relate to and connect with the other paragraphs in my composition?**

- How should I design and customize each paragraph individually and all of the paragraphs collectively to respond to the particular disciplinary "landscape" in which they reside and to meet the expectations of the people whom they will serve?

PlusONE/Shutterstock.com

ChameleonsEye/Shutterstock.com

Why you should design your paragraphs and pack them with evidence and detail

Your readers will dwell within the intellectual space of your writing, so design your paragraphs to come together as a functional, attractive, efficient dwelling.

What kinds of dwellings will your readers find functional, attractive, and efficient? They like designs that are sturdy and well supported. Since academic readers expect evidence-based writing, paragraphs that are designed to be packed full of evidence, support, and research are greatly preferred. The evidence you use as the building material for your paragraphs can range widely from primary to secondary sources, from texts to data. But what *does not vary at all* is the need to use abundant support. Houses with well-supported rooms sell for top dollar in this neighborhood, and Hannah knows how to design paragraphs that her readers are eager to buy.

Becoming a college writer requires developing your awareness of an array of different things: audience, genre, discipline, convention, and so on. This means that you want to also develop your awareness of paragraph designs in ways that respond to different writing situations. Be careful to avoid one extreme or another, or a one-size-fits-all approach to paragraphs. Some contexts call for paragraphs with a lot of evidence and a little bit of analysis. In some cases, you might need to build an argument with a number of premises and interpretations. The purpose of paragraph design is to respond to specific situations, and, although all academic writing requires significant support, paragraphs that are mostly lists of quotes or evidence might not be well designed for the purpose. On the other hand, paragraphs that are mostly opinion or analysis with little supporting evidence are typically not well designed either.

HANNAH
California State University, San Marcos

When he first told us not to use the five-paragraph format, I panicked a little bit inside because that's what I knew. That was my comfort zone. This was my cookie cutter way of getting a good grade. And now that he took that away, I was freaking out because now I didn't know what to do — now I didn't know what to rely on. Once you step out of that five-paragraph format, you're able to [find], "I can do this by myself, I don't need those crutches." A paragraph doesn't have to be eight to eleven sentences long and take up a whole page. A paragraph is just an idea and formatting that idea and stating it. …I used to feel the body paragraphs were the least important part of the paper because my teachers always focused on the getting the introduction right or getting the conclusion right. Now, I feel like the body paragraphs are the most important part because that's where your evidence is, that's where your thoughts are. So developing those and creating those into something that can be deep, and thoughtful, are the most important part. That's where I spend most of my time now in my paper. It used to be on my introduction and my conclusion, now it's on my concrete idea, the meat. I focus on the meat now.

PRACTICE Find three sample paragraphs from three different sources: one of the model papers in Lesson 25, a reading assignment given to you by your instructor, and an editorial in an online news source. Describe the differences between these paragraphs in terms of length and shape. More important, describe the differences or similarities between the three paragraphs in terms of the use of evidence and support. What percentage of each paragraph is evidence and support?

21.2 [HOW]

How you should design your paragraphs and pack them with evidence and detail.

Paragraphs are designed both internally and externally. The internal contents of each paragraph are your first consideration. Then you must design the relationships between your paragraphs. You could argue that *an effective college composition is a well-designed collection of evidence-based paragraphs*. The previous section argued that college writing is largely a matter of *paragraphing*, which means designing paragraphs packed full of support, evidence, detail, or research. The previous section aims to clarify your understanding of what paragraphs are and how they work so that you can successfully apply the six practical dimensions of paragraphing below.

1) Design your paragraphs to provide organization, structure, and relationship throughout your text.

The architectural metaphor used in the previous section emphasizes the importance of *design* when it comes to constructing your paragraphs. That metaphor addresses the practical aspect of composing paragraphs: They contain and organize thoughts, like rooms contain and organize people and furniture.

Perhaps the most obvious way to compose and arrange your paragraphs is to use an outline, which is like a floor plan for a building. Since a paragraph is a collection of sentences about one idea, then each of these ideas is a subtopic that, in turn, supports the main idea of the entire composition.

An outline is thus a plan to organize the subtopics for each paragraph. This enables you to see at a glance how the various subtopics and their associated paragraphs will relate to each other. Outlines are typically formatted in a single page or screen, although I like to use a whiteboard. When you are outlining, you have begun to think in terms of *paragraphing*, which develops, organizes, and structures your composition as a whole.

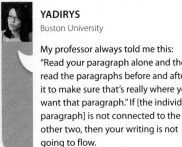

YADIRYS
Boston University

My professor always told me this: "Read your paragraph alone and then read the paragraphs before and after it to make sure that's really where you want that paragraph." If [the individual paragraph] is not connected to the other two, then your writing is not going to flow.

Some students do not use a formal or deliberate outline. Yadirys revises the organization of her paragraphs while drafting by carefully examining the relationship of each paragraph to the ones adjacent to it. Many students like to freewrite loose drafts, often made up of fragmented responses to readings and research that do not yet cohere or offer an obvious, logical structure. If so, it might help to use a *reverse outline*, which means that you jot down in the margin next to each paragraph a word or two that describes what the paragraph seems to be about (its subtopic). Then you can pull back and look at how each of the margin notes might be placed into a more formal outline. At that point, you can delete segments that don't fit, conduct additional research to fill in missing gaps, and write new sections to connect all of the pieces together. On the next page, Samantha uses a reverse outline to organize her paragraphs.

SAMANTHA
California State University, San Marcos

I think that the art of arranging paragraphs is something that maybe isn't talked about as often as it should be. . . . Sometimes, when I'm proofreading, I'll print it out and I will write the general thing that I'm trying to say in each of these paragraphs. When you look at just those general subtopics, it's, "Okay, do these ideas flow from one to the other, or is this just a random train of thought that's disconnected?" In doing that you realize, "Okay, there's nothing connecting these two paragraphs and maybe I need to insert either a closing statement to the previous paragraph or maybe I need to include a whole other paragraph so that way my ideas can flow in a logical manner."

Every academic writing rubric I have seen includes "effective organization" as a defining characteristic of success. Your paragraphs are the primary device used to organize your writing. This means you should consider the function, placement, and contents of each paragraph individually and all of your paragraphs collectively. Paragraphs are not merely mechanical containers for your thoughts and sentences. Paragraphs are devices for organizing your ideas and providing structure, which makes them essential for connecting with your readers and making meaning.

Since paragraphs are defined by their physical form, they are most effective when the *form* is well matched to its specific *function*. Introductions and conclusions are different from body paragraphs because each has a different function. So each paragraph might look different, depending on its purpose in your composition. A particularly evidence-heavy paragraph might include a block quote — so it will look and function differently. *Designing* your paragraphs thus involves both the sequencing of your ideas as well as determining the functions of different segments.

PRACTICE Create a reverse outline of Kendra's Komodo dragon report on pages 434–38 by jotting down three to five words to summarize each paragraph. Then look back at the pattern of ideas in your reverse outline. How do Kendra's paragraphs provide (or fail to provide) structure and organization to her report?

2) Design your paragraphs with topic sentences that focus each subtopic.

NICOLE
California State University, San Marcos

Well, what defines a paragraph (and it immediately popped in my head, because it's been instilled in me since I was young) is your topic sentence, your content, and your transition sentence, within every paragraph. But a really good paragraph is tight and condensed, and it doesn't digress away from the topic. Each paragraph has its own separate [sub]topic, and it's almost as if each paragraph is its own separate entity. It's separate but together — I guess kind of like a community because you have your individualized people, but there's still a community.

In Nicole's analogy, a composition is made up of paragraphs the way that a community is made up of individuals. The essence of both, for Nicole, is that they are "separate but together," which means that each paragraph is defined by a tight focus on an individual subtopic.

PHILLIP
Santa Fe College

As far as writing a paragraph, I've been taught that you have your topic sentence opening up the paragraph, which is going to relate directly back to your thesis statement. And that topic sentence is going to provide the framework for the paragraph. As you write each paragraph, every sentence thereafter needs to come back to that topic sentence. So, one sentence just leads right into the other.

As Phillip describes, a well-known convention for each body paragraph is to begin with a "topic sentence" that serves as a subtopic or mini-thesis for that paragraph. This convention prompts writers to place a topic sentence at the very front of each paragraph as the first thing they do when composing a paragraph. A topic sentence is therefore defined as a single sentence that functions as the mini-thesis for each paragraph (though it doesn't have to come at the beginning). Since a paragraph is defined as a collection of sentences about a central idea, then a topic sentence helps focus each paragraph and separate the ideas between paragraphs into logical, structured segments, which enable flow and comprehension for your readers. Consider the paragraph below from Deonta's sociology paper. How effectively does his topic sentence connect to the rest of his paragraph? Would you make any changes?

> In examining the point about cultural capital it is important to consider the work of Lamont and Lareau. They define cultural capital as "institutionalized, i.e., widely shared, high status cultural signals (attitudes, preferences,

formal knowledge, behaviors, good and credentials) used for social and cultural exclusion" (Lamont, Lareau 45). They then go on to talk about the four forms of exclusion, which are self-elimination, over-selection, relegation, and direct exclusion. Lamont and Lareau do not believe that cultural capital exists as a tool that only the elite can use. They believe that cultural capital can also be used for exclusion by the lower class and use the example of being street smart as a high-class marker for people of low socioeconomic status.

Sometimes you might begin writing a rough draft of a paragraph without a clear focus or a topic sentence. Other times you might have outlined a specific subtopic that kickstarts your paragraph as the first sentence you write. Either way, as you revise and refine each paragraph, it is important that you eventually locate a focus, since a paragraph is defined by its attention to a central, unifying idea.

In academic writing, each paragraph should explore a related subtopic that is arguable and in need of support, and a topic sentence is an effective way to declare the claims or key ideas you will discuss within a paragraph. For some inexperienced writers, their paragraphs can contain too many generalizations and not enough specific support or details. Unsupported generalizations are easy to write. Thus, weak paragraphs often have too many topic sentences or they paraphrase a topic sentence repeatedly without adding something new. In general, each paragraph should present one clear, definitive claim in the form of a topic sentence. Then the rest of the paragraph is made up of abundant, concrete evidence to support the central idea. Which leads us to the next point.

How you should design your paragraphs and pack them with evidence and detail

PRACTICE Highlight or underline each topic sentence in each paragraph of Kendra's Komodo dragon report in Lesson 25. Does she consistently use topic sentences in each paragraph? Does she ever have more than one topic sentence in a paragraph? Does she locate a topic sentence in the same place in each paragraph or is there variety? Do you find Kendra's use of topic sentences effective for her particular context and genre? Why or why not?

3) Design your paragraphs with abundant evidence and detail to support each topic sentence.

HANNAH
California State University, San Marcos

For me the difference between college writing and high school writing is quantity, it's the length of writing. In high school, you're allowed to add fluff into your piece. . . . [In college], you can't put fluff in there — everything has to be concrete to what you're trying to prove. So, that's the biggest difference.

THOMAS
Red Rocks Community College

To become a successful writer, you need to be able to provide the evidence to back up what it is that you're trying to say. It doesn't really work anymore for you to say, "Oh, I think this, or I feel this way" when you're writing an academic paper. You need to have solid sources.

The title for this lesson says that you should pack your paragraphs with evidence and detail, and both Hannah and Thomas recognize this as essential to college writing. As practical advice regarding college paragraphs, nothing may be more important

than this: *Body paragraphs should include about four parts evidence for every one part of generalization.* For every general, interpretive sentence you have in your body paragraphs, you will need at least four or five concrete, detailed, well-researched, evidence-based sentences that provide support. High school paragraphs are too often the inverse, with lots of generalization and little concrete support. Inexperienced writers often include four generalizations in each paragraph but only one sentence of supporting evidence, often in the form of a single quote.

Examine Nicole's model paragraph on the facing page. The first two sentences provide a mini-thesis. Those topic sentences make a generalization that is essential to giving the paragraph a function and purpose, so do not think that all generalization is bad and all evidence is good. Generalization is absolutely essential; without generalization or interpretation, evidence and detail have little purpose.

The most common problem is when there is *too much generalization* and *not enough support*. Generalization is easier to write because it can come from off the top of your head, rather than from careful attention to supporting evidence. Generalization tends to arrive more easily through stream-of-consciousness, whereas support requires methodical concentration. Notice the ratio of generalization to evidence in the model paragraph on the facing page. You might not even need to read or understand what Nicole is saying to identify the pattern of support, quotes, and citation to see how she grounds each sentence beyond the first two in concrete evidence. How many sentences are general compared to the ones that provide a concrete reference?

The magical realism genre is often examined with a lens of decolonization. Through this lens, narrative centers have been challenged by the establishment of this genre. Within the framework of this decolonized theme, the magical realism narrative operates as an agent that creates "a new decolonized space for narrative," and this new space is one that has not been previously "occupied by the assumptions and techniques" of a cultural center (Faris 135). Magical realism's "defocalized narrative" incorporates supernatural elements that breach cultural centers (Faris 133). In the breaching of these centers, the genre challenges "the dominant discourses of the privileged centers . . . in a way that redefines the future of humanity" (Faris 134). The magical realism genre's challenging of dominant discourses redefines and creates a new — somewhat canonized — space for the genre itself; therefore, "the genre undermines the right to represent the world" (Faris 133).

Too often, high school paragraphs are comprised of four sentences: (1) a topic sentence, (2) an additional generalization, (3) a direct quote sprinkled on top to look like research, and (4) more generalization to conclude and transition. College writing is necessarily more complicated. If there is only one principle that you take from this entire lesson on paragraphs, I recommend this one: *A college body paragraph is comprised of one topic sentence that is directly supported by at least four sentences providing concrete evidence or details from careful research or in-depth knowledge.* Be aware, though, that different paragraphs have different purposes that might call for different amounts of evidence and generalization. For example, concluding paragraphs often contain more analysis and interpretation and not as much evidence and support.

PRACTICE Highlight or circle the sentences used as evidence in a sample body paragraph of Kendra's Komodo dragon report in Lesson 25. Does she provide abundant evidence in the sample paragraph? Is there a balance between claims/generalizations in the paragraph and evidence/support? Do you find Kendra's use of evidence effective for her particular context and genre? Why or why not?

4) Design your paragraphs with transitions to connect subtopics.

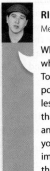

RICHARD
Metropolitan State University of Denver

When I think about paragraphs as a whole, I take into consideration flow. To me, flow is getting from point A to point B, to point C to point D, as painlessly as possible. And it's important that one paragraph leads into the next and there isn't just a sudden jump (if you're not using subheadings). So it's important to move the reader along through your writing as you progress into the deeper elements of the paper.

College paragraphs are built internally out of a unifying generalization and abundant concrete support. But paragraphs also work externally to provide structure and relationship throughout the composition as a whole. Thus, when you design your paragraphs, you must consider how the ideas connect not only within each paragraph but also between all of the paragraphs. Transitions are the most obvious devices to help create connections between paragraphs, and they can take a number of forms such as logical connectors, repeated hooks, and key terms. A transition can be an entire sentence at either the beginning or the end of a paragraph, or both. Most frequently, a transition is embedded in a phrase in the conclusion of the preceding paragraph.

How you should design your paragraphs and pack them with evidence and detail

Transitions make it easier for readers to follow your thoughts smoothly and rhythmically from one paragraph to another. They promote flow because they organize and structure your thoughts logically.

KARINA
University of Florida

Transitional words — I hate them, but it gets the flow of the paragraphs going — just connections. If you do use transitional words, it doesn't have to be the cheesy ones, like *first*, *second*. If you use them, I think it really does help with the body of the essay a lot. ... I always read out loud after I'm done writing because I think of essays, like songs, have to have a rhythm and they have to flow.

The most common transitions are introductory logical connectors (*thus, therefore, consequently, in other words, in conclusion*). Chronological connectors are often used as well (*first, second, finally*). A subtler transition is a *hook*, which occurs when a writer repeats a word or phrase from the concluding sentence of a preceding paragraph to the opening sentences of the following paragraph. Many academic writing assignments prompt students to define or redefine key terms that are currently being debated and researched; so, key terms can often effectively transition between sentences at the borders between paragraphs. Like the repetition of a chorus or theme throughout a song or symphony, key terms and their synonyms can promote continuity to connect your paragraphs and encourage flow for both the writer and reader. For example, the words *rhythm* and *flow* connect Karina's quote with the previous paragraph, and the words *first* and *second* connect Karina's quote with this paragraph.

PRACTICE Highlight or draw a box around each transitional phrase or sentence in each paragraph of Kendra's Komodo dragon report in Lesson 25. Does she use transitions between each paragraph? Does she use transitions in exactly the same way each time, or is there variety? Do you find Kendra's use of transitions effective for her particular context and genre? Why or why not?

5) Design your paragraphs with movement, direction, and development to advance your ideas.

So far, the recipe for a college paragraph includes each of these ingredients:

- Physical formatting like indents and white space to compose and separate each paragraph visually

- An outline or sketch of how each paragraph functions and relates to the others

- A generalization or topic sentence that might be reiterated at the conclusion of the paragraph

- At least four or five sentences of solid support and evidence from careful research

- An intentional transition from one paragraph to the next

The result is a physical product that will typically appear to be longer and more substantial than the paragraphs that many writers composed in high school. But a paragraph is much more than a static, mechanical form to be slapped together according to a mindless recipe. A paragraph is an intentional design that you thoughtfully craft to respond to a particular rhetorical context. Therefore, there is one additional element to add to your college paragraph recipe: *movement*.

TARA
Boston University

A paragraph to me is very different now than it was in high school because I used to write my papers like: topic sentence, a little introduction, quotation, quotation, and then conclusion. I don't think that way anymore. I like for each paragraph *to add something more*.

GINA
Metropolitan State University of Denver

I think that the paragraph is really the biggest place of expression in a paper. It's the place where not only you make your arguments but also prove to your audience that whatever you've put forth in your introduction is something that they can kind of sink their teeth into, in the body of the paper. When you're thinking about somebody reading what you've written, as they get to the end of a paragraph, they should be nodding . . . and then they move on to the next paragraph. As you see somebody read a paper of yours, if they're reading and they're not nodding, you may not have done your job yet. Sometimes I'll have friends read things that I've written [and] I'm looking for the nod. I'm looking for that this-is-a-good-paragraph kind of nod: "You've done your job. I'm with you where you're going." So, I think that paragraphs do that.

In becoming a college writer, Tara has redefined her idea of a paragraph from a formula to a function. For her, a paragraph has become a more abstract but meaningful concept, which she approaches as adding "something more" or adding a new idea to her text. Tara's paragraphs are thus designed to add something and to move her ideas forward. *Movement* is more abstract than the other pieces of the paragraph recipe, so it might take some extra focus.

Your paragraphs should have movement and direction; they should develop and unfold like events in a story. Your readers will expect to gain something from the experience of their reading, which means that they expect to be moved from one place to another, thanks to your work. This movement may not be particularly dramatic or even melodramatic — they are not likely to be moved to tears. But each paragraph should have some kind of movement or direction from beginning to end. When Gina concludes that successful paragraphs should make your readers nod in agreement, she identifies the importance of movement throughout your paragraphs. As she says, nodding is a sign from your readers that they are "with you where you're going," which implies *movement*.

If you begin each paragraph with a generalization, typically in the form of a topic sentence, and you support that generalization persistently throughout each subsequent sentence, then you have provided movement and direction. It's like your topic sentence is the floor of a room, and each additional sentence is a wall that combines to form the room. Maybe you have a concluding sentence that works like the ceiling, capping off the room. So there's development here; you built something in a conscious direction (from the ground up) that results in something new that was not there before.

Rough paragraphs often lack development or direction because they merely circle around a subtopic without carrying the reader forward, from one place to another,

How you should design your paragraphs and pack them with evidence and detail

from beginning to end. Rough paragraphs also often start developing one idea but then leap to another idea altogether, which means that it might be better off as two paragraphs.

Paragraphs can move in all sorts of directions: from general to specific, from one point on a time line to another, from one scholar's perspective to another. Paragraphs can even change directions through comparison or contrast. However you move, there should be some kind of development from the first sentence, to the middle of the paragraph, to the end. Your reader should be rewarded with some sense of accomplishment, of an idea accumulating focus or support, of a concept being clarified or explained, of understanding and knowledge growing throughout the paragraph. Ask yourself:

- How do the sentences within the paragraph connect and relate to each other?

- What kind of pattern of direction connects each successive sentence in the paragraph?

- Is your argument or analysis moved forward from the first sentence to the last sentence of the paragraph?

- Do each of the sentences that make up the paragraphs seem to be pulling in one direction? Are they working together toward a common purpose and function?

- Is the development of the paragraph more than simply one sentence slapped on top of another?

In other words, have you designed the interior of your paragraph to have a function, style, purpose, or development? And have you accomplished that development

by packing your design with evidence and detail?

PRACTICE Study a sample body paragraph of Kendra's Komodo dragon report in Lesson 25. Describe in three sentences the beginning, middle, and end of the sample paragraph. Describe your sense of the movement or progress of that paragraph from your perspective as a reader. Do you discover new ideas? Do you feel as if the paragraph put in place another piece of a puzzle? Does the paragraph have direction? Does it move?

6) Improve your paragraph designs by Revising Repeatedly from Feedback.

I really like what Gina said previously about learning from the body language of her audience as they read through her text. Are they smiling or clenching their jaw? Are their eyes widening or wincing? Gina has learned that her paragraphs are working when readers nod their heads, and she knows where to revise when they don't. She demonstrates that **RRFF** applies to every aspect of your writing and every lesson in this text. By revising a paragraph when she fails to get a nod from a reader, Gina improves as a college writer.

HYESU
University of Florida

Sometimes I'll write paragraphs one, two, three, and then I'll decide that paragraph three belongs better in the beginning. If I do change the location of the paragraphs, then I have to rewrite and revise sentences here and there. So revision for me is mostly about finding inconsistencies [between paragraphs], making sure that my argument is coherent.

Hyesu's revision process focuses primarily on paragraphs at the macro level, on the structure and relationships between them. As a more micro-level revision, Salhuana applies Spanish transitional words to her English paragraphs to make connections as she revises.

PRACTICE Study a sample body paragraph of Kendra's Komodo dragon report in Lesson 25. Write down a single sentence of feedback that Kendra might use to revise and improve that paragraph. Describe how your suggestion might potentially be applied to your own writing.

SALHUANA
Red Rocks Community College

The body is obviously very important to give my support or my information, and it is difficult to do that. So, it's many things, [including] how the ideas flow — I start reading and reading and reading and say, "No, these don't flow. No, I cannot. I need very good transitions, how [to connect] this paragraph to the next one?" I think this is one of the reasons I use many, many drafts.... In Spanish, we use *sin embargo*, that means "however," and "to tell the truth" is *decir la verdad*, or "as a result" is *como resultado*. So, there are many words, many transitions that I like to use, and I use them a lot because my first thought is in Spanish.

21.3

Exercises: paragraphs

21a Integrate the video.

Samantha sets the tone and focus of this lesson when she declares, "I think that the art of arranging paragraphs is something that maybe isn't talked about as often as it should be." Write a substantial paragraph or two, with a topic sentence or mini-thesis, through which you respond to Samantha and other videos in the lesson as you form your own approaches to developing paragraphs. You can watch the Lesson 21 Essentials Video, or you can browse the embedded clips in the online edition of this lesson. You might begin by identifying the moments that stand out to you the most. Which student videos seem to make the most sense to you? With whom do you agree? Disagree? What patterns do you find among the student sound bites? Which ideas were the most instructive or helpful to you? What surprised you? How have your own ideas about paragraphs come into focus through the videos?

21b Create a journal entry or blog.

Your instructor might ask you to keep a writer's journal throughout this class. This journal could be handwritten or composed on a computer; it could take the shape of a text-based blog or a video blog.

To prepare a journal entry on Lesson 21, describe your thoughts and approaches to the key term, *paragraphs*, trying not to glance back at the material in this lesson, at first. Not referring to this material initially will help you see what you have internalized so far. After carefully composing your initial thoughts, look back at some of the ideas and definitions other students gave in Lesson 21 or in the online database of interviews. For example, in his interview, Hussain defines a paragraph and its boundaries according to a specific idea or requirement from the assignment prompt: "I think the distinction between paragraphs is when you change an idea or you change the focus. When I go from paragraph to paragraph, it's usually [because] I'm changing what I'm focusing on or I'm changing a specific point that I'm addressing in the prompt."

You might wish to disagree with some of this lesson, or you might want to modify or expand on some of its advice. For example, consider integrating additional thoughts, notes, and lessons from your instructor and your class meetings into your journal entry. It might help you to imagine that you are giving advice to your future self about writing. What from this lesson and from discussions about writing might benefit you down the road?

21c See yourself as a writer.

In a page or two, describe the evolution of your sense of paragraphs since you began writing. Where and when did you start to develop your strategies for paragraphs? Tara and Cara have some very specific ideas about the differences between their high school–and college-level paragraphs. According to Tara:

> A paragraph to me is very different now than it was in high school because I used to write my papers like: topic sentence, a little introduction, quotation, quotation, and then conclusion. I don't think that way anymore. I like for each paragraph *to add something more.*

Cara notes:

> In high school, you have to have three paragraphs, and each paragraph has to have so many sources and it's very, very structured. But I feel like once you get to the college level, you have a better understanding of what the purpose of that structure is. So you can tailor that structure to your subject matter, to the sources you're using — You can just make it your own because once you understand how that structure works, you can own it, and use it, for powerful writing.

What was your sense of paragraphs before you began reading this lesson? What is your approach now that you have finished this lesson? Have your approaches to writing paragraphs changed, as they have for Tara and Cara? What major events, assignments, and papers have influenced your sense of paragraphs along the way? What particular teachers or classes have reshaped the ways you develop paragraph? In what ways can you imagine your sense of paragraphs changing beyond college?

21d Invent your writing.

Section 21.2 of this lesson discusses six ideas for developing paragraphs. In five complete sentences, map out how five of these six concepts could be applied to a writing assignment you are working on in this class (or in another class, if you are not currently writing in this course).

21e Analyze student writing.

Study the opening two or three paragraphs or segments of a couple of model projects in Lesson 25 or in the LaunchPad. You might compare very different models, such as Dan's video and Nicole's paper, or you might read similar work, such as Nanaissa's and Vinh-Thuy's papers. For each writer, describe in a sentence or two the kind of paragraphs each of these authors seems to write. How do these models, compare to the more predictable and robotic approaches critiqued throughout this lesson? In what ways do the model papers seem alike? Different? Which approaches to paragraphs in the models seem most effective?

Your instructor might ask you to apply this analysis and these questions to your classmates' writing instead (or in addition to the model projects).

21f Revise repeatedly from feedback.

Mark declares that "an ideal paragraph would have a targeted topic sentence that says, 'This is exactly what's happening,' and then back that with a direct example." This lesson discusses a recipe for academic paragraphs that focuses on the relationship between claims and support, between a "targeted topic sentence" and "direct example," in Mark's words. Examine a writing assignment you are currently working on and consider when and how you should revise your paragraphs, especially using the recipe in section 21.2.5. Perhaps most important, to complete this exercise, take an early draft of your writing to the writing center, a peer workshop, or your instructor's office hours and ask: "Do my paragraphs fit this particular prompt, assignment, genre, and mode? Are my paragraphs well designed for the particular context? Are there places where my paragraphs are formulaic and could be improved? Does each paragraph provide abundant evidence, detail, and support? Are there logical connections and transitions between the paragraphs?"

LESSON 22

Sentences

Develop your own active, economic style.

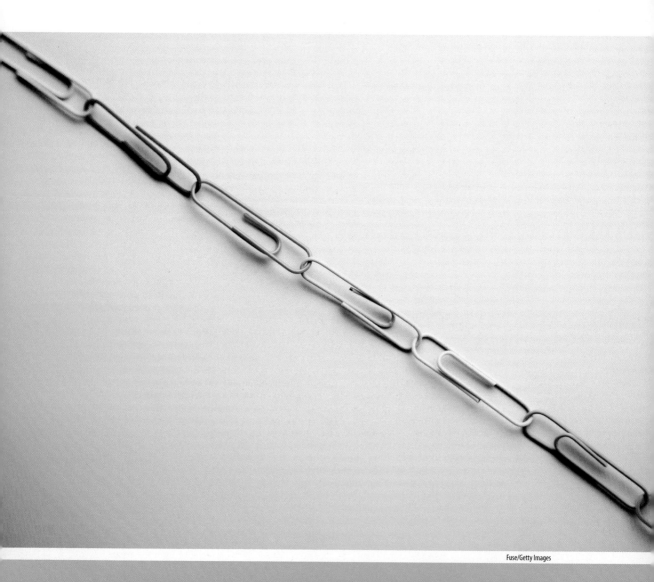

Visit the LaunchPad for *Becoming a College Writer* to watch the Lesson 22 Essentials Video.

22.1 [WHY]

Why you should develop your own active, economic style.

ELIZABETH
Palomar College

The most helpful thing a writing teacher has done for me is to teach me to say as much as possible with as few words as possible.

Many students do not know that there is a big difference between sentence style and sentence error. It's common to think that a sentence is either correct or incorrect, when, in fact, most of the choices you make will be more a matter of *preferred style* rather than *correct grammar*. Think of sentences more as "the material that I use to craft meaning" as opposed to "a grammatical unit with rules that I must follow." You will also find that good style is the best way to achieve good grammar because high-quality thoughts lead to high-quality sentences. This lesson addresses sentence style, while the next lesson takes a look at sentence grammar and punctuation.

There are many dimensions to style, and it's important to match your sentence style to the appropriate context. For example, you know tone and vocabulary are very important. In general, you wouldn't write a highly charged emotional rant in a college writing assignment, and you know to avoid slang, casual vocabulary, and profanity, too. In most cases, you want to write in a style that would sound appropriate in a professional setting.

Engage your readers by crafting professional sentences.

Be aware that a professional style is neither inherently correct nor incorrect on its own; style is a matter of community preference, and it is a very important indicator of membership in (or exclusion from) a community. As such, sentence style is somewhat like clothing fashion: It changes from group to group and over time. For example, necktie widths and patterns are constantly changing, as well as the shape and size of lapels on business suits. Professional attire for women in the 1950s almost exclusively demanded skirts and dresses, but that has since changed dramatically. Cara highlights a similar evolution in language.

CARA
Metropolitan State University of Denver

The way we talk now versus "It's 1901 and there's grammar rules" are two very different things. Language continues to change and evolve, and, if it doesn't, it dies. So, I would say you're killing the English language with prescriptive grammar.

You might be surprised to learn that sentence style has undergone some dramatic changes in fashion and preference. Consider,

Emancipation Proclamation
AND HIS

Whereas On the Twenty-second day of September, in the year of our Lord one thousand eight hundred and sixty-two, a Proclamation was issued by the President of the United States, containing among other things the following, to-wit:

"That on the first day of January, in the year of our Lord one thousand eight hundred and sixty-three, all persons held as slaves within any State, or designated part of a State, the people whereof shall then be in rebellion against the United States, shall be then, thenceforward and forever free, and the executive government of the United States, including the military and naval authority thereof, will recognize and maintain the freedom of such persons, and will do no act or acts to repress such persons, or any of them, in any efforts they may make for their actual freedom.

"That the executive will, on the first day of January aforesaid, by proclamation, designate the States and parts of States, if any, in which the people thereof respectively shall then be in rebellion against the United States, and the fact that any State, or the people thereof, shall on that day be in good faith represented in the Congress of the United States by members chosen thereto at elections wherein a majority of the qualified voters of such State shall have participated, shall, in the absence of strong countervailing testimony, be deemed conclusive evidence that such State and the people thereof are not then in rebellion against the United States."

Now, therefore, I, ABRAHAM LINCOLN, President of the United States, by virtue of the power in me vested as Commander-in-Chief of the Army and Navy of the United States in time of actual armed rebellion against the authority and government of the United States, and as a fit and necessary war measure for suppressing said rebellion, do, on this first day of January, in the year of our Lord one thousand eight hundred and sixty-three, and in accordance with my purpose so to do, publicly proclaim for the full period of one hundred days from the day first above mentioned order, and designate as the States and parts of States wherein the people thereof respectively are this day in rebellion against the United States, the following, to-wit:

ARKANSAS, TEXAS, LOUISIANA (except the parishes of St. Bernard, Plaquemines, Jefferson, St. John, St. Charles, St. James, Ascension, Assumption, Terre Bonne, Lafourche, St. Mary, St. Martin, and Orleans, including the city of New Orleans), MISSISSIPPI, ALABAMA, FLORIDA, GEORGIA, SOUTH CAROLINA, NORTH CAROLINA and VIRGINIA (except the forty-eight counties designated as West Virginia, and also the counties of Berkley, Accomac, Northampton, Elizabeth City, York, Princess Ann and Norfolk, including the cities of Norfolk and Portsmouth), and which excepted parts are, for the present, left precisely as if this Proclamation were not issued.

And by virtue of the power and for the purpose aforesaid, I do order and declare that all persons held as slaves within said designated States and parts of States are and henceforward shall be free; and that the executive government of the United States, including the military and naval authorities thereof, will recognize and maintain the freedom of said persons.

And I hereby enjoin upon the people so declared to be free, to abstain from all violence, unless in necessary self-defence, and I recommend to them that in all cases, when allowed, they labor faithfully for reasonable wages.

And I further declare and make known that such persons of suitable condition, will be received into the armed service of the United States to garrison forts, positions, stations and other places, and to man vessels of all sorts in said service.

And upon this act, sincerely believed to be an act of justice, warranted by the Constitution, upon military necessity, I invoke the considerate judgment of mankind, and the gracious favor of Almighty God.

In testimony whereof, I have hereunto set my name, and caused the seal of the United States to be affixed.

Done at the City of Washington, this first day of January, in the year of our Lord one thousand eight hundred and sixty-three, and of the Independence of the United States the eighty-Seventh.

By the President: ABRAHAM LINCOLN.

WILLIAM H. SEWARD, Secretary of State.

NOTE.---The rest of the slaves were afterwards freed by Legislation and Constitutional Amendments.

---

for example, one of the most famous pieces of American writing from over one hundred years ago: the Emancipation Proclamation by Abraham Lincoln, excerpted above.

Nobody writes like that anymore. So much has changed. Abraham Lincoln's sentences are grammatically correct, but contemporary readers would find them very difficult to comprehend, primarily because they are long and wordy. If you wrote sentences in Abraham Lincoln's style, your instructor would probably dislike it and might think that you are inflating or padding your sentences to meet a required assignment length. Style changes not only across time

but also cultures. According to Nanaissa, her U.S. college professors prefer a much more direct style compared to her teachers in France.

NANAISSA
Lansing Community College

In French, we like poetry and not saying things directly, and here people [complain], "You're too wordy. Just say it directly." So that's a problem [for me] because [the style is] short and precise, and in French you play with words — you need to show that you know the language.

Matthew's first language is Spanish, which, like French, prefers a different style. For Matthew, English is more direct and logical compared to Spanish, which he finds relatively poetic and aesthetic.

MATTHEW
Palomar College

When I write in English, I want to become better at logic instead of the aesthetic of writing. When I write in Spanish, it just sounds beautiful with metaphors and similes and hyperbole and all that, because that's how it is in the culture. But, when I write in English, people are used to just writing to the point. . . . Academic writing must be precise, the point has to be clear, so the audience knows what you're really talking about.

It's probably easy for you to envision how sentence style changes from culture to culture, language to language, and country to country. Even if you don't know the language, you can probably *hear* some of the differences in style between spoken English, Spanish, and French, for example. As a college writer, you will need to "travel" between different disciplinary contexts such as the humanities, social sciences, and sciences, like you might travel between England, Spain, and France. Adjusting to different disciplinary cultures in college is like adjusting to different national and ethnic cultures around the globe: You want to learn how to speak the language. And, of course, speaking the language means learning how to understand and use appropriate sentence style. This is why the early lessons defined writing as a dynamic relationship between a writer, audience, and topic — and why *context* has been emphasized so much throughout this textbook. Appropriate sentence style adjusts to rhetorical context.

The sentence style used to write a lab report isn't exactly the same as the style used in a literary analysis.

Respect your readers by being precise and making every word and sentence count.

YADIRYS
Boston University

My professor would [cross] out complete sentences, saying "This is not right. You need to be more precise, like you're talking too much here. You're not making your point." So for college I feel like you need to make a point in every single sentence. There's a reason for each sentence to be there in college writing, when in high school there's not that much of an importance to sentences.

Yadirys suddenly became aware that every sentence matters in college writing and that nothing should be filler. When you think carefully about each sentence and you work hard to make every word count, you convey respect for your readers, and they will respond positively to that. When you craft your sentences with precision, it shows that you value the time and energy that your audience invests in reading your work. Harley and Yadirys pore over every choice that they make when crafting their sentences. How do you think their instructors will respond?

HARLEY
Red Rocks Community College

It's also painful because you really have to think a lot about your word choices and how your vocabulary states your purpose for your paper. To me, that [requires] a lot of brainpower. You have to spend a lot of time thinking about every sentence and every word that you use.

Direct, concise sentences are now the preferred style in most academic writing. This is also called having an "economic" style because it is spare and thrifty, as opposed to ornate and exorbitant. My students are eager to learn how to write error-free sentences; they ask me time and again how they can learn to "fix their grammar." As we discussed above, style is very different from simple grammatical correctness, and getting your style nailed down should really come first. Understanding how to compose a paper with both a great style and no grammatical errors begins with understanding five ideas:

1) **Preferred style and grammatical correctness are different things.**
2) **Economic, professional sentence style is currently preferred for most college writing.**
3) **Weak sentence style and grammatical sentence errors most typically result from unclear thinking, not from a sudden loss of grammatical knowledge.**
4) **The way to improve your sentence style in the short term is to Revise Repeatedly from Feedback with particular attention to sentence structure.**
5) **The way to improve on mechanical and grammatical errors in the long term is to keep a journal about the mistakes you make and work to improve on them methodically.**

Today's preferred economic style is believed to be "cognitively efficient," which means it is easier for readers' brains to process: It's more readable. Whether or not this style is actually more cognitively efficient might not matter as much as the fact that most readers find it easier to read.

Lesson 23 on sentence errors discusses the final point (#5) above, as does Lesson 16: Proofreading. Ugly sentences typically come from unclear thinking, not lack of grammatical knowledge. So when you locate an unraveling sentence in your own writing, see if you can first reboot the thought by restating the ideas more simply or clearly, and then your sentence style is likely to straighten itself out. Sometimes, however, the idea is there and it really is the presentation of it that needs some work. If that's the case, keep reading to learn about Richard Lanham's "Paramedic Method" for saving injured sentences.

22.2 [HOW]

How to develop your own active, economic style.

Most writing teachers I know have been greatly influenced by Richard Lanham's research on academic sentences, which he published in the form of his famous "Paramedic Method."[1] Many textbooks, like this one, have incorporated his advice because it is so insightful and effective. I have reworked Lanham's "Paramedic Method" in my own ways, based on what has worked well for my students over many years of teaching sentence style. It gets its name because, like a paramedic who runs down a checklist of vital signs when first arriving at the scene of an injured patient, you can run down the seven-step checklist below to diagnose and fix the injured sentence. (By the way, Lanham's original published method includes nine or more steps, but I have reduced and rearranged them to seven.)

[1] Richard Lanham, *Revising Prose*, 2e (New York: Macmillan, 1987).

1) Build from a dynamic verb.

AMY
Boston University

Active voice for me was really difficult to overcome, but, once I did it, it helped my writing so much. It's so easy to write passively because people usually speak that way. But active voice, it's strong verb usage for me — if I can use one strong verb that will really convey what I'm trying to say instead of five words with a "to be" verb. One time, a professor had us write papers, and we couldn't use "to be" at all or any kind of passive language, and I think that definitely helped.

The heart of the English sentence is actually the verb. If you have a strong, robust, active, dynamic verb, then your sentence is likely to be healthy as well. Weak verb forms lead to weak, wandering sentences. Professional, active, economic sentences need a really smashing verb. For example, look at the verbs in the table of contents of this textbook. There are many "instructive" active verbs: clarify, approach, interact, support, reflect, focus, craft, and so on. These verbs are punchy, dynamic, informative, and revealing.

The weakest verb forms are words that merely indicate a state of being or verbs that have been transformed into nouns. The forms of the English verb "to be" (*am*, *is*, *are*, *was*, *were*) and its synonyms (*exists*, *happens*, *occurs*) do not convey any specific information; thus, they are vague and not dynamic. When you convert a verb into a noun, it also dilutes the power of the action and leads to longer sentences. "The consultation with Steve" is weaker and more indirect than "Steve consults" because it transforms the essential action *consults* into a noun in the form of consultation and removes Steve from the action.

If you waste the heart of your sentence on a weak verb, then the rest of your sentence will have to kick and struggle to wrestle substantial thought out of the rest of the sentence.

WEAK VERB, WEAK SENTENCE
It is because Nicole revised repeatedly from feedback that she became a college writer.

STRONG VERB, STRONG SENTENCE
Nicole revised repeatedly from feedback to become a college writer.

2) Start the sentence with a concrete subject/agent.

If the verb is the heart of the English sentence, then the subject is the face because it's most likely the first thing we recognize, and it is typically located at the very front of the sentence. By now, like Amy, you probably have been given many lessons in school on "passive voice" and you have learned that you should avoid it because passive voice is, by definition, an un-economic, indirect, passive way to construct a sentence. Passive voice is defined by taking the object of the sentence and placing it awkwardly into the subject of the sentence, as in, "My leg was bitten by the dog" (passive voice) instead of "The dog bit my leg" (active voice). The *agent* in this thought is actually the dog because the dog is doing the action: biting. So, to be active, you want to write the dog, not the leg, in the subject position in the sentence.

Students have now been so often drilled in the apparent evil of passive voice that they often think that it is grammatically incorrect. However, there is nothing grammatically wrong with passive voice; it breaks no rules. Passive voice is just a *less effective* sentence style than active voice, most of the time. For many years, passive voice was the preferred style of lab reports because it conveyed a sense of objectivity: "The beaker was filled to 500 ml." If you are writing a scientific report, check with your instructor about the use of passive voice, which is losing favor as the preferred style in those contexts, too. The passive voice is also common in criminal justice writing, where the agent (or subject) is not always known or there are important legal reasons for not referring to the subject. Otherwise, passive voice is currently an unpopular sentence style because it is indirect, which leads to longer, wordier sentences.

MARK
Palomar College

You know, it's not poetry, but you're still playing with words and still there's a power in words and you want that to come across. You don't just want to smash a bunch of consonants together. . . . If you open five sentences in a row with I, it's obviously not going to flow at all. So you do want to think about what words you open each sentence with.

Mark recognizes that the way you start your sentences influences the quality that follows, and, if you start with a weak subject, you might be off on the wrong foot. If you use passive voice or you start a sentence with an indefinite (it, there) or universal (society, everyone, the world) subject, then your sentence will lack a concrete agent who is performing a definite action. The very weakest way to start an English sentence would

be with "It is . . ." or "There are . . ." because you have wasted the heart (the verb) and the face (the subject) of the sentence and *conveyed zero meaning*. The result is that the rest of the sentence is likely to struggle. This does *not* mean that "It is" and "There are" are always wrong. It does mean that they should be used sparingly.

WEAK SUBJECT, WEAK SENTENCE
<u>It is</u> because Nicole revised repeatedly from feedback that she became a college writer.

STRONG SUBJECT, STRONG SENTENCE
<u>Nicole</u> revised repeatedly from feedback to become a college writer.

3) Begin directly.

JENNA
California State University, San Marcos

Sometimes you can get stuck in the same vocabulary ruts over and over, and you're using the same introductory phrases and you're using the same adjectives to describe things.

Fatigue can lead to laborious opening phrases, as Jenna points out. Anxiety can also inflate the beginning of your sentence, when you are nervous about reaching a word count. Introductory clauses often delay the start of the sentence and disrupt momentum by pushing the verb and subject deeper into the sentence. Most clauses are more effectively located after the noun and verb, although there's something seemingly "intellectual sounding" about a stuffy, long-winded windup like "Four score and seven years ago" in front of "our fathers brought forth on this continent a new nation." Today, we would be more likely to say, "Our ancestors founded a new nation eighty-seven years ago."

If you have a lengthy clause or a lot of words at the beginning of your sentence, before you arrive directly at your subject and verb, try to trim things back or move the idea to the end of the sentence, after the subject and verb are established. In short, begin directly.

LENGTHY OPENING CLAUSE, WEAK SENTENCE
<u>With a great deal of help from her professors and from the various tutors in the writing center,</u> Nicole revised repeatedly from feedback to become a college writer.

DIRECT START, STRONG SENTENCE
Nicole revised repeatedly from feedback to become a college writer with the help of professors and tutors.

4) Trim overgrown vines of conjunctions, prepositions, and subordinate clauses.

CHASE
Santa Fe College

One of the biggest problems that people make when they start a paper or even a blog or anything is that they think longer is better. . . . It doesn't make for an interesting article when it doesn't make for an easy read. The best paper isn't the one that's the longest, it's the one where you've cut all the fat.

One of the easiest ways to overinflate a sentence is to pump it up with lots of conjunctions and prepositions.

See Chart A in Lesson 23 for more on independent and dependent clauses.

Wordy sentences often result from weak verbs and indefinite subjects, as described in steps #1 and #2 above. When writers waste their verbs and subjects on weak action and unclear agents, then the rest of the sentence is doomed to twist together rambling chains of prepositions, conjunctions, and subordinate clauses to scrape together some sort of meaning. An effective way to "cut all of the fat" (as Chase calls it) from your sentences is to circle or highlight all of the conjunctions and prepositions. Circling draws your attention to these bloaters, so that you know where to trim.

Read the problem sentence aloud and emphasize all of the underlined words to see how breathless and cloudy the style becomes. When sentences are long and overgrown, it becomes cognitively difficult for readers to hold all of the pieces in their head — it is easy to lose track of the actual subject and verb, especially if they are weak or unspecific. The result is low readability. The cure is to tighten the verb and subject, and to prune back overgrown conjunctions, prepositions, and subordinate clauses.

OVERGROWN PREPOSITIONS AND CONJUNCTIONS, WEAK SENTENCE
It <u>is because</u> Nicole took the time to revise <u>and</u> proofread her essays more closely <u>in</u> college <u>than</u> she did <u>in</u> high school, <u>which</u> resulted <u>in</u> her success <u>and</u> rewards <u>as a</u> college writer <u>in</u> the field <u>of</u> writing <u>on</u> topics assigned <u>by</u> a teacher <u>or</u> professor.

CONCISE SENTENCE, STRONG SENTENCE
Nicole revised repeatedly <u>from</u> feedback to become a college writer.

5) Avoid inflated words.

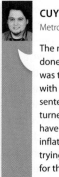

CUYLER
Metropolitan State University of Denver

The most helpful thing a teacher has done to help me improve my writing was to tell me to be more economical with my language and use simple sentences where I can. [When] I turned in my first paper he said, "You have pretty language, but it's so over-inflated that I can't tell what you're trying to tell me." And so, my project for the rest of the semester was learning to speak more directly.

Mark Twain is famous for saying, "Don't use a five-dollar word when a fifty-cent word will do," which pretty much sums up the contemporary American preference for direct, active, economic, professional style. A classic example of this problem would be if I utilize the word *utilize* instead of the more efficient word *use*. The tendency to *utilize* inflated language is understandable because, to someone who is new to advanced academic writing, the language of college and of your instructors can *sound* so sophisticated, and you know that you should avoid common, casual language and slang in most circumstances.

The pressure to use sophisticated vocabulary can also lead to problems with word swapping — using a thesaurus to find a replacement word or a synonym for a word you dislike. If you don't really know the replacement word, you might not recognize that it doesn't fit quite right, and you run the risk of misapplying a term whose definition you don't fully understand. Writers who use five-dollar words because they *actually* know the definition run the risk of sounding pretentious if a simpler word would work instead.

On the other hand, professionals who have developed advanced vocabulary for complex ideas can and should use such terms because they speak directly to the ideas within professional contexts among colleagues. Out of context, however, such terminology can become jargon or inflated when it doesn't exactly fit.

INFLATED WORDS, WEAK SENTENCE
Nicole recursively performed reexaminations upon her intellectual machinations resulting from the meta-critical reverberations from interlocutors to infuse her ascent as a progenitor of scholastic prose.

DIRECT WORDS, STRONG SENTENCE
Nicole revised repeatedly from feedback to become a college writer.

6) Use a variety of sentence structures.

MARC
Boston University

Sentence structure seemed like a new thing to me when I came to college because I'd never heard it described that way. You never really hear in high school: "This sentence is a compound sentence, and this sentence is complex." You're never really critiqued or marked down for having the same kind of sentence throughout your paper. But in my rhetoric class this year, sentence structure was a big part of the overall grade.

Today's preferred economic style enhances clarity and readability, but taking it to an extreme can distract your readers. If all of your sentences follow exactly the same pattern, or if you edit all of them ruthlessly down to only the bare bones, then you might go too far. Variety is also important to effective sentence style. Chart B in Lesson 23 explains three basic sentence structures: simple, compound, and complex. Mixing it up between those three modes will add variety to your sentence style and make your writing feel organic and dynamic.

As you apply the Paramedic Method in steps 1 through 5, don't get carried away and reduce your style to something so austere that it lacks flavor. "Variety is the spice of life," and it's also important to sentence style, as well as key to developing your voice as writer, which is covered in the next section.

REPETITIVE STRUCTURE, WEAK STYLE
Nicole revised repeatedly. She emphasized her own voice. She integrated sources consistently. Nicole grew as a college writer.

SENTENCE VARIETY, STRONG STYLE
Nicole revised her work repeatedly, which led to her growth as a college writer. Her writing integrated sources consistently, but she maintained her own voice along the way.

7) Own your voice.

GRETCHEN
Boston University

The style of writing in high school was very boring. I look back on those papers and I read them and I'm so bored reading them. They sound awful. The sentences are either really, really long, or really, really short. There's no variation, there's no tone. And in college I think I developed my own voice in my writing.

One of the most wonderful things about writing is that it is deeply human, which means that each writer has a distinct "voice" in print, the way that singers do out loud. Whether you're conscious of it or not, your writing will be distinct from that of your classmates, and your instructors are so attuned to written words that they can often tell your signature style, your voice, from others in the class.

In this lesson you have received a lot of advice on preferences for sentence style. And, in the next lesson, you will read even more prescriptive rules for composing sentences. But even within the potentially restrictive and corrective domain of college writing, your voice will inevitably come through and be distinct from others. Everyone in the class might aim to write the same kind of active, economic sentences this lesson suggests, but, even so, your voice will be unique.

Developing a comprehensive writing style means that you should reflect on and identify with your individual writer's voice. Consider and discuss the stylistic moves that you make with your sentences that seem unique, effective, or exciting. So many of the students interviewed in this textbook discussed at length the importance of finding and developing an individual writer's voice. Once you begin to analyze and tinker with the components of basic and generic sentence styles, then you can become more self-aware of your signature voice and style. Developing, strengthening, and *owning* your individual writer's voice is perhaps the ultimate goal of deepening your understanding of sentence style and how sentences work.

22.3

Exercises: sentence style

22a Integrate the video.

The gist of this lesson is probably contained between Elizabeth's opening insight on being concise and Gretchen's concluding advice on voice. Write a substantial paragraph or two, with a topic sentence or mini-thesis, through which you respond to Elizabeth, Gretchen, and other videos in the lesson as you develop your own voice through economic sentence style. You can watch the Lesson 22 Essentials Video, or you can browse the embedded clips in the online edition of this lesson. You might begin by identifying the moments that stand out to you the most. Which student videos seem to make the most sense to you? With whom do you agree? Disagree? What patterns do you find among the student sound bites? Which ideas were the most instructive or helpful to you? What surprised you? How have your own ideas about sentences come into focus through the videos?

22b Create a journal entry or blog.

Your instructor might ask you to keep a writer's journal throughout this class. This journal could be handwritten or composed on a computer; it could take the shape of a text-based blog or a video blog.

To prepare a journal entry on Lesson 22, describe your thoughts and approaches to the key term, *sentences*, trying not to glance back at the material in this lesson, at first. Not referring to this material initially will help you see what you have internalized so far. After carefully composing your initial thoughts, then look back at some of the ideas and definitions other students gave in Lesson 22 or in the online database of interviews. For example, in her interview, Yadirys reports:

My professor would [cross] out complete sentences [saying], "This is not right. You need to be more precise, like you're talking too much here. You're not making your point." So, for college I feel like you need to make a point in every single sentence. There's a reason for each sentence to be there in college [writing], when in high school there's not that much of an importance [to] sentences.

Does Yadirys seem to capture what this lesson and college sentences are all about? You might disagree with Yadirys or other voices in this lesson, or you might want to modify or expand on some of the advice. For example, consider integrating additional thoughts, notes, and lessons from your instructor and your class meetings into your journal entry. It might help you to imagine that you are giving advice to your future self about writing. What lessons from this lesson and from discussions about writing might benefit you down the road?

22c See yourself as a writer.

In a page or two, describe the evolution of your sense of sentences since you began writing. Where and when did you start to develop your strategies for sentences? Vinh-Thuy aims to develop a sentence style that flows and is easy to read because he sees himself as a writer, with something to say that he is working hard to explain to his readers:

That's why you're writing the paper, you're trying to educate someone or share something with someone. You want them to be able to get it as if it was like a conversation or like a lecture where they can just understand everything and then go through and then think about it instead of stopping after each paragraph or each sentence, and then having to go back. So, I think it's really important that it's smooth.

Becoming a college writer for Vinh-Thuy means developing a "smooth" conversational sentence style. How does that compare to your ideas about sentence style? What was your sense of sentences before you began reading this lesson? What is your approach now that you have finished this lesson? Have your approaches to writing sentences changed? What major events, assignments, and papers have influenced your sense of sentences along the way? What particular teachers or classes have reshaped the ways you develop a sentence? In what ways can you imagine your sense of sentences changing beyond college?

22d Invent your writing.

Section 22.2 of this lesson discusses seven ideas for developing sentences. The first five work together to form the "Paramedic Method." But the last two, on sentence variety and voice are different. In three complete sentences, map out how (1) the Paramedic Method, (2) sentence variety, and (3) your voice as a writer could be used to improve a writing assignment you are working on in this class (or in another class, if you are not currently writing in this course).

22e Analyze student writing.

Study the opening two or three paragraphs or segments of a couple of model projects in Lesson 25 or in the LaunchPad. You might compare very different models, such as Dan's video and Nicole's paper, or you might read similar work, such as Nanaissa's and Vinh-Thuy's papers. For each writer, describe in a short paragraph the kind of sentences each of these authors seems to write. How do these models illustrate the principles and approaches discussed throughout this lesson? In what ways do the model sentences seem alike? Different? Which sentences in the models seem most effective? Do the sentences need help from the Paramedic Method? Is there sentence variety? Does the writer's voice come through in their sentence style?

Your instructor might ask you to apply this analysis and these questions to your classmates' writing instead (or in addition to the model projects).

22f Revise repeatedly from feedback.

This lesson discusses a "recipe" for academic sentences. Examine a writing assignment you are currently working on, and consider when and how you should revise your sentences, especially using the advice in section 22.2. Perhaps most important, to complete this exercise, take an early draft of your writing to the writing center, a peer workshop, or your instructor's office hours and ask: "Do my sentences fit this particular prompt, assignment, genre, and mode? Are my sentences well designed for the particular context? Are there places where my sentences are formulaic and could be improved? Does my voice come through in my sentence style?"

Grammar

Learn from your grammatical mistakes and don't be intimidated.

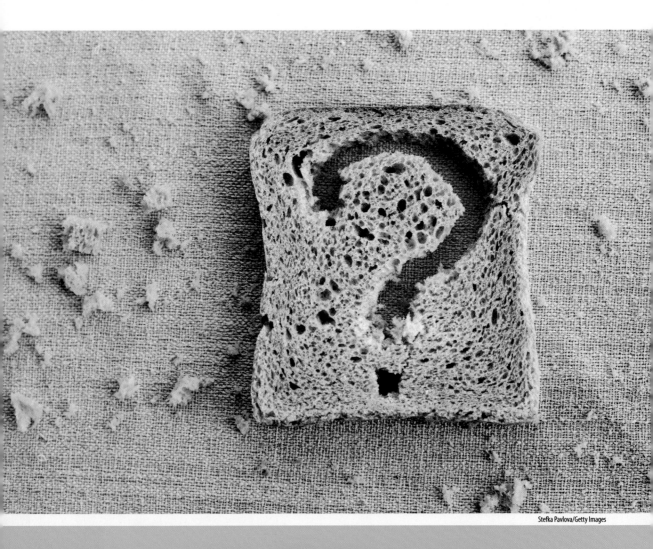

Visit the LaunchPad for *Becoming a College Writer* to watch the
Lesson 23 Essentials Video.

23.1 [WHY]

Why you should learn from your grammatical mistakes and not be intimidated.

Too many students are insecure about their writing skills because they misunderstand the nature of their errors and how to fix them. Grammatical correctness is often a frightening monster because it has a legacy of being taught through contempt and intimidation: Students who made grammatical mistakes were considered inattentive at best or illiterate at worst. If you are reading this sentence, you are neither inattentive nor illiterate.

The truth is that grammatical correctness is a skill like any other: If you work methodically and practice consistently, you will improve dramatically. When I stop playing soccer for a couple of months, I get instantly exhausted when I start back. But after a couple of weeks of playing regularly, I don't seem to tire out much at all.

Since **Revising Repeatedly from Feedback** is the key to college writing, then your sentence grammar will improve as you revise through a methodical program of informed feedback. Each time you have a feedback session with a writing instructor or writing center tutor, ask this question: "Can you help me identify one or two grammatical mistakes that I seem to make repeatedly so that I can write them down and work to improve on them?" In other words, ask a professional to help you put together a customized regimen for improving your sentence grammar, one concrete step at a time. Avoid trying to solve every problem at once.

A focus on one or two grammatical problems will help you improve quickly.

Once you make some progress, continue to build momentum by working on additional aspects of your sentence grammar, one step at a time. You are likely to be surprised by how fast you will improve and how short your list of problems actually is. When you involve your instructors directly in a specific program for grammatical improvement, they are almost certain to be impressed with your maturity and commitment. They will be further pleased to be a part of your development and success.

Step one is to identify patterns in the types of grammatical and mechanical mistakes that you tend to make. Each writer has individual strengths and weaknesses, so you want to work on specific issues that are stumbling blocks for you. Step two is cataloguing your grammar program in writing in a journal, as outlined on the next page.

Writing down a list of grammatical issues that you are working to improve upon will help you grow over time.

Exercise b in every previous lesson asks you to keep a thoughtful, reflective journal about your development as a writer. Writing down specific goals as a writer is essential to steady improvement. Such methodical reflection is the key to getting the most out of each session of drafting-feedback-revision. It's how you integrate the lessons from a particular experience to transfer to future situations.

When you write down a specific grammatical concern you will begin to focus on it, prompting you to seek advice and models to help you improve. Once you start paying attention to a problem, then you can work in a concentrated way to solve it.

When it comes to a program or regimen for grammatical improvement, it is important to understand the nature of college writing errors. You have been taught writing in school for years. Some of those lessons stuck with you, but many of them did not. You have actually been developing grammatical knowledge since you were a baby. Most of what you know about grammar you learned verbally, listening to and speaking the language as you grew up. When you make a grammatical error, it typically is *not* because you do not know grammar, but because you have not yet internalized a few specific aspects of it.

Most grammatical and mechanical errors are the result of unclear thinking; so the solution to a bad sentence is most often straightening out the thought so that the words will follow.

Students, by definition, are supposed to be stretching and challenging their abilities as they learn and develop. College errors are frequently the result of trying to do something new that you haven't done before. As such, many thoughts are likely to be new to you, so it's to be expected that you might struggle with your sentences as a result.

To some extent college writing and academic discourse are like new languages for you to learn. More accurately, they are like a new dialect, a new way of speaking within a language you already know. The more practice and exposure you have with the dialect of college writing, the clearer your thoughts will be when writing college assignments, and the easier it will become to avoid errors. In other words, the more often you **Revise Repeatedly from Feedback**, the less often you will make grammatical mistakes.

The most effective way to improve on specific grammatical concerns is to do so with your own sentences, in the context of an actual writing assignment.

You probably passed most of the grammar quizzes and standardized tests you had, but you didn't deeply apply those lessons because they were taught through worksheets and workbooks outside the context of your own writing. I was taught grammatical correctness based on someone else's sentences, not my own, which did not work very well for me. So, the third and final step in your grammatical exercise routine is to practice these lessons on your own writing, within the context of a real assignment that you are submitting as a part of a class.

Examples of correct and incorrect forms like those in the next section of this lesson (**Punctuation, Grammar, and Mechanics A–Z**) can help illustrate the problem so that you can discuss it, but the real improvement will result from a deep focus on and manipulation of your own sentences, especially if there is an eventual grade or important purpose at stake.

Understand the benefits and limitations of computer grammar- and spell-checkers because they can point you in some good directions, but they are far from perfect.

Spell-checkers and grammar-checkers are a double-edged sword. On the one hand, they can do more harm than good if they create the impression that they can handle all of the thinking for you and solve all of your problems. On the other hand, these applications continue to become increasingly powerful and effective with each new version. So, the key for a contemporary college writer is to understand the benefits and limitations of these checkers and to use them to help you improve your intuitive understanding of grammar and correctness.

For example, many precollege high school writing classes focus a great deal on avoiding passive voice. Since the year 2010 or so, grammar-checkers have become pretty good at identifying passive voice, which I think is impressive. However, you still have to understand the concept of passive voice to understand and apply the alert that the grammar-checker is giving you.

Once you have highlighted some of your personal grammar targets by writing them down in your journal, then every aspect of your writing (research, drafting, feedback, proofreading, etc.) can come together to focus intensely on finding solutions and realizing improvement. Once you have entered a specific concern in your writing journal, even grammar-checkers will begin to reinforce the lessons you are working to integrate.

My generation was taught grammar in elementary school through grammar textbooks. The current generation of college writers is likely to be learning a lot more from their interactions with grammar-checkers than dense paper textbooks. Consequently, students and teachers alike need to be increasingly aware of the ways grammar-checkers *are* and *are not* "teaching" grammar.

So, here's how to use a grammar-checker to complement your writing journal:

1) **Do not automatically accept a suggested correction from a grammar-checker without working to understand the problem.**
2) **If you do not understand the problem indicated from the grammar-checker, use the checker's "help" or "explanation" functions to clarify, and then use resources like the next section in this textbook to further explain (see section 23.2).**
3) **Notice patterns to the errors pointed out by the grammar-checker. If you repeat the same mistakes, then write that pattern down in your journal so that you will improve.**

23.2

Punctuation, Grammar, and Mechanics A–Z.

I have listed from A to Z the most common concerns that my students ask about, in roughly their order of importance and frequency. In the following pages in the print book, I have reduced this advice to a single chart for each grammatical topic to highlight only the most important concerns for immediate comprehension and use. Additional exercises and samples are available in the LaunchPad, although I strongly argue that it is much more effective to practice these grammatical forms on your own sentences rather than someone else's.

Grammar at a Glance

A. Independent and dependent clauses

B. Sentence structure and variety: simple, compound, and complex

C. Four ways to punctuate two independent clauses

D. The big three sentence errors: run-ons, fragments, and comma splices

E. Commas

F. Semicolons

G. Quotation marks

H. Spelling and homonyms

I. Active and passive voice

J. Indention and block quotes

K. Misplaced modifiers

L. Subject-verb agreement

M. Pronoun agreement

N. Apostrophes

O. Capitalization

P. Italics, underlining, and boldface

Q. Parallelism

R. Gender-specific language and cultural awareness

S. Consistent verb tense

T. First, second, and third person

U. Parentheses and brackets

V. Colons

W. Hyphens and dashes

X. Formatting a period as terminal punctuation

Y. Formatting question marks and exclamation points as terminal punctuation

Z. Ellipses

CHART A

Independent and Dependent Clauses

Definition

An **independent clause** is a complete thought that includes a subject (a noun and supporting words) and a predicate (a verb and supporting words). A **dependent clause** is a phrase that does not contain a complete thought, so it must *depend* on an independent clause to make sense.

Form

Subject and noun predicate and verb, with dependent clause.

✗ Students who revise a lot will grow as writers. Especially when they respond to informed feedback.

✔ Students who revise a lot will grow as writers, especially when they respond to informed feedback.

Advice

To determine if a clause is independent or dependent, physically cover up different segments and ask yourself, "Can this thought stand on its own?" The example sentences include a noun phrase in the subject (underlined in green) that includes what appears to be a verb ("revise") but that word is actually used to modify the noun. The predicate (underlined in purple) contains the verb, which is a combination of the auxiliary verb "will" and the verb "grow." In the ✗ sample above, it is wrong to punctuate a dependent clause (underlined in brown) as its own sentence. The dependent clause is subordinate. It contains the word "they" (which is a pronoun that might look like a subject) and the word "respond" (which is a verb that might be mistaken for a predicate). But, it's not the words themselves that determine grammatical role in a clause; it's how they are used in each sentence that matters.

Closely Related

Sentence Variety, Sentence Errors, Commas, Semicolons

CHART B

Sentence Structure and Variety: Simple, Compound, and Complex

Definition	There are three basic sentence structures: simple, compound, and complex. A **simple sentence** is the same thing as an independent clause. A **compound sentence** contains two or more independent clauses that are joined together using proper punctuation. A **complex sentence** contains at least one independent clause and one dependent clause. College writers most often will want to offer sentence variety, which means that they use a variety of sentence structures instead of repeating the exact same form too frequently.
Simple Form:	Subject predicate.
Compound Form:	Subject predicate, conjunction subject predicate.
Complex Form:	Subject predicate, with dependent clause.
	✗ Nicole says that peer review is the key to her success as a writer. Her classmates and friends give her helpful feedback. She spends a lot of time incorporating their advice into her drafts. Nicole will grow stronger as a writer. That is the purpose of a college composition course.
	✔ Nicole says that peer review is the key to her success as a writer. Her classmates and friends give her helpful feedback, and she spends a lot of time incorporating their advice into her drafts. Students like Nicole who invest time and thought in the revision process will grow stronger as writers, which is the purpose of a college composition course.
Advice	The ✔ example includes a simple sentence, a compound sentence, and complex sentence. The ✗ example repeats the same simple sentence structure five times, and the results are difficult to read. The sentences in the ✗ example sound like they come from a grammar-school textbook, which is not what you want when it comes to college writing. (By the way, the previous three sentences were simple, compound, and complex, too.)
Closely Related	Sentence Variety, Sentence Errors, Commas, Semicolons

CHART C

Four Ways to Punctuate Two Independent Clauses

Definition	There are at least four ways to **punctuate two independent clauses** in order to prevent fragments, run-ons, and comma splices: (1) use two periods to break them into two sentences, (2) use a comma and coordinating conjunction, (3) use a semicolon with no coordinating conjunction, or (4) revise one of the clauses into a dependent clause.

**Form 1
Two Periods**

Subject and predicate. Subject and predicate.

✗ Vinh-Thuy revises his writing process to fit each assignment. Which still requires at least one visit to the writing center.

✔ Vinh-Thuy revises his writing process to fit each assignment. He always takes a draft to the writing center.

**Form 2
Comma +
Conjunction**

Subject and predicate, conjunction subject and predicate.

✗ Vinh-Thuy revises his writing process to fit each assignment; but he always takes a draft to the writing center.

✔ Vinh-Thuy revises his writing process to fit each assignment, but he always takes a draft to the writing center.

**Form 3
Semicolon**

Subject and predicate; subject and predicate.

✗ Vinh-Thuy revises his writing process to fit each assignment, however, he always takes a draft to the writing center.

✔ Vinh-Thuy revises his writing process to fit each assignment; however, he always takes a draft to the writing center.

Form 4
Revise into Complex Sentence

Subject and predicate**,** with dependent clause here.

✘ Vinh-Thuy revises his writing process to fit each assignment, his approach still requires at least one visit to the writing center.

✔ Vinh-Thuy revises his writing process to fit each assignment, which still requires at least one visit to the writing center.

Advice

In order to have sentence variety, you will need different approaches for handling two closely related independent clauses. Sometimes you will want to combine them into a compound sentence, and other times you might revise one of the clauses into a dependent clause to produce a complex sentence. Either way, you need to be clear on the proper way to punctuate these sentences to avoid common sentence errors, including run-ons, fragments, and comma splices.

Closely Related

Sentence Variety, Sentence Errors, Commas, Semicolons

CHART D

The Big Three Sentence Errors: Run-Ons, Fragments, and Comma Splices

Definition	A **run-on sentence** contains two or more independent clauses that have not been joined together using proper punctuation. A **sentence fragment** does not contain a complete thought; thus, it is not an independent clause. A **comma splice** joins two independent clauses together without a proper conjunction.
Form 1 **Comma + Conj.**	Subject and noun predicate and verb, <u>conjunction</u> subject and noun predicate and verb. ✗ Vinh-Thuy revises his writing process to fit each assignment. Which still requires at least one visit to the writing center. ✔ Vinh-Thuy revises his writing process to fit each assignment, <u>but</u> he always takes a draft to the writing center.
Form 2 **Semicolon**	Subject and noun predicate and verb; <u>no conjunction here</u> subject and noun predicate and verb. ✗ Vinh-Thuy revises his writing process to fit each assignment <u>but</u> he always takes a draft to the writing center. ✔ Vinh-Thuy revises his writing process to fit each assignment; he always takes a draft to the writing center.
Fixing a Comma **Splice: Revise into** **Complex Sentence**	Subject and noun predicate and verb, <u>with dependent clause</u>. ✗ Vinh-Thuy revises his writing process to fit each assignment, he always takes a draft to the writing center. ✔ Vinh-Thuy revises his writing process to fit each assignment, <u>which still requires at least one visit to the writing center</u>.

Advice

To achieve sentence variety, you will want to uses different approaches for punctuating or revising compound sentences. However, you must understand the rules for doing so in order to avoid fragments, run-ons, and comma splices. You can use a comma and a coordinating conjunction (such as *for, and, nor, but, or, yet,* and *so*), but you cannot use a semicolon and a coordinating conjunction. Words like *however* and *therefore* are actually not coordinating conjunctions; thus you use a semicolon, not a comma, to separate those independent clauses within a compound sentence. If you use no punctuation at all to join two independent clauses in a compound sentence, then you have made a run-on sentence. If you punctuate an isolated dependent clause like an independent clause, then you have created a sentence fragment.

Closely Related   Sentence Variety, Sentence Errors, Commas, Semicolons

CHART E

Commas

Definition	A **comma** is a punctuation mark that is used to separate words, phrases, or clauses that might be confusing or difficult to read if they were left together. There are five main uses for a comma, each described below.

Form 1 **To Separate Three or More Items in a Series**	This sentence requires a comma between three or more items in a series that includes a first item, a second item, and a third item. ✗ Nanaissa's writing process includes brainstorming researching and revising. ✔ Nanaissa's writing process includes brainstorming, researching, and revising.
Form 2 **To Separate Nonessential Words and Clauses**	Subject and noun predicate and verb, with dependent clause. ✗ Vinh-Thuy revises his writing process to fit each assignment which still requires at least one visit to the writing center. ✔ Vinh-Thuy revises his writing process to fit each assignment, which still requires at least one visit to the writing center.
Form 3 **To Separate Two or More Independent Clauses in a Compound Sentence**	Subject and noun predicate and verb, conjunction subject and noun predicate and verb. ✗ Vinh-Thuy revises his writing process to fit each assignment but he always takes a draft to the writing center. ✔ Vinh-Thuy revises his writing process to fit each assignment, but he always takes a draft to the writing center.

Form 4 **To Announce a** **Quotation**	This sentence requires a comma to indicate that someone said, "A comma is needed to separate a direct quotation from introductory words." ✗ In her interview, Nicole said "I like to get a lot of peer feedback." ✔ In her interview, Nicole said, "I like to get a lot of peer feedback."
Form 5 **To Follow a** **Convention**	Month day, year City, State Salutation at the beginning of a correspondence, ✗ July 11 2019 Boston MA Dear Professor Burton ✔ July 11, 2019 Boston, MA Dear Professor Burton,
Advice	Many students who struggle with commas have been told, "read the sentence aloud, and when you feel the need to take a breath and pause, then a comma probably goes there." That can be good advice, but that technique can be even more effective when you combine it with understanding forms #1, #2, and #3 above because then you can double-check your intuition with an actual rule. Forms #4 and #5 above are technical conventions, and you just need to recognize those rules to use commas correctly in those situations. And, of course, it's important to keep the overarching concept in mind, namely: **Use commas to separate words, phrases, or clauses that might be confusing or difficult to read if they were left together.** (Notice how many different uses of a comma were demonstrated in this advice paragraph itself!)
Closely Related	Sentence Variety, Sentence Errors, Commas, Semicolons

CHART F

Semicolons

Definition	A **semicolon** is like a comma; both punctuation marks are used to separate words, phrases, or clauses that might be confusing or difficult to read if they were left together. A semicolon is used in situations where a comma might be confusing, such as (1) when the items in a series separated by commas already contain a comma, and (2) when separating two or more independent clauses in a compound sentence without a coordinating conjunction.
Form 1 **To Separate Items in a Series that Already Contains Commas**	This sentence includes a series of cities and states, including City1, State1; City2, State2; and City3, State3. ✗ *Becoming a College Writer* includes interviews with students from Boston, MA, Denver, CO, and San Diego, CA. ✔ *Becoming a College Writer* includes interviews with students from Boston, MA; Denver, CO; and San Diego, CA.
Form 2 **To Separate Two or more Independent Clauses in a Compound Sentence without a Coordinating Conjunction**	Subject and noun predicate and verb; no conjunction subject and noun predicate and verb ✗ Vinh-Thuy revises his writing process to fit each assignment, however, he always takes a draft to the writing center. ✔ Vinh-Thuy revises his writing process to fit each assignment; however, he always takes a draft to the writing center.
Advice	Notice how confusing the first ✗ sentence above is without semicolons: When punctuated only with commas, it's unclear if the sentence is referring to the entire state of Massachusetts, Colorado, and California, or is only referring to a specific town in each state. Words like *however* and *therefore* are actually not coordinating conjunctions; thus you use a semicolon, not a comma, to separate those independent clauses within a compound sentence. You can use a comma and a coordinating conjunction (such as *for, and, nor, but, or, yet,* and *so*), but you cannot use a semicolon and a coordinating conjunction.
Closely Related	Commas, Sentence Variety, Sentence Errors

CHART G

Quotation Marks

Definition	**Quotation marks** are used in pairs, and they come in two forms: double, which look like "this," and single, which look like 'this.' Quotation marks are primarily used to identify *the exact words* you are quoting. A pair of single quotation marks are used inside a pair of double quotation marks to indicate an embedded quote within a primary quote. Quotation marks used to indicate an emphasis on a word or term itself and to indicate that a word or phrase is admittedly in doubt or contested are called "scare quotes." Quotation marks are also used to enclose the titles of shorter works, such as short stories, songs, presentations, and poems.
Form 1 Identify Exact Words in a Quote	This sentence encloses "the exact words written by someone else" inside a pair of double quotation marks. ✗ Nicole says that the most helpful thing someone has ever done to improve my writing was to "not let me slide on my mistakes." ✔ Nicole says that "the most helpful thing someone has ever done to improve my writing was to not let me slide on my mistakes."
Form 2 Identify a Quote within a Quote	This sentence uses single quotation marks inside double quotation marks to indicate " 'the exact words quoted by someone else' inside the exact words of a larger quotation." ✗ In her Interview, Nicole said, "I've heard my teachers discuss, "voice," and "your voice" and "finding your voice." ✔ In her Interview, Nicole said, "I've heard my teachers discuss, 'voice,' and 'your voice' and 'finding your voice.' "
Form 3 Indicate a Term or Phrase that is in Doubt	This sentence uses a pair of quotation marks to indicate that "this specific term" is doubtful or in question. ✗ In her interview, Nicole is unsure at first whether or not she considers herself a *writer*. ✔ In her interview, Nicole is unsure at first whether or not she considers herself a "writer."

Form 4 **Indicate Special** **Emphasis**	This sentence uses a pair of quotation marks to emphasize *"*this specific term*"* and *"*this specific term.*"*
	✘ This book tries to separate the definition of the term revision from the word proofreading.
	✔ This book tries to separate the definition of the term *"*revision*"* from the word *"*proofreading.*"*
Advice	It's important for you to use pairs of quotation marks very carefully to enclose *only the exact words* from the original source you are quoting. Use pairs of single quotation marks for quotes embedded within other quotes to separate one person's words from another's. Punctuation used *before* a quotation goes *outside* of the pair, but punctuation located at the end of a quotation goes *inside* the pair. For example, introductory commas and colons precede the first quotation mark in a pair, but commas and periods at the end of a quotation are located inside the pair.
Closely Related	Commas, Colons, Terminal Punctuation, Apostrophes

CHART H

Spelling and Homonyms

Definition	A **homonym** is a word that sounds the same when spoken but has different spellings and different meanings. A contemporary study by Lunsford and Lunsford shows that pure misspellings are on the decline, but homonym and "wrong word" errors are increasing. This trend is almost certainly due to spell-checking applications. This means that it's increasingly likely that college writers will type a word that a spell-checker will not catch, even when the word is technically misspelled, because the writer typed the wrong spelling for the way the word is being used. Andrea A. Lunsford and Karen J. Lunsford, "Mistakes Are a Fact of Life," *CCC* 59, no. 4 (June 2008): 781–806.
Commonly Misspelled Homonyms	it's = contraction of words *it* and *is*. It's a shame he failed to spell-check. its = possessive for indefinite pronoun *it*. He understood its meaning. no = negative. There's no place like home. know = to understand. I know how to avoid homonym errors. there = a place. I will meet you there. they're = contraction of words *they* and *are*. They're at it again. their = possessive for plural pronoun *they*. Their papers were excellent. to = preposition indicating direction. Nicole went to the writing center. too = also or abundant. I like it, too. He wrote too many pages. two = number. Nicole met two friends at the writing center. your = possessive for second-person pronoun. Your paper is well written. you're = contraction of words *you* and *are*. You're a strong writer.
Advice	The key to avoiding misspellings and homonym errors includes four steps: (1) understand how spell-checkers work and their limitations, (2) develop the habit of searching online for definitions of words that you might be confused about, (3) be aware of common homonym errors like the ones listed briefly above, and most important, (4) write down the spelling and homonym errors you make to keep from repeating them (see section 23.1 as well as Lesson 16: Proofreading, section 16.2.9).
Closely Related	Lesson 16: Proofreading

CHART I

Active and Passive Voice

Definition	**Passive voice** occurs when the object of the action is the subject of the sentence and the agent of the action is the object (in the predicate). Passive voice is not grammatically incorrect, but it often leads to wordy and unclear sentences. In most but not all situations, active voice is better because it puts the "doer" of the action more naturally in the front of the sentence and the "recipient" of the action more comfortably at the end. The "recipient" of an action in a sentence is called the direct object of the sentence. Lesson 22 covers using **active voice** and avoiding passive voice in detail.
Form 1 Passive Voice	The recipient of the action in the sentence performs an action on the agent of this sentence. ✔ **The paper was revised, based upon feedback from the writing center, by Vinh-Thuy.**
Form 2 Active Voice	The agent in the sentence performs an action on the direct object of this sentence. ✔ **Vinh-Thuy revised the paper based upon feedback from the writing center.**
Advice	In most cases, sentences written in passive voice are as awkward as running a race while carrying a sack of potatoes. Follow the advice in Lesson 22 to avoid problems with passive voice. Many students have been taught to look for forms of the verb *to be* as a cure for unwanted passive sentences. *To be* forms include *is, are, was, were, am*; however, the presence of one of those words does not necessarily mean that the sentence uses passive voice. You really need to understand how an agent and direct object function in a sentence to handle active and passive voice effectively.
Closely Related	Lesson 22: Sentences

CHART J

Indention and Block Quotes

Definition	**Indention** is a formatting feature in which the writer moves a line of text farther away from the left margin than the rest of the body text. The first line of each paragraph is normally indented about 0.5 inches. A hanging indent, which is most often used for bibliographies and lists, indents subsequent lines rather than first lines. **Block quotes** are a formatting feature that indents every line of a long quote. The exact format for using a block quote depends on the specific documentation style, such as MLA, APA, or *Chicago* styles.
Form 1 Paragraph Indention	The first line of a normal paragraph is indented 0.5 inches, and the best way to do so is to use the tab key/function on your word processor. In most academic papers, long quotations that would consume four or more lines are often formatted as a block quote to enhance readability, like this quote from Nicole's below:

> **The best thing about college writing is that it's liberating: you can go anywhere with your writing. The worst thing about college writing is that sometimes my teachers will only mark the first ten errors, assuming that I'll connect earlier errors to the later sentences.**

If the paragraph continues after the block quote has concluded, then the next sentence should not be indented. |
| **Form 2 Bibliography Indention** | Taylor, Todd. *Becoming a College Writer: A Multimedia Text*. Bedford/St. Martin's: Boston, MA. 2018.

✗ Never use the space bar in your word processor to format indentions.

✔ Use your word processor's formatting features to format indention and block quotes, especially the tab function/key to indent each new paragraph. |
| **Advice** | Be sure to check with your instructor regarding specific expectations for each project that you must format. For example, if you are formatting an online document, indenting each paragraph may be unnecessary, since paragraphs may have extra white space between each segment instead, as this textbook does. |
| **Closely Related** | Lesson 17: Publishing |

CHART K

Misplaced Modifiers

Definition	A modifier is defined as a word or phrase that provides more detail or description in a sentence. So, a **misplaced modifier** adds description, but the target of that description is unclear because it is either at a distance within a sentence or is missing. To fix most misplaced modifiers, reword the sentence so that the additional description is adjacent to its target, which sometimes means that you need to explicitly add a target to the sentence that was previously implied. Dangling modifiers are often in the form of a dangling participle, and, as you can see, the word *dangling* indicates that the modifier is not connected tightly enough to its target. There are many forms of misplaced modifiers, as the examples below illustrate.
Simple Adjective Modifier	✗ Vinh-Thuy's thoughts were effective and received high praise, <u>revised</u>. ✔ Vinh-Thuy's <u>revised</u> thoughts were effective and received high praise.
Simple Adverb Modifier	✗ <u>Effectively</u>, Vinh-Thuy revised his conclusion. ✔ Vinh-Thuy revised his conclusion <u>effectively</u>.
Prepositional Phrase Modifier	✗ Vinh-Thuy's thoughts were complicated <u>on his writing</u>. ✔ Vinh-Thuy's thoughts <u>on his writing</u> were complicated.
Participial Phrase Modifier	✗ Vinh-Thuy received a high mark on his paper, <u>having revised effectively</u>. ✔ <u>Having revised effectively</u>, Vinh-Thuy received a high mark on his paper.
Dependent Clause	✗ Vinh-Thuy's paper, <u>which included a $50 prize</u>, was nominated for an undergraduate research award. ✔ Vinh-Thuy's paper was nominated for an undergraduate research award, <u>which included a $50 prize</u>.

Advice

Locate all modifiers as close as possible to the targets they describe. Imagine circling the modifying word or phrase and connecting the circle to the target word, and then ask yourself if there could be confusion about that connection. ✘ 1 above could be misread to think that the *praise,* not the *paper,* was revised. ✘ 2 makes it unclear whether the word *effectively* means *basically* or *successfully.* ✘ 3 makes it unclear that Vinh-Thuy's thoughts were about his writing specifically because it could be that his thoughts in general were different under the influence of his writing. ✘ 4 suggests that the paper revised itself effectively. Vinh-Thuy's paper, in ✘ 5, did not include a $50 prize.

Closely Related   Pronoun Agreement, Dependent Clauses

CHART L

Subject-Verb Agreement

Definition	**Subjects** and **verbs** must agree in number: singular subjects use singular verbs (e.g., *He writes.*) and plural subjects require plural verbs (e.g., *They write.*)

**Form 1
Singular Subject**

A singular subject requires a singular verb.

✗ Only one student in all of my classes know how to write a sonnet.

✔ Only one student in all of my classes knows how to write a sonnet.

**Form 2
Plural Subject**

Plural subjects require plural verbs.

✗ All of the students in my class knows how to revise repeatedly from feedback.

✔ All of the students in my class know how to revise repeatedly from feedback.

Advice

Most college writers have no problem when it comes to subject-verb agreement in simple sentences. The trick is when the subject or verb has an unusual construction. The prepositional phrases "in all of my classes" and "in my class" above illustrate some of these challenges because the verb must agree with the noun (in green above), not intervening words like those in the prepositional phrases. Compound subjects with constructions using the words *and, either/or, neither/nor* can be tricky. Collective nouns such as *everyone, team*, and *group* can be confusing. And verbs in the form of a contraction might throw you off, too (e.g., *He doesn't.* versus *They don't.*)

Whenever I'm confused, I try to sound it out by trying out the construction with a "placeholder" plural subject compared to a singular one. For example, if the verb in the sentence is a form of "to run" I will actually say out loud "They run" compared to "She runs." Then I determine if the subject is plural (like "They") or singular (like "She"). I then pick the corresponding plural or singular verb. If that doesn't clear things up, consult online advice for explanations and clarity. And if that doesn't work, ask a writing center tutor or your instructor for help.

Closely Related

Pronoun Agreement

CHART M

Pronoun Agreement

Definition

A **pronoun** takes the place of a noun, and the noun it replaces is called the *antecedent*. A pronoun must agree with its antecedent in number (singular or plural), person (1st person, 2nd person, or 3rd person), and gender (when relevant).

**Form 1
Singular**

The antecedent agrees in number and person with its pronoun.

✘ I benefit from the effort invested in our revisions.
You benefit from the effort invested in our revisions.
Nicole benefits from the effort invested in their revisions.

✔ I benefit from the effort invested in my revisions.
You benefit from the effort invested in your revisions.
Nicole benefits from the effort invested in her revisions.

**Form 2
Plural**

Antecedents agree in number and person with their pronouns.

✘ We benefit from the effort invested in my revisions.
They benefit from the effort invested in our revisions.
Nicole and Vinh-Thuy benefit from the effort invested in our revisions.

✔ We benefit from the effort invested in our revisions.
They benefit from the effort invested in their revisions.
Nicole and Vinh-Thuy benefit from the effort invested in their revisions.

Advice

Pronouns are very common, so it's important to get them right. In the examples above, the pronouns used in the subjects of those sentences (*I, You, They, We*) are called *personal pronouns*, and they function like nouns. The pronouns used in the predicates above are called *possessive pronouns*, and they function like adjectives. Notice how the possessive pronoun "her" must also agree in gender with its antecedent, Nicole. But the other possessive pronouns are gender neutral. You'll also notice that you could contort the meaning of each of the ✘ sentences to make a certain amount of sense. The point, however, is to make your sentences as clear as possible by direct agreement between pronouns and their antecedents.

Closely Related

Subject-Verb Agreement; Gender; First, Second, and Third Person

CHART N

Apostrophes

Definition	An **apostrophe** is a single punctuation mark that does one of three things: (1) indicates possession, (2) forms a contraction, or (3) makes a plural in the rare case of typographical letters and numbers. Below are some examples of the many forms for using an apostrophe.
Form 1 **Singular Possession** **Plural Possession** **Possession for Nouns Ending with** *s*	Nicole's, the dog's, the city's Students', the dogs', the Taylors' Deloris', the class', the Moss'
Form 2 **Familiar Contractions** **Rare Contractions**	I am → I'm, they are → they're, will not → won't of the clock → o'clock, madam → ma'am
Form 3 **Plural Letters**	A's and B's, P's and Q's, catching some z's
Advice	If you get cross-eyed about the more unusual aspects of using apostrophes, then take a quick glance online to be sure to get it right. The plural possession and possession for nouns ending in *s* is easier than it seems: Just add an apostrophe at the end. Sometimes you will see writers using *Moss's* instead of *Moss'* to indicate possession belong to the Moss family, but there's actually no complete agreement on that approach. I say just keep it simple: Add an apostrophe and no additional *s* to the end of a word ending in *s* to indicate possession, whether it's plural or not.
Closely Related	Quotation Marks

CHART O

Capitalization

Definition	**Capitalization** is used in three primary ways: to indicate (1) the beginning of a sentence or a quote, (2) a specific or proper name, (3) essential words in a title, or (4) the pronoun *I*.
Form 1 **To Begin a Sentence or Quote**	✗ she said, "usually, I freewrite a lot before an essay." ✔ She said, "Usually, I freewrite a lot before an essay."
Form 2 **Specific or Proper Name**	✗ leasa burton, Spring, south korea, president Truman ✔ Leasa Burton, April, South Korea, President Truman
Form 3 **Important Words in a Title**	✗ *Becoming A College Writer, Exile on main street* ✔ *Becoming a College Writer, Exile on Main Street*
Form 4 **The Pronoun *I***	✗ In my writing classes, i teach students to revise. ✔ In my writing classes, I teach students to revise.
Advice	If you are unsure about the more unusual aspects of using capitalization, then take a quick glance online to check your work. The general rule of thumb about whether or not to capitalize the name of a thing is whether or not the word is precise and specific. For example, you know that the month of April is capitalized, but what about the word *river*? If the word refers to something specific, such as the *Illinois River,* then it is capitalized. If the word is imprecise like *across the river,* or *that river,* then it is not capitalized. In cases where there is a lack of standards or agreement on capitalization, then make a choice and be consistent.
Closely Related	Lesson 16: Proofreading

CHART P

Italics, Underlining, and Boldface

Definition

Italics, <u>underlining</u>, and **boldface** are three related ways to format text to convey different kinds of emphasis. In recent years, italics has become the more prominent of the three, since it is the preferred way to format the titles of books and to indicate words that are foreign to English usage. At one point, writers were either supposed to use italics or underlining, but not both. Underlining and boldface should be used sparingly in academic writing, most typically only when a specific style guide requires them for headings, subheadings, and titles in your documents.

(1) Italicize Publication Titles Every Time

Todd Taylor wrote *Becoming a College Writer*. He once worked for a newspaper called *Creative Loafing*. His favorite album is *Exile on Mainstreet,* and his favorite song on that album is "Tumbling Dice."

(2) Italicize for Emphasis, Other Languages, and Words as Terms

I *strongly* encourage college writers to revise repeatedly from feedback.
This textbook is a *de facto* companion to an undergraduate career.
I don't think that you are using the word *inconceivable* properly.

(3) Use Bold or Underlining When Required by a Formatting Style

Level-1 APA Heading is Centered, Boldface with Capitalization.
Level-2 APA Heading is Left-Justified, Boldface with Capitalization.
Level-3 APA Heading is indented, boldface without capitalization.
Level-4 APA Heading is indented, boldface, ending with a period.
Level-5 APA Heading is indented, italics, ending with a period.

Advice

If you are unsure about the more unusual aspects of using italics, boldface, and underlining, then take a quick glance online to be sure to get it right. Otherwise, when in doubt, use italics. Either way, use these features strategically. If your project has sections with subheadings; use them correctly and consistently for titles of larger works; and use them sparingly in the body of your text.

Closely Related

Quotation Marks, Lesson 16: Proofreading

CHART Q

Parallelism

Definition	Items in a series must be parallel in grammatical form, which means that each item in a series must use the same forms and same parts of speech.
Example 1	When I write, I verb adverb, verb adverb, verb adverb. ✘ When I write, I brainstorm quickly, revise repeatedly, and proofread my paper. ✔ When I write, I brainstorm quickly, revise repeatedly, and proofread carefully.
Example 2	I go to the library to find either noun or noun. ✘ I go to the library either to find books or meeting with librarians. ✔ I go to the library either to find books or meet with librarians.
Example 3	To verb, to verb, and not to verb — that's my Tennyson-inspired motto. ✘ To strive, to seek, and not yield — that's my Tennyson-inspired motto. ✔ To strive, to seek, and not to yield — that's my Tennyson-inspired motto.
Advice	Parallel structures have a rhythm to them, and that rhythm is disrupted when the grammatical construction is unparallel. The incorrect sentence in Example 1 replaces the final adverb with a noun. Note that in Example 2, the series needs to contain only two items (or more) to require parallelism. The incorrect sentence in Example 2 swaps a participle phrase for a noun. The last example is subtle because the final verb is not in the infinitive form like the other two members of the series, as indicated by the lack of the preposition *to*.
Closely Related	Lesson 16: Proofreading, Sentence Structure

CHART R

Gender-Specific Language and Cultural Awareness

Definition   Assume that your readers are from a variety of genders and cultures. You do not want to insult anyone by making assumptions about them, so you should use gender-neutral pronouns and terms whenever possible and respect cultural differences in the ways people refer to themselves.

Form   ✗ When a student revises repeatedly, he is more successful.

✔ When students revise repeatedly, they are more successful.

✗ The chairman of the steering committee has a great responsibility.

✔ The chair of the steering committee has a great responsibility.

Advice   Decades ago, the standard, abstract, single-person pronoun was the masculine forms *he, him,* and *his,* but the new standard is to use the plural forms *they, them,* and *their* whenever possible, as illustrated in Sample 1 above. Even if the gender is known, the current standard is to avoid gender-specific words like *chairman* or *chairwoman,* since neutral terms like *chair* work just as well. You will want to pay attention to how people wish to self-identify and to use the language they prefer.

Closely Related   Lesson 16: Proofreading, Pronoun Agreement

Consistent Verb Tense

Definition	The most obvious **verb tenses** are past, present, and future: *Nicole* **wrote**. *Nicole* **writes**. *Nicole* **will write**. But there are a dozen or more variations, including past perfect, infinitives, future perfect, and so on. You want to maintain a consistent verb tense as much as possible, but you should not be afraid to shift tenses when necessary. If you shift verb tenses in a paragraph or sentence, you should do so thoughtfully and intentionally because surprising or unnatural shifts in verb tense can disrupt your readers.
Past Tense	✘ When the students revised repeatedly, they are more successful. ✔ When the students revised repeatedly, they were more successful.
Present Tense	✘ The students revise repeatedly, and they will succeed. ✔ The students revise repeatedly, and they succeed.
Future Tense	✘ The students will revise repeatedly so they succeeded. ✔ The students will revise repeatedly so that they will succeed.
Shifting Tense	✘ Students revise repeatedly, and they will succeed. ✔ If the students revise repeatedly, they will succeed.
Advice	In most college writing situations, you should use a consistent tense throughout the entire document and be especially wary of shifting verb tenses in a sentence or paragraph. Also recognize that different disciplines and classes can have different expectations. Literary criticism is often written in the present; for example, you might write about Shakespeare's moral themes as if he were speaking to us today. In contrast, in an historical class, even on Shakespeare, you need to write about the past in that tense. The first ✘ sentence above shifts from past to present tense. The second ✘ example flips from present to future tense. The third ✘ sentence starts out in future tense but flops back to the past. It's sometimes necessary to shift tenses to convey your complete meaning, but you must clue your readers. The problem with the fourth ✘ sentence is that it lacks the "If" as a signal of a shift in tense that is coming.
Closely Related	Lesson 16: Proofreading

First, Second, and Third Person

Definition	The easiest way to identify this usage is through pronouns. **First person** refers to the singular self: *I write*. **Second person** addresses a singular other: *You* write. **Third person** is used for talking about someone other than me or you: *Nicole writes*. There is also first-person plural (*we*) and third-person plural (*they*), but there is no standard English second-person plural, which is why the informal *ya'll* and *you guys* are so common. Like other forms of consistency and agreement, you do not want to shift from first to second or third person abruptly. And, more important, you generally want to avoid first and second person in college writing because they can be too informal.
First Person	✗ When I revised repeatedly, you were more successful. ✔ When I revised repeatedly, I was more successful.
Second Person	✗ As you revise repeatedly, they are more successful. ✔ As you revise repeatedly, you are more successful.
Third Person	✗ Once they revise repeatedly, I will be more successful. ✔ Once they revise repeatedly, they will be more successful.
Advice	In most college writing situations, you should use the third person consistently throughout the entire document. However, this does not mean that either first person or second person is categorically wrong. In fact, your writing can be awkward if you avoid situations in which first person or second person would be more natural. For example, if you created and administered a set of survey questions for interviewees to respond to, the passive voice ("a set of questions was generated") would be less effective than first-person active voice ("I generated a set of questions"). Second person is the most unlikely form to use in conventional academic writing — it can be disruptive like the awkward moment when an actor accidentally looks straight into the camera.
Closely Related	Lesson 16: Proofreading, Pronoun Agreement

CHART U

Parentheses and Brackets

Definition	Like quotation marks, **parentheses and brackets** are used in pairs to enclose something. Unlike quotation marks that enclose something central, parenthesis and brackets, by definition, indicate things that are less important, tangential, or ancillary. Parentheses are used to enclose either a sidebar comment or a utility element, like citation information. Square brackets primarily indicate that words within a quote have been edited.
Parenthetical Comments	✘ I complemented Vinh-Thuy on his paper's imagery, he laughed nervously at this. ✔ I complemented Vinh-Thuy on his paper's imagery (he laughed nervously at this).
Citation	✘ Nicole said, "I've heard my teachers discuss 'voice,' and 'your voice' and 'finding your voice'" Taylor 455. ✔ Nicole said, "I've heard my teachers discuss 'voice,' and 'your voice' and 'finding your voice'" (Taylor 455).
Brackets	✘ Nicole said, "My professors have discussed 'voice,' and 'your voice' and 'finding your voice'" (Taylor 455). ✔ Nicole said, "[My professors have discussed] 'voice,' and 'your voice' and 'finding your voice'" (Taylor 455).
Advice	The safest route is to avoid using parentheses and brackets for purposes other than mechanical necessity. However, it's essential that you recognize when and why parentheses and brackets are necessary. Your in-text citation style will almost certainly require parentheses. If you edit a quote and fail to provide brackets indicating the differences between your words and the quoted sources, then you have misrepresented the original quotation. Notice how the terminal punctuation goes outside the closing parenthesis.
Closely Related	Quotation Marks, Lesson 24: Citation

CHART V

Colons

Definition	The **colon** has two simple functions: (1) to introduce a list, phrase, or clause and (2) as a mechanical separator in conventional formats such as the time of day, formal salutations, and two-piece titles.
Introduce a List	✗ The three priorities I have in mind are: to strive, to seek, and not to yield. ✔ I have three priorities in mind: to strive, to seek, and not to yield.
Introduce a Clause	✗ The news was dramatic (he would resign immediately). ✔ The news was dramatic: He would resign immediately.
Time of Day	✔ 10:25 pm
Formal Salutation	✔ To Whom It May Concern:
Two-part Titles	✔ *Becoming a College Writer: A Multimedia Text*
Advice	Don't be intimidated. A colon is simple: It introduces something with emphasis. A colon is also used to format a couple of mechanical conventions, but those are easily understood, too. The biggest wrinkle with using a colon is to avoid placing it after a verb, as illustrated in the first ✗ sample above.
Closely Related	Hyphens and Dashes

Hyphens and Dashes

Definition	**Hyphens and dashes** look similar, but their functions are different: A hyphen glues two words together, but a dash breaks words and ideas apart. A hyphen is typed using one single, short, horizontal stroke as in the word *email*. A dash is a longer line that connects parts of a sentence — the way a hyphen connects parts of a word. The dash in the previous sentence is also called an *em dash*. Hyphens are absolutely necessary for certain words (such as *mother-in-law*) and to avoid confusion when two words combine to form an adjective (*your well-written paper*). An em dash is used to interrupt a thought or sentence abruptly. An *en dash* is longer than a hyphen and shorter than an *em dash*, and it's used to indicate a span across time or things.
Hyphens	state-of-the-art, off-site, twelve-year-old, high-class wardrobe
Em Dashes	The sentence started just fine — I thought to myself — but then it fell apart.
En Dashes	9:00am – 11:20am, Part Two – Part Five, 1st – 3rd Grade
Advice	It's unlikely that you will write a substantial college paper without using a hyphen, but many instructors and editors feel that dashes are unnecessary in college writing. The phrase *beautifully written paper* does not require a hyphen, whereas *well-written paper* does because adverbs ending in –ly do not need a hyphen when used as a compound adjective.
Closely Related	Colons, Parentheses and Brackets

CHART X

Formatting a Period as Terminal Punctuation

Definition	You know what a **period** is and how to use it to end a sentence. But formatting periods correctly in academic writing can be tricky because of other ending punctuation such as parenthetical in-text citations, quotation marks, and abbreviations.
Period and In-text Citation	When using a period in a sentence with a parenthetical in-text citation, the period always goes *outside, after, beyond, and to the right* of the final, closing parenthesis. ✘ Nicole said, "I've heard my teachers discuss 'voice,' and 'your voice' and 'finding your voice'." (Taylor 455). ✔ Nicole said, "I've heard my teachers discuss 'voice,' and 'your voice' and 'finding your voice'" (Taylor 455).
Period and Ending Quotation	When using a period in a sentence that ends with a quotation, the period goes *inside, before, and to the left* of the final quotation mark. ✘ Nicole said, "I've heard my teachers discuss 'voice,' and 'your voice' and 'finding your voice'". ✔ Nicole said, "I've heard my teachers discuss 'voice,' and 'your voice' and 'finding your voice.'"
Period and Ending Quotation	When using a period in a sentence that ends with an abbreviation, the period combines with the final abbreviation and goes *inside, before, and to the left* of the final quotation mark. ✘ Jules said, "It's seven o'clock a.m.". ✔ Jules said, "It's seven o'clock a.m."
Advice	There can be nuances to terminal punctuation in a college paper with many quotes, but most of the confusion can be solved with two principles: (1) Terminal punctuation goes *before* a final quotation mark or (2) *after* the final parenthesis in an in-text citation. As a footnote: I also advise you to avoid the popular, casual construction of a series of "one-word sentences." Just. Don't. Do. It.
Closely Related	Formatting Question Marks and Exclamation Points as Terminal Punctuation, Quotation Marks

CHART Y

Formatting Question Marks and Exclamation Points as Terminal Punctuation

Definition	You know what **question marks and exclamation points** are and how to use them to end a sentence. But formatting these punctuation marks correctly in academic writing can be tricky because of other ending punctuation involved with parenthetical in-text citations, quotation marks, and sentences that ask questions or make exclamations themselves.
In-Text Citation	When the sentence itself asks a question or there is an exclamation in a sentence with a parenthetical in-text citation, the terminal punctuation always goes *outside, after, beyond, and to the right* of the final, closing parenthesis.
Question Mark	What does it mean to "Revise Repeatedly from Feedback" (Taylor 7)**?**
Exclamation Point	I am a here to declare that "the key to writing is to Revise Repeatedly from Feedback" (Taylor 7)**!**
Quote Ends with Question Mark or Exclamation Point	When a quotation with a question mark or exclamation point ends a sentence, the terminal punctuation always goes *inside, before, and to the left* of the final quotation mark. ✔ **He began the book by asking, "What is the key to college writing?"** ✔ **She finished the book by declaring, "I know the key to college writing!"**
Advice	There can be nuances to terminal punctuation in a college paper with many quotes, but most of the confusion can be solved with two principles: (1) Terminal punctuation goes *before* a final quotation mark or (2) *after* the final parenthesis in an in-text citation.
Closely Related	Formatting a Period as Terminal Punctuation, Lesson 24: Citation

CHART Z

Ellipses

Definition	In academic writing, an **ellipsis** is most typically three periods that are used to indicate that words have been edited out of a quotation. In popular or conventional writing, writers sometimes use ellipses to suggest that they are pausing or waiting to try to connect thoughts. Since college writing is most often supposed to be coherent when complete, the "searching for a thought" ellipsis is usually out-of-place. However, the "I edited out words from a quotation" usage is very important because you must quote from your sources accurately and with integrity.
Full Quote	In her interview, Nicole said, "I've heard my teachers discuss 'voice,' and 'your voice' and 'finding your voice.'"
Ellipses in the Middle of a Sentence	In her interview, Nicole said, "I've heard my teachers discuss . . . 'finding your voice.'"
Ellipses at the End of a Sentence	In her interview, Nicole said, "I've heard my teachers discuss 'voice,' and 'your voice.' . . ."
Advice	Be very careful when you remove words from an original quote. You might also consider the use of brackets to revise quotations. In MLA style, ellipses used inside a sentence should be formatted using a space between each of the three periods. However, ellipses used at the end of a sentence in MLA style should be formatted using no space after the final word and then one space between each of the four periods.
Closely Related	Terminal Punctuation: Period, Lesson 24: Citation

Citation

Approach citation as a research tool, not as a threat.

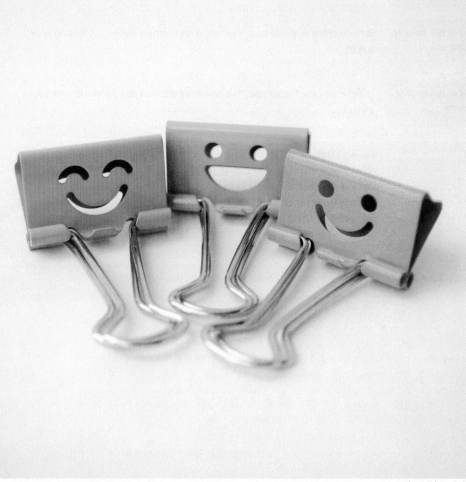

ESSENTIALS VIDEO

Visit the LaunchPad for *Becoming a College Writer* to watch the Lesson 24 Essentials Video.

24.1 [WHY]

Why you should approach citation as a research tool, not as a threat.

Out of the twenty-five lessons in this book, citation is probably the most widely misunderstood aspect of college writing. For the vast majority of students, citation is all about avoiding cheating and plagiarism. Students cite for fear of the nuclear threat of an honor court trial. And, if fear of cheating isn't your first thought on the topic of citation, then the potential tediousness of proper citation style, punctuation, and mechanics is probably at the top of your list instead.

This negativity is backward. The purpose and function of citation is to help build knowledge through carefully documented research. A side effect of citation systems is that students must cite diligently in order to give credit for the intellectual work of others, but even before that, the purpose and function of citation is for students to create meaning by connecting their ideas with the work of others. That's not tedious at all.

When scholars glance over a book or article for the first time, they often scan the bibliography before reading the text itself because bibliographies are so important to providing context for the writing and research. When scholars study a bibliography, they are not doing so thinking "I wonder if this text is plagiarized?" They are looking to start connecting with the text in a meaningful way.

Citation is, therefore, more a system for building knowledge and conducting research than it is a way to prevent or prosecute plagiarism. When the punitive aspects of citation are foregrounded as a threat, then the constructive core purpose of connecting research sources can too easily get lost in the background. The eight principles of citation below aim to help you approach citation as an important research tool, not a threatening academic burden.

1) Mark a citation trail for others to follow because that's how knowledge is made.

Research and knowledge are built incrementally and cumulatively. What we know today is a result of what we learned years before, which was likewise dependent on the knowledge that preceded it. Since college writing as a genre is research based, then college writers are adding their voices to intellectual conversations that have been going on for a while. Citation is, thus, a written system that documents the history of ongoing conversations: who said what and when so that others can follow and contribute.

The primary function of citation and bibliography, then, is to clearly mark a trail for others to follow so that they can benefit from a path that was cut by a previously intrepid researcher. As a student, you should almost gleefully *want* to leave tracks for your readers to follow because you want your readers to appreciate the research that you have put together. If you ever find yourself feeling like you want to conceal your tracks regarding a source that you consulted, then something is very wrong.

Your citation and bibliography are a badge of honor that you should proudly display as the documentation of your hard work. You want to clearly indicate your research sources because you were smart enough to locate and integrate them, and you want your readers to be able to easily follow your thoughts — so leave tracks.

2) Cite from the very first moment in your very first draft.

Most writers these days use a word processor and the Internet extensively, which means that they are almost certain to use their computer's copy, cut, and paste functions to gather sources even in the earliest stages of their writing processes. Since the bibliography is physically located at the end of a research project, and since stopping to format citations can disrupt the flow of early drafting, writers have for decades tended to worry about citation near the submission deadline instead of from the very beginning.

Times have changed dramatically. Copying and pasting from an electronic resource into your document is so quick and easy now that gathering citation information as you go, from the very first draft to the final version, is no longer a significant disruption. However, the much more prominent concern is losing track of your sources as you are churning through your research and drafting processes — copying and pasting is now so lightning quick that we often do it automatically without being fully aware.

If you put off dealing with citation and bibliography until the end of your writing process,

you are taking a giant risk that you will not be able to find your sources again, often under the significant pressure of an immediate deadline. It is *much* easier, far more reliable, and much more efficient to grab citation data immediately, when you first encounter a source, than it is to try to piece it all together at the end, under the gun. In the early drafts, you don't have to format the citation and bibliography perfectly, you just need to be sure that you grab the information and store it at the end of your document (*not* in a separate file) from your very first draft. I require my students to place a preliminary bibliography in every single draft, especially the first one, because college writers want to leave an obvious citation trail of even their earliest steps, so that their readers can follow along.

3) When in doubt, cite.

Picture holding a short bibliography from one student in your left hand. Then picture holding in the other a long bibliography, with a dozen or more sources, from a different student. What's your impression of one student compared to the other? Which student seems more likely to receive a better grade?

Citation makes you look smart. Abundant citations from a variety of sources make you look very smart. Your best bet, when in doubt, is to cite. There is very little risk in citing. How much do you stand to lose if you fail to cite? Citing is what researchers do; integrating sources and referring to external, concrete evidence defines college writing. In other words, citation is fundamental to college writing.

Now, you probably have a sense that it's possible to cite too much — to "over cite." If your paragraphs are composed of nothing but direct quotes from other people, then you might not be effectively integrating your sources with your own thoughts and analysis. Your own thoughts must drive the paper after all. But the solution to that problem is *not* to cite less but to reconstruct the paragraph with more of your own ideas. Including fewer quotes or less material from outside sources might strengthen your paper, but that is very different from citing less. In twenty years of teaching college writing, I have very rarely seen students who cite too much, whereas I see students who cite too little almost every day.

My students ask me all of the time, "Do I need to cite _____?" — to which I always reply, "When in doubt, always cite because it makes you look smart and you have nothing to lose."

4) Adjust your citation style according to your discipline and requirements.

You are probably aware that there are a variety of citation styles to choose from, such as Modern Language Association (MLA), American Psychological Association (APA), *Chicago Manual of Style*, and Council of Science Editors (CSE). Your instructors will typically tell you which style they want you to use, but, if they don't tell you, then ask if they have a preference — it makes you look prepared and ahead of the game, and it indicates that you are already working to connect your sources and your readers.

When I was in college, it seemed to me at first that switching between these citation styles was a cruel game: Why couldn't everyone just use the same style? It turns out that there's a good reason. Citation styles reflect the disciplinary and methodological contexts within which writers and researchers work. The more scientific styles (APA and CSE) foreground the date of publication by citing that information in-text

and near the front of the bibliography. MLA is often preferred in the humanities because that style foregrounds the author's complete name and the titles of works.

These differences emerge from different disciplinary and methodological perspectives and different ways of conducting research. The sciences care more about *when* information was published. The humanities care more about *who* published the work. Citation styles, thus, respond to expectations and perspectives of their audiences because they are integral parts of making meaning (and not afterthought busywork).

5) Use a citation generator and do not try to memorize the details of citation style.

You now have the benefit of citation- and bibliography-generating software applications. Use them! Memorizing the minute details of citation style is a waste of time and mental energy. You have much more important things to learn. Even so, you should have a basic understanding of the differences between the major citation styles (MLA, APA, and *Chicago*). And you need to know that bibliographic (works-cited) entries are slightly different for a book, journal article, website, and so on. Such basic understanding enables you to use a citation generator properly; it also enables you to use online and print resources like you will find in this lesson to locate help and detailed explanations.

You should work diligently to cite properly, which means that you are still responsible for your bibliography and you can't blame the computer or your software for problems. But, citation generators are very effective tools for formatting your bibliographies correctly. Let them help you.

Why you should approach citation as a research tool, not as a threat

Citation styles are evolving rapidly in response to digital technologies, which means that the rules are constantly shifting, and only experts know them completely. Your college library's website probably has citation generators built into various search engines. There are professional software applications out there, and free Internet help is available, too.

6) Each citation should have three parts.

Every time you cite a source, you should do three things: (1) Signal that the contents of the sentence is from a source, (2) provide an in-text link to an entry in your bibliography, and (3) place a complete entry for the source in your bibliography. Each citation is like a tripod: If one of the essential three pieces is missing, it fails. Each of these three citation components is described in practical detail in the next section, and each leg of the citation tripod is color-coded below so that you can see how the three parts work together:

Signal phrase
In-text citation
Corresponding MLA Style Works-Cited Entry

In Becoming a College Writer, I say that the signal announces to the reader that the sentence is based upon a particular source, with the signal often being located at the very beginning of the sentence. The in-text citation offers a brief code that links the sentence within the body of the text to an entry in the bibliography, most typically in the form of a parenthesis including the author's surname and either page number or year of publication (Taylor 366). The bibliography is a list of citations placed at the end of the document that gives the full publication details of each citation so that readers can locate the source themselves.

Taylor, Todd. *Becoming a College Writer*. Boston, MA: Bedford/St. Martin's, 2019.

So the tracks you leave with each citation begin with a signal in the sentence, which leads to a brief in-text reference, which leads to the complete entry in the final bibliography. When your readers can connect the signal to the in-text citation, then link the in-text citation to a specific entry in the bibliography, and lastly follow the entry in the bibliography to the actual source itself — you have blazed a trail for your readers to follow! Winner!

7) When your voice changes, informed readers will recognize it immediately.

Think about a skill you know so well that you will never forget it. Maybe it's a basketball jump shot, cooking a spaghetti dinner, or writing an essay for school. Now imagine you are watching someone learn for the first time that skill you know so well. Your experiences are so vast and have been developed over so many years that as you watch a rookie try to perform the skill you have mastered, you will instantly recognize when they make a mistake or things are going wrong. Maybe they don't hold the basketball correctly, they don't stir the spaghetti properly, or they write a poem instead of an essay.

When you use words from a source that are not your own, your instructors will recognize it immediately in almost every case. Your instructors are experts at written language, and they have read mountains of research. They tend to eat, breathe, and sleep books and writing. Thus, they are very attuned to authors' voices, and it is as obvious as a bright neon sign to them when an author's voice suddenly changes.

Most of the time, student writers unintentionally incorporate other people's words. Students sometimes word-swap using a thesaurus, which isn't necessarily wrong, but it can startle your readers because of a sudden shift in vocabulary. *The biggest problem comes from paraphrasing incorrectly, when you try to rephrase ideas from a source in your own words, but the vocabulary from the original source remains too prominent in your paraphrased sentence.* You should know that when this happens, your instructors are almost certain to notice and the impression will be bad. The next two sections examine correctly citing direct quotes (24.2.B) and paraphrasing (24.2.C) in detail.

8) Visual elements and compositions also require citation.

A photograph, table, or chart that you include in your writing from another source must be cited the same as any other resource reference. Someone else performed the intellectual work to create that photograph, and someone else performed the intellectual work to place it within the original source and publish that source. So, you need to leave a trail that signals the citation and links back to the original source of that visual element. Just because a citation is visual and not textual does not mean that it does not require attribution.

Additionally, just because you might be presenting your work visually rather than on paper does not mean that you do not have to cite your sources. If you are delivering a talk accompanied by projected slides, then you should include a bibliography on your last slide. If you give a speech without slides, you should print out a bibliography to share and perhaps reference at moments during your talk. Citation always makes you look smart.

Even Hollywood films acknowledge sources and the intellectual contributions that went into the production. For example, there's often an extensive list of musical recordings listed at the end of the film in *the credits*. Filmmakers don't dare leave anyone out of the ending credits; doing so even in that nonacademic genre is a deeply offensive professional sin — even the caterers get listed.

PRACTICE Find a scholarly resource online or in print that includes an extensive bibliography. Your instructor might provide you with this model, or it might come from something that you are currently researching as part of a writing assignment. Describe in a short paragraph your impression of the author and the work. How does the author's integration of citation and resources influence your reading of the work? Describe the ways in which the sample you are analyzing demonstrates the central concept of this lesson: Citation is a research tool, not a threat. Which of the eight principles in 24.1 do you recognize in the sample?

24.2 [HOW]

Citation Mechanics.

I have listed the most common citation concerns that my students ask about, in MLA, APA, and *Chicago* styles. Additional exercises are available in the LaunchPad, although I strongly argue that it is much more effective to practice these citation forms on your own writing rather than on someone else's.

In the charts that follow, keep an eye on the information that is underlined. Once you have mastered the basic citation format, the underlining will help draw your attention to portions of a citation that are different from the basic form.

CHART 24.2.A

Signal

Definition	Section 24.1.6 describes the three essential components of each citation: signal, in-text citation, and bibliography. A signal announces to your readers that they are about to encounter a citation, source, or reference that you are integrating into your writing. The purpose of a signal is to make it clear as a bell that you are referring to someone else's ideas.
	Signals are accomplished in three different ways, which are often used in combination: (1) quotation marks, (2) in-text citation, and (3) direct attribution. You must use at least one of these signals whenever you cite, and you must also provide a link between in-text citation and a bibliographic entry.
Signals 1 and 2 Quotation Marks and In-Text Citation Provide Signals (MLA In-Text Style)	When you use three or more words from a source, always put those words in quotations marks, "Just like these five words" — just as you would for longer direct quotes.
	The guiding concept seems to be that citation is primarily a "system for knowledge building" (Walker and Taylor 30).
Signals 2 and 3 In-Text Citation and Direct Attribution Provide Signals (APA In-Text Style)	Even when you paraphrase an idea from someone else, you must signal and cite the source.
	Walker and Taylor argue that citation styles and systems are used to advance research (2007, p. 30).
Advice	Although, you must use at least one signal (quotes, in-text citation, or direct attribution) whenever you cite, you generally should use at least two or three of them. Remember, you want it to be clear as a bell that you are citing — and a bell is a pretty clear signal (which is most often rung more than once).
Closely Related	In-Text Citation, Bibliography, Paraphrase, Direct Quote, MLA, APA, *Chicago*

CHART 24.2.B

Direct Quote

Definition	In terms of academic citation, a direct quote is defined as using quotation marks (or a block quote) to indicate precisely which words come from a source. Direct quotes are safe and easy to create. As easy as they might be, you must still carefully attribute the source with an in-text citation and bibliographic reference. You face three challenges with direct quotes: 1. You must put quotation marks around the words *exactly* as they are used in the source. 2. You cannot use a quote out of context, which means to apply the quote to a situation for which it was probably not intended. 3. If you use too much direct quotation, you can frustrate your readers.
Transcript of Nicole's Interview	"I go back again and I edit and revise and peer review. You want to make sure that you have your body paragraphs and your intro and your conclusion. But, basically, lots of peer review, lots of peer review before I turn in my paper."
Incorrect Direct Quote	In *Becoming a College Writer*, Nicole claims that she uses "many rounds of peer review" to proofread her bibliographies (Taylor 157).
Correct Direct Quote (MLA In-Text Style)	In *Becoming a College Writer*, Nicole claims that she uses "lots of peer review before" she submits her writing assignments (Taylor 157).
Advice	There are two problems with the incorrect direct quote: (1) Nicole's interview doesn't actually use the words "many rounds," as the quotation marks suggest. (2) The quote is taken out of context because Nicole was not talking about her bibliographies; she was talking about her use of peer review in general.
Closely Related	Paraphrase, Summary, Signal

CHART 24.2.C

Paraphrase

Definition	In terms of academic citation, a paraphrase is defined as restating someone else's ideas in your own words *while clearly attributing the source with an in-text citation and bibliographic reference.* If you fail to make it clear that you are paraphrasing someone else's words or thoughts, then your reader cannot follow your research trail (24.1.1) and you have committed plagiarism. You will need to become comfortable paraphrasing in your college writing because you want to include abundant sources and evidence in your work. If you only use direct quotes, then your writing might be difficult to read or become needlessly lengthy. However, when you paraphrase, you must cite the source, even though you are using your own words to represent someone else's ideas.
Transcript of Nicole's Interview	"I go back again and I edit and revise and peer review. You want to make sure that you have your body paragraphs and your intro and your conclusion. But, basically, lots of peer review, lots of peer review before I turn in my paper."
Incorrect Paraphrase	In *Becoming a College Writer*, Nicole claimed she based the revisions of her paper on lots of peer review before she turned in her writing assignment (Taylor, 2019, p. 458).
Correct Paraphrase (APA In-Text Style)	In *Becoming a College Writer*, Nicole claimed she based the revisions of her paper on abundant advice from her classmates (Taylor, 2019, p. 458).
Advice	If you have three or more words that are exactly or nearly the same as the original text, you must either make them a direct quote or reword them substantially to paraphrase correctly. In the incorrect paraphrase above the words "lots of peer review before" should be in quotation marks. Even though the incorrect paraphrase above has a correct in-text citation, it is still incorrect because, without those quotation marks, the writer is claiming those words were original, but they belong to Nicole.
Closely Related	Direct Quote, Summary Signal

CHART 24.2.D

Summary

Definition	A paraphrase restates someone else's ideas in your own words, as does a summary. There is no official separation between a paraphrase and a summary, just a general rule of thumb that a paraphrase typically restates a shorter passage (sentence or paragraph) while a summary encapsulates a larger body of writing (many paragraphs, an article, chapter, entire book).
	The problem can be that writers don't think they need to cite a summary because it is in their own words. You absolutely do! In order for your readers to know what you are summarizing so that they can benefit from consulting the original source too, they must know the source you are summarizing.
	For each summary, you must signal, provide in-text citation, and provide a correct bibliographic entry!
Incorrect Summary	*Becoming a College Writer* provides 25 lessons that cover the essentials of college writing — none more important than the need to Revise Repeatedly from Feedback.
Correct Summary (APA In-Text Style)	*Becoming a College Writer* provides 25 lessons that cover the essentials of college writing — none more important than the need to "Revise Repeatedly from Feedback" (Taylor 2019).
Advice	The incorrect summary attempts to signal and cite appropriately, but the title alone, *Becoming a College Writer*, will not correspond to the author's last name in the bibliography! Furthermore, even though the summary is referring to the use of RRFF throughout the entire book and not a specific page, those are still someone else's words that need to be put into quotation marks (as the correct summary does). A page number is not needed in the in-text citation because the summary refers to the entire book.
Closely Related	Direct Quote, Paraphrase, Signal

Citation at a Glance

CHICAGO CITATION

MLA OVERVIEW

In-Text Citation

Explanation

There are three essential components of each citation: signal, in-text citation, and bibliography. An MLA in-text citation has two purposes:

1. To link the current citation to a bibliographic entry for the source, and
2. To point to specific page numbers, paragraphs, or places so that the reader can find a specific quote, sentence, passage, or paragraph in the original source.

Each time you cite, ask yourself, "Can the reader easily link from the cited sentence to a corresponding bibliographic entry?" That's the primary purpose of your in-text citations: to give readers a guide to the material you use to support your writing.

If you develop your works-cited list as you work with new sources, it will be easier to link those entries to your in-text citations and to clearly mark a trail for your readers.

In the examples below, the pieces of the citation are underlined. If the author or source is named in the text, it does not need to be repeated in parentheses.

MLA In-Text Citation with No Author Listed in the Sentence Itself (No Direct Attribution)

MLA in-text citation style requires you to put the author's last name and a page number (when relevant and available) in an in-text citation when your sentence does not directly attribute the author(s).

Overall, this is a book about food, drink, and drug crusaders (Goodwin 30).

MLA In-Text Citation with the Author's Name Listed in the Sentence (Direct Attribution)

You do not need to include the author's last name enclosed in the parentheses at the end of the sentence when you signal their names in the sentences, like the example below. Notice that you still need a page number to locate the direct quote.

Pollan discusses the relationship between obesity and fast food, citing data on chronic diseases. He says, "The health care crisis probably cannot be addressed without addressing the catastrophe of the American diet" (30).

No Author	When there is no listed author, editor or organization, use the full title within your signal, or use a shortened version (the first word) in parentheses.
(Direct Attribution)	In "The Facts on Junk Food Marketing and Kids," the eating habits of children are examined in relation to advertisements.
(No Direct Attribution)	As a result, kids see about four thousand ads per year encouraging them to eat unhealthy food and drinks ("Facts").
Quoted In	When you want to use a statement that is from someone being quoted by the author in a citation, use the tag "qtd. in" in your parenthetical citation.
	Jeff Levi of the nonprofit Trust for America's Health said, "We need to create environments where the healthy choice becomes the easy choice, where it's possible for people to bear that responsibility" (qtd. in Neergaard and Agiesta).
Closely Related	Signal, Bibliography, Paraphrase, Direct Quote, MLA, APA, *Chicago*

MLA OVERVIEW

Sample Works Cited

Definition	A bibliography is a list of sources referenced in your writing, called "Works Cited" in MLA style. It is essential that you are very careful and precise with your Works Cited entries, because a mistake could mean that you and your readers are not able to find the source.

- Your final bibliography should be alphabetical by author last name.

- You should build your bibliography as you go. This will help you with in-text citations and will keep you organized.

- If your entry runs onto more than one line, MLA requires the additional lines to be indented. You can indent the additional lines by selecting the entire entry and moving the lower slider (the one that says "hanging indent" when you hover over it) on the ruler at the top of your document.

Below is an example of a properly formatted bibliography.

Form: MLA "Works Cited" Bibliography	Works Cited
Newspaper Article	Conly, Sarah. "Three Cheers for the Nanny State." *The New York Times*, 25 Mar. 2013, p. A23.
No Author Listed	"The Facts on Junk Food Marketing and Kids." *Prevention Institute*, www .preventioninstitute.org/focus-areas/supporting-healthy-food-a-activity /supporting-healthy-food-and-activity-environments-advocacy/get -involved-were-not-buying-it/735-were-not-buying-it-the-facts-on-junk -food-marketing-and-kids.html. Accessed 21 Apr. 2017.
Book	Goodwin, Lorine Swainston. *The Pure Food, Drink, and Drug Crusaders, 1879–1914*. McFarland, 2006.
Online Journal	Gostin, L. O., and K. G. Gostin. "A Broader Liberty: J. S. Mill, Paternalism, and the Public's Health." *Public Health*, vol. 123, no. 3, 2009, pp. 214–21, doi:10.1016/ j.puhe.2008.12.024.
Two Authors	Schillinger, Dean, and Cristin Kearns. "Guidelines to Limit Added Sugar Intake: Junk Science or Junk Food?" *Annals of Internal Medicine*, 21 Jan. 2017, http://annals.org/aim/article-abstract/2593852/ guidelines-limit-added-sugar-intake-junk-science-junk-food.

Dissertation	Nestle, Marion. *Food Politics: How the Food Industry Influences Nutrition and Health.* U of California P, 2013.
Online Magazine	Sunstein, Cass R. "It's For Your Own Good!" *The New York Review of Books,* 7 March 2013, www.nybooks.com/articles/2013/03/07/its-your-own-good/.
Journal Article	Rosi, Alice, et al. "How to Improve Food Choices through Vending Machines." *Food Quality and Preference,* vol. 62, Dec. 2017, pp. 262–69.
Organizational Author	U.S. Department of Agriculture and Department of Health and Human Services. *Dietary Guidelines for Americans 2015–2020,* Skyhorse Publishing, 2017.

Closely Related	MLA Overview: In-Text Citation, MLA Citation Charts

MLA WORKS CITED

The Basics — by Author

Explanation	Think of MLA citation as a fill-in-the-blank form. Once you gather all of the items you need, it's easy to put them in the blanks. Before you begin, there are a few key pieces of information you need to collect:

- Author or authors

- Full title of the selection and the work it's from

- Name of the publisher and the date of publication

- For a digital source: the medium and location of the material

In the models below, the author or authors are underlined in red. You'll notice that the last example has no author listed, so there is no underlining.

Basic Form	Author's Last Name, Author's First Name. "Selection title in quotation marks." *Title of the Work in Italics*. Publisher, date of publication, URL or page number.
1. Single Author	Albright, Horace. "The Paradox of the Park." *National Geographic*, May 2016, pp. 54–91.
2. Two Authors	Groopman, Jerome, and Pamela Hartzband. "Putting Profits Ahead of Patients." *The New York Review of Books*, 13 Jul. 2017, http://www.nybooks.com /articles/2017/07/13/putting-profits-ahead-of-patients/.
3. Three or More Authors	Wolf, Mary Ann et al. *Leading Personalized and Digital Learning: A Framework for Implementing School Change*. Harvard Education Press, 2017. Note: When there are more than two authors, the Latin "et al." is used to show that others contributed to the work.
4. Editor as Author	Wall, Cheryl A., editor. *Changing Our Own Words: Essays on Criticism, Theory, and Writing by Black Women*. Rutgers UP, 1989.
5. Organizational Author	Human Rights Watch. *World Report of 2015: Events of 2014*. Seven Stories Press, 2015.
6. No Author Listed	"Policing Ohio's Online Courses." *Plain Dealer* [Cleveland], 9 Oct. 2012, p. A5. Editorial.
Closely Related	MLA: Printed Sources, MLA: Online Sources

MLA WORKS CITED

Printed Sources

Explanation

For printed sources in MLA style, note that a single selection is treated in the same way, regardless of the whole work it comes from. You need to collect:

- Author or authors
- Full title of the whole work and the selection (if used)
- Publisher name (for books)
- Date of publication
- Volume and issue number (if relevant)
- Page numbers (if relevant)

Note: When citing a newspaper article that starts on the front page but continues later in that section, use a plus sign to show that it is more than one page, rather than listing several pages out of sequence.

Underlining (below) highlights how titles (of selections and of whole works) and page numbers are handled for different print sources.

Basic Form 1

Author's Last Name, Author's First Name. "Selection title in quotation marks." *Title of the Work in Italics*. Publisher, date of publication, page numbers.

7. Book

Taylor, Todd. *Becoming a College Writer: A Multimedia Text*. Bedford/St. Martin's, 2019, pp. 64–83.

Basic Form 2

Author's Last Name, Author's First Name. "Selection title in quotation marks." *Title of the Work in Italics*, volume or issue number, date of publication, page numbers.

8. Magazine Article

Bryan, Christy. "The Rise of Eyes." *National Geographic*, Feb. 2016, pp. 42–57.

9. Newspaper Article

Sherry, Allison. "Volunteers' Personal Touch Turns High-Tech Data into Votes." *The Denver Post*, 30 Oct. 2012, pp. 1A+.

10. Journal Article

Matchie, Thomas. "Law versus Love in The Round House." *Midwest Quarterly*, vol. 56, no. 4, Summer 2015, pp. 353–64.

Closely Related

MLA: The Basics — by Author, MLA: Online Resource

MLA WORKS CITED

Online Sources

Explanation

Before you start to cite an online resource, gather a few key pieces of information.

- Author/authors
- Full title of article/essay
- URL or DOI
- Volume, issue number, and date (if applicable)

A DOI, or **digital object identifier**, is a unique number assigned to a piece of content. While URLs can sometimes change or break, a DOI is intended to be a permanent connection to the source.

In the first three examples below, the title of the publication and the name of the publisher are underlined to show where and how to include this information. In the final example, the underlining highlights the elements that are significant for journals and other similar publications: the volume and issue numbers and the database where you found the source.

Form 1:
Online Resource, no Volume or Issue Number

Author's Last Name, Author's First Name. "Title of the Work in Quotation Marks." _Publication name in italics_, Publisher, Date of publication, Full URL or DOI.

11. Online Newspaper or Magazine Article

Belluz, Julia. "Why Harassment Trainings Don't Stop Harassment." _Vox_, 14 Nov. 2017, https://www.vox.com/science-and-health/2017/10/24/16498674/corporate-harassment-trainings-dont-work.

12. Blog Post

Eakin, Emily. "_Cloud Atlas_'s Theory of Everything." _NYR Daily_, NYREV, 2 Nov. 2012, www.nybooks.com/daily/2012/11/02/ken-wilber-cloud-atlas.

13. Entire Website

Transparency International. _Transparency International: The Global Coalition against Corruption_, 2018, www.transparency.org.

Form 2:
Online Resource with Volume or Issue Numbers

Author's Last Name, Author's First Name. "Title of the Work in Quotation Marks." _Publication name in italics_, volume, edition number, date, and pages. _Online database name_, Full URL or DOI.

14. Journal Article in an Online Database	Maier, Jessica. "A 'True Likeness': The Renaissance City Portrait." *Renaissance Quarterly*, vol. 65, no. 3, Fall 2012, pp. 711–52. *JSTOR*, doi:10.1086/668300.
Closely Related	MLA: Printed Sources, MLA: The Basics — by Author

MLA WORKS CITED

Multimedia Sources

Explanation

In a book, the edition number follows the title. In an e-book, the medium is expressed as the edition (Nook ed., Kindle ed., etc.).

When citing a film or television show, you'll want to include:

- The director or producer

- The names of the lead actors

- The production company

If you are focusing on the movie as a whole, the title comes before the names of the participants. If you're discussing a film or television show in the context of a particular actor or director; however, you should list them first as you would a normal author.

For an audio recording, include the record label. Like the production company or publisher, this is the group that actually creates the content, so it's an important key to tracking a source. If you include a piece of art, you'll want to add the location of the museum or name of the collection to your citation.

Notice that the date is used in all multimedia works, but in a photograph or piece of fine art, it appears earlier in the citation.

In the Form 1 examples below, the author is underlined (you'll notice it doesn't always appear at the beginning). In both forms, the date of publication is underlined (usually, but not always at the end of the citation) and so is the location of the source. In Form 2, we have also underlined the selection title and collection title, the features that set this form apart.

Form 1

Author's Last Name, Author's First Name. *Title of the Work or Collection in italics*, Museum name or production company, Date of publication. Full URL or location.

15. E-book

Beard, Mary. *SPQR: A History of Ancient Rome*. Nook ed., Liveright Publishing, 2015.

16. Photograph

Bradford, Mark. *Let's Walk to the Middle of the Ocean*. 2015, Museum of Modern Art, New York.

17. Film	*Wonderstruck*. Directed by Todd Haynes, performances by Oakes Fegley, Julianne Moore, and Millicent Simmonds, Amazon Studios, 2017.
18. Television Show	Marshall, N. (Director), & Martin, G. (Writer). (2012, May 27). Blackwater [Television series episode]. In D. Benioff, F. Doelger, C. Strauss, D. Weiss (Executive producers), *Game of Thrones*. Croatia, HBO.
19. Digital Game	Firaxis Games. *Sid Meier's Civilization Revolution*. Take-Two Interactive, 2008.
Form 2	Author's Last Name, Author's First Name. "Selection title in quotation marks." *Title of the Collection in italics*, Production company, Date of publication.
20. YouTube Video	Swaniker, Fred. "Reimagining Leadership." *YouTube*, 24 July 2017, https://www.youtube.com/watch?v=M0MvdurXvpU.
21. Audio Recording	Maroon 5. "Don't Wanna Know." *Red Pill Blues*, Interscope Records, 2017.
Closely Related	MLA: Printed Sources, MLA: Book, MLA: Online Sources

MLA WORKS CITED

Social Media Sources

Explanation	When citing a social media source, you always need a URL and a date, as well as elements that are standard in bibliographies, such as authors and titles. Given the nature of social media platforms, some sources may need alternative or additional elements. For example,

- The author of a post or comment may be a person's actual name, a screen name, or an organization.

- When citing a tweet, include the entire tweet within the citation.

- When citing a short Facebook post, include the entire post. If it is longer, include a brief, summative title of the post instead.

- When citing a comment on a blog post or other online content, note the title of the post, along with the publisher.

In the models below, the name of the social media platform (or the name of the website, in the case of Internet comments) is underlined because this is an element that does not appear in other types of citations.

Form: Social Media	Poster's name or organization name. "Title of the Work in quotation marks". Social media platform, publication or publisher, Date of publication. Full URL.
21. Tweet	Curiosity Rover. "Can you see me waving? How to spot #Mars in the night sky: https://youtu.be/hv8hVvJlcJQ." Twitter, 5 Nov. 2015, 11:00 a.m., twitter.com/marscuriosity/status/672859022911889408.
22. Instagram Post	Natgeo (National Geographic). Post. Instagram, 22 July 2016, instagram.com/p/BIKyGHtDD4W/?taken-by=natgeo.
23. Facebook Post	Bedford English. "Stacey Cochran explores Reflective Writing in the classroom and as a writer: http://ow.ly/YkjVB." Facebook, 15 Feb. 2016, www.facebook.com/BedfordEnglish/posts/10153415001259607.
24. Internet Comments	hannahcraine. Comment on "The Pizza Thought Experiment." *NYR Daily*, NYREV, 26 Nov. 2017, http://www.nybooks.com/daily/2017/11/26/the-pizza-thought-experiment/.
Closely Related	MLA: Multimedia Sources, MLA: Online Sources

MLA WORKS CITED

Other Sources

Explanation	Some sources don't fit easily into categories and are best addressed according to their specific characteristics.

- A **dissertation** (or thesis) is typically the final paper or project completed as part of earning a master's degree or a PhD.
- **Lectures** might include special events on campus, book readings, or even just the material your professor covers in class every day.
- **Interviews** might include ones that are published in print, ones that are conducted on the radio, TV, or online, and interviews that you yourself might conduct to gather primary research.

All three of these citations include the type of source, something that MLA does not usually require. In this case, it is necessary because these sources are often unpublished, which means that they are not easily found or identified through the other citation information. The location of that information varies, so confirm that you are including it in the correct location for each source type.

If one of these sources has been published, you can cite it as you would any other print or digital source. When you cite an interview that you yourself have taken, do not list your name but use "Personal interview" as the type of source instead.

In the examples below, we have underlined three key pieces of information: the Sponsoring Institution or Interviewer Name, the location (of the source or of the sponsor), and the type of source.

Form: Academic Works	Author or Interviewee's Last Name, Author or Interviewee's First Name. "Title of the Work." Sponsoring Institution or Interviewer Name. *Name of Publication in Italics*, Publisher, Date of publication. Full URL or location of the sponsor. Type of source.
25. Lecture	Taylor, Todd. "On Writing an Introduction." UNC Chapel Hill, Chapel Hill, NC, 6 Apr. 2018. Lecture.
26. Interview	Jaffrey, Madhur. "Madhur Jaffrey on How Indian Cuisine Won Western Taste Buds." Interview by Shadrach Kabango. *Q*, CBC Radio, 29 Oct. 2015, www.cbc.ca/1.3292918.
	Akufo, Dautey. Personal interview, 11 Apr. 2016.
27. Dissertation (Unpublished)	Abbas, Megan Brankley. "Knowing Islam: The Entangled History of Western Academia and Modern Islamic Thought." Dissertation, Princeton U, 2015.
Closely Related	MLA: The Basics, MLA: Printed Sources, MLA: Online Sources

APA OVERVIEW

In-Text Citation

Explanation

There are three essential components of each citation: signal, in-text citation, and bibliography. An in-text citation has:

1. To link the current citation to a bibliographic entry for the source,
2. To reveal how current the source is, and
3. To point to specific page numbers, paragraphs, or places so that the reader can find a specific quote, sentence, passage, or paragraph in the original source.

Each time you cite, ask yourself, "can the reader easily link from the cited sentence to a corresponding bibliographic entry?" That's the primary purpose of your in-text citations: to give readers a guide to the material you use to support your writing.

If you develop your references list as you work with new sources, it will be easier to link those entries to your in-text citations and clearly mark a trail for your readers.

In the examples below, the pieces of the citation are underlined. If the author or source is named in the text, it does not need to be repeated in parentheses.

APA In-Text Citation with No Author Listed in the Sentence Itself (No Direct Attribution)

APA in-text citation style requires you to put the author's last name, the year of the publication, and a page number (when relevant and available) in an in-text citation when your sentence does not directly attribute the author(s).

Overall, this is a book about food, drink, and drug crusaders (Goodwin, 2018, p. 30).

APA In-Text Citation with the Author's Name Listed in the Sentence (Direct Attribution)

You do not need to include the author's last name enclosed in the parenthesis at the end of the sentence when you signal their name in the sentences, as in the example below. Notice that you still need a page number to locate the direct quote.

Pollan (2010) discusses the relationship between obesity and fast food, citing data on chronic diseases. He says, "The health care crisis probably cannot be addressed without addressing the catastrophe of the American diet" (p. 30).

No Author	When there is no listed author, editor, or organization, use the full title within your signal, or use a shortened version (the first word) in parentheses. Also note that the example below requires the indication n.d. when the source does not provide a publication date.
(Direct Attribution)	In "The Facts on Junk Food Marketing and Kids" (n.d.), the eating habits of children are examined in relation to advertisements.
(No Direct Attribution)	As a result, kids see about four thousand ads per year encouraging them to eat unhealthy food and drinks ("Facts," n.d.).
Quoted In	When you want to use a statement that is from someone being quoted by the author in a citation, add the phrase *as quoted in* to your parenthetical citation. Jeff Levi of the nonprofit Trust for America's Health said, "We need to create environments where the healthy choice becomes the easy choice, where it's possible for people to bear that responsibility" (as quoted in Neergaard and Agiesta, 2013, para. 14).

Closely Related	Signal, Bibliography, Paraphrase, Direct Quote, APA, MLA, *Chicago*

APA OVERVIEW

Sample References List

Definition	A reference list is a list of sources referenced in your writing, called "References" in APA style. It is essential that you are very careful and precise with your reference list entries because a mistake could mean that you and your readers cannot find the source.

- Your final bibliography should be alphabetical by author last name.

- You should build your bibliography as you go. This will help you with in-text citations and will keep you organized.

- If your entry runs onto more than one line, APA requires the additional lines to be indented. You can indent the additional lines by selecting the entire entry and moving the lower slider (the one that says "hanging indent" when you hover over it) on the ruler at the top of your document.

Below is an example of a properly formatted references list.

Form: APA "References" Bibliography	**References** Conly, S. (2013, March 25). Three cheers for the nanny state. *The New York Times*, A23.
Newspaper Article **No Author Listed, No Date Listed**	The facts on junk food marketing and kids. (n.d.). *Prevention Institute*. Retrieved April 21, 2017 from http://www.preventioninstitute.org/focus-areas/ supporting-healthy-food-a-activity/supporting-healthy-food-and-activity -environments-advocacy/get-involved-were-not-buying-it/735-were-not -buying-it-the-facts-on-junk-food-marketing-and-kids.html
Book	Goodwin, L. S. (2006). *The pure food, drink, and drug crusaders, 1879–1914*. Jefferson, NC: McFarland.
Online Journal	Gostin, L.O. & Gostin, K.G. (2009). A broader liberty: J. S. Mill, paternalism, and the public's health. *Public Health*, 123 (3), pp. 214–21. http://dx.doi. org/10.1016/j.puhe.2008.12.024
Two Authors	Schillinger, D. & Kearns, C. (2017, January 21). Guidelines to limit added sugar intake: Junk science or junk food?" *Annals of Internal Medicine*. Retrieved from http://annals.org/aim/article-abstract/2593852/ guidelines-limit-added-sugar-intake-junk-science-junk-food

Dissertation	Nestle, M. (2013). *Food politics: How the food industry influences nutrition and health*. Berkeley, CA: University of California Press.
Online Magazine	Sunstein, C. R. (2013, March 7). It's for your own good! *The New York Review of Books*. Retrieved from: www.nybooks.com/articles/2013/03/07/its-your-own-good/
Journal Article	Rosi, A., Zerbini, C., Pellegrini, N., Scazzina, F., Brighenti, F. & Lugli, G. (2017, December). How to improve food choices through vending machines. *Food Quality and Preference*, 62, pp. 262–69.
Organizational Author	U.S. Department of Agriculture and Department of Health and Human Services. (2017). *Dietary Guidelines for Americans 2015–2020*. New York, NY: Skyhorse Publishing.

Closely Related	APA Overview: In-Text Citation; APA Citation Charts

APA REFERENCES

The Basics — by Author

Explanation

Think of APA citation as a fill-in-the-blank form. Once you gather all of the items you need, it's easy to put them in the blanks. Before you begin, there are a few key pieces of information you need to collect.

- Author or authors

- Full title of the selection and the work it's from

- Name of the publisher (for books)
  the date of publication

- For a digital source: the medium and location of the material

In the models below, the author or authors are underlined in red. You'll notice that the last example has no author listed, so there is no underlining.

Basic Form

Author's Last Name, Author's First Initial. (Date of Publication). Selection title in roman. *Title of the work in italics*. City, State abbreviation: Publisher, page number. DOI or Retrieved from URL

1. Single Author

Albright, H. (2016, May). The paradox of the park. *National Geographic*, pp. 54–91.

2. Two to Seven Authors

Groopman, J., and Hartzband, P. (2017, July 13). Putting profits ahead of patients. *The New York Review of Books*. Retrieved from http://www.nybooks .com/articles/2017/07/13/putting-profits-ahead-of-patients/

3. Seven or More Authors

Bekelman, J., Halpern, S., Blankart, C., Bynum, J., Cohen, J., Fowler, R. . . . & Emanuel, E. (2016). Comparison of site of death, health care utilization, and hospital expenditures. *JAMA*, 315 (3), 272–83. http://dx.doi.org/10.1001/ jama.2015.18603

Note: When there are more than seven authors, list the first six authors followed by a comma. Then, include three ellipsis dots and the name of the final author.

4. Editor as Author

Wall, C. (Ed.). (1989). *Changing our own words: Essays on criticism, theory, and writing by black women*. New Brunswick, NJ: Rutgers University Press.

5. Organizational Author	Human Rights Watch. (2015). *World report of 2015: Events of 2014*. New York, NY: Seven Stories Press.
6. No Author Listed	Policing Ohio's online courses [Editorial]. (2012, October 9). *Plain Dealer*, p. A5.

Closely Related	APA: Printed Sources, APA: Online Sources

APA REFERENCES

Printed Sources

Explanation	For printed sources in APA style, you need to collect

- Author or authors

- Date of publication

- Full title of the whole work and the selection (if used)

- Location of publication and publisher name (for books)

- Volume and issue number (if relevant)

- Page numbers (if relevant)

Note when citing a newspaper article that starts on the front page but continues later in that section, you should list each page number, separated by commas.

Underlining (below) highlights how titles (of selections and of whole works) and page numbers are handled for different print sources.

Basic Form 1	Author's Last Name, Author's First Initial. (Date of publication). Selection title. *Title of the work in italics*. City, and State of Publication: Publisher, page numbers.
7. Book	Taylor, T. (2018). *Becoming a college writer: a multimedia text*. Boston, MA: Bedford/St. Martin's, pp. 64–83.
Basic Form 2	Author's Last Name, Author's First Initial. (Date of publication). Selection title. *Title of the Publication in italics*, volume (issue number), page numbers.
	Note that for magazines and journal articles, you do not use p. or pp. before the page numbers.

8. Magazine Article	Bryan, C. (2016, February). The rise of eyes. *National Geographic*, 42–57.
9. Newspaper Article	Sherry, A. (2012, October 30). Volunteers' personal touch turns high-tech data into votes. *The Denver Post*, pp. 1A, 1C.
10. Journal Article	Matchie, T. (2015, Summer). Law versus love in The Round House. *Midwest Quarterly*, 56(4), 353–64.

Closely Related	APA: The Basics — by Author, APA: Online Sources

APA REFERENCES

Online Sources

Explanation	Before you start to cite an online resource, gather a few key pieces of information.

- Author/authors

- Full title of article/essay

- URL or DOI

- Volume, issue number, and date (if applicable)

A DOI, or **digital object identifier**, is a unique number assigned to a piece of content. Having a URL or DOI makes it easy for your reader to find your sources, but URLs can sometimes change or break. A DOI is intended to be a permanent connection to the source.

In the first three examples below, the title of the publication is underlined to show where and how to include this information. In the final example, the underlining highlights the elements that are significant for journals and other similar publications: the volume and issue numbers and the database where you found the source.

Form 1: Online Source without a Volume or Issue Number	Author's Last Name, Author's First Initial. (Date of Publication). Title of the work. *Publication name in italics*. [Additional information if needed] DOI or Retrieved from URL
11. Online Newspaper or Magazine Article	Belluz, J. (2017, November). Why harassment trainings don't stop harassment. *Vox*. Retrieved from https://www.vox.com/science-and-health/2017/10/24/16498674/corporate-harassment-trainings-dont-work
12. Blog Post	Eakin, E. (2012, November 2). *Cloud Atlas*'s theory of everything [Blog post]. *NYR Daily*. Retrieved from www.nybooks.com/daily/2012/11/02/ken-wilber-cloud-atlas
13. Entire Website	Transparency International. (2018). *Transparency International: The Global Coalition against Corruption*. Retrieved from http://www.transparency.org

Form 2: Online Source with Volume or Issue Numbers	Author's Last Name, Author's First Initial. (Date of publication). Title of the work. *Publication Name in Italics*, volume (edition number), and pages. Full URL or DOI
14. Journal Article in an Online Database	Maier, J. (2012). A "True Likeness": The Renaissance City Portrait. *Renaissance Quarterly*, 65(3), 711–52. http://dx.doi.org/10.1086/668300
Closely Related	APA: Printed Sources, APA: The Basics — by Author

APA REFERENCES

Multimedia Sources

Explanation	In a book, the edition number follows the title. In an e-book, film, or television show, the medium is expressed as the edition (Nook edition, Kindle edition, etc.). When citing a film, you'll want to include: • The director or producer • The country where the film or episode was made • The studio or distributor For a television show, the information is similar, but you'll need the writer of the episode as well. For an audio recording, include the record label. Like the production company, or a publisher, this is the group that actually creates the content, so it's an important key to tracking a source. If you include a piece of art, you'll want to add the location of the museum to your citation. In the Form 1 examples below, the URL or location is underlined. In Form 2, we have also underlined the selection title and collection title as the features that set this form apart.
Form 1	Creator's Last Name, Creator's First Initial. (Date of publication). *Title of the work or collection in italics*, [Format]. Full URL or location: Museum name or production company (if applicable).
15. E-book	Beard, M. (2015). *SPQR: A History of Ancient Rome* [Nook edition]. Retrieved from Amazon.com.
16. Photograph	Bradford, M. (2015). *Let's walk to the middle of the ocean*. [Photograph]. New York: Museum of Modern Art.
17. Film	Haynes, T. (Director). (2017). *Wonderstruck* [Motion picture]. United States: Amazon Studios.
18. Television Episode	Marshall, N. (Director), & Martin, G. (Writer). (2012, May 27). Blackwater [Television series episode]. In D. Benioff, F. Doelger, C. Strauss, D. Weiss (Executive producers), *Game of Thrones*. Croatia, HBO.

19. Digital Game	Firaxis Games. (2008). *Sid Meier's Civilization revolution* [Video game]. New York: Take-Two Interactive.
Form 2	Author's Last Name, Author's First Initial. (Date of publication). Selection title. [Medium]. *Title of the collection in italics*, Full URL or location: Production company (if applicable).
20. YouTube Video	Swaniker, F. (2017, July 24). Reimagining leadership. [Video file]. Retrieved from https://www.youtube.com/watch?v=M0MvdurXvpU
21. Audio Recording	Maroon 5. (2017). Don't wanna know. On *Red pill blues* [MP3]. Los Angeles, CA: Interscope Records.
Closely Related	APA: Printed Sources, APA: Book, APA: Online Sources

APA REFERENCES

Social Media Sources

Explanation

When citing a social media source, you always need a URL and a date, as well as elements that are standard in bibliographies, such as authors and titles. Given the nature of social media platforms, some sources may need alternative or additional elements. For example:

- The author of a post or comment may be a person's actual name, a screen name, or an organization.

- When citing a tweet, include the entire tweet within the citation.

- When citing a short Facebook post, include the entire post. If it is longer, include a brief, summative title of the post instead.

- When citing a comment on a blog post or other online content, note the title of the post, along with the publisher.

In the models below, the format is underlined because this is an element that does not always appear in other types of citations.

Form: Social Media

Poster's name or organization name. (Date of publication). Title of the Work. [Format]. Retrieved from URL

22. Tweet

Curiosity Rover [MarsCuriosity]. (2015, November 5). Can you see me waving? How to spot #Mars in the night sky: https://youtu.be/hv8hVvJlcJQ [Tweet]. Retrieved from http://twitter.com/marscuriosity/status/672859022911889408

23. Instagram Post

National Geographic [@Natgeo]. (2016, July 22). [Photograph of a tiger's face, close-up, by Steve Winter]. Retrieved from http://instagram.com/p/BIKyGHtDD4W/?taken-by=natgeo

24. Facebook Post

Bedford English. (2016, February 15). Stacey Cochran explores reflective writing in the classroom and as a writer: http://ow.ly/YkjVB. [Facebook status update]. Retrieved from http://www.facebook.com/BedfordEnglish/posts/10153415001259607

25. Internet Comments

hannahcraine. (2017, November 26). Re: The Pizza Thought Experiment [article comment]. Retrieved from http://www.nybooks.com/daily/2017/11/26/the-pizza-thought-experiment/

Closely Related

APA: Multimedia Sources, APA: Online Sources

APA REFERENCES

Other Sources

Explanation	Some sources don't fit easily into categories and are best addressed according to their specific characteristics.
	• A **dissertation** (or thesis) is typically the final paper or project completed as part of earning a master's degree or a PhD.
	• **Lectures** might include special events on campus, book readings, or even just the material your professor covers in class every day.
	• **Interviews** might include ones that are published in print, ones that are conducted on the radio, TV, or online, and interviews that you yourself might conduct to gather primary research.
	All three of these citations include the type of source. In this case, it is necessary because these sources are often unpublished, which means that they are not easily found or identified through the other citation information. The location of that information varies, however, so confirm that you are including it in the correct location for each source type. If one of these sources has been published, you can cite it as you would any other print or digital source. When you cite an interview that you yourself have taken, you list it only in your in-text citations. Do not include personal interviews in your References in APA style. In the examples below, we have underlined three key pieces of information: the sponsoring institution or interviewer name, the location (of the source or of the sponsor), and the type of source.
Form: Academic Works	Author or Interviewee's Last Name, Author or Interviewee's First Initial. (Date of publication). Title of the work. [Type of source]. Sponsoring Institution, Full URL or location of the sponsor.
26. Lecture	Taylor, T. (2018, April 6). On writing an introduction. [Lecture presented at UNC Chapel Hill], Chapel Hill, NC.
27. Interview	Jaffrey, M. (2015, October 29). Madhur Jaffrey on How Indian Cuisine Won Western Taste Buds. [Interview by Shadrach Kabango]. In Q. Ottawa, Canada: CBC Radio. Retrieved from: http://www.cbc.ca/1.3292918
28. Dissertation (Unpublished)	Abbas, M. B. (2015). *Knowing Islam: The entangled history of Western academia and modern Islamic thought*. [Unpublished dissertation]. Princeton University, Princeton, NJ.
Closely Related	APA: The Basics — by Author, APA: Printed Sources, APA: Online Sources

CHICAGO OVERVIEW

In-Text Citation

Explanation

There are three essential components of each citation: signal, in-text citation, and bibliography. An in-text citation has two central purposes:

1. To link the current citation to a bibliographic entry (notes) for the source, and

2. To point to specific page numbers, paragraphs, or places so that the reader can find a specific quote, sentence, passage, or paragraph in the original source.

Each time you cite, ask yourself, "Can the reader easily link from the cited sentence to a corresponding bibliographic entry?" That's the primary purpose of your in-text citations: to give readers a guide to the material you use to support your writing.

If you develop your Notes list as you work with new sources, it will be easier to link those entries to your in-text citations and clearly mark a trail for your readers.

In the examples below, the pieces of the citation are underlined. Remember, if the author or source is named in the text, it does not need to be repeated in parentheses.

Chicago In-Text Citation

Chicago in-text citation is very simple. Each time you cite a source, you add a reference number at the end of the sentence in which you cite the material, outside of any punctuation. These numbers refer to the numbered Notes at the end of your paper, where you will provide a more complete citation.

Numbers should be added consecutively. Your first citation will be followed by a superscript 1, the next by a superscript 2, and so on.

Goodwin notes that overall, this is a book about food, drink, and drug crusaders.[1]

Chicago In-Text Citation with Dashes

When you are citing material in the first half of a sentence that is separated by an em dash (or two hyphens), you should put the superscript number before the dash, so that it stays with the material you are citing.

Pollan argues that health care and diet are inextricably connected[3] — though diet can be seen as only one small part of a much larger social crisis.

Closely Related

Signal, *Chicago* Overview: Sample Notes List, Paraphrase, Direct Quote, APA, MLA, *Chicago*

CHICAGO OVERVIEW

Sample Notes List

Definition

In *Chicago* citation style, you have the option to include two different source lists at the end of your document. The first, which you must have, is the Notes. The numbered entries in this list correspond to the superscript in-text references that you added throughout your paper.

- Your sources should be listed in the order in which they appear in your paper.

- You should build your Notes list as you go. This will help you with in-text citations and will keep you organized.

- Notes entries should be indented on the first line only. Entries in the bibliography should use a hanging indent. You can indent the additional lines by selecting the entire entry and moving the lower slider (the one that says "hanging indent" when you hover over it) on the ruler at the top of your document. This list will ultimately appear at the end of your paper.

The second source list you might include is a Bibliography. The Bibliography should come after your Notes and includes works that are relevant to your paper but are not specifically cited. Entries in the Bibliography should be listed alphabetically by author last name.

Form: *Chicago* "Notes"

Notes

Newspaper Article

1. Sarah Conly. "Three Cheers for the Nanny State," *New York Times*, 25 Mar. 2013.

No Author Listed, No Date Listed

2. "The Facts on Junk Food Marketing and Kids." Prevention Institute, accessed April 21, 2017, http://www.preventioninstitute.org/focus-areas/ supporting-healthy-food-a-activity/supporting-healthy-food-and -activity-environments-advocacy/get-involved-were-not-buying-it/ 735-were-not-buying-it-the-facts-on-junk-food-marketing-and-kids.html.

Book

3. Lorine Swainston Goodwin. *The Pure Food, Drink, and Drug Crusaders, 1879–1914* (Jefferson, NC: McFarland, 2006): 34–37.

Two Authors

4. Dean Schillinger and Cristin Kearns. "Guidelines to Limit Added Sugar Intake: Junk Science or Junk Food?" *Annals of Internal Medicine*, American College of Physicians, 21 Jan. 2017, http://annals.org/aim/ article-abstract/2593852/guidelines-limit-added-sugar-intake-junk -science-junk-food.

(continued on next page)

Dissertation	5. Marion Nestle, *Food Politics: How the Food Industry Influences Nutrition and Health.* (Berkeley, CA: University of California Press, 2013), 17.
Online Magazine	6. Cass R. Sunstein, "It's For Your Own Good!" *New York Review of Books*, 7 March 2013, http://www.nybooks.com/articles/2013/03/07/its-your-own-good/.
Online Journal	7. L. O. Gostin and K. G. Gostin, "A Broader Liberty: J. S. Mill, Paternalism, and the Public's Health," *Public Health* 123, no. 3 (2009): 214–21, doi: 10.1016/j.puhe.2008.12.024.
Journal Article	8. Alice Rosi et al., "How to Improve Food Choices through Vending Machines," *Food Quality and Preference* 62 (Dec. 2017): 262–69.
Organizational Author	9. U.S. Department of Agriculture and Department of Health and Human Services, *Dietary Guidelines for Americans 2015–2020* (New York: Skyhorse Publishing, 2017), 18–19.

Closely Related	*Chicago* Overview: In-Text Citation; *Chicago* Citation Charts

CHICAGO NOTES

The Basics — by Author

Explanation

Think of *Chicago* citation as a fill-in-the-blank form. Once you gather all of the items you need, it's easy to put them in the blanks. Before you begin, there are a few key pieces of information you need to collect:

- The author or authors

- The full title of the selection and the work it's from

- The name of the publisher and the date of publication (for books)

- For a digital source: the medium and location of the material

In the models below, the first entry shows the formatting for the Notes section, while the second shows how to format the source in a Bibliography. Author or authors are underlined in red. You'll notice that the last example has no author listed, so there is no underlining.

Notes Form

\#. Author's First Name Author's Last Name, "Selection title in quotation marks." *Title of the Work in Italics* (City of Publication: Publisher, date of publication), URL/DOI or page numbers.

Bibliography Form

Author's Last Name, Author's First Name. "Selection title in quotation marks." *Title of the Work in Italics*, City of Publication: Publisher, date of publication, URL or DOI.

1. Single Author

1. Horace Albright, "The Paradox of the Park," *National Geographic*, May 2016, 54–91.

Albright, Horace. "The Paradox of the Park." *National Geographic*, May 2016.

2. Two to Three Authors

2. Jerome Groopman and Pamela Hartzband, "Putting Profits Ahead of Patients," *The New York Review of Books*, July 2017, http://www.nybooks .com/articles/2017/07/13/putting-profits-ahead-of-patients/, 17.

Groopman, Jerome, and Pamela Hartzband. "Putting Profits Ahead of Patients." *The New York Review of Books*, July 2017, http://www.nybooks.com/ articles/2017/07/13/putting-profits-ahead-of-patients/.

3. Four or More Authors	3. Kyra Doumlele et al., "Sudden Unexpected Death in Epilepsy Among Patients with Benign Childhood Epilepsy with Centrotemporal Spikes," *JAMA Neurology* 74, no. 6 (2017): 645–649. doi:10.1001/jamaneurol.2016.6126. Doumlele, Kyra, Daniel Friedman, Jeffrey Buchhalter, Elizabeth J. Donner, Jay Louik, Orrin Devinsky. "Sudden Unexpected Death in Epilepsy Among Patients with Benign Childhood Epilepsy with Centrotemporal Spikes." *JAMA Neurology* 74, no. 6 (2017): 645–649. doi:10.1001/jamaneurol.2016.6126.
4. Editor as Author	4. Cheryl Wall, ed., *Changing Our Own Words*: *Essays on Criticism, Theory, and Writing by Black Women* (New Brunswick, NJ: Rutgers University Press, 1989), 27. Wall, Cheryl. ed. *Changing Our Own Words*: *Essays on Criticism, Theory, and Writing by Black Women*. New Brunswick, NJ: Rutgers University Press, 1989.
5. Organizational Author	5. Human Rights Watch, *World Report of 2015: Events of 2014* (New York: Seven Stories Press, 2015), 11. Human Rights Watch. *World Report of 2015: Events of 2014*. New York: Seven Stories Press, 2015.
6. No Author Listed	6. "Policing Ohio's Online Courses," editorial, *Plain Dealer* (Cleveland, OH), October 9, 2012. "Policing Ohio's Online Courses" Editorial. *Plain Dealer* (Cleveland, OH), October 9, 2012.
Closely Related	*Chicago*: Printed Sources, *Chicago*: Online Sources

CHICAGO NOTES

Printed Sources

<table>
<tr>
<td>Explanation</td>
<td colspan="2">For printed sources in Chicago style, you need to collect</td>
</tr>
</table>

- Author or authors
- Date of publication
- Full title of the whole work and the selection (if used)
- Location of publication and publisher name (for books)
- Volume and issue number (if relevant)
- Page numbers (if relevant)

When citing a newspaper, page numbers may be omitted because they may vary from one edition of the paper to another.

Underlining (below) highlights how titles (of selections and of whole works) and publication dates are handled for different print sources. The first model in each row is for the Notes; the second is for the Bibliography.

Basic Form 1

1. Author's First Name Author's Last Name, "Selection Title," in *Title of the Work in Italics*, volume and edition numbers (Place of Publication: Publisher, Date of publication): page numbers.

Author Last Name, Author First Name. "Selection Title." *Title of the Work in Italics*, volume and edition numbers. Place of Publication: Publisher, Date of publication: inclusive page numbers.

7. Book

1. Todd Taylor, "Lesson 6: Evidence," in *Becoming a College Writer* (Boston, MA: Bedford/St. Martin's, 2018), 64–83.

Taylor, Todd. " Lesson 6: Evidence." In *Becoming a College Writer*. Boston, MA: Bedford/St. Martin's, 2018.

8. Magazine Article

3. Roff Smith, "London Down Under," *National Geographic*, February 2016, 90–109.

Smith, Roff. "London Down Under." *National Geographic*. February 2016, 90–109.

Basic Form 2	3. Author's First Name Author's Last Name, "Selection Title," *Title of the Work in Italics*, Date of publication, page numbers.
	Author Last Name, Author First Name. "Selection Title." *Title of the Work in Italics*, Date of publication, inclusive page numbers. URL if applicable.
9. Newspaper Article	4. Allison Sherry, " Volunteers' Personal Touch Turns High-Tech Data Into Votes," The Denver Post, October 29, 2012. https://www.denverpost .com/2012/10/29/volunteers-personal-touch-turns-high-tech-data-into -colorado-votes/.
	Sherry, Allison. "*Volunteers' Personal Touch Turns High-Tech Data Into Votes.*" *The Denver Post*, October 29, 2012. https://www.denverpost.com/2012/ 10/29/volunteers-personal-touch-turns-high-tech-data-into-colorado-votes/.
10. Journal Article	2. Thomas Matchie, "Law versus love in The Round House," *Midwest Quarterly*, 56, no. 4 (Summer 2015): 353–64.
	Matchie, Thomas. "Law versus love in The Round House." *Midwest Quarterly*, 56, no. 4 (Summer 2015): 353–64.
Closely Related	*Chicago*: The Basics — by Author, *Chicago*: Online Sources

CHICAGO NOTES

Online Sources

Explanation	Before you start to cite an online resource, gather a few key pieces of information.

- Author/authors

- Full title of article/essay

- URL or DOI

- Volume, issue number, and date (if applicable)

A DOI, or **digital object identifier**, is a unique number assigned to a piece of content. Having a URL or DOI makes it easy for your reader to find your sources, but URLs can sometimes change or break. A DOI is intended to be a permanent connection to the source.

In the first three examples below, the title of the publication is underlined to point out the difference between a website that is also a periodical name and one that is not. In the final example, the underlining highlights the elements that are significant for journals and other similar publications: the volume and issue numbers.

Form 1: Online Resource without a Volume or Issue Number	1. Author's First Name Author's Last Name. "Title of the Work in Quotation Marks," *Publication name in italics*, Nonperiodical website name (if different), Date of publication, Full URL or DOI. Author's Last Name, Author's First Name. "Title of the Work in Quotation Marks." *Publication name in italics*. Nonperiodical website name (if different), Date of publication. Full URL or DOI.
11. Online Newspaper or Magazine Article	1. Julia Belluz, "Why Harassment Trainings Don't Stop Harassment," *Vox*, November 14, 2017, https://www.vox.com/science-and-health/2017/10/24/16498674/corporate-harassment-trainings-dont-work. Belluz, Julia. "Why Harassment Trainings Don't Stop Harassment." *Vox*, November 14, 2017. https://www.vox.com/science-and-health/2017/10/24/16498674/corporate-harassment-trainings-dont-work.

12. Blog Post	2. Emily Eakin, "*Cloud Atlas*'s theory of everything," *NYR Daily* (blog), November 2, 2012, www.nybooks.com/daily/2012/11/02/ken-wilber-cloud-atlas.
	Eakin, Emily. "*Cloud Atlas*'s theory of everything." *NYR Daily* (blog). November 2, 2012. www.nybooks.com/daily/2012/11/02/ken-wilber-cloud-atlas.
13. Entire Website	3. "Transparency International," Transparency International: The Global Coalition against Corruption, 2017, http://www.transparency.org (accessed December 20, 2017).
	"Transparency International." Transparency International: The Global Coalition against Corruption. 2017. http://www.transparency.org (Accessed December 20, 2017).
Form 2: Online Resource with Volume or Issue Numbers	4. Author's First Name Author's Last Name. "Title of the Work in Quotation Marks," *Publication name in italics*, volume and edition number (date): page numbers, Full URL or DOI.
	Author's Last Name, Author's First Name. "Title of the Work in Quotation Marks." *Publication name in italics*, volume and edition number (date): page numbers, Full URL or DOI.
14. Journal Article in an Online Database	4. Jessica Maier, "A 'True Likeness': The Renaissance City Portrait," *Renaissance Quarterly* 65 no. 3 (2012): 718, http://dx.doi.org/10.1086/668300.
	Maier, Jessica. "A 'True Likeness': The Renaissance City Portrait." *Renaissance Quarterly* 65 no. 3 (2012): 711–752. http://dx.doi.org/10.1086/668300.
Closely Related	*Chicago*: Printed Sources, *Chicago*: The Basics — by Author

CHICAGO NOTES

Multimedia Sources

Explanation

Multimedia sources vary wildly, so each of the sources below has its own form to ensure that you are capturing all of the key information for each source. In an e-book or film, include the medium at the end of the citation (Nook edition, Kindle edition, DVD, etc.).

When citing a film, you'll want to include:

- The director or producer
- The country where the film was made
- The studio or distributor

For an audio recording include the record label. Like the production company, or a publisher, this is the group that actually creates the content, so it's an important key to tracking a source. If you include a piece of art, you'll want to add the location of the museum to your citation.

In the examples below, we have underlined the location and the date, as this information varies from one source to another. You'll also notice that there are two separate dates included when you're citing a film, so be sure to include both of them!

Form 1

1. Author's First Name Author's Last Name. *Title of the Work or Collection in italics* (Location: Publisher, Date of publication), Format.

Author's Last Name, Author's First Name. *Title of the Work or Collection in italics*. Location: Publisher, Date of publication. Format.

15. E-book

1. Mary Beard, *SPQR: A History of Ancient Rome* (London: Liveright, 2015), Nook edition.

Beard, Mary, *SPQR: A History of Ancient Rome*. London: Liveright, 2015. Nook edition.

Form 2

2. *Title of the Film*, directed by Director's Name (Filming date; Location: Studio or Distributor, Year of Release), Format.

Title of the Film. Directed by Director's Name. Filming date; Location: Studio or Distributor, Year of Release. Format.

16. Film	2. *Wonderstruck*, directed by Todd Haynes (2016; United States: Amazon Studios, 2017), DVD.
	Wonderstruck. Directed by Todd Haynes. 2016; United States: Amazon Studios, 2017. DVD.
17. Television Episode	*Chicago* does not specify a format for television shows in particular, so you should cite these as you would a film.
Form 3	3. Author's First Name Author's Last Name, *Selection Title in Italics* (Date: Location, Production Company), format. URL.
	Author's Last Name, Author's First Name, *Selection Title in Italics*. Date: Location, Production Company. Format. URL.
18. YouTube Video	3. Fred Swaniker, *Reimagining leadership* (July 24, 2017: Euston, Tedx–Spotlights), video file. https://www.youtube.com/watch?v=M0MvdurXvpU.
	Swaniker, Fred. *Reimagining leadership*. July 24, 2017: Euston, TedxSpotlights. Video file. https://www.youtube.com/watch?v=M0MvdurXvpU.
Form 4	4. Artist's Name, *Selection Title in Italics*, recording date, track number on *Title of the Collection in Italics*. Production company, Format.
	Artist's Last Name, Artist's First Name. *Selection Title in Italics*, Recording date. Track number on *Title of the Collection in Italics*. Production company. Format.
19. Audio Recording	5. Maroon 5, *Don't Wanna Know*, recorded 2017, track 14 on *Red Pill Blues*, Interscope Records, MP3.
	Maroon 5. *Don't Wanna Know*. Recorded 2017. Track 14 on *Red Pill Blues*, Interscope Records. MP3.
Closely Related	*Chicago*: Printed Sources, *Chicago*: Book, *Chicago*: Online Sources

CHICAGO NOTES

Social Media Sources

Explanation	When citing a social media source, you always need a URL and a date, as well as elements that are standard in bibliographies, such as authors and titles. Given the nature of social media platforms, some sources may need alternative or additional elements. For example: • The author of a post or comment may be a person's actual name, a screen name, or an organization. If both a real name and screen name are available, include both with the screen name in parentheses. • Include the first 160 characters of the text of the post where you would normally put the title. • Unless a social media source is cited frequently or extensively, you do not need to include it in your Bibliography. In the models below, the format is underlined because the formatting varies slightly from one type of social media to another.
Form: Social Media	Poster's name or organization name (Screen name), "First 160 characters of the text," Format, Date of post, URL.
20. Tweets	1. Curiosity Rover (@MarsCuriosity), "Can you see me waving? How to spot #Mars in the night sky: https://youtu.be/hv8hVvJlcJQ," Twitter, November 5, 2015, 11:25 a.m., http://twitter.com/marscuriosity/status/672859022911889408.
21. Instagram Post	2. National Geographic (@Natgeo). "@stevewinterphoto @natgeo We can save the tiger, we can do better. When the buying stops, the killing can too… #bigcatsforever." Instagram photo, July 22, 2016, http://instagram.com/p/BIKyGHtDD4W/?taken-by=natgeo.
22. Facebook Post	3. Bedford English, "Stacey Cochran explores Reflective Writing in the classroom and as a writer: http://ow.ly/YkjVB." Facebook status update, February 15, 2016, http://www.facebook.com/BedfordEnglish/posts/10153415001259607.
23. Internet Comments	4. hannahcraine. "I wouldn't have guessed as much!," November 26, 2017, comment on Manzotti, "The Pizza Thought Experiment," http://www.nybooks.com/daily/2017/11/26/the-pizza-thought-experiment/.
Closely Related	*Chicago*: Multimedia Sources, *Chicago*: Online Sources

CHICAGO NOTES

Other Sources

<table>
<tr>
<td>Explanation</td>
<td>Some resources don't fit easily into other categories and are best addressed according to their specific characteristics.</td>
</tr>
</table>

- A **dissertation** (or thesis) is typically the final paper or project completed as part of earning a master's degree or a PhD.

- **Lectures** might include special events on campus, book readings, or even just the material your professor covers in class every day.

- **Interviews** might include ones that are published in print, ones that are conducted on the radio, TV, or online, and interviews that you yourself might conduct to gather primary research.

All three of these citations include the type of source. In this case, it is necessary because these sources are often unpublished, which means that they are not easily found or identified through the other citation information.

If one of these sources has been published, however, you can cite it as you would any other print or digital source, including information on the publisher and where you found the source.

In the examples below, we have underlined three key pieces of information: the sponsoring institution, the location (of the source or of the event), and the type of source.

<table>
<tr>
<td>Form: Academic Works</td>
<td>

1. Author or Interviewer's First Name Author or Interviewee's Last Name. "Title of the Work" (type of source, Sponsoring Institution or Interviewer Name, Location, Date of publication or event).

Author or Interviewer's Last Name, Author or Interviewee's First Name. "Title of the Work." Type of source, Sponsoring Institution or Interviewer Name, Location, Date of publication or event.

</td>
</tr>
<tr>
<td>24. Lecture</td>
<td>

1. Todd Taylor, "On Writing an Introduction" (lecture, University of North Caroline, Chapel Hill, Chapel Hill, NC, April 6, 2018).

Taylor, Todd. "On Writing an Introduction." Lecture presented at University of North Caroline, Chapel Hill, Chapel Hill, NC, April 6, 2018.

</td>
</tr>
</table>

**25. Interview
(Unpublished)**

2.   Dautey Akufo, interview by author, Kansas City, April 11, 2016.

Personal interviews are not included in the bibliography. Remember that published interviews are cited as any other digital source. (See *Chicago*: Online Sources for more.)

**26. Dissertation
(Unpublished)**

3.   Megan Brankley Abbas, "Knowing Islam: The Entangled History of Western Academia and Modern Islamic Thought" (PhD diss, Princeton University, 2015).

Abbas, Megan Brankley. "Knowing Islam: The Entangled History of Western Academia and Modern Islamic Thought." PhD diss, Princeton University, 2015.

Closely Related

Chicago: The Basics, *Chicago*: Printed Sources, *Chicago*: Online Sources

Writers Like You

Part Five is made up of a single, very important lesson, containing interviews and sample papers from six featured students. Studying the strategies and habits of other writers like you will give you a head start in developing your own approach to being a successful college writer.

Lesson 25 | **Student Interviews and Sample Papers** Learn from the moves other writers make.

Student Interviews and Sample Papers

Learn from the moves other writers make.

Visit the LaunchPad for *Becoming a College Writer* to watch the Lesson 25 Essentials Video.

25.1 [WHY]

Why you should study the moves other writers make.

When their teams are not practicing or competing, coaches often spend many hours carefully studying film recordings of their players and opponents in action. Fans like to watch highlight clips of athletes making big plays (or big mistakes). They will slow down key moments, play them backward, freeze-frame a split second, and replay key moments from different angles. Why?

You will understand the inner secrets, fundamental laws, or changing nature of an important ability.

Filmmakers, sculptors, musicians, and painters often begin their formal education and training by studying and sometimes duplicating the work of famous predecessors. Painters are renowned for making homages to other painters within their new work. Most movie directors are fanatic students of influential earlier filmmakers and know their historical films backward and forward. A musician might listen to an inspirational composer to prepare for a performance or help write a new piece of music. Why?

You will learn to make similar moves, especially when you notice an approach, treatment, or strategy that solves a problem you face.

The print edition of this book features six model papers from six different academic

disciplines, involving six distinct genres and methods; and the LaunchPad offers nearly 100 additional sample papers. Like coaches studying film or painters studying masterpieces, you should carefully study the work of other students to identify and understand the moves they make and the rhetorical strategies they pursue. Such careful study will help you make similar moves and decisions when facing similar challenges and problems in your writing.

In Lesson 2, I outlined five habits of experienced writers. The first habit listed is to develop a network of people to write with. The six students featured in the print edition of this book, combined with the other students in the online version, provide you with a virtual network of writers with whom you can compare experiences. Yes, you can learn a lot directly from your teachers, but you are probably aware that you learn a lot from your peers, too. Your peers occupy a different but potentially very powerful position in terms of your thinking and learning. You can learn a lot from your classmates, and I don't mean just borrowing their notes when you miss class. Students inevitably model thoughts and behaviors for each other, and a big part of learning involves noticing how your peers are acting and thinking.

There are nearly 100 students in this textbook, which means there are inevitably one or two of them, at the very least, who are like you. There will also be many others who have different perspectives from which you can learn a great deal. So, browsing the interviews within this collection will help

417

Why you should study the moves other writers make

you deepen your understanding of yourself as a writer by comparing your experiences and perspectives with others. Some of the interviews will say things that confirm your approaches to writing and thinking, which will reinforce your strategies and build confidence. Some of the interviews will say things that surprise you and that you might disagree with, at least at first — which is potentially of equal value, because it exposes you to new ideas and challenges you to examine your thoughts and habits in depth.

Learning that takes place solely between a teacher and you, as a student, can be too one-dimensional, too much like a monologue and not enough like a dialogue. Learning that takes place in a variety of ways, modes, and contexts, especially between classmates and peers, is often very successful. This book in general, and this lesson in particular, aims to help you learn by comparing your experiences with a wide array of other students, many of whom you will be able to identify with and learn from.

25.2 [HOW]

How to learn from the moves other writers make.

The table of contents of this book is organized according to key terms that define college writing for most teachers and students. In order to study the moves that the writers make in the sample papers, you can use the vocabulary in the table of contents to examine different dimensions of each paper. If you are struggling with a particular aspect of college writing (for example, you are having trouble with conclusions), you could browse a number of papers, comparing how each seems to approach a conclusion.

If you are looking for a more general or holistic understanding of the moves a particular writer makes in a particular paper, you probably want to begin by thinking in terms of our definition of *writing* as "a dynamic relationship between an author, audience, a topic, and the sources they use":

- ***What moves does the author make to define what they do and who they are?*** Who does the **author** seem to be? How are they positioned? Do they work within their major or discipline or outside it? What does the interview reveal about the author? What does the writing itself seem to reveal about the author?

- ***What moves does the author make to reach their audience?*** Who is the **audience** for the paper? How do you know? How specific or general does the audience seem to be? What evidence in the writing, tone, style, genre, or vocabulary seems to try to meet the audience's expectations?

- ***What moves does the author make to select and establish the topic?*** How is the **topic** connected to the author and the audience? What is the topic? How wide or narrow is the scope of the topic? Why did the author seem to select this topic? How did the audience seem to influence or determine this topic?

- ***What moves does the author make when they select and use evidence?*** How does the writer select, arrange, and use **sources**? What genre is used and why? What methodology is used and why? In what discipline or department is the paper written?

Everyone has a way that they like to browse the Internet. Some people start browsing with a search engine like Google. Others have extensive websites bookmarked as familiar starting points for their sessions. If you are browsing for class, maybe you begin in a scholarly database or archive. Maybe you go to your favorite news site, check the headlines and then explore from there. Students often launch their browsing within social media websites, looking for connections among their friends or interests. Likewise, you might have different ways to browse the collection of interviews in the LaunchPad, depending on the purposes of your search or your browsing habits.

I recommend that you compare your experiences with the other student writers in the LaunchPad by browsing on instinct at first. Who struck you as particularly insightful or intriguing? Who seems to be a lot like you and could share helpful advice and ideas? Who seems very different and, thus, potentially enlightening through contrast? You have by now probably watched some of the Essentials videos in each lesson, and some of the students in those videos probably caught your attention more than others. If so, look them up in the LaunchPad interviews and see what more they have to say.

Think of these interviews as a large social event with everyone in the same room. As you mingle, some conversations are going to be more interesting than others. You may discover a bond between you and someone else. If so, you will want to get to know them better by learning more about them — through their video interview or sample paper, or through both. It's like browsing the sales rack in a clothing store or the shelves of a bookstore: You might have some idea what you are looking for at first, but you find your attention suddenly drawn to something you like but did not initially anticipate.

Of course, your browsing and studying aren't always accidental and exploratory: Sometimes you have a specific problem to solve or work to complete. You might be struggling with a thesis or looking for ways to improve your writing process. All of the videos are listed under major thematic headings so that you can search for key terms, which can lead you to someone in the collection of students who can share a perspective that helps you out.

Remember, the print edition of this book only has six featured student papers. There are nearly 100 more online for you to meet and learn from.

In the following student papers and in the LaunchPad, we have replaced the students' last name with "Lastname" to preserve both their formatting and their anonymity.

INTERVIEW A

Nanaissa: Undeclared major

Meet Nanaissa. At the time of the interview, she was a freshman at Lansing Community College and had not yet chosen a major. However, she was very interested in architecture and fine art and was taking classes in art history and English. Like each of the six students featured in the print edition of the book, Nanaissa was selected because her advice and perspectives on college writing seemed particularly helpful to students like you. Even so, you should read Nanaissa's advice and study her model paper carefully and critically, not assuming everything she says or writes is perfectly correct (or at least correct for you). Her interview transcript was edited to eliminate confusing or contradictory moments and reorganized to group together moments where the same topic is discussed.

Writing across Languages

I can speak other languages, so I see writing as an international thing because whatever language you speak, there is a structure that you have to respect. That's the easy part for me. It's only the little things that wouldn't sound natural in English that I have to correct. For example, you say "the blue car" or "the car blue." I'm always inversing the order and other people always catch it because, when I read it, I can't see it. That's why I always look for help. Even if you are the best writer in the world you always need someone to check your paper. But whatever language you speak, the structure is the same, which makes it easy to adapt.

My mom took me to a bilingual school when we were living in Belgium. So, I was speaking English, doing everything in English. Then I had to travel again and I spent a long time not speaking the language, but I was glad to see that I could still speak English and other languages native to the countries I had lived in. I practiced alone, in my room; I bought some books in English to try not to lose it. Now, I'm just practicing the English I learned when I was a baby. I really want to improve it and be a good bilingual and, if possible, multilingual person.

French is my native language, but I also know English; Spanish; Bambara, the language I spoke when I was living in Mali, an African country; and Japanese. In a French high school, you have to be able to speak English but it was a really basic level. I wouldn't call that practicing my English, but I had British friends whom I practiced with. There were many Americans in Mali, too, and I would always go to the American clubs trying to practice my English.

When I first arrived in America, I was translating most of the things I was saying. Now, I'm trying to think directly in English. A language is also a culture, so I have to totally forget about my French for a moment and only speak in English. Sometimes I'm speaking and something in French just pops out, but I can control it.

Different Styles of Writing

I see writing as a way to guide people through what I want to say. In France, we like poetry and saying the same thing in many different ways. Here [in America] people are like, "you're too wordy, just say it directly." So, that's the main problem. Americans like short and precise and the French like to play with words.

The structure in French is way more detailed — so, writing in English is easier. There are less rules but, as long as the reader understands and there's still a topic sentence and a thesis, it's okay. In France, teachers are more precise; they need more details, more structure and organization. I prefer writing in English even if I know I'm not perfect at it.

In French, we call it a *problématique* because it's usually a question you're trying to answer. Here we call it a thesis and it doesn't have to be a question. In French, it's a question you ask yourself and the audience so they can think about it. We also have a topic sentence. We just call it *un introduction* or *un paragraphe*. I think in French when I'm structuring my paper because I really like the idea of a question: "Why is it so?" I always come back to my thesis after each paragraph to make sure it answers my question. I guess I'm still attached to the French system.

When you wrote a paragraph it had to have an introduction, an example, the idea, and the argument. In America, it's an idea, a paragraph, an idea, a paragraph. You don't have the obligation to add a source; to give an — well, it's better to give an example — but there is no obligation to do so. In France, a paragraph could be good but the structure that we had to have was not always about understanding the paper, it

was more about respecting the rules. Even if the *problématique* is a question, at the end of your conclusion, you have to present a clear answer to show that you are confident about what you are saying. Even if you don't agree, you have to give an answer.

In France an introduction has to be half a page. It has to have a catching phrase, then the definition of what you are going to talk about, then an example, then the *problématique*, and then saying exactly what you are going to write about. It's really structured and detailed, and you have to do it in a really nice way because the reader is not supposed to see how structured it is. You need to show that you can play with words. And here [in America] the professor went through the introduction and conclusion lessons really fast. It was the French system that helped me understand what and how I had to do it, but here we were so free that sometimes I felt a little lost. So, I'm writing my conclusion how I learned to in France, which is giving your answer and ending the topic. If you want to be a little dramatic, finish with a tiny question. It's not opening a new subject, but making the reader think about what you wrote after they are done reading the essay.

I always write my thesis at the last moment unless I really know what I want to write about. If I'm not sure, I write about what I want and find a thesis that fits into it. It's exactly the same pattern. I know what I want to write about; I'm going to do research that will help me prove what I want to say. Usually I even do research about things I already know because I want somebody serious and who has credit to say it. That's what I did for my paper. We can always turn what somebody says into what we want it to mean. Somebody who says, "This chair is yellow," you can say, "Yeah, it's yellow because of the sun. So, it's bringing joy in this room." And somebody can just take another aspect of the chair. You have to know your words and play with the words.

In French, it doesn't matter what you think. When you write a paper, there must be outside support, professional support, too; we don't even really see your writing [as your own ideas]. With English, I was like "Whoa! I can write what I think? And I won't be punished for that?" I got punished a lot because I write with too much passion in French. My teacher knew I was a good writer, but I didn't stick to what the French want when you write in high school. So, I prefer the Americans' freedom when they write.

Artistic Freedom

In France, we never wrote about what we thought. We wrote about what we had to write. In high school — I've always been out of the box — I liked saying what I thought and questioning what we weren't supposed to question. Some teachers really didn't like that and I had bad grades because of it. I really liked writing, but writing in school was different. I felt depressed like, "Oh, I'm not going to make it. I just can't write." And that was not the problem, the problem was I didn't write what the French school wanted me to write.

There is a really famous high school in France and you have to be the best. They don't have an average. If you are not the best among the hundreds of students who applied, you are not going to be accepted. Even if you have an A-plus; if somebody has an A-plus-plus, you won't be taken. For private school, I guess, it's the same thing everywhere, but even in public school. They don't want average students. As if they

didn't want to encourage average students. I was struggling because I don't like being singled out and feel that I'm useless, but I was working hard. I didn't like it because students are not objects; they are people who just work hard and must be encouraged. Even if you are an average student and you dream about being a doctor, when the advisor is laughing at you, you may give up on your dreams. That's what happened to most of the students I knew who didn't even graduate middle school. For high school you need a diploma and you're called an elite — a part of the elite.

I feel better in America because, as long as we respect the structure, there is more freedom when we write. And that's normal because when you're writing you need to learn how to make the reader understand what you are saying; that's the main point of writing. So, the American system is focusing on what's important, not on what we want you to write. It's teaching students how to express what they want to say and not what the audience wants to hear because sometimes it just doesn't work. If you don't want to write about something you are not going to do a good job. I just want to like what I'm doing and be passionate about what I'm working on. I don't want to work hard and get a bad grade in the end. I would just feel depressed. I want to work hard and make sure I get the grade I think I deserve.

When I really like something nothing can stop me. No one wanted me to come to America. No one wanted me to become an architect, but I always fight for what I want.

Art & Writing

In France, art is really important, so I took many art classes. I did sculpture, photography, interviewing people. . . . I really love video montage. I did so many things . . . drawing . . . painting. I tried a little bit of everything. I'm still drawing. I always have my little paper and my pencil on my bed and before I go to sleep I have to sketch something.

When I write, I feel that I'm with my camera pointing at what I want the reader to see. The world is vast. I could focus on the sofa and someone could focus on the light. So, I'm just pointing the camera in the direction that shows what I want the reader to see. It may sound like I'm trying to control every-thing but writing is not something random. It's proving a point and not writing just to write. You have to have an intellectual basis.

Even when I sculpt I think about writing. They are linked together. Sometimes it's feeling like God because you really go into detail and you start to understand why you put this here. When I had to sculpt an entire body I realized how a certain part didn't fit properly and I had to correct it; I do the same thing with writing. You can't just say, "Just try that and it's going to work." You have to try it, check if it fits, and if it falls just start it again. Writing is a lot of work. If you really want to do it well, you have to have total control of everything.

Advice on the Writing Process

I think that if I really like what I'm writing, I can touch most of the audience. In my class, I was told that I had to pay a lot of attention to my audience. Some people may not be interested in what I'm writing because they may not be the right audience. I can be writing about hunting, and some people are against killing animals this way, but if I manage to find a nice way to explain my argument, probably, the person against it

could even change his mind. If — just by reading your paper — someone can meet you halfway and try to understand what you're saying, you did a great job; even if it was not the right audience. Writing for an audience is forgetting about what you want to write; it's only writing to them, and some-times you need to do that. When you want to prove a point you must only think about the audience and the way you are going to talk to them. It's you, you are the one writing the paper, not the audience.

I'm always afraid of assignments because there are a lot of things I have to do and I want to make sure I don't miss anything. I always underline the most important points and then I write them down to make sure I really get what I have to do. Because I'm an artist, I try to respect those rules but also do it the way I want it to be. It may sound a little selfish but, when I do something, I want to like what I'm doing. I'm going to look for a topic that I, personally, like and that I can write without struggling, or feeling like I'm doing something I don't want to. When I don't want to write about a topic, the reader is going to feel it and I don't want that to happen.

I look for feedback when it's closer to the end. When it's only a draft, because I'm not an English speaker, I know they won't under-stand everything and it will be frustrating to have someone ask me, "Okay, what are you trying to say?" So, I work on my English, work on my structure, and then I look for feedback. When you don't know what you're doing, and don't ask for help, it doesn't go well. You are the one writing the paper. You have to work a lot before asking for someone else's opinion. Otherwise, it would be a two-person paper.

At the beginning of your paper you have to be selfish and know what you want to do.

Then you have to accept feedback. It's hard; sometimes people are going to be like, "I don't understand. Why are you writing that? There is no point in you writing that." Listen to what they have to say because it will help you become a better writer.

As an architect, I won't be the one living in all of my buildings. So, I have to know how to listen to people, but, as an architect, I know what a building needs and I know what's going to work out or not. So, I need to find a way to make people agree with what I'm saying, even if they can't totally understand it.

We all have to study. We all have classes we have to take. So, the best way to do it is to trick ourselves to like it, and do what we have to do in the best way possible. We don't have anything to lose. It's time-consuming. It's tiring, but knowing that we are doing something good is a really great reward. "

Problem-Solution Paper

The portion of Nanaissa's interview that discusses her model paper is included below, before the paper is presented. Nanaissa was selected as one of the six featured students in the print companion because of her self-reflection and thoughtfulness about both her writing and about language in general.

High School in France: The Filter before College

" I didn't like the assignment when she gave it to us. It was a problem-solution assignment; we had to find a problem and find a solution. My main problem was that every time I had to write a paper it was about American problems and I didn't know anything about America. When I wrote the paper it was my fifth week in this country and I felt a little frustrated. First, I wanted to write about how people see tall people. Then, I wanted to write about women's role in society now; how women are going to work and men can stay with the kids, but it was too complex and too much research. I would have liked to work on it, but I didn't have enough time; I only had a week to write the paper. Instead of complaining about how I didn't fit into American society, I wrote a paper explaining why I was here. Because even if I was complaining, I was happy to be here. I knew that I would gain more staying here than going back to France because I really struggled with their system. You can interview any French student and it's exactly the same testimony about how selective and elite their system is. Here, as a student, I feel really respected. It was a big cultural shock. I was really surprised to see how many people were willing to help me. So, I just wrote about all my bad memories of France. I only focused on the negative side because it was only a three-page paper, I had to focus on something, and that was the point that I needed to express. I was questioning myself. I couldn't really point out why I came to the U.S. and I was relieved when I wrote the paper because it gave me all my answers. I didn't want to ask myself these questions but I wanted to write the paper as sincere and as best as I could.

I wanted America to realize that they have a great system. In Europe they're like, "Oh, American high school, they have the worst level ever." It's not a matter of level, of being the best or not, it's about being encouraged and being self-confident. I couldn't talk the first three weeks in class. I was just sitting there because I was afraid of talking and making mistakes. I was like, "I'm in front of native speakers. I can't speak English." In France we were taught that it's better not to talk than make a mistake. Writing a paper is not something I do in a moment; I'm constantly thinking about it because I want it to be good. When I think about what I want to write, I always have paper in my pocket where I write down the few ideas that I have. Sometimes, part of my thesis just pops into my mind, and sometimes I ask myself questions until an answer pops up. When I finally start working, I take the paper where I wrote down all my ideas, and start putting everything in order paragraph by paragraph.

I went to the writing center a lot and I told them to be really crude and just tell me if it was good or not. I was used to being told the truth, and I didn't mind them telling me that my paper was bad. I was glad they did. They thought it was not an interesting paper for my audience, and they wanted me to write about the tall people. In the end, I was the one writing the paper. It was too self-focused. It was too, "Okay, I am tall. Who else is tall in there?" I didn't like it. Even if it's personal and I'm the one writing the

paper, it has to touch other people reading it. I can't do something I don't like to do; if I do it, it wouldn't be good and I hate doing something bad. I want everything I do to be really good.

I can write a paper on tall people, but it was just not the time. My heart was not in it. I had to find what my heart wanted to write about. I didn't know anyone in Lansing. I was alone trying to adapt to this new system, afraid to even go outside and figure out which bus I was supposed to take. I was always asking myself, "What am I doing here? I could be in France and with my friends and do all the things I know." But I'm not that person. I like adventure and discovering everything, and this paper was simply, "Okay, I'm here, and this is part of the reason why I'm here."

People in my class weren't really interested. They were like, "Education. We are in class in here. Why would we read about that? We are tired of coming to school, so why are we writing about school?" But because I, personally, really liked the topic, this time I didn't let it go. The paper about tall people I let it go because I agreed I wasn't motivated by the topic. For this one, all I had to do was find a way for the audience to like it. I rewrote it a little bit and the teacher really liked it because it was something international. She said, "Well, that's what touched the audience because we are educators and we want to know how it works overseas." I didn't write for the audience, but I was glad it was fitting for the audience.

It was a new experience because I was only writing what I wanted to write about, which was different from the French system. Even if I'm still attached to it, I'm starting to forget about it — not forget, but liberate myself from the system.

NANAISSA: PROBLEM-SOLUTION PAPER

Nanaissa Lastname

High School in France: The Filter before College

I graduated from *Lycée Français Liberté,* a high school in France, in June 2011. This might not seem momentous, but only five of my twenty childhood friends had graduated from high school. Of the five, only three are attending college. In the online French newspaper *20 minutes,* French sociologists and education specialists, Christian Baudelot and Roger Establet denounced teachers and the high school system for not helping their students efficiently. They stated that, "The number of school children in great difficulty increased [from] 15% in 2000 to 20% in 2009; it is huge. We are in an 'elite system' that has always favored the select few and dropped those who cannot keep up" (Baudelot and Establet). The French educational system has always been called an elite system by its people. According to the *Oxford Dictionary,* this means that "it only values a group of people considered superior by the society" ("Elite"). Teachers who believe in the elite system claim that "college is not for everyone." Therefore, they have their students constantly competing and under constant pressure to make sure only the best will have the opportunity to attend college. Moreover, once a student shows difficulty in keeping up in class, the instructor strongly recommends that the student drop out of school at sixteen, the age when school is no longer compulsory in France. Most teachers are seen by French students as an obstacle to success. The negative attitude of the teachers and the lack of student services in high school are preventing students from continuing on to college.

This elite attitude is clear from how the teachers in French high schools behave. They will only point out (and severely punish) mistakes the students make. They never positively reinforce their successes. This causes students to feel insecure and

weakens their self-esteem. The online French newspaper *Le nouvel observateur*
and British journalist Peter Gumbel, who has lived in Paris since 2002, attest
that French high school students are generally more anxious, intimidated in the
classroom, and have a strong fear of failure. Both sources emphasize that France is
the only country where the instructors mark the "off-topic answer" (a term used
when a student has not provided the expected answer) as an "offense punishable
with a zero" ("L'ecole Casse"; Gumbel). The point is, a student who has low self-
esteem and is constantly punished will not believe he/she can move on in his/her
education. Due to the harshness of the teachers, students will tend to drop out of
school to escape ridicule.

What is more, the lack of student services compels students to seek parental
aid. When parents are the only support, students with uneducated parents will
be at a loss. *L'express*, a famous French newspaper, reports 150,000 young people
are leaving school each year without any qualifications (Masson and Dycke).
This means they did not even attend high school. In an average French high
school, there is no obligation to have a program to help what the French call
"students in difficulty." Usually, these students have uneducated parents, and
French parents have a very important role in their children's education. A study
of French students in *The Journal of Developmental Psychology* by Michel Duyme
reported a "positive correlation between parental social class and the academic
success of their children" (qtd. in Becker). It can be drawn from this that students
from a high intellectual background will be more likely to succeed because their
parents went to school and can guide them. For instance, parents with a higher
level of education tend to encourage their children to read, usually French classical
literature, and are able to discuss it afterwards. This style of literature is usually
studied in French high schools. Thus the child will have already made his mistakes

and had the "right answers" explained at home. The combination of uneducated parents and the lack of support services at school leaves these students feeling that they are walking a high wire without a net. Consequently, such students have a tendency to give up on their studies because they know they do not have the tools to succeed.

In addition, the instructors impose a need to excel, which creates a very strong spirit of competition among the students and, in turn, adversely affects their health. Coming to school with the feeling that you are going to wage a merciless war against your classmates is stressful. I remember my history teacher, "Mrs. Wicked," always showing the best paper and comparing it to the others. She was criticizing all the mistakes we made, in a very humiliating way, by reading aloud what we wrote on our papers and even mocking our errors. This ridicule is very harsh for young students. To avoid the discomfort, students competed against each other for the best grades. In February 2009, I did not have the best grade and the resulting embarrassment still brings a bitter taste to my mouth. I was singled out by all the class and the teacher so much that I thought this would prevent me from going to college and would ruin my life. I was in such a panic, I could not sleep for a week, and I became ill. Peter Gumbel, the author of *On Achève Bien les Ecoliers*, or in English *We Are Killing Our Schoolchildren*, stresses how this constant competition is unhealthy and hard for students to handle. His research shows that "71% of students in France are regularly subjected to irritability, 63% suffer from nervousness. One in four had a stomach ache or headache weekly and 40% complained of frequent insomnia" (Gumbel). He is not alone in his findings. A recent French study by the Association of the Foundation for Students (AFEV) shows the damaging effects of academic pressure on the morale of students. In this study, the damage was also manifested by "43% of the students having a stomach ache before going to class" (qtd. in Masson and Dycke). This stressful atmosphere has a negative effect on students' self-confidence and health, causing a lack of motivation to continue with their education.

When all is said and done, more often than not, failure of French high school students is due to the system rather than the student. I believe this is wrong. Failure should only be due to a student's lack of serious effort. The system is unfair and should be corrected by questioning the role of the professors and creating efficient student services. There is no benefit in limiting educational opportunities to only the so-called "elite." American exchange student Daisy Belle Nguyen came to France and immediately she realized, "The system's goal [was] to fish out the '*elite*' and wash away the rest." She found that shocking because it is totally contradictory to the American philosophy of education (Nguyen). My personal retort against this tiring French system was simply to remove myself from it. Even though the option was available to me, I did not want to go to a French college. I preferred to leave my home country, my native language, and the lifestyle to which I was accustomed in order to leave behind the extreme, competitive atmosphere of the French educational system as well. I know that I will have to overcome linguistic and cultural differences. I am not afraid because I know I will have all the help I need. As far as I'm concerned, there is no perfect high school system. It is, however, worth pulling estimable aspects from one system of education to benefit another. The American education system helps students build themselves up by giving them several ways to be supported, including extended office hours and the opportunity to send e-mail to teachers. Feeling secure and supported develops students' self-confidence. The French should learn a lesson from this positive aspect of the American high school system.

Works Cited

Becker, Lara. "The Problem of Underachievement in the French Educational System." *Lehigh University*, 1 Jan. 2011, preserve.lehigh.edu/cgi/viewcontent .cgi?article=1003&context=perspectives-v15.

Baudelot, Christian and Roger Establet "En France, une proportion d'élèves faibles bien trop élevée" Translated by Nanaissa Lastname, Ministère de l'éducation, June 2009, www.education.gouv.fr//L-elitisme-republicain-L-ecole-francaise -a-l-epreuve-des-comparaisons-internationales.

"Elite, 1." *OED Online.* Oxford Dictionaries UP, 2012, www .oxfordlearnersdictionaries.com/us/definition/english/elite_1.

Gumbel, Peter. "Un système élitiste qui malmène son élite" Translated by Nanaissa Lastname, *Acadomia*, 5 Jan. 2011, www.acadomia.fr/dossierdumois/article/r/ ecole-un-systeme-elitiste-qui-malmene-son-elite.

"L'ecole casse-t-elle nos enfants?" Translated by Nanaissa Lastname, *Le nouvel observateur*, 30 May 2012, www.nouvelobs.com/education/20100902.OBS9318/ exclusif-l-ecole-casse-t-elle-nos-enfants.html.

Masson, Elvira and Emilie Dycke. "L'idéal éducatif français reste très élitiste." Translated by Nanaissa Lastname, *L'express.* 05 Sep. 2011, www.lexpress.fr/ education/rentree-scolaire-l-ideal-educatif-francais-reste-tres-elitiste_1026953.html.

Nguyen, Daisy Belle. "A Foreigner in the French Education System." *La Peniche.* 16 Apr. 2006, lapeniche.net/a-foreigner-in-the-french-education-system/.

Kendra: Environmental Science major

Meet Kendra. At the time of the interview, she was an environmental science major at Michigan State University and was interested in going on to graduate school to continue studying science. Like each of the six students featured in the print edition of the book, Kendra was selected because her advice and perspectives on college writing seemed particularly helpful to students like you. Even so, you should read Kendra's advice and study her model paper carefully and critically, not assuming everything she says or writes is perfectly correct (or at least correct for you). Her interview transcript was edited to eliminate confusing or contradictory moments and to help to clarify her discussions of writing in the sciences. Kendra's research paper follows the interview. However, she also completed an oral presentation based on this paper. An audio version, including her presentation slides, is available in the LaunchPad for *Becoming a College Writer*.

What Is a Writer?

I used to think a writer was someone who chose to write because it was something they were passionate about, but writing is really involved in everything — you can't get away from it. Everyone writes. I feel it's a good skill to have no matter what field you are going into. You can't avoid it.

When I first entered college I thought writing was just an assignment you were given and you had to do it how the teacher wanted it. I found, though, that you're in college to further your passion so that you can get a career in it, so you should pick topics that you are interested in and make your paper answer your own questions rather than a teacher's when you can. After my first freshman class I tried to do it the teacher's way and I realized it wasn't as fun and I wasn't getting as much personal gain as I wanted. So I told myself from now on I'm going to make it fit me, and make it interesting to me, and then writing isn't a hassle; it's not a chore. It's something I enjoy and I'm learning from.

Since I've been in college, I've written personal narratives about my life, I've had to read papers and then summarize them, or write summary papers or reviews. I've had to write scientific papers. I've had to write papers where I'm asking people to fund me to write about a topic. That's more of a persuasive, "here's why I need your help," type of paper. I've written papers where I've had to argue the opposite of what I may personally believe, and I've had to argue for something I might personally not believe in, but I still have to write a good paper on it and make other people believe I think that way. And I think the variety of writing I've had is good. You might not like a certain genre, but playing around with all the different types of writing helps you find one that you do like.

Going between them is difficult. You have to kind of change your mind-set and approach for different types of papers. But you can always ask other people who may have just written that type of paper or your teacher what you need to do to set yourself up for the type of paper you are writing.

What Makes a Good Writer?

I think a writer — a good writer — has to be able to review their own papers. Someone who doesn't just sit down and write a final draft. They have to get peer edits because when you write down what you are thinking in your head, you might not notice the errors, but other people will.

I think when you're writing in a class, a lot of people come up with the first idea and they just run with it. I like to think about being different, being original, and popping out more ideas makes me a stronger writer. Because if you're just writing the same thing as someone else, it might not be as interesting. If you're going to put the effort into writing a paper you might as well make it interesting.

Approaching Different Topics

I like to look at the topic as like a house and there are different ways to get in. I personally try to find the hardest way to get in — the most obscure, original idea to approach a topic. You would think a lot of people would just walk in the front door of a house but I like to think: "What if I climbed in through an attic window or tried the basement door?" So I try to think: "What would be the most common way to approach this topic? And then what are more original, different ways — spins — on the topic?"

Research for a scientific paper can be taken two ways. You have to do research on a topic to find out more about it and to see if it's a topic that you really want to look into. Then you have to personalize your research so that you can write a paper that is exciting, that is a new and fresh idea that looks at something in a different way.

Know Your Audience

The difference between entry-level writing and scientific writing is the audience and what they already know about the topic. Scientific writing is a lot more structured. There's creativity that you need to add to the topic, but there are different ways of adding it. In a paper for another discipline, it might be your writing style or a different perspective that shows your creativity, but in scientific writing your writing has a specific structure that it has to follow. The paragraphs go in a certain order and there is a certain way of writing them. So you have to be more creative with your topic and your research beforehand to really make the paper yours, and to make it stand out to your audience.

I think the audience changes with the type of writing you are doing. If you are just writing a story or a personal experience, you have to add a lot of the background information so that people can follow it. But as I started doing more scientific writing I learned that the audience is usually professionals looking to get more knowledge on a subject, and they already have a lot of background knowledge so you can just cut that out. It's good to know your audience so that you keep their interest. If you don't have enough information, they won't be able to follow your argument and if you have too much they might think: "I already know all this. I'm going to move on to something else."

STUDENT PAPER B

Scientific Journal Paper

The portion of Kendra's interview that discusses her model paper is included below, before the paper is presented. Kendra was selected as one of the six featured students in the print companion because of her creative approach to scientific writing and her decision to adapt her final report into an oral presentation.

The Structure of Scientific Writing

I feel like that is very strict with scientific writing; that you can't stray too much. That doesn't mean there is no creativity; you just have to find different ways of fitting it in. I would say all scientific writing follows the same structure. There is the abstract — how your experiment went, your methods, and then the most freedom you can put is at the end with your conclusions and what you would like to see come out of further experiments. I write the five segments starting with the introduction, the methods, materials, the research and conclusion, and then with the conclusion you can explain further what you'd like to see come out of what you've done.

The most recent paper I wrote was on Komodo dragons. It was like a scientific journal paper, where I had to write as if I was going to submit it to the journal. I wrote it for Zoology 428, which was a herpetology class. I had to write something that was interesting. I could have picked any reptile or amphibian, just something I personally thought was interesting and wanted to further research. And I had to write it as if I was going to submit it to the *Journal of Herpetology*.

I personally thought that Komodo dragons were interesting and I wanted to look into their method of predation, and their prey, and how it was so efficient. So I had to think of a topic. The predation of Komodo dragons had been a question in the science world that had been tossed around, so I had to think of something more specific, like a specific angle of approaching it. I couldn't just use Komodo dragons as my topic. I had that as my topic, but then I had to find specifics, so I started with that and I thought of the question of how they kill their prey, and I decided to look at if Komodo dragons were venomous or not and how their mouths affected their ability to take down prey.

The Process of Scientific Writing

Once I found a specific topic, I started researching, seeing if there was enough research done on this already that I could write a paper. Because I couldn't personally do the research myself (I didn't have any Komodo dragons to research on) I had to look at other research that had already been done and analyze that. And I did find five sufficient articles, so I thought that was good enough to start. My school has a subscription to all these scientific journals, so I could just go to the library and search what online articles they had and what subscriptions they had to different journals. I used Web MD to find them. I just typed in komodo dragons and venom and went through all the articles, reading their abstracts to find out if they would be sufficient enough for what my topic was.

Once I found them all, I had to read them. I found more than I needed, just in case one didn't fit, I would still have enough to write my paper. So I got about ten articles and I read through them all, which was a little bit tedious — science writing isn't the most enjoyable thing — so sometimes you just have to like highlight and reread and try to find what the conclusion was. So, I think abstracts helped a lot with that, just summarizing everything: "so they found this, where can I find that in the paper?"

Once I had that, I looked at their findings and whether or not they applied to mine. And I started with what my question was, whether or not Komodo dragons were venomous and how their teeth affected that. And I looked at each paper and whether or not it supported or answered that question to get a general census on where it was going. And I had papers on both sides, so I kind of had to compare and contrast them to see how they answered my question.

The question for scientific articles is like the thesis for other types of writing. It's the main point you need to have before you can start writing. It ties everything together. With scientific writing there is a method of getting your question and turning it into a hypothesis, and how you tested it so that other people can follow the same ways that you tested the hypothesis and what the results

were. Even if you don't answer that question, you still have to write the whole process of getting that question, finding the answer, and what the answer was so that people with the same questions or similar questions can use that same process.

The procedure doesn't have a lot of room for personal input. It has to be exactly how you did it so that other people could do the same research and test if they get the same result to that question, or your hypothesis, as you did. It's like note taking — just exactly how you did something so that it could be repeated. Having the universal conversions of things is important so that even those in other countries could follow the same instructions. It's like an instruction manual of how to do the exact same work you did to find if your results were just a chance or if this is really related to the question — if it answers the question and it's significant or not.

I had to use the methods from three different sources. I looked at how they did their studies and what they found. And I could have written small samples of each of their papers, but I chose instead to mix them together and write one methods section that included all of their methods. I put all three sources into each section of my paper. And I had my conclusion, and wrote based off whether or not I thought the sources concluded that Komodo dragons were venomous.

The result section is where you state exactly what your findings were. You can't put your own assumptions on what it means. You have to state it without any bias to what the answer would be. You have to state your results just as they were without saying: "The results were this and it led to this. It led us to believe that this is why this is happening." Later you can explain what you *think* it leads to and what you *think* further studies of those results would help you to find. The results section is just what you found, whether your hypothesis was right or not, and you can't put any personal biases or assumptions on it.

The discussion is where you can put more of a personal assumption or the larger picture and how your results play in. You base the format of your scientific paper on the journal that you most likely would submit it to. So if you're writing on neurobiology, you would look up a neurobiology journal and see how they title and format their journal so that it's similar because not all journals are the same. And my paper was supposed to be for the *Journal of Herpetology*, so that was the format that I tried to follow.

Reflecting on the Process

After I got my paper back, there were some annotations from the professor. Things that maybe other people had caught but I thought I fixed and maybe didn't follow up with them. It's a little frustrating to see that he caught the same thing as someone else

that I thought I had fixed. So, I think making sure you are following up with everyone who wrote a little review or note to make sure that you are fixing the problems is good. I didn't follow up with everyone that reviewed mine and then my professor did catch things that I had thought I had fixed.

Overall, I think I did very well. I got a good grade. The topic I chose was interesting to me. So I personally had fun writing it and enjoyed the research. Scientific writing isn't the most fun thing to do but if you're interested in it, it makes it easier. I would say making sure you set up enough time before-hand is another good thing. Toward the end I was feeling a little pressured, to get this in, to get it done in time. I don't think that helps writing at all.

Although I did do well, I wish I would've maybe set out a little bit more time. If I know I have to write this intro tonight, just do it then and don't have it mushed together at the end because you put it off. It's definitely worth it if you write it when you scheduled out to write it so that you have enough time. But other than that, I thought it was a rewarding experience. I learned a lot and it made me a stronger writer. "

Kendra Lastname 1

Professor Kieta

Komodo Dragons: The bite, bacteria, venom, or a combination?

Abstract

Using three key sources on the topic to stand in for field or laboratory research, this paper examines the question of how Komodo dragons successfully subdue their prey. The close examination of the mechanics of the reptile's teeth and jaw, combined with a chemical analysis of blood, saliva, and mouth swabs, all combine to indicate that it is the combination of tactics rather than a single, principal factor that allow for the effectiveness of the Komodo dragon as a hunter.

Introduction

Scholarship has not yet come to a unified consensus on some of the defining characteristics of an important member of the reptile world: the Komodo dragon (*Veranus komodoensis*). There is a "popular notion" (1) that this animal kills its prey primarily by means of a poison released with its bite. However, an equally fervent group of scholars believe that it is the "unique hold and pull-feeding technique" (3) that accounts for the success of the Komodo dragon in subduing prey. It can be seen, however, that Komodo dragons do not rely exclusively on either of these characteristics, but instead rely on an intricate combination of variables in order to subdue their prey effectively, one that includes dentition, jaw shape, and the application of bacterial agents to which the Komodo dragons themselves are immune.

Being unable to conduct experiments on actual representatives of *Veranus komodoensis* (Komodo dragons), evidence has instead been drawn from three material sources on the topic. The Materials and Methods section has been synthesized from these three studies to provide a clear view of the approaches taken by each. A thorough exploration and analysis of these sources provides a reasonable body of support for the claim that Komodo dragons do not, in fact, ultimately rely on any singular approach to subduing their prey, but rather a calibrated balance of multiple techniques.

Materials and Methods

Both Fry et al. and Moreno et al. closely examined the teeth and jaw of the Komodo dragon using digital scanning methods (magnetic resonance imaging, CT scanning, and a scanning electron microscope). Moreno et al. also created fine element models in order to conduct their load-bearing experiments. These models were calculated to be proportional to the bone density and muscle force found in the Komodo dragon.

Additionally, Fry et al and Montgomery et al. both conducted experiments on the potential for venom and other significant bacteria within the Komodo dragon. Fry et al. made a "surgical excision of the mandibular venom gland" (1), dehydrated the samples of the gland, and tested for bacterial content. This test was performed on a single, "terminally ill animal at the Singapore Zoo" (1).

Montgomery et al., however, collected saliva, oral swabs, and blood "from 23 Komodo dragons in Komodo National Park" in Indonesia over a number of years (2). An additional 13 samples were obtained from captive dragons at the Gembira Loka Zoo in Indonesia (2). Bacteria within the oral swabs was encouraged to grow by the addition of trypticase soy agar, MacConkey agar, and TSA (2) before being analyzed. Saliva samples were diluted with saline and injected into mice, whose subsequent reactions and deaths were recorded. Finally, the blood samples "were analyzed for antibodies to the bacterial species that killed the mice" in the hope of sufficiently explaining the presence of the debilitating bacteria within otherwise healthy reptiles.

Results

The most straightforward results of the three papers analyzed were those of Moreno et al. Through the use of models, their research confirmed that the Komodo dragon attacks its prey with "the application of quick jerks" rather than the "bone crushing behavior" most common in other lizards in the same family (3). These quick, jerking movements allow the Komodo dragon to more efficiently rend the flesh of its prey. However, Moreno et al. also point out that when presented with "lower and more dispersed stress," or stress that comes from a wider variety of angles, even if it is exerting less force, caused a "catastrophic failure" in the structure of the jaw. This would seem to indicate that the jaws of Komodo dragons are not designed to restrain persistently struggling prey.

Fry et al. had similar results, finding that "the skull of *V. komodoensis* [Komodo dragons] is poorly adapted to resist the erratic forces generated in a sustained bite and hold attack on large prey" (1). Their research suggests instead that Komodo dragons open wounds by biting and pulling on prey simultaneously, which they suggest is similar to how some sharks and sabered cats kill their prey (1). They concluded, however, that "the bacterial species identified were unremarkable" (1) and do not feel that bacteria is a contributing factor in the success of Komodo dragons in taking down their prey.

In these results, Montgomery et al. departed significantly from Fry et al. The research in Montgomery et al. focused exclusively on the bacterial element and evidence from their experiments clearly shows that "the Komodo dragon is infected with a wide variety of bacterial species in its saliva" which "cause high mortality among mice injected with dragon saliva" (2). This study "support[s] the hypothesis that infliction of wounds in prey animals by the Komodo dragon provides a strong opportunity for wound contamination by…pathogenic bacteria" (2).

Discussion

Although the three studies (Fry et al., Moreno et al., and Montgomery et al.) do not cover identical features of the Komodo dragon, they explored interrelated features that all contribute to the successful killing of prey.

While Fry et al. conclude that there is insufficient evidence to support the use of bacterial agents in weakening prey and "reject the popular notion regarding toxic bacteria utilization" (1), Montgomery et al.'s extensive study, "Aerobic salivary bacteria in wild and captive Komodo dragons," offers sufficient proof that it is, in fact, a key element in the takedown of prey. Their greater sample size and broader tests, incorporating not just the venom gland but also the saliva and blood chemistry, allows for greater weight to be given to their conclusions regarding bacterial intervention in bringing down prey. While Fry et al. and Montgomery et al. disagree on the point of bacterial intervention, however, Fry et al.'s intense focus on dentition and jaw strength, particularly with regard to gape angles, actually complements the case that Montgomery et al. are making. Fry et al. readily prove that Komodo dragons are not successful at containing erratic prey, which supports the notion of Montgomery et al. that the prey of Komodo dragons is at least partially subdued by a bacterial agent.

It is clear from a combined analysis that it is the important interplay between the force and directionality of the Komodo dragon bite and the efficacy of the salivary bacteria to induce sepsis that allow the Komodo dragon to so effectively bring down its prey. There is a strong case to be made that rather than relying on any one method, the Komodo dragon relies significantly and simultaneously on both the bite and the bacteria in order to successfully subdue food and enable it to continue to succeed as a predator.

Literature Cited

1. Fry, B. G., S. Wroec, W. Teeuwissed, M. J. P. Van Oschd, K. Morenoc, J. Inglef, C. McHenryf, T. Ferrarac, P. Clausenf, H. Scheibg, K. L. Winterh, L. Greismana, K. Roelants L. Van er Weerdd, C. J. Clementek, E. Giannakisl, W. C. Hodgsonh, S. Luzm, P. Martellin, K. Krishnasamyo, E. Kochvap, H. F. Kwokq, D. Scanlonb, J. Karasb, D. M. Citronr, E. J. C. Goldsteinr, J. E. Mcnaughtans, J. A. Normana. 2009. A central role for venom in predation by Varanus komodoensis (Komodo Dragon) and the extinct giant Varanus (Megalania) priscus. *Proceedings of the National Academy of Sciences of the United States of America*. 106:8969–8974.

2. Montgomery, J. M., D. Gillespie, P. Sastrawan, T. M. Fredeking, G. L. Stewart, 2002. Aerobic salivary bacteria in wild and captive Komodo dragons. *J. Wildl. Dis*. 38:545–551.

3. Moreno, K., S. Wroe, P. Clausen, C. McHenry, D. C. D'Amore, E. J. Rayfield, E. Cunningham. 2008. Cranial performance in the Komodo dragon (*Varanus komodoensis*) as revealed by high-resolution 3-D finite element analysis. *J. Anat*. 212:736–746.

INTERVIEW C

Deonta: Sociology major

 **Meet Deonta.** At the time of the interview, he was applying to law school, although he began his college career planning to study pharmacology. He attended the University of North Carolina, Chapel Hill. Like each of the six students featured in the print edition of the book, Deonta was selected because his advice and perspectives on college writing seemed particularly helpful to students like you. Even so, you should read Deonta's advice and study his model paper carefully and critically, not assuming everything he says or writes is perfectly correct (or at least correct for you). The interview transcript was edited slightly to unite similar ideas and correct minor errors.

Being a College Writer

For me, college writing seems to be defined by the ability to write across various different subjects. At a liberal arts school you are required to take classes that are outside of your major that will prepare you for things that you may or may not be doing in the future. By having you write about various subjects, you learn different writing styles and how to read and think critically about different materials. It's a great preparation for real-life situations. I also think that college writing is defined by the ability to proofread your own work and make edits on your own without somebody else there to do it for you.

I do consider myself a writer. Throughout high school I always had to write — not at a college level where it's much more academic, though. We were given topics and strategies. In college, they say, "Here's the prompt; pick a topic that relates to the prompt and write about it. Stay within these limits." I consider myself a writer because I've been able to work through those topics and those limits, and I've done pretty well so far.

Collaborative Writing

When I write by myself, I'm picky about what and how something is said. When I'm doing collaborative writing, other people are involved and you can't really control the language they use, how they use it, or how they format it. It's been hard, but I've learned to deal with that.

In spite of the challenges, I enjoy collaborative writing because the groups are so diverse that you learn a lot of new vocabulary, new styles of writing. You also see how other people write and how their thought process works out. It's a great opportunity to take advantage of. It's also helped me learn things from other people that have helped me improve as a writer.

Thinking about Audience

When I think about audience, I think about how I've progressed as a college writer when it comes to an audience. Throughout high school you are writing for your teacher, but in college it might not just be for your

How to learn from the moves other writers make

professor. You may have another target audience, or you may have to think about the topic and what kind of audience would be reading something of that nature. With English papers it's been literary analysis and putting other texts in conversation with each other. You have to think about the audience that read the text that you are writing about, how they perceive it, and how they might think about it. With sociology papers I've done proposals for new ideas and we had to think about what kind of audience would be interested in these ideas. How would they conceive the ideas? How would they respond to them?

Citing Your Research

When it comes to citations, the hardest part for me are in-text citations. When do you do them? How are you supposed to do them? For the bibliography, I normally just use a citation website to make a list. Then, it's just going back and making sure that everything — quotes or paraphrases — are correctly cited. That's probably the hardest part for me because you don't want to go to honor court or anything like that for plagiarism.

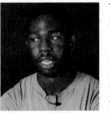

The Importance of Proofreading and Feedback

I like to revise my papers at least twice but I typically go to the writing center, or I'll talk to the professor or the TA to get their feedback. When I do my revising, I look for how well the paragraphs flow and how they connect to each other. I make sure that my paper is organized and that my thesis and conclusion are strong.

When I was in high school, I used to think that papers were introduction, three

paragraphs, and conclusion but, since I've been in college, I've learned that a paper is going to have more than three paragraphs. I've learned that you need to make sure that there is a connection from one paragraph to the next and that they are well organized, in a way that makes sense for the paper and also that makes sense to the reader. Paragraphs are going to be somewhat long because they are the meat of the paper; it's alright if they take up half a page or so. I try to make sure to get the main idea of my topics in the paragraphs along with supporting evidence, quotes from the text, or the research that I'm putting in conversation with the main idea, and make sure that the topic is also related to the prompt within the paragraph. I look for all of those things when I'm editing.

When I was in high school I didn't do a lot of proofreading. I had a bad habit of writing papers the day before they were due. Proofreading wasn't something I did a lot of but, now that I've been in college, since I've been planning out papers and doing them in advance, I've started to proofread after I've made the final revisions. Once I've made sure that everything is the way I like it, I'll go back and proofread the paper and see if there are any spelling, grammar, and punctuation errors. I'll go to the writing center, or I'll have a friend proofread it, to see if there are other mistakes that I just didn't catch.

What's helped me become a strong writer is the feedback I get from the professors and being able to talk about how I can do better on the next paper, or what it was in this paper that didn't work and why it didn't work. That's helped me improve my writing and it has enabled me to make relationships with people that I may not have been connected with before. When I'm writing papers in other courses, I can go talk to them and they'll be able to give me feedback. They also tell me things that they've done throughout their own writing process, and share tips with me.

The best piece of advice that I've gotten since writing college papers is to revise repeatedly based upon informed feedback. That's probably the advice that I would give any other college student that asked. Revising based on informed feedback, not only gives you feedback on your writing, but also gives you feedback on the topic that you are writing about and how you can become a stronger writer in those subjects. "

Sociology Paper

The portion of Deonta's interview that discusses his model paper is included below, before the paper is presented. Deonta was selected as one of the six featured students in the print companion because of his thoughtful approach to research and his careful integration of sources.

Planning My Writing Process

" When I'm given a prompt and I start planning my writing process, I simply look at the things that I have planned out before the paper is due, and I look for pockets of free time. I try to use that time well for my writing process. I normally schedule brainstorming one day and then organizing the next day so that I don't feel overwhelmed doing it all in one day. I try to write the paper after completing the brainstorming, planning, researching, and organizing stages. I try to write the paper three or four days in advance, that way I can still make edits and revise it, and possibly go to the writing center to get another person's point of view on the paper. And if there is anything else that I am missing I can make additions to it.

When I write a first draft, I simply think about my time constraints and what else I have to do during that day. I like to sit down and get my first draft all done at one time. I don't like to have to do it over multiple days because that's when I like to make my revisions. If I'm doing my first draft and making edits as I go along, it takes longer than it should. So, I typically go to the learning center, or somewhere quiet; that way I'm not distracted and I can focus on what I'm doing.

My Writing Process

When it comes to picking a topic, I normally think about what I'm interested in, how that relates to the text, how I'd be able to write about that in relationship to the text, whether or not it's going to require research, and how many sources I would need. I also try and keep in mind the page limits that we are given, and other limitations as far as the topic is concerned, so that I know I'm not just broadening the topic to a point where I can't make a conclusive argument about it.

When I have to start brainstorming, I like to sit down on my bed listening to '90s R&B and hip-hop. I get a notepad and pen and the prompt, and I just start to think about things that interest me and how they relate to the topic. I just write that down and think: "Well, am I going to need to do research?" So, I need to get to the library. Then, "Is the paper allowed to have research as a component of it?" So, then I think: "Well, I should email the professor and make sure that research is okay for the paper before moving any further with that." I'll make bullet points, and subpoints about how the idea relates to the paper, and then I try to map out the ideas in a bubble diagram. I normally go with the topic that interests me the most and the one with most substance.

After brainstorming I might try to write a rough draft of my thesis. Throughout high school, I always thought that the thesis was this strict thing that had to be perfect. It had to be done at the start of the paper, and I spent too much time on it. Now that I'm in college, I've learned that the thesis may not be perfect the first time, that you can always redo it. As long as you have an idea of what you want to talk about, you can write the rest of the paper and come back to the thesis later. I've even been told that some people put the thesis at the end of the paper, but I'm not really sure how to do that yet. As far as what the thesis is to me, I think it tells the reader what they are going to be reading about in the paper, how you are going to talk about it, and why it's important.

When I do research, I normally do it after I'm done brainstorming, after I've decided what I'm going to write about and made the bullet list of the topics that I want to talk about. I begin by researching the topic I chose or other texts that relate to the topics. I typically do this using Google Scholar, school search engines, and sometimes I go to the library and sort through the shelves. I ask the librarians for help looking for a certain book or books that are related to a certain topic that I am looking for. After that, I read through the books or the online articles that I found and take out the points that I think are important and I'll compile a list with all of it. I also keep a list of the search engines that I used to get the information, for when I make my citations page.

As I was writing and putting the text that I was supposed to be writing about in conversation with the research that I'd found, a new topic came to mind. So, I had to go back and do more research and figure out how I could incorporate it into the paper.

Social Inequality 1

Deonta Lastname

SOCI 423

Final Paper

The Reproduction of Social Inequality through AVID

UNC Honor Pledge: I certify that no unauthorized assistance has been received or given in the completion of this work.

Introduction:

This paper seeks to examine the effectiveness of the AVID program at reducing social inequality. In examining how effective AVID is at reducing social inequality, this paper will look at cultural capital, tracking, the segregation that takes place in AVID, and the lack of activity during the summer. This is important because AVID is an effective way of reducing the educational gap during the school year, but it is not as effective at reducing social inequality. I believe that AVID is an effective method of reducing the achievement gap during the school year, but I believe that it fails at doing anything about the achievement gap during the summer and while it tries to address the issue of social inequality, I feel that there are still aspects of the program that reproduce social inequality through the instillation of the achievement ideology and tracking.

In examining the point about cultural capital it is important to consider the work of Lamont and Lareau. They define cultural capital as "institutionalized, i.e., widely shared, high status cultural signals (attitudes, preferences, formal knowledge, behaviors, goods and credentials) used for social and cultural exclusion" (Lamont, Lareau 45). They then go on to talk about the four forms of exclusion, which are self-elimination, over-selection, relegation, and direct exclusion. Lamont and Lareau do not believe that cultural capital exists as a tool that only the elite can use. They believe that cultural capital can also be used for exclusion by the lower class and use the example of being street smart as a high-class marker for people of low socioeconomic status.

In examining the tracking aspect it is important to consider the work of Hallinan and Oakes. In Hallinan's work, he focuses on how tracking was theorized to work and how it actually works in practice. In theory tracking is meant to increase the effectiveness and efficiency of instruction. It is supposed to do this by allowing teachers to change their instruction to fit the ability level of their students. Over time tracking has changed from assigning students to academic, general, or vocational tracks to assigning students to advanced, honors, regular, or basic level courses. Hallinan believes that the regular and higher level courses are similar to the academic track while the basic and lower level courses are similar to the general and vocational track. He further argues that tracking is inequitable as it related to race, ethnicity, and socioeconomic status and uses these demographics for discriminatory purposes.

The work of Entwisle, Alexander, and Olson is also important to consider in evaluating the AVID program. In their work, *The Nature of Schooling*, they examine whether or not schools have actually been effective at reducing the achievement gap. They look at previous studies such as the Coleman Report to show that schools actually do have an effect on students' achievements. They found that the achievement gap closes during the time that schools are open but during the time that schools are closed for the summer, the achievement gap widens. In their work they mention Heyns who found that "(1) the gains children made in the school year exceeded those they made in the summer, and (2) children's summer gains were inversely related to their socioeconomic status" (Entwisle, Alexander, Olson 225). The rest of this evidence presented will back up the claim that while the

AVID program does help to reduce the achievement gap during the school year and provides students with cultural capital, it fails to reduce this gap outside of the school and reproduces social inequality through its practice of tracking and reinforcing the achievement ideology.

Data and Methods:

AVID stands for advancement via individual determination and is a program that seeks to close the achievement gap and prepare students for college and other postsecondary forms of education. The AVID program has existed for over 35 years and has spread to 46 states in the U.S. and 16 other countries and territories. Over 60,000 educators are provided with training and methodologies that are meant to develop students' critical thinking, literacy, and math skills. The program seeks to close the achievement gap by "teaching skills and behaviors for academic success, providing intensive support with tutorials and strong student/teacher relationships, creating a positive peer group for students, and developing a sense of hope for personal achievement gained through hard work and determination"[1] (AVID). As of 2016 seniors in the AVID program were 59% Hispanic, 14% African American, 14% White and 13% other. 74% percent of these students came from low socio-economic status, 86% came from underrepresented races/ethnicities and 57% had parents that had no college experience.[2] To gather further information and evidence to support my claim, I volunteered at Beasty Shell High School as an AVID tutor in a 9th grade classroom. The school had a total of 363 ninth graders, with 2 of these students being American Indian or Alaska Native, 81 Asians, 32 African Americans, 38 Hispanic/Latino, 25 students of two or more races, 185 Whites.[3] The classroom that I primarily observed for the collection of my data consisted of one White male teacher, four Hispanic/Latino males, four Hispanic/

Latina females, three African American/Black males, three African American/Black females, one White male and one Middle Eastern female.

Cultural Capital:

The AVID program does a good job of providing its students with cultural capital. It does this by giving students their own unique note-taking system, implementing programs such as dress for success and having a day when all of the AVID students wear matching shirts, and doing things such as college tours and college fairs and alternative spring breaks in places like Paris. These things fit Lamont and Lareau's definition of cultural capital because they confer a particular set of values to the students that would be associated with the upper class and are used to exclude people of lower classes. The best example of this that I noticed during my observations is the dress for success day that AVID students are required to participate in. AVID students at Beast Shell High School have their dress for success day on the first of each month. At this time they are required to wear business professional attire. They are not required to wear a full suit, but the males are expected to wear a button-up shirt, slacks or dress pants, dress shoes and a tie while the females are expected to wear a business casual dress and shoes, or dress slacks and dress shirts with dress shoes. Providing the students with access to college representatives and giving them the ability to visit colleges through the use of college fairs and campus visits is another way in which the AVID program provides students with cultural capital. Having the ability to connect with college representatives and visit college campus is a privilege that is disproportionately enjoyed by the middle and upper class and since AVID students are disproportionately from families that are of lower socioeconomic status and have no college experience, this is one way that AVID seeks to fight social inequality. In regards to providing cultural capital, AVID is effective in trying to fight social inequality.

An instance of cultural capital being transferred to a student on an individual basis that I noticed was one day when I came into the school to find Teacher K talking with an AVID student, named Hide, and another school employee. The two were having a conversation about school and sports that went as follows:

Teacher K: It is too late for me to do anything for you this season but if you can promise me that you will keep your grades up and come to school like you are supposed to next year, I will make sure that you get a chance to play on the team.

Hide: Yes sir, I will do that as long as I'm on the team.

Teacher K: Alright, I mean it, I am putting my neck on the line for you and I am going to be hurt if you let me down, so the first time you decide not to come to school and do not have a legitimate excuse for why you did not show up, it is over.

During this conversation, there was definitely a tension between what Hide, the young black male saw as valuable and what the Teacher K thought was valuable. Teacher K was really pushing education as being valuable, which would be an idea that resonated more within the middle and upper class while Hide, who seemed to be of lower socioeconomic status, was pushing sports as being more valuable. To further help illustrate his point about education being more valuable, Teacher K introduced me to the student and used me as an example of how valuing education can take you to high places in life such as an elite four-year public college.

Tracking:

Throughout my time volunteering at Brell High School during the semester, I noticed that most of the students tended to be in the lower track courses. Within the class that I volunteered, I noticed that the students were disproportionately tracked into the lower level courses. I did not notice this trend at first but as the semester went on, I started to take note of it and recorded the number of students in honors and advanced courses and which subject they were in honors and advanced courses for. Over the course of the semester, I noticed the Hispanic/Latino students in the class were more likely to be in the higher track course than were their black counterparts. The Hispanic/Latino students were in courses such as Math 2, honors English, honors Biology, and honors World History whereas the black students tended to be in the basic level Math, English, Biology, and World History courses. The only exception to this was a black female student, Sally, who was in honors English, honors world history. I noticed that the questions that the honors students would ask were more complex than the questions that the students in the basic level courses would ask and that their assignments seemed to be much more engaging. On February 2nd, 2017 I worked with two students who had English questions. Chad, a young black male was in basic English, while Tierra, a Latina female was in honors English. Chad had a very simple question about sentence structure and making topic sentences while Tierra had a much more complex and engaging question. Tierra's question involved her doing critical thinking and analysis of a primary text in order to come up with a way to depict what the quote signified.

On February 20th, 2017 I noticed another example of the black students being disproportionately tracked into the lower level courses. On this day I worked with a group of five students that consisted of two Latino males, two Latino females, and one black female. The two Latino males were not in honors math, but by being in Math 2, they were in an advanced level of math for ninth graders. Over the course of the rest of the semester working with the other students in the classroom, I noticed that these two Latino males were the only students in the classroom who were in a higher track for math. From volunteering in one non-AVID ninth grade classroom once during the semester, I found that in comparison to the AVID classroom that I normally volunteered in, almost all of the students in the class were white and all of them were in honors English. The assignment that they were doing in comparison to the assignments that I noticed the AVID students doing was also much more engaging and complex. The students in this non-AVID classroom were given the task of analyzing a play by Shakespeare and also picking one scene from the play and depicting it in a four-panel illustration. The students in this class also seemed to be of higher socioeconomic status than the students in the AVID class, as these students all had their own laptops, most of which were Apple MacBook's. Upon completion of the assignments, these students were allowed to do work for other classes and were even encouraged to do so. This did not happen in the AVID classroom that I volunteered in.

These examples support Hallinan's thoughts on tracking. They further illustrate his point about the placement for tracking relating to race, ethnicity and socioeconomic status. Comparing the AVID classroom and the non-AVID classroom illustrates Hallinan's fourth point about assignment to tracks that "a greater proportion of minority and low-income students are assigned to the lower tracks" (Hallinan 219) and his fifth point about assignment to tracks being that "higher social status is associated with placement in a higher track" (Hallinan 219). These examples further support the points that Hallinan makes about the effects of tracking. They show that there is more time spent planning the activities for the higher level tracks and that the quality of the instruction increases, as well as the engagement level of the class and the work. They also illustrate his point that "students in high-ability tracks learn more and at a faster pace than those in lower-ability tracks" (Hallinan 219). Furthermore, my findings are consistent with the findings of Oakes who also found a relationship between student ethnicity and tracking in the mixed schools that she studied for her work *The Distribution of Knowledge*. She also found that white students were more likely to be tracked into the high level courses while students of color were disproportionately tracked into lower level courses.

Seasonal Learning:

Throughout my time volunteering in the AVID program, I never once heard any of the students mention what they would be doing over the summer. This is important to note because while AVID does a good job of helping to close the achievement gap during the school year, from what I have observed and heard it does not seem to have a plan for continuing to close the achievement gap during the time that schools are closed. This is concerning because according to a study done by Entwisle, Alexander, and Olson the achievement gap widens during the time that students are not in schools, and this is due to factors such as socioeconomic status and the level of parents' education. With 74% of AVID students coming from low socioeconomic status and 56% coming from parents with no college experience it is concerning that I never heard any of the students mention what they would be doing for the summer since this is the time when the education gap widens the most because students who come from higher socioeconomic status have access to the things that give them an advantage over students of lower socioeconomic status.

Achievement Ideology:

The AVID program further reproduces social inequality through its reinforcement of the achievement ideology. The program seeks to produce students that are self-determined and hard working. In doing so it reinforces that achievement ideology, which is the idea that if one works hard they will be successful no matter what circumstances they come from throughout their life. The brothers in Jay MacLeod's

Ain't No Makin' It are a perfect example of how the achievement ideology works. This is a group of young black men growing up in a poor neighborhood and they believe that through their hard work they can make it out and be successful. They have also internalized the idea that when they fail it is their fault and that it does not have anything to do with their outside circumstances. AVID can be seen instilling the achievement ideology in its students through the mission of AVID as a whole. Part of the program's mission is to "develop a sense of hope for personal achievement gained through hard work and determination" (AVID). Something that I have noticed within the AVID classroom that I volunteered in is that there is no real consequence for the students not coming to class prepared. I have noticed that when they do not do their work, it is on them. In order to keep them from being a distraction to the class, Teacher K would assign these students to the group that he thought they needed to be in the most whether they wanted to be in that group or not. This can be considered a reinforcement of the achievement ideology because it puts the blame on the students and Teacher K would not listen to their excuses or accept them. He would just give the students a zero for not having their tutorial forms. In doing so it forces the students to internalize their failure and think that it is their fault.

Conclusion:

Throughout my time volunteering at Brell High School, I came to the conclusion that the AVID program does not reduce social inequality. The evidence shows that AVID does a good job of providing cultural capital, but it is not doing enough to reduce social inequality in general. The program continues to perpetuate racial segregation and in comparison with the non-AVID classroom that I visited, the AVID program continues to disadvantage its students by not placing them in as many higher track courses as their non-AVID counterparts.

The program continues to disadvantage students by pushing the achievement ideology on them and not making them aware of the surrounding social and cultural issues that affect their educational outcomes and life circumstances. The findings suggest that schools are making attempts to reduce social inequalities, but there are still things that need to be done in order to completely do away with social inequality.

When I started my observations, I was expecting to find that the AVID program was a perfect solution to fixing the problem of social inequality. When I went through training for the program, they talked about how successful the program was at sending students to college and how likely AVID students were to return for their second year of college. The program was made to seem like it was a fix all program that was pushing for the success of minorities, but after further research and studying I found that some of the things that AVID was doing (such as instilling the achievement ideology in students) were not things that would be helpful to the students.

Problems that I came across in my work were not having access to other AVID classrooms. I feel that having access to more AVID classrooms would allow me to have more points of comparison and would have allowed me to collect more data for the tracking argumentation that would have allowed me to provide more detailed statistical evidence. I also feel that my work would have benefitted from having more points of comparison that were not AVID classrooms so that I could have gotten a better feel of the things that the school was doing in its attempt to reduce social inequality. In order to build on this work, researchers should focus on the tracking that occurs with AVID students versus their non-AVID counterparts. Something else that researchers should focus on in order to build upon this study of how effective AVID is at reducing social inequality is the job placement of students upon graduation from high school and college. By doing so, it would help provide a fuller picture of the lasting effects of being an AVID student.

Works Cited

"AVID's Mission Is to Close the Achievement Gap by Preparing All Students for

   College Readiness and Success in a Global Society." *Data and Results*. N.p., n.d.

   Web. 25 Apr. 2017. <http://www.avid.org/data-and-results.ashx>.

"AVID's Mission Is to Close the Achievement Gap by Preparing All Students for

   College Readiness and Success in a Global Society." *What Is AVID?* N.p., n.d.

   Web. 25 Apr. 2017. <http://www.avid.org/what-is-avid.ashx>.

"Enrollment Data." *Chapel Hill Carrboro City Schools*. N.p., n.d. Web. 25 Apr. 2017.

   <http://www.chccs.k12.nc.us/enrollment/enrollment-data>.

Entwisle, Doris R., Karl L. Alexander, and Linda Olson. "The Nature of

   Schooling." *The Structure of Schooling: Readings in the Sociology of Education*.

   By Richard Arum, Irenee R. Beattie, and Karly Ford. 3rd ed. Thousand Oaks,

   California: Sage, 2015. 223–33. Print.

Hallinan, Maureen. "Tracking: From Theory to Practice." *The Structure of Schooling*.

   N.p.: n.p., n.d. 218-24. *UNC Course Reserves*. Web. 21 Mar. 2017. <https://ares

   .lib.unc.edu/ares/ares.dll?SessionID=W075739573S&Action=10&Type=10&

   Value=109041122>.

Lamont, Michele, and Annette Lareau. "Cultural Capital." *The Structure of Schooling:

   Readings in the Sociology of Education*. By Richard Arum, Irenee R. Beattie, and

   Karly Ford. 3rd ed. Thousand Oaks, California: Sage, 2015. 44–59. Print.

MacLeod, Jay. *Ain't No Makin' It: Leveled Aspirations in a Low-income Neighborhood.* Boulder, CO: Westview, 2009. Print.

Oakes, Jeannie. "The Distribution of Knowledge." *The Structure of Schooling: Readings in the Sociology of Education.* By Richard Arum, Irenee R. Beattie, and Karly Ford. 3rd ed. Thousand Oaks, California: Sage, 2015. 259–67. Print.

[1] http://www.avid.org/what-is-avid.ashx
[2] http://www.avid.org/data-and-results.ashx
[3] http://www.chccs.k12.nc.us/enrollment/enrollment-data

INTERVIEW D

Nicole: English major

Meet Nicole. At the time of the interview, she was an English major and a junior who had transferred from a two-year college to a large state university, California State University, San Marcos. Like each of the six students featured in the print edition of the book, Nicole was selected because her advice and perspectives on college writing seemed particularly helpful to students like you. You should read Nicole's advice and study her model paper carefully and critically, not assuming everything she says or writes is perfectly correct (or at least correct for you). Her interview transcript was edited to eliminate confusing or contradictory moments.

College Writing and Voice

I think college writing is worth the challenge because it opens you up to a way to express your voice. You have your opinions, you have your voice; then, with college writing, there's so much more to learn. It roots your voice; it grounds your voice. And it's a way for people to comprehend what you're actually thinking and what you're trying to get out there: the message you're trying to push.

When I think of "voice," I think of the individual. Voice is linked to the individual. It's a piece of you; it's your personal style; it's your rhetoric. But voice isn't something that I have come up with on my own. I have heard it in college — I've heard my teachers discuss "voice," and "your voice" and "finding your voice" — and I've heard writers discuss their voice and how they found their voice, and what they use their voice for. I think that for me, personally, voice is linked to combating injustices and rising to the occasion and speaking to those injustices. Then, that can

turn into a change or a possible solution for those injustices. For me, this comes from my own personal experiences in life, in general. We all have our own personal experiences, and that kind of molds who we are and the voice that we carry and what our voice is interested in. For me, growing up, I have encountered and I have seen a lot of injustices; so, my voice just inevitably attached to that. My voice, I've learned, is a way to fight and oppose those injustices.

On campus, a lot of students use their voice to oppose injustice. For instance, right now, there's a publication on our campus that is circulating extreme hate speech about different races, about gender, about sexual orientation — but our staff can't shut the publication down because that's an infringement on freedom of speech. So, a lot of students have used their voice as a way to oppose this hate speech on campus. And that's just one example. There are so many injustices in the world, not just in our nation — I think a voice is a great way (I almost want to say the only way) to oppose those injustices.

My Story as a Writer

When I was in elementary school, I began writing about the howling wolves outside at night and the crickets in the field and just random stuff. . . . Fast forward to junior college, where I had a huge, personal tragedy, in which I lost a family member who was really young. That took away everything that I thought was stable. Everything became a question after that; so, I took to writing. I took to poetry, and at first my poetry was absolutely horrible. It didn't make sense, and it was very much misinterpreted because I didn't know how to communicate what was going on inside me, but I expressed it someway. Horrible poetry at first! But, the more I learned, the more I was interested in writing poetry and meter and content — so, the more I learned, the more I was able to communicate what I was feeling inside.

Writing is my love. I can sit in a writing class for hours or write all afternoon and not realize that five hours went by — I think if you have that, then you are going to progress as a writer because it is your passion, and if you have your passion, it doesn't feel like work — it's just your love. So, with school, I was able to become a better writer.

To call myself a "writer" has been a struggle for me. I remember when I first arrived at the four-year university that I transferred to . . . I was in a creative writing class and the teacher said that we are all writers, but I remember not feeling like I was a writer — I just didn't — I refused to be called a "writer." I guess I linked it to the idea that a "writer" has to be published, a "writer" has to be accomplished. . . . So, anyway, I've come to this: If you're speaking about a writer in terms of a professional or a profession, then,

no I'm not yet a writer. But, if you're speaking about "writer" as a form of a verb, then, yes, I'm a writer.

The Value of Feedback and Writing Workshops

The most helpful thing that someone has ever done to improve my writing was to not let me slide on my mistakes — to not overlook my mistakes, to give honest feedback, not just: "I like that!" That might be honest feedback, but what did you like about it? And what didn't you like about it? What does this mean to you? So, in essence, any and all feedback is helpful to my writing.

You know, a teacher doesn't necessarily have to be someone in the classroom. I'm a firm believer in that: Everyone is a teacher and everyone is a student. You have your friends, acquaintances, peers, and even random strangers — all of that can be a teachable moment or a lesson that you needed to learn.

In student-based writing workshops, when you get a group of students together, they are not going to be shy about telling you what they feel about your piece. Those are really helpful to me . . . that just occurred over the summer for me: I went to these workshops and I was able to get a lot of feedback from other students.

The best thing about college writing is that it's liberating: You can go anywhere with your writing. The worst thing about college writing is that sometimes my teachers will only mark the first ten errors, assuming that I'll connect earlier errors to the later sentences. Sometimes teachers tend to overlook your errors, and I would rather that they point it out so that I can correct it and not continue to make the same mistakes.

My Identity as a College Writer

My greatest strength as a college writer is content and my use of quotes. I believe my greatest weakness as a college writer is clarity: Sometimes in peer review or in essays that I have turned in, there are points that are misinterpreted or the reader is confused. That tells me that there is a dichotomy there: I need to expand or include more evidence. . . . I need to find a way to get my point across so that it's not misinterpreted.

I enjoy reading poetry a lot. I enjoy reading — I'm probably going to sound like a dork — but I enjoy reading essays and articles. As a child, growing up, I enjoyed reading novels — I loved, loved, loved reading novels! But in the last several years, I have kind of backed away from the novel and clung more to essays and articles — and I'm in love with poetry right now. I still write poetry. I love writing essays, where I can include theory . . . and all that good stuff. I enjoy writing nonfiction stories; I've been published a few times at school. And I did a tribal publication workbook for a class on one of the Indian reservations in our local community. I've done volunteer work as a ghostwriter on a grant team. I would love to do something with my writing after college; I'm just not sure where it's going to take me. I don't really have a specific plan. I guess I look at it as if my writing is going to be the vessel to take me wherever it is that I'm going.

Advice for Writers like You

The difference between writing in high school and writing in college: In high school, they give you your topic, always. In college, they let you choose your topic, which is even harder than having a teacher give you your topic. When you get to college and the teacher says, "Write on whatever you want to write," now you have the process of finding all of your passions and then narrowing down that passion to one topic that you want to write about — and then, on top of that, narrowing down that one topic to categories that you want to address. For me, I found that just nerve-wracking because I had never had so much freedom in my writing.

My approach to writing a college assignment paper is lots of freewriting . . . a lot of freewriting! I literally dump my thoughts onto the page; I don't worry about grammar; I don't worry about mechanics; I don't worry about logic, clarity, or comprehension. I do a lot of freewriting, and then I go back to the freewriting and organize and do somewhat of a "post outline" to my freewriting. Then, that sets up the outline of where I'm going to take it from there — that's how I organize: lots of freewriting and then pre- and post-outlining. It's a series of days. So, say you have two weeks before your assignment is due, I will just start freewriting every single day because every day you're learning more information and you're researching more; so, you're going to have new ideas. As I'm freewriting I also wanted to include my sources — you need to mark and document your sources as you're freewriting because it's difficult to go back and find all of those sources. So, it's a process — I'm not sure how many hours it takes . . . but it takes days, possibly weeks, to compile all of your freewriting, and then after that, the way I organize it is to pull out the claims that are most significant to what I am choosing to write about. I will separate my claims and organize it into those claims. Then . . . I go back again and I edit and revise and peer review. You want to make sure that you have your body paragraphs and your intro and your conclusion. But, basically, lots of peer review, *lots* of peer review before I turn in my paper.

When I think about integrating sources into my writing, it's more so of an internalized thing, where I'm not so much aware of what I'm doing or why I'm choosing certain sources . . . but, when I do choose a quote from a source, I make sure that it's parallel or backs up a claim in my paper. You don't just want to drop a quote into the paper. You want to introduce your quote: Why are you using this quote and how is it relevant to the point you just mentioned? That's how I decide which quotes or which sources I am going to incorporate into my paper.

A lot of times sources will come from previous items I have already read, from articles I have read in the newspaper, from scholarly journals, articles from library databases. When I read, I do a lot of underlining and a lot of boxing words and highlighting and side notes, then marking pages so that if I ever do need it, I can go back to it. But, a lot of times when I'm reading, I don't even have a paper in mind as I'm underlining. Say I have a paper two weeks later, then I remember back and say, "Oh, I was just reading this article a couple of weeks ago, and it links up exactly to what we're talking about in this assignment"—so, I will go back to that source and pull that quote and then use it that way.

I have been taught that you never want to write your introduction first, and I have learned that lesson because, as you write your paper and you have five or six awesome body paragraphs and then you have your conclusion at the end, and then you go back

and read your paper, your introduction has nothing to do with what you just discussed in your body paragraphs.

I don't really like to include my thesis at the end of the first, introduction paragraph, like we were taught. If it's a three- to four-page paper, possibly I will because it's such a short assignment that you kind of have to include your thesis at the end of your introduction, but I usually like to include my thesis in the second paragraph. . . . I don't know why; maybe it's just me trying to go against the grain.

To develop your thesis, you need your topic and you need your opinion on that topic and you combine both the topic and your opinion to create your thesis. . . . I've always just kind of flowed with that formula for a thesis.

I learned this in school: Look at the conclusion as the "so what?" For instance, you have Occupy San Diego going on right now, it's a worldwide movement, and there have been conflicts with the protestors. Your conclusion: so what? Why does this matter? What's the point? That's how I approach a conclusion: on that "so what?" factor.

It's been instilled in me since I was young: A paragraph includes a topic sentence, content, and a transition sentence . . . within every paragraph! But a really good paragraph is tight and condensed, and it doesn't digress away from the topic. And each paragraph has its own, separate topic. It's almost as if each paragraph is its own, separate entity; at the same time, it still flows together in a way — separate but together — kind of like community because you have your individualized people, but there's still a community.

There are mistakes that I find I am still working on with grammar, and I do find that I struggle with grammar. There are grammatical facts that I do know and can explain, but then there's a lot of grammar and mechanics that I have internalized in a way where I'm doing it correctly, but I can't tell you what I'm doing because I don't know — it's just internalized. But I also feel like I have internalized incorrect forms of grammar and mechanics, which is very difficult for me to grasp now, and that's what I struggle with regarding grammar right now. I have a tendency to use passive voice and to repeat that passive voice, even though recent teachers have marked this on my paper. This semester I keep making mistakes with the semicolon.

Literary Criticism

The portion of Nicole's interview that discusses her model paper is included below, before the paper is presented. Nicole was selected as one of the six featured students in the print companion because her advice to students seemed particularly wise and because her model paper represented one of the main types of college composition, namely, literary analysis.

The paper I wrote on Márquez's short story evolved out of a writing class. Our teacher had us read Márquez's story, and she said that she didn't want us to spend a lot of time searching for sources. So, she provided 10 to 15 books that we could choose from; so, the entire class chose which books they wanted to incorporate into their essay. That's what I did: I examined the fifteen books . . . previously I had read a few articles on magical realism; so, I had an opinion on where I wanted to go with this assignment. When I finally arrived at the sources, it was easier to choose which books I wanted to incorporate into my assignment because I had already read about magical realism.

So, after we chose our sources, we just "had at it." We did our rough drafts — I'm still thankful for this — any teacher who does peer review workshops, I am very thankful for — our teacher did many peer review workshops. We were required to write two rough drafts, and both of those drafts have to go through a peer review. Two students in the class will review your work and provide constructive criticism — and they're all suggestions and you don't have to follow it — then I work with that criticism. After the two rough drafts, I wrote out my final draft and turned in the paper.

The struggle I had with the Márquez assignment was that I was initially looking at the story through a Marxist lens, which wasn't so appropriate for the story. In my initial rough draft another student caught that and explained that I needed to expand more or go another route. So, when I went back to my paper and started revising and looking at the Marxist theory in my paper and I tried to expand, I realized that I couldn't expand; so, I had to go another route.

That last step before turning in your paper: I like to read it over several times, and I like to read it out loud just to see the flow of it. If I'm reading out loud and I kind of trip on one of my sentences, then I realize that there needs to be a correction there. Before I turn in my final draft, I like to go through the assignment and make a break between each sentence to make sure each sentence is flowing into the next. When you do that, you can see if you are digressing, if you are going off topic, and then you can fix it. So, right before I turn in my assignment, I read it out loud and then I do the sentence-break exercise.

Whenever I hand in an assignment, I am always thinking about what I could have or should have edited — no matter what, even if it's an A+ assignment — it's still on my mind: "Oh, I could have done this and added this here, and I could have used that source." I find myself always kind of wanting to edit my work, no matter what.

Usually I freewrite a lot before an essay, but this semester has been really busy. With this assignment, I didn't do as much freewriting as I could have done. But, for the most part, it was my usual process: the freewriting, the outlines, the sentence breaks, the reading out loud, the peer review, the rough drafts — the whole nine yards.

I would say that the weaknesses in this paper would be some of my sentence structures. I'm still having a lot of trouble with that. I've learned that I have internalized a lot of my knowledge of grammar and mechanics, both good and bad — so, I'm still having trouble with sentence structure problems that I have internalized incorrectly. I think my greatest strength in this paper would be just how deep I went into the topic or the content . . . I think?

Nicole Lastname

Magical Realism: A Postcolonial Narrative

Magical realism is a blend of magical-like elements rooted in the foundation of reality. This binary blend borders the uncanny, while placing emphasis on the supernatural. The culturally-hybrid genre is infused with elements oscillating on the seam of reality and fantasy; however, these transcendent elements also serve in challenging the meta-narrative. Within this process, the magical realism genre becomes a lens of decolonization. Magical realism is "postcolonial writing" created by one "who learns the master's language," and then uses this language "to undermine some of its masters assumptions" (Faris 28). The magical realism elements in Gabriel García Márquez's "The Handsomest Drowned Man in the World" works as a postcolonial narrative serving as a decolonizing agent.

The magical realism genre is often examined with a lens of decolonization. Through this lens, narrative centers have been challenged by the establishment of this genre. Within the framework of this decolonized theme, the magical realism narrative operates as an agent that creates "a new decolonized space for narrative," and this new space is one that has not been previously "occupied by the assumptions and techniques" of a cultural center (Faris 135). Magical realism's "defocalized narrative" incorporates supernatural elements that breach cultural centers (Faris 133). In the breaching of these centers, the genre challenges "the dominant discourses of the privileged centers . . . in a way that redefines the future of humanity" (Faris 134). The magical realism genre's challenging of dominant discourses redefines and creates a new—somewhat canonized—space for the genre itself; therefore, the genre "undermines the right to represent the world" (Faris 133).

Márquez's culturally hybrid narrative examines one center and details the development, when another center is introduced. The story drops into the lives of a community residing within the "twenty-odd wooden houses . . . on the end of a desert like cape," and the reader is immediately presented with subtle images that piece together the community's shared ideology. The community lives in a barren desert town made of "only twenty houses" and "stone courtyards with no flowers." The community's geography seems bleak, complacent, desolate and lonely, which symbolically represents the village's shared and socially-constructed center of ideology.

When the drowned-dead man washes up on the cape's shore, the wooden housed community constructs a centered ideology for the dead man they eventually name Esteban. By giving the drowned man a name, the village people have given a defined meaning to the drowned man — with a name there is meaning, and without a name the bounds of meaning are infinite. The village people, however, have chosen the drowned man's meaning — they have constructed his ideologies just from his appearance alone.

The seemingly coincidental ideologies the community creates for the drowned man are actually built of the exact ideologies the community lacks. As the plot progresses, readers can see the progression of Esteban's socially-constructed ideology. Within the village's initial introduction to the drowned man, the women of the community instantly describe him as being bigger, taller and more beautiful, than any of the men in the village, and he possibly had the ability to "keep growing after death." He is also thought to "have had so much authority that he could have drawn fish out of the sea simply by calling their names."

The beginning of the story describes how "the first children who saw the dark and slinky bulge approaching through the sea let themselves think it was an enemy ship," and this first sentence implies their community is somewhat under attack. Following this implication, the village's people create this larger than life character—the village's savior; the village protector—out of the drowned man they name Esteban. Before the village people claim him, they imagine Esteban, in life, being "condemned to going through doors sideway, cracking his head on crossbeams," and this vision implies death is Esteban's saving grace, just as he is the village's symbolic representation of a savior.

According to Mikhail Bakhtin, the magical realism genre has a carnival spirit-like quality, and this "carnival spirit offers the chance to have a new outlook on the world, to realize the relative nature of all that exists, and to enter a completely new order of things" (qtd. in Danow 33–4). Esteban serves as the catalyst in the village's paradigm shift, as he—even in death—teaches the village a lesson about life and community. The entire narration outlines the relationship that builds between this drowned man and the village. By the end of the story, Esteban and the village people have a sincere connection; however, what is not mentioned speaks louder than what is mentioned. After the village people create a narration for the drowned man, his funeral is the finalizing event in the paradigm shift among the village's people.

As the village people say their goodbyes to Esteban, they all vow to "create wider doors, higher ceilings, and stronger floors so that Esteban's memory could go everywhere without bumping into beams." The village's people also promise to "paint their house fronts gay colors" and "break their backs digging for springs among the stones" just to plant "flowers on the cliffs for future years." The community defines their vows and promises in the name of Esteban; however, these same vows and promises seem to be what the village people yearned for all along. These promises from the village's people are also the hybrid results of ideology created by the collision of two socially constructed ideological centers.

The story examines the process of ideological centers being challenged, and creates a hybrid of culture and ideologies that transcends previous meta-narrative centers. Throughout the magical realism narrative, the reader begins to question the reality found in the supernatural moments, where magic seeps into realism; however, this "questioning of realism makes way for . . . [hybrid and multi-culturally infused] forms of representation" (Faris 133). Through strategic use, the elements within the culturally hybrid story of magical realism present a culturally, ideological decolonized perspective.

Works Cited

Danow, David. *The Spirit of Carnival*. Kentucky: University Press, 1995.

Faris, Wendy. *Ordinary Enchantments*. Nashville: University Press, 2004.

Márquez, Gabriel García. "The Handsomest Drowned Man in the World."
   Cardinal Hayes, 3 Oct. 2011, www.cardinalhayes.org/ourpages/
   auto/20011/11/3/1156299380289/English%209%handsomestman/
   gabrielgarciamarquez.pdf

INTERVIEW E

Vinh-Thuy: Chemistry major

Meet Vinh-Thuy. At the time of the interview, he was a chemistry major at Red Rocks Community College and he eventually went on to graduate from a four-year university. Like each of the six students featured in the print edition of the book, Vinh-Thuy was selected because his advice and perspectives on college writing seemed particularly helpful to students like you. You should read his advice and study his model paper carefully and critically, not assuming everything he says or writes is perfectly correct (or at least correct for you). Vinh-Thuy's interview transcript was edited to bring similar topics together and to eliminate any moments that seemed confusing.

Freedom in College Writing

I think that there are people who are in science, and they seem to think that because they are in science they don't have to write, and that they will never have to write. Then I ask them, "When you get your PhD, when you go out there and work for the National Science Foundation — and let's say you want to save the whales in Norway — how are you going to get people to agree with you?" You have to write a proposal. You have to stand up there and present a multimedia project. You have to stand out there and talk about it. I wish that other science majors — like myself — could see the value in writing; the value in composition class.

Most of the people I talk to are always saying, "Once I'm done with school, I'm done with writing. That's it, no more writing from then on." They don't see that writing is such an important part of your life. It's something

that's life-long, right? Let's say you're writing about photosynthesis — I'm not going to become a botanist, so that's probably the last time I'll approach that subject — but I'm never going to get away from writing. So why not just embrace it?

I think college writing is being able to freely express who you want to be. In high school it's really hard to write about what you want to be because you are kind of discovering yourself. I've taken two English composition classes and in both classes they have really encouraged me to write about what I want to say, not what they want to hear. I think that's what's really great about college writing, is that you really do have that freedom to explore whatever it is you want to explore, no matter how weird or strange or out there it might be. At the end, your professors — at least the ones I've come into contact with — will always read it and will always give you positive feedback or constructive criticism for it. Because they never give you a rubric saying they want you to write about the color yellow. You can write about the entire rainbow if you wanted to. Whatever it is that you wanted to write about, they'll listen to you.

I had to write an assignment for my botany class, which was basically anything you want to write about in botany, it just has to be a certain length, it has to be a certain amount of sources. Both my English classes were the same way.

So, there is always a theme but within that theme there is a huge amount of freedom and there is a huge amount of directions in which you can take it. I've never actually had a class where it was just basically you had to write about one thing and one thing only. It was always about giving you a theme or giving you a direction and letting you go wherever you want with that direction. More often than not, the professors are always happy to accommodate whatever it is that you would like to do on that particular assignment.

Breaking from Tradition

The traditional format, you know—intro, three body paragraphs and conclusion—that you learn in high school. For the longest time I thought that was the only way to write. Whenever I read an essay like that in high school, I thought that was the way to write and I thought that if somebody followed that formula to the dot, they would write a really well-rounded essay. There was an English teacher who told me my head was in the clouds when I wrote a different way. She told me I should go ahead and get back down. I thought, *Well, okay. I guess, she should know, she's an English teacher*. So, I

just decided from then on I would write the standard formula.

When I first entered a college writing class, I wrote like that, and the professor said: "Well, this is correct, I'm not going to fault you for writing like this. But you won't find professional essays written like this." She had me look through a copy of our textbook and I realized that none of the people in it write like this, you know? They might begin with a conclusion or they might begin with, "This is how I feel about something," and the rest of the essay would be proving that statement.

So, when I think of a boring essay, I think of reading an anatomy textbook, which is: your scapula is located here, your femur is located here, and your tibia is in front of your fibula. It's very dry and when you read it you feel like the author is saying: "I like apples because they are red." Not, "I like apples because they remind me of a time during my childhood when my mom was making apple pie." An essay that's to the point and has no creative value to it — that's not how you would write an essay. An essay is not a math formula. You don't just plug numbers in and get an answer, you know, it doesn't work that way.

I think that an essay is really a story. It has an argument, and therefore it's a story. So, an introduction should tell your reader where you're at, or maybe have your reader ask that question when they read it. Where are they? You know, at what point of the story are they? And your conclusion should be something to wrap up what it is that you've been arguing about, but it doesn't necessarily have to be a happy ending, it doesn't have to be the be all and end all. It can be

How to learn from the moves other writers make

the terminal point of your argument, but it can continue to ask questions. I think how to go from where you start the story to where you end your argument should be points, or should be certain things that can support your overall argument.

Writing is not about the three body paragraphs, and it's not about the conclusion. You don't necessarily have to start with the intro, you don't necessarily have to end with the conclusion, and you don't necessarily need to have X amount of evidence. When you write something, you should write about what you really feel like writing. It could be confined within a theme, but even if I give you a theme — let's say, colors — there are so many different colors you could write about and you can pick out a color that means something to you. An essay is not about an intro, it's not about body paragraphs, it's not about conclusions; it's about writing what you really, really like, and writing passionately about what you like and what you really believe in. When I write something that I didn't put all of my mental capacities into, I didn't put my heart and soul into, it doesn't feel like something somebody should read. Because if I can't even read through that and be proud of it, it's not worth somebody else's time, honestly.

Paying Attention to Sources

When writing a traditional research paper, like my botany paper, I have to really pay attention to the sources. When I write a research paper, I read through the primary literature and I pay attention to the context of what it is I'm extracting from the work — are the ideas still loyal to the original work? It's especially important in science. Science isn't based on the abstract most of the time. Science is based on facts, and when you extract something, you want to extract it where the idea of it is still loyal to the writer, but you also don't want your essay to consist of just these disjointed chunks of facts. I learned ways to use words so that you can link these two thoughts together. For example, if you find three different sources and they all have some similarities, you can construct a paragraph around them, or you can construct an idea around them. The main thing that I really try to be careful about is not to take the original author's work, extract it, and then change it to fit my thesis because that's not the point.

In terms of finding the sources, it's actually a lot harder than it sounds and it took me a lot longer than I thought it would. When I did the botany paper, I was lazy and I decided to wait about three days before the sources were due to look at them, and I realized that you need a lot of time because there are a whole lot of sources out there. If you type photosynthesis into JSTOR, for example, which is the database for scientific journals, you will get over 50,000 results. All the results will have photosynthesis in there, but you really have to read through it to make sure that it is what you really want to say.

A lot of the research into finding sources is seeing if your sources help you to write your paper. There's an advanced search section, and I usually check these different buttons to try and get key words to match what it is that I am researching about, but even then, it takes sitting down. It takes reading through all these different sources, and it takes really having to read the authors' work in order to see if their intent matches yours, and if you can use their intent and keep it whole in your research paper.

Thinking Creatively

I find myself adding very creative elements to my academic writings. I think it comes to the fact that I am very introverted. I've actually asked myself this question many, many times, "Why do you write like this?" When I write I'm much more opinionated than I am in person. It might not seem like it but I'm a pretty quiet person at school and at home. I don't really have much to say and I don't really want to say much. But when I write, it allows me to put my thoughts and the opinions I don't get to voice on paper. I can edit it to a point where it's a very fluid and a very effective argument. I think that's why I write the way I do because I don't get to project what I really feel in the inside to the outside too much because I'm a little introverted.

Writing as a Non-Native English Speaker

My advice to non-native English speakers is to read. I know that sounds weird to say that the key to writing is through reading, but when I first came to America, I picked up my first Charlie Brown book and read through that thing. I didn't understand anything, but I got "hello" and I got "how are you?" and I got "Charlie Brown," but it made me furious that I couldn't understand the other words. The Vietnamese alphabet uses the same set of Latin alphabets, so I thought, "Why can't I understand this construct?" So I just sat down and practiced and practiced, and just trained myself.

Through reading you learn so much. It doesn't have to be a book, you know, you could read Wikipedia, you could read the newspaper, but reading helps you to see how other people construct their writing and then you can infer upon that for your own writing. If you never read, then you don't really know what it's like to read through something that's been written passionately, or to read through something that somebody wrote with all their heart. Take me for example, I thought essays were supposed to be a certain way, but it was through reading different things that I finally saw that essays weren't about being an intro, three body paragraphs, and a conclusion. It was about so much more. It was about writing what you really liked and writing about something that you really feel passionate about.

The role of mechanical correctness is pretty important, and I can tell you first-hand that I have not mastered English grammar by any means whatsoever. I feel like mechanical correctness is really important because if a comma is placed in the wrong place you will say something different. Whenever I write an essay, the main thing that I usually have an editor look at is, "Do you see any repeating grammatical mistakes?" Because I do make them and I sometimes don't put a comma or I'll sometimes forget to conjugate a word correctly. So I think that rhetoric and grammar is a crucial thing that we should really focus on; it is one of those things I do have to pay attention to.

It is not something that just comes out, and I really have to read the paragraph, read it, sound it out, you know, hold the essay in front of me and read the entire essay slowly to see if I've made any grammatical mistakes. It comes from the fact that I wasn't born in America, and English grammar is really difficult when you are not a native speaker. It's something that you train yourself, and even when you train yourself you do make mistakes time and time again.

The Writing Center and Editing Process

My strategy for correcting my paper is I hold it up and just read it very slowly and I read it multiple times. I read it right before I finish just to catch any silly mistakes. Then I wait a couple of days and I read it again. Reading out loud was something that sounds so simple, but before my professor told me to do it, I never actually did it. I would sit there and just read the paper and then I would think I edited it. It would look fine and I'd get the paper back and there's all these missing commas, and misuse of semicolons, and misuse of colons.

Reading it over and over, out loud, really helped me. Having a second pair of eyes look at it was really helpful because sometimes even if you read it aloud, you read it the way that you think you wrote it but it's not the way that it appears on paper. I'll be sitting in the writing center and I'll read my sentence the way I think I wrote it, but the tutor would say: "That's not what you wrote, though." It really takes both reading it out loud and having a second pair of eyes.

I find the writing center really useful because it allows me to edit my paper and it allows me to obtain different ideas. For example, there was this one paper that I had to write in my second semester English composition class, a research paper on how one can tell culture of a country through food. I had a difficult time trying to end the paper and I am really passionate about different Asian cuisines, and Korean, Japanese, and Thai, and Vietnamese, and Indian cuisine. I was trying to use all those cuisines to tell about the different cultures of these different nations, and I had a really difficult time trying to piece together a conclusion.

When I went to the writing center, they helped me ask, "What are the similarities between all these different cuisines and all these different foods? And how can you piece that together into a conclusion?" So they helped me with different ideas, and they also helped me with grammatical mistakes. I do like the fact that they don't just tell you out right: "Oh, you know sentence one, you need a comma here; sentence two, you need a semicolon; sentence three, you need to put this in parenthesis — but they tell you if there are any repeating patterns and then you can pick out the rest. They'll mention, "Okay, you're having a lot of comma splices, fix that." Or they'll say, "You're using the wrong *whose* and *who's*." I do like that aspect.

Usually, I can whip out a draft really quickly and then I'll take that draft to the writing center and see if my ideas are solid, if my sentences are flowing, and if my ideas are flowing. Then I'll go back and edit by myself, and rewrite. Sometimes I need help at the very end. Sometimes I can do the draft, and I feel really good about it and I'll do my second draft and I'll actually have to go to the writing center for the third draft; for the very final draft. Sometimes I go in the middle. There is no one time in which I go into the writing center. It's all about how well I can write that particular essay, or particular paper, and then I'll go in at the point where I really do need help, whether it's starting the paper or ending the paper, or gathering enough evidence.

Multimedia Essay

The portion of Vinh-Thuy's interview that discusses his model paper is included below, before the paper is presented. Vinh-Thuy was selected as one of the six featured students in the print book because of his exploration of genres and his determination to revise repeatedly and creatively to improve his writing. His interview was edited to eliminate confusing or contradictory moments.

My professor gave us a choice at the end of the semester for a rewrite for our final portfolio. I took the essay and I just thought: "How can I rework this?" And I spent two weeks on it and I couldn't rework this essay to what I wanted, and then I remembered my very first stage of writing the "sky essay." I had this idea of writing about Shenandoah Mountain and I thought, "Well, where can I take this?" And that's how it came about. So, this essay is the final draft of the sky essay and it is nothing like the original one. It's about how the sky is a metaphor for all my memories.

My professor said, "If you really feel that strongly about rewriting this, you should go ahead and do it," and I thought, "Well, I can't make the original essay into a fluid entity. So what I'm going to do is take my original idea and try to write around that." That gave

birth to that paper and I got a better grade in that paper, but that's beside the point. I'm much more proud of this paper than I am of the original draft because that was a mess of thoughts that I just pieced together into an essay. This one was a coherent narrative and I thought that the visuals really supported the text.

It was interesting piecing them together. I sat down and looked through the pictures and thought, *How can I tell a story?* I opened up a Word document — it wasn't anything fancy — and I dragged all the pictures onto there. I split the screen and I had my essay on the right and I had my Word document with the pictures on the left, and I just read the essay and I looked at the pictures and said: "Well, how can I match this with this?" If I couldn't, I moved the pictures to another place. That's how I put it together.

Vinh-Thuy Lastname

04-19-2010

ENG 121-008

A Journey of Self-Discovery

Two summers ago, I met Uncle Aaron for the very first time. He was a small, round and amiable man who gave the greatest hugs in the world. Even though Uncle Aaron was Dad's older brother, I seldom heard stories about him. Nevertheless, with the start of my college career approaching, Dad thought it was time for me to meet Uncle Aaron. He pestered me all-month long with tactics ranging from guilt trips, to long lectures, to even docile pleas. I did a good job of ignoring them until Dad offered me something I couldn't refuse: a MacBook (on the condition that I would partake on this trip). I agreed.

Two days before the trip, I spoke to Uncle Aaron for the first time. His gentle yet firm voice on the phone reminded me of my Buddhism teacher back in Vietnam. We exchanged typical casual pleasantries, obligatory questions and statuses in life. As the conversation was about to close, Uncle Aaron suddenly asked me if I liked to hike. Despite living in Colorado, I've never hiked before, but I told him I did anyway. "Great!" was his reply.

"We'll go to my favorite spot the morning after you arrive, Vinh-Thuy."

That morning came sooner than I expected. I crawled out of bed and put on my clothing. Walking downstairs, I quickly glanced over to see Uncle Aaron stuffing a waffle down his mouth. "We have to get there before the sunrise," he said while munching loudly.

Taking heed, I inhaled some pancakes and raced out the door. A little while down the road, I turned to Uncle Aaron and quietly asked, "If you don't mind me asking, Uncle, where is this special spot?"

"Shenandoah Mountain," he said smiling.

We arrived at the foot of Shenandoah Mountain at a quarter to five. The sky above was still dark, almost eerily gloomy like those surrounding villains' castles in Disney classics. I stepped out of the truck and waddled my way through invisible shrubs in the dark. "This way nephew!" yelled out my uncle.

I quickly dashed over to him, and we began our hike up the mountain. Huffing and puffing (so out of shape!) my way along the trail, I looked beyond the horizon, towards the backdrop of mountains on the other side. I noticed tiny glimpses of light peeking gently out behind the mountains, like little children peeking out of their blankets. To my right, cloud silhouettes float atop the sky's black-gray canvas, slowly drifting towards the source of light. Like a beacon of hope, the light became a sign that life would soon return to the eternal blue above. "I remember this…" I thought to myself.

It was after a night of prom, after-prom, and late night Denny's. Aidan, my boyfriend, and I decided that we'd do the "usual prom thing" and watch the sunrise from Red Rocks Amphitheater. We got there at a quarter to five and sat atop a large boulder. I had my head against his shoulder while we quietly waited for the sunrise. The sky was gloomy and dark; ghostly cloud silhouettes floated helplessly above, seemingly blinded by the absence of light. Like the clouds, I also had no sense of direction. Now that the school year was ending, I wondered where life would take me. Sure, I had a college choice, and yes, I had a career goal

How to learn from the moves other writers make

in mind. Nevertheless, I wondered if those were really the directions for my life. Had I chosen the right paths? Would they take me away from Aidan? Would they lead me somewhere meaningful? Or would I drift helplessly amongst the gloomy future? At that moment, I was lost.

Just then, I noticed a squeeze on my hand. "Can you see it?" Aidan looked at me smiling.

As I looked in the direction he pointed, I noticed the gradual sunrise, its rays of light pierced outward behind the mountains. The sun's rays slowly lit up the sky, from gray, to blue-black, to dark blue. The gloomy mask of the sky now dissolved to reveal its gentle cerulean face. To my right, amongst the clouds, now alive with vigor, a flock of birds flew towards the sunrise. I woke up from my daydream then; the self-berating, self-pity and questions stopped. Inspired by this scene of renewal, I realized that even if the paths I've chosen lead me towards a dark and gloomy future, a bright and shining tomorrow is always around the corner. All too often in life, I made decisions diplomatically, always wagering and scaling the best options. The sky showed me that it's all right to make mistakes, to fade, or to lose a bit of life, as there's always a brighter tomorrow. "It's pretty isn't it, Vinh-Thuy?" Aidan said with the sweetest smile.

"Sure is," I replied softly.

"Are you excited for college, nephew?" Uncle Aaron's voice brought me back to Shenandoah Mountain. "Y-yes, Johns Hopkins was always a school of my dreams."

The sun had completely risen by now and smiled gloriously down at Uncle Aaron and me. I stopped near a patch of wildflowers and took in a deep breath. "Takes your breath away, doesn't it?" Uncle Aaron sighed as he touched my shoulders.

"Sure does."

We decided to take a quick break beside a tree trunk. As Uncle Aaron fidgeted with his backpack, I munched on some trail mix and lay down on the grass. My eyes were fixated on the sky again, this time noticing streaks of white across its cerulean face. I took my hands and traced the white plumes as memories of my childhood came rushing back.

It was the summer before my family immigrated to the U.S. I was nine years old then and Mom wanted to take me to Can Tho, her hometown. We went on a red-gray charter bus, stuffed to capacity with people with luggage. The environment was hectic as babies cried, old women yelled, old men smoked their lives away, and vendors patrolled the walkway selling roasted peanuts. To save money, Mom and I shared a seat; I sat on her lap with my eyes fixated on the scenery outside.

Along the trip, I noticed rice paddies as far as the eyes could see, water buffaloes hard-at-work churning up soil, and small elderly women picking rice with skillful dexterity. Upon reaching the city of Minh Thuan, I noticed plumes of white smoke across the clear blue sky. I took Mom's hand playfully and traced a smiley face in the sky with her fingers. "What are you doing, Vinh-Thuy?" I remember Mom asking.

"Since you told me that Grandma was in heaven watching down on us, I thought I'd draw a smiley face just in case she couldn't see me smiling from way down here."

I like to think, even to this day, that Grandma saw that smiley face. Even though I have grown out of the habit, I hope she can still see how happy I am down here.

Passing the "Welcome to Can Tho" sign, I could sense restlessness on the bus. Likewise, my legs were itchy and all I wanted was to get off this stinky moving furnace. When we got to our destination, Mom and I left the bus station and walked onto a beaten trail. Passing a "chicken grass" forest, we walked further in and crossed a makeshift monkey bridge. From afar, my mom's old childhood home came into view.

It was an old and rickety bamboo house atop a lotus lake. I found myself spending most of my time out in the back, against the pole scratched with Mom's heights at various ages. I would often stare into the beautiful and clear cerulean sky of Can Tho. Like the bluest of waters, it reminded me of an undisturbed Sea of Eden as white clouds float calmly to the melody of the wind. As such, all the harmonies of serenity seemed to meld together creating this eternal blue canvas unfolding before my eyes. It struck me then that the sky above Can Tho mirrored the humility and simplicity of its inhabitants. The people here were simple and humble folks; they worked from sunrise to sunset and never took anything in their life for granted. Neither the noises of construction nor the angry hustle and bustle of the Saigon traffic was present. Likewise, the perpetual dust, smog and pollution covering the sky of Saigon was also absent. If the sky above Saigon and Can Tho were the same sky, how can it have two faces? It hit me then that the sky is like a mirror of the world below. For Saigon, it showed an industrialized metropolis filled with dusts as mopeds raced about, debris as old buildings give way to new ones, and gloom as citizens scatter about, too busy to worry about anything but themselves. In contrast, everything slowed down in Can Tho; things flowed according to nature's clock and the organic way of life prevailed. As my realization came full circle, a ray of sunshine pierced through the clouds.

I opened my eyes and saw Uncle Aaron standing with his hands on his hips, looking out towards the horizon. "Thank you for taking me here. It's truly gorgeous," I said.

"I knew you'd like it. I used to come here every weekend when I was younger and could hike more easily," he said lightly laughing.

We got back on the trail and began our ascent once again.

"Vinh-Thuy, I'm sorry I couldn't make it to your graduation," Uncle Aaron said suddenly with slight guilt in his voice.

"Oh, i-it's alright. Dad told me you were busy with work so I understand. We live far away after all," I said trying to ease his guilt.

"I want you to know that I wanted to be there very badly."

"I know, Uncle."

I turned to him and smiled and he hugged me across my shoulders.

We were almost at Shenandoah Mountain's peak when I noticed a hot air balloon to my left weaving in and out of the clouds. From afar, it looked like a fish swimming freely in the ocean, dancing capriciously in its cerulean waters. As my eyes traced its path, the swaying of the balloon brought me back to the day of my graduation ceremony.

My graduation commenced on a beautiful day. The sky was crystal blue and there was not a cloud in sight. I sat in the second row with the rest of my class's salutatorians exchanging funny looks with my best friend, Madison, our graduating class's valedictorian. Up on the stage, the honored speaker congratulated us on our achievements and reassured us that the "best has yet to come." As I looked at my friend's faces, I saw the bright smiles and their eyes glistening with hope. I saw my parents in the back rows, like other parents, with black-and-gold balloons in their hands. The balloons swayed back and forth in the gentle wind creating a wave of colors on the horizon. From afar, it looked like we had an army of supporters and fans (in a way, our parents had always been our supporters and fans). Beyond the balloons, the clear blue sky lent its beautiful metaphor down to us. The sky that day was like an empty canvas and mirrored the soon-to-be graduates. Armed with our education and very own empty canvases, we were to each move onto different paths, lives, and goals. Filled with energy, I was ready to take on the world, ready for anything.

"Vinh-Thuy Lastname!" the announcer, struggling to properly pronounce my name, called out. I quickly walked up to the stage, clumsily tripping on the steps. I hugged my principal as she handed my diploma and salutatorian certificate. Quickly shuffling my feet down the line, so as not to hold anyone up, I was greeted by Madison with a bouquet of flowers and a great big hug. I looked back to the crowd to see Mom with tears streaming down her face and Dad nodding approvingly. Against the backdrop of the blue sky, they stood amongst a sea of swaying balloons, smiles and joyous tears. I wondered then how different my graduation commencement would have been had the sky turned gray, or worst yet…started to rain. Surely, some smiles would have turned into frowns and superstition would have led some to conclude that this was a "bad ending" or a "horrible beginning." Would we have had to cancel the graduation commencement? The ambience surely would have changed and my memory of this day, different. It is peculiar how the sky can affect any setting; how something can turn sour just because the sky changed its face. Walking down the steps, I wondered how this "start of a new chapter in my life" could have been "ruined" had the sky put on its gloomy mask.

The snapping of a twig beneath my feet brought me back to reality. Approaching the summit, Uncle Aaron and I were nearing the conclusion of our hike. A sense of nostalgia suddenly came rushing as I looked back down the mountain, at how far I've travelled. We stood atop Shenandoah Mountain for a while, silently taking in the view and the fresh air. This hike with Uncle Aaron had taken me back to my past and reminded me not only of my wonderful memories, but also of a presence that has always been a part of my life. I came to the realization that the sky is as much a part of me as I am a part of it. In a way, the sky comes to be a part of everyone. We sit underneath its hold, forever hugged by its boundless existence, its influence eternal. Not a day goes by when we are not touched in some ways by the sky. Together, we forged good times as well as bad times. Its bears us many good memories and reminds us of many bad ones. Walking back down Shenandoah Mountain, I looked upward again at the eternal blue above me. The realization that this day, like every other day, had been shaped by the sky above filled me with indescribable emotions.

INTERVIEW F

Dan: Professional Writing major

Meet Dan. At the time of the interview, he was specializing in environmental science and professional writing at Michigan State University. Like each of the six students featured in the print edition of the book, Dan was selected because his advice and perspectives on college writing seemed particularly helpful to students like you. Even so, you should read Dan's advice and study his model film carefully and critically, not assuming everything he says or writes is perfectly correct (or at least correct for you). His interview transcript was edited to eliminate confusing or contradictory moments as well as moments when he seems to have misspoken.

Breaking the Rules in College Writing

When I was initially taught how to write, there were a set of rules that I had to follow, and you were graded and judged based on how well you followed those rules — not how well you changed the rules — not how well you came up with new ways to do things, but how well you stuck to a guideline. I did that from the moment I knew how to write until end of high school. Then, as I started to fall in love with writing and really enjoy communicating through writing, those rules sort of became extremely evident to me. I saw those rules in a new light, and I just sort of delved into breaking them. When I came to college I did my first couple of papers by following the rules because I thought that's how I'd be graded, and I did terrible on the papers. Now, I don't know if it was because of the change in academia or just the change of the times in general, you are rewarded by the ways that you are able to effectively break the rules. So, no longer can you just write an intro with a thesis in it, a few paragraphs, and a conclusion.

That was a great place to start because it helps you start thinking about the writing process and how to organize your thoughts. But, now, if you stick to that sort of format it's not going to do well because nobody wants to read that, even if it's an academic paper. So, writing has evolved for me: from understanding the rules, to really understanding the rules, to not understanding why I am following the rules, and then breaking the rules — breaking them really effectively. That's how writing has evolved since I learned how to do it.

In my eyes, college writing is defined by how effectively you are able to communicate, no matter what you are writing about. It's about your delivery. You can't communicate well by sticking to these rules of intro, three body paragraphs, and a conclusion. College writing, in many ways, disagrees with high school and middle school for teaching that. College writing is more about exploring new ways to understand writing, exploring new ways to produce writing. You are rewarded in college writing

483

How to learn from the moves other writers make

by how well you are able to change things, to communicate your point in new ways. Every piece of content can be produced and delivered in a different way; there are different delivery methods for each production. That is what college writing is about to me.

A Content Strategist

I don't call myself a writer any longer because, even though I think writing is everything, I also think film is writing; audio is writing; graffiti is writing. I think all of that is writing. What I call myself now is *Content Strategist*. That is my nerdy term for it. It's understanding what content you have and need, and coming up with the best strategy to produce and deliver that. To me, originally, a writer was someone who sat in their loft apartment in New York on a typewriter and sent their book in every couple of years and made a whole bunch of money. I was like: "I want to do that. That sounds great!" Now, I'm realizing that's not what a writer is. The people who are actually producing and really contributing to the creative class, to academia, to the business world; those are content strategists. It's strategizing how to produce content, how to deliver that content, and eventually how to maintain that content.

In high school, we were always taught that every paragraph has to start with a topic sentence and every word and sentence within that paragraph has to relate back to that topic sentence. I think that's ridiculous. Keeping in mind your topic is vital; understanding what you need to cover, is vital; but more importantly you need to figure out what you want to say about

that topic and how you are going to say it. So, what do I want to say about the topic and what do I want to do with that topic is more important. Nowadays, that's what I've learned at least.

Genre as the Evolution of Writing

Genre, to me, is proof that new digital technology is an evolution of writing. They are not new ways of writing. They are not this brand-new thing that no one thought of. The Internet, for instance, is just an evolution of producing content and storing content. Genre is evident of that because, when all you had was stone tablets and things like that, genre was whatever you were recording. When you move to books you get romance novels and things like that; then you move to the digital world, all you are doing is opening up vast amount of genres. You're not really changing anything, you're just expanding things.

I think genre in academia is really important; to understand what your genre is, and how it needs to look, and what it needs to do, that's vital. If you're not living within the purposes or the rules of that genre, your content is not going to work for your audience because that genre is what they are expecting. In academia, genre is vital. When you move toward the digital world genre explodes and becomes something that you can readily change. When you think about content management systems, you can write "press release" and then all you've got to do is parse that out and you can reproduce it as a future story on your website. Digital technology makes weaving between genres easier.

Rhetorical Significance

I hate theses because writers all too often think, "Okay, here is my thesis. All I've got to do is make sure that everyone understands what my thesis is and then I have to give a little bit of proof of my thesis and I'm done. I got it." A thesis and writing are much more than that. What should replace the term *thesis* is *rhetorical significance*. What is the rhetorical significance of your production? Not, "what is the thesis?" Not, "I want to prove the color red is the best color." Rhetorical significance is What do you want to prove? Why do you want to prove it? How do you want to prove it?

If you have to write a thesis statement for your paper, what you've got to do is write it briefly, figure out what you want to prove, but then moreover, figure out strategies for proving it and explain to yourself why you want to prove it. Then, you can really make a piece of content that is valuable and effective.

Scope

Scope, for me, has to be toward the end of the writing process. If you, right when you start off your process, say, "All right, I'm going to only produce this three minute video. That's it." If you start with that, all you are going to do is think about how you have to edit 82 videos into three minutes. You have to let scope just come eventually and stay within the constraints of "I want a thousand word essay." Produce the content with a scope that is rhetorically effective. Say what you need to say as briefly as you need to say it, but let the scope just organically work itself out and eventually it will.

Once you've figured out what you want to say, how you want to say it, and why you want to say it, the scope of the project will come. In so far as scope, your project could be huge and I think that's a good thing. The scope of the project should be as big as you want it to be and then, slowly narrow it down as you go and it will organically work itself out.

The Writing Process

Research is the first step of every production or piece of writing. I always start with research because, as you are researching, connections start to surface and you start to think, "Okay, that fits with this other piece I just read. Let's sort of start." You start writing the paper in your head as you are researching. I also think that researching your audience, the delivery you are planning on producing and the genre, is important. All that research is vital to writing well and effectively because it all plays a huge role in producing writing. Research should be the first step, and it also should be the thing that I am consistently going back to as I am producing. Who is my audience? What do they need? What's the genre supposed to look like? What is a memo supposed to look like? Then, I'll put the things that I researched about my topic in as well.

The writing process starts with brainstorming, which is perfectly evident in what I was talking about insofar as breaking the rules once you learn them. In high school, you are taught that there are four or five ways you could brainstorm. You can create a web that connects things. You can get things all on a list. You can do a Venn diagram. There's only a couple of ways you can brainstorm and there's only a couple of ways you can do it right. Those principles that are taught are really valuable and have been valuable to me, but the actual brainstorming process changes every time. It changes based on what I'm producing, what the content actually is, what the content is that I have, what research I have found, and what I want to say. So, the brainstorming process, though it generally starts in writing, starts with figuring out what I have in my head now and putting it on paper. "What do I have to work with now?" And then, "What do I need to go find?" is my brainstorming process as far as writing goes.

As far as the digital word goes, brainstorming becomes much more difficult but also much more fun. As I delve into film, I started getting into storyboarding. I think storyboarding is brilliant and my brainstorming process for everything now is more or less a storyboard; when I'm writing and even when I'm designing a website. Now, I'm using these storyboarding techniques. So, scene one: What needs to appear? When does it need to appear? What does it need to look like? That's paragraph one; that's point one. I just get everything out on the storyboard — whether it's writing it on a computer or actually drawing it — and then I sort of figure out the moves I need to make to transition between those storyboards. That's my brainstorming process, which is, now, more of a storyboarding process for everything.

The relationship between brainstorming and outlining, traditionally, has been: you brainstorm first and you take that disorganized brainstorm and you organize it into an outline with point A, subpoint A, B and C. That rendered either one of those things completely useless because I'd end up combining them either way. I would create a brainstorm web of a thousand things and then I would just not even think about it when writing my outline; I'd just re-brainstorm. I think that combining those two things is important, and it works for me because I continuously edit my outlines and my storyboards. I'm doing my brainstorming as I'm structuring it, and I'm fixing and changing things all the time. Because it's indefinitely editable — your storyboard or your brainstorm — they could be sort of combined into one. You can always change it.

In college, we learn that everything is a draft. You never ever, ever have a final draft. Everything is always in a process. Even once you publish something in a book, if you want to republish it somewhere else, you're probably going to change it in some regard. So, drafting is vital. That's what I do, I get something there and I chunk it down and figure out where those pieces of content need to go. When I'm producing something, I'll turn it in as finished as I can, but it's never finished. I have never, with a piece of writing, in my entire life, said: "Yep, that's done. That's as good as it ever could be." It's never going to be perfect because things are always changing. So, there is always a way that you can adapt that content, that piece of writing, to better suit an audience; a genre; an evolution in thinking. Drafting is a forever process.

In high school, all you ever had to do was produce your first draft, revise it, proofread it, turn it in, get some notes from the teacher, make those changes, and then turn it back in and you get a 100 percent. That was revising and it was disappointing because it never taught you how to actually do your own changes and make your own revisions. Now, revising is more: Get something on the page and start reading through it all. "Yea that's a good point, let me figure that out a little more, let me kick away some of the weeds around it, delete some stuff," or "read it through, you know, that's a good point, but it's not going to help me deliver my rhetorical expression in any way, so I'm just going to delete that." Revising is a systematic thing. I'll put something on the page, read through it, cut what I can and bring out what I can, get to the bottom of the page, done, do it again and just keep doing it. I do the same thing with every sort of digital expression as well. I'll finish a video; I'll watch it through and as I am going through I'm like, "Okay, no, that needs to change. That — okay, you know what, he just said — in an interview, for instance — he just said something really cool and I think he said something about that earlier. So, I need to go back to the original film and find out where he talks more about that one point because I must have missed that. So, I need to go find that and bring it back."

You are not your audience. Even though something might work for you, and you might think, "Okay, that works," you might be entirely wrong; someone else might not get it. The audience might not get it because they don't have the thoughts that you have in your head. It's really important to involve other people in my writing because it helps me figure out what I am saying effectively and what I'm saying not so effectively. So, when I'm producing something I actually care about, I'll always send it to people. Sending it as I go: "What do you think of this?" or "How's this look?" I've sent dozens of videos to one of my professors who does a lot of video at my school and in the email I'll say, "Listen, I know this is crap but does this work? Does this one part work? What do you think of this? How can I change it?" Involving other people, at least to get another eye on it, and asking specific questions about certain parts of the content, is really important to me.

Including resources was always the most frustrating thing for me in high school because it was like, "All right, I've written this paper. It's pretty good, but oh, now I have to quote the author three times somewhere. Okay, I'll throw that one in there and that one in there and there." Now, it's more important to me. It's not just, "Oh, yea I need to make this look better. So I'll throw in some resources." Now, in college writing, it builds on *ethos*. It makes you more effective as a communicator to prove to yourself and your audience that you've done your research, that you understand the topic and that you are bringing in other people's thoughts. You are not "Here's my thoughts." You are "Here's my thoughts and here's some experts," or "Here's some research that agrees with my thoughts." It should never be "Oh, this paper doesn't have enough resources. I need to go get three more sources." It should be "You know, this point is a good point but who am I to say that? Okay, I need to go find someone else who's said that. Hopefully an expert who's also made that same point and then I'll bring in some research, in that regard, bring in some sources." It's no longer just "Let me throw a source in that paragraph 'cause I have to." It's now "This topic is perhaps something that all people won't agree with right off the bat, just because I'm saying it. So, let's see who else has said it and I'll cite something there."

487

Polish Your Work

At work we had to create an annual report video and I got one of the newer colleagues to do it because she needs to take my place eventually. She had storyboarded and made all the right moves. She submitted it to our boss and he didn't like it because he didn't know much about film. He didn't know the steps required to take something from not effective to effective, and she made some really effective moves. The content of the video was high quality and she did a great job. Then, I went in and really polished things. I grabbed things, dragged them out an extra second, made the words appear to the beat of the song, changed the color of some things because they didn't fit quite as well, cutting half a second of that person's word because she trails off in the interview and we don't need to hear that, and submitted the same video to the boss. He was like "Yea, this is great. We are going to use it."

In proofreading — when creating a video — it's about going back and making things fit perfectly. There's a whole puzzle that fits together and there is only one way in that regard. Once you've created something — there's several ways to create something — there's really only one way to go back and make those things perfect, by dragging and cutting things. You can make people completely lose your point if you are not polished.

My Plea to Content Strategists . . .

I would like to make a plea to writers, to content strategists, soon to be content strategists, or current content strategists to challenge things. Challenge convention. Understand convention completely, immerse yourself in the conventions of writing and production and then break the rules and fail. Fail a hundred times while you are breaking the rules but in some ways you'll find something that really worked for you. You'll break the rules in a way that is extremely effective. So, challenge the boundaries of writing, I'd say.

STUDENT PAPER F

Video Essay

The portion of Dan's interview that discusses his model writing is included below, before the transcript of the video essay is presented. Dan was selected as one of the six featured students in the print book because of his use of media and his thoughtful reflection on his own composing process.

The class was called digital rhetoric; it was a writing class at my school. We got the prompt months before finishing the actual project. The prompt was to tell the story of my evolution as writer and how the digital world had affected that. I thought the prompt was really interesting, and I started writing it as a paper and thought to myself "This is okay, I could get this done as an okay paper and get a good grade, but I'm really interested in this, so a paper is really not enough for me." So I scrapped the paper and decided to make a movie.

I started with the narration. I broke the paper down into a script, recorded the audio — it took me about 18 takes to get it right. And then I tried a 100 different things, including delving into animation. Then, I just grabbed a flip-cam and began shooting random things that did not work at all. About two days before the project was due, I went into the documentary lab, listened to it again, and sat there for about three hours doing nothing.

The day before it was due I came up with the idea of the dry-erase board approach. It took a little while, but it started to click. I storyboarded it out for about two hours, and then filmed and edited in the lab for about twelve hours. Five or six cups of coffee later, I finally finished it and watched and was really proud of it, because it really did rhetorically what I wanted to do in the first place. It was just really interesting that I started with a paper, and it didn't work. So, I turned the paper into a script, turned that script into an audio production, and eventually turned that audio production into a full video that's really gotten some traction. "

TRANSCRIPT OF DAN'S VIDEO PROJECT

Go to the LaunchPad for *Becoming a College Writer* to see Dan's final video.

My Digital Life

00:05 When I was young, I used to write with a wood, Ticonderoga number 2 pencil. My penmanship was terrible, my writing was unreadable, thus, ungradable, and teachers warned my parents that I would need some "special care" if I was to succeed in the public education system.

00:21 It was suggested, and I don't recall how, that I attempt to write with a mechanical pencil, the more or less progression of the traditional pencil. Like a switch, my penmanship suddenly improved. My writing was appreciated and teachers no longer assumed that I had a low mental capacity. Most importantly what happened, and I didn't know it at the time, was that I was embarking on a journey of continuous writing "upgrades" that would eventually bring me to my current spot in the digital world.

00:52 My name is Dan, and I am a digital communicator. That's a rather loaded term I know, but I think a bit of background on my relationship with writing might clear things up.

1:03 In grade school, when I had days off, I'd often head into work with my mom or dad. At my mom's office, I'd occupy my own eight-hour workday not with coloring books and crayons, not with arts and crafts materials, but with a dusty old typewriter that was being held for both frugality and nostalgia.

1:22 Being only about six, I had no typing ability, but I would bang on the keyboard all day, creating intricately brilliant stories about characters that existed in my mind. What really was on the paper was nonsense that was void of spaces, punctuation, and well, words.

1:40 On days that I'd go into the office with my dad, he'd sit me down at the table in his office, grab me one of the dozens of laptops his company had in a closet, and I'd type words. Lists of thirty, maybe forty words that would take me hours. Pecking away at each key, I spelled colors, numbers, simple words, and I was proud of my work.

2:01 Writing became a staple of my childhood, a pencil at the piano with my sister, a goofy name on a video game against my brother. Writing implements became artifacts, around which my fondest childhood memories revolved. Some digital, some not.

2:17 As I grew older, and my family grew less cool (at least, twelve year old me thought they did), I found an Internet service that captivated my generation for years: AIM. AKA, American Online Instant Messenger. I used the service to chat with new and old friends, make plans, talk drama, and most importantly, solve problems.

2:39 After hours per day typing away on AIM, I became a rather advanced typist, but more importantly, I saw my words having an effect on people, a pleasure speech hadn't yet allowed me to take part in. Behind the computer screen, I acted as a psychiatrist for the life threatening problems my friends had. Like getting braces or breaking up with Bobby. And I decided that I was quite good at this problem-solving thing. And at fourteen, I was determined that I would be a psychiatrist.

3:10 My new career trajectory left something of a lull in my digital life. But once I arrived at college, that changed. After a full year of transferring six times, I found professional writing. I met people with digital abilities I didn't even know existed. And I wanted to hop on that bandwagon. So I did.

3:31 I became almost entirely digital. In four years, I've owned three laptops, two desktops, an iPhone, two iPods, a Nook, and an Xbox. Let it be known that I did use my own money to pay for most of them. With each of these tools, I produced videos, articles, press releases, e-mails, newsletters, web content, art, promotional materials, music. I do almost any communication, and I do it digitally. That is why I am a digital communicator.

my digital life

With each tool... newsletters
articles videos
press releases
emails
promo stuff music
web content

▶ ▶| 🔊 3:51 / 3:07

4:00 So what does that mean? Why do I do everything digital? Well, I suppose it's because it's only natural. I, like much of my generation, am constantly bombarded with new technologies, new abilities, new mediums, and it'd be ignorant to ignore all of them. I produce digitally because that's just the way things work nowadays. It is the progression of the handwritten word. Digital work is on its way to almost entirely eliminating the physical text. So, I produce digitally because that's what this is: a digital era.

4:36 Bookstores are going out of business, public libraries are threatening extinction, while sites like YouTube, Facebook, and WordPress are flourishing on the web. Digital literacy is in demand for the vast benefits that go along with it. I have an intimate relationship with writing and communication and I always want to do it. That's why I, like most magazines, books, and newspapers, am going digital and will continue to be a digital communicator.

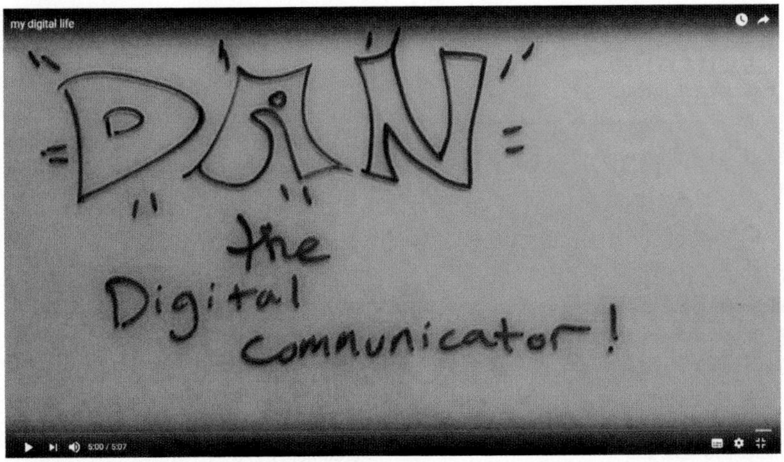
my digital life
"DAN"
the
Digital
communicator!
5:00 / 5:07

Index

LaunchPad
macmillan learning

Additional video material may be found online in LaunchPad when the ⊙ icon appears.

I

ideas
    advancing through paragraph design, 308–310
    expressing your, 21–22
    grammar and clarity on, 328
    mapping, 163–164
    organizing into patterns, 184, 188–192
    paragraphs based on, 302–306
    paraphrasing, 370
    ranking, 187
    structuring, 185–188
imagery, 96
images
    formats for, 240
    for publishing, 245–247
IMRAC structure, 191
indention, 344
independent clauses, 331
    comma splices with, 335–336
    commas with, 337
    punctuation with two, 333–334
    semicolons between, 339
information overload, 71
informed readers, 213–215
ink colors, 243–244
in narrative essays, 96
insights
    in literary analysis, 93
    in rhetorical analysis, 92
    topic selection with potential for, 47–49
Instagram posts
    APA citation style for, 398
    Chicago citation style for, 411
    MLA citation style for, 384
instructors. *See also* prompts, assignment
    clarifying assignments by, 24, 57
    engaging, 33–34
    feedback from, 19–20, 30
    names of in document headers, 241
    publishing and, 236
    researching expectations of, 31
    revising help from, 213–214
    topic selection and, 47
    writing to please, 38
integrity, 79
Internet, 419

comments, APA citation style for, 398
comments, *Chicago* citation style for, 411
comments, MLA citation style for, 384
publishing through the, 236
search engines, 72–74
interviews, 419
    APA citation style for, 399
    Chicago citation style for, 412, 413
    with Dan, 483–488
    with Deonta, 441–444
    generating your own primary evidence with, 75–76
    with Kendra, 431–432
    MLA citation style for, 385
    with Nanaissa, 420–424
    with Nicole, 457–461
    with Vinh-Thuy, 468–473
in-text citations, 366
    APA, 386–387
    Chicago style for, 400
    as citation signals, 368
    MLA, 374–375
    for summaries, 371
introductions, 278–295, 460
    clichés and dysfunctional approaches in, 291–293
    context for, 279–280
    designing, 279
    French style for, 421
    goals of, 281–282, 284
    key word definitions in, 287
    in lab reports, 191
    main points in, 286–287
    mirrored triangles design on, 280
    moving from general to specific in, 286
    in oral presentations, 100
    organization of, 290
    previewing structure in, 288
    providing context and application in, 285–286
    thesis statements in, 273
introductory clauses, 320–321
isolation booth technique, 196, 197
issue numbers, 379
    in APA style, 395
italics, 351
its, it's, 342